HARVARD MIDDLE EASTERN STUDIES

Out of Print Titles Are Omitted.

* Published jointly by the Center for International Affairs and the Center for Middle Eastern Studies.

† Published jointly by the Center for Middle Eastern Studies and the Joint Center for Urban Studies.

HARVARD MIDDLE EASTERN STUDIES 3

THE IDEA OF
THE
JEWISH
STATE

SECOND EDITION

THE IDEA OF
THE
JEWISH
STATE

Ben Halpern

Second Edition

HARVARD UNIVERSITY PRESS
Cambridge, Massachusetts

1 9 6 9

Distributed in Great Britain by Oxford University Press, London

Library of Congress Catalog Card Number 71–89969
SBN 674–44201–6

Manufactured in the United States of America

DEDICATED TO GERTRUDE

PREFACE TO THE SECOND EDITION

Since 1961, when this analysis of the rise of Israel was first published, a fascinated world has witnessed swift, drastic, and altogether dramatic changes in the fortunes of the Jewish state. In making the study once more available to readers, a revision was obviously required in order to take account of recent events. Also, a number of significant works which appeared too late to be used in the first edition may now be utilized.

New information derived either from events or from research, and bearing on the central themes of this book, has not, however, necessitated any substantive alteration of its conclusions. The "idea of the Jewish state" expressed itself under new conditions in essentially the same ways as were apparent before such recent upheavals as the 1967 Six Day War. As for the important historical studies that became available after the first edition was completed, they have made it possible to state with certainty some conclusions which were then advanced as more or less conjectural.

This new edition has also profited from critical comment on the original publication. An effort has been made to eliminate ambiguities made apparent by critics' remarks; this guidance is gratefully acknowledged. Some critics pointed out that the study was almost, but not quite, one of several things which they might, respectively, have preferred it to be: a general history of Zionism, or of Israel, or a general diplomatic history of the Palestine problem, covering the developing viewpoints of all parties concerned. The study is not intended as any of the above.

Although it deals with parts of all these topics, this book does so in order to illuminate its own special problem: the development of the modern notion of Jewish sovereignty from the stage of a myth, with no more than emotional definition, to a rationally elaborated ideology, and from that stage to an institutional reality. Because of this focus, other questions touched on cannot always receive full, well-rounded treatment. They concern us primarily as they bear on changing attitudes and opinions within that movement which successfully embodied the idea of Jewish sovereignty in the state of Israel.

Apart from supplementary material, this revision includes one major deletion. The "Appendix on Methods, Assumptions, and Terms" that appeared in the first edition has been omitted. This methodological appendix was so briefly presented that its usefulness was doubtful. The terms in question are in any case sufficiently intelligible in their common usage as to be understood in the context of this study without specific explanation of the technical signification intended.

In the perspective of the last few eventful years, the special subject of this study seems to have become critically important, and not merely intrinsically interesting. Nothing in current Middle Eastern politics has been so blatantly disregarded by outside area specialists and policy planners as the elementary precaution of studying seriously Israel's "self-image," the springs of its "political culture," its public opinion, and decision-making. Men who constantly preached sensitivity to the special values of the Arab East and consideration for the inherent restrictions imposed by tradition and public pressure on Arab leadership tried to manage the Israelis without troubling to understand them. The costs to everyone directly and indirectly involved are all too clear.

In presenting this new edition, the author hopes that his study of the idea of the Jewish state may contribute to a better understanding of the reality.

Ben Halpern

Brandeis University, February 1969

PREFACE TO THE FIRST EDITION

THIS book is the first half of a projected two-part study of Israel. It attempts a systematic explanation of a central theme in the history of the young nation: the development of the idea of the Jewish state from a vaguely defined aspiration towards national sovereignty, pursued by an ideological movement, to the achievement of statehood and the exercise of sovereignty by representative national institutions. It deals, in large measure, with what might be called the external relations, first of the Zionist movement and then of the Jewish state. The study is to be completed by a comprehensive analysis of the developing social structure and domestic problems of Israel, which will be treated in a second volume.

Any study of Israel and its problems and prospects is of high and general interest, small as the nation is. There is hardly another land or people to which so much of the world is bound with sentimental bonds so diverse and often so conflicting. The Christian nations of Europe and the Americas and large Moslem communities in Asia and Africa regard Palestine as a Holy Land. The Jews scattered throughout the globe not only revere Zion as the center of their religious tradition and as their ancient patrimony; they are also deeply concerned with the historic purpose to which Israel is dedicated — the attempt to solve the worldwide Jewish problem. For Christians everywhere, too, that attempt raises questions of conscience that became acute and irrepressible through the genocidal slaughter of six million Jews in Europe.

Besides this, the territory over which the state of Israel maintains its sovereignty is a crossroads of international interests and imperial strategies, and, at the same time, a crux of pan-Arab ambitions. Consequently, the severe disputes that pit world powers against one another in the Eastern Mediterranean today are inextricably involved with the bitter local quarrel of Israel and the Arab states. Whoever is directly concerned with Middle Eastern oil or with Suez — and this includes the whole European and North Atlantic world as well as Eastern Asia and Australasia — is necessarily concerned also with this intractable complication. No otherwise rational or practicable solution for any problem in this critical area can be successfully attempted without considering how hatred for Israel may distort the probable Arab reactions. Nor can any such proposals be made, taking the "problem" of Israel into account, without understanding what may be Israel's probable reaction to an anticipated new situation.

It must be added that Israel, as a Jewish state, is a source of the same kind of moral and intellectual perplexity that the extraordinary history of the Jews has always aroused. The successful establishment of the Jewish state in a country where only recently Jews lived in very small number seems as puzzling to historical understanding as the millennial survival of the Jewish Diaspora. The restoration of Jewish sovereignty seems to challenge moral understanding no less severely than the Jewish Exile.

It is not surprising, therefore, that Israel, its background, and its contemporary problems have been treated in a voluminous literature. The books and pamphlets on this subject are divided into two types. There have been a large number of polemical volumes which have sought to justify or condemn the very existence of Israel or to impugn or exalt the character of its institutions and policies. In fact, so common is this approach to the subject that any new book is expected to take the same form and answer the same questions. A second type of literature exempts itself from such far-reaching demands by confining itself to narrowly defined special problems of economics, social psychology, or political science.

This book (as well as its projected sequel) attempts not the analysis of special, technical problems but a general explanation of Israel as a whole. The study is inevitably concerned, accordingly, with questions regarding the character of Israel, the aims it sets itself, and the probable effect of objective circumstances upon its future development and attitudes. It also must consider historically and analytically the very issues which are debated by the advocates and opponents of Israel's existence or policies — nor does the author claim to be neutral on these questions.

But it is not within the scope or intention of this book to answer or to examine directly any questions concerning the justification of Israel's existence, character, institutions, or policies. This study attempts no legal or ethical analysis of the issues involved in the rise of the Jewish state; nor, in its discussion of political and diplomatic developments, does it aim at a comprehensive account of these events, or, assuming the role of the tribunal of history, undertake to show what errors were made, or what other policies on one side or another would better have served justice or the interests of world order or the strategies of the major powers.

The aim of this book is not judgment but explanation; and while its method (the method of systematic historical explanation) is comprehensive, its subject (the development of the idea of the Jewish state from an ideological conception to a political institution) is circumscribed. We are concerned not with how the problems that arose during Israel's establishment and early history might best have been solved, but with how the solutions that were adopted came to be what they were. It is, perhaps, necessary to make this clear at the outset, for much of the material presented for the purpose of explanation may be pertinent to the questions that are foremost in the minds of readers interested in judgment. Any answer to such questions that a reader may derive from the discussion that follows will be supplied by himself out of elucidations that have a somewhat different and more restricted aim.

While this study attempts a systematic explanation, instead of a graphic survey of its subject, it is, at least in intent, written for the general reader with no more than the intelligent layman's acquaintance with the material treated and the methods employed. Certain usages, as well as the organization of the book, have thus had to be adapted for a dual role: to achieve a certain degree of rigor in argument together with a certain degree of ease in presentation.

An effort has been made to use terms in a way that will be intelligible without specific definition, even in those instances where technical definitions are respected. Those terms which, for one or another reason, are technically defined by the author in a way not familiar to most social scientists, or whose usage here does not respect their common technical definition, are indicated (for the benefit of scholars and out of consideration for the general reader) in an appendix on methods, assumptions, and terms. All citations, and only citations, are given in the end notes; while everything intended as an aid for the general reader is on the page before him. Foreign terms and special concepts that are familiar to readers of modern Jewish history, but not necessarily so to others, are explained in the text or in footnotes at their first appearance; and the Hebrew transliterations correspond to those far from rigorous usages which the reader is most likely to encounter if he pursues this subject further in contemporary periodicals. A large part of this book is devoted to the analysis of documents in their historical setting; the pertinent documents or excerpts are reprinted in the text.

The book is organized chiefly as a series of discussions of historical problems. This involves a certain unavoidable amount of repetition, or of deviation from chronological sequence. An attempt is made to keep both to a minimum by arranging the formal discussion of each problem, as far as possible, in the order of its historical emergence as a topic of major significance.

The first two chapters constitute a kind of overture to the whole, in which the setting of the problem is outlined and the development of the main theme is recapitulated in a consecutive narrative exposition. Chapter I outlines the rise of the modern Jewish problem, which was so signal a feature of general Occidental history in the nineteenth and twentieth centuries, and describes the divergent ideologies and groupings within the Jewish community. Having thus sketched the general and the Jewish environments in which Zionism developed and in which it advocated its idea of Jewish sovereignty as the solution for the Jewish problem, the exposition, in Chapter II, analyzes the successive formulations of this idea, in response to historical contingencies, which were selected from among logically possible alternatives by various Zionist factions and by the Zionist consensus.

Following these introductory chapters, the historical analysis of the idea of the Jewish state is presented in two major divisions. In adjusting their ideas to external pressures, the Zionists faced essentially different situations within the Jewish community and beyond it. Accordingly, one part of the analysis (Chapters III–VII) traces the successive reformulations of the idea of Jewish sovereignty undertaken by Zionists in the endeavor to obtain the approval and support of the Jewish community. The other part (Chapters VIII–XII) traces the successive reformulations of the idea in the debates and negotiations of the Zionists with the powers, political interests, and international bodies that concerned themselves with the questions of Palestine and Zionism.

A natural climax, but not the conclusion of the analysis here undertaken, is Israel's declaration of independence on May 14, 1948. The nature of Israel's sovereignty, and particularly its relation to the purpose of solving the Jewish problem, did not cease to be problematic at that point; they still remain to a significant degree open questions today. The recent developments in the definition of Israel's relations, as a sovereign state, to Jews abroad and to foreign nations are traced in this volume through the Sinai campaign of 1956 and the international developments directly connected with it in the following year; only in a few details does the study, for the sake of rounding out a conclusion, refer to anything that happened after 1957.

This book, as a whole, constitutes an introduction to the second part that is to follow. What we have described as the historic purpose of Zionism and of Israel — to solve the Jewish problem by means of the restoration of Jewish sovereignty in Palestine — was pursued directly through the efforts, analyzed in this book, to create and maintain Jewish sovereignty as such. The same purpose may be traced in its indirect expressions and effects as the Jewish state encounters the problems of education, religion, culture, and communal relations and seeks political and economic equilibrium under the testing conditions of its local environment and the specific impact of mass immigration; and these topics will be treated in a second volume.

In any book which draws so largely upon the researches of other scholars, full acknowledgment of intellectual debts is impossible. The citations give only inadequate recognition to those whose results are most directly relied on to support the author's conclusions.

More personal debts require more specific acknowledgment. The author is under deep obligation to the Center for Middle Eastern Studies at Harvard, its Director, Sir Hamilton A. R. Gibb, and its staff and fellows for an environment in which both stimulation and leisure were amply provided for this work. He is particularly grateful to the Associate Director, Derwood W. Lockard, for taking upon himself not only large responsibilities but many petty labors essential for the publication of the volume. A special debt, too, must be acknowledged to Mrs. Kay Pease, and to Miss Carolyn Cross and Mrs. Martha Smith for their unfailing helpfulness in the preparation of the manuscript. The book has benefited immeasurably from the patient editorial care of Miss Ann Orlov of the staff of the Harvard University Press.

The author is indebted to the librarians of many institutions, notably to the Widener Library at Harvard; but special acknowledgments are owed to the Zionist Central Archives and Library in Jerusalem for the use of archival materials and to the Zionist Archives and Library in New York for the use lavishly made of their excellent special collection.

The courtesy of publishers who have kindly given permission for substantial quotation from material copyrighted by them is acknowledged for excerpts from the following sources: The American Jewish Committee and the Jewish Publication Society, quotations from *Louis Marshall: Champion of Liberty*, edited by Charles Reznikoff; Miss Hannah Bodenheimer, quotations from her book *Toldot Tokhnit Bazel*; Mr. Hayim Hazaz and *Partisan Review*, quotations from his story "The Sermon"; the Jewish Publication Society, quotations from *Selected*

Essays by Ahad Ha'am, and from *Theodore Herzl* by Alex Bein; Routledge and Kegan Paul, Ltd., quotations from *Ten Essays on Zionism and Judaism* by Ahad Ha'am; World Publishing Company, quotations from *Theodor Herzl, a Portrait for this Age*, edited by the late Ludwig Lewisohn.

I cannot conclude without expressing my deep personal indebtedness to two eminent scholars who have shown me great kindness for many years and especially during the preparation of this book. The project itself was initially undertaken at the suggestion of Professor Harry A. Wolfson, and he was good enough to give it his customarily perceptive reading. Dr. Jacob Robinson, whose published and unpublished work on the subject considered in this volume have been a constant reliance, generously gave the manuscript the meticulous reading which has been so valuable to many of his friends and colleagues. For these and for untold other favors, I thank them both.

Cambridge, May, 1960　　　　　　　　　　　　　　　　　　*Ben Halpern*

CONTENTS

MAPS

Part One

ZIONISM: BACKGROUND AND DESCRIPTION

1 THE SETTING OF MODERN JEWISH HISTORY

I<small>T</small> is often said that "modern Jewish history" begins with the emergence of the Jewish Problem. The Enlightenment in eighteenth-century France and Germany raised this problem among intellectuals by its critical examination of the traditional status of the Jews. The French Revolution, through the Emancipation of the Jews, created a new institutional status that was intended to solve the problem but, in fact, converted it from an intellectual issue into a dominant political and social reality in modern Jewish history.

Before the Emancipation, the position of the Jews was undoubtedly beset with problems, both for Jews and Christians, but on each side there was nevertheless a consistent idea, expressed in appropriate institutions, which constituted an agreed interpretation of the Jewish position: the Jews thought of themselves as suffering Exile until God pleased to grant them Redemption and restore them to Zion; the Gentiles interpreted the Jewish fate in terms of the myth of the Wandering Jew, doomed to persist until the Second Advent in Exile and subjection. Either of these diametrically opposed versions of the same belief could satisfactorily rationalize not only the Jewish fate in general but the specific institutional patterns that grew up in those European countries where significant Jewish communities continued to exist after the fifteenth century. Expelled from countries where an effective central rule was established — from England at the close of the thirteenth, France at the close of the fourteenth, and Spain at the close of the fifteenth century — Jewish communities remained chiefly in Italy, Germany, and Poland, areas of decentralized authority during the sixteenth and seventeenth centuries. Their residential rights were usually conditional, contractually defined, and limited to specified zones of settlement. They lived as a tight, secluded community with only marginal contacts with their Gentile milieu. They fostered an independent traditional culture. Their economic activities were restricted by special laws and by the jealously guarded privileges of Christian guilds and merchants. Such special treatment was in harmony with the view accepted by both Jews and Christians that the position to be accorded to the Jew should be defined on the basis of his religious difference.

In European society generally the growth of secular principles underlying social and political status was well advanced in the late eighteenth century. The special laws applying to the Jews because of their religious difference appeared anomalous to many intellectuals in that era of Enlightenment. The discussion of this question among intellectuals was followed by the recognition of the Jews as citizens and the removal of existing legal restrictions enacted by the French National Assembly on September 28, 1791. Emancipation was not fated to be completed in one spontaneous act of grace, but it became a cause for which the Jews themselves had to conduct a stubborn, protracted battle. By 1860, nevertheless, the equality of the Jews was generally effective in Europe as far east as the Russian Empire and as far south as Rumania; but there the old pattern of special restrictions still prevailed.

In those countries where the Jews were emancipated during the nineteenth century, emancipation removed disabilities and ameliorated many hardships. But it also ended the consensus that had existed among the Jews and the Christians, each according to their own interpretation, as to the nature of the Jewish position in the world. The Christian proponents of emancipation rejected the old institutional status of the Jews and proposed a new one based on the recognition of the Jews as citizens; but in later years this status and the principles upon which it rested were in turn questioned by Gentile opponents. In the Jewish community, too, the Emancipation led to ideological differences about the proper principles and institutions of the Jewish status.

Among the ideologies that grew up, Zionism was one of the relatively late developments. It appeared as a criticism of the solution of the Jewish problem based on civic emancipation alone; and it was an effort to reestablish continuity with those traditional conceptions of the nature and goal of Jewish history that had been discarded by Jewish disciples of the Enlightenment.

I

Pre-Emancipation Jewry displayed a remarkable unity, continuing over vast stretches of time and space. Their solidarity rested upon an effective consensus that united them among themselves and set them apart from the environment in regard to both religious culture and communal organization. The effectiveness of their consensus depended not only on the intensity of their attachment to common values and sentiments, but also on the great scope for freedom in the intellectual definition of their beliefs and the great elasticity in the structure of their communal organization. Without an elaborate body of dogma or a powerfully organized center and hierarchy of religious authority, the Jews throughout a long history and a global dispersion maintained a consistent uniformity of religious practice and persisted as a sharply distinct religious entity. Without secular power, or their own land, or even a strongly organized machinery of self-government that continuously comprehended all or any appreciable part of the Jewish people, they carried on an orderly communal life on a worldwide scale under the most extreme and varied conditions. They persisted through centuries as a distinct ethnic entity everywhere subject to a majority that at best tolerated but never really understood their existence.

The lack of much of the formal paraphernalia of solidarity commonly found in strongly organized bodies enabled the Jews, perhaps, to bend with the winds that blasted their course through history; but what enabled them to stand was a complex of values to which the Jews showed an unexampled attachment. The uniformity of religious behavior and flexible order of communal organization, the pillars upon which Jewish unity stood, depended upon a voluntary, not a compulsory discipline. The ground upon which the whole structure rested was an extraordinary organization for the preservation, cultivation, and transmission of a religious culture. The Hebrew language, maintained as a language not only of ritual and prayer, but also of all branches of scholarship, of communal law, of correspondence between Jews in all corners of the world, and of personal and communal records, was part of this groundwork. The system of universal education in the national language and tradition, which produced a universal ability to understand the essentials and a universal willingness to respect the instructions of Jewish learning and to base communal relations and individual behavior upon it, was also part of this groundwork.

A most significant part of the groundwork of Jewish unity, from our point of view, was that aspect of Jewish culture in which the Jews were most self-conscious, their conception of themselves and their place in God's plan of history. The historic, eschatological myth of the Exile and Redemption of the Jews, cultivated by successive generations in every country to which Jews came in their wanderings, and binding them in a self-conscious union of fate and destiny, was a major theme in the culture and education of all Jews. Ritual, instruction, turns of speech, and elaborate recitals and philosophies collaborated to impress it upon the minds and hearts of Jews. The Exile might be mild or harsh, and the relations with the Gentiles open or barred; in any case, Jews remained always conscious of an irreducible alienhood — their duty as well as their burden — in all lands but the ancestral home. However ancient and intimate their bonds with any other land, their destiny and true home, they knew, were elsewhere. So, too, the Return to Zion might seem remote or become immediate, be actively attempted or awaited in abnegation: the Land of Israel remained the ultimate as well as original homeland of the Jews. Its qualities and historical associations often had more meaning for Jews than the places in which they were born.

Such were the values and such the channels of transmission through which the unity of the Jews was maintained. In major sections of the Jewish people the structure and its supporting processes remained substantially intact to our own times. This was the case in the relatively stagnant Jewish communities of Western Asia and North Africa and to a great degree in the Jewish communities of Eastern Europe, in spite of the massive changes in circumstances experienced there.

The Jews entered their "modern period" in the course of an immense increase and rapid redistribution of population. Hard conditions and harsh treatment, culminating in mass expulsions and forced conversions, had reduced the number of Jews to about 1,500,000 in the fifteenth century. In the eighteenth century the population began to rise from this low point, reaching about 2,500,000 in 1800; and, in an expansion of explosive proportions, it increased to over 10,000,000 by 1900 and well over 16,000,000 at the outbreak of World War II.[1]

This unprecedented population growth, in itself a factor that fundamentally changed the conditions of Jewish living, was not equally distributed among all the widely separated communities of the Jewish Diaspora. It was concentrated chiefly in the Jewish communities of Eastern Europe, the great reservoir of Jewish natural increase, and in the new Jewish communities of Western Europe and countries overseas which grew through the flow of migration from Eastern Europe. Of the 2,500,000 Jews in the world in 1800, about three-fifths resided in Europe and two-fifths in the Ottoman Empire and North Africa, reversing the ratios that had prevailed a century earlier. By 1850, "the total number of Jews . . . amounted to 4,750,000, of whom 72 per cent inhabited Eastern Europe and the Balkans, 14.5 per cent Central and Western Europe, and 1.5 per cent America, while only 12 per cent inhabited the Near East and North Africa."[2] Thereafter, immigration to the Western Hemisphere, mainly from Eastern Europe, grew to massive proportions. By 1938, when there were believed to be almost 17,000,000 Jews in the world, almost 8,000,000 lived in Eastern Europe. In the Americas, there had grown up communities of well over 5,000,000 Jews, constituting over 30 per cent of the Jewish people. In the continents of Asia and Africa, the number of Jews had increased to 1,500,000 (though declining to a proportion of less than 9 per cent) largely through the immigration of European Jews to Palestine and the Union of South Africa.[3] Thus, the source of the extraordinary increase of Jewish population had been chiefly the natural increase of Eastern European Jewry; and its effect had been not only to make that Jewry by far the largest segment of world Jewry, but to supply the immigrants who constituted the next largest segment, the Jews of the United States and other Western Hemisphere countries.

So large a relative increase in numbers must in itself have served to induce sharp changes in the life of European Jewry. Certainly, the movement of masses of immigrants to new countries and widely different environments did so. But, another factor, the impact of critical changes in the political environment and cultural milieu, radically altering conditions of life in the countries where Jews had long resided and impelling them to move to new countries, not only induced changes in Jewish life; it forced the Jewish community consciously to face the need for change and to consider the problems of its historic destiny. Only in the Near Eastern and North African communities (and not in all of them) did changing political and cultural conditions fail to reach a critical intensity of impact. In Eastern and Western Europe and in the Americas, the Jewish communities were continually confronted with the pressing need to consider how they might best adjust to irreversibly altering conditions.

To be sure, political vicissitudes and changing social and cultural conditions were something of a constant factor in the historical experience of the Jewish people. Hence, when the partition of Poland in the late eighteenth century brought new groups of Jews under Russian, Austrian, and Prussian rule, such a change of masters could in itself, no doubt, have been adjusted to by the Jewish community without any major impact on its institutions or values, as similar political changes had been in the past. So, too, when nineteenth-century political upheavals in such places as Algeria or Rumania, at opposite ends of the Ottoman-North African complex of countries, caused Jewish refugees to emigrate, these, too, were emergencies, similar to others in the past, that the Jewish community was equipped to meet in terms of its traditional values.

However, two new conditions now accompanied such events, particularly in Europe — the Enlightenment and the Emancipation of the Jews. Under their influence, the instability of the environment penetrated into the internal relationships of the Jewish community. The principles of emancipation and enlightenment were taken up by advocates within the Jewish community, and produced lines of division in European Jewry. Thus, the Jewish community in the West was set off from the Jewish community in the East, and new partisanships and fissions were created within the organized body of each Jewish community that experienced the historic change.

In Western and Central Europe and in the new overseas countries, a radically new condition in Jewish history developed. Adjusting to a new social and political situation and cultural climate, Jews discarded some of the values and practices that had always constituted the framework of Jewish unity and no longer preserved those supporting processes by which it was sustained. In spite of this, the Jewish consensus showed itself sufficiently strong and sufficiently flexible so that these aberrant tendencies were contained within the bounds of Jewish unity. Remaining within a single consensus, however, the new variants of Jewish belief and organization produced divisions in the unified body.

Differences and even total breaches in Jewish unity were far from unknown, of course, in past history. The Sephardic and Ashkenazic sections of traditional Jewry, for example, were different in many details of ritual and in their internal social relationships, as well as in their degree of openness to the Gentile cultural milieu and of involvement in the Gentile political and social environment. The range of difference was wide enough to include Spanish Jews, brought up as Marrano Christians, who returned to Judaism, after their flight to Italy or Holland, filled with devotion but devoid of Jewish background, and Polish Jews, immersed from childhood in an intensely Jewish environment and hardly aware of any world outside their own. An extensive uniformity of religious practice established, and an intensive communication of traditional Jewish culture maintained, unity throughout the range defined by such extremes. On the other hand, in the past when the basic uniformity of religious practice was broken, as in the anti-Talmudic Karaite movement, or when the traditional culture and the Hebrew tongue were neglected, as in some Hellenistic Jewish communities, the deviant groups left the Jewish fold abruptly or by gradual stages, and the remaining community continued to be united by the old bonds. Under the influence of the Enlightenment and Emancipation in Europe, the uniformity of religious practice among Jews was broken and the traditional culture through which they communicated was in some areas neglected; yet the deviants remained united — inside the Jewish fold — and introduced divisions within it.

In the West, a religious reform spread from Germany in the mid-nineteenth century and introduced into Judaism a measure of denomi-nationalism similar to that of Christendom, breaking the traditional unity of religious practice. The new sectaries of Reform Judaism did not secede nor were they excluded by the Jewish consensus, as had happened in parallel cases earlier; and, as a result, the persisting unity of Judaism, no longer founded on the familiar, traditional uniformity of practice, became problematical at its foundations. The reaction of traditionalists in the West to this new challenge, while it did not lead to schism (which might have restricted the unity of the Jews to its old basis), led not only to intellectual but to organizational division within the Jewish community. For, following a Christian pattern themselves, the Western traditionalist Jews (beginning to be called Orthodox, a title not previously used among Jews) claimed from Gentile authorities the right to secede from Jewish community organ-izations dominated by religious innovators, and they set up parallel Jewish community organizations of their own.

Not only was the uniformity of Jewish religious practice and the universality of Jewish communal organization now challenged, but the transmission of Jewish culture which supported the whole structure of traditional Jewish unity became increasingly ineffective. In the aftermath of Enlightenment and Emancipation, the Hebrew language and traditional Jewish education ceased to be the universal heritage of Jews in the West and no longer served as channels of communication accessible to all Jews.

As for the historic eschatological myth of Exile and Return, this, too, suffered a dilution of meaning as significant in its effect as the decline of Hebrew and of traditional education. In the climate of liberalism that prevailed during the days of the French Revolution, Gentile opponents of Jewish emancipation could not directly defend the religious discrimination that existed under the *ancien régime*. Hence, they developed an argument against granting citizenship to the Jews that could be defended in terms of liberal principles, con-tending that the Jews constituted not just a different religion but a separate nation from the majority in the countries where they lived. In a defensive reaction stimulated by such polemical assertions,

Western Jews solemnly declared that the Jews were not a separate nation but a purely religious body; and accordingly they denied any intention or desire to return to Zion.

Long before the Emancipation made the Jewish Problem acute, the Age of Enlightenment, as early as the seventeenth and into the eighteenth century, had begun to affect at least the mood in which absolute rulers defined their policies toward the Jews. On the one hand, a certain distaste developed for an institutional status which, like that of the tolerated Jew, rested upon a palpable myth; on the other hand, the uncertainty of the Jewish status made it possible to deal with the Jews in the manner most congenial to enlightened absolutism — as a problem to be solved rationally and practically.

In the revolutionary upheavals of the late eighteenth and the early nineteenth centuries, the republican rebels tried to reconstruct all of society in precisely this way. The emancipation of the Jews was only one item in their grand project for the emancipation and enlightenment of all mankind.

The violence these revolutionary changes did to established institutional values, to ancient sentiments and vested interests, was matched by the vehemence of counterrevolutionary movements throughout Continental Europe in the nineteenth century. And as the Jewish emancipation was symbolically identified with everything that was found offensive in the liberal revolution by its foes, the traditional hostility to the Jews, transformed into modern anti-Semitism, now assumed the organized purposefulness of a major political movement. Thus, the Jewish Problem, posed in the clear light of eighteenth-century Enlightenment as an issue requiring rational solution, continued to be kept alive by the anti-Semitic irrationalism of the nineteenth century, which, in the twentieth, sought to bring it to a final inhuman solution.[4]

Such was the pattern of the development of Gentile approaches to the Jewish problem in Western countries. In those countries, the status of the Jews was redefined by their gradual emancipation, during a series of political struggles that extended into the second half of the nineteenth century. Political anti-Semitism then grew up as a counterrevolutionary movement, hostile to the *status quo* especially in respect to the Jewish position but also in regard to the democratic structure and liberal attitudes of contemporary society as a whole.

In Eastern countries and in particular in the Russian Empire, the liberal reconstruction both of the whole social and political system and of the status of the Jews was slow and halting, or was totally aborted. Hostility to civic equality as a solution of the Jewish problem consequently developed among Gentiles not in opposition to but as a defense of the *status quo*; though in some respects it borrowed principles developed in the reaction against the successful establishment of liberal institutions of the West.

Whenever the absolute despotism of the Russian Czars was influenced by the Enlightenment, their policy towards the Jews resembled that of the prerevolutionary absolute monarchs of the West. They tried to "reform" the traditional Jewish position by administrative measures, instituting secular education in state-sponsored schools, appointing state-approved Rabbis, and seeking to transfer Jewish colonists to farm areas and into agricultural and mechanical trades, without, however, granting the Jews civic equality and allowing them to arrive at a new social and cultural adjustment in freedom.

More characteristic of the attitude of the Eastern European regimes was a policy of simple restriction and repression, intended to maintain the traditional subjection of the Jews. After the partition of Poland the Czarist regime sought to prevent the settlement of Jews in "Holy Russia" and confined them to a "Pale of Settlement" in its newly acquired western provinces. Sometimes, however, the advocates of restrictive policies employed tactics or arguments of a postrevolutionary flavor. When Rumania, obtaining its freedom from Ottoman rule, was called upon by Western powers to extend freedom and equal citizenship to its Jewish subjects, it evaded these demands by using an old argument from the armory of opponents of the emancipation of the Jews: it declared the Jews an alien people in Rumania.[5] In order to remedy the inequities that this policy entailed, the Rumanians were prepared in the 1860's and 1870's to cooperate in organizing the mass emigration of Rumanian Jews to America or to Palestine. So, too, in Russia the alternative to oppression which the authorities were often ready to make available to the Jews was emigration on a large scale.

Failing to introduce effective reforms of political and social status, the doctrines of the Enlightenment and the Emancipation failed, also, to effect any historic internal divisions among the Eastern European Jews. At the core of the Jewish community, the traditional structure of religious practice and all-embracing communal organization remained intact, the traditional channels of communication and education were kept open, and the traditional historic and eschatological self-image retained its force.

The innovators, who constituted a fringe group in the community, did not appear as religious reformers altering the uniform traditional practices, nor did they disturb the traditional shape of communal relations, or successfully substitute Russian culture and Western education for Hebrew and Jewish learning. Minor efforts to achieve some of these results produced incidents of conflict in the Eastern European community but no real institutional change. Many of the advocates of Enlightenment in Eastern European Jewry during the nineteenth century themselves fostered a new secular Hebrew literature, rather than turning to Russian or Rumanian as the medium of communication among Jews. They created, in the latter half of the century, a "modernized" type of Hebrew school; and instead of seeking to reform the Jewish religion, they were usually distinguished from the traditionalists mainly by the laxness of their observance and the uncertainty of their beliefs. Nor, finally, did they feel any ideological compulsion to renounce demonstratively the intention of the Jewish people ever to return to its ancestral homeland. Thus, the Enlightenment within Eastern Jewry during the nineteenth century created only an active intellectual and social ferment in the community but produced no clear-cut internal division.

Only in the closing decades of the century was Eastern European Jewry to experience its internal division arising from the impact of the modern Jewish problem. Not enlightenment and emancipation, but nationalism and social radicalism were the ideas that produced this change.

II

Not only the situation of the Jews but their national tradition offered obvious analogies with the new nationalist ideas that developed among other suppressed peoples in Europe during the nineteenth century. Indeed, as we have seen, opponents of the enfranchisement of the Jews at various times and places turned with a common impulse to the idea that the Jews, as a separate nation, should find their freedom in a land or region of their own, instead of being admitted to equal citizenship in Gentile society. But this very fact caused Jews seeking emancipation to deny that they were a distinct nationality, and to suppress nationalist notions, at least where explicitly presented as a possible solution for the Jewish problem.

However, throughout the nineteenth century the stimulus of European nationalist movements was responded to by Jews aware of the analogies between nationalism and the traditional Jewish self-image. Traditionalists like the Sephardic rabbi, Judah Alcalay (1798–1878) and the Ashkenazic rabbi, Zvi Hirsch Kalischer (1795–1874), observing at close hand the nationalist uprisings of Balkan or Central and Eastern European peoples, and stung, moreover, by such reminders of Jewish insecurity as the ritual murder trial in Damascus in 1840 * or the enforced conversion of the Mortara child in Rome in 1858,** argued that the divinely appointed time had come for the Jews, too, to seek actively the liberation of their people in the form foreseen by tradition, through returning to the Holy Land. The nationalism of these men was a direct reading, as they saw it, of the contemporary significance of the tradition which, in them, was never shaken. There were also occasional Western intellectuals like Moses Hess (1812–1875) who, having witnessed the same events, responded in a similar way and turned to an eclectic Jewish nationalism and traditionalism of their own. For such men, the nationalist doctrine, adopted out of dissatisfaction with the conventional contemporary solutions of political, social and religious problems, both general and Jewish, was a bridge by which they hoped to reunite their advanced modern principles with the historic Jewish tradition.

The early and mid-nineteenth century also saw a relative increase in the rate of resettlement of Jews in Palestine. The miniature community that had always been maintained there by a constant influx of pious Jews now grew to proportions which, though still small, presented new problems of economic maintenance and legal security. Immigration into Palestine, moreover, on occasion seemed to offer a suitable method to provide for the Jewish refugees ejected by political disturbances from the countries of North Africa or Southeastern Europe during this period.

The Jewish community throughout the world had always contributed as a pious duty to the support of the Jews in Palestine. But

* Father Thomas, superior of the Franciscan convent in Damascus, disappeared on February 5. He had been seen in the Jewish quarter on the previous day, and monks of his convent spread the rumor that the Damascene Jews had killed him in order to use his blood in their alleged rituals. At the instance of the French consul, the governor of the city arrested a Jewish barber and seven communal leaders and put them to the torture. Some confessions were obtained in this way, some prisoners died, and the governor imprisoned others and sought to obtain permission for executions. These incidents aroused widespread protests among Jews and Christians throughout the world, and a collective note of nine consuls brought about the release of the prisoners by Mohammed Ali, then ruler of Syria. When Turkey regained control of the territory shortly afterwards, the sultan issued a firman pronouncing the charge of ritual murder a libel against the Jews.

** Edgar Mortara of Bologna, then six years old, having been baptized during an illness by a Catholic nurse, was taken from his home by papal gendarmes and brought up in the Roman church. Worldwide protests had no effect.

the new tasks which arose from the growth of the Palestine community and particularly from proposals to establish a haven for the resettlement of Jewish refugees there required methods other than the traditional charity. Moreover, as Western countries acquired new influence in all Ottoman affairs, so the Western Jewish communities undertook greater responsibilities for their coreligionists in the Ottoman and North African area and, among them, for the community in Palestine. Having achieved success more or less fully in the emancipation and enlightenment of the Jews at home, they conceived it as their duty to extend the same benefits of secular education, economic security, and political and social equality to the Jews in more backward areas.

The Damascus affair of 1840 found the Western Jews able to give only improvised assistance to their coreligionists in the East. When the Mortara case shocked Western Jewry into renewed activity almost twenty years later, it brought about their organization for continuous assistance on an international scale. The Alliance Israélite Universelle was founded in 1860 as an agency for the defense of Jews against deprivation of rights and for the relief of economic and other social hardships throughout the world. While it had members and constituent committees throughout Europe and beyond, it was essentially a philanthropic agency of Western Jewry, and, with its center in Paris, particularly an organization of the wealthy and influential Jews of France.

The nationalist views of men like Alcalay, Kalischer, and Hess found expression not only in exhortation and debate. They were in close touch with the improvised and permanent agencies of Western Jewry that concerned themselves with the troubled areas of the Jewish world in the mid-nineteenth century, and they had some influence in securing the support then given to the growth of Palestine Jewry. Moreover, sporadic efforts to organize groups specifically devoted to resettlement in Zion also had some success at this time.

In the later 1860's and 1870's, however, the oppression of Jews in Rumania posed the question of emigration on a far larger scale and with far more pointed political implications, so that new ideological and practical issues arose. The Rumanian authorities and some Jews favored the mass emigration of Rumanian Jewry as a political solution for a problem that the former insisted and the latter conceded would not be solved by emancipation; but this was a position which, when so plainly put, a body like the Alliance Israélite Universelle could not accept. Among the Jews who accepted mass emigration as a solution for the problem, particularly in Rumania itself, debate arose over whether the destination should be America or Palestine.

During the same years, some of the Russian Jewish intellectuals, especially the Hebrew writers among them, at home and abroad, began also to develop a direct attack upon the way of life of Western Jewry under the aegis of Emancipation and Enlightenment. However, it was the pogrom wave of the 1880's which brought these tendencies to a head and produced in Dr. Leo Pinsker's (1821–1891) *Auto-Emancipation* the first fully-formed articulation of a Zionist doctrine directly stated as a solution for the Jewish problem and openly proposed as a substitute for Emancipation, which it explicitly rejected as a possible solution.

The Hovevei-Zion ("Lovers of Zion"), as the new Russian movement called itself, had an historic impact that was essentially ideological in nature. Because the idea sprang up among intellectuals, for whom the Jewish problem was a matter of acute concern, it was formulated as a critique of and an alternative to an earlier solution of the Jewish problem, Emancipation. Arising from disillusionment with Emancipation, it expressed in a new form the eschatological tradition, and reunited its adherents with the still largely traditionalist community of Eastern European Jewry. Thus, Hovevei-Zionism was able to found a popular movement which in the 1880's and 1890's spread to all parts of the Jewish world.

However, owing to the limits which circumstances imposed upon the scope of its activities, the ideological character of Hovevei-Zionism was blurred and its challenge was blunted. The Turkish regime reacted sharply against the initial political approaches and the implicit political potentialities of Hovevei-Zionism. The movement, unable to muster large resources through its own efforts, had to solicit the aid of Western Jewish organizations and benefactors for the settlers whom it sent to Palestine. In the interests of these settlers, upon whose success the Hovevei-Zion concentrated their hopes and attention, the challenging implications of the Zionist idea were muted.

In 1896, Theodor Herzl's (1860–1904) *Judenstaat* renewed the challenge in a new and sharper form. Not only did he clearly and explicitly defend Zionism as an ideological alternative to Emancipation; he demanded immediate political activities to obtain international recognition of the Jewish claim to Palestine and attacked any small-scale resettlement in Palestine until such recognition had been obtained. Still more challenging was the character of the Zionist organization which he subsequently established. The Hovevei-Zion before him had established Zionism as a popular movement, but the nature of their aims and activities made them dependent upon the support, and responsive to the demands, of their Western Jewish benefactors. The popular organization which Herzl established had one paramount aim and activity, to serve as the representative of the Jewish people and, in this capacity, to obtain political recognition for Jewish nationalism from the great powers and from the Turks. Thus, the World Zionist Organization at its very birth forced ideological issues. The subsequent history of Zionism, particularly in Eastern Europe, was accompanied by a succession of ideological divisions.

Religious reform had been the occasion in Western Europe for a break with the traditional elements of Jewish unity, and the new kind of unity thereafter achieved had to provide for the first time for a form of denominationalism among the Jews. In Eastern Europe, on the other hand, it was Jewish secularism, not Jewish sectarianism, which began to challenge the traditional framework of Jewish unity. Nationalism and social radicalism, not religious reform, were the new doctrines and the new organized forces which Eastern European Jewry had to include within its consensus.

The challenge to traditional forms was provoked not by the successful emancipation of the Jews but, after the decisive collapse of trends toward emancipation, by other massive changes that shook the Jewish community and particularly its intellectuals. In Western Europe counter- and post-Emancipation ideas such as created modern political anti-Semitism and social radicalism among Gentiles had their influence on Jewish intellectuals, too, but they led only to abandonment of the fold. In Eastern Europe, where the Emancipation was not instituted, a critical attitude to the ideas of enlightened liberalism did not have this effect upon Jewish intellectuals. Other factors of change, the political pressures that provoked waves of emigration and the increasing impoverishment, congestion, and "proletarianization" of the rapidly growing Pale of Settlement, produced new ideologies — Zionism first, followed by Socialism — which found expression within the Jewish community rather than leading to its abandonment.

The core of the Eastern Jewish community, then, remained the tradition, with its uniformity of religious practice and its elastic community organization, its historic and eschatological myth of Exile and Redemption, and its well-established channels of communication to all of Jewry throughout the ages and in all parts of the globe, the Hebrew language and the system of traditional Jewish education.

Jewish nationalism, from the 1880's on, found acceptance within the field dominated by this nucleus, in spite of the laxness of religious practice of some Zionists, because they did not propose an opposing religious code; and in spite of their insistence on a rational solution for the problem of Jewish Exile, because their proposed solution was a reaffirmation of the traditional historic and eschatological myth abandoned, in effect, by Western Jewry; and, finally, because they were no less concerned with Hebrew and Jewish education than were traditional Jews. Consequently, not only secularists but religious Jews participated in the nationalist movement from its inception.

The effect of this partnership, however, was to create, eventually, organizations expressing the differences between religious and secular partisans of Zionism and between Zionist and anti-Zionist factions among religious Jews. Conflicts arose, first within the Hovevei-Zion movement and later within the World Zionist Organization, which caused the traditionalist Zionists to organize, in 1893 and in 1901, as a separate faction in the nationalist movement under the name of Mizrachi (an abbreviation for *merkaz ruhani*, or spiritual center). During Herzl's life, and while the World Zionist Organization was controlled by his successor, David Wolffsohn (1856–1914), the issues between Mizrachi and the secular Zionists were blunted because the movement, concentrating its attention on its diplomatic goals, deliberately avoided discussion or direct pursuit of nationalist cultural aims.

Organizational separatism had been a device adopted by Orthodox Jews in the West, as we have noted, in defense against the domination of the community by adherents of more liberal religious views. Efforts to organize Orthodox Jewry on a world scale and bring Eastern traditionalists into an effective union with Western Orthodoxy came to a head in 1912. In the Zionist Congress of 1911, the rise to power of a faction that demanded greater attention to nationalist cultural aims (as well as more attention to "practical" colonization in Palestine) caused some of the Mizrachi to leave the Zionist Organization. Together with Orthodox groups who had consistently opposed Zionism as a secularist threat to religion, they formed Agudat Israel, a union of Orthodox Jewry which developed a clearly marked anti-Zionist ideology. While the movement was worldwide, it was naturally strongest in Eastern Europe where traditionalism had no rivals as the authentic representative of Jewish religion.

The general political oppression and the peculiar hardships of Jewish life in the Russian Empire produced not only Zionists but social radicals among young Jewish intellectuals in Eastern Europe. They participated from the 1870's in the revolutionary movements that sought to overthrow Russian despotism for the benefit of all the people, and particularly of the Russian peasant. Such preoccupations meant in many cases disregard of the Jewish plight as a minor ill of society. In the course of time, however, the number of Jewish workers in Russian towns grew considerably through the expansion of industry and commerce. Jewish radicals found a broad field for activity in organizing a Jewish proletarian movement. In 1897, the very year when Herzl convened the first Zionist Congress, these men founded the Bund (*Der Algemeyner Idisher Arbeter Bund in Rusland un Poiln*), the socialist and trade union organization of the Jewish workers in Russia and Poland.

The Eastern European Jewish radicals, in many cases, shared far fewer of the traditional, institutional values of the community, especially at the beginning, than did the secular Zionists. Nevertheless, they found that they, too, if they wished, could remain within the bond of unity of Eastern European Jewry. This was possible because the Jewish nationalists had demonstrated that secular versions of Jewish values could be given institutional forms acceptable by the consensus. Some of the radicals were themselves Zionists. Others, while opposed both to Zionism and to traditional values, established themselves as a valid variant of the common *ethos* by following in the paths opened up by Zionism. They learned to appeal to Jewish folk solidarity as a bond of unity which, as the Zionists had shown, persisted even when the uniform religious practice was no longer observed. If they did not accept Hebrew and the traditional culture as channels of communication and consensus, they found acceptance within the community by becoming the protagonists of a conceivable alternative, the Yiddish language and Eastern European folk culture. Thus, social radicals — some Zionist, but more anti-Zionist; usually secularist, but occasionally also religious — found a place in the rapidly changing community and increased its internal divisions.

Founded in the same year as the World Zionist Organization, the Bund conceived itself as the ideological rival of Zionism in the Eastern European community. Soon, however, there crystallized groups of Jewish radicals who opposed the anti-Zionism of the Bund. A variety of Socialist Zionist parties were formed, some organized as factions within the World Zionist Organization, others shunning such an association with the *bourgeoisie* as "class collaborationism."

In addition to the Zionists, Orthodox Zionists and various Socialist Zionist parties, and the anti-Zionist Orthodox and Socialist organizations, the ideological spectrum of Eastern European Jewry was enriched by a variety of other groups often opposed to the Zionists.

Some of the latter parties stressed the need for autonomy in the Diaspora instead of emigration as the means of solving the Jewish problem, while others, the "Territorialist" parties, favored emigration, but to some more suitable land for Jewish colonization than was, in their opinion, Palestine.

In Western Europe, on the other hand, Zionism often had to deal not so much with rival organizations set up in the form of parties as with general communal agencies, many of them established before Zionism. But here, too, Zionism, especially in critical moments that focused attention on ideological issues, encountered opponents in the Jewish community whom it had to overcome or to conciliate in the pursuit of its aims.

Such were the conditions under which the Zionist movement sought to represent the whole Jewish people and to obtain from the international community, on its behalf, those rights and conditions which it regarded as essential for solving the Jewish problem by establishing a sovereign Jewish nation in Palestine.

2 ZIONIST CONCEPTIONS OF SOVEREIGNTY

ISRAEL, the Jewish state, is, of course, the child of Zionism. Zionism is one of a group of modern nationalist movements which sought to gain for a people in full measure those attributes which characterize a modern nation.

What the attributes of a modern nation are may be more clearly defined as an ideal than generalized from the description of "national groups," for many peoples who are considered to represent nationalities or who claim the title of nationality lack one or another of the typical "national" traits in part or in full. Ideally, then, a modern nation possesses a land of its own and a language of its own, and exercises independent sovereignty. Nationalities that have a "consciousness of kind" rooted in a common past but lack one or another of the above attributes or possess them only in part have been prone in modern times to develop nationalist movements, aiming to acquire or recapture the missing elements and so to raise the people to the status of a nation in the full modern sense.

It is well to begin with these commonplaces, because the subject of our study is a far from typical case. By placing Zionism against the background of a common type to which it belongs, we may hope to understand it better as a particular instance.

Thus, as a modern nationalist movement Zionism adopted the standard nationalist aims, and sought to acquire or recapture for the Jews, in full measure, the attributes of a national land, language, and sovereignty. But in view of the gross differences between the Jewish situation and that of other nationalities, Zionism from the beginning added certain obviously necessary supplements to the standard list. A minimum general statement of the Zionist aim would include "securing the survival of the Jewish people" or "solving the Jewish problem" by establishing the Jews in Palestine with all the attributes of a modern nation: land, language, and sovereignty. Moreover, the statement would be inadequate if it did not also add that Zionism aimed at major demographic and occupational shifts in the distribution of the Jews. In more specific terms, the national tasks undertaken by Zionism included the following: not only to develop Hebrew as a secular literary language but to make it the spoken tongue of the Jews; to direct Jewish migration to Palestine and establish a community there which would be free from the social and cultural problems that attended the Jewish status as a dispersed minority people in the Diaspora; and to carry out all the transformations in social and economic distribution, create the appropriate social institutions, and foster the cultural changes necessary for such a program.

If there is any purpose to which a typical modern nationalist movement seems absolutely and unconditionally committed, it is the conquest and the unrestricted exercise of political sovereignty. The other major aims of nationalism — such as the exclusive control of the land and natural resources, or the secure establishment and cultivation of the national language and culture — are not infrequently thought of as means to national ends. The pursuit of such aims may be deliberately restricted or suspended for reasons of policy. Independent India, for example, still recognizes the English language as an official language; and, on the other hand, it has serious difficulty in deciding how its own numerous native languages, instead of creating cultural and social cleavages, may be used in order to create a sense of All-Indian nationality, founded upon the deepest and widest possible social consensus. In the same way, new national states with underdeveloped resources may prefer to encourage investment by granting concessions to foreigners rather than to keep exclusive national control of their resources without the funds to develop them. The Sultan of Morocco and the President of Tunisia retained their repute as nationalists so long as they remained symbolic leaders of the struggle for political sovereignty, even though they wished to follow a policy that would not discourage foreign economic ties. But leaders who incline to be "moderate" in regard to the conquest or exercise of national sovereignty itself are usually given a quite different reception. Such proponents of political compromise are decried as "lackeys" of colonialism and imperialism. The nationalist movement, as though by a mass instinct, rejects them in the same way that the logic of a mass revolutionary impulse passed by Kerensky and swept on to Lenin. It seems to be the very hallmark of a modern nationalist movement, or of a new nation, that it never thinks of its political sovereignty as subordinate to other specific ends.

Nationalists, of course, often speak of a higher significance in their struggle for national sovereignty, and dream, as Giuseppe Mazzini did, that, after liberation, their nation is destined to play a quasi-Messianic role in the historic progress of mankind. Nehru's conception of India as a balance wheel of global politics, a moral force upon whose strength world peace depends, certainly affected his course of action on many occasions. Colonel Nasser dreamt of a role for himself and his people in Arab and world affairs in a way that undoubtedly determined his use of national sovereignty in many instances. But such "subordination" of national sovereignty to higher ends has one important characteristic: the role assigned by Mazzini to Italy, Nehru to India, or Nasser to the expanding Arab Republic could never possibly require that these nations yield or restrict their freedom of sovereign decision. On the contrary, only by acting with complete freedom and self-determination, guided only by the dictates of national individuality, could they conceivably perform the heroic roles allotted to them.

For a true subordination of the demands of national sovereignty to "higher ends," we must seek elsewhere in the modern world. We may find it in nations too well established to need to be nationalist, as in the agreements of the NATO powers, of Benelux, or of the European coal and steel pool. We may also find it, on the other hand, among the more docile of the Communist satellite republics "liberated" after the last war by Soviet armies; but, precisely because of this renunciation of full independence, we consider them to be a phenomenon characteristically different from the typical new nationalist state.

Thus a fierce determination to achieve and preserve national sovereignty seems almost to belong to the very definition of nationalism. Yet there appears to be no inherent reason why sovereignty could not sometimes be subordinated in a true and effective sense to other national ends, just as the national language and the national control of resources have been. In abstract logic, at least, this should be contained within the range of possibilities of the nationalist idea.

In the ideology of the State of Israel, and in the history of the Zionist idea, we have in fact just such a case. Political sovereignty has not been an absolute and unconditional purpose of the Zionist movement at all times without exception, though certainly it was viewed essentially in that light by some almost always and on some occasions by almost all. As a general rule most Zionists, and in some respects almost all Zionists, valued national sovereignty not for its own sake alone, but also as one of the instruments needed for the attainment of other ends of the nationalist movement.

The reasons for this peculiarity in Zionism are easily understood. Other nationalist movements arose among peoples occupying the land where they wished to be free. Consequently, the nationalist myth of freedom, with its call to expel the foreigner, could appeal to powerful popular feelings of rage and envy arising from the continual frictions that mark the relations between peoples when one rules and the other is forced to be subject. Zionism, however, could not evoke an overpowering wave of popular emotion by a simple outcry against the foreign tyrant, for it proposed not to free the Jews in the countries where they were oppressed but to bring them into a new country.

Focusing innumerable resentments in a single myth of liberation and directing them against a concretely visible image of an enemy, nationalism is usually able to brush aside or absorb alternative ideologies that may exist among a subject people. But for Zionism neither the problem it sought to solve nor the enemy it proposed to overcome could come to focus in a single image of mythic concreteness, appealing immediately and intimately to every sort and condition of Jew. The oppression of the Jews was experienced in various forms and degrees in many different lands and under widely differing conditions, while, as we shall see, the Zionist mythos arose from and intimately expressed a particular variant. Hence, from the outset, Zionism was only one among several rival ideologies, and by no means certain to dominate the others because of its mass appeal.

Sovereignty is not only the lack most acutely felt in the ordinary nationalist myth. It also epitomizes every other national aim in nationalist ideologies. Emotional primacy here gives rise to logical precedence. The other national aims, cultural and economic, often seem hardly more than logical consequences of the attainment of political independence. Sovereignty is regarded as a condition precedent for pursuing other aims, but is not related to them as means to end in the value systems of nationalists. Once the people rules itself, national control of resources, national economic reform, or even the more perfect cultivation of the national literature and arts, should follow almost automatically as mere details: this, at least, seems to be the working principle frequently adopted by nationalists. But if it could be shown that the pursuit of political sovereignty, or its free exercise once achieved, interfered with the attainment of national economic or cultural ends, nationalists would not ordinarily agree to defer or restrict the political in favor of the other national aims. On the other hand, since a national cultural revival is generally believed to stimulate the urge to independence, nationalists often favor concentrating attention on this national aim as an immediate objective; but if, for some reason, this is not felt to be the case, they can sacrifice less important cultural (or economic) aims to the primary value of asserting national sovereignty. "When I hear the word 'culture,'" the Nazi leader said, "I reach for my pistol."

Such unquestioned supremacy of the aim of sovereignty could not gain the general consent of all Zionists. The Jewish situation and the Jewish problem were such, prima facie, that other than strictly political aims seemed to many to deserve prior attention. Zionism had first to bring the Jewish people into that land where it hoped ultimately to exercise sovereignty. Also, many felt that it was a primary task to transform Hebrew into a "living language" so that it might be the medium for crystallizing an active national will. For such Zionists the achievement of political sovereignty did not seem to be logically precedent to other national aims. Nor was it conceived as an absolute principle epitomizing all other national ideas and absorbing all other passions of the national movement. If the occupation of land or rejuvenation of the national language rather than political sovereignty engaged immediate attention as the nationalist aim of logically precedent importance, it also became fixed in the feelings of those who most ardently devoted themselves to it as the primary national value. Logical precedence here gave rise to emotional primacy. Thus, different factions arose in the Zionist movement stressing one or another nationalist aim, and one or another aspect of the Jewish problem which this aim was particularly designed to remedy, with no general agreement on the primacy of political sovereignty over other national aims. Such factions, accordingly, evaluated and defined the nationalist aim of sovereignty itself in different ways.

This point can also be stated in the following way: Zionism could afford to be ideologically reasonable, because it was not bound to the nationalist myth of an autochthonous populace aroused to rebellion against foreign rulers. It could regard sovereignty, like any other national aim, either as end or as means, according to circumstances. A Zionist leader could sometimes propose to moderate, modify, or defer the conquest of political sovereignty without serious loss of popular support, as shown by the brilliant career of Chaim Weizmann (1874–1952). For, in the Zionist movement, unlike other nationalist movements, this did not involve frustrating an endemic complex of popular passions which found effective, concentrated expression in the demand of sovereignty.

In Zionism, then, any one of the three major nationalist aims, land, language, or sovereignty, could be made the primary value and the most general end from which all the others were logically derived. Each of these aims, in turn, was valued because it was conceived as the logical means for dealing with the intolerable situation which lay at the roots of the Zionist myth and idea: the Jewish problem, as it became acute for a generation of moderns. Whether land, language, or sovereignty were the particular principle valued as the primary aim and as the logical end of all nationalist policy was a judgment that depended on how the Jewish problem was conceived by one or another type of Zionist, and which of these major nationalist aims seemed, accordingly, the most logical as a direct solution for the problem.

To Theodor Herzl, the Jewish question was most painfully apparent as one of "Judennot" — the plight of the Jews: the civic disabilities, economic restrictions, social oppression and popular hatred suffered by the individual Jews.[1] His critic, Ahad Ha'am,* emphasized that in addition to "Judennot" — the "problem of the Jews" — there existed another, even more important aspect of the Jewish problem, the "problem of Judaism." For what he, as a modern man, found most intolerable in the Jewish situation was the dissolving consensus of the Jewish people because of the loss of faith among the "enlightened" and the apparent irrelevance to modern conditions of the faith of the Orthodox.

For Zionists of the type of Ahad Ha'am, the primary, immediate objective of the nationalist movement, the national aim that was logically demanded by the situation, was to revive a secular Jewish culture through the medium of the Hebrew language, and so to re-establish the consensus of the Jewish people, as the prerequisite condition for pursuing other national aims. They had varying attitudes to other nationalist activities — such as encouraging emigration from the Diaspora and resettling the land in Palestine — which were logically related to the Jewish problem conceived as one of *Judennot*. Only under special circumstances did a small group develop who were ready for far-reaching compromises regarding land (including immigration) and sovereignty as national aims, if permitted to cultivate the national language and culture in Palestine. But if a secular

* Ahad Ha'am ("One of the People"): pseudonym of Asher Ginzberg (1856–1927); Hebrew publicist and editor; leader of B'nei Moshe, 1889–1896.

Jewish culture were to be revived, this end itself required as its necessary means resettlement, under conditions of relative autonomy, by a small, devoted nucleus that could constitute a soundly based, well-rooted Jewish society in Palestine; for only the spontaneous life of such a national entity could give substance and elasticity to the new secular Jewish culture. Nor did "cultural Zionists," as a rule, remain insensitive to the need for solving the "problem of the Jews" as well as the "problem of Judaism" in Palestine. But since this was not what they valued as a primary aim, they could consider the problem skeptically. Well aware of the oppression of the Jews and their need to emigrate at once from the centers of severest hardship, the cultural Zionists might doubt that Palestine, in their own day, could provide for this necessity. They might feel that only after the Jewish people had been rejuvenated and invigorated by its revived culture, could it undertake — if at all — the long, historic task of resettling en masse in Palestine and reclaiming sovereignty there. They might even feel that the Jewish settlement in Palestine would always remain a relatively small enclave in that country, though sufficiently established and independent to develop its own authentic culture; while the mass of the Jewish people, continuing in the Diaspora, would be consolidated by the cultural influence of the nucleus.

All these, however, usually remained nuances of belief rather than principles around which groups were organized. What has been called "cultural Zionism" appealed to men in whom the undermining of tradition and the disillusioning impact of the modern Jewish situation had created a state of intellectual disorientation. Such a condition was traumatic in its effect, but it was an emotional upheaval which extended, not to the whole people, but only to intellectual groups. Consequently, cultural Zionism did not emerge as the ideological principle of a partisan, political grouping in Jewish life. The nearest it came to becoming a full-fledged ideology was at its inception in the 1890's when, in the ebb of the Hovevei-Zion movement, Ahad Ha'am himself, together with a group of friends, sought to revive the nationalist spirit by organizing the elite secret society of "B'nei Moshe." * Apart from this effort, cultural Zionism — in which language became a primary aim — exercised its influence not as a power-oriented organization but as a pervasive idea that affected groupings organized around other principles. The national aims of

* "B'nei Moshe" (Sons of Moses) was a secret order on Masonic lines organized in 1889 in the hope of reviving the Hovevei-Zion movement by giving it a disciplined controlling group of men devoted to the Hebrew culture and national cause.

land and sovereignty, on the other hand, were primary principles around which Zionist partisans organized themselves.

The Zionists who considered most pressing not "the problem of Judaism" but "the problem of the Jews" — the need for immediate mass migration and, at the same time, for escaping the plague of anti-Semitism and alienhood which dogged the Jews' footsteps wherever they went as a minority — may be roughly divided into two groups. Both groups agreed that the terms of the problem dictated a single solution — a territory where the Jews could concentrate as a majority and exercise national sovereignty; as Zionists, moreover, they specified Palestine as the Jewish territory. But one group considered sovereignty itself the primary national aim: they believed that before an effective demographic concentration in Palestine could begin, the establishment of the Jewish claim to sovereignty there was essential. The other group felt that settlement of the land was the first task, and that only on the basis of effective occupation by Jewish settlers could the claim of Jewish sovereignty be sustained. The history of organized Zionism is essentially a record of the debates between these two views and of the successive achievements along each of the two lines.

The distinction between the two groups was not made at once. The earliest Zionists of real historic significance, the Hovevei-Zion and BILU * groups of the 1880's, did not develop any true ideological debate over the question of the precedence of the Zionist hen or the Zionist egg: whether concentration in the land logically preceded sovereignty or vice-versa. They were prepared to try both approaches, as occasion permitted. In the very beginning, some of the BILU group made their way to Palestine without preliminaries, while others went to Constantinople to seek from the Porte the necessary authority and facilities for the settlement of their members.[2] Just at that time the Turks, turning against Britain, turned decisively also against projects for Jewish immigration and resettlement in Palestine, with which the British had long been somewhat vaguely associated. And not only the Jewish Zionists, but Laurence Oliphant (1829–1888) and Edward Cazalet (1827–1883), who were promoting plans for Jewish resettlement in Palestine, were decisively turned down.[3] Thereupon, also, the Turks began to enforce far stricter regulations than before in order to discourage Jewish immigration.

* BILU: acrostic of "Beit Ya'akov l'khu v'nelkha" — "House of Jacob, come, let us go" (Isa. 2:5). A student and youth organization organized in Russia in 1882 for immigration and settlement as farm workers in Palestine.

Under these circumstances, the Zionist movement of the eighties and nineties disregarded political aims and methods. It went ahead with immigration and resettlement in Palestine regardless of legal status and in spite of legal restrictions. The achievements of the movement were disappointing, however, and, in assessing the inadequate results, the question of the tactics that should be adopted in resettling Palestine became an issue of ideological debate. On the one hand, the "cultural Zionists" argued from the premise of the slow and insecure resettlement to the conclusion that Palestine could not solve "the problem of the Jews" under existing circumstances. Consequently, the immediate task was to solve "the problem of Judaism." On the other hand, when Theodor Herzl formulated his own version of Zionism, he, too, drew major ideological conclusions from his analysis of the shortcomings of the earlier resettlement projects. He set up a programmatic tenet disavowing any settlement of Palestine by "infiltration," and contending that a charter for colonization must be secured before colonization should be undertaken at all.[4]

The Basle program, adopted by the First Zionist Congress in 1897, laid down a compromise formula in which these differences of opinion, or of nuance, were elided or harmonized. The first sentence of that program, generally used as a slogan to stand for the whole, declared the Zionist aim to be "the establishment of a home (*Heimstaette*) for the Jewish people secured under public law in Palestine."[5] This formula, together with the additional proviso that "all those Jews who could not or would not assimilate" were to go to the Jewish homeland, was used by Herzl as his own short definition of Zionism.[6] But the Basle program, in addition to stating the aim, also formulated in four paragraphs the means to be employed. Taking these in reverse order, we find that the Zionist movement committed itself to the following immediate objectives: preparatory steps toward securing the "governmental acts of approval" (*Regierungszustimmungen*) needed to achieve the Zionist aim; the strengthening of Jewish national consciousness; the organization of all Jewry through local and general institutions, consonant with the laws of each country; and the "appropriate" (*zweckdienliche*) resettlement of Palestine by Jewish farmers, artisans, and entrepreneurs.

There was little room for doubting what Herzl, and the Congress at large, meant by the significant insertion of "appropriate." It was made sufficiently clear that, in the Zionist view, further colonization should really stop until a proper basis "under public law" had been secured by diplomacy.[7] Yet the formula also provided houseroom in the Zionist organization for those who contended, as some did during the Congress, that the "practical" work of resettlement should go forward without interruption. Nevertheless, the enthusiasm engendered by the Congress was all centered on the new approach, then elevated to a doctrinal principle, which held that the negotiation of a political status in Palestine — the aim of sovereignty — was the royal road to the triumph of Zionism, and hence to the solution of the Jewish problem. The recognition given to the practical work of colonization — the aim of land — was a concession to vested interests and to counsels of caution which aroused no enthusiasm at the time; hence they had not the force of a principle.

But times changed, and with them evaluations. As the obstacles to practical colonization by Herzl's predecessors had engendered disappointment and only a new approach was able to arouse enthusiasm, so the frustration of Herzl's diplomacy led in turn to a mood of depression. This reached a traumatic climax in the Sixth and Seventh Zionist Congresses in 1903 and 1905. Failing to progress in his negotiations for a charter for Palestine and oppressed by the growing need for Jewish emigration, Herzl turned to East Africa as a "Nachtasyl," a temporary national home, until Palestine should become available. This proposal was bitterly opposed in the Sixth Congress, and its rejection by the Seventh Congress, after Herzl's death, split the organization.[8] Out of the despondency of that time, however, a new principle arose to engender enthusiasm: the principle, this time, of colonization regardless of legal or any other obstacles, until the desired political status should become practicable as a crowning achievement of Zionism. In the wake of the Russian upheavals following the Russo-Japanese war, a wave of rebellious young Zionists went to Palestine and achieved two triumphs of mythic impact: they established Hebrew as a spoken language and they created a prototype of the Jewish farmer-worker in Palestine.[9] Following 1908, the World Zionist Organization, soon to be dominated by the late Herzl's opponents, the Practical Zionists, undertook a program of specific experiments and projects of actual colonization, under whatever legal conditions they could obtain at that time. But the critical success of Practical Zionism was, after all, its negotiation of the Balfour Declaration and the Jewish national home clauses in the Palestine Mandate after World War I, the long-sought-for charter that Herzl had set as Zionism's first aim.[10]

After the charter had been secured, ideological dispute within the Zionist movement did not cease but continued to rage over the question whether political sovereignty or the effective occupation of the land should be defined as the immediate objective of the Zionist movement. The debate over this point even after the charter was gained revealed the ambiguity essentially involved in sovereignty as a Zionist aim, when this sovereignty applied to a country the Jews did not yet effectively occupy.

It became clear, in the very heat of arriving at an agreed formula for the Balfour Declaration and in the ensuing debates, that Herzl's formula for the aim of Jewish sovereignty was subject to conflicting interpretations. That this was the case had been apparent even at the First Zionist Congress, where the question that led to the most pointed definition of rival opinions had been precisely the formulation of the aim of sovereignty.

In order to facilitate negotiations with the Turks, as well as to still fears of hostile reactions against the existing colonies by the Turks or against the Hovevei-Zion societies by the Russian government, the drafting committee headed by Max Nordau (1849–1923) had avoided an outright demand for a Jewish state in Palestine, just as Herzl had learned to do in his first Constantinople negotiations.[11] Instead, the committee proposed a formula stating that Zionism aimed to obtain a "legally secured home for the Jewish people in Palestine."[12] This seemed to many delegates to water down unduly the formulation of the ultimate aim of Zionism, to obscure the Zionist intention to set up a Jewish state, and to blur that decisive difference from previous attempts at resettlement which gave the Zionist movement its *élan*. Those delegates argued that the formula could be interpreted as claiming no more than the normal rights of private individuals to buy real estate and develop it; and they demanded that in order to stress the essential character of a Zionist charter the congress should demand "a home for the Jewish people, secured by *international law*, in Palestine." Such phrasing seemed to Herzl impolitic, in view of the Turks' suspicion of foreign intervention and their fear of new movements for national independence, as well as narrower than was necessary in order to imply that Zionism sought to restore Jewish sovereignty in Palestine. Instead Herzl proposed the formula finally adopted — one which he felt made clear the distinction from normal rights of individuals to purchase and develop real estate — that Zionism aimed to achieve "a home for the Jewish people secured under *public law* in Palestine."[13] This left open certain major questions: was the "sovereignty" Zionism aimed at nothing more than the charter, that is, a concession to develop large, continuous areas of Palestine and maintain communal autonomy there, or did Zionism intend at some future date to claim the right to independence of a people occupying its own land?

Major ideological differences which developed after the Balfour Declaration revolved around the question whether to leave this matter open, as Herzl had done, or to close it by a new definition. The first course — the course Herzl had adopted — was advocated by his erstwhile opponents, the Practical Zionists, while the latter course — from which Herzl had dissuaded the First Congress — was pressed by those who saw themselves as his heirs, the Revisionist-Zionists, headed by Vladimir Jabotinsky (1880–1940).

The differences which arose on these issues are not to be explained solely as ultimate or temperamental in character, as though they were based merely on the arbitrary preferences of contending groups for full or for restricted national freedom. Apart from the irrational preferences they may reflect, the opposing formulations of the Zionist aim of sovereignty each had its own rational connection with the other aims of Zionist nationalism and with the different ways in which the rival parties visualized the achievement of those aims. The Revisionists contended that Zionism should now go beyond the deliberately vague Basle formula and declare that it demanded as its ultimate goal (*Endziel*) "a Jewish State within its historic boundaries" — that is, extending over the entire area of the Mandate, including Transjordan. In taking this position, they were not moved by sheer fetishism of the myth image of the state, however much they cultivated it as a movement fetish. The political tactics they proposed had above all a logical connection with their views about the way in which Zionism should proceed to settle the country, now that they had a charter for the purpose in the form of Balfour Declaration; about the attitude the Zionist Organization should take in its negotiations with the British and other authorities concerning the interpretation and implementing of the charter, and in particular concerning its territorial extension; and, also, about the proper Zionist policies for dealing with the opposed interests of Arab nationalism.[14] The majority of Zionists, who favored retaining the Basle formula unchanged, were motivated not by opposition (in most cases) to the ultimate establishment of a Jewish state as the final expression of the national aim of sovereignty. They differed from the Revisionists, and also differed among themselves, about the ways in which Zionism should proceed to settle the country, now that they had a charter for the purpose in the form of the Balfour Declaration; about the attitude the Zionist Organization should take in its negotiations with the British and other authorities concerning the interpretation and implementing of the charter, and in particular concerning its territorial extension; and also about the proper Zionist policies for dealing with the opposed interests of Arab nationalism.

Thus, for most participants, the quarrel concerning the *Endziel* was not really over the ultimate sovereignty of the Jewish state, even though it revolved about the question whether this should or should not now be stated as the Zionist aim. The quarrel was really about the kind and degree of authority exercised by themselves, or the kind of "colonization regime" instituted by the Mandatory power, that the Zionists required in the interim period of immigration and colonization.

If one were to set up a paradigm of the mental construction represented by Zionist Revisionism, one would have to begin with a characteristic perception of the Jewish problem. This extreme of Zionism arose out of a view which regarded the Jewish problem as first and foremost "the problem of the Jews," of their rightlessness and oppression, and of their rejection even by emancipated and enlightened Gentile society. The Jewish problem, as viewed by men like Pinsker, Nordau, Herzl, and Jabotinsky, was overwhelmingly the problem of anti-Semitism, which they came to regard as ineradicable so long as Jews persisted as a distinct group among Gentiles. However, when the Jewish nation rose to claim its rights to sovereignty in its ancestral homeland, the other nations would ultimately recognize this right, because, in this age of Enlightenment, they no less than the Jews must be interested in curing the plague of anti-Semitism. Thus Jews and Gentiles alike would agree to a supreme political act of emancipation, the grant of a charter under public law, which would once and for all make possible a rational solution of the Jewish problem.[15]

Such a solution was visualized by these men in the form of a vast, planned project of social engineering eliminating virtually at one blow, or in a series of stages, the "problem of the Jews."[16] Zionists of this type tended to envisage the transfer of the Jewish nation to Palestine as a rapid, large-scale movement. Such a conception could only be put into effect if the "colonization regime" to be established by the charter (or by the "suzerain power") met rather stringent requirements. All the powers of a modern state — or rather the extraordinary powers (exceeding what a modern democratic state often permits itself) characteristic of a colonial concessionaire — would not be too much to equip the proposed Jewish company for such a task. Moreover the determined cooperation of the governments of the lands from which Jews were to come, as well as of that controlling the land in which the company would colonize, was no less essential. Such were the prerequisite means to the grand project of mass transfer envisaged by those Zionists; and such is the actual denotation of the aims comprehended under the Revisionist slogan of the Jewish state as the avowed *Endziel* of the Zionist movement. In this extreme position of Zionist nationalism, the sovereign Jewish state was not, as in other nationalisms, to be the condition precedent for achieving all other national aims; but extraordinary powers, approaching or even exceeding those common in many sovereign states, were to be exercised by a Jewish company so that, with international cooperation, the other Jewish national aims — immigration, occupation of land, and social integration — might first be achieved, with the independent, sovereign Jewish state coming thereafter as the crowning, ultimate achievement.

We see, then, that even for the Zionists most markedly political in their approach, the aim of sovereignty was connected pragmatically with the other aims of their Zionist ideology, and not set apart as an absolute condition of all of them, as a fetishistic demand flowing directly from irrational or mythic sources. Thus, on occasion, the most extreme political Zionists could modify or mitigate their demands of sovereignty, or subordinate the exercise of sovereignty to other national aims which at the moment seemed more pressing. We have already noted how at the First Zionist Congress, Herzl and Nordau argued for a formulation of the Zionist aim regarding sovereignty which would allow the greatest flexibility in negotiation, and permit the future, with its unpredictable circumstances, to determine the ultimate kind and degree of authority that would characterize the Jewish state.

Not only Herzl and Nordau, but Jabotinsky, too, demonstrated repeatedly how the peculiar situation of Zionism forced the most "extreme nationalists" to mitigate, defer, and subordinate the demand of sovereignty. Like other Zionists in the period before the First World War, he treated the aim of Jewish sovereignty in Palestine as a maximum program to be worked for at some more suitable juncture of events in the future, while other, minimum but more immediate, objectives — land and language — were pursued at once. He worked ardently for Hebrew as the spoken language and language of instruction of the Jews in the Diaspora; he supported the immigration and resettlement in Palestine of pioneers who built positions of Jewish strength in the country, without waiting for suitable legal political guarantees and regardless of unfavorable local conditions;

and he argued for the organization and legal recognition of the Jews in Diaspora countries, particularly in Russia, as a distinct nationality, like the Poles or Ukrainians.[17]

These activities could perhaps be dismissed as coming before Jabotinsky fully worked out his doctrine of "monolithic" Zionism. But his attitudes in the later period of his life no less clearly demonstrated readiness to treat the question of sovereignty in a far from fetishistic manner. He *opposed* the autonomous organization of a Jewish self-defense corps, or of the Jewish school system in Palestine under the Mandate, since he insisted that both must be organized by the Mandate government, made subordinate to its officers, and operated under its immediate authority and directions.[18] The reason for this refusal, on the part of a Jabotinsky, to approve the exercise of Jewish quasi-sovereignty, the growth of a state within the Mandate state, was, of course, that he felt that such a policy would interfere with a more important objective: to make the establishment of the Jewish state the direct aim and responsibility of Mandate policy. If the Jews undertook to defend, educate, and colonize themselves, this would only make it easier for the mandatary to avoid the responsibility for creating the Jewish state. Jabotinsky, at times, almost despaired of Britain's being won over fully to the Zionist program, as he had originally despaired of Turkey, and was inclined to seek allies elsewhere. But the idea of an alliance with an existing sovereign power, as a prerequisite for "evacuating" the mass of Jews to Palestine and for setting up the Jewish state on the basis of a Jewish majority, was his ruling idea. While he was sometimes sympathetic to the view that positions of power should be built by Jews in Palestine without waiting for such an alliance, he was ready to oppose Jewish autonomy if he felt it gave Britain an excuse for not acting directly to build the Jewish state. In the interests of the grand alliance that would make possible the great evacuation, he was inclined to regard as "expendable" any nuclei of sovereignty, as well as of economic or social power, that could be built in Palestine by the Jews alone.[19]

The great majority of Zionists, who supported Weizmann's "organic" Zionism against Jabotinsky's "monolithic" Zionism, refused to define a Zionist *Endziel*, preferring to build the Jewish national home, man by man, farmstead by farmstead, under the increasingly modest interpretations of the Balfour Declaration and the Mandate.[20] It hardly needs demonstrating that they were prepared to modify and moderate the Zionist demand for sovereignty, to consider it a means as well as an end, and to subordinate it sometimes to other national aims.

Jabotinskian Zionism was led, in the final analysis, to disparage the slow growth of a Zionist community in Palestine as "expendable" in the name of a "political offensive" that was to achieve the mass evacuation of Jews from Europe. The premise with which organic Zionism began was quite the opposite. Weizmann's Zionism tended to regard any particular set of political conditions as nonessential for the real immediate aim of Zionism, the aim which could never be given less than the most concentrated and the most purposeful attention. That aim was the gradual building up on sound social, cultural, and economic foundations of the Jewish settlement in Palestine, against the time when the political future of the country would have to be determined. Any formulation of Zionism which could possibly halt the growth of the existing community by forcing issues such as that of the political sovereignty of the country, any view which regarded the existing community and the status it had achieved as, in the last analysis, expendable in a dubious struggle to obtain better political conditions, was opposed by Weizmann. On the other hand, Weizmann, and especially the settlers in Palestine who swung to his view, nurtured with great care every seed of autonomy and of political organization of the Jewish community itself: its independent school system, self-defense corps, institutions of self-government, and above all, its network of agricultural settlements.[21]

Thus both the "extremists" and the "moderate" majority among Zionists were prepared to regard "sovereignty" as either end or means, and, considered as means, as either "expendable" or as "indispensable" — depending upon the definition given to the term "sovereignty." The verbal line of division between the "extremists" and the "moderates" was over the question whether the Basle program of the World Zionist Organization should or should not be replaced by a formal avowal of the aim of a Jewish state. What actually divided them, however, was not a verbal but a pragmatic issue, hinging on the practical effects of adopting a new formula.

The Revisionist proposal to stake everything on this redefinition logically implied the view that the indispensable means to the Zionist national aim was such a colonial regime in Palestine and such policies regarding the Jews everywhere as would make possible a rapid mass migration to that country: specifically, a Mandatory policy unequivocally directed to this end and implemented by officers sympathetic to it; a world-wide Jewish company endowed with extraordinary powers to control immigration; and a policy in the countries whence Jews emigrated favorable to their orderly mass evacuation. For the sake of these goals, the indispensable means both to the solution of the Jewish problem and to the creation of the Jewish state, the Revisionists were prepared to consider expendable the autonomous institutions of the Jews in Palestine, and, in the last analysis, the community itself.

The great majority of Zionists, on the other hand, considered that the achievement of the Zionist aim — the aim of a Jewish state devoted to the solution of the Jewish problem — required as its indispensable means the sound establishment and the steady development, the expansion and extension, of the existing settlement in Palestine: specifically, the selective immigration of pioneers qualified to establish farm settlements and a Jewish working class; the gradual investment of capital not in speculative but in productive enterprise; and the organic growth of Jewish autonomous economic, political, social and cultural institutions. As long as they were given what they thought to be acceptable conditions for continued work along these lines, the majority of Zionists — however ardently they wished for a firm pro-Zionist Mandatory policy — were ready to regard any particular form of colonial regime in Palestine as, in the final analysis, expendable.

Just as the Zionist extremists, so the more characteristic form of Zionism had a logical relationship to the way in which the Jewish problem was perceived and its solution imagined. Indeed, the "organic" Zionists may be divided into two groups, according to their view of the Jewish problem. Some saw the problem as primarily a "problem of Judaism." For them, the question was essentially one of finding a new basis of validity for a Jewish culture that had lost its religious sanction, and of establishing a new consensus for a secularized Jewish people. An autonomous community in Israel spontaneously generating a characteristic Jewish culture was regarded as an indispensable means for the solution of the Jewish problem so conceived. But the idea of creating that community through a process of mass evacuation and rapid resettlement was at best irrelevant to the cultural end the community had to serve, and at worst antagonistic to it, since it was likely that nothing but a new Babel would emerge from such a mass migration.[22]

Others among the great majority who favored "organic" Zionism saw "the problem of the Jews," not "the problem of Judaism," as the main problem to be solved. However, they could not accept the view that the proper political conditions were the only indispensable means needed for solving "the problem of the Jews," while all economic, social, and cultural preconditions were mere matters of detail. Their dissent arose either from skepticism about the idea of mass evacuation or from opposition to it. Skepticism about a mass migration to Palestine as a practical possibility was widespread in the period following Herzl's unsuccessful diplomacy, when the main current of Jewish emigration flowed from Europe to countries other than Palestine; and it remained strong in the early days of the Mandate, when Palestine proved unable at first to absorb a large influx. At such times the idea took shape of a selective immigration to Palestine, motivated by the Zionist idea, as the indispensable preliminary means to lay the groundwork for eventual mass immigration. Only after the select community should establish sound social and economic, as well as cultural foundations, only through building up its own powers of self-government — all this on the basis of whatever legal recognition it could obtain — would Zionism be able to claim larger political authority, and, in the end, be equipped socially, economically, and culturally to solve the "problem of the Jews." Moreover, when the Revisionists, in the thirties, revived the idea of a mass evacuation of Jews through an agreement with Poland, it was condemned by their opponents as a proposal to surrender Jewish rights to a hostile government.[23]

The political conditions that had been attained under the Mandate were so much superior to the situation in Palestine before the First World War that no matter how they were restricted in application there were, at first, great and demanding tasks immediately available to challenge enthusiasm — or to solace the bitterness of those who had suffered the anti-Jewish ferocity of the postwar days in Europe. Then, too, the great mass of migrants continued in the early twenties to seek other havens than Palestine; and when the United States began to be closed, the path of least resistance still led to Canada or South Africa or to South America sooner than it led to Palestine. Thus, even when Transjordan was closed to Jewish development and when tests of "economic absorptive capacity" were imposed upon Jewish labor immigration, the scope for development works immediately available in Palestine was still greater than the Jews could handle with the immigrant manpower and capital resources at hand. Moreover, if a clear political decision were to be challenged, another claimant, the awakening Arab nationalists, bid fair to win the award of Palestine rather than the Jews, who were in a distinct minority.

However conditions began gradually but decisively to alter. The Jewish need and capacity for developing Palestine began to strain against the increasingly restricted legal and political possibilities. On the other hand, Arab nationalism and the general development of world affairs began ever more insistently to press the political issue.

The stream of Jewish immigration in the late twenties and the thirties turned overwhelmingly towards Palestine. The omens of this change became apparent not long after the First World War in the new American immigration acts which foreshadowed a period when Jewish emigrants and refugees would find doors closed against them in all parts of the world. In the thirties, the era of Hitler, Jewish fugitives from Central Europe found in Palestine, before all other havens, their major hope of resettlement. And the culmination of this growing and spreading crisis came in the Second World War, when the Jewish community of Palestine, alone in the entire world, was unreservedly ready for anything that might rescue the doomed Jews of Europe from methodical extermination and offer them a new home.

With a progression equally rapid and fateful, the trend of world politics sharpened the political issues surrounding Palestine to the point where final decisions would have to be made. The original stimulus that the First World War had given to Arab nationalism was succeeded by the far stronger encouragement of the Era of Appeasement, when Arab policy found itself in the position it has been able to exploit more or less continuously ever since: it was wooed by both sides in a global conflict. In Palestine, the rival claims of Zionism spurred Arab nationalism to still greater energy and persistence in seeking, while the Arabs still formed a majority, to force from the British government final policy decisions on the question of sovereignty.

A specific context channeled the influence of these forces upon the ideological positions of the majority of Zionists: they made their impact through their effects upon the development of the existing community under the Mandatory regime. By successive restrictions, the prospects for further growth of the Jewish settlement in Palestine were narrowed to the vanishing point. Restrictions began, indeed, to be applied from the very beginning of the Mandatory regime, and, they were a precipitating cause of the ideological division between Revisionism and organic Zionism as early as 1925. However, in the course of time the majority of Jews, while determined to continue building and to defer final political decisions as long as possible, were nevertheless more and more acutely aware that the scope within which they could build was continually contracting — and that final political decisions might be upon them before they were prepared. These threatening prospects became imminent realities when the British government adopted the policy of the 1939 White Paper. In pursuance of the principles of this document, the Zionists were permitted to buy land freely only in 5 per cent of Palestine and that, too, in an area where Jews were most thickly settled; after the admission of a maximum of 75,000 additional Jews over a period of five years, Jewish immigration was to cease, unless the Arabs were "prepared to acquiesce in it"; and, British policy set itself the objective of establishing within ten years an independent "Palestinian" (i.e., Arab) state, if conditions permitted.[24]

Moreover, the mounting persecution of Jews in Europe confronted the Jewish national home with the imperative demand that, rather than continue preparing for the function it was intended to perform in solving the "problem of the Jews," it begin performing that function. The Evian Conference of 1938 focused a harsh light upon the inability and unwillingness of the rest of the world to offer Jewish refugees a haven,[25] and every moment in those tense prewar days made the need to escape more desperate. The war and the extermination of the Jews that soon began involved the deepest and most human passions not only of the Jews but of all of the world in any way concerned with the "problem of the Jews." At the same time the strategies of war reinforced the very calculations which had led Britain to issue the White Paper and close Palestine to Jewish refugees.

Under these pressures, new attitudes developed among various Zionist ideological groupings regarding the aim of national sovereignty. Among the majority of Zionists, during the long crisis of the Hitler era, there developed the position defined by the Biltmore program of 1942, which came to fruition in the proclamation of the State of Israel in 1948.

The Biltmore formula, subsequently adopted in substance by the great majority of Jews, Zionist and officially non-Zionist alike,[26] was in many ways the kind of definition of the aim of sovereignty long demanded by the Revisionists. The Revisionists took it as such, and rejoined the World Zionist Organization in 1946, disbanding the New Zionist Organization they had formed in 1935.[27] Yet the seeming general acceptance of a Revisionist formula, forced by the trend of events in 1942, actually veiled continuing sharp differences among the Zionists on the practical attitudes to be taken regarding Jewish sovereignty in Palestine after the war.

The Biltmore program,[28] denouncing the 1939 White Paper in Winston Churchill's words as "a breach and a repudiation of the Balfour Declaration," called for fulfilment of the underlying purpose of the Mandate for Palestine. That purpose it declared to be to establish Palestine as a Jewish commonwealth. In order to bring this about, however, it made proposals which differed radically from the position the Revisionists had originally taken. Far from relying on the Mandatory power to create the conditions which would establish the Jewish state, the Biltmore conference demanded that full powers to achieve this aim be delegated to the Jewish Agency for Palestine. The Agency was to be authorized not only "to direct and regulate immigration into Palestine," as the Revisionists, too, had demanded, but "to develop to the maximum the agricultural and industrial possibilities and the natural resources of the country, and to utilize its uncultivated and unoccupied lands for Jewish colonization and for the benefit of the country as a whole." In other words, all powers for the development of the country were to pass into the hands of the autonomous institutions of the Jews, built up over the years in Palestine and throughout the world in order to cooperate in implementing the Mandate. The mandatary, confidence in whom had dwindled to the vanishing point, was to retain only the ultimate sanctions of sovereignty for a certain time. When the war ended, masses of Jews, whose survival the conference prayed for, would be rapidly resettled in Palestine by the Jewish Agency. After a Jewish majority had been established in the country, the Jewish commonwealth would take over the remaining powers still exercised by the mandatary.

Like many another position taken on legal and moral grounds, the Biltmore program contained an internal contradiction, for it implicitly assumed that reality was opposed to its demands. It was obviously out of lack of confidence in the mandatary's willingness to be responsible for turning Palestine into a Jewish commonwealth that the Biltmore conference demanded the necessary powers to enable the Jewish Agency to do this. Those who drafted this demand were not naive enough to suppose that the mandatary, who was unwilling to be directly responsible for making Palestine a Jewish state, would be easily induced to let the Jewish Agency do it, while itself exercising authority in Palestine solely to keep order against Arab resistance. They knew too well that, in fact, the set policy of Britain was to write off its obligations to the Jews through the White Paper and to use its authority to subdue Jewish resistance. Accordingly, a crucial question of tactics arose: how did the Zionists propose, in practice, to achieve the Biltmore aim? The Biltmore program merely defined a "maximum objective" upon which there was massive agreement. Under the cover of its general formulas, there were ideologically based differences regarding the tactics to be used in accomplishing the Biltmore objectives, or regarding alternative "minimum objectives" that might be resorted to.

Roughly speaking, there was a fourfold division on the question of alternatives to the Jewish commonwealth: there were those Zionists who opposed this formula outright, and stood for some kind of binational Jewish-Arab state in Palestine; there were those, on the other hand, who insisted that not simply Palestine, but Palestine on both sides of the Jordan must be established as a Jewish state; there were those who on no account would agree to set up the Jewish state in anything less than the whole of Palestine west of the Jordan; and finally, there were those (and they turned out to be the bulk of the Zionists) who were prepared, if it seemed essential on behalf of other national aims, to set up the Jewish state in part of Palestine. But whatever the ultimate aim regarding the form and extent of statehood, each group found itself further perplexed by problems concerning the tactics to be adopted in achieving its goal. For none of the four variants of the Zionist aim regarding sovereignty was likely to be realized if the policy in force at the time went unopposed.

The idea of a binational Jewish-Arab state had among its supporters many who were inclined to regard Zionism as a solution not primarily of "the problem of the Jews" but of the "problem of Judaism." But the most active binationalist lobbying was occasioned by the approach of the political crisis in Palestine, at a time when the "problem of the Jews" was rapidly taking the grim shape of the Hitler refugee.[29] No Jew in that period could formulate a Zionist theory or a solution for the Palestine problem which did not provide for the immigration of Jewish refugees to Palestine. How to reverse the political trends which were closing the doors of Palestine against the refugees became for the binationalists, as well as for all other Zionist ideologists, a cardinal question of tactics.

The binationalist solution was proposed by Zionists who, on various ideological grounds, were most sensitive to the need for obtaining Arab consent to the form of statehood that should ultimately be established in Palestine. For some the reason was the kind of religious pacifism, for others the kind of socialist internationalism that gave them their basic ideological orientations. In either case, an acute tactical problem arose. For, however much they might castigate other Zionists for insufficient efforts to seek agreement with the Arabs, the Zionist binationalists knew that their own best efforts were not likely to secure Arab agreement to a binationalist state in Palestine, or to any further Jewish immigration.[30] The socialists sought an ideological escape from the dilemma in their hope for the ulti-

mate emergence of socialist governments in Europe and for a socialist overturn in the Middle East which would bring to power new
forces amenable to a binationalist solution. In the meantime, they opposed the Biltmore program, as well as the implied alternative of
partition, which would introduce a political division between Jews
and Arabs as a final solution of the Palestine problem.[31] The religious
pacifists looked to enlightened public opinion in Britain and the civilized world at large with similar hopes. They proposed, in the end,
that, with the support of such a consensus, Britain should impose
a just solution of the Palestine problem upon both Jews and Arabs.
Such a solution, they thought, should establish a binational state
with certain guarantees of continued Jewish immigration.[32]

At the opposite extreme were the Revisionists, who had never
believed that Jewish policy could expect to obtain Arab consent until
after the Jewish state was established.[33] Despite a vague tendency
to be satisfied with the Biltmore program — which ultimately led
some Revisionists to leave their own organization — the Revisionists
as a body continued to differ with other Zionists in their demand for
a Jewish state extending over both sides of the Jordan. Moreover,
the official Revisionist organization was under pressure from more
extreme groups. For, during the critical decade preceding the rise
of the Jewish state in 1948, the loosely connected paramilitary *Irgun
Ts'vaï Le'umi* * pursued objectives and adopted tactics of its own to
which the official Revisionist movement had to adjust ideologically.

The Revisionist tradition laid great emphasis upon a political
and diplomatic "offensive" in favor of Jewish demands in Palestine.
The Revisionists, like other Zionists, urged their claims on the legal
basis of the Balfour Declaration and the Mandate, and made their
appeal to the conscience of the global community, particularly of
the Western Allies. While arguing the same case before the same
tribunal, the Revisionists — and particularly some of their associated
groups — conducted their own propaganda independently of and
even in opposition to that of the Zionist organization.[34] One Revisionist offshoot, the Fighters for Israel's Freedom or "Stern Group", lost
hope in the West and, following an example set by Jabotinsky, was
ready to try alternative alliances. Some of its leaders did not hesitate to seek ties with an Axis partner, Fascist Italy, during the war,
and after the war's close some leaned toward a working arrangement
with the Soviet Union.[35]

* *Irgun Ts'vaï Le'umi* ("National Military Organization"): founded in 1937
by a group of leaders of the Zionist Revisionists and of their autonomous youth
movement.

But major emphasis was also laid by the Revisionists, and particularly by their splinter groups, on a new tactic of armed resistance to British policy. They initiated a campaign of terrorism with the avowed aim of undermining British rule and forcing the mandatary to abandon Palestine.[36] There was no lack of ideology to justify and rationalize the choice of these tactics; but in addition they had behind them the force of powerful emotional needs which were widespread in the Jewish community in Palestine and throughout the world. The resistance of Revisionist-inspired guerillas to Britain differed from the tactics of resistance adopted by the Hagana,* in giving direct and uninhibited expression to these deep passions. The terrorists justified their tactics by rational arguments claiming to prove that they were the only effective way to secure Jewish national aims in Palestine.[37] But they served another, primary purpose in venting national resentment and rage. Thus, Revisionists advocated retaliation instead of strict self-defense in 1936–1939 as a more effective way to stop Arab attacks upon the Jews. But the isolated bombings carried out in Arab areas by Revisionist splinter groups succeeded above all in satisfying an incompletely suppressed Jewish desire for revenge. The Revisionist campaign to smuggle Jewish refugees into Palestine, to the extent it was effective, saved Jewish lives. It also responded to a deep human need of the community to do *something* to help its martyred brethren and to defy the British blockade against those who could escape from Europe. The terrorists' campaign against the British Mandate undoubtedly degenerated on occasion into a simple vendetta between the opposed Jewish and British forces, and it paid little heed to the balance of loss and gain to the Jewish cause from particular actions. But it satisfied a deepseated desire of the community to assault and humiliate the authors of the White Paper, because of whom Jewish refugees and the Jewish community in Palestine were subjected to the most violent and unforgivable assault and humiliation.

The great majority of Zionists could not accept the ideological premises or the tactical conclusions of either of the two extremes. The attitude of some binationalists, who wished to defer final political decisions on Palestine until a socialist overturn brought about governments in Europe and the Middle East with whom an Arab-Jewish agreement on Palestine would be possible, was rendered meaningless by events. The anticipated end of the war confronted Zionists with the very moment of decision and it was pointless to

---

* *Hagana* ("Defense"): the semisecret militia of the Jewish community in Palestine under the Mandate.

wait any longer. Other binationalists, as we have noted, proposed that Britain and the world community impose on both Jews and Arabs a binational solution of the kind which, in the opinion of these spokesmen, they should have agreed to voluntarily, if they had been reasonable men. But neither Britain nor the world community showed much inclination to impose a solution which would be opposed by both instead of only one of the claimants to sovereignty in Palestine. Besides, it showed singularly little appreciation of the nationalist frame of mind to suggest to Zionists that they should fight for a policy that would deprive the Jews of their right to determine their own destiny. No ideology which had originated in the idea and myth image of auto-Emancipation, as did Zionism, could conceivably — except in ultimate defeat — struggle to have outsiders decide its fate in disregard of its own will.

As to the tactics of terror and the ideological rationalizations by which Revisionist splinter groups supported them, the bulk of Jewish community in Palestine was also opposed to these in spite of the emotions to which they could appeal. The basic assumption upon which most Zionists in Palestine tended to decide questions of ideology and tactics was that the existing community, its chance to grow, and the strength it had already achieved were not expendable — least of all, after the extermination of six million Jews in Europe — but were the indispensable means to the realization of all Jewish national aims. The community could not be persuaded to expose these fundamental assets to destruction for no more than irrational gratification; certainly not so long as it had other hope of success.

But, on the other hand, as early as 1932 so representative a figure as the brilliant young Labor Zionist leader, Hayim Arlosoroff (1899–1933), concluded from his chillingly cogent analysis of Zionist prospects that the Jewish national aim could no longer conceivably be accomplished by a gradual "evolutionary" or "organic" progression from stage to stage.[38] The moment soon would come, if it had not already done so, when the community must do something more than conserve and build up its strength. It would soon have to risk its strength, to throw it into the balance, in order to force a new political conjuncture that would make possible the achievement of the Jewish national aims.

This conclusion was reached by many Zionists in the thirties and became inescapable for many more after the White Paper of 1939. Yet the extent and the forms of resistance to British policy were carefully considered by the leaders to whom most Zionists gave their confidence. Their calculation of gains and losses was based on the assumption that the existing community in Palestine was the one indispensable asset and element of strength possessed by the Zionist movement. Moreover, while the "activist" campaign of physical resistance to British policy was, of necessity, conducted by an illegal organization, its tactics had to be compatible with the principles on which the official Zionist leadership was conducting a legal and political campaign for Jewish national aims. Thus, the Hagana did not announce an all-out campaign to drive the British out but engaged in acts of armed resistance primarily in order to circumvent or to sabotage the blockade against Jewish refugees. This blockade the Zionist leadership had publicly repudiated as essentially illegal, and contrary to the basic purposes of the Mandate itself — an attitude in which the Zionist movement could claim the support of the Permanent Mandates Commission and the sympathy of large segments of international public opinion. The occasion for defining this complex position in a programmatic form arose with the Second World War. The Jewish community in Palestine at once claimed its place as a national entity on the side of Britain and her Allies, for the Jews had been singled out by the Nazis as their chief enemy and foremost victim. In this connection David Ben-Gurion formulated the official Zionist policy of fighting the White Paper as though there were no war, and fighting the war as though there were no White Paper.[39]

In establishing these limits for "activism," the majority of Zionists, as we have noted, rejected the idea of seeking to overthrow British rule directly by an armed uprising. The movement relied on efforts of persuasion and of pressure, legal, political, and moral, to determine the final political destiny of Palestine in a form favorable to Zionist aims. The position the Zionists defended in the Biltmore program was that of the Balfour Declaration which, they contended, had not only been finally repudiated by the White Paper but had been continually whittled down and disregarded from the moment British officials began to administer Palestine. They asked, then, for the reassertion of the Balfour Declaration in its full and original significance, for the explicit determination that Palestine was to be established as a Jewish commonwealth, and for the delegation of full powers to the Jewish Agency to establish a Jewish majority in the country in order to give substance to such an adjudication.

We have noted the implicit contradiction involved in demanding that Britain yield powers to the Jews to carry out a program for which it was determined not to be responsible. Another contradiction was implicit in demanding, on the basis of the Balfour Declaration,

that an area named "Palestine" be established as a Jewish commonwealth. What was referred to as "Palestine" in the Biltmore program
did not include the whole area to which the Balfour Declaration was
originally intended to apply. It included only Palestine west of the
Jordan, for in 1922 the Zionist movement had felt forced to acquiesce
in Winston Churchill's decision to set up Transjordan as a separate
amirate and "postpone or withhold" the application of the Jewish
national home clauses to "the territories lying between the Jordan and
the eastern boundary of Palestine. . . ." [40] Moreover, the possibility
that a Jewish state might have to be established in only part of the
remainder of Palestine, west of the Jordan, was undoubtedly present
in the minds of those who framed the Biltmore program. The
Twentieth Zionist Congress, in a resolution concerning the Royal
Commission Report of 1937, expressed the same contradiction quite
explicitly. In one paragraph it took note of the finding of the Palestine Royal Commission "that the field in which the Jewish National
Home was to be established was understood, at the time of the Balfour Declaration, to be the whole of historic Palestine, including
Trans-Jordan." In another paragraph it empowered the Executive
to negotiate with Britain in order to explore the possibilities of securing a more favorable partition of Palestine west of the Jordan than
the one proposed by the Royal Commission.[41] When the Biltmore
program now declared for the establishment of "Palestine" as a Jewish commonwealth, it was an implicit assertion that Transjordan
should not have been excluded from the scope of Jewish development; for the Balfour Declaration had committed Britain to "view
with favour" and "facilitate" the establishment of the Jewish national
home in the whole of Palestine, not in part of it. It was, above all,
an intimation that the Zionist movement would contest the legal
validity of any attempt to restrict still further the area of the Jewish
commonwealth and confine it to only a part of Western Palestine,
rather than all of it.

But the original acquiescence in the closing off of Transjordan
had been forced by practical considerations, rather than by the persuasiveness of the legal grounds upon which it might be based. In
the same way, in 1942, the Zionists knew very well that practical
and political considerations rather than legalities would probably
determine whether the Jewish commonwealth would be reconstituted
in all or in part of Western Palestine, or indeed whether it would
be reconstituted at all. The Biltmore program based itself on practical grounds rather than on an interpretation of the original intent of
the Balfour Declaration when it refrained from raising an issue con-

cerning Transjordan. But by asserting the right to reconstitute all of Western Palestine as a Jewish commonwealth, it was asserting a legal rather than a practical political claim. For such a claim could only be practical if Britain, or some other mandatary, were prepared to keep order for the period until a Jewish majority could be established in the whole area. Neither Britain nor any other mandatary was available for this purpose; and events pressed for a speedy and final determination of the form of statehood to be established in Palestine.

Foreseeing the inevitability of such a moment of decision, Hayim Arlosoroff in the thirties had regretfully rejected the idea of a partition as the means for establishing an independent Jewish polity in Palestine.[42] If Palestine were to be partitioned, only those parts of it where Jews formed a majority would become available for establishing a Jewish state. Surveying conditions in 1932, Arlosoroff found that the areas of Jewish settlement and concentration were too scattered and too small to form a strategically and economically viable state, or one capable of absorbing the mass immigration that alone could solve "the problem of the Jews." In the years that followed, it became increasingly obvious that the issue of sovereignty was imminent and that Jews would be able to claim only what they effectively occupied. Zionist colonization policy during that time was clearly directed, among other objectives, to staking out a claim to an area that would be viable in the event of partition, and filling out as far as possible the discontinuities of Jewish settlement in that part of Palestine where Jews could hope to prove a majority.[43]

By 1942, an area of Jewish settlement that was at least conceivable as a viable state had begun to take shape. Partition was now a defensible if not a desirable alternative to the nominal goal of the Biltmore program. To some of the leading architects of that program, it began to seem increasingly important to take the bull by the horns and choose partition rather than continuation of the Mandate as the policy of Zionism. After the Labor Party came to power in Britain and instead of revoking the White Paper policy adopted it, in essence, as its own, this mood became the dominant mood in the Zionist movement.

The problem of Palestine and the form of its future government was referred to the international community by Britain under the pressure of resistance in the country and of refugee smuggling into the country that followed the war. The United Nations, in the Second Session of the General Assembly on November 29, 1947, resolved

on the partition of Palestine, the establishment of territorially interlocking Jewish and Arab states — joined together, moreover, in economic union — and the establishment of an internationalized area including Jerusalem.

Thus, recognition of the aim of Jewish sovereignty, although over
a sharply reduced area in Palestine and under very unusual conditions,
was achieved by means of a moral and legal appeal to the international
community. The outlines of the Jewish state allocated in the partition
of Palestine were defined in accordance with the area of effective
settlement by Jews, supplemented by a reserve of wasteland in the
Negev which was effectively settled by neither Jews nor Arabs. In
this way, the program of "organic Zionism" was, after a fashion, vindi-
cated.

On the other hand, it was not through the tactics of "organic
Zionism" that, in the moment of decision, the British determination
to impose the White Paper policy was undermined so that the issue
was submitted to the UN. The tactics of "activism" on the one hand
and "terrorism" on the other set the stage for this development.
The former undoubtedly differed from the latter in a significant respect — for, unlike the terrorist groups, the activists refused to stake
the existence of the whole community on outright rebellion, but
used controlled violence chiefly against the immigrant blockade.
Yet the time came when they too had to risk everything in the fight
for sovereignty. For the international judgment in favor of partitioning Palestine was not fated to be smoothly carried out — nor even
to be enforced at all by the international community. The Palestinian
Arabs and the Arab nations, by violence, and the British, by passive
resistance, threatened to thwart its realization. And in the face of
this determined opposition, the UN, under the lead of Washington,
seemed inclined to back down and abandon its own decision. In
these circumstances, Israel was proclaimed an independent state on
the eve of the British evacuation and was plunged immediately into
a desperate war for its very life.[44]

The proclamation of the State of Israel at once placed the principle of sovereignty in quite a different perspective from the peculiarly
ambiguous situation of Zionist doctrine before that time. Sovereignty
now became for the Israelis, as for all other peoples on their own
land, the jealously guarded natural right to determine their national
destiny and defend their territorial integrity. The fact that Israel
was born under the fire of armed foes and that the international
community abandoned it, in the Israeli view, to its own defenses,

made even more fierce the insistence of Israelis on their prerogatives of sovereignty.

At the same time, the special conditions under which Israel was created and continued to exist caused somewhat different views of some aspects of Israel's sovereignty to find support in the international community. Israel itself gave symbolic recognition to the unusual relationship of the international community to the new state, by proclaiming in its Declaration of Independence that, in establishing human rights and fundamental freedoms in its constitutional structure, it would carry out the injunction laid upon it by the UN Partition Resolution. But other instances in which international or foreign interests claimed to be legitimately concerned with Israel's exercise of sovereign rights were not so cordially received, as we shall see.

It scarcely needs noting that this was the case in regard to the stubborn attitude of the Arab nations, who persisted in denying Israel's sovereign existence and did everything within their power to undermine it or to block its international acceptance. Apart from this, however, Israel's relations with her Arab neighbors were governed after 1949 by Armistice Agreements and were affected by UN resolutions in which a number of UN bodies were involved. On numerous issues, these bodies felt entitled to delay or bar actions, particularly in demilitarized zones within Israeli territory, which are normally the sovereign right of nations and which Israel felt to be legitimate under the terms of the Armistice Agreements. Moreover, in attempting to conciliate the Arab-Jewish dispute, UN officers — or even foreign powers indirectly concerned — felt entitled to propose to Israel particular policies in a way which showed no great respect for the country's sovereignty. Since Israel, from the day of its birth, has been heavily dependent on foreign aid and investment as well as on international good will, it has been possible for those who could influence the sources of such support to exert sharp pressure. This, in fact, was repeatedly done to induce Israel to make concessions of various kinds on behalf of Arab refugees, and to try to extract from Israel other gestures — the unilateral cession of territory or even the restriction of Jewish immigration — which it was presumed might bring about a more peaceable attitude in the Arab states.

Under such pressures, the response of Israel has been, as might be anticipated, to make its free exercise of sovereignty a point of honor. Even though it yielded from time to time on certain matters — particularly on questions where differences regarding the interpretation of its treaty or other international obligations were involved, or where humanitarian issues arose — it stood adamant against all concessions of territory or of internal policy affecting its security and strategic position. At the same time, the Israelis were acutely aware that they had won in warfare sovereignty over a greater area than they effectively occupied by peaceful civilian development. The question of immigration thus became pressing; and in connection with that question, echoes of old ideological positions regarding sovereignty as both end and means continued to be heard. The formal sovereignty won by Israel left a more substantial and secure sovereignty as an end still to be achieved by means of mass immigration and the colonization of waste and border areas. On the other hand, by means of Israel's established formal sovereignty it now became possible to undertake the national aim of mass migration to the homeland and, it might be hoped, bring about the definitive solution of "the problem of the Jews."

The extermination of six million Jews in Europe and the creation of the Jewish state in war and not in peace set the terms in which the Israeli public defined its attitude anew to "the problem of the Jews" and the role of the new state in solving it. Old Zionists or refugees who escaped the slaughter in Poland and Germany by settling in Palestine took what had happened in their old homes, the total destruction which hardly anyone had believed in before it took place, as conclusive evidence that "it could happen" anywhere, no matter how apparently secure the Jewish position. The rapid removal of every possible Jew from all possible countries to Israel seemed to them the urgent demand of the time. The needs of Israel itself, the defense of its sovereignty and rapid strengthening of its economy, also required that the waste places be settled, that the population be expanded, and that the immigration include not only penniless refugees from concentration camps or from "backward countries" but the skill, capital, and manpower of the Jewry of the West.

Thus, for the national aim of achieving Israel's sovereignty in the fullest sense, the mass migration from all corners of the Jewish world was regarded as an essential means. But even more, the Israeli public profoundly felt, was it essential for the Diaspora Jews themselves. The time had come to "liquidate" the Jewish Diaspora, to commence the ingathering of the exiles — to employ the sovereignty of Israel as the means for the great purpose in whose name it had been won: for the final solution of "the problem of the Jews"; or the Jewish problem *tout court*.

So it was that Israel's Declaration of Independence, after a preamble which stressed in paragraph after paragraph the right and the need of Jews in the Diaspora to return to Palestine, proclaimed: "The State of Israel will be open to the immigration of Jews from all countries of their dispersion." [45] So, also, among the first of its fundamental laws, Israel enacted the Law of the Return and the Nationality Law.[46] These remarkable enactments gave every Jew, wherever he lived, the unquestioned right to enter Israel as an immigrant and become, immediately upon entry, an Israeli citizen. In the triumphant conquest of its sovereignty, Israel gave symbolic expression to what remained its characteristic and peculiar Zionist aim. It made its hard-won sovereignty subordinate to a higher national aim: to the solution of the Jewish problem.

Part Two

ZIONISM AND WORLD JEWRY

3 THE RISE AND RECEPTION OF ZIONISM IN THE NINETEENTH CENTURY

The political ideas expressed by the concepts "national home" or "Jewish commonwealth" were neither uniformly nor unequivocally defined, even if we had no more to consider than Zionist theory itself. They were used as slogans in a political contest; and, in the struggle for advantage, each rival ideologist sought to appropriate the same popular conceptions by introducing his own shades of interpretation into them. But when opposing theorists engage in such dialectic, each is forced, at least, to take account of the other's usage; and he may have to modify his own so that it can be rationally defended against the other's, or effectively counteract its emotional appeal.[1]

Moreover, the Zionist debate was not conducted in a closed circle. The public whose conversion was desired was the whole Jewish public. Consequently, although the "Jewish national home" and the "Jewish state" were terms invented and advocated by the Zionists alone, they were not free to formulate those ideas as they saw fit, without regard for the understanding of their concepts and the reactions to them among other Jews. The influence of Jewish non-Zionist and anti-Zionist ideas and attitudes must be understood in a historical-sociological analysis of Zionist political ideas.

Such influences to which Zionist theories responded were both traditional and contemporary. The Zionist conception of the Jewish homeland in Palestine always had overtones recalling traditional conceptions of Zion. As we shall see later, in these reminiscences of ancient symbols Zionism perceived itself as a rebellion against tradition quite as much as a continuation of it. Zionism also had to define and redefine its ideas and continually elaborate its mythic symbols in response to the rival opinions of its contemporaries. A constant dialectical development was required in order to oppose the anti-Zionists more effectively or find a suitable basis for compromise with the non-Zionists in the community.

These necessities were, perhaps, more pressing for Zionism than for other nationalist movements. As noted earlier, nationalism ordinarily develops in countries ruled by foreigners. The initiation of the movement by rebellious intellectuals, consequently, meets a ready response among the mass of the people; for they, too, are kept in constant, though latent, rebelliousness by a subjection never consecrated by including the rulers in a common social consensus. Just as any idea rapidly takes on overtones of meaning reflecting the experience of those to whom it is effectively communicated, so the ideologies of the nationalist elite, when communicated to a responsive mass, soon absorb the experiences and impulses, the frustrations and resentments, to which the mass is sensitive. In this way nationalism establishes itself as a new focus of social consensus for the subject people — an active consensus, which in many cases did not exist before, and which now fuses together the ideologies of the elite with the myth images of the mass in a single historic force and purpose.

Jewish nationalism, however, could not simply arouse a subject people against its oppressors. The Jewish situation was not that of a people oppressed in its own country by a foreign garrison and administration, or by landlords and nobles who had imposed their rule after conquest. The latent impulse of the mass of Jews in extremity was not to rebel — but to take flight, to emigrate. For the oppressors of the Jews were either the autochthonous majority of the land, or foreign rulers who enjoyed the support of the majority in their anti-Jewish policies. Consequently, while the emotional mood of Zionist rebellion might be echoed in some of the myth images of the Jewish mass, the positive Zionist proposals could not arouse such a concerted impulse as would establish an unquestioned consensus. In fact, Zionism aroused debate perhaps quite as much as it created a consensus.

Moreover, the Jews did not need to wait for Zionism to create an active consensus among them. The Jewish tradition, for one thing, was never reduced to a mass of mythic material, as happened to the traditions of many subjugated peoples; it always defined a clear historical (or transhistorical) purpose and exercised a decided historical force.[2] Even if the tradition was a strictly conservative force among its most orthodox adherents, there was always an active rather than passive consensus among Jews, a purpose in history imposing a definite discipline upon Jewish attitudes and a definite direction upon Jewish impulses. In its relation to both Jewish tradition and the Jewish mass, then, Zionism was not called upon to activate a latent historic impulse. It had, instead, to overcome Jewish history and impose a new pattern upon the Jewish consensus.

Nationalist movements usually prefer to regard themselves not as historic innovations, but as movements for the *revival* of a national culture and the *restoration* of national sovereignty. Even when it is obvious that in actuality they have relatively insignificant ties to tradition, nationalists may seek to reconstruct bonds with the past, however great the effort of imagination and propaganda required to make them seem plausible. The attempted revival of Gaelic in Eire, the insistence on Gothic rather than Roman type faces during periods of nationalist enthusiasm in Germany, and the concerted drive for the adoption of Hebraic cognomens in newborn Israel are extreme and, perhaps, trivial examples. But the same tendency also manifests itself in territorial disputes based on the assertion of historic rights.

The attempt to reconstruct a tradition is facilitated in some ways by the decline of culture among suppressed and, particularly, degraded peoples. In such cases there may be no significant historical conceptions already established in the popular consensus which nationalism must seek to overcome in order to dominate. The nationalists frequently appeal simply for the revival of a culture that had fallen into oblivion or declined to the level of archaism or dialect; they strive to restore a sovereignty that had faded to a pale and ineffectual memory. The main opposition with which these ideologists have to contend is often the resistance of popular lethargy.

In this respect the problem Zionism faced from its very birth was quite different. Before Zionism arose there were already two distinct and well-established ideological positions, which we may call the ideologies of Western modernism and of Eastern traditionalism. For each of these ideologies, Jewish culture and Jewish sovereignty — which became the central concerns of Zionism — were significant problems, and each, in its historical development, had manifested a characteristic attitude toward those ideas. So, when Zionism undertook to revive a Jewish culture and restore Jewish sovereignty, it had not only popular lethargy to contend with. In its effort to implant its own attitudes in the popular consensus, it had to oppose other attitudes toward Jewish culture and Jewish sovereignty that had already more or less firmly taken root.

The position which Zionism eventually established in relation to its ideological opponents was not quite the same among Western and Eastern Jews. Certain rough distinctions are immediately obvious.

First, in the East the idea that the "problem of the Jews" must be treated as a national problem became dominant, and ideological issues between Zionists and anti-Zionists developed within a broad consensus on this point. In the West, whether or not the Jewish problem was a national problem remained an ideological issue between Zionists and non- and anti-Zionists.

The second distinction is a corollary of the first. In all countries, the characteristic Zionist attitude toward the "problem of Judaism" implied a return to the cultural situation characteristic of the East and a repudiation of the cultural trend of the West, which in the Zionist view had departed too far from the ethnic tradition.

Thirdly, in the West, Zionists and their opponents, who were divided over the national character of the problems "of the Jews" and "of Judaism," could unite in their practical concern for the settlement in Palestine. In the East, the latter was the bone of contention.

For a more accurate understanding of these differences and of the situations that produced them, we must consider, first, the circumstances under which Zionism emerged as an historic force.

I

The familiar division between Eastern and Western Jewries did not exist before the movement to emancipate the Jews in the late eighteenth century. Those whom we have learned to call Western Jews since that time are the Jewish communities that were effectively emancipated. Such communities, to the west of the Oder, adjusted their institutions to a status of civic equality. Their culture and customs responded to all the trends of general European culture since the Enlightenment. On the other hand, the title of "Eastern European Jewry", while superficially denoting the Jews south of Vienna and east of Prague, Breslau, and Koenigsberg, refers essentially to communities that were never effectively emancipated in the nineteenth century.[3]

Zionism arose as a historic force in response to the situation characteristic not of Western but of Eastern Jewry. In ideological terms, it was a reaction against the Emancipation, a denial of it as a rational solution of the Jewish problem.

Before this historic reaction, ideas subsequently crystallized by Zionism were not unknown. The doctrine of the emancipation of the Jews involved the view that their earlier status of subjection was no longer permissible; consequently, a "Jewish problem" existed. Given the existence of this problem, it was logically possible to seek a solution for it in two different ways: by granting the Jews a new status of equality either individually, as citizens of the countries where they lived, or collectively, as a modern nationality. The first to consider the latter possibility seriously, once the emancipation of the Jews began to be discussed in Western Europe, were not Jews but Gentiles.

That the Jews were a "nation" and not merely a "church" like other churches and that consequently their enfranchisement presented a particularly difficult problem was felt, among others, by ardent advocates of Emancipation like Abbé Henri Grégoire.[4] However, this view was far more likely to be stressed by opponents of the Jews, who did not wish them admitted to civic equality, for in their case it served a polemical purpose.[5] In the climate of opinion created by the French Revolution, it was common ground, accepted by every enlightened person, that a democratic nation, constituting itself anew, must respect the principle that all its members were equally endowed with the rights of man. Moreover, through the separation of church and state, religious differences were eliminated as obstacles to equal citizenship. On the other hand, it was also a valid position for all sides in the debate that an alien could be excluded from the rights of citizenship in a state where he happened to live, since he ought properly to exercise those rights in the nation to which he really belonged. Thus, if "church" was really equivalent to "nation" in the case of the Jews, there was a defensible case for denying them citizenship in France or in the Batavian Republic.

It was on this point that the Jews saw their advocates and opponents divide. The former urged that Jews be admitted to full citizenship in the countries where they lived; the latter argued, in effect, that through their long history as a distinct nation the Jews had already chosen to exclude themselves from the bodies politic of the lands in which they lived. As a practical conclusion from this, it was sometimes proposed to settle the Jews apart from the Gentiles as colonists in thinly populated, underdeveloped areas in France, Austria-Hungary, or Southern Russia. It was also suggested on occasion that it would be best for the Jews to be emancipated not as individual citizens in European countries, but as a people in Palestine.[6] Such ideas of segregation and resettlement, put forward somewhat tentatively or even simply for polemical effect in the discussions arising directly in the wake of the French Revolution and its Napoleonic expansion, crystallized into seriously elaborated proposals among Russian and, to a degree, among Polish revolutionaries [7] in succeeding decades.

The movement for emancipation and the ensuing debates caught the Jews of Europe unprepared. In their initial reaction, the Jews did not universally welcome the release from the old regime which was held out to them by the new. Within the familiar old restrictions they had built up institutions securing their traditions, and the uncertain benefits of the new regime left one thing quite certain: that much held dear by traditional Jews would have to go by the board in order that they might be emancipated.[8] But as the debate among the Gentiles unfolded, the actual alternatives open to the Jews became clearer. Their old status, including the positive values they had built into its framework of restriction and deprival, was no longer a defensible position. The arguments *pro* and *contra* the Jews took place between the new alternatives — individual enfranchisement or collective segregation — formulated in the course of the emancipation debate; and it was in these terms that Jews were now called upon to defend their own interests as best they could. That they adopted the arguments of their defenders rather than of their detractors is not surprising; especially since the alternatives to emancipation which were proposed — regional colonization or restoration to Zion — bore very little semblance of practicability, and merely served in fact as a pretext for retaining the disabilities of the old regime.

Thus it was that, more at first out of compliance with the prevailing climate of opinion than out of such inner conviction as later matured in the religious Reform movement[9] — even, indeed, out of sheer submission to a peremptory demand such as Napoleon placed before the assembly of Jewish notables in 1806[10] — some Jews responded to the debates on their emancipation by formulating two new principles. The Jews, they said, were not a nation but a religious confession like any other — and if they were not yet completely like any other church, they would, under freedom, become so. As for the hopes of a Messianic Restoration of the Jews, some explained these away as symbolical or abstract, and others proposed that the whole theme be wiped out of the Jewish liturgy.[11] So, even before Zionism arose, Western Jews, hoping to solve the Jewish problem by emancipation, formulated views implicitly opposed to Zionism.

However, throughout the nineteenth century, there were Jews as well as Gentiles who suggested solutions for the Jewish problem which were akin to Zionism. Even though Emancipation became the established basis of the Jewish community in the West, Western Jews were not wanting who, like their Gentile contemporaries, adopted a critical attitude to liberalism and the Enlightenment as a whole, and also to the Jewish Emancipation. From such a point of view, it was logical and natural to develop notions which anticipate the Zionist ideology in all but one respect: they were not intended to supplant but to complement the Emancipation.[12] Because of this difference and, above all, because they gave rise to no movement of historic consequence, leading continuously to the establishment of Israel, we call them "proto-Zionist" rather than "Zionist."

Moses Hess conceived his view of a Jewish Zionist mission out of the conviction that the liberal, bourgeois, rationalist revolution had exhausted its historical function and brought mankind to a dead end. The whole world needed for its revival a fresh restatement of eternal verities, a religious rebirth, in fact, in which the Jews were called upon to play a crucial part: it was their historic mission to give the essentially social doctrine of Judaism a new and spontaneous development in free and sovereign self-expression in Palestine.[13]

Such proto-Zionist doctrines remained nothing but stimulating eccentricities of opinion, favored by Jews more or less "marginal" in their relation to the community of Western Jewry. The more representative Western Jews were no less aware than the proto-Zionists of the setbacks to their dreams of redemption-through-liberalism. They, too, were sensitive to the anti-Semitic overtones in the Revolutionary and Napoleonic era itself, the reaction of 1815–1830, and the social upheavals of 1830 and 1848. But the Jewish emancipation seemed to them to be making steady strides, despite temporary retreats. As for the perfection of society as a whole, if this were the context of the discussion, then the Messianic role assigned to Judaism by the proto-Zionists was indeed a flattering idea, but the "representative" view of Western Jews was that it was a role to be performed in Europe. The idea of returning to Palestine in order to be able to live Judaism fully and spontaneously might be academically interesting, if it were not for the fact, that, in the minds of Western Jews, it was associated in a very practical way with the anti-Jewish propaganda of the opponents of emancipation. The Western Jews were still engaged, with confidence in their ultimate full success, in realizing their emancipation. The academic interest they might have in the theories and projects of both Jewish and Christian proto-Zionists was consequently mixed with disapproval because of the apparent practical effects of such discussion.[14]

A decisive historic difference made the Jews of Eastern Europe give to Zionism, when it developed among them, a wide and powerful response instead of the cool disinterest of the Western Jews. In Eastern Europe, Zionism arose in the context of an Enlightenment that had fallen short of its goal and an Emancipation that had been aborted — and of the Jewish problem that was defined by these circumstances. For those who had never stirred from the strict tradition, the problem was one of crude oppression which confined the Jews to a Pale of Set-

tlement too poor and too congested to maintain them. It was the problem of a constant pressure for emigration, rendered acute by the
coordinated pogroms that were condoned and abetted by the government. For the young and emancipated Jews who shared in the
Hovevei-Zion movement, it was a more complicated problem.

The movement to emancipate the Jews, as part of the general
Enlightenment, never went far enough or advanced steadily enough
in nineteenth-century Russia to inspire anyone with confidence in
its prospects. What it did succeed in doing was to raise up a thin layer
of enlightened young Jews. But this generation, reaching maturity
around 1860, pinned their faith on the ideal of Emancipation, both on
the emancipation of their own people and of the Russian peasant,
only to have their hopes cruelly and decisively disappointed in their
own lifetimes. The traumatic event that brought this disappointment
to a head was provided, of course, by the pogroms of the 1880's.
What was the emotional reaction of enlightened Jews to this shock
is illustrated by the diary notes of M. L. Lilienblum (1843–1910):

> May 7, 1881 . . . I am glad I have suffered. At least once in my life
> I have had the opportunity of feeling what my ancestors felt every day of
> their lives. Their lives were one long terror, so why should I experience
> nothing of that fright which they felt all their lives? I am their son, their
> sufferings are dear to me and I aspire to their glory.[15]

A similar description of the mood of that time is given in Abraham
Cahan's autobiography:

> As a result of the anti-Semitic riots there occurred such scenes as the
> following, for example: In Kiev a group of Jewish students came into a
> synagogue packed with mourning, weeping Jews. One of the group, a
> slender University student named Aleinikoff, got up at the reader's stand
> and addressed the people in Russian:
> "We are your brothers, we are Jews like you, we regret and repent
> that we considered ourselves Russians and not Jews until now. The events
> of the past weeks — the pogrom in Elisavetgrad, in Balta, here in Kiev,
> and in other cities — have shown us how tragically we were mistaken. Yes,
> we are Jews."
> It is needless to describe the impression that such words made on the
> community.[16]

The ultimate adjustment to this traumatic moment was not the
same for all intellectuals, of course. It was a "trauma," in fact, primarily for those who, since the turn to liberalism in Russia in the
60's, had hoped for a solution of the Jewish problem by Enlightenment. Others, younger men, in particular, who first awoke to dog-
matic enthusiasm in the revolutionary movements of the late 70's,

were sometimes too single-minded and too detached from the Jewish community for disillusionment. Some of these continued to fight for the revolutionary cause of the Russians, without regard for the cost to the Jews.[17] Others, who had seen not only Czarist authorities supporting the pogromists but revolutionaries calculating whether it might not be wise to do the same, and sometimes doing so, were open, in revulsion, to new ideas.[18] They found in Zionism the solution for what they now concluded was the inveterate and unalleviated Jewish problem. The personal situation which brought forth this new ideology, the crisis of disillusionment with the Enlightenment and Emancipation, was widespread enough so that Dr. Leo Pinsker's call for "auto-Emancipation" did not remain a mere eccentricity but evoked a wide response and consolidated a movement.[19]

In Russia, moreover, as in all of Europe to the east of Germany, there had always been a far stronger resistance of traditional Jewry to the ideas of the Enlightenment and to the various aspects of partial Emancipation than in Western Europe.[20] Thus, when Dr. Pinsker and other leaders of the new Hovevei-Zion movement declared Emancipation bankrupt and challenged the Jews to look to their own national resources for their national redemption, they initiated a *rapprochement* of the Zionist intelligentsia with the traditional leadership of Russian Jewry.

Moreover, the Zionists could present their movement as an expression of the powerful urge to emigrate from Russia to lands of freedom. The Zionist vision of social redemption, of the end of exile, was an echo of the dreams of masses who were on the move. As for the "official" leadership, dimly or clearly they sensed this: that in leaving Russia for the free West, the immigrants were going to lands of dangerous Enlightenment and "assimilation." The Zionist alternative, the prospect of migration to a home both free and Jewish, could not fail to attract them as a possible new safeguard against assimilation — though it was still prudent to wait until it became clear whether Zionism, too, were not merely a new subversion of tradition.[21]

Actually, of course, it turned out that the Hovevei-Zion could not divert the stream of migration to any significant extent towards Palestine; and the bridge to tradition had to be built through a long process of polemics and strife from the beginning. Yet the Eastern Zionists were not listened to with merely academic interest as had been Moses Hess. Their underlying assumptions and the problem they grasped were, in one form or another, the assumptions of the bulk of the people of their time and the problem felt most painfully by all Eastern European Jewry: for the Jewish masses attested by their migration that they did not regard Russia as a home or haven for them; and the crisis of Jewish tradition as well as the failure of the Emancipation and the Enlightenment was everywhere felt. Consequently Zionism for the first time established itself as a recognized faction in the community, whose views and activities must, at any rate, be taken seriously.

For all that, no one could safely have prophesied at that time that Zionism would last and become historically memorable and effective. The Zionists, bred on Western ideas, felt isolated and odd so long as they remained a faction virtually restricted to Eastern European Jewry, with its basic hostility to every manifestation of Westernism. Furthermore, all their efforts to affect the fate of the mass of Jews, and the course of their migration, in a tangible way remained fruitless, for the stream went Westward, and not to Zion. Then Herzl arose and with his bold style and large conceptions made a way for Zionism in the West, too, giving the Eastern Zionists a share in a national movement of Jews throughout the entire Diaspora. Moreover, he raised the failing spirits of the Hovevei-Zion, by turning their efforts from practical colonization, whose limits had been painfully encountered in that period, to a new road of international political action. To be sure, in a short time this road too came to the end of its resources, but in the early days of Herzl, before its contemporary limits were plumbed, the new approach rekindled enthusiasm and released new energies among the old Zionists — till a new generation arose, inspired by its own new vision of a road to Zion through labor, and reestablished Zionism's claim to become historic.

It remains true that, in his own Western Jewish community, Herzl, like Hess, was an essentially "marginal" figure; and if not for the prior existence of Eastern Zionism, he could not have achieved his decisive contribution towards making Zionism historic. For despite the long-drawn-out resistance of partisans of traditional institutions in Germany, to name only one example, what determined the situation and the character of Western Jewry was that the Enlightenment and the Emancipation had established a new cultural and institutional milieu in which the Jewish community now lived as of necessity. There was no failure of the Emancipation to be established, there was only sharp disappointment in the way it had been established: disappointment at the stubborn resistance to Jewish rights that was encountered from the start, at the "relapses" into anti-Semitism, and at the price which the Jews had to pay, in their own cultural confusion and communal disorganization, for so grudging a grant of freedom.

Such doubts and disturbance were transformed in the case of some individuals into a new proto-Zionist or Zionist ideology as a reaction to traumatic events. For Hess the Damascus and Mortara cases and the excitement of the Franco-Italian attack on the Holy Roman Empire,[22] for Herzl the Dreyfus affair set off such a reaction.[23] Each found a group of sympathetic readers with similar experiences among Western Jews. But the community as a whole could not take seriously any suggestion to seek a status other than civic emancipation in each country as its basis of existence — nor did any Western Zionist, until Herzl, forcefully present this position. But by the time Herzl arose to deny that the Emancipation was the solution of the Jewish problem, his Zionist proposals fell into a framework already established by the Hovevei-Zion societies that had spread among Jews from their origin in Russia. There the patent failure of the Emancipation had made Zionism something to be taken seriously by the community, a plausible alternative solution for a problem that urgently demanded to be solved.

Because Zionism was taken seriously in the East, Western Jews whom it attracted became not merely eccentrics, but adherents of a historic cause; and because of the accession of the Westerners, with their facilities for action, Zionism developed into something more than an episode — it became a historic movement. The Zionist movement now faced its first historic task: to convert its own basic views and attitudes into a national consensus shared by the entire people whom it hoped to revive. In this task, Zionism had to deal with substantially different problems in the Western and Eastern Jewish communities. It had to deal, first of all, with already well-formed and quite distinct attitudes of Western and Eastern Jewries to those ideas which were characteristically Zionist — the revival of Jewish culture as a solution for the "problem of Judaism" and the restoration of Jewish sovereignty in Zion as a solution for the "problem of the Jews."

While Jewish culture and Jewish sovereignty were matters of cardinal ideological significance for Zionism, they did not necessarily have equal importance for Western modernism or Eastern traditionalism. Before Zionism arose and sharpened these issues, "Zionist" ideas regarding Jewish sovereignty were sometimes voiced both among modernists and traditionalists. But Zionism could hardly have arisen at all if it had not sensed that, on those matters which it felt to be cardinal, the whole weight of the two already existing ideologies implied attitudes, nonrational as well as rational, which provoked the Zionists to rebellion. For Zionism, like any historic movement, was primarily a revulsion against what it found intolerable in the past. In the history of Zionist ideas, therefore, what is important is not the full range of the rather elastic views of its predecessors on questions Zionism regarded as crucial, but the more rigidly defined descriptions of those opposing views formulated by the Zionists themselves. And those formulations were molded under the polarizing force of the passion with which Zionists reacted to certain ideas, upon which, consequently, they demanded that everyone else take a definite, principled position.

When Zionism had confronted its ideological opponents with its own polemical descriptions of their views, these sometimes served as what a sociologist might call "self-validating definitions." Under the challenge of the fixed Zionist positions on Jewish culture and Jewish sovereignty, the modernist and traditionalist rivals of Zionism defined their own attitudes in more rigorous opposition — though the positions they took did not necessarily coincide point for point with the Zionist descriptions of them. Nor did Zionist ideology alone affect its rivals. The moods of the Zionist rebellion spread through mythic channels and exercised an influence not always parallel with the effect of Zionism as an intellectual challenge.

Our analysis begins, accordingly, with the traditionalist and modernist positions on Jewish culture and Jewish sovereignty as the Zionists perceived and reacted to them. The Hegelian dialectic provided the terms by which late nineteenth-century European parties liked to describe themselves in relation to their opposing ideologies. Zionism, too, regarded traditionalism and modernism as the "thesis" and "antithesis" of a Hegelian dialectic, with Zionism itself appearing as the "synthesis" of its historic predecessors. That is to say, Zionism recapitulated what it conceived to be the valid criticisms of tradition by modernism and of modernism by traditionalism. The element by which it hoped to transcend both was chiefly the new stress it laid on "auto-Emancipation" or, as we prefer to say, on sovereignty — a myth image whose conceptual content remained to be defined — as an indispensable requirement for the solution of the Jewish problem.

In the Zionist view, the valid historic contribution of the Western modernists had been the insistence that there was a Jewish problem that had to be solved rationally. The idea that the Jewish situation in the world is a problematic one is, of course, far from a modern discovery. According to the traditional view, the Jews are "in Exile," a conception which we today would unhesitatingly label as "ambivalent." Exile is a penance for which the Jews were singled out precisely because they are the "Chosen People." Hence, it is a sign of divine favor and a trial that must be piously and lovingly accepted. But Exile is also a penalty the Jews brought upon themselves and continue to suffer "because of our many sins." Hence, they must continually pray to be relieved of it and to be restored to Zion. To live in the light of such a conception is certainly to live problematically; but the problem involved is one which from the outset is conceived as beyond rational solution. It is at this point that what we have called modernism propounded a new idea: the modernists held that the condition of oppression and degradation involved in Exile could be and should be overcome by rational measures. This idea Zionism accepted and employed in its own criticism of traditionalism.

The conviction that the Jewish problem urgently demanded rational solution brought both modernism and Zionism not only into intellectual opposition but also into a sharp emotional antagonism to the traditionalists. Each expressed its hostility in its own characteristic way. But since modernism did not have to take care to distinguish its own attitudes from those of Zionism at a time when Zionism had not yet arisen, one finds the characteristic form of Zionist hostility to traditionalism prefigured by a number of incidental reactions of the modernists.

Moses Mendelssohn (1729–1786), in 1770, was asked by a "man of station" for his opinion on what seems to have been a "Zionist" plan for solving the Jewish problem. After praising the boldness and benevolence of the conception, Mendelssohn remarked:

The greatest difficulty which seems to me to stand in the way of the project is the character of my people [*Nation*]. It is not adequately equipped to undertake anything great.

The pressure under which we have lived for so many centuries has deprived our spirit of all *vigueur*. It is not our fault; but we cannot deny that the natural urge to freedom has completely ceased to be active in us. It has transformed itself into a monkish virtue and expresses itself in prayer and patience, not in action.[24]

A more violent antipathy to the traditional Jewish *ethos* of suffering was expressed by Ferdinand Lassalle (1825–1864). In 1840, when Jews in Damascus were put to the torture, young Lassalle, just turned sixteen, recorded his reaction in a furious diary entry (Thursday, May 21):

Oh, it is terrible to read, terrible to hear . . . A people that permits this is horrible, let it take vengeance or accept its [due] treatment . . . Even the Christians are amazed . . . at our failure to rebel and seek death on the field of battle rather than on the rack . . . Cowardly people, you deserve no better lot! The trodden worm turns, but you only bow the

deeper! You know not . . . how to bury your foes together with your-
selves and how to cut them to bits even in the death throes! You were
born to be slaves! [25]

Lassalle's youthful outburst foreshadows the characteristic emotional antagonism of Zionism against what it perceived as the supine-
ness of traditionalism. The expression of this attitude which crystallized
the Zionist rebellion into a fully formed myth image was H. N. Bialik's
(1873–1934) wrathful poem following the Kishineff pogrom of 1903.

> Descend then, to the cellars of the town,
> There where the virginal daughters of thy folk were fouled,
> Where seven heathen flung a woman down,
> The daughter in the presence of her mother,
> The mother in the presence of her daughter,
> Before slaughter, during slaughter, and after slaughter! . . .
> Note also do not fail to note,
> In that dark corner, and behind that cask
> Crouched husbands, bridegrooms, brothers, peering from the cracks,
> Watching the sacred bodies struggling underneath
> The bestial breath,
> Stifled in filth, and swallowing their blood!
> Watching from the darkness and its mesh
> The lecherous rabble portioning for booty
> Their kindred and their flesh!
> Crushed in their shame, they saw it all;
> They did not stir nor move;
> They did not pluck their eyes out; they
> Beat not their brains against the wall!
> Perhaps, perhaps, each watcher had it in his heart to pray:
> *A miracle, O Lord, — and spare my skin this day!* . . .
> They crawled forth from their holes, they fled to the House of the Lord,
> They offered thanks to Him, the sweet benedictory word.
> The *Cohanim* sallied forth, to the Rabbi's house they flitted:
> *Tell me, O Rabbi, tell, is my own wife permitted?* . . .
>
> Come, now, and I will bring thee to their lairs
> The privies, jakes and pigpens where the heirs
> Of Hasmoneans lay, with trembling knees,
> Concealed and cowering, — the sons of the Maccabees!
> The seed of saints, the scions of the lions!
> Who, crammed by scores in all the sanctuaries of their shame,
> So sanctified My name!
> It was the flight of mice they fled,
> The scurrying of roaches was their flight:
> They died like dogs, and they were dead! [26]

Out of their hostility to the pious, traditionalist acceptance of
Exile, the Zionists adopted a familiar formula for the intellectual
repudiation of a rival doctrine. They saw in the traditional conception

of a millennial restoration by the Messiah, following the completion of the Jewish penance, only a cover for timid inaction — that is, they debunked it as mere "ideology." This view is sharply yet subtly expressed in the episode which the contemporary Hebrew writer, Hayim Hazaz, entitles "The Sermon."

They do nothing, not an effort, nothing at all, just sit and wait . . . They invented a Messiah in Heaven, but not as a legend out of the past, as a promise for their future. That's very important, terribly important — and they trust in him to come and bring their redemption, while they themselves are *obliged* to do nothing at all and there you have it . . . How can men who are by no means simple, who are no fools at all, on the contrary, very shrewd men, men with more than a touch of skepticism, men who are practical, and maybe even a bit too practical, how can they believe something like that, *a kind of thing like that* — and not just believe, but trust in it, pin their whole life upon it, the whole substance of their life and survival, their national historic fate? . . . And quite seriously, in full earnest. For truly they believe with perfect faith . . . The whole thing is that they really believe! And yet, and yet, in the secrecy of their heart, you know, deep down, in some hidden fold, some geometric point down in their hearts — *somewhat* they don't believe, just the faintest hint; at any rate, that he will come now, at this very moment, that he will come during their own lives, in their day, and this, of course, is the core of the matter. . . See? . . . This is a Jewish trait, too, a very Jewish trait! to believe with perfect faith, with the mad and knowing faith of all the heart and all the soul, and yet *somewhat* not to believe, the least little bit, and to let this tiny bit be decisive . . . Redemption is the chief of all their desires, the whole substance of their hopes, and yet they have bound themselves, locked their hands and feet in chains, and sealed their own doom, guarding and observing their own sentence with unimaginable pedantic strictness, not to be redeemed forever and ever! . . . What is this? A *Weltanschauung?* Historic wisdom? Or is it perhaps what one dare not hint: simply their own fear of redemption? . . . Ye-e-s, such is that wild, enthusiastic, moonlit fantasy of theirs . . . the fantasy they need for such practical purposes, for their well-understood ends . . . Because they don't want to be saved! . . . That is the deliberate intent of this myth, that is its practical effect, consciously or unconsciously, not to be saved, not ever to go back to the land of their fathers.[27]

Considered in terms of its logical sources, the Zionist hostility to traditionalism derives from the view that the Jewish problem can and must be rationally solved, and it expresses a consequent irritation with attitudes based on a nonrational view of the problem. But this is not the only kind of denunciation of traditionalism to which the same underlying opposition can logically lead. While Western modernism, as we have seen, also occasionally revolted against traditionalist passivity, it was far more characteristic of modernism to express its hostility in other terms. Obscurantism, not passivity, was

the vice the modernists most frequently condemned in the representatives of traditional Jewry.[28]

To condemn obscurantism as the vice that prevented a rational
solution of the Jewish problem implied the view that the Gentiles
had adopted, or would adopt, rational attitudes toward the Jews, and
that the Jews must follow suit, or anticipate, by adopting corresponding rational attitudes. Consequently, in place of the vice of stubborn
obscurantism the modernists preached the virtues of reasonableness
and accommodation: the *acceptance* by the Jews of enlightened
standards of culture and institutions of civil society, of an emancipation offered (if not yet everywhere in fact, then at least in conception)
on the initiative of Gentile society. To condemn the traditionalists for
passivity, as Zionism did, implies quite different assumptions and
conclusions. It assumes that a rational solution of the Jewish problem
demanded action *initiated* by the Jews, not by the Gentiles, perhaps
even action by the Jews in the teeth of Gentile opposition. The virtues
which Zionism, accordingly, preached were those of boldness and
activity: the assertion of the individuality and the self-liberation — or,
as it was called, the auto-Emancipation — of the Jews. To this it was
hoped and expected that Gentiles would concur, but the initiative
necessarily had to be Jewish.[29]

Quite as sharp an opposition between the conceptions of modernism
and Zionism arose in relation to two other issues, Jewish culture and
Jewish sovereignty, on which both departed from the traditional views.

What would be the effect of enlightenment and emancipation upon
the individual tradition of Jewish culture and upon the traditional
vision of Jewish sovereignty was not, perhaps, a cardinal problem
but still a matter of concern to the modernists. One logical limit had
to be observed by any *Jewish* modernism in seeking a rational accommodation with enlightened Gentile society: it could not accept a
"solution" of the Jewish problem involving the total submergence of
the Jews. In the generation following Moses Mendelssohn, a solution of
this nature was proposed as a policy by some and adopted as an
expedient by many who sought to escape the Jewish problem by
conversion to Christianity.[30] The Jewish modernists wished to erect
a dam against such desertion by preserving those elements of Jewish
culture and Jewish autonomy which were consistent with the standards
of an enlightened Gentile world — and, of course, by discarding the
others.

The Talmudic literature as well as the Yiddish language appeared
at once to the Jewish Enlightenment as the kind of tradition that
must be discarded. The Bible and the Hebrew language, on the other

hand, deserved to be cherished on two accounts. These were, first of all, the classic foundations of the Mosaic cult, which the modernists defended as essentially rational. In addition, Biblical and Hebraic purism were valuable tools in the struggle against those strongholds of traditionalist obscurantism, the Yiddish "jargon" and rabbinic Talmudism. However, what actually happened in the wake of the Jewish Enlightenment in Germany was different from what was planned. Not only the obscurantist tradition and Yiddish language were discarded by the modernist reformers, but the projected neo-Biblical and neo-Hebraic Enlightenment culture swiftly vanished, remaining the hobby, at most, of a few scholarly specialists. Western Jews adopted the French and German cultural traditions as the most effective media of Enlightenment, while Jewish cultural individuality was restricted almost entirely to the synagogue.[31]

When Zionism arose in the 1880's, the modernist attempt to reconstruct a Hebrew literature and culture in a classical Biblical style continued to be pursued on any appreciable scale only to the east of Vienna. An element that made it seem more feasible to preserve Jewish cultural individuality in Eastern Europe was that both Austria-Hungary and Russia were multilingual and multinational empires, unlike France or Germany, where a single national language was the unquestioned vehicle of universal enlightenment. Yet, in Austria-Hungary and Russia, too, the modernists soon adopted the dominant national language and culture of the empire or the province as the most effective medium for general enlightenment. The Hebrew revival promoted by the Enlightenment rapidly dwindled to a cult to which it seemed only an eccentric few would remain devoted. The foremost Russian Hebrew poet of the Enlightenment, Judah Leib Gordon (1830–1892), expressed what was undoubtedly a general mood in these lines, written in 1880: [32]

> Still doth the Muse visit by night,
> Still the heart hearkeneth, the hand doth write —
> Fashioning songs in a tongue forsaken.
> What will I, what hope? To what end travail?
> For whom do I labor? To what avail
> The good years wasted, the pleasures ne'er taken?
> . . . Oh, tell me what future the shades forecast!
> Am I of all Zion's bards the last,
> And are ye not the last who e'er shall read?

The gloomy tone of these lines expressed the mood of those modernists who, as writers or readers, were personally committed to neo-Hebraic culture for its own sake, not merely for the sake of its supposed usefulness as a tool of enlightenment. Others, like Dr. Leo Pinsker, who later turned to a Zionist position, quite readily invested their hopes in the Russian language rather than the Hebrew language, when it seemed that enlightenment and emancipation of the Jews could be more effectively promoted in that way.[33] But when the Zionist reaction came, it echoed still another point of view, that had begun to be voiced in the seventies. The decline of Hebrew culture was not merely regretted in personal terms; it was feared as a danger to Jewish nationality. And, moreover, it became an ideological tenet that the abandonment of Jewish cultural individuality was a necessary result of Western modernism.[34]

On these grounds, the Zionists adopted toward the Enlightenment an attitude of condemnation like that of the traditionalists, who foresaw nothing but "shmad" (which translates roughly as "renegade apostasy") as the outcome of modernism. This traditionalist term of abuse was replaced in the nationalist vocabulary by another, "assimilationism," more neutral in its flavor but still heavily weighted with disapproval and bearing a connotation of "betrayal."

The common hostility of Zionism and traditionalism to the "renegade" tendencies of modernism was paralleled by a sense that the two were allied in defense of the Hebrew tradition. Significant differences divided them, of course, on this point. Tradition had cherished and succeeded in maintaining the Hebrew language as the medium of prayer and scholarship and also of general communication and solidarity between Jews and Jewish communities scattered in all quarters of the Exile. Zionism, however, wished to revive Hebrew as a spoken language so that the people — especially when it came together out of its Exile — would have a common mother tongue. In consequence of this, vernacular Hebrew would no longer be simply the vehicle of a "normative" religious culture such as had "created" Jews through successive generations. It would reverse that relationship for a more "normal" one. By expressing all the activities that spontaneously occur in a fully rounded society, it would become the medium through which the Jewish people would freely create its secular culture and thereby consolidate a national rather than religious consensus.[35]

All these, however, were differences which crystallized in the course of time. When Zionism arose, the far more significant feeling was one of alliance with the traditionalists against the "assimilationism" of the modernists.

What concerned the nationalists even more was the position to which modernism was led on the questions of Jewish sovereignty and the restoration to Zion. We have noted how the Western Jews, in defence of their emancipation, were led to adopt the view that the Jews were not an ethnic group but a religious denomination no different from Christian denominations — or if not yet quite as divorced from any ethnic quality as the Christian denominations, certain to become so under a regime of civic equality. This involved a series of related propositions: that the traditional Messianic hope of Jewish restoration in Zion was at most a symbol or an abstract notion, perhaps best interpreted as no more than the reign of divine justice throughout the world; that the traditional idea of Exile had now been superseded by the grant of emancipation; and that the dispersion of the Jews was a providential act, signifying that the Jews had a mission to set the Gentiles an example of a pure, rational, prophetic, monotheistic faith.

The nationalist rejection of these views and their implied emotional correlates was passionate and decisive. Ahad Ha'am summed it up for his generation in an essay which, because of its emotional as well as intellectual conviction, crystallized the nationalist consensus with mythic force, so that its title, "Slavery in Freedom," cast the verdict against the West in a stereotype formula. The idea of a Jewish mission to be forever dispersed among the Gentiles in order to teach them prophetic monotheism, he dismisses with contempt. The Jews, he notes, are *not* a missionary people and they have long since renounced any idea of spreading their gospel by mass conversions to Judaism.

In itself, therefore, our mission is an easy and a comfortable one. At least there is nothing disgraceful in being the teachers of the whole world, in regarding the whole human race, to the end of time, as pupils who slake their thirst at the fountain of our inspiration: more especially when this honorable task of ours involves no labor or worry on our part. We are like the Israelites at the Red Sea: the progress which emanates from the Scriptures is to fight for our mission, while we look on and rejoice. Now, this would be very well indeed, if the pupils on their side were amenable and docile, and paid the proper respect to their teacher. But in fact they are impertinent fellows, these pupils. They kick their teacher: they heap curses on him: they are forever besmirching his name, until his life becomes a positive burden to him. And so we are left face to face with the same question. We are no longer doing anything useful towards the fulfillment of our mission: the Scriptures, and consequently religious progress, are independent of us, and will do their work without us: we are nothing but a monument on the path of religious progress, which marches on to its consummation without our assistance.[36]

How can enlightened men of our time, Ahad Ha'am goes on to ask, who have learned from Darwin that no purposes, divine or otherwise, but only determining causes control the course of history, believe in such nonsense? The obvious answer is that they don't really believe it; they only pretend to believe. Thus, just as Zionist critics attacked traditionalism as mere ideology, they made the same analysis of modernist beliefs. The critique was even fiercer in this instance, for the debunking of traditionalism was often tempered by respect for the profound faith which Zionists acknowledged among Orthodox believers, but no such consideration palliated the polemic against modernism.

What, then, are those Jews to do who have nothing left but this theoretical religion, which is itself losing its hold on them? Are they to give up Judaism altogether, and become completely assimilated to their surroundings? A few of them have done this: but why should they not all adopt the same course? Why do most of them feel that they cannot? Where is the chain to which they can point as that which holds them fast to Judaism, and does not allow them to be free? Is it the instinctive national feeling which they have inherited, which is independent of religious beliefs or practices? . . . Try as they will to conceal it, seek as they will for subterfuges to deceive the world and themselves, it lives none the less; resent it as they will, it is a force at the centre of their being. But this answer, though it satisfies us, does not satisfy them. They have publicly renounced their Jewish nationality, and they cannot go back on their words; they cannot confess that they have sold that which was not theirs to sell.[37]

So the modernists of the West had paid for their formal emancipation by selling themselves into intellectual and moral slavery. They dared not admit what they must have known to be true, that their professed religious belief was an ideological pretense, nor to confess what they must have felt to be true, that their Jewish loyalties were, in fact, a sentiment of nationality. In his conclusion, therefore, Ahad Ha'am places Eastern traditional Jewry on a higher plane than the Western modernists.

I try . . . to give my weary eyes a rest from the scene of ignorance, of degradation, of unutterable poverty that confronts me here in Russia, and find comfort by looking yonder across the border, where there are Jewish professors, Jewish members of Academies, Jewish officers in the army, Jewish civil servants; and when I see there, behind the glory and grandeur of it all, a twofold spiritual slavery — moral slavery and intellectual slavery — and ask myself: Do I envy these fellow-Jews of mine their emancipation? — I answer, in all truth and sincerity: No! a thousand times No! The privileges are not worth the price! I may not be emancipated; but at least I have not sold my soul for emancipation. I at least can proclaim from the housetops that my kith and kin are dear to me wherever they are, without being constrained to find forced and unsatisfactory excuses. I at least can remember Jerusalem at other times than those of "divine service": I can mourn for its loss, in public or in private, without being asked what

Zion is to me, or I to Zion. I at least have no need to exalt my people to Heaven, to trumpet its superiority above all other nations, in order to find a justification for its existence. I at least know "why I remain a Jew" — or rather, I can find no meaning in such a question, any more than if I were asked why I remain my father's son. I at least can speak my mind concerning the beliefs and opinions which I have inherited from my ancestors, without fearing to snap the bond that unites me to my people. I can even adopt that "scientific heresy which bears the name of Darwin," without any danger to my Judaism. In a word, I am my own, and my opinions and feelings are my own. I have no reason for concealing or denying them, for deceiving others or myself. And this spiritual freedom — scoff who will! — I would not exchange or barter for all the emancipation in the world.[38]

Apart from the typical emotional revulsion against the modernists, these passages also convey a central nationalist doctrine: that emancipation is not a rational solution of the Jewish problem. The real danger to Jewish survival as a distinct group is not loss of religious belief, leading to assimilation. The Jews are an ethnic entity, and individual Jews consequently retain their loyalty and sense of solidarity even when no longer religious. However, modernism can injure the Jewish people severely. By forcing them to hide their natural ethnic feelings from others and even from themselves, it causes them to adopt false ideologies and to abandon their own historic myth. So, too, it leads them to rely on others to emancipate them, inculcating a false spirit of submission, instead of arousing the will to independence. This is the cardinal point in the Zionist critique; and in this regard, it condemns both traditionalism and modernism in almost the same terms. That pious acceptance of Exile which tradition exalted as a high penance, Zionism condemned as a supine surrender to oppression. So, too, the Zionists saw in the lofty Jewish mission proposed by the Western modernists only a high-sounding pretense, a "conventional lie" serving to hide "slavery in freedom."

The attitude of Zionism to modernism was, in other important respects, quite different from its attitude to traditionalism. The modernists were opposed because their views led to the abandonment of traditional Jewish culture and resulted in undermining the idea of Jewish independence and the will to achieve it. The Zionists had only this hope for the modernists: that they might be brought back again to the ranks of unestranged and uninhibited Jews.

The traditionalists, on the other hand, had never abandoned the heritage of Jewish culture or the historic myth of Jewish independence. They had been the mainstays of both, and preserved them alive through the centuries. At the same time, in the Zionist view, both Jewish culture and the idea of Jewish independence had been reduced by the traditionalists to a state of suspended animation in which they might be preserved, but were unable to be active and effectual. The Zionist hope, as to the traditionalists, was to persuade them to accept new views of Jewish culture and Jewish sovereignty based on the pursuit of independence as an immediate aim.

Reverting to the Hegelian formula, we may say that the Zionist "synthesis" stood directly opposed to the "antithesis," modernism, and sought a *rapprochement* with the original "thesis," traditionalism. For with modernism, Zionism shared the general principle that the Jewish problem required an immediate, rational solution; but it differed sharply — and emotionally — on the nature of the problem and the solution. With traditionalism, Zionism shared, as an emotional bond, the common vision of a solution by which the Exile would be transcended. Its task was to persuade the traditionalists to seek the desired solution immediately by inducing them to take a rational view of the existing situation.

Behind this difference in attitude lies the fact that Zionism arose as a historic movement in response to the situation of Eastern, not of Western Jewry. United with Western modernism in its resolve to achieve an immediate rational solution of the Jewish problem, Zionism found a different solution — because it addressed itself to a different situation. Opposed to traditionalism because it was impatient to solve the Jewish problem immediately and rationally, Zionism sought essentially the same solution, because it saw itself in the same situation: in exile. What seemed rational in terms of the Jewish situation as Western modernism saw it, and as the Western Jews defined it institutionally, seemed simply unrealistic in terms of the situation of Eastern Jews, as enlightened young men began to understand it after the 1880's.

II

These differences directly affected the different manners in which Zionism was received into the consensus of Western and Eastern Jewries. In the East, the crucial experience of the 1880's, and similar experiences that followed, made not only Zionists and traditionalists but the succeeding generations of Eastern modernists perceive their situation as one of national conflict. Even where Zionism led to the development of new ideologies opposed to its own tenets, some of the mythic components of the Zionist view — especially the stereotype of "assimilationism" — were accepted by the general consensus. In the West, however, the basic experience behind Zionism never dominated the consensus of the community. The Zionist myth was shared only by those won over to the Zionist ideology; and they often saw it as their primary task to bring their own community back into the consensus of Eastern Jewry.

For in the West, it was modernism that had had a dominant effect upon the communal consensus. With the rise of modernism, traditional Judaism did not, indeed, disappear; there was, in fact, an ideological revival of Jewish Orthodoxy in reaction against the doctrines of the modernists. Where modernist theologians like Abraham Geiger (1810–1874) demanded that traditional Jewish law and custom, as well as doctrine, bow to reason and contemporary history (which two they tended to identify), Orthodox theologians like Samson Raphael Hirsch (1808–1888) propounded the opposing view that the Torah, as a revealed law and doctrine, transcended history.[39] But at the same time Western Orthodoxy shared the basic experience of the modernists and bowed to the force of their formulations. They, too, recognized that emancipation had established a new fundamental status for the Jews, that no return to the ghetto was possible, and that Jewish "secular" life must be conducted in a spirit of thorough accommodation to the standards of enlightenment which contemporary history had adopted. Only religion, and particularly the traditional ritual law, was defended against history, while a broad secular realm was recognized within which the Jews must live as fully and individually integrated nationals of the countries where they enjoyed civic equality. The characteristic attitude of Western Orthodoxy was summed up by S. R. Hirsch in the formula, "Torah together with *Derekh Eretz*." Interpreted, this meant the preservation of the traditional, particularly ritual, laws as above history, together with a full acceptance of prevailing non-Jewish contemporary standards in all secular affairs.

Before Zionism arose as an organized ideological movement and made a matter of principle of the idea of Jewish sovereignty, attitudes on this question could vary in spite of a basic acceptance of the Emancipation. Indeed, the 1860's saw a kind of proto-Zionism in Western Europe which took on almost the aspect of a historic movement: a theory of Jewish restoration was propounded, groups were organized and propaganda conducted on behalf of the return to Zion. It was among the Orthodox Jews of Germany and its bordering areas that this activity was most marked, in spite of the dictum of the leading Orthodox theorist, S. R. Hirsch, that the restoration to Zion was an event that could only occur beyond the bounds of history.

But two things must be noted about the proto-Zionism of those Western Orthodox Jews. The first is the striking fact that the movement enjoyed its greatest success and found its intellectual leaders among those in a "marginal" position in relation to Western Jewry, since in most cases they lived in the outskirts of the German cultural area (in Silesia or northern Prussia, or in Hungary) and shared as much in the life of the East as of the West.[40] Yet the hopes of these proto-Zionists were pinned on Western Jewry — and the second striking characteristic of the movement reflects this orientation. The proto-Zionists of the 1860's did not begin with a programmatic assertion that the Jewish problem remained unsolved in spite of emancipation. They did not question the fundamental status of the Western Jews as an emancipated community, but sought an essentially religious supplement to emancipation through the restoration of the Jews in Zion.[41]

Because it did not clearly challenge emancipation as the fundamental principle of Jewish status, the proto-Zionism of the 1860's fell short of becoming a historic movement based on ideological principles. It remained essentially a mythic variant within the attitude system of Western Orthodox Jews, a system that accepted emancipation as a principle that could solve the problems of Jewish secular status. No serious challenge of this view arose among Western Jews until Herzl. But, at the same time, the ideas of emancipation and enlightenment did not inspire intellectual enthusiasm for long. For while they had a decisive effect upon the Jewish consensus at a mythic as well as a rational level, their effect was a decisively negative, iconoclastic or, one may say, "antimythic" one.

Moreover, the rationalistic, egalitarian attitudes implied in the doctrines of Emancipation and Enlightenment hark back to the time when the German Classicists, particularly Lessing, Schiller, and Kant, were fresh and current; and even then they were questioned by some German intellectuals.[42] But it was only during the middle decades of the nineteenth century, one or two generations after the heyday of Classicism in German intellectual circles, that Emancipation and Enlightenment were taken up and defended most vigorously by Jews as their own ideology and the principles of their communal status. By that time German Romanticism, a reaction against the Enlightenment, and German left-wing Hegelianism, a revolt against the bourgeois limits of Liberalism, were the intellectual fashions of the time. These were the ideas and attitudes that interested those Jews who were primarily free intellectuals, while the doctrines of Enlightenment and Emancipation, which the spokesmen of the Jewish community stoutly defended, seem no more than "philistine" platitudes [43] — true enough, to be sure, but not important.

On the other hand, the fashionable intellectual ideas of the time could not have any great influence upon the Western Jewish consensus. The group of young scholars who first projected the scientific study of Jewish life and history, the initiators of the *Wissenschaft des Judentums*, did in the beginning conceive of the Jews, in the vein of contemporary German Romanticism, as an ethnic entity with a folk culture whose historic and universally significant expression was Jewish religion.[44] Similar ideas continued to influence the historical writings of Heinrich Graetz and the philosophies of Jewish history of the time, especially that of Moses Hess. But for the most marked Romantic reaction against the Enlightenment view, and for the only outright rejection of the Emancipation of the Jews, we must look not to Jews but to Gentiles. In its counterrevolutionary attack on the French Revolution and its intellectual source, the Enlightenment, the clerical and nationalist Romanticism of Western Europe produced modern anti-Semitism; for the Jewish Emancipation was regarded as an inherent and symbolically prominent expression of the revolutionary Enlightenment, and was repudiated as violently as was its source.[45] Under the circumstances sympathy with antirationalist and antiliberal ideas, for which clerical Romanticism in France or nationalist Romanticism in Germany supplied a social milieu, could only detach Jewish intellectuals from their Jewish milieu. It led to purely individual expressions, varying in intensity: to conversion or Jewish self-hatred or to a paradoxical and completely detached preference for the Judaism of the Ghetto over the reformed Judaism and emancipated Jewry of their contemporaries.[46] No Romantic theory of Jewish nationality could gain a hearing in a Jewish community actively opposed to the anti-Semitic Romanticism of the Gentiles.

Nor could any Jewish ideology opposed to the Emancipation arise out of the other fashionable ideological trend, left-wing Hegelianism. Even though the revolutionaries of the mid-nineteenth century wished to transcend rather than reverse the French Revolution, and hence developed no political anti-Semitism,[47] they were almost as hostile to "Jewish" Liberalism as were the reactionary Romanticists. Karl Marx's identification of Judaism with Capitalism [48] expressed a common attitude among left-wing intellectuals. Such a stereotype left room for no rational solution of the Jewish problem except the disappearance of the Jews in the classless society after the social revolution. It made Jewish left-wing revolutionaries disregard the contemporary Jewish problem as insignificant rather than develop new ideological positions regarding it.

The Jewish community, for its part, had to defend its fundamental position ideologically even if it meant adhering to ideas that did not enter the mainstream of intellectual fashion. Marx's scornful identification of Judaism with Capitalism and the general disdain among intellectuals for the philistinism of the community did not deter the Jewish consensus from accepting the standards of *bourgeois* society as its own. The rabbis and theologians developed Idealistic philosophies which sought to justify accommodation to contemporary conditions as a Jewish mission.[49] The community at large took assurance from the Liberal ideology, to which it was attracted by a kind of social tropism. The disdainful intellectuals, for their part, pursued their own tropisms and in accommodating to the fashionable ideas of the time lost touch with the Jewish consensus.

What was radical in the Zionism of Theodor Herzl, as in the doctrine of Leo Pinsker before him, was that it was bold enough to reject Emancipation as the principle of Jewish status and the solution of the Jewish problem. These Zionists were moved by an intuition of fundamental significance: that accommodation to Gentile standards, whether of the *ancien régime*, the bourgeois, or the classless society, was not a satisfactory basis for solving the Jewish problem; and, in particular, that anti-Semitism must be taken seriously, that it would persist and dog the footsteps of the Jews wherever they went seeking toleration. Only the "auto-Emancipation" of the Jews in an independent society of their own could make possible a rational solution of the Jewish problem.

This underlying assumption made a fundamental difference in the attitudes of Zionist intellectuals. It meant, first of all, that instead of accommodating to conditions constituted by others, by Gentile society, the Jews must seek autonomously to establish the conditions of their own national existence. A necessary corollary of this view was that the Zionist intellectual had to find his way back to the Jewish community and win over the Jewish consensus to his views. This conclusion, which Herzl took some time to reach, was expressed in the formula that Zionism must "conquer the communities." [50] But even while it freed them from submission to the conditions of Gentile society, Zionism also enabled Jewish intellectuals to bring into Jewish ideologies all the fashionable ideas of European culture. Having rejected the Emancipation as an adequate principle of Jewish status, Zionist intellectuals were not bound to a range of ideas essentially akin to those of the old-fashioned Enlightenment. They could give free play to all contemporary ideologies of the right and the left in proposing new principles for Jewish autonomous existence.[51]

Zionism did not succeed in "conquering the communities" in the West. The non-Zionist opposition, signalized by the Munich Jewish community's effective protest against convening the first Zionist congress in their city and based on ideological principles in statements issued by rabbis in Germany and even in far-off America, remained in control of the Western Jewries. Zionist intellectuals, like Herzl and Nordau, who sought a national consensus to respond to their appeal had to find it in those communities whose myth still perceived Jewry as an ethnic entity, the communities of Eastern European Jewry.

Some Western Zionist intellectuals, moreover, built into their ideology fashionable ideas repudiating rational Idealism. Zionism, through its rejection of Emancipation and Enlightenment as the adequate principles of Jewish life, enabled these men to seek what we now call existentialist doctrines in Jewish tradition and not outside it, and an organic community in the Jewish people, not outside it. The tradition of Orthodox Judaism, especially the mysticism of the Hassidic movement, was the new intellectual heritage, and the community of Eastern European Jewry was the new organic community they discovered.[52]

Thus the over-all effect of the rise of Zionism in Western Europe was not the conquest of the communities there by the ideology of Zionist intellectuals. The effect was rather that Western Zionists, won over by the Zionist myth, found themselves in a new communion with Eastern Jewry. The assumption of the West had been hitherto that the Western situation of Emancipation and the Western principles of Enlightenment were the fundamental defining conditions of Jewish life in modern times; and that if Eastern Jewry did not yet live under those conditions, this was the result of backwardness that time would overcome. The new, Zionist assumption was that the Eastern situation of ethnic community, and the principle of auto-Emancipation that was demanded by such a situation, were the true defining conditions of the contemporary Jewish problem; and that the principles of Western Jewry represented a detour from the true course of Jewish history, and led to no rational solution of the Jewish problem.[53]

The Zionists did not succeed completely in conquering the Eastern communities either. Even more than in the West, the rise of Zionism provoked a multiplication of opposing ideologies. But the underlying myth of Zionism did pervade the consensus of Eastern Jewry and was widely effective there. The general emotional reaction of Zionism to the historic events that gave it birth in Eastern Europe was shared by many others, modernist and traditionalist alike; and the forms in which the Zionist rebellion was symbolized communicated a common sentiment and thus exerted an influence well beyond the Zionist group.

The most characteristic emotional mood of the Zionist myth was its militancy; and what militant Zionism found most odious in Eastern traditionalism and in Western modernism was their passive or accommodating submission to outer compulsions. But militant and rebellious moods in the face of oppression were, in fact, far from foreign to either traditionalists or modernists. Certainly, in Eastern Europe, the modernist youths who hoped to create by revolution a new Russia in which the Jewish problem would disappear (together with the Jewish community) did not lack militancy. In 1882 and in subsequent crises, they fought during pogroms in self-defense groups just as the young Zionists did; and their myth of revolutionary idealism provided the young Zionists with many figures of heroism. And in the West, the organization of Jewish self-defense in Eastern Europe found ready support among leaders of the community some of whom were anything but Zionist.[54]

Resistance to pogroms found no less support in the traditionalist community. The self-defense groups could count not only on the cooperation of young workmen in the pious, poorer quarters but on the sympathy of traditionalists too old or too respectable to fight themselves. That it was Jewish militancy rather than Zionism which evoked this response is clear, because there was a similar warmth in the reaction of many traditionalist Jews in Russia — as well as of pillars of the Jewish community in the West — to the young Jewish social revolutionaries and terrorists.[55] The views of these violent men were anathema and their actions damnable to such conservatives; if for no other reason, then simply because they imperilled the whole community. Yet it was balm for the helpless and humiliated anger of those who witnessed pogroms, from near at hand or from afar, to see the oppressor hurt. So, too, traditionalist Jews did not need to accept the Zionist view that the Jewish problem must be rationally solved in order to feel a lift of pride (often mixed with distaste) when Jewish students suddenly undertook to display an un-Jewish prowess in duelling and athletic games.[56] The adulation of Herzl in the crowded towns of Eastern Europe was certainly shared by many a Jew who had only a slight idea of his views, or who opposed them, but was moved by the legendary figure of this "King of the Jews." [57]

From having touched a responsive chord among both modernists and traditionalists by its myth of militancy, Zionism still had a long course to cover in order to conquer the communal consensus for its more specific tenets. But among Eastern traditionalists and modernists alike, Zionism found understanding and acceptance of other aspects of its myth, of the way in which it perceived the critical experiences of its times, while it provoked sharp differences in the ideological conclusions that it drew.

Zionism strengthened its bonds with the traditionalists, in its mood of *rapprochement* with the past, by molding its own symbols and symbolic actions in the style of tradition.[58] Among the effects of the Zionist mood was a new appreciation of some of the traditional holidays, especially those that recalled heroic episodes in the national history or celebrated Palestinian harvest or sowing seasons. The first pamphlet issued for mass distribution in 1891 by the Zionist secret society B'nei Moshe was a Russian brochure on Hannuka, the festival of the Maccabees; [59] and the observance of the spring festival of Lag Ba'Omer as a Palestinian Arbor Day was accepted by the community throughout the Diaspora after the Zionists initiated this practice. Just as traditionalist Jews collected funds for Palestine in little tin boxes dedicated to "Rabbi Meir Baal ha-Ness," so the Zionists collected funds for Palestine in little blue-white boxes dedicated to the "Keren Kayemet le-Israel." Not only the name of the fund (and the colors of the box) struck a traditional note, but its statutes and purposes were in the authentic style. For the Keren Kayemet was a fund for the purchase of land in Palestine as the inalienable possession of the Jewish people as a whole; and the provisions under which it proposed to lease its holdings vaguely recalled ancient Biblical laws, commandments which tradition regarded as only fallen into disuse since the Jews left the Holy Land but still representing a sacred duty for all Jews to carry out. So, too, when new settlements of farmers were established in Palestine in the 1880's and 1890's, when Hebrew and Yiddish folksongs began to sing their praises,[60] and one of these songs, "Hatikva," became a Zionist anthem; and when a new blue-white flag with a mystic six-cornered Star of David was adopted by the Zionists as the Jewish flag, all these adaptations of traditional materials and traditional styles penetrated far beyond the circle of avowed Zionists, and, indeed, were rejected only where clearly opposed ideologies arose.

Ideological issues which prevented the full *rapprochement* of traditionalism and Zionism soon did arise. The cultural program of those Zionists who were primarily concerned with solving "the problem of Judaism" could not be considered merely a matter of new Zionist symbols and ceremonial acts, of mythic variations in the traditional style, which traditionalists could accept as permissible innovations. It represented a full ideological attack on the very basis of traditionalism; for it proposed not merely to revive and reinvigorate, but to reform and reconstruct Jewish education, the Hebrew language and literature, and, indeed, the whole historic and ethical institutional structure of the tradition.

To such an enterprise the traditionalists could feel themselves drawn only in the early stages, and only in the hope that what began as a turn against the Enlightenment might end as a full return to tradition. When Ahad Ha'am set up his quasi-Masonic Zionist cultural order of B'nei Moshe, traditionalists joined it, and they proposed that the secret society bind itself at least to a *pro forma* acceptance of the most characteristic traditional customs; that much, as a beginning.[61] In the agricultural settlements founded in Palestine in the 1880's, pious Jews were largely represented; and they hoped for the revival of ancient traditional rites in the colonies.[62] So, too, the early peda- gogical projects of the "cultural Zionists" in the Diaspora found many of the traditionalists ready to cooperate.[63]

But it soon appeared that the Zionist *rapprochement* to tradition was not to be a one-sided movement. The revived tradition which the cultural Zionists envisaged was one that would meet the prodigal sons of Jewry halfway. It would have to be elastic enough to express without compromise of conscience the mood of nationalists who were, after all, stamped with the mark of the Enlightenment and who iden- tified with Jewish tradition historically, not ecclesiastically. The demands of the traditionalists in regard to ritual and education were more than such men could meet, while, on the other hand, the ideological position of the secular Zionists provoked the Orthodox to set up their own ideological opposition.

Orthodox opposition to the secular Zionist cultural program in the course of time developed two forms, one Zionist and one anti- Zionist, each with its own ideology. Those who became Religious Zionists were united with other Zionists not only in their political aims but in sharing membership in the World Zionist Organization, while they differed with them in regard to the religious-cultural question. The Orthodox anti-Zionists, on the other hand, rejected membership in the World Zionist Organization on religious grounds, and at the same time developed a religious ideology politically opposed to Zionism.

These ideological divergencies developed rather slowly. Theodor Herzl regarded the Zionist Organization as having one function above all: to serve as an institutional and symbolic embodiment of the sovereign will of the Jews, as a kind of provisional "Government-in- Exile" or, to use his own phrase, as a "gestor negotiorum."[64] Conse- quently he did not wish to have it divided or diverted by issues not related to the main goal — the hope of giving substance to its symbolic sovereignty. In his day, the Zionist Organization not only avoided disputes over the religious-cultural question but also eschewed any serious program of cultural activity.[65] At the First Zionist Congress a general reference was made to the need to "stimulate national consciousness," but the Organization undertook no specific responsibility for a revival of Jewish culture. The cultural activities of Zionists in Palestine and in the Diaspora were not forced as ideological issues that had to be decided by the Congress until the last years of Herzl's leadership. Thereupon, the Orthodox Zionists were organized under the name of Mizrachi as a distinct party in the movement.[66] They proved unable to prevent the Zionist Organization indefinitely from considering the issue of cultural activity, and, in any case, they could not prevent cultural activities by Zionists outside the scope of the Congress. But they successfully insisted on the right of the Orthodox Jews to autonomy and segregation in cultural and religious activities of their own, if they could not achieve compliance with traditionalist standards by all Zionists. Granted this minimum demand, they remained within the Zionist Organization and, later, within the Jewish Community which was set up in Palestine under the Mandate.[67]

When the Tenth Zionist Congress of 1911 brought the Practical Zionists to leadership and approved, as part of their program, the initiation of cultural activities by the Zionist Organization, it precipitated the formation of an anti-Zionist Orthodox movement, Agudat Israel, which was based on an ideology rejecting both the Zionist Organization and Zionist political aims.[68] The idea of seceding from Jewish communities which were not dominated by traditionalists had been advocated since the latter half of the nineteenth century by Western Orthodox groups, accepting Christian ideas of ecclesiastical organization. Prussia and Hungary, in the 1870's, made it legally possible to withdraw from the Jewish community without renouncing Judaism and to organize separatist Orthodox communities paralleling the community organization dominated by other Jewish "denominations." [69] This idea was now extended, in 1912, to the scale of world Jewry. The failure to prevent the Zionist Organization from sponsoring non-traditionalist cultural activities made part of the Religious Zionists leave the World Zionist Organization; and together with anti-Zionist traditionalists in the East, and in alliance with the separatist Orthodoxy of the West, they formed the ultra-traditionalist world organization of Agudat Israel. The separatism characteristic of Agudat Israel as a world organization was also applied in Palestine. When an organized community of Palestine Jews was created in the twenties, the partisans of Agudat Israel would not join it but tried unsuccessfully to gain recognition as a separate Jewish community.[70] In Eastern Europe, however, the idea of communal separatism did not take root. In this dominantly traditional environment, the Western idea of a denominational organization of Jews remained foreign. Here Agudat Israel adopted the same position on the religious-cultural issue, in effect, as the Religious Zionists. They, too, while remaining within the general Jewish community, conducted an autonomous school system in Eastern Europe, side by side with the several systems of secular Hebraists, Yiddishists and of Mizrachi, the Religious Zionists.[71]

The doctrine of the World Organization of Agudat Israel paralleled in a significant detail the doctrine of Theodor Herzl regarding the Zionist Organization. He had regarded the World Zionist Organization as embodying the sovereign will — or the will to sovereignty — of the Jewish people; as a *gestor negotiorum* empowered, in view of the political disorganization and impotence of the people, to represent the Jewish "nation" and act on its behalf. The Zionist Organization was entitled to assume authority on behalf of the Jews until, by its own successful action, a normal situation was achieved making possible the replacement of the organization by a regularly constituted Jewish state. In accordance with this view, Herzl dismissed intransigent opposition to Zionism as a form of resignation from the Jewish people.[72]

So, too, Agudat Israel held that all those who did not submit implicitly to the laws of Jewish tradition, as interpreted by the rabbinical authorities whom it recognized, had thereby fallen away from the divinely appointed course of Jewish destiny, and it might be said they had disenfranchised themselves from the Jewish people by denying its Law. Consequently, when Agudat Israel was formed as a world organization of "Torah-true" Jewry and when it refused to participate, in the Diaspora or in Palestine, in the general Jewish communal organization, or in the Zionist Organization, which pretended to embody the principle of Jewish sovereignty, these were only superficially acts of secession. More properly, in the view of these traditionalists, what had been done was to reestablish the principle of Jewish authority upon its legitimate basis, the strict tradition. For just as Herzl regarded the Zionist Organization, even in its infancy, as the legitimate *gestor negotiorum* of the legally disabled Jewish people, so Jacob Rosenheim, the ideologist of Agudat Israel, believed he had created anew the organ of legitimate communal authority in Jewry by establishing a disciplined world organization of "Torah-true" Jews. By its mere existence, Agudat Israel had once more set the

Jewish people upon the true path, and if it held to its course those who had fallen by the wayside would eventually repent and return.[73]

Not only in the principle of its organization, but also in its attitude to the return to Palestine did the new traditionalist opposition to Zionism adopt ideological views which, in their opposition, reflect the theories of the adversary. A movement based on Jewish tradition is hampered when it attempts to set up as doctrinal principles beliefs which had been traditionally regarded as within the realm of permissive speculation, or even of imaginative elaboration. The latter, according to Maimonides' express statement, had always been the status of the various beliefs which are to be found in the Jewish eschatological tradition concerning the sequence of Messianic events such as the return to Zion and the restoration of Jewish sovereignty.

Some of our Sages say that the coming of Elijah will precede the advent of the Messiah. But no one is in a position to know the details of this and similar things until they have come to pass . . . Hence there is a divergence of opinion on the subject. But be that as it may, neither the exact sequence of those events nor the details thereof constitute religious dogmas. No one should ever occupy himself with the legendary themes or spend much time on midrashic statements bearing on this and like subjects.[74]

In spite of Maimonides' excellent advice, however — and despite the Talmudic anathema on those who "calculate the end of days" — Jews throughout their Exile have occupied themselves with the legendary themes of the Redemption, adopting doctrines concerning the sequence and details of these events as principles of action, if not (except in pseudo-Messianic movements) as religious dogmas.[75] So, too, the traditionalist proto-Zionists of the mid-nineteenth century, followed by the Religious Zionists in the nineteenth and twentieth centuries used one kind of midrashic statement and similar "legendary themes" to justify their position, and traditionalist anti-Zionists, in turn, justified their views with opposing statements and interpretations.

In neither camp was a particular interpretation of this kind adopted by the movement as its stated position, for the whole topic was too firmly classified by tradition as essentially mythic to be publicly proclaimed an ideological principle by a traditionalist movement. But leading theorists among the religious proto-Zionists, such as the rabbis Judah Alcalay and Zvi Hirsch Kalischer had very actively advocated the interpretation that the resettlement of Palestine, the cultivation of its soil in accordance with Biblical laws, and even the rebuilding of the Temple were initial, preparatory stages of the Messianic times.[76] These were duties which the Jews were obliged to carry out before the

Messiah would come, and they were prerequisite for his advent. Thus, the Zionist mythos of auto-Emancipation, the idea that Redemption depended on the active initiative of the Jews, was prefigured in the generation preceding the rise of historic Zionism in the form of a traditionalist interpretation which had been current repeatedly in the past. After the rise of Zionism, the same sort of traditionalist argument from Biblical proof texts and midrashic statements continued to be employed by such Religious Zionist leaders as Rabbi Abraham Isaac Hacohen Kuk, (1865–1935) though, of course, the movement as such did not formulate a binding doctrine on what was recognized as a mythic point.[77]

Against this interpretation, traditionalists of an anti-Zionist bent emphasized two other common interpretations. The first was the stereotyped suspicion of all attempts to "force the End," to bring about the Redemption by human intervention, a suspicion that had sharpened since the pseudo-Messiahs Sabbethai Zevi in the seventeenth and Jacob Frank in the eighteenth century had led their followers into antinomian excesses and apostasy.[78] It was in this vein that Samson Raphael Hirsch took care to remark, concerning the Messianic promise, that Jews must attempt no action on their own initiative to restore their sovereignty, but must pursue their mission in Exile, awaiting the Redemption solely through divine intervention.[79] This view, which was not much more than an academic rebuttal of an academic proposition before the rise of Zionism, took on the aspect of an ideological position when men like Jacob Rosenheim used it as an argument against organized Zionism, and phrased it in the terminology of Western philosophy.[80]

In addition to Rosenheim's ideology of anti-Zionism, based on stressing the mission of Dispersion, there was another "Palestine-oriented" ideology within Agudat Israel, defended by Isaac Breuer (1883–1946). Here, too, the argument, although clothed in modern philosophical phraseology, was conducted in terms of an interpretation of "legendary themes" concerning the role of Zion in history and eschatology that had been current at various times in the tradition. This view did not oppose the proto-Zionist and Zionist interpretation which regarded the building of a normal Jewish community in Palestine as a prerequisite for the Redemption. Instead, it argued that precisely because the community in Palestine had this crucial function, it had to be a holy community. The existence of a secular or non-Orthodox Jewish community in Palestine was a positive danger: for in the Diaspora, it was the Gentiles alone who impiously claimed the divine attribute of sovereignty; in Palestine, the Jewish community itself, even in its embryonic stage, would make that claim. If the "Torah-true" Jews everywhere should shun the communal institutions of the non-Orthodox Jews, in Palestine they must do more — they must oppose and try to abort the creation of the unbelieving community. Failing this, it was the duty of Agudat Israel to concentrate upon building up a separatist "Torah-true" community in Palestine until it could hope to become dominant there.[81]

These quasi-ideological positions, for the reasons we have indicated, were not formulated as doctrines binding upon Agudat Israel. Not being entirely compatible between themselves, they alternately determined the position of the organization regarding "practical work" in Palestine. And while neither was strictly formulated as an ideological position, both were freely employed in the polemics between Zionists and anti-Zionists. This debate, often carried on in the traditional style and always with traditional ideas, was conducted on behalf of the Zionists by the Mizrachi, and it had no direct effect upon the ideas of other Zionists regarding the Jewish state. Indirectly, however, the issues debated between the traditionalists involved the whole Zionist movement and its idea of Jewish sovereignty. The demands regarding religious and cultural questions raised by the Orthodox in the forum of the Zionist Organization were not unaffected, in formulation and in intensity, by the need of the Mizrachi movement to defend itself against Agudat Israel in another forum, the forum of the traditionalist community.

Much the same relationship developed out of a similar situation within the Eastern Jewish community in regard to the other "party" or "trend" that was formally organized at an early date in the World Zionist Organization. Like the Religious Zionists, so, too, the Labor Zionists defended a special ideological position in the Zionist movement. This position was held not only by a group that remained within the Zionist Organization, but by another group that was ideologically opposed to membership in the organization. Against those Jewish radicals in Eastern Europe who opposed membership in the Zionist Organization or who were ideologically opposed to Zionism itself, the Labor Zionists engaged in an ideological battle based on conceptions and methods of argument that had no direct relevance for other Zionists but were the common terms of discourse recognized among radical groups at the time.

The issues that the Socialist Zionists had to debate arose in relation to Marxist theory and the principles of Russian revolutionary organization. The basic element in the Jewish situation, from a socialist point of view, was that the Jews had no significant proletarian or peasant classes, which were the recognized beneficiaries of revolutionary action according to the existing stereotype. This in itself predisposed Jewish Socialists to ignore the Jewish situation (even when they might accept the views of some Austrian Socialists, or of Marx and Engels themselves, about the importance of the "national struggle" of other peoples) and to accept the doctrine that the Jewish problem would be solved as an incidental result of the general revolutionary struggle of the workers and peasants.[82]

But this was precisely the kind of doctrine which the Zionists, in their repentant return to their own people, could not tolerate. The absence of Jewish workers and farmers was given quite a different interpretation by them. The very fact that the Jews had no significant workers' and farmers' class was the core of the Jewish problem. It was this special situation to which Jewish Socialists must address themselves, both in order to analyze it scientifically and, through this analysis, to delineate a rational solution for the Jewish problem.

In the analysis they developed, the Socialist Zionist and other nationalist radicals among the Jews in Eastern Europe originated new conceptions and hypotheses within the Marxian system of scientific socialism, and new tactical "theses" within the Russian revolutionary movement. Jews had few proletarians and few farmers, according to the "new" analysis (which had, indeed, many precursors) because of a history of exclusion from the land and from guild-dominated trades. This very common observation led Socialist Zionists like Ber Borochov (1881–1917) to develop not only a special theory of Jewish history, but a new general Marxist principle.[83] In addition to the analysis of the class conflict within each nation, a correct Marxist analysis of history required attention to the conflict between the same classes of different nations. Whereas the interclass struggle arises from "the relations of production," the intraclass national struggle arises from competition for "the conditions of production," for what Borochov called a "strategic base" — land, natural resources, access to channels of trade, and the sovereign control of all these. The peculiar principle of Jewish history had been the exclusion of all Jewish classes from control of the conditions of production, for, as an exiled people, they were without a strategic base. Consequently, the history of the Jews was one of continual migrations. Called in to fill "interstitial," pioneering roles in new territories (to bring trade and capital to backward agrarian and new mercantile economies), they were driven out when the economy matured and competitors for the same roles arose among the national majority. Therefore, the solution of the Jewish problem depended on establishing a Jewish strategic base, a homeland where

Jews would be the national majority. Only in this way, moreover, would a Jewish working and peasant class arise, allowing the Jews to take a normal part in the class struggle.

Although these innovations in Marxist theory had little more direct effect upon the ideas of other Zionists concerning Jewish sovereignty than did the novellae with which the traditionalists debated among themselves *pro* and *contra* Zionism, the controversy had significant indirect effects. The question of socialist principles in the creation of the Jewish state became an issue at the Zionist Congresses, just as the religious question did. So, too, the growth of a partisan socialist version of Zionism produced reservations among the Labor Zionists upon their acceptance of the full consensus that Zionism aimed at. For some Socialist Zionists, the Marxist condemnation of "class collaboration" meant that participating — and, what is more, participating voluntarily — in a general organ of Jewish national authority such as the bourgeois Zionist Organization was impossible. Others, however, defied this stereotype and worked within the Zionist Organization, but formed a (or usually more than one) separate "trend" or "party" and strove to give a socialist character to the organization and to the Jewish resettlement in Palestine from the start.[84]

Thus, as an ideological challenge, the introduction of Zionist ideas had the same effect among Socialists as it had among traditionalist Jews. It led to ideological divisions and new barriers; it divided not only Socialists into Zionist and anti-Zionist partisans, but also the Zionist Organization into Socialist and bourgeois, or General, Zionist parties. It followed a course, then, quite similar to that of Religious Zionism. But in another respect, as an emotional force, the effect of the Zionist myth, or of the experience expressed by Zionism, upon the modernists in Eastern Europe was far more decisive than the reception of the new Zionist militancy among the traditionalist community.

As a mythic force, the Zionist mood penetrated and infiltrated the traditionalist community along paths that had long been trodden out in the tradition. That symbolisms of Zion were familiar to traditionalists need hardly be mentioned. They were so familiar as perhaps to be trivialized. If the new Zionist variations of them added anything, it was possibly a freshness of feeling, partly arising from the new forms of ceremony that were devised, partly from the new vitality that the Zionist mood infused into the old forms. The mood of militancy was always present in the tradition though perhaps suppressed or formalized. When a traditionalist accepted Zionism he gave release to the militancy that was latent in the community, and this was perhaps more significant than his acceptance of the new forms of Zionist militancy.

Among the modernists in the Eastern European Jewish community, however, the Zionist mood achieved a far more significant result. It achieved a real, new consensus in the community, so that ideological anti-Zionists among the modernists yielded to the mythic force of the Zionist attitude by an outright reversal of opinion. The Zionist tag of "assimilationism" became a stereotype to which even the anti-Zionists bowed in Eastern Europe; and that it was, indeed, a case of yielding is proved by the reluctance with which this change of heart was undergone.[85]

Militancy in itself was not a new mood for the modernists. We have noted a few illustrations of a "militant" mood among Western modernists that sound like prefigurations of Zionism itself. But it is needless to seek out these byways of Western modernism for our proof. The Jewish struggle for Emancipation in the West was fought with a militancy no less bold and proud than that of Zionism.[86] Of course, the militancy of Western modernism was a militant demand to share the Enlightenment and Emancipation of all Western society, a proud insistence on being included. A formulation of Jewish militancy which stressed that freedom must be achieved apart from the general freedoms of the whole society, and that Jews must, for this reason, organize separately and take action separately, was not characteristic of Western modernism. In the early years of the Emancipation, notions of this sort were voiced and had seemed, at least, logically possible and emotionally natural, but soon they were ideologically excluded. By the time Zionism arose, modernism no longer had any place for such formulas as permissible mythic variations. To recapture them required a true change of heart. In these respects Enlightened modernists in Eastern Europe did not differ, in the beginning, from Western modernists.

The pogroms of 1881 turned some young Jewish intellectuals from the revolutionary cause of the Russian peasant to the national cause of the Jews. But in those years, Jewish revolutionaries were a very minor and quite a new phenomenon. The decades which followed saw socialism attract a far larger following among Jews, not restricted at all to intellectuals but including young people of every kind of background and, in particular, young Jewish workmen. The Jewish Socialist movement now consisted not of a handful of young missionaries who preached the revolution to the Russian peasant, but of Jewish units and organizations comprising Jewish "rank and file" as well as leaders. But in addition to sheer numbers there was another element which cannot be ignored: the new awareness of the Jews as a separate entity, a sensitivity to their special situation and their special problems, which prevailed after the 1880's.

The logical end to which this new awareness led was the recognition of the Jews as a separate people in the multinational Russian and Austro-Hungarian Empires. As an ideological principle, this view was resisted by young Jewish intellectuals brought up on a Marxist tradition that had no place for the Jews. But, notwithstanding this ideological block, the Socialist leaders who came into contact with Jewish laborers ultimately yielded to the mythic rejection of "assimilationism" and recognized the ethnic integrity of Eastern European Jewry. The anti-Zionist Socialist leaders, who began with little more than the thesis that socialist defense of Jewish laborers was justified and who wished to employ the Yiddish language in their propaganda only until they could teach the Jewish workers Russian, ended, more or less, as Diaspora nationalists. Their anti-Zionism remained in their opposition to the return to Zion and to the Hebrew language. But their own view had undergone a striking change from the time that they had hoped to see the Jews, together with Jewish problem, happily disappear in the classless society of the Russian people. Now they had become devotees of the Yiddish language and the new Yiddish literature, and ardent proponents of cultural autonomy for minority groups; or even of personal national rights for the members of nationalities dispersed too thinly over Russia or the Ukraine to claim the recognition of their language and culture in a region or in localities where they were significantly represented.

Neither in their Yiddishism nor in their advocacy of Jewish cultural autonomy in the Diaspora did these Socialists set up ideological barriers that clearly divided them from the Zionists. The contrary was true: by championing a Jewish national language, even if not Hebrew, and Jewish cultural autonomy, even if not sovereignty in Zion, the Jewish Socialists had bowed to the consensus of opinion and accepted the Zionist attitude epitomized in the use of the word "assimilationist" as a term of condemnation and abuse. Whether Yiddish or Hebrew should be favored as the Jewish national language, and whether or not — or to what extent — national minority rights should be fought for and exercised in the Diaspora until the return to Zion could be completed, were issues on which Zionists disputed among themselves, not issues on which all Zionists opposed all anti-Zionists. But on one question the anti-Zionists, and particularly the Jewish Socialists of Eastern Europe, confronted the Zionists with a clear and uniform ideological challenge. All anti-Zionists were opposed to all Zionists in rejecting the cardinal belief that only through the restoration of Jewish sovereignty and, moreover, only in Palestine could the Jewish problem be solved.

Ideologically, this was the central issue between Zionists and non-Zionists as well as anti-Zionists, and in Western as well as Eastern Europe. But two curious facts must be noted; first, that the ideological arguments of Zionists for the choice of Palestine as the place where the Jewish problem must be solved were exceedingly flimsy, and they can hardly explain the emotional conviction of the Zionists on this point; second, that the real reasons for the unbending Zionist fixation on Palestine were mythic and historic attachments, taken over by the Zionists from other parts of the Jewish community. For there were preexisting connections which bound not only Zionists but their opponents, and Western as well as Eastern Jews, in a practical as well as sentimental, contemporary as well as inherited, involvement with the Land of Israel.

4 ATTACHMENT TO ZION: TRADITIONAL BONDS AND INVOLVEMENT OF JEWISH ORGANIZATIONS

I⊤ is a commonplace observation frequently made about Zionism that its bond to Zion is an irrational attachment, not a rational conclusion. This generalization is usually developed into far too rigid corollaries. The rational ideologies of Western modernism, it is said, completely severed the tie to Zion. Even Western Zionists like Theodor Herzl only chose Palestine for the Jewish national home as a concession to the Eastern Zionists, still under the thrall of tradition. As for the traditionalists their relation to Zion is presented in only one light: as a living, fervent, and unambiguous attachment, sometimes dormant, because an immediate return was impossible, but never complicated by emotional or intellectual reservations. As proof no further evidence is needed than the pleas to be restored to Zion which recur constantly in Jewish ritual observance. The depth and massive impact of this traditional attitude may be taken for granted. It is necessary, however, to consider some mythic and ideological complications in the attitudes to Zion prevalent during the period when Zionism had to define its own position.[1]

I

"Zion" is, of course, a place name for an actual country with a well-known geographical location; yet it functioned as a markedly utopian conception in the myths of traditionalists, modernists, and Zionists alike. For all of them, the symbol "Zion" expressed an ideal, a historical vision whose exact physiognomy was not defined by what appeared on the map of Palestine. Its character was far more significantly defined by the specific content of another idea, the idea of "Exile." For it was Exile, not Zion, which the Jews experienced as a concrete historical reality. The utopia of Zion was delineated according to the perceived nature of Exile, for it reflected, as in a negative image, the reverse of everything rejected in the actual Jewish situation in the Diaspora. For the traditionalists, "Zion" meant the Holy Land, but the Holy Land transfigured by the Messianic return which would heal all the ills of Exile. For the modernists, "Zion" became a symbol detached from its original geographic denotation; it was an honorific title that could readily be applied to any country where Jews lived in anticipation of the full solution of the Jewish problem through their emancipation. For the Zionists, the utopian image of "Zion" once again referred to Palestine alone, but to a Palestine which tended to have no specific qualities other than the postulated one of being the only place where the Jewish problem could be solved. Each conception of "Zion" reflects a particular view of the nature of the Jewish "Exile."

The traditional idea of Exile — a penance imposed as a sign of chosenness and, at the same time, a due penalty for sin — is an ambivalent idea, as we have already noted. The attitude of traditionalists to their Exile was a mixed one, compounded of a pious and loving acceptance of the penance and of fervent prayer to be relieved "speedily, in our day" of the penalty. Such a mixture is obviously unstable. Historical circumstances could, and did on occasion, cause such a sharp rejection of Exile that it altogether excluded any measure of acceptance, or, on the other hand, make acceptance so complete that rejection almost disappeared. Such changes naturally affected the utopian — that is, the inversely related — image of Zion.

One could easily write a history of traditional Jewry in terms of a cycle based on the mutations of these ideas.[2] When oppression in the Exile reached an intolerable pitch, Messianic enthusiasm rose in intensity and there were movements for an immediate return to Zion. The idea of Exile was so thoroughly rejected that, in their enthusiastic conviction of being redeemed, the chiliastic sectaries abrogated the fast of the Ninth of Ab, in which the destruction of the Temple is mourned. These Messianic attempts, however, not only failed to achieve the Restoration to Zion, ending the Exile in fact and not just symbolically, but (a development paralleled in the movements of religious and chiliastic enthusiasm in other faiths as well) they led to emotional excesses and perversions of belief that, in the case of Jewish pseudo-Messianism, did not stop short of apostasy. In reaction against such results, the pendulum swung back to a new acceptance of the penance of Exile — and to a deep-rooted fear and suspicion of projects for an immediate return to Zion or restoration of Jewish sovereignty. Such ideas were condemned as pseudo-Messianic attempts to "force the End."[3]

Yet even in periods when the Messianic Zion seemed remote and attempts to bring it near were regarded with suspicion, the ties of traditional Jewry with the actual, physical Zion remained close. In the cult of Exile which traditionalist Jews built up in reaction to the seventeenth-century pseudo-Messianism of Sabbethai Zevi, the Land of Israel played a central, paradoxical role. The Jews must sanctify the Exile by their penance and not seek a final safety from its oppression by a premature Return to Zion; this was the view that grew up. But in the holy exercises of Jewishness — that is, in the penance of Exile — the Land of Israel was far from being excluded. In fact, it occupied a privileged position in the ordeal of Exile. For, in Jerusalem the doors of heaven stood open to prayer more than in other places; and the other holy cities of Palestine, too, Hebron, Safed, and Tiberias, were efficacious in themselves to perfect the piety and wisdom of a Jew who came there, whether as a pilgrim or, still better, as a settler devoting his life to pious works. While an attempted return to a Messianic Zion was feared by the consensus of the time as a dangerous idea, to go to observe the rites of Exile in the actual Zion was an act of high merit. It was not only the most efficacious way of performing the penance of Exile by which the Messianic advent would in due time be merited; it also, if one may say so, augmented the fund of Jewish illumination and holiness and increased the power of the Jewish people residing in unholy lands to hallow the Exile by their penance.[4]

The most characteristic attitude of the Enlightenment toward the Jewish Exile was to deny it as an idea and suppress it as an experience. This was in sharp contrast to the traditional attitude. No matter how strongly the *acceptance* of Exile was stressed at any time by traditionalists, they had still viewed it as a punishment for sin; and even though tradition said that the Jews were dispersed because they are the Chosen People, only when they were gathered in again would they be redeemed. All these themes, which are inherent in the paired traditional images of Exile and Zion, were either denied or neutralized in the Enlightenment literature.

Even so conservative a representative of the Enlightenment as the Hebrew philosopher of history, Nahman Krochmal (1785–1840), contributed to a rational deflation of the traditional drama of sin, penance, and redemption. He replaced this pattern with a natural cycle of the origin, efflorescence, and degeneration of peoples continually recurring in history. What marked out the Jews from other peoples, in his theory, was that the national ideas of other peoples were relative, proper to their particular time and place in history, but the Jewish national idea is the Absolute, God Himself. Hence, Jewish history does not end with a single cycle, like the history of other peoples, but continues over and over again to rise, flower, and decay. Nevertheless, the character and causes of the unending Jewish cycle are explained by no different mechanisms from those that explain the single historical cycle of each of the other peoples, by mechanisms and causes that are entirely natural. Thus what the tradition calls the national sinfulness which caused the beginning and the persistence of the Exile, and which arises from a free choice between good and evil, is converted by this rational theory into an inevitable, quasi-biological phase of cyclical decay.[5]

In the same way, Enlightenment theory tended to eliminate the idea of divine punishment from the concept of Exile, leaving only the idea of a mission for which the Jews were chosen, and for the sake of which they were dispersed. Traditionalism, too, of course, had a conception of a Jewish "mission," though not the name. What we have called the traditional "cult of Exile" prevailed at times when fear of pseudo-Messianism was acute; accordingly, it was strongly stressed that God and God alone would determine the time and manner of the Messianic advent. At the same time, no one thought of denying that human acts were relevant to the Redemption. Such historical developments as, for example, the spread of monotheism through Christianity and Islam or the grant of civil emancipation to the Jews were interpreted as preparations for the Messiah in which the Gentiles served as the agents of God's purposes.[6] But the most significant active human role in the traditionalists' divine drama of history was that of the Chosen People. In the sense in which it could be said that men shared in bringing about the advent of the Messiah, this mission was to be accomplished directly or mystically by the Jews: by the purging of their sins through oppression and by their practice of Jewish sacred devotions even in the unholy lands of the Dispersion — and, of course, in the Holy Land during the Exile of the divine Presence. In the idea of a Jewish Mission developed by the Western modernists, on the other hand, the Jewish role was neither direct nor mystical, but indirect and rational — or one might say symbolic rather than substantive. The function of the Jews was not to play a protagonist's role in the divine drama, but to serve, at most, as a modest kind of Greek chorus. Not their devotion or suffering, but precisely the growing illumination of the Gentiles was the process by which the Messianic era was being brought about; and, until the final act was concluded by the real protagonists, the Jews were set in the Diaspora to live among the cast of actors as a sect apart, an example of pure, rational, monotheistic faith, testifying that the triumphant consummation of the drama was still to come.[7]

As for the penalties associated with the Exile — and the strong consciousness of Jewish sinfulness — these were no longer considered essential elements in God's plan. To be sure, the favorite mythic symbol to represent the divine mission of the Jewish Dispersion was Deutero-Isaiah's graphic image of the Suffering Servant.[8] Suffering is, indeed, a natural metaphorical association of ideas with the notion of a divine mission. But the actual suffering which constituted the concrete historical experience of Exile was not accepted by the modernists as a divine decree inherently connected with their mission. On the contrary: the most fundamental article of their belief was to regard the oppression of the Jews as an expression of human (that is, Gentile) error or ill-will which they were determined to overcome rationally. Thus the idea of Exile was separated, for the modernists, from the idea of Dispersion, and "Exile" came to mean no more than the civil disabilities and other inequities of the Jewish position. When the Gentiles became sufficiently enlightened to emancipate the Jews — and this was thought either to have occurred already or to be imminent — then the Exile would be at an end, leaving the dispersed Jews only their mission, free from penalty.[9]

The shortfall of emancipation and the "relapses" into anti-Semitism in the nineteenth century were experienced by the traditionalist Jews as only another manifestation of Exile, for they had never abandoned that idea. The modernists, however, having implicitly renounced the idea, were forced to suppress the natural inclination to experience anti-Semitism and discrimination as part of the familiar image of a divinely ordained Exile. Instead they chose to perceive it as a passing eccentricity of events; for they would explain it away as a consequence of still insufficient enlightenment among the Gentiles or of backwardness among the Jews.

The latter explanation had the more important ideological consequences for the Enlightenment. One of the features of Jewish backwardness, in the eyes of the modernists, was a superstitious attachment to Zion. In the long correspondence of the Hebrew writer, Joseph Perl (1773–1839), with the Austrian authorities, which went on for over twenty years, one of his recurrent complaints was that Jewish obscurantists were conducting clandestine fund collections for the community in Palestine.[10] Not only the cultural backwardness of supporting a community with no more productive function than that of prayer annoyed such a modernist as Perl; he also disapproved of the diversion of Austrian funds to a foreign land. We have noted how Napoleon and other early nineteenth-century authorities brought pressure or made specific demands on the Jews henceforth to consider Zion a foreign land, and set this as part of the price of toleration or emancipation. This price not only Reform Judaism but other enlightened modernists readily paid.

Yet even while renouncing the idea of a Return to Zion, now declared foreign to Jewish hopes, the modernists retained Zion as a symbol. This they did in the same way that, by substituting universal Messianism for a personal Messiah, the Messianic symbol was retained: "Zion" became, in a strict sense, a utopia, fading from a name historically and geographically definite to a generic symbol. Under the magic of an Emancipation identified with the Messiah, any place in the Diaspora which the Jews wished to think of as home and not Exile was readily perceived as the new Zion.[11]

Even in the Enlightenment's phase of neo-Hebraic revival, which aroused a literary interest in Biblical Palestine together with Biblical Hebrew, the image of Zion was sublimated to a rationalistic abstraction. This effect emerges quite clearly from the very popular Biblical romances of the Lithuanian Hebraist, Abraham Mapu (1808–1867). There Zion is imagined as representing a Golden Age of the Jews, directly opposed to their decadent present. Instead of being rootless, defenseless peddlers and middlemen, fearful and cunning, the ancient Judeans were shepherds, farmers, soldiers, dwelling in staunch independence in the bosom of Nature. Nevertheless, in the program of the Enlightenment for the recovery of the pristine Jewish virtues, the actual Land of Israel played no part; for the reform of Jewish occupations and character was a goal the modernists hoped to attain in the Diaspora itself, in the very countries where the rootless Jews lived. As for the image of Zion, painted, for example, by Mapu, they construed this as no more than a symbol of the classical past. In this way the physical Zion was reduced — or sublimated — to a true utopia: in relation to the future of the Jews, it did not exist.[12]

Zionism begins with a new awareness of Exile as a fact, reversing its denial as an idea and suppression as an experience by modernism. At the same time, Zionism could not accept, but indeed revolted against, a traditional commitment to Exile as a penance to be lovingly borne. Instead it perceived Exile as an intolerable condition for which a rational solution must be sought — in the return to Zion. But what the image of Zion came to mean for Zionism reflects those aspects of

Exile for which it was proposed as a rational solution: the "problem of the Jews" — their unresolved oppression and their rootlessness — and the "problem of Judaism" — its crisis after the collapse of traditional beliefs. To remedy these two problems, Zionism proposed that the Jews must overcome their cause, the abnormal condition of Exile, and gain freedom by regaining the normal conditions of national existence, particularly their own land. They needed a place where they would no longer be a perpetual minority and where they could revive their own culture on a secular basis.

But if Zion were simply the reverse image of Exile in its two aspects, the problem of the Jews and the problem of Judaism, this entailed certain very difficult questions. There was, first of all, the problem: why Palestine? If all that was needed was simply a land where Jews could be the majority, why would not any territory do? Herzl, in the beginning, was quite as ready to accept Argentina as Palestine for the territory of the Jewish state; and although he was won over more and more by the irrational attachment to Zion of his followers, his basic analysis of the Jewish problem had nothing in it which logically required Zion as the place where the solution had to be found.[13]

If the source of the Jewish problem is the fact that the Jews live as unwelcome guests in lands occupied and ruled by others, the solution obviously demands a land not occupied and ruled by others, where Jews could establish themselves as hosts — a territorial vacuum, that is. Ber Borochov made a specific attempt to prove that Zion and no other country in the world was the one place where, by historical necessity, the problem of the Jews would be solved.[14] And the essence of his proof was precisely this argument: that Palestine alone, of all countries, was a natural territorial vacuum to which no other people was attracted and which only a people in the peculiar condition of the Jews would ever claim as the base of a national economy and culture. But this argumentation, too, had a very brief life, and a much franker answer was given by other Socialist Zionist theorists: in the works of J. H. Brenner (1881–1921) and Berl Katzenelson (1887–1944), it is made quite clear that nothing in the physical nature and political circumstances of Palestine made this the chosen land of Zionism. What they saw in Palestine was a place to make a last attempt to establish a sound and worthy Jewish life, after having abandoned in disillusionment all solutions for the Jewish problem in other countries.[15] Why it should be in Zion rather than anywhere else that this last ditch fight should be made, they did not even attempt

to explain; and in a theory which relies so much on the heroic freedom
of man's decision, it is natural that such arbitrariness should be
accepted.

Ahad Ha'am, who considered the problem of Judaism — the search
for a new basis for preserving the individuality of Jewish culture —
to be the question Zionism was called upon to solve, was able to prove
to his own satisfaction (and with far more telling arguments than
Borochov's) that Palestine was *not* a suitable place for solving the
problem of the Jews, the concrete suffering of an oppressed minority.
His argument was quite simply that Palestine was not a vacuum, but
it was occupied and ruled by other peoples with definite national
interests in the land, and that Jewish mass immigration was not a
process that existing historical trends could conceivably bring to
completion in Zion in the foreseeable future. But Ahad Ha'am, in
turn, gives no serious consideration to the question why Zion must
be chosen as the place for solving the spiritual problem of Judaism.
His very telling analysis of the crisis of Jewish culture between the
Scylla of traditionalist ossification and the Charybdis of disintegration
and assimilation leads only to the conclusion that Jews need to
establish somewhere, even in miniature, an autonomous secular community with a certain degree of social and economic self-sufficiency.
Logically, what such a solution required was an unoccupied territory,
a vacuum, free from non-Jewish domination. This alone would provide
the conditions for a Jewish culture that need not be so defensive
that it could permit no spontaneity, but would be capable of expressing individuality freely without undue influence from a foreign environment. As to why the autonomous community *had* to be established
in Zion — on this point Ahad Ha'am merely tells us that in their
vigorous youth the Jews could create a national center; now, in their
age and weakness, they can only rely on the attraction of the old
historic home. In another place, he remarks in passing that to seek
a new national language would be like destroying one's memory.[16]

A similar argument along somewhat different lines is far more
emphatically, though quite as vaguely, stated by A. D. Gordon (1856–
1922). He conceives of Jewish culture as a plant which originally
sprang up from roots in Zion. Uprooted, it became moribund, and to
restore its health it needs to be replanted in its native soil.[17] While
Gordon sometimes argues philosophically as well as metaphorically,
this particular thesis, no matter how often reiterated, remains a mere
assertion and is neither supported by evidential proof nor derived
from other basic assumptions of Gordon's system. As to the evidence,
a critical historian has no difficulty in showing that the fundamental

ideas of Jewish tradition may have originated in the desert or the Diaspora quite as much as in Zion, and are, in fact, quite independent of any geographic location.[18] And when related to the other basic conceptions of his own doctrine, Gordon's analysis of the problem of Judaism may prove no more than the need for rerooting the Jews in a natural environment, not necessarily a particular environment, in order that they may draw once more upon the generalized cosmic energy with which he believed such contact infuses national culture.

Basically the tie of the Zionist idea with Zion is not theoretical at all. It is an "existential" reality, a historical fact which Zionism does not question but knows itself to embody. The fundamental movement of Zionism, emotionally even more than intellectually, is away from the Enlightenment and back toward tradition. Turning from a concept which, to its mind, had dissipated the elements of Jewish individuality, Zionism naturally bound itself to the traditional symbols of Jewish individuality. If it preached restoration of the sovereignty of the Jews in a land of their own, it was symbolically obvious that the right land was their own land, the Land of Israel. The Zion that Jews remembered in their prayers for centuries was inevitably that Zion in which Zionism sought a solution, even if a rational solution, of the Jewish problem. It was the only place in which Jews felt any sentiment of national ownership.[19] Particularly was this true of those concerned primarily with the "problem of Judaism."

But once one had settled on Zion as the place to solve the Jewish problem, the actual nature of Zion had to be considered rationally. What advantages or drawbacks Palestine in fact presented as a site upon which to build a Jewish nation was a question upon which ideological differences arose. For most Zionists, this debate came after a decision irrevocably taken on symbolic grounds. For others — particularly those concerned primarily with the "problem of the Jews" — the symbolic values won out over practical values only after much hesitation; or else they were set aside in favor of "practical" considerations, and a Zionist became a Territorialist and sought to found a Jewish ethnic settlement in some place believed to be more richly endowed or less encumbered politically than Zion.

But it should not be imagined that symbolic values alone caused the historic fixation of Zionism upon Zion. There were tangible historical grounds, apart from Zionism, which placed Palestine concretely in the line of Jewish migration toward the end of the nineteenth century. Zionism itself was at first as much a consequence as it later became a major contributing cause to this development. Moreover, the pre-Zionist settlement in Palestine had become a standing

concern of European Jews and Jewish organizations during the nineteenth century. A rational program for the welfare and growth of
the Jewish community in Palestine, embracing aid to immigrants
and economic and educational reform, was actively pursued before
Zionism arose by groups who became non-Zionists or anti-Zionists,
after the rise of Zionism. To this complex of circumstances the attachment of Zionism to Zion is in no small degree indebted. On the other
hand, the rise of Zionism, and of its political proposals regarding the
development and ultimate status of Palestine, caused repercussions
of various kinds among Jewish groups already concerned with the
community in the Holy Land. The reactions of these groups and their
successors were, in turn, factors that Zionism had to take into account
in evolving the specific forms of its own ideas and activities.

II

The Zionist bond to Zion, as we have seen, involved an attempt
to graft upon the stock of the traditional attachment to the actual
country a modernist rationale which had no real relationship to the
actual country. In terms of the rational requirements of Zionist ideology, "Zion" need have meant no more than it meant for the modernists: a place where the "Exile" would be ended and the Jewish problem
solved. But while the modernists were capable of applying the name
"Zion" to any country in which Jews were emancipated, the Zionists
insisted not only that a national ingathering in *one* country was essential to solve the Jewish problem, but that the historic Land of Israel,
and that land alone, was the utopian Zion. In this attachment to the
actual Zion, the Zionists shared and relied upon a bond that the
traditionalists had always kept alive.

The bond was not one of prayer and mythic imagination alone,
but had always been a bond of pilgrimage and settlement, and of
continuous communication between the Diaspora and the Jewish
community in Palestine. Recurrent catastrophes sometimes reduced
the numbers of the Jewish community in the Holy Land to miniature
proportions, just as they repeatedly decimated the general population
of the country. Even when Palestine enjoyed a period of relative
continuity under a single regime, as during more than two hundred
years of Mameluke rule following the collapse of the Crusader kingdom
and four hundred years of Ottoman rule thereafter, the local political
conditions were anything but stable. During the Mameluke period,
Palestine was one of the loosely held, outermost Eastern provinces
of these war lords of Egypt, and it was repeatedly harried by Mongol

tribesmen and threatened by Turkish rulers to the northeast. During the Ottoman period, too, Palestine was a border province, always open to incursions of Bedouin tribes to the southeast and of Mameluke rebels to the southwest. At all times local feuds and uncertain tenure of local authority made life hazardous.[20] Yet even in those days of perpetual unrest and economic decline, immigrants continually replenished the Jewish community.

The expulsions from Britain and France brought groups of uprooted Jews to Palestine in the beginning of the thirteenth century, even while the Saracens and Crusaders still fought over its possession. In the second generation after the expulsion from Spain, when Ottoman rule had been established in Palestine, Portuguese Marranos and refugees from the Papal states sought a haven in Palestine. Refugees came from the disturbed regions of Eastern Europe, too, at the close of the seventeenth century and thereafter. Not only the sporadic social upheavals and Messianic revivals in the Diaspora, but a constant impulse of piety led scholars and men and women of sufficient means to come to end their days in the Holy Land. And, by the end of the eighteenth century, Jewish immigration to Palestine out of religious motives was no longer an individual and spontaneous matter, or even an episodic venture of chance groups. Rival factions of the Hassidic movement, as well as the outstanding opponents of Hassidism, the disciples of Rabbi Elijah of Vilna (1720–1797), regarded the settlement of their representatives in the holy cities as a significant advantage in prestige for their movement, a valuable gain in the odor of sanctity. In consequence the immigration of pious Jews of the Ashkenazic community was not only encouraged but virtually organized as well as supported during the late eighteenth and early nineteenth centuries.[21]

Neither conditions in Palestine nor the kind of immigrant who came favored a large or steady growth in the Jewish community, despite the continuing influx. During the Ottoman period, Jewish subjects of the Sultan moved freely in and out of Palestine from other parts of the far-flung Empire, from North Africa to the Balkans — as did also Moslems and Christians. The Ottoman Empire was hospitable, moreover, to refugees from Christian Europe. But the Jewish immigrants and residents were drawn to Constantinople, Damascus, or Cairo, where economic and political conditions were far more favorable, rather than to Palestine. Of those who settled in the Holy Land, only a small part were supported by the local economy as tradesmen, artisans, or farmers. A disproportionate part of the community was made up of old people, especially widows, and impecunious scholars, dependent on donations from abroad. The Ashkenazic immigrants, who began in the eighteenth century to become an increasingly important element in the community, were economically dependent in an even higher proportion than the rest. The difference in language, customs, and conditions of trade and production in Palestine from their old homes in Eastern Europe made it harder for them than for the Sephardic or Arabic-speaking Jews to become self-supporting within the Palestinian economy.[22]

Under the circumstances the Jewish community, like the population of Palestine as a whole, while it responded with remarkable rapidity to locally favorable conditions by rising sharply in numbers, continually was driven down by catastrophes or dropped off under the attrition of chronic hardships to miniature proportions. The whole population of Palestine, a region that in Roman times had probably supported three million, was in the neighborhood of three hundred thousand at the beginning of Ottoman rule and did not grow larger in a period of three centuries.[23] The variations which took place did not substantially increase the total for any significant period of time, but caused a temporary increase of the population in one part of Palestine together with its decrease elsewhere, as conditions of economic stability and political security varied from place to place. The Jewish population experienced not only sudden shifts of concentration, as when earthquake, plague, and pillage drove the community of Safed to seek new homes in Jerusalem or fiscal exactions caused an exodus from Jerusalem to Gaza, but also occasional very rapid general rises of population, favored by transient conditions. Thus at the height of its flowering in the sixteenth century, the Jewish community of Safed was variously estimated as counting from twelve to forty, or even seventy thousand tax-paying households — or, at the more reasonable estimate, forty thousand persons. In the mid-eighteenth century the growth of the community in Jerusalem to a reported figure of ten thousand aroused the ire of the local authorities, who took drastic measures to reduce their number.[24] These manifestations of a capacity for growth were neither lasting nor continuous, for the community was always driven back to a very low figure. The approximately six thousand Jews who were reported to Sir Moses Montefiore (1784–1885) to be living in Palestine in 1839 were equal in number to the community at the beginning of Ottoman rule in the sixteenth century or to those living in Palestine in the late thirteenth century — and there were times when oppression or natural calamities drove the number still lower.[25]

The political instability and economic decline of Palestine as a whole, and the special difficulties of adjustment confronting the Jewish community, made up as it was of a large proportion of dependent persons and new immigrants, were well understood by the Jewish leaders of the time. Their awareness of these difficulties led them sometimes to adopt negative conclusions. Realizing that the Jewish community could only be maintained artificially by subsidies from abroad and that constant vigilance was required to ward off threats from greedy authorities and hostile neighbors in the Holy Land, the Palestinian leaders often were opposed to ill-considered immigration. Jews abroad, especially Ashkenazim, were strongly advised on more than one occasion not to come to Palestine if they were young and needed to support themselves; those who were old and of independent means were counselled to invest their funds at home, in Europe, in ventures from which they could expect to derive a secure income to maintain them in the Holy Land.[26] The leader of one group of religious devotees immigrating to Palestine was gravely disturbed when his pilgrimage was joined by a following of refugees, simple poor people seeking a new, secure home in Palestine.[27] Such attitudes of caution were opposed, of course, to the traditional tendency to favor immigration to the Holy Land unconditionally; but they were dictated by a realistic concern over the difficulties of financing the needs of almost a whole community by appeals to Jews abroad, and a desire to keep this problem within manageable limits.

Conditions in Palestine guaranteed that one aim of this "restrictionist attitude" — if one may so describe what was merely a characteristic reaction rather than a considered "policy" — would be realized. The uncertainties of life in Palestine kept the community small. But the smallness of the community was not enough to achieve the other aim of the Jewish leaders: to reduce the dependence of the community on funds from abroad. In addition to its chronic condition of economic dependency, extortionate demands by the local tax farmers or eruptions of hostility threatened the community on numerous occasions with bankruptcy, or with expulsion, and appeals to Jews abroad became necessary. In the course of time both the Sephardic and Ashkenazic communities directed their appeals not only to Constantinople or to Austria-Hungary and Poland, where their kinsmen and townsmen lived, but more and more to the wealthy and influential Jewish communities of Western Europe and, later, of the United States as well.[28] In the nineteenth century, the growing influence of the West in Near Eastern affairs caused the Western Jewish communities to play an increasingly important role in the Holy Land, as well as in other parts of the crumbling Ottoman Empire where the

Jewish question arose in a new form. The characteristic attitudes of
the Western Jews, as well as the general influence of the West in
the area, significantly altered the conditions of the Jewish community
in Palestine, and so too the attitude that had to be taken to its problems.
Hence, they also altered the nature of the bond between Diaspora
Jewry and the "actual Zion," the Jewish community in the Holy Land.

The first effect of the new conditions was a renewed growth of
the Jewish community, no longer sporadic but steady, cumulative,
and relatively large. In 1856, sixteen years after Sir Moses Montefiore
had been given a count of 6,500 Jews in Palestine, their number had
risen to an estimated 10,600; and in 1876, twenty years later, a study
by a British Jewish delegation found a Jewish population of 13,920
in Jerusalem alone, more than double the number of 5,700 reported
in 1856.[29]

The growth of the Jewish community cannot be attributed to
improved economic conditions or other general factors benefiting the
country as a whole. All reports of the time agree in painting the
general situation of Palestine in the blackest colors. "For centuries
the country has been declining and it is still declining," wrote the
American consul in Jerusalem in 1880. "The population and the wealth
of Palestine has not increased during the last forty years," he declared.[30] The increase in the Jewish population was based, then, on
a specific factor: from 1840 on, European consuls were stationed in
Jerusalem and they, together with the ambassadors of the Western
powers in Constantinople, extended their protection to non-Ottoman
Jewish pilgrims and settlers who came to the Holy Land.[31]

The relatively sharp increase in the Jewish community, unaccom-
panied by any expansion of economic activity in the country at large
and made up in growing proportion of Ashkenazim, whose adjustment
to the local economic situation was particularly difficult, raised in a
more acute form the problem of maintaining the community. To some
extent, the Jewish settlers (particularly, no doubt, those born in the
country) took up productive trades; and furthermore, the sums
collected abroad for the support of the community were substantially
increased by a more systematic effort.[32] But despite these palliatives,
the difficulties of maintaining a steadily growing community of de-
pendents forced a new consideration of economic as well as political
means to solve a problem that could no longer be ignored.

The problem could no longer be ignored, moreover, because of
the increasing reliance of the Palestine community upon Western
Jews for both financial and political assistance. And when Western
Jews assumed a major responsibility for the settlement in Palestine,

they brought to this task a new attitude, one that could not possibly reconcile itself to economic and political dependency as a basis of communal existence.

Even while engaged in the final battles to establish beyond question their emancipation at home, leaders of Western Jewry also found themselves involved in the defense of equal rights under the law as a solution of the Jewish problem in foreign countries. The Ottoman Empire in particular, from about 1840 on, was felt by French and British Jews, and soon also by German, Austrian, and even American Jews, to demand their attention. The rights of Jews in Turkey and in its autonomous principalities were their concern almost as much as was the completion of the Jewish emancipation in their own countries. This was a natural consequence of the special position European powers began to occupy in Ottoman affairs.

From the time the European powers in concert intervened to end Mohammed Ali's rebellion against the Sublime Porte in 1840, the influence of Western powers was felt with increasing effect in the whole area from North Africa to the Balkans. The same attention which Russia had been able to grant to Greek Orthodox and France to Roman Catholic interests in the Ottoman realm, Britain began to extend not only to Protestants (of whom there were few) but to Jews — especially to those Russian Jewish settlers in Palestine whom, in 1847–1849, the Russians agreed to release to British protection.[33] The consuls and ambassadors of the other Western powers, too, had occasion to intercede with the Porte when Jews who were citizens of European countries or under their protection were molested by officials or by the populace in countries of the Ottoman realm.[34]

But the growth of European influence was itself a major indirect cause of unrest in the area, out of which arose difficulties for the Jews that then required Western intervention. For by direct expansion of European authority into formerly Ottoman territory, and through the encouragement given to nationalist rebellion by Western democratic and Russian Pan-Slavic ideas, the old order was undermined. In the troubled conditions that followed in territories slipping from Turkish control, the Jewish problem arose in an acute and modern form, and Western Jews were called upon to alleviate and if possible to solve it.

When war broke out with the French in Algeria in the 1830's and with the Spanish in Morocco in 1859, the Arabs, who had habitually treated the Jews of these areas with abusive contempt, now treated them as potential or actual allies of their enemies. The ensuing pillage and violence confronted the Jews of France and England, first of all, with the responsibility for providing refugee Jews with immediate relief and for finding them new homes.[35] After the wars, however, the problem became one of reconstructing a secure status for North African Jewry. The effect of the French conquest of Algeria had been to abrogate old ghetto institutions of the Jewish community, and the French Jews now took up the fight to win for their brethren a new status fully equal to the emancipation of their own community. In spite of some opposition, most of the Algerian Jews themselves willingly accepted a new status of French citizenship. In other North African countries, not integrated into metropolitan France, the Western Jews sought with varying success to safeguard the rights of their brethren by special provisions in the peace treaties ending the wars or by arrangements with the protectorate authorities.[36] In any case, the effect of the European incursion had been to bring immediate suffering upon the Jews, and to upset their old institutions — both of which conditions made it the duty of the Jews in the metropolis to seek a new, secure status for their North African brethren, a status which they naturally conceived along the lines of their own emancipation.

The impact of European influences had similar repercussions at the other end of the Ottoman realm, in the Balkan principalities. Under the pressure of European powers, the Ottoman Empire was forced to yield rights of autonomy to its Balkan, Christian-populated principalities of Serbia and of Wallachia and Moldavia. The Jewish community in those provinces not only suffered from the customary inconveniences of a despised minority in a war-torn area. It was also the victim of one of the first manifestations of a peculiarly modern form of the Jewish problem which has since become widely familiar.

In the Rumanian provinces (as in a different way, too, in Algeria) the Jews found that they had more to fear from a rising nationalism than from the traditional disabilities that they had known for generations. Under the Ottomans, the Jews, together with other non-Moslems, had occupied a subordinate but tolerated status. Rebelling against this status, the Greeks, Slavs, and Rumanians fought for the Western democratic principle of nationality. But when the Rumanians won this fight, with the aid of European powers, and obtained at least a status of autonomy under Ottoman suzerainty, they adamantly refused to grant the Jews among them the Western status of Jewish emancipation. Stubbornly resisting Jewish claims on this score, they did not fall back for justification on the traditional discrimination against Jews on religious grounds. Instead they based their discrimination on the modern principle of nationality. Adopting the same line as did foes of the Jews in the first struggles over emancipation, they declared the Jews were a foreign nationality, aliens in the land of their birth. If an alien status formally imposed on the Jews seemed a hardship and created a problem, they were prepared to accept as an alternative — the evacuation of the Jews from their country and their resettlement elsewhere. This solution the Western Jews rejected on principle, and they insisted on the natural rights of the Jews in their native lands, invoking international guarantees; but, nevertheless, they were forced to concern themselves with the emergency requirements of a sporadically continuing flow of refugees.[37]

The Rumanian attitude continued to occupy the attention of Western Jewish leaders throughout the nineteenth and into the twentieth century; that is, even after Rumania became fully independent. When the question first arose, Rumania was part of the Ottoman Empire. For contemporary Western Jewries, the Rumanian situation was part of a complex of Ottoman problems which was their responsibility because of the rights of intervention the Western powers possessed under treaties and, in particular, the capitulations. The most disturbing problem of the Ottoman area, and one which precipitated not only a transient flurry of activity but the permanent organization of Jews to protect their brethren abroad, was the series of ritual murder charges levelled against Jews and the outbreaks of violence which accompanied them.

Such incidents, to be sure, were based on ancient religious prejudices and occurred not only in Turkish provinces but throughout the Jewish world, from Russia to the United States. But beginning with the Damascus and Rhodes affairs of 1840 and erupting in mounting frequency through the 1870's, this ancient prejudice caused continual outbreaks, in which Christians of the Eastern churches were particularly active, against the Jews in the Ottoman realm. The violent hostility to Jews of Christian *rayahs* in the Ottoman Empire was not unconnected with the mounting nationalist unrest among those subject peoples, and the combination of clericalism with nationalism produced an anti-Semitic mood of a distinctly modern character.[38]

The reaction of the Jews to the unrest in the decaying Ottoman Empire was a similar mixture of traditional measures with modern attitudes. The same world-wide solidarity which Jews had always demonstrated in times of distress now, too, led British and French Jews to cooperate in financing the relief and resettlement of Algerian refugees or the feeding of famine-stricken Polish or Persian Jews; or to join with other Jews throughout the world in intercessions to their own governments and other influential quarters in such matters as the Damascus affair in 1840 or the Mortara case in 1858.[39] At the end of that nearly twenty-year period, the Western Jewish communities, who at first met these emergencies as they arose by the improvised measures of eminent individuals like Sir Moses Montefiore or Adolphe Crémieux, organized internationally to give continuous attention to the rights and interests of the Jews throughout the world.

In reaction to the Mortara affair, a permanent Jewish organization for this purpose, the Alliance Israélite Universelle, was organized in 1860 with its center in Paris and constituent committees in many countries. Somewhat earlier, American Jewry, a young and small community, established its Board of Delegates of American Israelites, which was also a direct response to the Mortara affair and sought too "to elevate the social condition of Israelites in countries where the laws discriminated against them." [40] Following the Franco-German War of 1870, the branches of the Alliance in some countries outside France were set up as independent organizations devoted to the same end; and in this way were founded the Anglo-Jewish Association in 1871 and the Israelitische Allianz in Austria in 1872.[41] German Jewry in 1901 established its own Hilfsverein der deutschen Juden.[42]

These organizations, cooperating to the same end, aimed to carry out a traditional Jewish duty — mutual aid on an international scale — but they were guided also by the principles of a modern ideology. They strove to extend the Emancipation and Enlightenment they had achieved at home to countries which had not yet adopted this rational solution of the Jewish problem, including especially the provinces and successor states of the Ottoman Empire, and among them the Holy Land.

The methods adopted by the champions of Emancipation for Jews abroad differed from traditional methods, since their new ideology made them reject solutions that satisfied traditionalists. (On the other hand, their methods were not clearly distinguished from those afterwards adopted by Zionism, until the Zionist ideology arose and forced a distinction to be made.) Traditionalists did not rebel against a status of chronic oppression, and resorted to remedial measures only when oppression became acute. The exactions of established authorities, whether they were feudal lords in Europe or rapacious pashas in Palestine, were met by help from abroad, if they were too great for the local purse, or by intercession with the higher authorities. And if these methods failed, or if the trouble came not from the authorities but from the collapse of authority, then Jews helped each other find new homes elsewhere. For in the traditionalist Exile, no status was expected to be too secure nor was any home in the Diaspora trusted to be permanent.[43]

When the Western Jews sought to apply the principles of their own emancipated status to territories of the Ottoman realm or of Eastern Europe, they hoped to remedy not only the acute but the chronic oppression of the Jews and to replace it by equality and freedom. But only in Algeria, which became an integral part of France, could the new status be sought directly.[44] In the Ottoman Empire itself, no more could be attempted than to gain greater security under the system of capitulations, or under Imperial decrees, issued in order to please European powers and granting the Jews the same degree of official toleration as other non-Moslem subject populations.[45] These were techniques that resembled the mediaeval appeals for specific grants of protection and, on the other hand, foreshadowed the later nationalist demands for minority rights. And when even these expedients failed, as in Rumania, then there remained only the resort to emigration [46] — this, too, a technique which recalled either the mediaeval search for havens of temporary refuge, or the later nationalist projects for a concentrated territorial settlement of the Jews in a country of their own from which they could no longer be expelled. Thus, the situation in the Ottoman regions, as in Eastern Europe, led the Western Jews, out of the desire to extend their own emancipated status to other Jews, into practical expedients that implied at least a compromise with, if not an acceptance of, rival ideologies.

In much the same way, unexpectedly complicated relationships with traditionalists and nationalists arose — particularly in Palestine — out of the attempt to apply another, equally important principle of Western modernism. Not only Emancipation, but Enlightenment was required for the solution of the Jewish problem, according to the doctrine of the Western Jews. The situation in Palestine presented a classic illustration of this point. A community almost entirely devoted to religious exercises and traditional studies which, whatever sanctity one might ascribe to them, were quite without practical utility needed one thing above all, in Western eyes: it needed an educational reform that would bring modern science and general culture and, above all, vocational training to make the young Jews capable of supporting themselves and their community. Led by the Alliance Israélite Universelle, the several Jewish organizations devoted themselves, wherever their resources and the influence of their governments could reach, to the establishment of hospitals, workshops, and, above all, schools — the humanitarian armory of the Enlightenment — for the benefit of the Jewish community.[47] These gifts were so obviously needed that, on the whole, they were warmly welcomed. But the ideology by which they were motivated (as well as the political implications of such cultural infiltration by French or German language institutions into Ottoman areas) also aroused some conflicts.

Nowhere were the conflicts more marked than in Palestine. They began with ideological differences between the old Ashkenazic settlers and their would-be benefactors. The Zionist settlers then appeared as allies of the Western effort to reform the economy and educational perspectives of the community in the Holy Land. And, in the end, the Zionists came into conflict with the Western Jews active in Palestine over the political and cultural objectives and methods of their common attempt to create a new basis for the Jewish community in Palestine. But, these conflicts apart, the record of Jewish activity in Palestine throughout the nineteenth century had created a new, intricately institutionalized bond with Zion, a structure into which the activities of the World Zionist Organization itself became integrated.

III

The ideas and prospects that appealed to practically all Jews concerned with the settlement in Palestine at the time when Western influence in the area began to mount are illustrated by the diary notes of Sir Moses Montefiore. During his second visit to the Holy Land, in 1839, Montefiore resolved to visit Mohammed Ali, who then controlled Palestine, in order to request

. . . that he will permit land and villages to be rented on a lease of fifty years, free from all taxes or claims of governors, the rent to be paid at Alexandria; that he will allow me to send people to assist and instruct the Jews in a better mode of cultivating the land, the olive, the vine, cotton and mulberries, as well as the breeding of sheep; finally, that he will give me a firman to open banks in Beyrout, Jaffa, Jerusalem and Cairo. I sincerely pray that my journey to the Holy Land may prove beneficial to the Jews; not only to those who are already there, but to many others who may come to settle in the Holy Cities, either from love for the Land of Promise, or from a desire to quit countries where persecution prevents their living in peace.[48]

Sir Moses' plan included, on the political side, the grant of a special status to the Jewish community which would not only free it from the authority of local tax farmers but allow a wide autonomy to be exercised. The security of the new legal status would benefit both the existing settlement and new immigrants, who would come to the Land of Israel to find a refuge from persecution as well as a home for their traditional culture. On the economic side, Montefiore not only planned to establish the Jews on the land and in productive industry, providing the education and expert guidance needed for such an undertaking. In a manner that foreshadowed Herzl, he also proposed to rebuild the economic health of the entire region. The increased production brought about by the Jewish settlement would of itself increase tax revenues and stimulate general economic growth, but Montefiore held out an even more enticing prospect as an inducement for granting the political concessions he desired. He indicated that he would establish banks in key cities which would expand credit in the whole area. And, lastly, on the educational side, Sir Moses built his whole project on a plan for introducing more modern and more practical studies into the schooling of young Jews in Palestine.

This frame of mind was by no means unparalleled in those years. Another interesting figure of the time was Rabbi Judah Bibas (d. 1852) of Corfu. This rabbi, under the immediate impression of contemporary Balkan nationalism, said quite plainly that it was time the Jews learned to employ arms so that, like the Greeks, they might take advantage of the democratic era to seek their sovereign freedom in Palestine. He held, furthermore, that it was now necessary not only to add secular studies to the sacred studies traditional among Jews, but that the circumstances might even demand neglecting the latter in favor of the former — for the Torah was like a normal diet for the Jews, to be taken regularly when well, but secular sciences were a medicine which they must take when ill.[49] These views of Bibas' were developed in the succeeding generation by Rabbi Judah Alcalay, the author of detailed political, economic, and organizational plans of operations to achieve the establishment of the Jewish State in Palestine.[50]

However, the attempts to put ideas of reform into effect caused differences to arise which, at some points, hardened into ideological principles. In the beginning, opposition arose not against the political objective of the Western Jews (to secure a new status on behalf of the Jews already in Palestine and of potential immigrants) nor against their economic plans (to establish Jews on the land or in new industries). It was the educational projects by which Western Jews hoped to make possible their economic reforms that first antagonized a part of the old settlers in Palestine.

The economic difficulties of the growing community in the Holy Land, and particularly in Jerusalem, were so acute that there was general approval for any measures directly intended to solve them. The rabbis and communal leaders themselves proposed to Western benefactors plans to establish industries and farms; to disperse the overcrowded residents of Jerusalem not only to new quarters outside the walls but also to outlying rural areas; or even to adopt a quite different expedient and support the emigration of such Jews as wished to leave the country and seek their living elsewhere.[51] However, the idea of encouraging Jews to adopt new occupations that could support them in Palestine involved the introduction of new educational methods and subjects of study. On this point the Western Jews encountered the stubborn resistance of one section of the traditionalist community in Israel; for while the Sephardic community accepted quite readily the new educational institutions of the Western benefactors, many of the Ashkenazim resisted such proposals bitterly and refused to have anything to do with them after they were established.

The roots of the opposition to educational reforms and secular studies may be traced to Eastern Europe. There, the Enlightenment program of reeducating the Jews according to the modern European standards had not come as one aspect of a successful Emancipation of the Jews. It was a program that enlightened despots attempted to impose upon the Jews while holding them in subjection. Only a small group of devotees of the Enlightenment among the Jews supported this program. That group, of course, hoped that Emancipation would follow. However, in most of Eastern Europe, Emancipation was a hope entertained by enlightened Jews but not widely supported by enlightened Gentiles, and the actual situation remained that of the *ancien régime*. Nothing compelled the East European Jews to regard emancipation as the status to which they must adjust willy-nilly. The bulk of the community remained true to traditionalism, accordingly, and attempts at the enforced enlightenment of the Jews through government-sponsored rabbinical seminaries and schools were resisted as a plot by hostile authorities to undermine traditional Jewish culture. Efforts of Jewish protagonists of the Enlightenment to advocate the new educational ideals within the community, and their eagerness to help the government impose them against the community's will, merely aroused a violent antagonism among the Jews to the whole movement of Enlightenment.[52]

Many of the leaders of the Ashkenazic community in Palestine in the first half of the nineteenth century had lived through this ideological conflict and fought to maintain the integrity of Jewish tradition against the despotic Enlightenment of the Austrian Kaiser or the

Russian Czar, and against enlightened Jews whom they regarded as renegades. They had learned to resist as both subversive and tyrannical attempts to reform the traditional methods of study. Thus when similar projects were proposed to them by Western benefactors whose good will and loyalty to Jewish tradition were unimpeachable they could not, like the Sephardim, approach these ideas with an open mind. They could not admit the obvious drawbacks in the very narrow concentration of their studies, as had Ashkenazic as well as Sephardic rabbis in earlier times,[53] for their reaction was determined by the conflict that constituted one of their own life experiences.

Consequently, in 1856 the Ashkenazim of Jerusalem rejected the offer of the Austrian von Laemel family to build a school where general studies would be taught.[54] They opposed the Evelina de Rothschild school for girls, initiated by Sir Moses Montefiore in 1855 and reopened under its new name by the British Rothschilds in the 1860's.[55] After these schools were nevertheless established, the ban on them was maintained by the Ashkenazic authorities in Jerusalem, and it was chiefly the Sephardim who took advantage of their facilities. A similar attitude held for the schools then founded by the Alliance Israélite Universelle, and even fiercer antagonism was shown when the early Zionists of the Hovevei-Zion movement began to establish modern schools in Palestine.[56]

Not only the condemnation of both modernist groups by the Ashkenazic traditionalists, but their common search for a rational solution of the problems of the Palestine community through agriculture, industry, and, above all, education made allies of the Western Jews and the early Zionists. When the Alliance Israélite Universelle was founded in 1860, the French Jews who were most active in it stood in continual correspondence with such proto-Zionist rabbis as Zvi Hirsch Kalischer and Judah Alcalay. The ideas of resettlement in Palestine and of the economic, political, and educational activities prerequisite to that aim were very close to such men as Charles Netter (1826–1882), the active leader of the Alliance. After the Crimean War there was a renewed interest in extending French influence in the Levant. French political writers suggested that not only the traditional protection of an autonomous Christian province of Lebanon but the support of an autonomous Jewish province of Palestine could serve this purpose.[57] Netter himself saw Palestine as a place in which to resettle victims of anti-Jewish disturbances in Persia or in the Balkans.[58] These tendencies were given a concrete, institutional expression when in 1870 the Alliance Israélite Universelle founded the agricultural school of Mikveh Israel, and in 1882,[59] when Netter brought in a group of refugee orphans from Brody as students.

As Zionism became a more sharply defined movement, with specific objectives not only stated but carried into effect through concrete activities directed toward the ultimate aim, the Alliance and other Western groups were no longer able to react to it merely with a diffuse sympathy. They had to define their position more clearly toward both the aims and activities of the new movement; and, thus challenged to convert general sympathy into specific commitments, they contracted their sympathy instead. Yet in one field, the field of education, the Zionist immigrants and the Western Jewish organizations remained closely allied. Children from the new farm settlements went to school at Mikveh Israel. For the rapidly increasing city population — particularly in Jerusalem — the Alliance and other Western organizations founded general and vocational schools; and here again both student body and teachers included a significant proportion of adherents of the new Zionist views.[60] After 1880, Zionist settlers and teachers, with the support of Zionist organizations abroad, began to establish similar schools, particularly devoted to cultivating the Hebrew language.[61] The instant antagonism which this aroused in the traditionalist community, as well as the educational purposes shared with the Western-sponsored schools, strengthened the bond between Zionists and modernists. The tie was close enough so that when the Hilfsverein der deutschen Juden planned to set up a technological institute in Haifa, they thought of a Russian Jewish fund as the sponsor. And, indeed, funds left by Wolf Wissotzky, patron and employer of Ahad Ha'am, in a trust of which Ahad Ha'am was one of the administrators, were allotted to the German organization for that purpose.[62]

This project, however, ended in an ideological clash that brought to a head the underlying differences between the Zionists and the Western reformers. The Zionists had long felt that the Alliance schools served as a medium of assimilation to French culture, if not a tool of French cultural propaganda. Western Jews, on the other hand, often regarded as chimerical the Zionist dreams of converting Hebrew into a modern spoken language and of making Jewish schools the nursery of a modern Hebrew culture. Battle was joined on this issue in 1913 when the Hilfsverein, which had hitherto accepted the standards of Hebrew training advocated by the Zionists more willingly than other Westerners, now proposed to make German instead of Hebrew the language of instruction for scientific subjects in the proposed Haifa Technical School. A teachers' strike which broke out throughout the country against this decision was a critical event in the movement to revive Hebrew as a spoken language.[63] After the first World War ended, the Zionist movement took over responsibility for the projected Haifa Technion and most of the other Jewish schools in Palestine, and formally established Hebrew as the language of instruction.

Of all the methods for improving the situation of the Palestine Jewish community, the proposals for economic development alone evoked no objection in principle but were favored by the traditionalists, by the Western Jews, and by the Zionists. To make the community more nearly self-supporting was an aim that everyone accepted. Differences arose only over the means to be employed toward this end (as when traditionalists rejected educational reforms the modernists thought essential for their economic plans) or over the broader purposes for which the economic projects themselves might serve as a foundation (as when the Zionists proclaimed the achievement of Jewish sovereignty in Palestine as the object of Jewish colonization).

Sir Moses Montefiore, perhaps the earliest modern Western sponsor of projects for the economic rehabilitation of the Jews in Palestine, found traditionalist Jews with ideas like his own on his early visits to the Holy Land.[64] Nor were all attempts at establishing farm settlements or new industrial enterprises initiated by Western benefactors. From the mid-nineteenth century, when security in Palestine improved owing to Western influence, well into the period of Zionist colonization, the old pre-Zionist Jewish settlers in Palestine continued to undertake isolated attempts at rural settlement or to develop new branches of enterprise on their own initiative. Sephardim and Ashkenazim alike gladly accepted Western aid in the establishment of an orchard, or a workshop, or the construction of a new housing development, and cooperated in turn with economic enterprises initiated by their benefactors, notwithstanding the opposition of some of them to the new Western schools. So, too, when Zionist settlers set up as farmers or began to work as artisans, the old settlement welcomed this accession of strength, whatever the quarrels between the two over modern Hebrew-language schooling or the observance of the Biblical sabbatical year in the farm settlements.[65] The relations between the Western patrons of the Palestine Jewish community and the new Zionist settlers were closer still, owing to their common interest in establishing Jewish settlements on the land.

It is true that the plans for agricultural settlement and economic development came in time to imply different and much broader perspectives from those that were most important at first. When the Palestinian rabbis petitioned Sir Moses Montefiore in 1839 to help settle Jews on the soil, they were concerned primarily with the existing community and its economic problems. In Montefiore's program, as we have noted, the development of agriculture and industry in Palestine was to provide for the support of new immigrants as well as those already in the country. This was an aim the rabbis undoubtedly shared, though they may not have stressed it. And while Montefiore's plan specifically referred to immigration, it is clear that he was not so possessed by the idea of a large-scale resettlement of Palestine that the economic rehabilitation of the existing community alone would seem picayune to him, as it logically would to a doctrinaire Zionist. Throughout his long life Sir Moses' absorbing interest in the economic welfare of the Jews living in Palestine never flagged. But sometimes his hope of persuading British Jewry to promote immigration to Palestine was reduced to a wistful desire; and at other times Sir Moses plainly preferred the resettlement of Jewish refugees in other countries than Palestine.[66]

Yet in the course of time, Jewish economic reconstruction in Palestine became overwhelmingly a program for the assistance of new immigrants rather than for the rehabilitation of residents. It grew to significant proportions, in fact, only when new immigrants became the chief concern. The immigrants who came, moreover, were largely brought in on a wave of Zionist impulses. Thus the rise of Zionist immigration coincided with, or brought about, a greater, more complex, and more institutional involvement of Western Jewry with the Palestine community and with the problems of immigration to Palestine than already existed before.[67] This situation, of course, contained the possibility of the ideological differences which became explicit with the appearance of Herzl. But, on the other hand, before Herzl came, Zionism had already entered into compacts of far-reaching cooperation and mutual accommodation with Jews of the West.

The first truly historic period of modern Jewish immigration to Palestine began at the time of the Zionist movement of the 1880's. In the forty years from 1840 to 1880 there had also been immigration, of course, and the Jewish community had increased from between five to ten thousand to a figure of about twenty-five thousand. The next roughly equal period, up to the beginning of the first World War in 1914, saw the Jewish population increase even more sharply, to a figure of around a hundred thousand. Not only the rapid increase in numbers, but the political motives and the objective political effects of the new immigration had a historic bearing that did not escape contemporaries. From the 1880's on, the Turks, who until then had fluctuated between benevolence and negligent obstruction in their attitude towards Jewish immigrants, now became set in their opposition — though they were far from perfectly efficient in preventing the growth of the community, and quite capable of being persuaded to relax their bans when suitably pressed or courted.[68] As for the Western Jews who traditionally supported the constructive economic and educational efforts of their fellow-Jews in the Ottoman Empire, and particularly in Palestine, the new political implications of such efforts in connection with relatively large-scale and ideologically motivated immigration to Palestine forced them, too, to reexamine their position.

The efforts of the Western Jews on behalf of their brethren in Ottoman territories had never been inseparable from political considerations. Some kind of diplomatic intercession with Turkish authorities had almost always been required in order to make possible even minor projects. In the decades after 1840 the Turks were often disposed to assent to requests from the West for the benefit of Jews, even though it frequently remained a difficult matter to induce local authorities to be quite so cooperative.

The general privileges secured to non-Moslems in this period, and the protection accorded them by Western powers, were concessions the Turks made not under duress but in relatively willing response. Those who demanded the enactment of reforms and privileges were not victorious foes but allied powers, who had rescued the Ottomans from rebels like Mohammed Ali or enemies like the Russians.[69]

To include the Jews under these decrees of rights was particularly easy and even appealing for the Porte. For while the grant of rights to Christian minorities, under Western protection, placed the Turks in the unhappy position of conceding their own past guilt, or the guilt of Moslems generally toward Christians, this was not the case with the Jews. It was the Christians in the Ottoman Empire, and above all the semiautonomous Christian principalities, who were guilty of the excesses against which Jews sought security. When the Sultan decreed the equality of the Jews with his other non-Moslem subjects, or when he condemned the ritual murder libels, he was not in effect letting Europe protect his own subjects against himself; he was, in a way, protecting a part of his own subjects against Europe. It was a role which, no doubt, was particularly gratifying when the Sultan was able to join the Western powers in international action against his recalcitrant Rumanian viceroys.[70]

There were similar reasons for the Porte to be hospitable to Jewish immigrants. Of primary importance was the fact that, in what amounted to a depopulated area, the Turks were interested in any new sources of taxable development. The period, moreover, was one in which the encroachments of Christian power forced many Moslems to emigrate, from the Caucasus and the Balkans on the East to Algeria on the West. These refugees the Sultan welcomed to such lands as Syria and Palestine, which they served not only to resettle but to garrison.[71] The political consequences of the upheavals in the frontier provinces of the Ottoman realm made Jews as well as Moslems in those countries fear for their security. When they, too, came to Palestine, not only their economic value but a certain similarity of fate with that of Moslems from the same areas may have made the Porte sympathetic to such immigrants. Consequently the efforts of Western Jews on behalf of immigrants from Russia or Rumania, Bukhara or Persia, Morocco or Algiers were not unwelcome at first in Constantinople, whatever the hostility in Palestine itself.[72]

The population and, generally speaking, the authorities in Palestine remained as ill-disposed to Jewish as to Christian settlers. In 1855 it was marked as an achievement when Sir Moses Montefiore obtained what his biographer believed to be the first permit granted to an Englishman to purchase land in Palestine.[73] It took Montefiore over four years to execute through local authorities the license he had obtained from the Porte to build on his plot in Jerusalem; and when in 1860 Sir Moses finally was able to use the legacy of Judah Touro to build houses outside the walls of Jerusalem, the Jews who ventured to occupy them knew they were taking serious risks.[74] Compared with the Arab fellahin, perhaps, Jews and others who enjoyed Western protection were enviably secure. Some of the earlier attempts to settle in rural areas probably relied on this fact. A fellah might undertake to work a plot for a share of the crop on behalf of an owner under consular protection in places where he would not otherwise dare to farm for fear of Bedouins or tax collectors. But the arguments against such an arrangement were that the fellahin themselves could not be trusted to leave the Jewish owner any return on his investment.[75] Whether this was so or not, no one could doubt that in the 1840's and 50's Moslem neighbors, as well as the authorities, would go as far as they dared in harassing non-Moslem settlers in rural areas. More than twenty years later, Laurence Oliphant noted the great difficulties which the German Templar settlements encountered in this respect.[76] The Jewish settlements founded from 1878 on had to circumvent official barriers before they could begin their development; and after these difficulties were overcome, they had to adopt a variety of special measures to protect their property and their tenancy from the incursions of their neighbors.[77]

Hence, the Western benefactors of Palestine Jewry were quite accustomed to tedious negotiations and to political problems that complicated every project of constructive assistance. By 1880, however, intercession by Europeans on behalf of non-Moslem Ottoman subjects, or consular protection for persons long resident in the Empire, met with hardening Turkish resistance. After the Congress of Berlin, the Turks grew decidedly suspicious of Britain, which became an immediate neighbor of Palestine by acquiring Cyprus and reoccupying Egypt.[78] Britain, the power that was previously the Sultan's chief European support and counsellor, now lost its influence. Russia was the traditional foe of Turkey, and Jewish immigrants from there were always suspect. Moreover, decades of renewed European activity in the Levant since 1840 had produced an economic revival of sorts, in Lebanon particularly — and after 1880, Western activity and Jewish immigration caused prospects of economic expansion to appear in Palestine as well. The Porte preferred to entrust the development of such potentialities to Lebanese investors and Arab cultivators rather than to Western-protected Russian or Rumanian Jews, with their ideas of an autonomous or sovereign Jewish status.[79] The relatively large influx from Eastern Europe in 1880, 1890, and 1905 was repeatedly stemmed by severe restrictions on Jewish immigration, land purchase, and permits for building, which remained essentially in effect until the First World War.[80]

Thus, Western Jews had to deal with a new political problem in their traditional constructive work in Palestine. Instead of a country in which the ruling power willingly recognized certain Western privileges and responsibilities, Palestine had become an area in which Turkey resisted not only Russian, but also British and French influence. Moreover, instead of working with a settled population alone, Western Jews found themselves involved with the political problems of facilitating immigration to Palestine, and of cooperating with immigrants with a Zionist ideology. It was a considerable ideological concession for the Western Jews to adopt emigration at all as a method for solving the Jewish problem. To do so meant conceding that in Rumania and Russia, or in Persia and Morocco, the solution of the Jewish problem by emancipation could not yet be achieved, and it was necessary, in defeat, to remove the Jews to more hospitable lands. The established Western Jewish organizations, notably the Alliance Israélite Universelle, did not, in fact, make themselves directly responsible for a policy of emigration. But, while continuing their own work of education and social welfare in Eastern and North African countries, they participated in conferences to set up special emergency or permanent organizations for the transfer and resettlement of Jewish emigrants. The latter activities were chiefly backed by individuals who could act with less consideration of ideology than could communal agencies: by Baron Maurice de Hirsch, who initiated large-scale resettlement projects in many far-flung countries; and, preceding him, by Baron Edmond de Rothschild, who sponsored the resettlement of Jews in farm colonies in Palestine.[81]

In undertaking the removal of large numbers of Jews from certain countries in order to transplant them elsewhere, Western Jewish philanthropists involved themselves with Eastern European ideological groups — with Zionists or with Territorialists. Both sides were forced by this partnership to temper ideological predilections in favor of pragmatic considerations; the Eastern Europeans, perhaps, in the greater measure. For in their case, the entire group and not an individual was committed to cooperation and was consequently obliged to reformulate its ideas.

IV

Two factors were decisive in bringing about cooperation between the two sides. The unprecedented scale of Jewish emigration from Eastern Europe, and the new problems that it brought home to Jews in Western countries forced the Western Jews to seek practical expedients, instead of relying on the unavailing ideology of Emancipation. Cooperation with the Zionists in resettling Palestine was one such expedient. On the side of the Eastern European Jews, it was the political difficulties and financial incapacity of the Zionist movement at home that forced them to seek support in the West.

That large-scale immigration from the East could mean unforeseen difficulties for Jews in Berlin, Paris, London and New York was realized with considerable shock in the 1880's. As a result of the pogroms, thousands of refugees accumulated in the border town of Brody. German, French, and British Jews, together with Gentile sympathizers, formed emergency committees to aid these unfortunates and help them find new homes.[82] But when the refugees arrived in German towns or in London, or even in New York and the American interior, the problems of accommodating the influx confronted a dismayed and unprepared community. European philanthropists who shipped immigrants together with funds for assistance to America soon began to receive agitated telegrams. The Americans insisted that they themselves must determine the scale and nature of the influx. Local committees began to turn back individuals or groups who might become public charges and to demand that only young, able-bodied, and skilled workers come to them.[83]

The first such reactions resulted from the unpreparedness of the Western Jewish communities, in spite of earlier emergencies of the same kind, to deal with the problems of the immigrant masses. In addition, they were reluctant to welcome into their own community Eastern Europeans with whose traditionalism and local customs they were out of sympathy. In time the responsibility of caring for fellow-Jews overcame such unworthy feelings, and moreover, the problem became more familiar and manageable. The first Eastern Europeans themselves blazed trails for the guidance and reception of those who followed, and the settled communities of Western Jews gradually organized to deal with the problem

Another difficulty did not vanish, however, but continued even more seriously to concern the Western Jews. The astoundingly rapid growth of the Jewish migration from Eastern Europe had a distressing, and even an alarming, effect on the attitudes of Western public opinion and government policy. In the end of the nineteenth and the early twentieth century, movements for the restriction of immigration gained momentum in countries like England and the United States. A particular animus against Jewish immigrants was frequently noticeable.[84] From the very beginning of the migration, contemporaries connected the Russian emigration with a new and dangerous development of anti-Semitism, now become international in its ramifications. The organized and semiofficial character of the Russian pogroms was quickly sensed; and Western Jews and Western liberals saw an extension and counterpart of Stoecker's Berlin anti-Semitism in the propaganda and organization of these outbreaks.[85] The potential damage to their own position involved in the growing hostility to Jewish immigrants was even more evident to Western Jews. When Herzl pointed out that Jewish migrants brought anti-Semitism with them, carrying it in their baggage wherever they went, he was making an observation that had occurred to many another Western Jew.[86]

The organization and direction of Jewish emigration from Eastern Europe, accordingly, became a problem of direct concern to Western Jews. If unable to send the emigrants on to another destination, they sought, at least, to disperse them widely through their own country in order to avoid the unhappy consequences they feared from slum concentrations.[87] They also sought to divert the stream to thinly settled territories like Argentina or Mesopotamia far from London and New

York.[88] In the same spirit, they added to their long-established concern with the welfare of the small settled community in Palestine a new responsibility for supporting and facilitating an expanded immigration and resettlement there. To this end they cooperated quite extensively with the new Hovevei-Zion movement.[89]

If the Western Jews had cogent reasons for cooperating with the early Eastern European Zionists, the latter had ever more pressing reasons for seeking the cooperation of the West. Not until 1890, almost a decade after its inception, was the Hovevei-Zion movement able to obtain permission to function openly and with official approval in Russia; and then too only in the guise of an Odessa Committee for aid to the Jewish settlement in Palestine, not as a national movement.[90] Such an uncertain legal status naturally restricted the capacity of the movement to act effectively, especially in view of the fact that it commanded no large funds, since it was based on a popular appeal and a membership of moderate means. Consequently, from the very beginning the Hovevei-Zion looked to the West, and particularly to the organizations that for the preceding decade or two had concerned themselves with Palestine, for political support and for funds. Dr. Pinsker did as Herzl did after him, and began his work by going on a mission to the West to convert the Jewish leaders to his vision.[91] He became the chief of a popular movement in the East only after returning from the West in defeat. After the expulsion of Jews from Moscow in 1891, leaders of the Hovevei-Zion organization hoped that an international organization, including the Alliance Israélite Universelle and backed by the funds of Baron Maurice de Hirsch, would sponsor their plans.[92]

These projects, however, never went beyond the stage of discussion. The Eastern popular movement was consequently able to accomplish little more than what its own small resources could encompass. Only one man, Baron Edmond de Rothschild, gave himself heart and soul to the project of Palestinian resettlement; and he worked independently along parallel lines rather than in full accord and mutual consultation with the Hovevei-Zion. In 1900, several years after Baron de Hirsch's death, the organization he had set up for the resettlement of Jews in the Americas and elsewhere took over the administration of the Rothschild-sponsored colonies in Palestine.[93] On the whole, however, the Western Jews did not place great faith in the prospects of large-scale colonization in Palestine, and devoted more attention to the possibilities in other undeveloped areas. The direct activities in Palestine of the Alliance and similar organizations were devoted primarily to education, vocational guidance, and social welfare. Their clientele was the increasing Jewish urban population rather than the farm settlements.

Yet, granted all these reservations, a close and ramified pattern of cooperation between Western and Eastern Jews grew up in the project to resettle Palestine. The Easterners initiated the founding of farm settlements which were later granted support by Rothschild; they stimulated the growth of an urban population which the Western organizations helped to serve. Furthermore, branches of the Hovevei-Zion movement were organized in the West, too, comprising not only Eastern immigrants but outstanding leaders of the Alliance, or the Anglo-Jewish Association; and these, together with the major western organizations, held council together from time to time about the political and economic problems of the growing Palestine community.[94]

The cooperation was never long without its conflicts. Between the Eastern Europeans and the Alliance and other Western organizations, the issue of education was sharply debated. With Baron de Rothschild, the Zionists soon came into disagreement over methods of colonization. They criticized the Baron's paternalistic administration because it undermined the initiative and independence of the settlers and because it ended in creating colonies in which a small group of Jewish planters were surrounded by a far more numerous aggregation of Arab farm laborers. The French schooling of the planters' sons, on the one hand, and the predominance of Arab village culture in the area of the Jewish settlements, on the other, seemed to doom the hope of an indigenous Jewish culture; and these conditions certainly gave no grounds for confidence that the hope of Jewish sovereignty, or of immigration sufficient to meet the existing needs for a safe refuge, was being significantly advanced.[95]

The Hovevei-Zion, and then later the Zionist Organization, took as their own specific objectives in the Palestine resettlement these very aims: to encourage the settlement not merely of Jewish planters, but of Jewish farm laborers in Palestine; to advance the cause of Hebrew culture and education in the settlements; and to defend the independent initiative of the Zionist settlers who continued to come to Palestine from Eastern Europe.

The one issue on which both Western and Eastern Jews tacitly agreed to be silent was the question of Jewish sovereignty itself and of the political means to achieve it. The urgent political task in the 1880's and 90's was one which fell far short of the Zionist ideal, and yet was fundamental to the activities of both the Eastern Zionists and the Western Jews: merely to keep the doors of Palestine open to Jewish immigrants and procure the right to buy land and settle it. All were agreed in their willingness to adopt any legal or semilegal arrangement or subterfuge that would accomplish these ends in the Ottoman Empire.

It was this point which Herzl in 1895 singled out in particular in his critique of the resettlement policy hitherto adopted in cooperation with Western leaders. In so doing he raised again the rallying call of the Jewish State and aroused once more, in redoubled intensity, all the mythic sources of Zionist morale.

Herzl, like Pinsker before him, was almost as ready initially to accept Argentina or another suitable territory as to choose Palestine for the Jewish national home. At the end of his brief career he left the Zionist Organization in crisis over his decision to explore the British offer of Uganda for Jewish colonization. In this open-mindedness, his attitude was similar to that of the Western Jewish philanthropists and organizations who shared his concern about the need for a properly directed Jewish resettlement policy; one that would remove Jews from the hotbeds of anti-Semitism and yet not evoke anti-Semitism in their new homes. Such Westerners lent their assistance to Jewish resettlement projects not only in the Holy Land but in many other territories as well.

But one significant element was present only in the case of Palestine. No other country became the object of a continuously existing popular movement. In the 1880's, simultaneously with the rise of the Hovevei-Zion movement, Jewish students in Russia organized a parallel movement, called Am Olam, to establish Jewish colonies in America. The organization never took root. The agricultural colonization and directed resettlement of Jews in America, as in all other countries outside Palestine where colonization projects were attempted or considered, was conducted by Western philanthropic agencies, without any significant cooperation on the part of a popular, ideological movement.[96] In the case of Palestine, on the other hand, the responsibility for resettlement was shared by Western philanthropic agencies with a popular movement. The membership of the Hovevei-Zion may have remained small and its ideology may have blurred, but the movement never ceased to be a significant factor both in the Diaspora Jewish community and in the affairs of the Palestinian settlement.

Herzl's initial plan was to win over to his views the outstanding Western leaders who were concerned not specifically with Palestine but with the general project of planned Jewish resettlement. He failed to convince Baron de Hirsch and the Rothschilds and the others of his thesis: that public, international arrangements, formally establishing adequate legal rights in a suitable territory as well as suitable understandings concerning the transfer of emigrants and their property, must be the first thing sought before any resettlement project could serve its true purpose – to solve the Jewish problem.[97]

But this thesis, stressing as it did the ultimate ideological premises that gave resettlement its historic meaning, was precisely what made so great and popular an impression. The Hovevei-Zion in particular regained their enthusiasm from it. For, while cooperation with the West on a nonideological basis gave them a practical stake in what was being achieved in Palestine, the slow pace of development and the obscurity of political status cast grave doubts on their chances of achieving the aim for which all the work was undertaken. In addition, not only was the road that could lead from the ongoing work to ultimate sovereignty hard to discern, but the goal itself had to be obscured, or suspended, in order that the work might be done. Herzl's decisive rejection of this impasse and his view that the Zionist aim must be proclaimed and negotiated restored the enthusiasm for a movement already pondering its clouded future.

Failing with the Western leaders, Herzl turned to the people. The people, in this case, meant not merely the oppressed masses of Eastern Europe whose problem it was that had to be solved by resettlement, but something more specific. It meant an already existing popular movement with the same ideological principles as Herzl's. Only the hope of resettling in Palestine, not the prospects of colonization in any other country nor the vague idea of resettlement in a country still to be nominated, had, in Herzl's day, been able to create a popular, ideological movement. And before Herzl resolved to turn from the wealthy to the people, from the benefactors to the beneficiaries, the "people" had already turned to Herzl. Zionist and student groups from near and far placed themselves at his disposal and offered him their leadership.[98] The result of this conjunction of ideas was that, in a surprisingly short time, the Zionist Congress – a project that had been discussed in a fitful way among Zionist societies for some time past – now took place in Basle in 1897 with Herzl as its leader and with the friends he attracted, particularly Max Nordau, in active attendance.[99]

That the Congress under Herzl became something far different from what another conclave of Hovevei-Zion societies might have been without him need not be stressed. The particular quality that he quite deliberately imparted to the Congress – in addition, of course, to the clear and positive political line — was the sense of representing the entire Jewish people. The Congress in Basle was imbued with the conviction that it expressed, in the only legitimate form then possible, the sovereign will of a people. "In Basle," said Herzl, "I founded the Jewish State."

If I said that aloud today, I would be met by universal laughter. Perhaps in five years, certainly in fifty, everyone will see it. The State is already founded, in essence, in the will of the people to the State; yes, even in the will of one individual, if he is powerful enough (the *l'Etat c'est moi* of Louis XIV). The territory is only the concrete manifestation; and even where it possesses a territory, the State is always something abstract. The Church State, too, exists without a territory, or else the Pope would not be sovereign.

In Basle I created this thing which is abstract and which is therefore invisible to the great majority of people . . .[100]

No conference of Hovevei-Zion, held in Eastern Europe under the surveillance of the Russian secret police and subject to the restrictive license under which the movement was permitted to exist, could have acted in this spirit; nor, in all probability, would any conference anywhere without Herzl have been inspired so to act. But, in return, the Hovevei-Zion did something equally decisive for Herzl. When he turned to the people and gave them the mantle of Jewish sovereignty, Herzl allied himself to a movement deeply committed and intricately involved in Palestine, implicitly accepting this and no other land as the Jewish national home. The question that Herzl had left open was settled. For, both the mythic force of tradition and the fixed principles of an ideology hammered out in argument against other territorial plans, both the stake already achieved in Palestine resettlement and the direction of future political aspirations, were decisively attached to Zion.

5 ANTI-ZIONISM AND NON-ZIONISM: EFFECTS UPON POLICY FROM FIRST ZIONIST CONGRESS TO BALFOUR DECLARATION

Every new idea necessarily calls forth a division. What determines the character of the idea in the end is whether it has a will to unity. But in the very emphasis of the element of nationality by our movement the will to unity is manifest.[1]

THESE words, written shortly before the Basle Congress by the young German "political Zionist," Dr. Max Bodenheimer (1865–1940), to the old Hovevei-Zionist, Professor Hermann Schapira (1840–1898), may well serve as a synoptic description of the effect of Herzlian Zionism upon the Jewish community. The first Zionists, the Hovevei-Zion in Russia, had also advanced a new idea and provoked some ideological division, but chiefly in the East, not in the West. Their controversial views about the Jewish question were less familiar or of less concern in the West than their quite uncontroversial practical endeavors. In the first years, the BILU attempt to obtain a political concession for resettling Palestine could have provoked Western Jews to ideological debate. But the speedy failure of this attempt, followed by the measures adopted by Turkey and Russia against the movement, made the Hovevei-Zion conduct their attempts at colonization thereafter without any proclaimed objective of sovereignty. In these practical efforts they found a large measure of Western support and cooperation. But Herzl stressed as an ideological issue precisely the manner in which the project of resettling Palestine should be prosecuted. The immediate effect was divisive; it evoked an ideological anti-Zionism in the West. However, after the political issues raised by Herzl subsided (or, in later periods, after Zionist victories converted certain political demands into accomplished facts), the "will to unity" which Bodenheimer saw as inherent in Zionism had its effect: anti-

Zionism was succeeded in the West by a renewal of the old cooperation under the name of non-Zionism. But, in the new circumstances, the name of "non-Zionism" was not merely a convenient way of grouping certain individuals; it corresponded to a position that was more or less definitely ideological.

We have noted that in Eastern Europe, Zionists and anti-Zionists did not differ over the essentially ethnic character of the Jewish community. On the other hand, neither the modernist nor the traditionalist anti-Zionism of the East could possibly turn into non-Zionism by cooperating in the practical work in Palestine; for both rejected such projects in principle. At most, anti-Zionist Orthodoxy could promote its own parallel resettlement in Palestine in direct opposition to the Zionists. Thus anti-Zionist ideologies remained a constant factor in the East, and no significant non-Zionism arose.

In the West, on the other hand, the major point on which Zionism was opposed was precisely the doctrine that the Jews were an ethnic entity and the Jewish problem a national problem. Western anti-Zionism was a reaction provoked whenever this doctrine was proclaimed so emphatically and with such publicity that it seemed to call in question the institutional basis on which Western Jewry existed. In principle, of course, Zionism always rejected the Emancipation, the institutional basis of Western Jewry, at least as a definitive solution of the Jewish question. Western Zionists regarded the Jewish community in Eastern Europe as the most characteristic expression of the modern Jewish situation. But, however gloomily the Western Zionists might view the ultimate fate of their own community, in practice they chiefly concerned themselves with the pressing problem of the Eastern rather than of the Western Jews.[2] The Eastern *Judennot* was the concrete problem they hoped to solve by means of resettlement in Palestine. And, on the other hand, long before Zionism, Western Jews who held, in principle, that their own community was the most characteristic expression of the modern Jewish situation, and that emancipation was the best and most rational way to solve the Jewish question everywhere had already concluded that, in practice, the immediate difficulties of Eastern Jewry required other remedies; among them, resettlement in Palestine.

Because of these conditions, anti-Zionism was not a constant but an episodic manifestation in Western Jewry. It arose when, in its concentration on crucial political aims, Zionism raised fundamental ideological questions regarding the Jews and the Jewish problem, and so drew general attention to doctrines which seemed to the West to undermine its institutional foundations. But when the political emphasis in Zionism subsided, either because of a Zionist defeat or because of an internationally recognized Zionist victory, and the stress shifted to practical resettlement in Palestine, the anti-Zionist tide ebbed. "Non-Zionism" appeared, as cooperation in the resettlement of Palestine was now resumed on the basis of a political status newly achieved by Zionism. And many, indeed, were those non-Zionists who, before the new status was won, had opposed it as vigorous anti-Zionists.

What made possible the attitude of practical cooperation called non-Zionism was the same "will to unity" which Bodenheimer regarded as inherent in the Zionist movement. For one basic premise united the non-Zionists with the Zionists. It was the unspoken belief that however defined or constituted, whether as a religious or ethnic community, the Jews throughout the world shared a common heritage and destiny, and their problems were a single indivisible responsibility. It was this that made possible a consensus between Zionism and non-Zionism in the Western Jewish community, just as it had made possible from the beginning the cooperation between Eastern Hovevei-Zionism and Western Jewish philanthropy.

I

The permanent and doctrinal confrontation of Zionism and anti-Zionism in the East caused the opposed ideological positions to be sharpened and clarified. For the tactics that lead to victory in a competition for popular favor are those that most effectively play on latent hostilities which either side can stir up among the people against its opponents. Thus, the constant principled opposition of Eastern anti-Zionism led to the elaboration and definition of many aspects of the general and partisan Zionist ideologies. Yet, at the same time, it contributed relatively little to the idea of the Jewish state.

On the other hand, in the West, Zionism was led by the kind of opposition it encountered in the Jewish community to accept far-reaching ideological adjustments and compromises. Sporadic as it was, Western anti-Zionism flared up in the very moments of political crisis when the full support of the Jewish community was essential; for in the struggle to gain practical advantages for the resettlement in Palestine, the whole community faced non-Jewish political institutions as a petitioner. What was essential here was to stress whatever was common between Zionists and their opponents, removing the divisions that came from pushing ideological positions to polemical extremes; and some of the same men who were anti-Zionist at such times could later become non-Zionist leaders, whose powerful support was counted on in the practical cooperation that succeeded the political dispute. Owing to these circumstances, Western non-Zionism exercised a great influence upon the way the idea of the Jewish state passed, in a succession of stages, from an ideological abstraction to a legal formula and political actuality.

The Basle Congress illustrates the relationship between the rise of political Zionism and the cycle of Western anti-Zionism and non-Zionism, though in an inverted form. Before political Zionism arose, the Hovevei-Zion movement, without provoking the anti-Zionism that was implicit in the Western opposition to its principles, had already made the compromises necessary for practical cooperation with non-Zionists. Herzlian Zionism, on the other hand, stressed that the immediate task was to obtain not only Turkish but international recognition, at least in principle, of the Jewish right to sovereignty in Palestine. Such an attitude was a goad which could turn the pragmatic non-Zionism of some Western friends of Hovevei-Zionism into a doctrinaire anti-Zionism — and, in fact, did so.

Herzl saw no great hindrance to his project in the emergence of ideological anti-Zionism.[3] His diplomatic campaign to acquire Palestine never advanced far enough to make the effects of a divided Jewish community upon its success a factor he had to consider seriously. Once he decided to work through the Zionist Organization, however, he had to achieve the solid, ungrudging agreement of those who were to embody, and authorize him to represent, the will to sovereignty of the Jewish people.

Concretely, Herzl's potential "constituency" was the dwindling Hovevei-Zion movement and its sympathizers who could be regrouped under the new banner. And while in the East even the tired veterans, not to speak of the disgruntled younger men, responded emotionally to the Herzlian concentration on the ideological, political crux of Zionism, the movement had, after all, invested a great deal in its cooperation with other elements in the Jewish community. In the West, in fact, the pillars of Hovevei-Zionism included men like Chief Rabbi Zadoc Kahn (1839–1905) of Paris or Joseph Sebag Montefiore (1822–1903) of London, noted for their active leadership in the Alliance Israélite Universelle or the Board of Jewish Deputies.[4] The suppression of the idea of Jewish sovereignty was the very thing that made their parallel leadership in Hovevei-Zion groups possible. Consequently, the immediate effect of Herzlian Zionism was to unsettle the Hovevei-Zion societies. Some — the British and a few of the German groups — refused to attend the Congress, and a number of their leaders emerged as outright anti-Zionists.[5] Others, especially the veterans in Eastern Europe who were attracted by the new doctrine or by its energetic leadership, were nevertheless concerned to maintain the existing organization. Consequently, the Basle program took account of "non-Zionist" opposition to some extent in order to soothe such old Hovevei-Zionists. But the formulas that resulted were only enough to assure the latter of the Herzlian "will to unity"; they could not prevent the emergence of sharply defined anti-Zionist positions, already provoked by the preparations for the Congress.

Herzl himself was anything but an ideologue, and he was entirely prepared to accept a revised formula if the Hovevei-Zion needed it to protect their political and legal position in Russia and in Palestine. But he was not in the least inclined to concede points of principle in order to keep the peace in the Jewish community, for the Zionist Organization, not the Jewish community, was the tool by which, at Basle, he hoped to gain his ends. When anti-Zionist opposition developed, rather than thinking of compromises to meet it in the hope of uniting the whole community behind him, Herzl responded with polemical counterattacks. These alienated his opponents even further, but served to sharpen the discipline and consolidate the organization of the Zionists as the chosen instrument of his policy.

In the beginning the eminent, scholarly rabbi of Vienna, Dr. Moritz Guedemann (1835–1918), responded with enthusiastic praise, perhaps more for the spirit and style than for the specific content of Herzl's presentation. Guedemann was a defender of tradition, who had unsuccessfully fought a proposal to eliminate from the liturgy of his own congregation references to Zion and to the hope of Messianic return.[6] What attracted him in Zionism was undoubtedly its revival of traditional moods and motifs. But faced with Zionism as a practical proposal, with plans to convoke a Congress, Guedemann hesitated, questioned, and finally formulated his opposition decisively in his pamphlet *Nationaljudentum*. His view — echoing S. R. Hirsch — was that the Messianic hopes and traditional prayers to return to Zion could have no immediate application but must be understood symbolically.

Herzl at first had placed high hopes in Guedemann and confided to his diary plans to make him "chief bishop of the capital city" in the Jewish State. After *Nationaljudentum*, however, he dismissed him as no more than the voice of his rich congregants, who paid his salary and thus determined his views.[7] In the same polemical vein, he describes the "Protest Rabbis," who publicly denounced the plans to hold the first Zionist Congress, as men who lived off the Jewish community, not for it; and he says that in their opposition to the sovereign will of the reawakening Jewish people they, in effect, seceded from Jewry. The Jewish people, for its part, would not stop them from leaving, and had no further interest in them. This was more than a casual gibe, for Herzl regularly made the same reply whenever the objection was raised that Zionism endangered the status of emancipated or "assimilated" Jews. If French Jewry were, indeed, an integral part of the French nation, and of that nation alone, with no ethnic bonds to other Jews, then the establishment of the Jewish state would not harm but rather help them. Those Jews who "could not or would not" assimilate in their present homes would transfer to the Jewish state, leaving the others behind, unencumbered thenceforth by embarrassing responsibilities for Jews who recognized an ethnic as well as a religious tie to their fellow-Jews.[8]

In line with this approach, Herzl's view regarding himself and other Zionists seems to have been relatively simple: they were among those who could not or would not assimilate in their present homes and, in all probability, would go to Palestine with the rest of the Jewish nation.[9] There was a fairly obvious implication: Herzl accepted the challenge of anti-Semites who denied that the Jews were Frenchmen or Germans like themselves. He expected a franker understanding with Gentiles because he refused, for himself and his fellows, to dispute this contention and, instead, proudly reclaimed his Jewish nationality.

The young Western Jews who joined Herzl's band of early Zionists, or who had anticipated him in their conversion to Jewish nationalism, took a very similar stand; yet certain shades of difference show their adjustment to the practical needs of building up a local Zionist organization, in Germany for instance. Dr. Max Bodenheimer, the first president of the German Zionist Organization, is an illustration of both the basic agreement and the shades of difference. Prof. Hermann Schapira, on the other hand, represents the sharper and more far-reaching differences that the older Hovevei-Zionist leaders had to overcome in helping to found the new organization.

Professor Schapira undoubtedly shared with other Hovevei-Zionists the general disappointment with the low state of their movement in the 1890's, at a time when there was large-scale Jewish migration overseas. The enthusiasm aroused by Herzl, particularly among Eastern students with Zionist ideas, made him feel that here was his hope for the future — such, at least, was the impression he gave some of these students, in spite of the academic distance he habitually maintained.[10]

Yet the great hopes he placed in a revived Zionist movement never made him forget the much greater historic significance which, in his view, attached to a united Jewish community.

Mr. Birnbaum, Mr. Nordau, and Mr. Schach may be the most splendid people and they may paint for themselves and for us the most beautiful pictures, but they are neither called nor capable to create a new Judaism for us. Only Judaism itself can live on and develop, not something newly fabricated which cuts the ground out from under its own feet.[11]

Schapira's great fear was the fear of disunion among Jews, the "spectre of modern party warfare" in the community. This danger, he thought, would come precisely from his young Zionist friends, whose enthusiasm might make them doctrinaire and so provoke a doctrinaire opposition.

You do not know enough of Judaism; nor, I believe, do you know enough of the Jews at all. You wish to heal and do not know where it hurts. The gravest illness of the Jews is their disunion and now you come and cause new splits.[12]

For Schapira explained the emergence of an anti-Zionist opposition on other grounds than Herzl. He, too, saw it as the product of fear, but he interpreted it as an ideological reflex provoked by Zionist doctrinaire utterances rather than debunking it as an expression of mean or mercenary motives.

We have no right to ascribe other than honorable motives to our opponents. These gentlemen believe they see a great danger approaching, and in order to ward it off they do not stop at such fearful sacrifices as the surrender of very important Jewish principles for the sake of saving Jewry itself. Indeed Guedemann's reduction of the most sacred principles to mere symbols is one of the most dangerous of remedies and could lead only to frightful consequences, and yet this good and honorable man knows no other way out of the predicament . . . I have held Dr. Guedemann in high esteem for many years, and from the impression I have received of his sincere love of Jewry, he must himself be deeply distressed, in private, at his success. Surely it was only in his fright that he offered us his vial of medicinal symbols, and he will have to permit me to paste on for him the label he forgot in his haste: Poison! External Use Only! . . . Therefore, instead of combating our opponents, I must again admonish you in no way to give occasion for conflict, so that our opponents may not be forced to use weapons which they themselves should know very well are all too dangerous; weapons they permit themselves to use only for "defense" in extreme need.[13]

The announcement that Zionism aimed at a Jewish state, and the principle that political concessions must be sought before anything else was done, were policies that Schapira opposed because he regarded them as a red flag waved in the faces of Jewish non-Zionists — not to speak (and he puts this as an afterthought) of the political effect in Turkey.[14] Instead, he proposed as a model a set of Zionist aims worked out in the light of years of experience of the Hovevei-Zion movement.

The aims of the "Zion" society are the following:

(1) to disseminate knowledge of Jewish history and the Hebrew language and literature among the Jews;

(2) to establish unity among all who believe in Judaism, without distinction, for the purpose of ameliorating the common situation of the Jews;

(3) to realize the idea of the settlement of Palestine by Jews; and

(4) to create a united center for all aspirations toward culture and education in the Jewish colonies that will be established. This will be achieved by founding a school of higher learning for training in all religious, scientific, and practical subjects with (a) a religious department, (b) an academic department, and (c) an agricultural-technological department, etc.[15]

For these activities, Schapira felt sanguine of obtaining the cooperation of the entire Jewish community — though hardly their participation in a body claiming to represent an embryonic Jewish sovereignty. He hoped further, in the spirit of Ahad Ha'am, that cultural development in Palestine, together with the common effort of "disseminating the knowledge of Jewish history and the Hebrew language and literature," would revive a free and creative consensus among the Jews, after it had been impaired and sterilized by religious division and by adaptation to different political and social conditions in different countries. As for the hope of Jewish sovereignty restored, if not stated as the public program of an organized body it could live on unhindered as the religious or quasi-religious aspiration of individuals.[16]

Professor Schapira's young correspondent, Dr. Max Bodenheimer, accepted neither these proposals nor the reasoning behind them. As to provoking doctrinaire opposition by stating clear doctrines, Bodenheimer welcomed rather than feared this. If he hoped, nevertheless, to see the Jewish community united, it was because Jewish unity was inherent in the national idea represented by the Zionist organization itself. As for the "Zionist aims" proposed by Professor Schapira, he could not take them seriously for what they were in fact — a statement of a Zionist ideology which, unlike his own stemmed from a primary concern with the "problem of Judaism" rather than the "problem of the Jews." Instead, he assumed that they were no more than an attempt to veil the true aims of Professor Schapira and other Zionists in the vain hope of avoiding conflicts and opposition. Not having understood the Ahad Ha'amist premises of Prof. Schapira's proposals, Bodenheimer, like Herzl, treated such suggestions as no more than counsels of timidity. In the final formulations of the draft which Bodenheimer brought to Basle, he took account of fears relating to Turkey and Russia by referring not to a "Jewish state" but to a "home secured by international law," and also made other insignificant gestures towards Schapira's views by introducing changes which he must have considered little more than verbal. The underlying assumptions of the draft, however, were clearly political-Zionist rather than Hovevei-Zionist or Ahad Ha'amist. In these respects, the "theses" formulated by Bodenheimer's Cologne group in consultation with other German Zionists were fully in accord with Herzl's own views.[17]

The theses differ from Herzl's pattern in one significant respect. Bodenheimer and his colleagues were sufficiently concerned about what a Zionist attitude might imply with regard to a German Zionist's present citizenship and status to think that this deserved specific mention. Moreover, they did not take Herzl's simple position that Zionism meant implicitly a kind of promissory renunciation of other than Jewish nationality, to be put into effect when the Jewish national home became open to those who "could not or would not" live either as oppressed Russian subjects or as Frenchmen or Germans "of the Mosaic persuasion." Consequently in the theses of the German Zionists a clause was introduced specifically in order to answer one of the arguments regularly raised against Zionism by anti-Zionists. In the first formulation, this read that

Bound together by common descent and history, the Jews of all countries constitute a national community. This conviction in no way infringes the active patriotic sentiments and fulfillment of the duties of citizenship on the part of the Jews, and in particular of the German Jews toward their German Fatherland.[18]

In later drafts, this clause was more generally phrased but, if anything, strengthened. The common bonds of the Jews which make them a national community are said to oblige them to give effective aid to their oppressed racial brethren (later still — to act in the common interest) to the extent that this does not infringe upon their duties of citizenship.[19]

In the Basle program itself this specific restriction was not inserted. On the other hand, the whole reference to those Jews who "could not or would not" assimilate in their present homes was also omitted. Since this expression carries the whole Herzlian implication that whoever was a Zionist had accepted the anti-Semitic challenge to declare himself for one or another exclusive nationality, its omission was perhaps not without significance.

The ideological problem involved was not one that could be dealt with by silence. Herzl himself recognized its existence and gave his initial response in his address to the Basle Congress. For what made the problem pressing was precisely the basic tactical premise of Herzlian Zionism: that the actual migration to Palestine was a second stage of Zionist activity, following a first period in which an essential preliminary goal had to be attained. Herzl defined this goal as the grant of a charter to establish a Jewish national home by international agreement. Ahad Ha'am, who also believed in a preparatory stage and preliminary goal of Zionism, defined it as the reestablishment of a Jewish social consensus expressed in a revived Jewish culture. At Basle Herzl made an approach toward recognizing this Ahad Ha'amist view which was shared by so many of the Eastern Hovevei-Zionists. He made a statement which was enthusiastically received as a token of reassurance by many Zionists who were dubious of the lack of Jewish culture in their new leader. "Zionism," he said, "is a return to the Jewish fold [*Judentum*] even before it becomes a return to the Jewish land." [20] For while the grant of a charter for colonization was the essential preliminary to an effective return to Palestine, the reconstitution of the solidarity of the Jewish people, of its will to sovereignty, was the essential preliminary to acquiring the charter; and the latter might follow the former by a considerable period. If, then, the immediate task of Zionism might prove to be the education and organization of the people quite as much as, or even more than, the diplomatic campaign for a charter, and if the preservation of Jewish solidarity in the Diaspora might be a duty of long duration, two questions of first ideological importance arose: how was the Zionist movement in the Diaspora to defend itself against the imputation of maintaining a "state within the state"; and what must be its attitude toward Jewish culture?

In spite of the influence of his Zionist friends, Herzl's answers to these questions never departed too far from his initial simple formulas. He assumed virtually total responsibility for the organization of the central institutions as well as the diplomacy of the movement.[21] Even if he had wished to, he could hardly have added the responsibility for solving what were essentially problems for the leaders of the local organizations. Moreover, he lived in hopes of a diplomatic victory that would soon make it unnecessary to take an ideological position regarding the right to preserve Jewish national solidarity in the Diaspora. As to Jewish culture, he vaguely said that while "we, the children who have returned, find much to redress under the ancestral roof, . . . we are not actuated by an arrogant desire to undermine that which should be revered." To balance this he reversed the proposition, stating that while "the Congress will concern itself with the spiritual means to be employed for reviving and fostering the national consciousness of the Jews," on the other hand, "we have not the least intention of yielding a jot of the culture we have acquired." [22] The problem was tabled rather than dealt with.

And so, too, was the question of the loyalty of Zionists toward the countries they implied they wished to leave. To this problem Herzl gave an answer that could be satisfactory only to one who believed that the removal of the Jews to Palestine was imminent.

But should the accusation that we are not patriotic figure among the more or less sincere arguments directed against our movement, this equivocal objection carries its own refutation with it [. . .] Nowhere can there be a question of the exodus of all the Jews. Those who are able or wish to be assimilated will remain behind and be absorbed. When once a satisfactory agreement is concluded with the various political units involved and a systematic Jewish migration begins, it will last only so long in each country as that country desires to be rid of its Jews. How will the current be stopped? Simply by the gradual decrease and the final cessation of anti-Semitism. Thus it is that we understand and anticipate the solution of the Jewish problem.[23]

But what if the solution of the Jewish problem were delayed? And what of those Jews who "could not or would not" assimilate even if the anti-Semitic movement were to decline or disappear, because their "Jewishness" was not a reflex of oppression but an historic attachment? If Herzl, in the fever of his political activity, could ignore these issues, men like Bodenheimer, in the slow struggle to organize, could not. They had to defend the right of Jewish solidarity and the right to a living Jewish culture not only on the assumption that the Jewish people would soon leave the Diaspora and settle *en bloc* in Palestine, but on the much more probable assumption that the Jewish people would, in the foreseeable future, continue for the most part to live in the Diaspora. Sharing Herzl's insight that the Jewish problem was a national problem, they had to defend not only the ultimate justice of a solution by the restoration of Jewish sovereignty in Zion; they also had to defend the immediate rights of the Jews to combine patriotism in their home countries with global Jewish solidarity, to participate in the cultural and social as well as political affairs of their homes and also to maintain special cultural and social as well as political affinities with Jews throughout the world. And they had to leave open the possibility that Palestine would never hold all the Jews who recognized an ethnic solidarity; but that the achievement of Jewish sovereignty in Palestine would indeed strengthen the ties of the world-wide people.[24]

In declaring the Jewish problem a national problem, Herzl accepted the ideological premises not only of anti-Semites, appealing to the mob, but of quite respectable opponents of the Jewish infiltration into German society; and this, indeed, was the basis of his hope for an internationally agreed solution of the Jewish problem, amicably and frankly compacted between Jews and Christians. It was the Gentile refusal to be consistently liberal that perpetuated the Jewish problem in enlightened Europe. For the Gentiles refused to recognize that citizenship alone should fully qualify for belonging to the nation, and they excluded their Jewish fellow-citizens from their national fellowship for lack of certain historic titles of social and cultural community. Instead of seeking to convince the Gentiles that this was wrong and inconsistent and so shame them into full enlightenment, as Jewish Liberals were trying to do, Herzl proposed to accept the Gentile attitude as an unalterable fact — and come to an honorable agreement on this basis.

This was the rational ideology of Herzl. The mythic appeal of his writing and oratory, however, lay in the conviction with which he emphasized that such an agreement must be, and would be, an *honorable* agreement. For it was implicit in Herzl's position that he accepted the Gentile assumptions regarding nationality not only as an intractable fact but as a just principle: a nationality was, indeed, not merely a body of fellow-citizens, but a union of men tied together by historic bonds of social and cultural communion. This insight need never have been formulated by Herzl, for it was ardently demonstrated by everything he did and by his manner in everything he said. The right he frankly conceded to the Gentiles to exclude Jews from their ethnic communion was paralleled by the pride with which he himself resumed his place in the Jewish ethnic communion.[25]

The Herzlian pride of return was what Western Zionism had to formulate ideologically. It was a task in which the Zionists could be quite as certain as Herzl of offending the Jewish opponents of Zionism, while they could hardly be as sanguine of pleasing the Gentile critics of the emancipation.

Against the Jewish advocates of Utopian Liberalism, the Zionists argued, like Herzl, that citizenship alone was no full admission to nationality — and even more flatly than he, for he left room for the conclusion that it was only the incomprehensible stubbornness of the Gentiles that prevented the full assimilation of the Jews. If the Gentiles had been ready to drop their social and cultural barriers, no attachment to their own tradition would have prevented Jews from complete assimilation, said Herzl plainly.[26] This conclusion, gainsaid by Herzl's own proud return, was now explicitly denied. Not only was the Gentile resistance no mere stubbornness but an historical necessity; there was also an historically necessary Jewish resistance to assimilation, a will to preserve their own ethnic segregation, which only hid itself behind the conceded right to religious difference. The Jews had a right to their ethnic identity. Patriotism was only one of the duties of a man of honor, and civic loyalty was not impugned by other, compatible loyalties beyond the state.

Jewish Liberals, too, recognized that much of what they did as a religious community — for example their international cooperation in defense of other Jews, national bodies to counteract anti-Semitism, and separate Jewish student corporations in German universities — really had the character of ethnic segregation. Moreover, while they contended that the Jews since the emancipation had lost, or were losing, their ethnic quality, they were aware that the whole past history of the Jews had been essentially that of an ethnic group. But these were facts ideology could easily cope with. The Liberals fought for the complete dissolution of the vestiges of Jewish ethnic tradition through the complete victory of emancipation. As for their self-protective segregation, to some extent this was justified as natural to a religious brotherhood; and what could not plausibly be explained in this way was interpreted as a provisional measure forced upon them by circumstances.[27]

Thus, the Zionist argument, that the failure of the emancipation to wipe out all nonreligious distinctions between Jews and Gentiles simply proved the Jews were more than a religious group, was conceded in practice but denied in theory by Jewish Liberals. So, too, the Zionist conclusion, that expressions of Jewish ethnic solidarity should not be deplored but strengthened, was likely to meet Gentile resistance. The effort to win recognition for Jews as a national minority in Eastern Europe would not go unopposed. The revival of Jewish national pride, not only in the act of removing Jews from Europe but even when they continued to live there, would be grist for the mills of anti-Semitism. Precisely in these practical matters, however, the Zionists found ways to cooperate with their Jewish ideological opponents, for the latter found their own justifications for policies in which the Zionists saw an expression of the ethnic will to survive.

II

A classic formulation of anti-Zionism was evoked by the preparations for the First Zionist Congress. It took the form of this press release,
issued to a number of papers in July 1897 by the famous "Protest
Rabbis":

The Executive Committee of the Association of Rabbis in Germany: Dr.
Maybaum (Berlin), Dr. Horovitz (Frankfurt), Dr. Guttmann (Breslau),
Dr. Auerbach (Halberstadt), Dr. Werner (Munich) made the following
announcement:

Through the call for a Zionist Congress and through the publication of its
agenda, such mistaken notions have been spread about the whole subject
of Judaism and about the objectives of its adherents that the undersigned
Executive Committee of the Association of Rabbis in Germany regards
it as proper to make the following explanation:

(1)   The efforts of so-called Zionists to found a Jewish national state
in Palestine contradict the Messianic promises of Judaism as contained in
the Holy Writ and in later religious sources.

(2)   Judaism obligates its adherents to serve with all devotion the
Fatherland to which they belong, and to further its national interests with
all their heart and with all their strength.

(3)   However, those noble aims directed toward the colonization of
Palestine by Jewish peasants and farmers are not in contradiction to these
obligations, because they have no relation whatsoever to the founding of
a national state.

Religion and patriotism both lay upon us the duty of asking all who are
concerned with the welfare of Judaism to stay away from the above-
mentioned Zionistic endeavors and most particularly from the Congress
which is still being planned, despite all the warnings against it.[28]

Points 1 and 2 succinctly express anti-Zionist doctrines in a form
which could satisfy both the rabbis who took a more conservative
and those who took a more liberal view of the sanctity of tradition.
The Zionist efforts to effect the return to Palestine and the restoration
of Jewish sovereignty were denounced in the name of tradition itself.
In their second point the rabbis by implication rejected Herzl's *volte-
face* in relation to the Emancipation and the anti-Semites. In pointedly
affirming Jewish loyalty to the Fatherland, they implied that since the
emancipation the Jews had relinquished any other ethnic loyalties
they might have had, and were bound to Jews beyond their frontiers
only by the permissible sympathy of coreligionists. This signified a
rejection of certain implied views: that citizenship was not all there
was to nationality; and that in other aspects of nationality, in their
historic social and cultural ties, Jews were not bound exclusively
to their compatriots — they had some social and cultural ties which
bound them in a world-wide ethnic bond with other Jews. In this

regard, point 2 stated the denial by anti-Zionists of an opinion that Zionists shared with anti-Semites and other critics of the emancipation. In another respect, it implied agreement of the anti-Zionists with a criticism of the Zionists by anti-Semites and other critics of the emancipation. For point 2 implied that if it were true, as the Zionists said, that Jews were bound the world over by ethnic bonds, then it would be justified to accuse the Jews of disloyalty to the country of their citizenship.

In contrast to these two anti-Zionist planks of the protesting rabbis' platform, point 3 states a position which may be called a virtual non-Zionism. Religion might be implied to be the only bond between Jews in different countries, and emancipation the definitive solution of the Jewish problem — but still there were countries where emancipation was not feasible, where the problem at any rate continued acute. The solidarity between Jews throughout the world, however it might be defined, demanded that fellow-Jews be aided to emigrate from the lands of oppression. And it was a particularly noble aim — though quite without relation to any idea of founding a Jewish state — to direct them to the colonization of Palestine.

The contradiction which is apparent between the anti-Zionist and non-Zionist points of the protest manifesto should not be considered just a random inconsistency, such as often occurs when people act upon complex motives. It is something that necessarily follows from the anti-Zionist premises themselves.

On an academic level, whoever wishes to explain Jewish solidarity as purely religious can deal plausibly enough with the theoretical objections likely to be raised against his position, such as those which point out the common descent, and the endogamy, or the separate languages and customs, or the historic tradition and myth of the Jews. The explanations, at any rate, satisfy their authors fully, which is the main point of an ideology.[29] But the international solidarity of Jewish coreligionists extended to countries whose legal institutions never regarded Jews as equivalent in all respects to their fellow citizens except for a distinction of religion, in the Western sense — and, so too, it extended to Jewish communities who never accepted that theory. The exercise of Jewish solidarity frequently involved, in such situations and in relation to such communities, helping to work out solutions which implied that an ethnic Jewishness existed. But precisely because the Jews were defined by Westerners as a religious group — and, in spite of all differences, a single religious group — the adherents of anti-Zionist views could not be consistent with their own principles if they confined their solidarity exclusively to Jews who

were their co-citizens. If the solidarity of coreligionists meant anything
at all, it had to extend to coreligionists of different countries. The most
the anti-Zionists could do was to seek to give these activities a character, or at least a nominal description, that would minimize whatever
ethnic qualities they might naturally possess.

Simply to combine together internationally in order to present
petitions to international conferences dealing with Jewish problems,
as Western Jews did early in the 1870's and still do as late as today,
may raise ideological problems It was natural to evade such issues in
the early days, before Zionism had established its organs of political
advocacy and representation deliberately and on principle as expressions of Jewish nationalism. However, in 1936, when the World Jewish
Congress was convened in order to attempt essentially the same kind
of international defense of Jewish rights as had been conducted for
over a century past, some of the non- and anti-Zionists invited to
participate denounced the proposed Congress in the most positive
terms: in itself, it was undesirable because Jewish international
organization and political activity implied an ethnic far more than a
religious bond; and its effect would be to make anti-Semitic charges
of an international Jewish conspiracy seem plausible. Yet not only had
similar organizations and activities been initiated by Western Jews
long before, but the very bodies who denounced the World Jewish
Congress in 1936 were later forced to create a new international
representative body of their own, because the situation after the end
of the Second World War required it.[30]

The basic predicament is further illustrated by the fight for
minority rights for Jews in the Diaspora. The Western Jews who
cooperated with Easterners in the *Comité des délégations juives* at
the peace conferences after the First World War did so, in many
cases, with great reluctance, because the case they were pleading was
formulated by their clients, the Eastern Jews, on the assumption that
Jews were a separate ethnic group with a collective title to certain
rights and liberties. But in the fight against Jewish disabilities in the
Balkans a generation earlier, Western Jews had themselves claimed
rights for their coreligionists based on the religio-ethnic *millet* system
customary in the Ottoman Empire, not on the Western principle of
the separation of church and state. So, too, at Versailles the situation
forced Western Jews — if they wished to express their Jewish solidarity
at all on the issue — to cooperate with their Eastern brethren in their
fight for what were called national minority rights. In effect, these
turned out to be hardly more than the traditional civil rights of an
emancipated Western citizen, though granted under the (ineffective)

guarantee of an international treaty system.[31] But the latter point itself, as well as the name "national minority rights," remained ideologically obnoxious to non-Zionist Western Jewish organizations, such as the American Jewish Committee. In planning for the post-war period in the 1940's, they sought to replace the minority rights system, imposed by treaty on especially sensitive areas where minorities considered themselves ethnic entities, by an International Bill of Rights, nominally applying to all countries and eliminating the explicit reference to ethnic minorities.[32]

The solution of the Jewish problem through emigration and planned territorial resettlement was another project in which Western non- and anti-Zionist Jews were led to cooperate even though it necessarily bore a strongly ethnic aspect. Here, too, there was the attempt to give an ideologically acceptable look to the activity, while at the same time satisfying its objective requirements and the requirements for cooperation with Eastern Jews, whom it chiefly concerned. The cooperation of Western and Eastern Jews in the "territorialist" movement is, moreover, directly involved with the developing relations between Zionists and non-Zionists; and many attitudes which were effective in the latter relationship, and thus helped determine the way the idea of the Jewish state became "institutionalized," were first worked out by trial in the former relationship.

III

As has been noted already, the idea of a territory, not necessarily Palestine, to which mass emigration might be sent, thus solving the Jewish problem in the countries of oppression, had occurred repeatedly to Western Jewish philanthropists and organizations. In the 1890's, shortly before the rise of the Herzlian Zionist movement, territorialist plans were canvassed with particular interest, and the major efforts of Baron de Hirsch in Argentina and elsewhere, outdoing even Baron Edmond de Rothschild's efforts in Palestine, made the question a live issue. A number of very pressing practical problems caused the acquisition of a Jewish territory to seem especially pertinent at that time.

The wave of migration in 1891, a year of economic distress and expulsions of Jews from interior Russia, was the second, if not the third or fourth, large-scale Jewish refugee movement with which Western Europe was faced. The Western Jews who had to shoulder the responsibility for aiding their destitute coreligionists approached the problem with the wisdom of their experience during the migration

of the 1880's and of earlier emergencies. The unpreparedness of Western Jews in 1880 was felt to be the reason why so substantial a part
of the funds raised to save Jews from Russia was spent instead on
sending them back to the land of their oppression. After that experience it was considered part of the task of aiding refugees to make
their reception in the new countries both easy and permanent. The
unplanned attempts to establish farm colonies in the 80's, which had
collapsed in America [33] and only been saved by the timely aid of
Rothschild in Palestine, would have to be succeeded by properly
conceived and properly financed schemes of colonization. The un-
controlled and unselected despatch or spontaneous flight of refugees
to the same places, which strained the resources of way stations and
caused immigrants to be barred from Palestine or sent back from
America, would have to stop. The Western European responsibility
for aiding emigrants could not rest at speeding them on their way,
but must include making sure that they went to destinations in which
both geography and social and political conditions guaranteed that
the Jews would remain — and that the Jewish problem would not dog
their footsteps.

A massive flow of emigrants in 1891 concentrated in the Charlottenburg railway depot of Berlin, and the Jews of this city consequently
took a leading part in organizing international Jewish assistance for
the refugees. At a conference on the problem held on October 21,
after over four months of experience with the refugees, a report of
a subcommittee on the "question of colonization" was delivered by
Karl Emil Franzos (1848–1904) from which one may learn a good
deal about the considerations influencing many Western Jews.

It is evident, first of all, that the question of principle whether,
and how far, Western Jews should be responsible for a project such
as the territorial colonization of their coreligionists was a constant
worry. The Berlin committee had already found it necessary to
defend itself against the imputation that its free-handed charity at
Charlottenburg (a liberality encouraged by the Prussian authorities,
who were anxious to keep the refugees moving out as fast as they
came in) was one reason why the emigration continued and increased.[34] It was easy to reject this charge, showing that Russian
oppression, not the benevolence of Berlin Jews, was responsible for
the mass flight, and arguing, as Franzos did, that simple humanitarianism, let alone a natural sympathy with one's coreligionists,
demanded that aid be freely given. Nevertheless, ideological scruples
continued to make the committee uneasy about the legitimate bounds

of its responsibility. Thus, Franzos said that, in principle, it might have met the demands of humane duty, and even of honor, if the Prussian Jews, who bore the major initial burden of the refugee mass at Charlottenburg, left all responsibility for their final settlement to the other Western Jews.

Yet, in view of the extent of the tragedy and the pitiful condition of the refugees, no one could feel he had done enough. The Berlin Jews could not take the refugees out of the darkness only to send them to a new darkness. "So we wished to provide, to colonize, like the others and together with the others." The magnitude of the problem — for Franzos expected a continuing flow of emigrants which would reach a million — was so great that only a state could properly handle it, as was done in the only modern parallel, the mass emigration after the Irish famine of the 1840's. This movement "was directed by a government, with the authority, the money, the credit, the administrative machinery of one of the richest and most efficient states in the world." The Jews had no state. "What is more, we are no longer a united people, the Jew in countries of modern culture today is a German, Frenchman, Briton of Jewish faith, and thank God that he is!" In spite of all that, without the funds, credit, machinery or authority of a state, the international brotherhood of Jews must find the means and the solidarity to solve the immense problem.[35]

The duty of providing for the refugees at their destination having been established, or at least vaguely justified, the question arose, "What should be the territory?" or more correctly, "What territory should the Berlin Jews choose for their *own* colonization project?" That the question was put in this peculiar way suggests that, in spite of the arguments by which Franzos had shown that charity to one's coreligionists should not remain at home, he still thought of the responsibility of the Western Jews as essentially parochial rather than national in character. The answers he gave to his own question, moreover, show that involved in this attitude was a quite deliberate avoidance of commitments that implied an ethnic ideological view of the problem.

Franzos spent little time demonstrating that Russian Jews should not be colonized in the enlightened countries of Western and Central Europe.

Europe was mentioned least often [in the deliberations of his subcommittee]. Quite correctly so, of course. I need not detail the reasons why we would not colonize in Germany, Austria-Hungary, France, and England. To be sure, occasionally one of these countries was suggested too. But what conceivable suggestions are not made! [36]

The unelucidated reasons against Jewish colonies in Europe are clear from earlier passages of Franzos' report. The first criterion for a suitable territory was the "slightest possible anti-Semitic trend," for Franzos assumed that Jews (and above all, as he felt forced to stress, Russian Jews) could go nowhere without provoking some hostility. Pertinent, also, was the fact that the aim of colonization should be to produce the edifying demonstration that Jews could become and remain a self-sustaining peasant class.

Other reasons spoke against Palestine. Palestine, of course, was the center of "a struggle of *Weltanschauung*, of the entire gamut of religious, political, national ideas among Jews." [37] Just because of their controversial character, the ideological issues concerning Palestine were not considered by the committee for which Franzos reported. However, he reports, under a number of heads, the opinions on the subject expressed to the investigating group in the petitions sent by Eastern Jews: (1) The petitioners were Jewish not only by faith but by nationality and language — meaning Yiddish, gentlemen! — and only in Palestine could they hope to bring up their children as good and pious Jews in their own tradition. (2) There was religious persecution everywhere, including America, and only in Palestine was there peace between all faiths. (3) The colonies in Palestine were prospering and no one returned from there as they did from America. (4) Even if things went badly in Palestine, all Russian Jews longed to go there for religious reasons and would be happy to live on bread and water in the ancestral land. (5) The Russian Jews were Easterners and would find it easier to accommodate themselves to the style of life of the Orient than to strange American ways. (6) The free political institutions of America, they feared, might lead astray many Jews unaccustomed to such license. (7) Many Russian Jews were going to Palestine with means of their own, and these could help their poor brethren, relieving the Committee of some of its burden. (8) In Palestine, and only there, would Jews persist as farmers, for they would want to cultivate the soil promised to their forefathers.

Of these reasons, Franzos assigned only to the last two any objective significance. As to the rest, he felt that his opinion could be given without entering into an ideological debate.

Would it be within the realm of partisanship from the standpoint of this assembly, which is not met in some Galician hideaway or convened by a Hassidic sect, if I say that the dread of learning a foreign language, the wish to keep Yiddish and preserve not just the Jewish faith but Jewish nationality cannot appeal to *us* as material grounds in favor of Palestine? [Applause]
As for the longing for Palestine on grounds of religion, this is an element

which my role as *rapporteur* forbids me to bring into the debate. How far this element may be considered a material ground for establishing colonies, I leave to each of you to determine.

But the *penchant* for Oriental customs, the revulsion against American liberty, the declaration that Russian Jews prefer the political institutions of Turkey to those of America! No, gentlemen, these are hardly material grounds in favor of Palestine; they are at most material grounds for our feeling obliged all the more, even when these times of stress and strain have long gone by, to concern ourselves with the Russian Jews in quiet times, too, so that we can introduce to them other views related to our own. [Applause] [38]

But setting these ideological matters aside, Franzos gave objective reasons why Palestine should not be chosen for the Berlin colony — a decision that was perhaps already precluded anyway by the applause that greeted Franzos' ironically omitted ideological remarks. The first objective reason was the Sultan's ban on Jewish immigration, and the resulting general difficulties in the country, which had already led the Alliance Israélite Universelle to finance the return of immigrants to Eastern Europe. The second objective reason was the high cost of land in Palestine (which in the ensuing period was bid up even higher by the competitive land-buying of Jewish immigrants). The final reason — apart from the ideological objection to the national character of Palestinian colonization which, once more, was "not mentioned" — was Franzos' suspicion that the Palestinian colony would not prove as safe as its sponsors believed.

As for other territories, Franzos, on behalf of his subcommittee, ruled out many on the following interesting principle: Since it was assumed that the colony was to be a project sponsored by the German committee for assistance to Russian emigrants and by that committee alone, the territory where it would be established had to satisfy two conditions. These were that (a) the means of the German group alone had to be sufficient; and (b) no other, similar group of French, British, or American Jews should be in a better position, because of geography or the political influence of their own government in the territory in question, to act as the sponsor of a colony.

Such parochialism was hardly dictated by the interests of the refugees themselves, and it could never have prevailed in any assembly which frankly considered the colonization of the Russian Jews an ethnic responsibility, an obligation which implied and gave point to the existence of a Jewish people. It is reasonable to see in it not only the deliberate rejection of precisely such implications of a national Jewish responsibility. One may also suspect some stress of peculiarly German national or imperial interests at a time when Germany first began to think in terms of colonial expansion, and when German Jews had become accustomed to consider the work of the Alliance Israélite Universelle as an activity promoting French interests.

Western Jews generally could not, of course, consider territorial colonization solely in the light of a suitable project to occupy the attention of local relief committees, and decide on its scope and location according to the means and specific patriotic impulses of the benefactors. Certainly American or British Jews, faced with the responsibility of the ultimate settlement of the refugees, not of their transit alone, had to take a diffcrent view and apply a different yardstick. They were under the pressure of mounting anti-immigrant feeling in their own countries and feared the menace of anti-Semitism. Their yardstick was the magnitude of the refugee problem and of its side effects, not the strength and interests of their own organization. To serve their purposes a territory, or territories, had to be able to divert from London or New York a major part of the refugees. To be sure, if this were not possible they also saw the material advantage of dispersing at least some immigrants from the slum concentration and the symbolic (or, as we would say, the "public relations") value of proving that at least some Jews could become farmers. But this was decidedly a "minimum objective," for only if it were pursued on a large scale could territorialist colonization cope with the problem of anti-Semitism threatened by the immigrant slum.

Even a small colonization project necessarily involved negotiating for definite political guarantees, though perhaps the political advantages might in that case accrue to a European protecting power, rather than to the Jewish colony in its own right. But a major colonization project, by its very nature, meant applying for such rights for the Jewish settlers as could naturally — and, if the colony succeeded, would inevitably — lead to something resembling Jewish national sovereignty. This was a probable consequence which Western Jews could easily anticipate and had to accept in seeking the political conditions indispensable for a large-scale colonization. While there was certainly no need for an explicit ideological concession on this point so long as the issue was not immediate, the Western interest in large-scale colonization in such countries as Mesopotamia, as well, of course, as Palestine and Argentina, constituted an implicit commitment not to let ideology stand in the way of cooperation when and if it did become an actual issue.

Pinsker and Herzl, on the other hand, not only accepted at once the pragmatic case for large-scale territorial colonization but they developed an ideology based on the restoration of Jewish sovereignty as the core of the solution for the Jewish problem everywhere. Furthermore, both men began by considering a territory as such, and not the specific territory of Palestine, as the object to be attained. Even after he had committed himself, through the Zionist Organization, to Palestine, Herzl still was ready to consider seriously the possibility of colonization in such a country as Mesopotamia.[39] But the bond with Zion had now been firmly established as a primary Zionist principle, and it became as much of an ideological compromise for him, or for other Zionists, to speak of colonization outside Palestine as for a non-Zionist like Cyrus Adler (1863–1940) to seek a territorial solution of the Jewish or the refugee problem at all. Only practical contingencies quite as urgent as the need of New York Jewry to counteract the growth of the East Side slums could bring the Zionist movement to consider a territory other than Zion. With the turn of the century, such contingencies had arisen in an acute form, and Zionism was faced with the test of choosing between ideology and "practicality," between Zion and one or another alternative territory.

The expedient of territorialism was forced upon Herzl by irresistible pressures, to which he was particularly sensitive because he knew his heart disease left him little time to work. There was first the fact of his ever more palpable failure to obtain a charter from the Sultan. Then, on the other hand, there was the renewed and overwhelming pressure of mass emigration from Eastern Europe, caused by the cycle of social upheaval and reaction that opened the twentieth century in Russia.[40]

These circumstances had led to numerous proposals at the Zionist Congresses, in particular by Davis Trietsch, to settle in areas contiguous to Palestine — "Cyprus, El Arish, Sinai" — if the Holy Land itself were not available, hoping at some more favorable juncture to spread into the ancestral home.[41] The attempt to circumvent ideological objections is obvious here, for two not altogether compatible arguments seemed to assimilate such countries to the Zionist idea: they were near enough to Palestine to be "Bible Lands" and share somewhat in the sacredness of Zion — at least, it could be so presented — and near enough, too, to make it plausible to think of expanding from there to Zion in the future. But what spoke for such an idea still more strongly than the sop to principle was that it seemed politically feasible. Whenever pressed for Jewish colonization in Palestine, the Turks suggested other parts of their territories — and, of course, the acceptance by the settlers of Ottoman citizenship.[42]

British willingness to negotiate about a Jewish colony in Sinai —

though the plan was eventually rejected by Egypt — gave Herzl his first substantial diplomatic advance toward tangible results. By the time Britain followed up with the proposal to settle in East Africa — a territory in which none but Britain had any formal authority — Herzl's desperation was heightened by the 1903 Kishineff pogrom.[43] East Africa had no possible association with the sanctity of the Holy Land, nor could even an ardent imagination conceive of a natural expansion from there to Jerusalem. Yet reluctant proponents of the plan still attempted to mitigate the surrender of principle by speaking of Uganda as a *Nachtasyl*, a temporary refuge in which Jews would train themselves for their ultimate purpose of establishing Jewish sovereignty in Palestine.[44] This line of reasoning, initiated by Herzl, may have had its effect on Herzl, too, for he wanted to be convinced. But he did not hide from himself the basic ideological renunciation which the Uganda plan required.[45] After the stormy Sixth Zionist Congress in 1903, where the plan aroused bitter protest, Herzl laid bare his heart to a few friends:

I want to tell you now what my speech before the seventh Congress is to be — if I live till then. By that time I shall have Palestine, or else I shall have recognized the complete futility of all further effort in that direction. In this latter case the summary of my speech will be: It was not possible. The ultimate goal has not been reached and cannot be reached within the calculable future. But we have a compromise achievement — this land in which our suffering masses can be settled on a national foundation with autonomous rights. I do not believe that for the sake of a beautiful dream or a legitimist flag we ought to withhold relief from the unfortunate. But I understand at the same time that this has brought a decisive split into our movement, and this division passes right through my person. Although I was originally a Jewish statist, no matter where, I did later on lift up the flag of Zion, and I myself became a lover of Zion. Palestine is the one land where our people can come to rest. But hundreds of thousands are waiting for immediate help. There is only one way of resolving this contradiction: I must resign the leadership. I will, if you so desire, conduct the next Congress; after that, elect two Action Committees, one for East Africa and one for Palestine. I shall not stand for election in either. But whoever should be elected can always have my counsel for the asking. And my best wishes will always follow those who devote themselves to the fulfillment of that beautiful dream.[46]

The Uganda proposal split the Zionist movement. After Herzl's death, some of those who favored accepting the alternative to Zion formed the Jewish Territorial Organization (ITO), under the leadership of Israel Zangwill (1864–1926). Among the territorialists the renunciation of Zion was not, in many cases, conceived as an ideological sacrifice. Quite the contrary: in separating themselves from

Zionism they formulated an ideological attack on the exclusive bond to Zion, and contended that not historic attachments but present conditions should determine the proper location of the Jewish homeland. The Jewish problem — or more accurately, the problem of the Jews, which primarily demanded a solution — would be rationally solved only by finding a land best suited for Jewish colonization by climate and geography and by its political and social conditions. Yet, even though, in following this line of argument, Territorialism developed a sharp ideological line dividing it from Zionism and rejecting Zion, the organization, at its inception, represented a preference for pragmatic over ideological considerations. Because of this, it enjoyed, from the beginning, the cooperation of Western Jews whose interest in territorial colonization was a sacrifice of their own ideological assumptions. In the evolution of this cooperative relationship, the Territorialist organization continued to show a marked ideological elasticity, and also to accustom its nonnationalist collaborators to a similar elasticity, afterwards extended into the relationship between Zionists and non-Zionists in the Jewish Agency for Palestine.

The willingness to forego ideological rigor was demonstrated at the very first conference of the new organization, held like the first Zionist Congress in Basle, from July 30 to August 1, 1905. A program for the new organization was proposed which read that "the aim of ITO is to acquire a territory on a basis of autonomy for those Jews who cannot or do not wish to remain in their present countries of residence." This was amended to refer to "a basis of *national* autonomy"; and the name officially adopted at the Conference for the new body was the Jewish Territorialist *National* Organization. But no sooner was the conference over than Zangwill, the newly-elected President, dropped the word "national" from both program and title of the Organization. It never appeared again.[47]

The reason for this practice was obvious. Zangwill was extremely anxious to attract to the new organization leading Jewish figures in the political, financial, as well as communal affairs of the Western countries. He consistently resisted, for this reason, all attempts to conduct the ITO on democratic lines and to give it the same character, both popular and partisan, which made the Zionist movement a folk movement. The Eastern Territorialists who pressed for democratic principles of organization were also the ideological rigorists; but on both points it was they who yielded to their leader. And, indeed, Zangwill was able to achieve the purpose for which he demanded these ideological sacrifices. Even more than the pre-Herzlian Hovevei-Zion, he attracted the support of outstanding nonnationalist Jews.

The work of the organization was largely conducted by its London members, and a man like Lucien Wolf (1857–1930), later famous as a determined foe of Zionism, was intimately involved in it. The executive committee of the organization was predominantly made up of notables like the Americans, Oscar S. Straus, Daniel Guggenheim, and Judge Mayer Sulzberger, and the Germans, James Simon and Paul Nathan, founders of the Hilfsverein der deutschen Juden, all cool or hostile to Jewish nationalism.[48]

So well understood was the pragmaticism of the Territorialist Organization, that Jacob H. Schiff (1847–1920) did not hesitate to propose a function for it directly at variance with its ideological goals.[49] He wrote to Zangwill that his own real wish was that Russian Jews might some day be free in Russia, just as Zangwill hoped ultimately to offer them freedom in a new Jewish territory. But in view of the urgency of the existing problem,

> . . . it behooves us to consider ways and means, the carrying out of which shall enable those of our co-religionists in Russia who wish to leave to find the land adapted for their prompt reception. It appears to me that in this existing emergency the Jewish Territorial Organization, if for the time being it will occupy itself with something which is immediately practicable and sidetrack its cherished project of finding a separate land of refuge where the Jew can live under autonomous conditions, can be of very great service to the momentous and pressing cause which we all have so very much at heart.

The "immediately practicable" undertaking that Schiff had in mind was what later became known as the Galveston Project. Its aim, shared by Territorialism, was to forestall the ill effects anticipated from the continued crowding of immigrants into slums, where, among other evils, there was the likelihood of provoking anti-Jewish feeling. But its method was the reverse of the Territorialist method. Instead of establishing the Jews in a solid mass, capable of sustaining itself apart from the Gentiles, they were to be dispersed widely in interior America on the theory that hostility to the Jews as a minority group was directly related to their numbers and concentration. In spite of the ideological inconsistency, Zangwill accepted a role for the ITO in carrying out the Galveston Project. And, after all, if Territorialism was resorted to because Zion seemed unavailable and the need for immediate relief was urgent, then it was reasonable, when no territory seemed available and the need remained urgent, to avoid if not dissolve anti-Semitism by dispersing the immigrants rather than segregating them in a concentrated body.

In the nine years of Zangwill's active leadership of the ITO, he paralleled the whole gamut of disappointments that had marked Herzl's nine years of Zionist activity. In Uganda, Canada, Australia, and Angola (Portuguese West Africa) Zangwill sought in vain for a charter to found an autonomous Jewish colony. Of his Western friends, some dropped out — often enough, in order to give more support to Palestine — and others advised him to keep the organization alive by transforming it into a general agency for aid to Jewish emigrants, converting into an avowed aim what he had accepted, in the case of the Galveston Project, as a temporary expedient. But this was going too far for Zangwill, and in 1914 he was ready to disband the ITO or resign its leadership. The war broke out, making this painful decision unnecessary, for, unable to meet, the organization passed into decline. Only in the East, where Territorialism was maintained as a small but solidly ideological movement, did its partisans keep the flame alive, to revive the movement in a new form in a later period.[50]

IV

In the decade before the first World War, Jewish ideologies and prescriptions for solving the Jewish problem had been considerably elaborated.[51] There were not only Zionism and Territorialism, on the one hand, as opposed to the reliance on Jewish civic emancipation, on the other. In addition, Eastern European Jews had developed the ideas of minority rights and a variety of subsidiary proposals, ranging from a region of concentrated Jewish settlement in Russia itself to state-supported facilities for individuals, however widely dispersed, to maintain their traditional culture and their Yiddish language and literature as an inalienable right. But together with the great cultivation of ideologies, the period was also marked by broad practical cooperation between Jews of widely differing ideologies, and between Jews of the East and the West. Not only the Territorialists but the Zionists in those years took a "practical" rather than doctrinaire turn; and since the Zionists were working in a single country rather than in all possible territories, and with a deeply rooted, historically founded popular consensus, their period of practical work yielded important, even crucial results. In this period of Practical Zionism, the habit of cooperation between Western and Eastern Jews of diverse ideologies, whose growth we noted in relation to Territorialism, was strengthened in regard to Palestine, too. The same observation may be made regarding the ideological opponents in Eastern Europe. For during a time when the ultimate objective of Zionism, the full solution of the Jewish problem through the restoration of Jewish sovereignty, seemed remote, Eastern Zionists devoted themselves to what they called *Gegenwartsarbeit*. This pursuit of "immediate" objectives concerned itself very successfully with the development of modern institutions of Hebrew and Yiddish education and culture in Eastern Europe. In this work their activities, considered as a necessary preparation for the ultimate Zionist aim, ran parallel to those of their ideological opponents, who denied that the final solution of the Jewish problem meant that all or a great part of Russian Jewry must go to Palestine.[52]

The practical cooperation and ideological elasticity of this period, particularly in the relations between Eastern nationalists and Westerners, were based, no doubt, on the patent inability of either ideological party to act successfully on its strict principles alone. The political Zionists turned to "practical" work in Palestine because they saw no way of getting their charter, and Westerners joined them in this activity because the urgent needs of Eastern Jewry would obviously not be solved by a speedy emancipation in Russia — and because, moreover, the demand for exclusion of certain kinds of immigrants was growing continually stronger in the West. The new situation brought on by the First World War changed all this radically. For the Zionists there opened up the possibility of an unprecedented advance to their goal, by the most direct approach, in the negotiations leading to the Balfour Declaration. They saw prospects of success through the outright recognition of their central ideological demand. For the nonnationalists, on the other hand, these prospects sharpened ideological differences all at once, and led to a recrudescence of doctrinaire anti-Zionism in the West.

The line-up of powers in the First World War presented a severe and troublesome difficulty to Western Jews in the Allied countries. The foremost problem that had concerned the leaders and organizations concerned with Jewish rights had been the situation in Russia. The American Jews, who by concerted pressure had induced their government to denounce its commercial treaty with Russia because of discrimination against Jews bearing American passports, and who had openly refused to aid Russia's projected bond issues because of its Jewish policy, set a standard of militancy that all Western Jews would have liked to emulate.[53] But despite the bitter insistence of men like Lucien Wolf, neither the French nor the British Jews could persuade their governments to endanger their relations with Russia in the days of the Triple Entente. And when the war broke out these men were obliged to cooperate in a campaign of patriotic propaganda in which Russia, as one of the Allies, could hardly be effectively criticized and the Allies as a body had to be extolled. This was a task which became exceedingly difficult when reports began to arrive of Russian administrative measures and pogroms against Jews in the border areas, while, on the other hand, other reports told of German measures, exceeding the bounds prescribed for an occupation force under international law, establishing Jewish rights in newly conquered provinces.[54] If it was a patriotic duty to win the support of Jews throughout the world for one's own government, then this was a duty that was made far easier for the Western Jews of Berlin than for the Western Jews of London and Paris.

Next only to the plight of Eastern European Jewry, the emergency which arose for the Palestinian settlement was a matter of concern to Western Jewry. In a country traditionally dependent on outside support, the war, cutting off Palestine from its sources of supply, brought a critical shortage both of food and funds. Added to this were the oppressive measures of the Turkish military governor, Jemal Pasha, who treated the Zionist Jews as potential enemies, imprisoning their leaders and expelling large numbers as foreign nationals.[55] Western Jews, particularly the Jews of Germany and Austria, allied with Turkey, and also the very influential Jewry of neutral America, worked to mitigate the wartime economic stringencies and counteract the effects of Turkish anti-Zionist measures in Palestine,[56] just as French and British Jews, together with American Jewry, worked to reverse the anti-Jewish policy of Russia. But in the case of Palestine these efforts enjoyed a considerable measure of success, while this could hardly be said regarding Russia. In fact, Jewish protests in London against Russian actions regularly met with denials or evasions by British representatives and British correspondents in Moscow who, as it turned out, were in close and cooperative contact with Russian official anti-Semites.[57] This did not make it easier to conduct Allied propaganda among Jews in neutral countries. As for the situation in Palestine, the fact that some effective assistance to the community was facilitated by Turkey made for good will; while, on the other hand, the awareness of the catastrophic results that could be precipitated by increased Turkish hostility was a constant check on tendencies to pro-Allied or pro-Zionist expressions in the neutral countries.

Not only did the British Jews find it difficult to propagandize their country's cause abroad, but they found themselves faced with an unpleasant domestic problem owing to the Jewish situation in the war. The Jews in London's Whitechapel included a considerable number of alien immigrants from Russia who were not called up for British military service. But, as nationals of Russia, an Allied country, these men were subject to official pressures to serve in their own native land's war efforts. The resistance of Whitechapel to such military service, hardened by constant reports of Russian anti-Semitic excesses, led to anti-Semitic symptoms in England itself and also to suggestions, defended by Herbert Samuel, that the government might resort to deportation.

All the Liberal instincts of Britain revolted both at this suggestion and at the situation which had evoked it. Placed in a false moral position by association with Russia and its persecution of the Jews from the beginning of the war, the British now found themselves directly involved in the secondary effects of that persecution. The pressure of Russian immigration had made Britain before the war adopt a policy of immigrant exclusion that vaguely offended the liberal and humanitarian consensus of the mother country of tolerance and free trade; now it had made Britain play the atavistic role of hectoring and pressing unwilling refugees into the service of their persecutors. It was felt that the recalcitrants of Whitechapel must be offered some more acceptable alternative than enforced service for a country which had virtually driven them out and still continued a vicious persecution of Jews. Let Britain offer naturalization to those who joined its own forces, and let it organize a Jewish Legion to march under a Zionist banner — these suggestions seemed far more worthy of Britain. Herbert Samuel, for one, was "very much impressed" by them, for Samuel from the very beginning of the war had favored a British Zionist policy for postwar Palestine and a compact between Britain and Jews throughout the world based on such a policy.[58]

The question of Allied relations with the Jews was, thus, a source of moral perplexity from the beginning of the war. But in 1916 the moral unease sharpened to a more practical and urgent discomfort. The need to bring America into the war on the side of the Allies became clearer from day to day. No influence that could hinder or advance that achievement was too small to be ignored, and the influence of American Jews was rated by the Western Allies as far from small. To seek to assuage Jewish hostility in America by reversing Russian anti-Jewish policies, as Lucien Wolf demanded, was impossible so long as the Czar ruled. After the Kerensky revolution, when it appeared that Jews would gain their rights in Russia, there still seemed to be need to make sure of Jewish sympathy. But there

seemed to be another way — and according to authoritative and un-
biased opinion, a more effective way — which the Russian Jews themselves publicly approved as soon as Kerensky made them free to
speak: the way of Zionism.[59]

The first to suggest this expedient as a suitable method to win
the sympathy of Jews had been the non-Zionist circles with whom
the Allied governments were in contact. In November 1915 a group
of French Jews had set up a *Comité français d'information et d'action
auprès des juifs des pays neutres*, and the government sent the
historian, Guillaume Victor Basch, on a propaganda mission to the
Jews of America. Not succeeding very well with the argument that
the Allied cause was an expression of essential Jewish ideals, Basch
made vague hints about Allied intentions to do something for the
Jews in Palestine after the war. On returning to Paris he tried, unsuccessfully, to persuade the *Comité* to set up an international committee to consider Jewish postwar rights and demands, a project being
actively agitated in America.[60] While the French Jews were not ready
to draw any conclusions from the Basch mission, French and British
government circles took note of the mission's failure. The latter, in
December 1915, had requested Lucien Wolf, a "distinguished Jewish
public figure who was familiar with Jewish attitudes in the neutral
countries and particularly in America," to draw up a plan for Allied
propaganda among Jews.[61] Declaring that he was no Zionist and regretted the development of the Jewish national movement, Wolf stated
that the Zionist movement could not be ignored. He suggested that,
without promising outright to set up a Jewish state, it might be possible
to turn the American Jews into "enthusiastic adherents of the Allies"
by appropriate proposals regarding the future of Palestine. The proposals suggested were essentially those being made to the British by
non-Zionist spokesmen, which Wolf formulated in specific terms in a
communication of March 3, 1916.

But if the way to win Jewish sympathy was to appease the Zionists, then it obviously made more sense to negotiate directly with
the Zionists themselves. This proposal was made to the British independently in October 1916 by James Malcolm. Through his activity
on behalf of Armenian nationalism and particularly of the Armenian
volunteers for armed service with Britain, Malcolm had met Zionists
engaged in parallel activities. Finding his friend, Sir Mark Sykes, in
a mood of depression one day over the Allied fortunes in neutral
America, as instanced by the Basch report, Malcolm immediately
suggested negotiating directly with the Zionists. He thus reawakened
Sykes' earlier interest in Zionism and helped establish new contacts

with the Zionist leadership out of which the Balfour Declaration then arose.[62]

Consideration of the future of Palestine and the possibility of a Jewish national restoration there after the war, both by the British government and the Western Jews, began long before the need to draw in neutral America became acute. At the end of October 1914, Turkey entered the war and, less than two weeks later, on November 9, the British Prime Minister, Mr. Herbert Asquith, said in the House of Commons that, "it is the Ottoman Government and not we who have rung the death-knell of Ottoman dominion, not only in Europe but in Asia." On the same day a member of the Cabinet, Herbert Samuel, spoke to the Foreign Secretary, Sir Edward Grey, about the future of Palestine and the possibility that "the opportunity might arise for the fulfillment of the ancient aspiration of the Jewish people and the restoration there of a Jewish State." [63] So, too, at the very beginning of the war both Zionists and non-Zionists were immediately aware that a new status for Palestine might emerge, and both began to think and take action looking toward the future. Tentative negotiations began at once along lines that were sometimes parallel, sometimes conflicting, and sometimes converging.

The first to take definite action was Herbert Samuel himself. His action was independent and without the knowledge of leading Zionists, whom he had apparently approached only for material describing the movement.[64] By January 1915 Samuel had sent to a few Cabinet members a memorandum outlining his proposals, and in March his revised memorandum was circulated and discussed. Even though the Foreign Secretary and other Cabinet members were quite friendly, several of them having become sympathetic to the Zionist idea years before during Herzl's and Zangwill's East African negotiations, sharp opposition by the Prime Minister closed out the issue for the time being. In the meantime, Herbert Samuel had come into closer contact with the Zionists; and his subsequent activities form part of the Zionist negotiations leading to the Balfour Declaration.

It is interesting to note how swiftly Herbert Samuel, coming to the question with a fresh mind, passed from a relatively simple to a rather more complex definition of his Zionist objective. He began with the idea of a Jewish state protected by an international guarantee of its neutrality, but almost at once realized that so long as the Arabs were a majority in Palestine the idea was impracticable. Examining other alternatives, such as French annexation, the *status quo*, and internationalization, he very quickly concluded that annexation of the territory to Britain with support of Jewish immigration, leading to Home Rule, was the best.[65]

The Zionists, for their part, had to take other circumstances into account which also favored a cautious formulation of their aims. When the war broke out, the headquarters of the World Zionist Organization were in Germany; and even though it was proposed almost at once to move to a neutral country in order to make possible continued work as an international body, the new headquarters in Copenhagen remained in closer contact with Germany than with Allied countries. Moreover, Palestine itself until near the end of the war was controlled by Turkey, and it was by no means certain at that time that this would not remain true when the war ended. The Zionists in Berlin and Constantinople, at any rate, could work on no other assumption. Zionists in Allied countries, who were free to assume the collapse of the Ottoman Empire after the war, could not conduct negotiations on this basis unless they were willing to disrupt the international Zionist organization. The broad, international character of Zionist diplomacy did, indeed, break down during the war. After 1916, at least, Weizmann and his friends in the Allied countries, together with the American Zionists, worked with little reference to the Zionist offices in Copenhagen and in Central Europe.[66]

However, even if they were willing to sacrifice the functional unity of the World Zionist Organization, there were other considerations which could influence Zionists in the West to temper their demands. To make a flat proposal that the Allies set up a Jewish State in Palestine after the war would not only fly in the face of the existing Arab preponderance; it would risk provoking Turkish reprisals against the Jewish community in Palestine. Moreover, the traditional Zionist formula, worked out in a form suitable for negotiation with the Turks, demanded only a national home secured under public law — which, for all practical purposes, meant the immediate right to colonize under a charter granted by a suzerain power leaving the independent Jewish state to be claimed when Palestine had a Jewish majority. This position originally adopted out of respect for Turkey's existing authority, was also one that took account of the small Jewish population that then lived in Palestine, and on these grounds was certain to recommend itself to a leader who, like Weizmann, regularly consulted the cautious, skeptical Ahad Ha'am.[67]

Another "moderating" influence was the necessity of negotiating for united action with the leaders of the French and British Jewish communities, who, in the main, were opponents of Zionism. In Novem-

ber 1914 and in February and April 1915, leaders of the World
Zionist Organization and of the British Zionists negotiated with the
Conjoint Foreign Committee of the Jewish Board of Deputies and
the Anglo-Jewish Association. The Zionists ended by asking whether
the Conjoint Committee would cooperate on the basis of the Basle
program, or, if not, to what extent it would support Zionist demands.
On April 27, the Committee replied that it could not accept the Zionist
formula, and then defined its own program for Palestine, which it
intended to pursue independently if the Zionists would not accept
its terms.[68] Even though negotiations continued for over two years,[69]
the Conjoint Committee did press separate proposals upon the British
government, not neglecting to stress that they and not the Zionists
were the authoritative representatives of British Jewry. The Zionists,
meanwhile, conducted a public campaign and made private contacts
on behalf of their own program. So, too, in France vague negotiations
between the Zionists and the French Jewish leaders, on one hand,
and between the latter and British Jewish leaders on the other,
continued inconclusively, while public evidence of the Jews' divided
views on the future of Palestine was not wanting.[70] In America, the
question of a united Jewish stand, not only on the future of Palestine
but on all Jewish postwar problems, was raised even more sharply.
A public ideological debate was provoked by negotiations which
began in 1915 concerning a Jewish Congress to formulate proposals
for the anticipated Peace Conference. This project not only was
opposed by the antinationalist leaders of the American Jewish Committee but was discouraged at the time by representatives of the
World Zionist Organization who feared the effects on their relations
with Ottoman authorities and on the welfare of the Jewish community
in Palestine. In the later years of the war, the movement for a Jewish
Congress gathered force once more, and the independent activities
of various American Jewish factions were forced into a common
channel.[71]

In all these negotiations, it is reasonable to suppose that the
collision of opposed viewpoints tended to sharpen differences, while
the never renounced intention of arriving at an agreement tended to
moderate differences. It would be interesting, but impossible, and
somewhat pointless in this context, to undertake a close textual study
of all available statements of Zionists and their Jewish opponents in
the light of such suppositions. In the process of framing the Balfour
Declaration, the debate within the Jewish community, outside Britain
at least, was considered by the British Cabinet only in a very broad,
general way as indicating the relative power, the pervasiveness and

intensity, of Zionist and anti-Zionist views. However the debate within English Jewry had a more specific influence. Once the Cabinet had set itself to formulate a policy on Palestine that could satisfy the Jews, it had to consider drafts independently presented not only by supporters but by opponents of Zionism in England. The traces of both views have been left on the Declaration.

The first formal draft for a British statement on Jewish interests in Palestine was proposed to the government by an opponent of Zionism, Lucien Wolf, on behalf of the Conjoint Foreign Committee. In it Wolf presented a formula which he had worked out in the course of negotiations with the Zionists during 1914–1915 as a basis of agreement which, in his opinion, took sufficient account of Zionist ideas.

Relying on the fact that the Tenth and Eleventh Zionist Congresses in 1911 and 1913 had been dominated by the Practical Zionists, Wolf contended that the Zionists did not really need to hold to the Basle program, for they themselves had adopted a different policy in the most recent Congresses.[72] This was a pointless argument to use, for the Zionists who negotiated with Wolf in 1914–1915 had been directly responsible for the overturn of 1911–1913 and knew best how to interpret it. The prevailing mood of the First Congress, in adopting the Basle program in 1897, had been opposed to colonizing Palestine so long as no charter had been granted for the purpose and the country had not been recognized by public law as a home for the Jewish people. In 1911, when there was no prospect of such a charter or such recognition, Weizmann and his friends were prepared to colonize on the basis of existing laws; but their Practical Zionism, aiming to build a larger and stronger Jewish community in Palestine, always hoped for an opportunity to alter its political status. The Zionists who in 1914–1916 were working in Germany or in Turkey still anticipated no change in this situation. But precisely because Weizmann wished to stake the Zionist future on an Allied victory, the time had come, from the point of view of Practical Zionism itself, to seek a new political status in line with the Basle program.

Much the same observation may be made about Lucien Wolf's attempt to present "cultural Zionism" as a more moderate aim which would satisfy the Eastern European Jews instead of a defined national status in Palestine. No one was cooler to Weizmann's negotiations with the "assimilationists" in London than Ahad Ha'am, the father of "cultural Zionism." For, his opposition to Herzl, too, had been one that was based on a difference concerning the sequence and importance rather than the substance of Zionist aims. Holding a political victory unlikely in the existing circumstances, he had considered it far more important to revive a vigorous national consensus against the time when there would be more propitious political conditions. But with all his native caution, Ahad Ha'am, too, knew that those days of 1916 were a critical political opportunity, and he urged the most precise and far-reaching political guarantees that could realistically be asked for.[73]

It was, of course, his own ideological views which Lucien Wolf had in mind in defining, as he did, a "Zionist" position with which his group could come to terms. This position he proposed to the Foreign Office on behalf of the Conjoint Foreign Committee on March 3, 1916:

In the event of Palestine coming within the spheres of influence of Great Britain or France at the close of the war, the Governments of those Powers will not fail to take account of the historic interest that country possesses for the Jewish community. The Jewish population will be secured in the enjoyment of civil and religious liberty, equal political rights with the rest of the population, reasonable facilities for immigration and colonisation, and such municipal privileges in the towns and colonies inhabited by them as may be shown to be necessary.[74]

Wolf's draft was discussed by Sir Edward Grey with the French and transmitted to St. Petersburg for a Russian opinion. Noting the probable inadequacy of the formula for its purpose of gaining Jewish sympathy for the Allies through an appeal to their Zionist sentiments, Sir Edward commented:

The only object of His Majesty's Government is to secure some agreement which will be sufficiently attractive to the majority of Jews to facilitate the conclusion of an understanding that would be assured of Jewish support. Having this consideration in view, it appears to His Majesty's Government that if the scheme provided for enabling the Jews, when their colonists have grown strong enough to rival the Arab population, to take in hand the administration of the internal affairs of this region (excluding Jerusalem and the Holy Places), then the agreement would be much more attractive for the majority of Jews.[75]

The French, in reply, were apparently cool to the whole idea, feeling that the proposed formula did not go far enough to achieve its purpose.[76] The Russians simply indicated that as far as Palestine was concerned, they were prepared to agree to any plan that would safeguard the rights of the Orthodox Church, and would make no objection in principle against Jewish colonization in that land.[77] At that very time, Sir Mark Sykes was in St. Petersburg with Georges Picot negotiating the postwar partition of the Ottoman provinces, and he discussed with Sazonov, the Russian Foreign Minister, "the possibility that Zionism might solve the Jewish problem of Russia." [78] In London, it appears, British officials suggested that a definite Zionist proposal be submitted, but the Zionist leaders feared the time was not yet ripe.[79] Months later, in October, James Malcolm's visit set off a series of events which established the contact between Sykes and Weizmann and Nahum Sokolow and eventually led to the Balfour Declaration. The idea that an Allied pro-Zionist postwar scheme might win Jewish sympathy had led to serious negotiation [80] with the Zionists themselves.

Formal definitions of the Zionist objectives, after the Samuel memorandum of early 1915, began to reach the British Cabinet in October 1916.[81] However, it was apparent then that the Asquith Cabinet would finally break up, as it did early in December. The new Lloyd George Cabinet was installed in the same month, and negotiations were soon resumed with the Zionists. Their heightened seriousness under the new regime was indicated when, at a meeting on February 7, 1917, Sir Mark Sykes induced the Zionists — who in their surprise hardly welcomed this extraordinary assignment — to undertake the diplomatic task of gaining Allied, particularly French, as well as Papal approval for a British pro-Zionist declaration.[82] When America entered the war in April, Balfour himself, on his visit to the United States, took decisive soundings on the American attitude.[83] Before the Foreign Secretary's return in June, the Zionists had already been informed that the British Government was ready to give concrete support to Zionist plans, as Dr. Weizmann duly announced at a special conference of the English Zionist Federation.[84] On the other hand, the alerted opponents of Zionism among British Jews had finally opened their public offensive against a pro-Zionist declaration, and when the Zionist formulas began to be considered by the Cabinet in July, they were presented against a background of anti-Zionist arguments and counter-proposals.[85] To these a recently returned Jewish member of the government, Herbert Samuel's cousin, Edwin Samuel Montagu (1879–1924), added his powerful voice.[86] As noted by Ahad Ha'am, the Cabinet drafted its own statement without much reference to the Zionist drafts.[87] Even less attention was ultimately paid to the proposals of the anti-Zionists. Yet no one can study the evolution of the final form of the Balfour Declaration without noting, in the separate line the British took for themselves, an intention to consider the sensibilities of both Zionists and anti-Zionists.

The principles which the Zionists wished to have expressed in the declaration were variously formulated in numerous different drafts, but may be summarized under several heads: (1) the recognition of Palestine as destined to be a Jewish state; (2) the recognition of a Jewish chartered company with powers to resettle Jews in Palestine in order to provide the necessary conditions for realizing Jewish national sovereignty; and (3) the recognition of linguistic as well as civil and religious rights of minorities in Palestine which should protect the national status of Jews and non-Jews in Palestine, whoever might be in the majority at a given time.[88]

As to the first point, there was hardly any attempt to obtain a statement explicitly containing the phrase "Jewish state." At an earlier stage of the negotiations, thinking it necessary to overcome British hesitation because of a possible clash with French interests, Weizmann had suggested what amounted to an immediate and direct assumption of power in Palestine by the Zionists.

If Great Britain does not wish anybody else to have Palestine, this means it will have to watch it and stop any penetration of another Power. Such a course involves as much responsibility as would be involved by a British Protectorate over Palestine, with the sole difference that watching is a much less efficient preventive than an actual Protectorate. I therefore thought that the middle course could be adopted: viz. The Jews take over the country; the whole burden of organisation falls on them, but for the next ten or fifteen years they work under a temporary British Protectorate.[89]

But by the time that specific drafts for a declaration were being drawn up, only Herbert Sidebotham proposed a version referring to the Jewish state as well as to a National Home for the Jewish people. He was then forced to explain in his draft that a Jewish state does not mean one with an exclusively Jewish population nor one which discriminates in favor of the Jewish and against other religions.[90] The final draft the Zionists intended to present to the Cabinet avoids these ideological entanglements, and also observes Ahad Ha'am's injunction to ask only for what could realistically be promised in the circumstances that would prevail immediately after the war.[91] They proposed that Britain accept "the principle of recognizing Palestine as the National Home of the Jewish people." The term "national home," derived from the Basle program's "Heimstaette," was, of course, more obscure as well as more realistic than the phrase "Jewish state"; and once it was introduced into ideological debate, British leaders were not slow to note its ambiguity. Lord Curzon's questions on this point caused Balfour to give an interpretation which Lloyd George records as follows:

As to the meaning of the words "national home," to which the Zionists attach so much importance, he understood it to mean some form of British,

American, or other protectorate, under which full facilities would be given to the Jews to work out their own salvation and to build up, by means of education, agriculture, and industry, a real centre of national culture and focus of national life. It did not necessarily involve the early establishment of an independent Jewish State, which was a matter of gradual development in accordance with the ordinary laws of political evolution.[92]

Since Weizmann anticipated a period of gradual development toward a Jewish majority, which would be an achievement that only Jewish efforts and not the British government could possibly guarantee, and since the British were equally clear about this division of responsibilities, he could realistically expect no more than a declaration granting Jews a chance to work toward a Jewish state. This was the commonly understood significance of the term "national home" among those who had a hand in the framing of the Balfour Declaration.[93]

The second point, the recognition of a Jewish chartered company, indicated the practical means which, with the support of a declared policy of "full and free" Jewish immigration and intensive settlement of public lands, would be employed to carry out the transition from the "national home" to the "Jewish commonwealth." The various drafts advanced by Zionists all included provisions on this point, and in several of them it was specified that the agency proposed would represent the worldwide Jewish people in its activities. As for the third point, in the most extensive draft the recognition of existing communities in Palestine and their rights of cultural and administrative autonomy was claimed for all nationalities, in others specifically on behalf of the Jews, and in the briefest dropped altogether. Finally, some of the drafts took pains to mention the need for an "integral Palestine" or for uniting "the whole area of historic Palestine under one administration." [94]

Sokolow had stressed that the proposed declaration, a unilateral British policy statement, was "not an agreement, neither is it a full programme." The draft must therefore be brief and general and eschew detail.[95] Seeking to abide by these instructions, the Zionist drafters on July 12 drew up a statement containing their three essential points: first, "the principle of recognising Palestine as the National Home of the Jewish people"; second, "the grant of internal autonomy to the Jewish nationality in Palestine"; and third, "freedom of immigration for Jews, and the establishment of a Jewish National Colonising Corporation for the re-settlement and economic development of the country." However, the British rejected this draft as too long and detailed, and sent Sokolow back with precise guidelines for a formula containing two points: "(1) the recognition of Palestine as the national home of the Jewish people, (2) the recognition of the Zionist Organisation." Thus, under date of July 18, 1919, Lord Rothschild requested a British declaration in the following form, strictly following the requirements set down by British officials: [96]

(1) H.M. Government accepts the principle that Palestine should be reconstituted as the national home of the Jewish people.
(2) H.M. Government will use its best endeavours to secure the achievement of this object and will discuss the necessary methods with the Zionist Organization.[97]

The spirit in which this draft was framed is quite clear, if one compares it with Zionist proposals. It consistently restricts the extent and the precision of the commitments made by the British government. Its spirit is one of a caution dictated by long experience in colonial administration. Even the briefest draft considered by the Zionists, on July 17, 1917, had added a specific reference to a chartered company as among the "methods and means" the British government would discuss with the Zionists.

But the revisions were not yet ended. The July 18 draft, though submitted for approval to President Wilson, had to yield to the criticism of Montagu, leading to the final version, forwarded on October 10 to President Wilson and promulgated, after some last-minute revision, on November 2, 1917. Described in the letter of transmittal as a "declaration of sympathy with Jewish Zionist aspirations," the document read:

His Majesty's Government view with favour the establishment in Palestine of a national home for the Jewish people, and will use their best endeavours to facilitate the achievement of this object, it being clearly understood that nothing shall be done which may prejudice the civil and religious rights of existing non-Jewish communities in Palestine, or the rights and political status enjoyed by Jews in any other country.[98]

The differences from earlier drafts are of two kinds. There are, first, changes in phrasing which tend even further to restrict the extent and mitigate the degree of Britain's commitment. Instead of "Palestine . . . reconstituted as the national home," there is reference to "the establishment in Palestine of a national home." Instead of using its best endeavors "to secure," the government would use its best endeavors "to facilitate" the achievement of the object. Also, all reference to the Zionist Organization is eliminated from the body of the declaration and relegated to the introductory sentence. Secondly, there were added two specific clauses, explaining that the "national home" policy would have no ill effects for two parties in interest, the non-Jewish communities in Palestine and the Jewish communities outside Palestine. Their obvious purpose was political, to give guarantees to groups who might think themselves adversely affected in order, if possible, to forestall or moderate their opposition.

There was a consistent direction of change in the differences between the first and final drafts, the first draft and Zionist proposals, and, for that matter, between the Zionist aims (the promise of a future Jewish state, of the legal means to achieve it, and of national rights for the existing community) and their own July 12 formula. The revision of the Declaration had been a long process and many hands had worked at it. But Chaim Weizmann and others have said that Jewish anti-Zionist pressure and it alone caused changes of serious consequence to be introduced in the Declaration.[99] Also, some of the alterations were, indeed, later interpreted in an anti-Zionist sense. It is pertinent, therefore, to consider just what effect upon the Balfour Declaration may be attributed to such pressures.

It is hard to assume that anyone hoped to satisfy the Jewish anti-Zionists by substituting "national home" for "Jewish state" in the Balfour Declaration. Their opposition not only to "national home" but to the even vaguer Basle formula of a "home secured by public law" was known to be almost as intense as to "Jewish state." So, too, the anti-Zionists were firmly opposed to any recognition of a Jewish chartered company with a "privileged" status, correctly seeing in this the medium which was intended to turn the "national home" into a "Jewish state" in the fulness of time. On the other hand, the formula proposed by Wolf gave an approximate equivalent of the Zionist demand for communal autonomy, as well as some title for claiming further immigration and settlement in Palestine — but in terms that strictly avoided any concession to the idea of a special national relation to Palestine.

There is no doubt that this ideological rigor was a reaction to the clearer ideological position taken by the Zionists in response to the political challenge of the times. It expresses itself in the abstract and anachronistic — sometimes dated, sometimes premature — nature of the arguments the anti-Zionists used. They argued not against the immediate effects of the formulas the Zionists proposed, but against their broader implications. Most extreme was the reaction of Edwin Montagu. It is said that he demanded, "How would he negotiate with the peoples of India if the world had just been told that H.M. Government regarded his national home as being in Turkish territory?" [100] The same point was put less picturesquely by Claude

Montefiore and David Alexander in their letter to *The Times* of
May 24, 1917: [101] The claim that the Jewish settlements in Palestine
possessed "a national character in a political sense," they argued, was
not a claim of purely local import, against which the Conjoint Committee would have had no objection. It was

> . . . part and parcel of a wider Zionist theory, which regards all the
> Jewish communities of the world as constituting one homeless nationality,
> incapable of complete social and political identification with the nations
> among which they dwell, and that for this homeless nationality a political
> centre and an always available homeland in Palestine are available . . .
> It follows that the establishment of a Jewish nationality in Palestine founded
> on this theory of Jewish homelessness, must have the effect throughout the
> world of stamping the Jews as strangers in their native lands, and of under-
> mining their hard-won position as citizens and nationals of those lands.

In a further extension of this argument, Montefiore and Alexander
make the significant but not immediately pertinent point that since
the Jewish religion was "the only certain test of a Jew," a Jewish
state would face the logical dilemma of founding itself on and
limiting itself by a religious criterion of citizenship (which obviously
no Jew would wish) or of failing to be Jewish in any spiritual sense
(an equally unacceptable alternative to all Jews).

With these arguments, the anti-Zionists hoped to eliminate any
promises of a "national home." They were equally concerned to
eliminate grants of the kind of colonizing powers the Zionists desired
for their chartered company. This, too, was opposed primarily because of its broader implications. The Jews should be the last to
seek a special position in any country because "in all countries where
they live the principle of equal rights for all religious denominations
is vital for them." To give the Zionists their chartered company would
be a severe setback to the fight for Jewish equality in countries where
equality was still to be attained, and make it hard to defend Jewish
equality where it already existed. Moreover, it would cause bitter
hostility among non-Jews in Palestine and throughout the Orient.

But all this did not mean that the hope of a Jewish majority,
perhaps even of a Jewish state, need be ruled out! Such a hope was
legitimate if the Zionists could pursue it without the ideologically
obnoxious legal recognition of a "national home" and a "Charter
Company." For "if the Jews prevail in a competition based on perfect
equality of rights and opportunity they will establish their eventual
preponderance in the land on a far sounder foundation than any that
could be secured by privileges and monopolies."

Whatever the effect of these arguments on the formulation of the

Balfour Declaration, it is clear from the outcome that it was neither an effect of intellectual persuasion nor of political impact. Neither of the principal objects of the anti-Zionist plea were won. The "national home" remained in the Declaration, and the "chartered company" though not mentioned there, for reasons not related to the anti-Zionist argument, was later provided for in a special article in the Mandate for Palestine. The secondary changes in the Declaration that were obviously meant to appease the anti-Zionists are placebos rather than concessions, matters of form, not of substance. One of the reasons why the anti-Zionists failed to achieve more substantial results was clearly that it was so obvious that not they but the Zionists represented the Jewish consensus.

On this point the British government had long before satisfied itself by the traditional methods and sources of diplomatic intelligence.[102] Not long after the Alexander-Montefiore letter appeared, confirmation of the accepted opinion was given by a close vote of the Board of Deputies of British Jews repudiating the anti-Zionist leaders.[103] Even the tone and character of the anti-Zionist argument itself all too plainly indicated how well the anti-Zionists were aware that the Jewish consensus opposed them. It was the Zionists who had all along fought for their cause openly, while the opponents, after working behind the scenes for so long, spoke publicly only after the issue had been virtually decided. Furthermore, the argument they made was morally enfeebled when they placed themselves in the position of fighting against obvious benefits for the anticipated refugee mass from Eastern Europe because of imagined dangers to their own secure position. This fatal weakness was evident to their Zionist opponents, to the anti-Zionists themselves, and above all to the non-Jewish community. French anti-Zionists who planned to oppose Sokolow's mission in Paris in April 1917 were convinced by Baron Edmond de Rothschild to reverse their position when he told them they should be ashamed to place their own interests above those of the Jewish millions in Russia.[104] Moreover, the validity of their professed fears was occasionally doubted by the anti-Zionists themselves. In a long letter arguing against Zionism, to be held confidential because (in 1918) the Zionist tide was too powerful to oppose openly, a leading French Jew, Jacques Bigart, remarked:

In fighting Zionism it has been contended that it gives substance to the views of anti-Semites, so that it is inherently suspect. This is an argument for journalistic polemics which I think should not be retained. The Jews in Western countries will not see their rights as citizens placed in question again simply because there may be in a corner of Asia some petty Jewish autonomous regime or a minor Jewish government under English or . . . suzerainty. We may forget this objection, even though it has a powerful effect on the minds of English and French Jews.[105]

What was apparent to Bigart in 1918 (and, indeed, to Alexander and Montefiore in their May 24, 1917, letter which, after all, did not oppose Jewish autonomy or even a Jewish state in Palestine, but only the special legal status that was demanded in order to achieve the latter) was equally apparent to others. In reply to the Alexander-Montefiore letter, James de Rothschild wrote to *The Times* that "We Zionists cannot see how the establishment of an autonomous Jewish State under the aegis and protection of one of the Allied Powers can be considered for a moment to be in any way subversive to the position or loyalty of the very large part of the Jewish people who have identified themselves thoroughly with the citizenship of the countries in which they live." [106] *The Times* itself, in a leading article on May 29, spoke up on behalf of the Gentiles: "Only an imaginative nervousness suggests that the realization of territorial Zionism, in some form, would cause Christendom to round on the Jews and say, 'Now you have a land of your own, go to it!' " [107] The anti-Zionist argument, in fact, not only expressed an anachronistic view of the immediate Jewish situation but it implied an appraisal of the anti-Semitic tendencies in Britain which reflected little credit on Gentile contemporaries. A hundred years before, in the fight against Emancipation, Gentile foes of Jewish rights had indeed thought of a Jewish national home as a pretext for refusing Jews citizenship. In 1917 only outright anti-Semites, eager to destroy a status that was generally recognized by all others, would be likely to seize upon such a pretext to justify an aim which they cherished in any case. When the Balfour Declaration retained the words "national home," and then explained this would in no way affect the emancipated status of Western Jews, it represented no substantive concession at all to Edwin Montagu, but only a somewhat gratuitous assurance that H.M. Government was not anti-Semitic.

If one could suppose that Jewish anti-Zionist arguments were the source of the other clause, explaining that non-Jewish civil and religious rights in Palestine were not affected by the national home, or of the change from "reconstituting Palestine as a national home" to "establishing a national home in Palestine," then similar observations might be made. To be sure, the case for attributing these changes to Montagu's objections is hardly as clearcut as for the clause regarding the rights of Jews outside Palestine. There were other reasons, quite obviously, for the assurance to the Arabs that their civil and religious rights would not be prejudiced. The need to forestall objections from this quarter was certainly appreciated by the Declaration's severest Gentile critic in the Cabinet, the seasoned colonial expert, Lord Curzon; while he quite explicitly said he was "not concerned to discuss the question in dispute between Zionist and anti-Zionist Jews." [108] Friends of the Declaration like Sykes and Milner were no less likely, in view of their own expert background, to see that some assurance to the Arabs was desirable. Sykes, in fact, had already said in February 1917 that he had had to restrain Arabs from an anti-Zionist campaign.[109] In view of later contentions that Arabs had no prior knowledge at all of the Declaration,[110] one may certainly suppose that their opinions on phrasing were not solicited. But men like Sykes, Milner, and Curzon were quite capable of imagining and very apt to take account of the kind of objection the Arabs might be expected to have. It may be, however, that, if not for Montagu's protests, one or another of the succession of drafts would have been accepted without the provisos safeguarding non-Zionist and Arab interests. Once a stipulation was made that the "rights and political status enjoyed by Jews in any other country" would not be prejudiced by the Declaration, it was obviously necessary to add a similar clause in favor of the Arabs. Neither the fact nor the phrasing — "civil and religious rights of existing non-Jewish communities" — of this clause needs any other explanation than the sensitivity to possible Arab reactions of men like Curzon, Milner, and Sykes. As for the change from "Palestine as a home" to "a home in Palestine," this is quite satisfactorily explained by the general tendency of the British drafters to restrict the scope of the government's commitment. If a more specific literary influence is desired, then the best place to seek it is in no other source than the Basle program, which speaks of securing "for the Jewish people a home in Palestine secured by public law."

One could nevertheless argue that both changes were of a kind that could meet, at least superficially, certain objections of the anti-Zionists. They had protested that recognizing the "national home" and incorporating a Jewish chartered company gave Jews undue privileges and discriminated against non-Jews. In rebuttal, Zionists always pointed out that the English character of England and the French character of France, etc., did not constitute unwarranted discrimination against men of other races who were British or French citizens. A similar disclaimer might be implied in attaching to the promise of a Jewish national home a clause regarding the civil and religious rights of non-Jews.[111] So, too, in place of a national status in Palestine at large, Lucien Wolf's memorandum had asked that municipal and local autonomy be granted in those parts of Palestine where actual resettlement warranted. By a very forced interpretation, one might interpret the phrase "a national home in Palestine" as hinting that Jewish self-rule in the beginning would be limited in actuality to the areas where they were settled, just as the anti-Zionists wished. But if such was indeed the intent of the two changes, then they could placate the anti-Zionists only in form, not in substance. For by including the reference to a "national home" (as well as by the form of transmittal of the Declaration to the Zionist Organization as a statement of sympathy with its aspirations) the status of the Jews in Palestine was placed in a distinct category from the local civil and religious rights which were guaranteed the non-Jews; and the autonomy anticipated for Jews, if in the course of time they took full advantage of the chance given them, did not fall short of the sovereignty of a state.

In sum, every change in the text of the Balfour Declaration which could conceivably be attributed to the influence of anti-Zionist Jews gave them no more than psychological satisfaction. The logical implication is in each case a denial of the ideological position of the anti-Zionists. The "national home" policy, says the final form of the Balfour Declaration if considered in relation to anti-Zionist contentions, *does not* endanger by its very nature the position of Jews abroad, *does not* give Jews an unduly privileged position discriminating against the legitimate rights of non-Jews, and *does not*, until such time as they become a countrywide majority, entitle the Jews to rule over non-Jewish localities.

On the other hand, the last two provisions were later interpreted by other opponents of Jewish claims, both Britons and Arabs, as implying restrictions on the national home policy. But there were, of course, other legal grounds and certainly other political factors by which these restrictions would in any case have been motivated.

6 THE JEWISH AGENCY AND THE JEWISH STATE

THE Balfour Declaration, when embodied in the instruments establishing the British Mandate in Palestine, converted some of the ideological premises of Zionism into internationally recognized legal provisions. We have seen that the Zionist conceptions, when restated by the British in the Balfour Declaration, were moderated, at least in form, in order to meet the objections of Jewish anti-Zionists in Western countries. In essentials, however, the Zionist positions were maintained and the anti-Zionist doctrines rejected in the Declaration and, thus, also in the Mandate.

Yet only a contingent right to a Jewish state was recognized in those documents; and the immediate activities which they authorized could also have consequences other than Jewish rule over Palestine. For example, without ever building up a Jewish majority in Palestine, Jews working under Mandate provisions could provide a refuge for European emigrants unable to gain admittance to America. This object, which the Zionists might regard as part of a larger nationalist campaign to solve the Jewish problem, could be considered by non-Zionists simply as a duty of benevolence towards one's coreligionists. Hence, Zionists and their ideological opponents in the West found themselves able to cooperate, setting aside their disagreements on ultimate principles on the assumption that such matters would not become critical in the near future.

The disagreements were only submerged, however, not eradicated; and within the Zionist movement, the neo-Herzlians, who wished to fight for a conclusive and not merely contingent recognition of the Jewish claim to sovereignty in Palestine, opposed forms of cooperation with non-Zionists which involved the indefinite postponement of this issue.

Ideological debate between some Zionists and non-Zionists arose not only in regard to the Palestinian resettlement but also in connection with their common campaign on behalf of Jewish rights in the Diaspora. The nationalist-minded leaders in this activity worked on the assumption that this, too — like the work in Palestine — was a task undertaken by the Jews through the world as a national entity. Such an assumption, as we shall see, is practically explicit in the status accorded by Article 4 of the Palestine Mandate to the Jewish Agency for Palestine, with which the Western non-Zionists affiliated themselves. On the other hand, the immediate activities of the Jewish Agency seemed likely to be more economic than political in nature. Moreover, the Zionist leadership of the Jewish Agency was inclined to make a distinction between the national character of what was being built in Palestine and the ethnic character of Jewish life in the Diaspora. Men like Weizmann had little faith in political guarantees for Jewish autonomy outside Palestine and little interest in political organization to achieve such guarantees.[1] Other Zionists, however, who took the lead in establishing the World Jewish Congress in the 1930's, no matter how reservedly they defined the nature of their organization, clearly implied that the Jewish people throughout the world were a national entity engaged in a political struggle for their rights in the Diaspora.[2] Consequently, the very same non-Zionists who cooperated in the work of the Jewish Agency for Palestine, disregarding the intimations of national status implied in the constitution of the Agency and in the maximum goal that it was entitled to strive for, simultaneously conducted a determined ideological struggle against the idea of the World Jewish Congress.[3]

The submerged political issues also arose in the work of the Jewish Agency itself. They were precipitated first by British attempts in the 1930's to interpret the obligations of the Mandate in such a way that Jewish immigration and Jewish settlement could be stopped short at a given point. On this issue, which involved the legal basis of the activities Zionists and non-Zionists conducted together in the Jewish Agency, the non-Zionists stood shoulder to shoulder with their partners and ideological rivals against the British attack. But it became apparent, to the Zionists at any rate, that after Britain had taken political decisions which virtually repudiated its obligations under the Mandate, no appeal to the old titles would suffice, but a new legal basis for the Zionist endeavor would have to be sought. They therefore reformulated their demand for political sovereignty in Palestine. The revival of the underlying political issues once more converted erstwhile non-Zionists into anti-Zionists, and some directly opposed, while others refused to support, the formulas of the Zionist demands in the early 1940's.

I

The World Zionist Organization, from the very beginning, was confident that it was entitled to represent the sovereign will of the Jewish people. At the same time it was inherent in the very aim of Zionism — to convert the Jewish will to sovereignty from a dormant to an active, and from a diffuse to an organized force — that the Zionist Organization should be regarded as a provisional body. It had eventually to replace itself, in order to succeed, by a regularly organized, authoritative body chosen by all the Jewish people, and not by its *avant-garde*. Theoretically, it might have been possible to hold that such a representative structure would be achieved only when the Jewish state was created in Palestine — though in fact there was no Zionist faction which unequivocally defended this view.[4] But even for purely practical purposes it seemed necessary, at least to the Zionist consensus if not to all Zionists, that the Jewish Company which, as envisaged by Herzl, would exercise authority in colonizing Palestine and building the Jewish state should also represent all sections of the Jewish people. The urgent need for funds in this stage of the Zionist plan was a weighty reason which convinced Zionist leaders from Herzl (or from Pinsker) to Weizmann that such a Jewish Company must include, at any rate, the wealthy and powerful non-Zionists of the West who had demonstrated their concern over the Jewish fate and future.

The idea that the Zionist Organization was acting only provisionally on behalf of the Jewish people and would in due time be replaced by a more fully representative body was introduced, in accordance with Zionist proposals, into the Mandate itself. Article 4 of the Mandate states that —

An appropriate Jewish agency shall be recognised as a public body for the purpose of advising and co-operating with the Administration of Palestine in such economic, social, and other matters as may affect the establishment of the Jewish national home and the interests of the Jewish population in Palestine, and, subject always to the control of the Administration, to assist and take part in the development of the country.
The Zionist organization, so long as its organisation and constitution are in the opinion of the Mandatory appropriate, shall be recognised as such agency. It shall take steps in consultation with His Britannic Majesty's Government to secure the co-operation of all Jews who are willing to assist in the establishment of the Jewish national home.[5]

The British government, in the subsequent period, does not seem to have concerned itself very closely with the negotiations by which

the Jewish Agency was extended to include non-Zionists.[6] Nevertheless, the phrasing of Article 4 could not but have acted as a challenge
to the Zionists to prove their claim of representing the Jewish popular
will, with the logically if not actually implied possibility that failure
in this respect might cause the opportunity of the Balfour Declaration
to be forfeited. The non-Zionists, on the other hand, were also challenged. Article 4 made the invitation to join the Jewish Agency seem
not only one extended by the Zionists but one in which Britain and
the other powers who endorsed the Mandate implicitly joined. Failure
to accept the invitation might conceivably be construed as a rejection
of the opportunities offered for work in Palestine [7] — work in which
the non-Zionists were interested regardless of qualms about the principles upon which the Mandate might be based and the ultimate
results to which it might lead.

Notwithstanding the reasons which both Zionists and non-Zionists
had for cooperating in the Jewish Agency, ideological conflict kept
them divided for years after the end of World War I. Ideological anti-
Zionism, moreover, showed considerable power precisely in the Eastern countries,[8] so that Zionism, when it demanded Western cooperation, could not present itself as the unquestioned representative of
the East, with its entire manpower ready to establish itself in Palestine. Indeed, the Jewish philanthropists of the West came into
conflict with the Zionists not only over the implications of the work
in Palestine, or in connection with the ideological aspects of international protection of Jewish minority rights in the Diaspora. They also
supported rehabilitation projects for the Jews in Europe which were
sometimes based on ideological premises opposed by Zionists and
conducted in cooperation with the ideological anti-Zionists of the
Eastern European countries.

The events of World War I had brought about a sharp shift in
centers of strength within the global Jewish community. When one
spoke of Western Jewish leaders now, it was no longer primarily the
French, German, or British Jews, and the great foundations of Baron
de Rothschild or Baron de Hirsch, but the powerful Jews of America
and their vast new philanthropic organization, the American Jewish
Joint Distribution Committee (JDC), that one had in mind. While
the Zionists, too, conducted fund-raising campaigns in the United
States, the American non-Zionist leaders controlled by far the larger
resources and employed them according to their own conception of
what the postwar rehabilitation of the ravaged Jewish communities
required.[9]

Some JDC funds went to prepare Palestine for immigrants or to relieve want there, but these were relatively small sums and they were not used according to any master plan drawn up by the Jewish Agency.[10] The bulk of JDC funds was spent to reestablish the Jewish communities in those very countries from which the Zionists expected a massive emigration. Zionists understood the need for emergency relief and reconstruction in Europe, but they strongly objected to the proportion of funds allotted to this purpose in comparison with the far smaller proportion given to what they regarded as the paramount task of a fundamental solution of the Jewish problem in the land of Israel. The differences were heightened by the fact that, following a policy of working through local leaders and institutions, the American philanthropists and social workers sometimes sponsored projects which were conceived and carried out in cooperation with Eastern European anti-Zionist leaders. The sharpest debate broke out over the very substantial assistance granted to the Soviet project of Jewish farm colonization in Crimea and the Ukraine at a time when the Communist liquidation of the Zionist movement in Russia was well under way.[11]

Regardless of the irritation caused by these quarrels with the Zionists, the association of American non-Zionists with the ultra-Orthodox, Social Democratic or Communist anti-Zionists of Eastern Europe could not develop into a united anti-Zionist movement based on common principles. The anti-Zionism of the ultra-Orthodox Agudat Israel was based on the rejection of any but a strictly traditionalist Jewish community in Palestine as being essentially illegitimate. The Americans, among whom Reform Jews were strongly represented, could not accept this as a principle upon which to establish a consensus.

The Social Democratic Bundists were modernists, to be sure, but their principles offered no greater basis of unity. To the extent they had become Yiddishists and Diaspora nationalists, they stressed in an even more obnoxious form the very ideological thesis which was the reason for opposing the Zionists, that the Jews were a national group. Some of the Zionist leaders, at least, were prepared to mitigate the feared impact of such ideas upon American Jewry by regarding Israel alone as the center of Jewish political nationality. This made the asserted ethnic character of Diaspora Jewry largely a matter of spiritual or cultural bonds. The Bundists, on the other hand, advocated a program of cultural autonomy which, to a Western eye, was hardly distinguishable from a program of political nationality for Jews in the Diaspora.[12]

Of course, the Bundists, before the Second World War, tended

to regard Yiddish-speaking or, even more narrowly, Polish Jewry
as a distinct national entity, whose cultural, let alone religious, connection with other Jews was of slight significance. Even more radical
in this respect were the Jewish Communists, who viewed with positive
suspicion, not only with disinterest, connections between the Soviet
Jews and Jews elsewhere. Moreover, they held not only the religious
element but also the ethnic element of Jewish consensus to be obso-
lescent.[13] Yet it need hardly be said that such attitudes toward
Jewish solidarity could not be accepted as an ideological premise by
the American Jewish leaders, who regarded the religious bond between Jews throughout the world as eternally valid.

The American basis for opposing Zionism was quite different from
that of the Eastern anti-Zionists. In one or another degree, most
Easterners accepted the same beliefs as the Zionists about the ethnic
elements in Jewish community structure — but these were precisely
the beliefs which the American non-Zionists feared and rejected. The
Bundists as well as the Communists opposed Zionism chiefly because
they regarded a program of emigration from Eastern Europe as
treason to the cause of Socialism, and Agudat Israel objected to the
large-scale resettlement of Palestine by unbelievers. Neither of these
viewpoints, naturally, commended itself to the wealthy, religiously
liberal leaders of American Jewry. Whether a Jew sought freedom
in Poland or in Palestine, was for them a question of convenience or
necessity, not of ideological principle, and they could no more deny
their aid to the one than to the other.

The cooperation between American Jewry and Eastern European
communities, including the anti-Zionist as well as Zionist leadership
of Eastern Jewry, was of precisely the same pragmatic type as that
contemplated for the Jewish Agency: the Americans worked with
the Easterners on practical projects without sharing common ideological principles. These projects could not, and did not, develop into
a full-fledged anti-Zionist alliance because no grounds for an ideological consensus were implicit in them.[14] Cooperation with Zionists
in Palestine implied exactly the same kind of relationship, and was
not foreclosed by the work of the JDC in Europe, which, not being
ideological, was not exclusive.

Cooperation between Zionists and non-Zionists in the work in
Palestine was, then, a matter of time. It needed time to pass from
the heat of debating ultimate ideological implications to the sober
planning of cooperation in the immediate tasks. It took time, too,
for the legal foundations of the work in Palestine to be fully established

through the medium of international conference and organization. It took still more time for the actual groundwork of cooperation to be laid out; and, in the case of the Zionists, this involved, further, the hammering out of a consensus through the arduous process of ideological controversy.

The political victories of the Zionists in the First World War brought them face to face with the real dimensions and character of a problem they had only considered imaginatively theretofore: how to carry out the transfer of the mass of Jews to their national home after the prerequisite recognition under international law had been achieved. Eastern Jews, who felt directly both the great pressure and the high enthusiasm for mass immigration in their own community — a community ravaged and uprooted by the war and then subjected to massacre, pillage, and humiliation in the postwar period — expected this population movement to be undertaken at once, and on a large enough scale to make its successful conclusion a reasonable goal for tactical, not only for strategic, planning. The same attitude was shared by such Herzlian Zionists as Nordau and Jabotinsky. The theory of these men provided for only two major stages in the Zionist strategy: (1) an opening campaign for the major indispensable means — international recognition of the Jewish claim to Palestine, and (2) a closing campaign for the major significant end — the solution of the problem of the Jews by a rapid, massive migration to Palestine and evacuation of anti-Semitic plague spots in Europe. Men with such expectations and theories could not be satisfied with the actual tactical situation of Zionism as it revealed itself in the early postwar period. For the immediate political effect of the Balfour Declaration and the Mandate was not sufficient to make a mass immigration possible, nor were the economic conditions of Palestine or the organized power of the Jewish people adequate for such a task to be undertaken at once.

As a result, a series of tactical disputes broke out, roughly speaking, between Easterners and Westerners in the Zionist Organization. The first insisted that the mass migration should be undertaken at once and the obstacles inherent in the actual legal, economic, and organizational position should be cleared by direct assault. The latter argued that further progress must be planned in terms of existing possibilities, and hence the present must be regarded as perhaps an intermediate and not a final stage in the development of the Zionist strategy. In the course of this debate, extreme positions, first advocated by Max Nordau and Louis D. Brandeis (1856–1941), were rejected and an intermediate position, advocated by Weizmann, was adopted.

The argument revolved in part about the idea of an extended Jewish Agency, which was one of the characteristic achievements of Weizmann's approach to Zionism.

At the first major international conference of Zionists after World War I, the London Conference of 1920, Max Nordau demanded a strenuous effort to overcome the restricted interpretation which was already being given to the terms of the Balfour Declaration and the Mandate. He proposed to regard the relations between the Jews and Britain as a clear alliance of interests, a compact in which the Jews had undertaken to create pro-Allied opinion during the war and to protect the Suez Canal from its eastward side in the postwar period. The first part of the compact had been kept. Now it remained for Britain to do its share by opening the doors of Palestine without restriction and giving effective aid to the immediate resettlement of six hundred thousand Jews. In this way a Jewish majority would be established rapidly, before Arab claims became pressing, and the Anglo-Jewish alliance could then be implemented fully by a Jewish State. Thus, in Nordau's view, the tactics of Zionism must now be to reopen the political question and drive through to a new formula that would give a legal and political basis for immediate mass immigration and the quick conversion of Palestine into a Jewish state.[15]

In contrast, Brandeis said, "The work of the great Herzl was completed at San Remo . . . (The nations of the world) have done all that they could do. The rest lies with us." [16] He, too, felt that it was necessary "to populate Palestine within a comparatively short time with a preponderating body of manly, self-supporting Jews." [17] Brandeis had been initiated into Zionism by a devotee of Herzlianism, Jacob De Haas, and indoctrinated with the view that prewar Practical Zionism was a relapse into the "infiltration" methods of the Hovevei-Zion. He had submitted to the Eleventh Zionist Congress proposals which revealed a bent for large-scale action based on clear political foundations.[18] But, since he believed that "the San Remo decision together with the appointment of Sir Herbert Samuel provides the open door," [19] he regarded the task of the Zionist Organization as one of economics and engineering alone, of raising funds in the Diaspora and investing them constructively in Palestine. This was not, moreover, a task that could conceivably be begun by a mass migration of half a million and crowned in a very short time by the creation of a Jewish state. For, essential preliminary activities in the Diaspora and in Palestine alike — widening the Zionist Organization and increasing its fund-raising capacity, purchasing land and clearing it of malaria, and training Jewish immigrants in trades that could make them self-supporting — clearly involved a comparatively lengthy transition period between the political victory of San Remo and the political consummation of the Jewish Commonwealth. In that period, according to Brandeis' prescription, the Zionist Organization was to disappear as a political organ. The idea of Jewish sovereignty which it had embodied was to lapse until revived in the Jewish state.

At the London Conference, Weizmann had no great difficulty in beating off whatever challenge Nordau's plan presented. Nordau had long been a lonely figure and came to the Conference with an avowed determination, long maintained, that he would *not* be involved in any position of specific responsibility in the movement.[20] Moreover, in the conditions which prevailed in 1920, no strong representation of Eastern Europe or of the Palestinian settlers was possible at the Conference.[21] The rejection of Brandeis' proposals, on the other hand, was a painful and difficult procedure at London, and later led to even more damaging conflicts in America.[22] Yet, ideologically considered, it was the position Nordau took that presented the more serious challenge to Weizmann in the ensuing years, and which had to be fought in order to lay the groundwork for the Jewish Agency. As for Brandeis' position, while Weizmann opposed the specific reorganization plan the American leader proposed, his own "synthetic Zionism" and, above all, his own conception of an extended Jewish Agency were very close in their ideological assumptions to those of his opponent.

The crux of the conflict with Brandeis was not over major strategy or over the major principles of Zionist tactics, but over the specific organizational reforms that the American leader proposed.[23] Since the political era of the World Zionist Organization was over, Brandeis argued, whatever legal questions might still arise in the course of achieving a Jewish preponderance in Palestine should be handled by the Jewish community in Palestine through such representative institutions as the Mandatory government would set up there. The political leaders of Zionism — with the exception of Weizmann and Sokolow — should retire from Palestine affairs and go back and build stronger Zionist Federations in the Diaspora, so that funds for necessary projects which could yield no return would be donated in greater amounts. The work in the Diaspora, too, should have no political flavor, and should be related strictly to constructive efforts in Palestine. As a consequence of these conclusions, Brandeis recommended that in Palestine the Zionist Organization should be headed by a group of experts in specific fields such as public health, agriculture, and industry, who should be chosen without reference to ideological commitments other than their willingness to work on the legal basis of the Mandate. And in the Diaspora, all Jews who were prepared to work for Palestine on this same basis should simply enter the Zionist Organization.

Brandeis' proposals were accompanied by rather insulting suggestions about some of the old leaders of the Zionist movement — such as proposing to establish a pension fund for them so that they could be more easily removed from active duty [24] — which in themselves were enough to make the plan impossible for a leader who, like Weizmann, was concerned to keep the confidence of the movement throughout the world. It also involved some unreal assumptions about the representative structures to be set up by the British for the whole population of Palestine through which the Jewish community could defend the legal claims of the Jewish people under the Mandate, when necessary. No one knew better than Weizmann how arduous the defense of these legal claims already had been and still was in spite of the victory of San Remo — a victory which he too rated very high.[25] He was hardly likely to abandon the existing machinery for a new machinery that did not yet exist.

Apart from this, however, Weizmann could not meet Brandeis on common grounds because of an underlying ideological — or, to be more precise, mythic — divergence regarding the relation of the Zionist movement to the Jewish people.[26] For Weizmann, a disciple of Ahad Ha'am and an Easterner with the instincts of the "ghetto" bred in his bone, the united will and consensus of the Jewish people was, after all, more fundamental than any legal principle or economic groundwork. The one indispensable achievement of Zionism had been to arouse this will and form this consensus, to give them a crystallized expression, mythic in the depth and significance of its effect, through the embodiment of Jewish sovereignty in the Zionist movement. What gave Weismann assurance in all his encounters with British statesmen before the Balfour Declaration was his conviction that he spoke "for those masses who have a will to live a life of their own." [27] Even after the political victory of San Remo, he was well aware of the political dangers, just as, later, after years of constructive endeavor, he could still doubt whether the positions that had been won were enough to assure that a Jewish majority in Palestine would ever be attained under the Mandate.[28] But an underlying faith was implied in Weizmann's skepticism. If the achievement of Zionism might be imperfect in his generation, all the more reason to strengthen the will to sovereignty in the people so that, if necessary, it might live on to seek new forms beyond the limitations imposed upon it by the conditions of the time. A major function of the Zionist Organization, then, must always be to express and perpetuate the will of the Jewish people to be master of its own destiny.

With deep-lying, barely formulated assumptions such as these, Weizmann, the "man of Pinsk," reacted instinctively and not only by calculation against a proposal which, like Brandeis', contemplated a lapse in the embodiment by the Zionist Organization of the principle of Jewish sovereignty. Neither the Zionist organization in Diaspora countries nor the Zionist work in Palestine could be conceived by him as completely determined in their scope and outlines by the legal limits of the Mandate or the economic limits of the day to day situation in Palestine. The need of the Jews in the East and their will to sovereignty in Palestine were dynamic forces capable of transforming the existing situation, and it was the primary function of the Zionist Organization to give expression to these forces.

It follows that Weizmann could not take the same view as Brandeis about the proper method for bringing into the work either experts or the wider public that had not previously been identified with the Zionist idea. He, too, felt that the Zionist political aim, in the intermediate phase that then began, was not to achieve new legal guarantees but to defend the existing ones, while the major emphasis must be laid on constructive work in the economic field. Success in this would secure the ultimate political destiny of the Jewish national home far more directly than would any political efforts. And for success in the constructive tasks that faced Zionism under the Mandate, the cooperation on a broad scale of men and agencies not previously connected with the Organization was vitally needed. In all this, he agreed with Brandeis. However, as one who thought of the Zionist Organization as still essentially the organ of an ideological consensus expressing the myth of Jewish national auto-Emancipation, Weizmann could not propose, as did Brandeis, that non-Zionists who rejected that myth should enter the Organization on the purely formal basis of the definitions laid down in the Mandate. Instead Weizmann favored an agreement between non-Zionist leaders and organizations and the World Zionist Organization in which both should assume equally the responsibilities provided for the Jewish Agency under the Mandate.

In such an association the Zionist Organization would continue to exist as an ideological organization expressing a will to sovereignty derived from sources more fundamental than the letter of the Mandate. A similar advantage, moreover, would be available to the non-Zionists. For, by entering into a partnership with the Zionists in which each partner retained his separate identity, the non-Zionists could clearly indicate that their cooperation on the legal basis of the Mandate did not commit them to any ideas about the broader implications of that document, in its ultimate fulfillment, such as had always been associated with the Zionist movement.[29]

It turned out, indeed, that the non-Zionists were as much impressed by the advantages to themselves of a looser association as was Weizmann on behalf of the Zionists, and they showed themselves more ready to cooperate on his terms than on Brandeis'. To be sure, working out the provisions of such an agreement meant more specific and protracted negotiations than might have been involved in simply opening the doors of the Zionist Organization on the basis of the Mandate as the final political definition of the Zionist aim. But it was also more effective, perhaps, in winning a broad consensus of the entire Jewish community, especially in the West, in favor of the work in Palestine.

The negotiations for the creation of an "extended Jewish Agency" were carried out by Weizmann over a period of many years in two separate encounters: with his own Zionist friends at the Congresses and inter-Congress conferences and with the non-Zionists in continual formal and informal discussions. The negotiations with the non-Zionists went forward in successive phases, taking their departure from the successive resolutions Weizmann was able to obtain at the Zionist conclaves.

The difficulty Weizmann faced at first was not so much the natural suspicion of Zionists when one proposed cooperating with men who had only recently distinguished themselves by their anti-Zionism; though this suspicion was expressed, too.[30] The major obstacle was the desire of Eastern Zionists, for quite different reasons than Brandeis', to establish a single body in which Zionists and non-Zionists would give up their separate organized identities. While Brandeis had hoped to open the doors of the Zionist Organization by dropping its political functions, the Eastern Zionists intended to bring all Jewry into a worldwide organ of Jewish political activity. Such a body, exercising popular authority more fully and more formally than could the Zionist avant-garde, would make itself responsible for achieving the goal of Zionism, among other national tasks. It would be based, moreover, on the democratic organization of Jewish communities throughout the postwar world. To be sure, those who supported this view expected that some of the very leaders of Western Jewry with whom Weizmann was negotiating would exclude themselves from the projected organs of Jewish autonomy. But they expected to be more than compensated for this loss by the massive power of an all-inclusive, self-taxing, representative body of world Jewry.[31]

At the Congress which followed the 1920 London Conference, taking place at Carlsbad on September 1–14, 1921, this point of view was reflected in a resolution which provided that

The Congress recommends to the Actions Committee to take the necessary steps, in agreement with the Executive of the American Jewish Congress, the Vaad Leumi of Palestine and other democratic Jewish organizations, for the convocation of a World Jewish Congress whose task it should be to organize all forces in the Jewish people for the upbuilding of Palestine as well as for the struggle for national rights in the various countries.[32]

This resolution, it should be noted, was not an outright decision but a recommendation of the Congress. Instead of adopting it definitively, the Congress referred it to the Executive for consideration jointly with the Actions Committee, the Zionist council intermediate between the Congress and the Executive. If it had been definitively adopted, it would have meant a decision to hand over the powers of the Jewish Agency under the Mandate to a worldwide Jewish authority in which Zionists and non-Zionists would merge, according to the Easterners' conception; not to a partnership, in which Zionists and non-Zionists would retain their separate identities, as Weizmann had proposed. But precisely because this would have been the implication, the Congress framed its resolution in the form of a recommendation to be further considered. Another resolution, adopted in a form that called for immediate implementation, was more in accord with Weizmann's approach. It provided that

The Zionist Congress addresses itself to the whole Jewish people with the demand that it lay the foundations for the upbuilding of the Jewish National Home in Eretz Israel through the Palestine Foundation Fund (Keren Hayesod) and so establish the Keren Hayesod as a general Jewish fund.[33]

Here, too, the myth of Jewish popular sovereignty found expression. The resolution included provisions for assessing Jewish incomes and property, and proposed to tithe Jews for the benefit of Palestine, in a traditional form of Jewish self-taxation. Moreover, the "non-Zionist" participation in the proposed "general Jewish fund" was to be based on individual contributions and on representatives chosen by vote of all contributors, not on a negotiated partnership with non-Zionist organizations. But a more realistic appreciation of the nature of this fund was implied in the provision that its Board of Directors should be constituted on terms of parity by nominees of the Zionist Organ-

ization and of a Council chosen by all contributors to the Keren
Hayesod. The latter constituency was expected to include a considerable number of Jews who were not willing to join the Zionist
Organization. In actuality, no Council could be organized and the
Keren Hayesod remained completely under the World Zionist Organization's control; but, at the same time, it did attract general support
from the beginning, and included prominent non-Zionists in its
leadership.[34]

In any case, the Keren Hayesod could have represented the
partnership with non-Zionists sought by Weizmann only in form,
not in substance. The fund became essentially a collecting not a
disbursing agency, and its influence on the actual construction of
the Jewish national home was therefore indirect and relatively small.
Cooperation on the scale and of the kind Weizmann wanted could
not be achieved without drawing non-Zionists far more fully into the
direct responsibility for work in Palestine. The next Congress (following a similar decision of the Actions Committee earlier in the year [35])
went a step further towards this aim, but still held to the more far-
reaching ideal of a World Jewish Congress.

The Thirteenth Zionist Congress, held in Carlsbad on August
6–18, 1923, adopted a resolution which provided: first, that the
Executive was to make earnest efforts to set up a World Jewish
Congress within three years and transfer to it the responsibilities of
the Jewish Agency under Article 4 of the Palestine Mandate (note
that Jewish national rights in the Diaspora were no longer mentioned); second, that in the meantime the Jewish Agency was to be
enlarged by adding representatives of those Jewish organizations that
accepted the legal basis of the Palestine Mandate.[36] A Labor proposal
that the non-Zionist representatives be "primarily" selected from the
representatives of contributors to the Keren Hayesod was evaded
by the device of referring it to the Executive,[37] for it was feared
such a proposal would prejudice negotiations with non-Zionist organizations. Thus, Weizmann was granted authority to go ahead immediately with his own program of a partnership with the non-
Zionists on condition that he would work for the creation at a later
date of a sovereign body directly representing the people as an integral
entity.

The Actions Committee and Congress resolutions of 1923 led at
once to serious negotiations with non-Zionists, but it took six years
to arrive at all the agreements and to clear up all the preliminary
questions involved in the final establishment of the enlarged Jewish
Agency. Not only did the preliminary conditions of the non-Zionists

have to be met by Weizmann, but, through him, the non-Zionists had
to be brought to accept the preliminary conditions of those factions
in the Zionist Congress without whose support the idea of the enlarged Jewish Agency could not be approved.

Such support was won when Weizmann succeeded in weaning
away some of his opponents, particularly the Labor Zionists, from the
notion that the enlarged Jewish Agency must serve as a direct expression of the idea of Jewish sovereignty. This view, which was held
by most Zionists, and particularly Eastern Zionists, in the early
twenties really comprised three logically separable attitudes. Involved
in it were the beliefs that Weizmann's policy of compromise hampered
not only (1), the rapid immigration of Jews, but also (2), the conversion of the Balfour Declaration into the full-fledged political victory
envisioned by Herzl, as well as (3), the creation of a fully active
national consensus of the Jews, expressed through a democratically
representative body. These were three attitudes shared broadly by
all of Weizmann's opponents at first. But when each of them was
made primary by a distinct partisan group, they turned out to be
mutually antagonistic. Consequently, it became possible for Weizmann to find allies among his erstwhile opponents.

For the Revisionists and others whose primary concern was to
turn the Mandate into a complete rather than partial political victory,
the idea of a World Jewish Congress was important as a symbol. It
indicated that the Jewish people throughout the world, and not only
the local Jewish community in the country, had a claim to Palestine.
On the other hand, if the union of all Jews in the Jewish Agency had
to be achieved by suppressing the political claim of a Jewish state
and resting content with an intermediate status which only allowed
the community in Palestine to grow, because non-Zionists would
subscribe to no more than this, then the Revisionists would repudiate
such a union. Their basic ideological commitment was neither to the
project of a World Jewish Congress nor to the autonomy of the
Palestinian community as such, though both symbolized the idea of
Jewish sovereignty which was the central value of their ideology.
They were primarily committed to the Jewish state, as the full realization of Jewish sovereignty. They were interested in a World Jewish
Congress, even in the Zionist Congress itself or in the Jewish community in Palestine, only if these bodies were dedicated to the direct
political struggle for achieving the State as their immediate tactical
objective.[38]

A second group, represented, for example, by the Radical Party
organized by Eastern European Zionists, was interested in a World

Jewish Congress per se, as a direct expression of the idea of Jewish national authority. As Zionists they desired, of course, a more definite political victory in Palestine and were concerned with the growth of the community there, but neither of these was for them the primary and immediate, indispensable tactical object to which the Jewish people should devote itself. That objective was none other than the democratic organization of the whole Jewish people throughout the world in a body giving direct expression to its united will. The World Jewish Congress, once organized, would of course devote itself to the realization of the national home promised to the Jews under the Mandate as well as to the realization of national minority rights for Jews in Eastern and Southern Europe and to all other positive, cultural and political, national aims of the Jews who sought to preserve themselves as a distinct nationality. With such a view, in which a democratically organized World Jewish Congress as the direct expression of the national will was a primary and essential element, this group was naturally as determined as the Revisionists in its opposition to the Weizmann conception of an enlarged Jewish Agency. For, in order to meet the demands of non-Zionists, Weizmann was ready to discard symbols and procedures inherently related to a sovereign national assembly.[39]

A third group, represented mainly by the Labor Zionist parties, saw as the primary, immediate tactical objective of Zionism the rapid immigration and settlement of Jewish workers in Palestine. Their strength included a large contingent of Eastern European young people, many of whom had crossed war-torn borders to enter Palestine, without regard to the policy of either the Zionist Organization or the Palestine Government, or who, though still in Europe, were desperately determined to immigrate. These were men and women who matured in the midst of traumatic conditions of revolution and counterrevolution in Eastern Europe, and whose urge toward Palestine was a deeply personal and emotional revulsion against a Jewish situation signalized by the postwar pogroms by Ukrainians and Poles.[40] They were opposed to Weizmann's policies in the early years, because under the restricted interpretation of the Mandate which he accepted the chances for rapid immigration too were restricted. This they blamed on the willingness of the Zionist leadership to compromise on the interpretation of the Mandate. Their natural sympathy was with those critics of Weizmann who demanded a firmer political line in Palestine and a form of organization of world Jewry that would directly and unambiguously express the idea of Jewish popular authority.[41]

But, under the prewar Turkish regime, when political conditions had been far more unfavorable to immigration, Labor groups had still made immigration and settlement the primary and immediate tactical objective of their Zionism. Their disappointment with the political status of the Mandate could not lead them, like the Revisionists, to disregard the growth of the Jewish community in Palestine until a more satisfactory status was won.[42] When convinced by the passage of time that Zionism was indeed in an intermediate and not in the final stage of its political consummation, they were led into an alliance with Weizmann by their essential kinship with his point of view. If the enlarged Jewish Agency could muster new non-Zionist support for the growth of a stronger Jewish settlement on the basis of the existing intermediate status, they welcomed such an agreement.

Nor were they disposed to take an intransigent stand regarding the form of organization of the enlarged Jewish Agency. They shared the Eastern European mythic attachment to symbolisms of national sovereignty and to the procedures of representative democracy in the Zionist Organization, just as did, for that matter, Weizmann himself. But to extend this symbolism to all sections of the Jewish people, to set up a democratic World Jewish Congress working both for the Jewish state in Palestine and Jewish national minority rights in the Diaspora, did not seem to them, as it did to the Radical Party, to be the primary immediate objective. If the non-Zionists would add their strength to the enlarged Jewish Agency only on non-democratic terms or under definitions that obscured the symbolisms of national status involved in such an organization, this seemed to them of less importance than the anticipated accession of strength in the upbuilding of Palestine. For it was in the growing Jewish community in Palestine, and in its developing organs of self-rule that this group saw the main hope for the full realization of the will to Jewish sovereignty.[43]

But before accepting the new partnership which Weizmann sought to negotiate, these men were particularly concerned to gain non-Zionist acceptance of the principles upon which the new Jewish community in Palestine was being built. For there was reason to expect that the rather unusual institutions of the Zionist-organized Jewish settlement would meet resistance from the non-Zionists. The long period which followed the decision of the Thirteenth Congress to proceed with formation of an enlarged Jewish Agency was devoted, accordingly, to the formulation and negotiation of specific demands made by Zionists on non-Zionists and by the non-Zionists on Zionists.

The Fourteenth Zionist Congress was held in Vienna in August 1925. By that time preliminary conferences of non-Zionists in New

York had set up a framework for detailed negotiations.[44] The resolution adopted in Vienna no longer mentions either national minority rights in the Diaspora or a World Jewish Congress, but proceeds to outline specific conditions relating to the work in Palestine which the Zionists asked the non-Zionists to accept:

I.   Recognising that it is desirable to provide facilities for more effective co-operation between all Jews willing to take part in the work of reconstruction in Palestine and the establishment of the Jewish National Home, in the spirit of the Balfour Declaration and the Mandate;

Considering that to this end it is expedient to broaden the basis of the Jewish Agency, and on the understanding that the activities of the Agency shall be based on the following inviolable principles, namely:
   (a)   A continuous increase in the volume of Jewish immigration;
   (b)   The redemption of the land as Jewish public property;
   (c)   Agricultural colonisation based on Jewish labour;
   (d)   The Hebrew language and Hebrew culture;

The Congress declares as follows:

I.   The Congress would view with favour the establishment of a Council of the enlarged Jewish Agency for Palestine under the following conditions:

(a)   The Council of the Jewish Agency, which shall consist, when complete, of approximately 150 members, shall be composed, as to one-half, of representatives of the Zionist Organisation, and as to the other half, of representatives of Jewish communities in various parts of the world.
(b)   The method by which the various communities shall appoint their representatives shall in each case be settled by agreement in accordance with local conditions, and shall, so far as possible, take the form of democratic elections . . .

VII.   In order to secure continuity in the political and other work of the Jewish Agency, the Congress directs the Executive to ensure the election of the President of the Zionist Organisation as the President of the enlarged Jewish Agency.[45]

It was four years after the Fourteenth Zionist Congress adopted the above resolution before the enlarged Jewish Agency came into being. The non-Zionists, with the aid of a Commission of Experts, minutely examined the principles upon which the Jewish resettlement was built before they agreed to be bound by them.[46] The Zionists went through a series of bitter debates before they agreed to the final formulations. Notwithstanding long and tedious discussion of details and procedures, these formulations remained essentially what they had been in 1925.

The enlarged Jewish Agency came into being in 1929, on the eve of the Great Depression. The expanded financial capacity which it brought to the Zionist work in Palestine was therefore far below what had been hoped for, at least in the first years.[47] Moreover, the direct involvement of non-Zionists in the other aspects of the Jewish Agency in Palestine was much less significant than their formal title of equal partnership would indicate. Non-Zionist participation in the current activities of the Jewish Agency Executive never succeeded in drawing new Jewish organizations and communities as such into an intimate relationship with the project of building the Jewish national home. Such intimate concern with the settlement of Palestine continued to be limited — as in the case of the Keren Hayesod — to individual non-Zionists, though to be sure they were more numerous, more prominent, and more responsibly involved than before. On the other hand, when the original non-Zionist leaders who joined the Jewish Agency dropped out one by one in the natural course of events, they were not replaced by new non-Zionists, and the Jewish Agency reverted gradually to what it was at first — another name for the Zionist Organization.[48]

Nevertheless, the creation of the enlarged Jewish Agency, in quite unexpected ways, fully satisfied the expectations that had been laid upon it. After the Depression had lifted somewhat, this was shown in regard to fund-raising. The response of Jews throughout the world, and particularly in America, to the vastly increased financial demands of the Jewish Agency in the Hitler years far exceeded the level of contributions that the Zionists had previously achieved. That the rebuilding of Palestine was accepted by the whole leadership of the Western Jewish community, among other Jewish needs, as their direct responsibility, instead of resting solely on the influence of Zionists, who devoted themselves to this alone, unquestionably made the far larger sums easier to collect. There were Zionists who argued, to be sure, that under the conditions of the time they could have achieved still greater results by independent fund-raising campaigns. On the other hand, the institution of joint campaigns impressed upon the Jewish community an attitude of support for the national home as a noncontroversial matter on which there was a general consensus.

If the enlargement of the Jewish Agency did not bring an expanding circle of non-Zionist organizations and organized Jewish communities into a formal, permanent partnership with the Zionist Organization, it had another, no less important effect. It caused the major, most representative Jewish organizations and communal institutions in the Western countries, with whose leaders the Jewish Agency compact was negotiated, to be unable to take a principled, unreservedly anti-Zionist stand thereafter.[49] The attitude most naturally taken by such bodies after 1929 was a kind of benevolent neutrality which, without binding the organization as such to active participation in the Jewish Agency, led to support on collateral lines. Zionism itself was neither adopted nor opposed but considered an issue on which the members were entitled to think and act individually, while the leaders of the major Jewish organizations were also leading men in the Jewish Agency or, even more often, in the various Zionist organizations. If not a partnership of organizations, there was, then a personal union of Zionism, or of the Jewish Agency, with the major organizations and community organs in the Western countries through an interlocking leadership.

The fact that the Balfour Declaration and the Mandate had been internationally recognized itself tended to produce a similar effect. Yet even after these events the several schools of anti-Zionism continued as organized movements in Eastern countries. The Jewish Communists, of course, followed the political line of the Soviet Union and opposed every aspect of the Jewish national home, and particularly the emigration of Jews. The anti-Zionism of the Social Democratic Bund or the ultra-Orthodox Agudat Israel varied in intensity; in the case of the latter, cooperation with Zionists was achieved on such issues as Jewish rights at the Wailing Wall, and an attempt was made to associate them with the Jewish Agency.[50] Nonetheless, all anti-Zionist groups in the Eastern countries remained separated from Zionism by a continuous, organized, ideological opposition. In the West, these anti-Zionist groups did not exist as an organized force, but they were represented by men and organizations sympathetic with their point of view. Here, however, the consensus created by the negotiations for the enlargement of the Jewish Agency was sufficiently effective to gain the adherence even of leaders sympathetic to the Eastern European Social-Democratic and ultra-Orthodox movements. Men like the Orthodox Rabbi Leo Jung and the Socialist Abraham Shiplacoff (1877–1934) joined the new partnership.[51]

The characteristic evolution of non-Zionist opinion in the West is best illustrated by the successive ideological positions adopted by one of the central organs of American Reform Judaism.[52] Established in 1889, the Central Conference of American Rabbis (CCAR) in the following year adopted Reform principles, rejecting any Messianic vision of returning to Zion and of restoring Jewish sovereignty. After the Basle Zionist Congress in 1897 the CCAR specifically condemned the Zionist doctrine in toto. There were, nevertheless, some Reform rabbis like Gustav Gottheil (1827–1903), Max Heller (1860–1929), Judah L. Magnes (1877–1947), and Stephen S. Wise (1874–1949) who were prominent Zionists. In 1906, 1912, and 1917 the CCAR adopted resolutions declaring that Zionist ideas were incompatible with Reform doctrine, implicitly condemning these rabbis.

Yet time and events had their effect. Younger rabbis were turning in ever greater numbers to Zionism, while the world outside, through the Balfour Declaration, granted the movement recognition and sympathy. Some of the Reform stalwarts led by Dr. David Philipson (1862–1949) tried to organize an anti-Zionist demonstration against the Balfour Declaration in 1918 but eventually gave up the attempt in deference to the remonstrances of leading laymen like Louis Marshall (1856–1929).[53] Soon after, the suggestion that the Reform movement might cooperate with the Zionists in building the Jewish settlement in Palestine, if the more far-reaching ideological implications could be avoided, was not only voiced by individuals but began to be embodied in CCAR resolutions.[54] And, indeed, when the 1928 Conference of non-Zionists in New York formally adopted the plan for the enlarged Jewish Agency, Dr. Philipson and other erstwhile anti-Zionists gave their blessings to the enterprise in emotional addresses.[55] Even after that, it took until 1935 before the increasingly numerous contingent of Zionists among the Reform rabbis could carry a CCAR resolution that explicitly revoked earlier condemnations of Jewish nationalism and declared the pro- or anti-Zionist positions adopted by Reform rabbis to be entirely a matter of personal conscience.[56]

That is where matters rested. The Reform movement as such was officially sympathetic to the Jewish national home and prepared in principle to cooperate, as a non-Zionist body, with the Zionist movement in such forms as the Jewish Agency. An increasingly large majority of Reform rabbis were Zionists and often active Zionist leaders. The cooperation of the CCAR as a body with the Jewish Agency remained an academic suggestion. The Agency did not develop further as a firm and formal partnership between organizations but maintained *ad hoc*, personal ties with non-Zionist organizations through their authorized leaders. In the period following the 1935 resolution, new resolutions were passed which placed the CCAR behind the Zionist movement on issues that seemed to the dwindling minority of anti-Zionists once more to involve questions of principle. Such were the CCAR resolutions during the Second World War supporting the creation of a Jewish Brigade and endorsing the results of the American Jewish Conference, which had proposed a Jewish Commonwealth in Palestine.[57] While the opponents of these measures were unable to reverse the stand of the CCAR, their resistance (and also the policy of the Zionist rabbis) caused the general principle to be maintained that the CCAR remained a non-Zionist organization: views favoring or opposing Zionism continued to be regarded as matters of individual conscience. Accordingly, the large Zionist majority committed the CCAR to particular, *ad hoc* measures of cooperation with the Zionists, but made no effort to build up permanent forms of organizational union between the Reform movement and the Zionist movement.

While other Jewish organizations and representative institutions in the West did not always start from as firm an anti-Zionist position as the CCAR, the kind of benevolent neutrality toward Zionism with which this body ended was characteristic. Thus, on the basis established by the Balfour Declaration and the Mandate, Zionism acquired in the West a favorable climate of opinion and a network of institutional support drawing in the entire community through channels that called themselves non-Zionist.

II

The foundation for the consensus between Zionism and ideological non-Zionism was the belief that questions of fundamental significance would not arise in a program of cooperation based on the legal formulas of the Mandate, if realistically interpreted. Weizmann's successful battle within the Zionist movement for the acceptance of the Balfour Declaration as an intermediate and not a final phase of the Zionist endeavor helped to establish this belief. Even while negotiating the Balfour Declaration, Weizmann had taken occasion to deny that it was "the endeavour of the Zionist movement immediately to create a Jewish State in Palestine." [58] The pressure of British caution and Arab hostility caused the Zionist leader so often and so emphatically to repeat his moderate estimate of Zionist aims in the existing intermediate phase of the movement that a non-Zionist leader like Louis Marshall could understandably come to the same conclusions as Weizmann's Zionist opponents: [59] he concluded that the moderate Zionist leader did not really believe there could be a final phase in which Palestine would become a Jewish state. He thought Weizmann would in the end be satisfied with a status of relative autonomy and opportunities for reasonable growth of the Jewish settlement such as Zionism already enjoyed during the existing intermediate phase defined by the Mandate.

Thus, in seeking to persuade other non-Zionists to cooperate with the Zionists, Marshall argued:

You probably know that I am not a Zionist. I am, however, greatly concerned in the rehabilitation of Palestine, and I regard it to be the duty of every Jew to aid in that cause. Political Zionism is a thing of the past. There is nobody now in authority in the Zionist Organization who has the slightest idea of doing anything more than to build up the Holy Land and to give those who desire a home there the opportunity which they cherish.[60]

The basis for such an assumption is indicated in Marshall's record of a conversation with Brandeis in September 1919:

He admits that two things are necessary before there can be any immigration into a Palestine whatsoever, (1), to eradicate the prevailing malaria . . . and (2), the creation of industries . . . He expresses confidence, however, that . . . Palestine could support a large population. He several times spoke of six million people. I called his attention to the danger of using such figures, first, because of its effect upon the Jews of Eastern Europe politically, and secondly, because of its effect psychologically upon the great mass of the Jews of the world, who would actually believe that it would become feasible for half of all the Jews of the world to transplant themselves into Palestine. I called his attention to the fact that the two problems which he regarded as conditions sine qua non to the migration of the Jews to Palestine could not be accomplished in fifty years and without an enormous expenditure of money. To speak therefore of a Jewish population of six million was in my judgment playing with fire and would only excite the imagination of those who would find their hopes shattered . . . He at once admitted that I was right and thanked me cordially for having pointed [to] the danger. The entire organization is anxious to let the people know that it is premature to contemplate a large Jewish settlement in Palestine, and it is evident that there will be an effort made to delay immigration by calling attention to the unsanitary conditions now prevailing and the necessity of establishing industries before immigration can be safely undertaken.[61]

Marshall's judgment regarding the Zionist appraisal of their position was, of course, far from being groundless, though it is so clearly biased in accordance with his own wish. In 1931 Weizmann's constant stress on the limits which a realistic Zionist policy must observe during the intermediate phase of its program carried him, in an unguarded moment, to an outright renunciation of the aim of a Jewish majority as being unrealistic even as a final phase of the Zionist program.[62] The Zionist leader attempted to retrieve his error in making such a statement, but, failing to make his retraction effective, was defeated for the first time in his candidacy as President of the Zionist Organization. But even if one were to dismiss his attempted retraction as mere politics and regard his original statement as a well-considered opinion instead of an impulsive slip, the difference in attitude from Marshall's view is obvious. The Zionist leader may have been prepared ultimately to accept something less than a Jewish majority and a Jewish state in Palestine if all efforts to secure these failed. Nevertheless he took the legal basis of the Mandate as an opportunity to work immediately for a Jewish majority and a Jewish state. Marshall, on the other hand, confident that all efforts to achieve a Jewish majority and a Jewish state in Palestine would fail, was willing to work for something less than these on the legal basis of the Mandate, trusting that the ideological issues concerning statehood would never arise in practice.

Cooperation with the Zionists on the legal basis of the Mandate, as it turned out, involved political conflicts in which the non-Zionists, out of loyal adherence to the position they had adopted, had to array themselves on the side of the Zionists against British policy. For, the period following the creation of the enlarged Jewish Agency brought a succession of decisive events which radically altered all assumptions regarding the work on behalf of the Jewish national home.

There was a radical change, first of all, in the pressure of Jewish emigration from Europe. One of the reasons that from the beginning had inclined non-Zionists like Marshall to cooperate in the Palestine project through the Jewish Agency had been the mounting scale of Jewish emigration and the bad conscience of American Jews over their inability to keep the doors of America open to their refugee "co-religionists." This was a longstanding preoccupation of Marshall's, as one may see from his letter of January 20, 1914 to Nathan Straus (1848–1931):

As you know, I have for many years given serious thought to the subject of immigration. Until now, we have been enabled to keep open the doors of opportunity, but the time has come when I greatly fear that restrictive immigration laws will be passed, with the result that, to a considerable extent, the storm-tossed children of Russian and Roumanian Ghettos will be unable to receive admittance here. The operation of the alien laws in England has been equally discouraging, and the difficulties attending immigration into South America, South Africa, and other distant lands, are of so formidable a character, that but few can travel thither. Hence it becomes the bounden duty of those of our people who have been blessed by Providence with worldly possessions, and who are at the same time imbued with the sentiments of love and loyalty for Judaism and its institutions, to concentrate their efforts toward the development of that land, which, after all, should rouse the most tender feelings in the heart of every Jew.[63]

In the postwar years Marshall's fears were borne out by the passage of the "infamous Johnson bill." He then repeatedly urged American Jewish support for Palestine on the grounds that, his own country having closed its doors, the need for a haven for European Jews in

Palestine had become even more urgent.[64] But the pressure of the 1920's was insignificant in comparison with the desperate need for asylum of Jews fleeing the Hitler menace in the 30's and 40's. Thus, one of the most effective motives that had caused non-Zionists to support the enlarged Jewish Agency became a far more powerful reason for defending it against the political threats that arose to the free exercise of Jewish rights under the Mandate.

The creation of the enlarged Jewish Agency itself was the signal for a series of Arab attacks that kept Palestine in a state of intermittent political turmoil until the Second World War. The Arab uprisings were followed by successive British investigations leading to the adoption of new policies that tended to restrict or deny rights which the Jewish Agency claimed under the Mandate.[65] The non-Zionists were, consequently, placed in a position, which was not without its difficulties, of having to share in the Zionist political struggle against the mandatary .

The 1929 riots took the form of a Moslem uprising against the Jews occasioned by a dispute concerning religious observances at the Wailing Wall. However, British investigating commissions treated the outbreaks as a reaction against Jewish activities in building the national home which Arabs considered prejudicial to their interests. The 1930 White Paper issued by the British government thereafter echoed the view that the immigration, land purchase, and settlement policies of the Zionist Organization were already, or were likely to become, prejudicial to Arab interests. It understood the mandatary's obligation to the non-Jewish community to mean that Palestine's resources must be primarily reserved for the growing Arab economy and proposed to restrict the further growth of the Jewish national home by this yardstick.[66]

To both contentions not only the Zionist but the non-Zionist leaders of the Jewish Agency reacted with shock and outrage. They expressed their bitterness by resigning as a body. A British Cabinet committee then met with the Zionist and non-Zionist leaders to discuss the situation and find a way to renew cooperation. This was achieved by the MacDonald letter, in which the two causes of complaint on the part of the Jewish Agency were alleviated. The implications that existing practices of the Zionist Organization in regard to immigration, land purchase, and settlement were, indeed, prejudicial to legitimate Arab interests were denied, and it was stated that the Government's obligation to protect non-Jewish, as well as Jewish, interests was not understood to require at that time freezing the Jewish national home at its existing stage of development.[67]

If the Zionist embitterment at the Passfield White Paper of 1930 needs no comment, it is instructive to consider the reasons why the non-Zionists, too, felt outraged, as well as the ideological consequences of the measures of protest in which they, consequently, joined. The idea that the Jewish national home might be prejudicial to the legitimate interests of the Arabs in Palestine had been one of the arguments of such men, or their predecessors, in opposing the issuance of the Balfour Declaration in the very beginning. Rejecting objections on this score, the British Government and the nations of the world had defined what constituted the legitimate interests of the Arabs in Palestine by means of the clauses of the Mandate protecting the "civil and religious rights" of existing non-Jewish communities (Preamble) and of all inhabitants of Palestine, irrespective of race and religion (Article 2).[68] The obligations of the mandatary to protect the civil and religious rights of all existing communities in Palestine, both Jewish and non-Jewish, and also to develop self-governing institutions, were paralleled by or, more probably, subordinated to another obligation, to help secure the establishment of the Jewish national home. By the latter obligation, the mandatary was bound not to any of the existing communities in Palestine, but to the Jews throughout the world who were willing to assist in the establishment of the Jewish national home (Article 4).[69] The non-Zionists had just entered the Jewish Agency in good faith, and had thus entered also into a relationship with the mandatary on the terms the latter had defined. Before they had committed themselves to this step they had examined, among other questions, whether the activities of the Zionist Organization, in law or in fact, prejudiced the legitimate interests of the Arabs, as they had once feared they might. They had, of course, accepted the well-established principle that the obligation to facilitate the growth of the Jewish national home was part of the basic law for Palestine and that the limits within which the interests of the Arabs were legitimate could not therefore be stretched so far as to preclude building the national home. Their studies had also convinced them that, in fact, the activities of the Zionists had not, on the whole, prejudiced but advanced the legitimate interests of the non-Jewish community.[70] In reaching these conclusions, they had not only based themselves on what they considered objective facts. They had gone at least half-way to meet the Zionists and all the way to meet the mandatary and the international community in terms of the principles the latter had previously established.

They were bound, then, to resent the sudden abandonment by the mandatary of positions which they had accepted in good faith as defining their legal relationship. The British intimations that the Jewish community in Palestine was not entitled to grow freely as of right but only on sufferance by the Arabs, who could bring about restrictions by no better legal argument than violence, was a repudiation of a contract that the non-Zionists had freshly signed. As for the charges that the development of the national home had already had, or would necessarily have, prejudicial effects upon the Arab economic position, the non-Zionists had satisfied themselves on this point before joining the Jewish Agency. On both legal and factual grounds, then, their opposition to the Passfield White Paper of 1930 was as strong as the Zionists'.

The effect of this episode was to commit the non-Zionists to far more precisely formulated definitions of Jewish rights in Palestine than they might otherwise have reached. Their hope in joining the Jewish Agency had been that questions of the ultimate political status of Palestine would not arise, and all attention would thus be concentrated on practical work in terms of the status quo. But the political focus of the investigations and discussions following the 1929 riots made a current issue of the final status that Jews wished to attain in Palestine. Whether they welcomed it or not, Jewish groups concerned in the Palestine project were called upon to define their ultimate objectives. On July 14, 1931, presiding over the Second Meeting of the Jewish Agency Council, Dr. Cyrus Adler presented a definition of the national home for which he claimed the status of a contract binding upon both Zionists and non-Zionists.[71] While Adler's statement was hardly binding on the Zionists, it undoubtedly may be regarded as an authoritative explicit formulation of a final status for Palestine to which the non-Zionists had implicitly agreed in entering the Jewish Agency.

The definition consists of quotations from two official sources. The first is a famous passage from the Churchill White Paper of 1922:

When it is asked what is meant by the development of the Jewish National Home in Palestine, it may be answered that it is not the imposition of a Jewish nationality upon the inhabitants of Palestine as a whole, but the further development of the existing Jewish community, with the assistance of Jews in other parts of the world, in order that it may become a centre in which the Jewish people as a whole may take, on grounds of religion and race, an interest and a pride. But in order that this community should have the best prospect of free development and provide a full opportunity for the Jewish people to display its capacities, it is essential that it should know that it is in Palestine as of right and not on sufferance. That is the reason why it is necessary that the existence of a Jewish National Home in Palestine should be internationally guaranteed, and that it should be formally recognised to rest upon ancient historic connection.[72]

For a briefer definition, Adler referred to a statement by Norman
Bentwich, Attorney General of Palestine:

A national home connotes a territory in which a people, without receiving
the rights of political sovereignty, has, nevertheless, a recognized legal
position and receives the opportunity to develop its moral, social, and
spiritual ideals.[73]

This, then, was the limit of what the non-Zionists felt they were
committed to by their adherence to the Jewish Agency, and the far-
thest they were prepared to go with the Zionists. Negatively, it meant
a refusal to advocate, or agree to, an independent state of the Jews
in Palestine. On the other hand, it also meant a proclaimed intention
to resist the freezing of Jewish development in Palestine either by
establishing an Arab state there or by a unilateral, hence arbitrary,
decision of the mandatary to consider that its obligations concerning
the Jewish national home were at an end. What, in fact was implied
by this non-Zionist formulations was that the intermediate position
in which Palestine found itself should remain, in essence, its final
position; that the Holy Land should never become a Jewish, Arab,
or any other kind of sovereign state, but always remain an international trust. The Mandate had stated no term or conditions for con-
cluding the contingent right granted to the Jews to build up a
majority and receive their sovereignty in Palestine, or for deciding
what final status the actual achievement of the Jews entitled them to.
The implicit meaning of the non-Zionist position was to suggest a
new interpretation for the failure of the Mandate to state when or
under what conditions the final accounting and settlement must be
made. It suggested that the rights granted to the Jews under the
Mandate were permanent and not provisional, and the status they
enjoyed was not contingent at all, but definite.

III

In the early 1930's much could still be left implicit. The British,
at that time, only implied that they might consider their obligations
to the national home terminated, and no Jew, whether Zionist or
non-Zionist, was compelled to formulate his own position in terms
of a clear British renunciation of this part of the Mandate.

The Arab revolt of 1936–1939, and the British investigations and
policy statements which it produced, completely altered the situation.
The new premise of British policy was stated in the Peel Commission's
declaration of 1937 that the Mandate had from the very beginning
been based on a mistaken assumption.[74] The obligation towards the

Jewish people — which the Peel Commission now recognized was the primary obligation of the Mandate — could not be reconciled with the obligation toward the Arabs, at least so long as that people remained adamantly opposed to the Jewish national home.

While this premise was not always so openly avowed in the policy documents issued by Britain in the later 1930's, conclusions were drawn which clearly implied it. The Mandatory obligations toward the Jewish national home were virtually liquidated by a series of restrictions on Jewish immigration and land purchase whose underlying doctrine was given a final definition in the White Paper of 1939.[75] The new policy made concessions to the Arabs by freezing the Jewish national home at its existing proportionate position in relation to the whole territory and population of Palestine.

On the other hand, it also made the establishment of an independent (Arab) state of Palestine, after a transitional period, depend on agreement between Jews and Arabs. Thus it perpetuated the same impasse which had led Britain to consider the Mandate itself unworkable. The Peel Commission had proposed the partition of Palestine and the creation in it of a Jewish and an Arab state as a solution for this problem. This was the only British proposal that provided for any real growth of the Jewish national home in the near future. While the proposal of partition was abandoned officially by the British government shortly after it was made, it remained far more than an academic possibility from the moment it was first officially broached.

All Jewish organizations concerning themselves with the national home were forced by the events and statements of the late 1930's to consider their own positions anew. They were challenged not only by the White Paper and its repudiation of obligations toward the national home, but also by the proposal for a solution by partition. On the first issue the unity between Zionists and non-Zionists remained intact. On the second, their underlying ideological division revealed itself once more.

Zionists and non-Zionists alike vehemently denounced the freezing of Jewish development by the White Paper as a "breach of faith" on the part of the mandatary.[76] The same unity which had been shown in rejecting the 1930 White Paper was once again demonstrated, for Zionist and non-Zionist alike agreed in defending the legal rights and position which they had shared on behalf of the Jewish people through the Jewish Agency.

But the proposal to partition Palestine and set up a Jewish State in order to continue the development of the national home in part

of the country was another matter. It raised, as an immediate possibility, the question of restoring Jewish sovereignty, of setting up a
Jewish nation defined in the fullest degree and the most formal
manner as a political entity. Such a possibility required a readjustment
of the ideas of even the most extreme Zionists. In 1930, appearing
before the Shaw Commission in London, Jabotinsky had stated that
his party's aim was to set up a Jewish state, and then defined that
conception as follows:

[A Jewish State] does not necessarily mean being independent in the
sense of having the right to declare war on anybody, but what it means
is first of all a majority of Jewish people in Palestine, so that under a
democratic rule the Jewish point of view should always prevail, and
secondly, that measure of self-government which for instance the State
of Nebraska possesses. That would satisfy me completely as long as it is a
local self-government, and as long as there is a Jewish majority in the
country.[77]

Such a proposal involved not only perpetuating British control over
Palestine indefinitely, but a long period in which the building up
of a Jewish majority would have to depend on Britain's acceptance
of that aim as its own. While another Revisionist spokesman had
referred to mass immigration for twenty-five to thirty years as the
condition required to achieve a Jewish majority, Jabotinsky at that
time spoke of 30,000 immigrants a year for the next sixty years as
his desideratum.[78] But by the 1940's it was clear to the Revisionists
that no one but the Jews themselves could be counted on to pursue
the aim of Jewish sovereignty for long periods. They now favored a
different approach. They reverted to the Nordau plan of twenty years
earlier, and proposed that the United Nations grant an international
loan and technical assistance for the transfer of one million Jews to
Palestine within a single year after the end of the war. The Jewish
majority in Palestine was to be established at once. Thereafter the
Jewish people throughout the world would be in a position to conduct
the further resettlement of its homeland independently.[79]

   A similar shift of position was necessitated for the whole consensus
of Zionist opinion, since British policy in the thirties was a cogent
demonstration that the Jews could rely on none but themselves, over
long periods of time, to guarantee the full development of the Jewish
national home. The official formulation of this conclusion, upon which
it proved possible to obtain a consensus, was the Biltmore program.
This, as we have seen, called for the grant of full authority to the
Jewish Agency to carry out the rapid development of the national
home into a Jewish commonwealth based on a Jewish majority, with

the mandatary simply keeping order in the interim. The leaders who pushed through the new policy statement could not but have been aware that it was unrealistic in assuming that Britain would agree to keep order in Palestine, under the proposed arrangements. Men like Ben-Gurion were prepared, therefore, to fall back on another policy; they were ready for the immediate assumption of authority in a suitable area within which Jews already commanded a majority, thus accepting a partition. Other Zionists opposed partition either because of the implied restrictions on the scope for growth, or because they hoped alternative solutions might ultimately be concluded with the agreement of the Arabs. But, obviously, no Zionist found the partition plan unacceptable because of the fact that it involved the restoration of sovereignty in Palestine to the Jews.

This very point made partition unacceptable in principle to most non-Zionists — though by now there were already leaders among them who refused to be bound by such a principle. At the Fifth Jewish Agency Council Meeting in August 1937, the American non-Zionists opposed partition vehemently.[80] They maintained their opposition through the catastrophic years that followed and in the plans that they drew up for the postwar period. It became quite impossible, nevertheless, to assume that Great Britain could be persuaded, after so many years, to resume the obligations toward the national home which its final White Paper of 1939 had so definitively rejected. Yet the non-Zionists continued to stand on their legal position instead of seeking a political solution. The American Jewish Committee proposed that the *status quo ante* be restored, by a new international trusteeship embodying the substance of the Mandate.[81] Recognizing, however, that no trustee could be expected, in the light of the Mandatory experience, to exercise this charge forever, the Committee vaguely proposed that "within a reasonable period of years" Palestine should become "a self-governing commonwealth" — by implication, neither Jewish nor non-Jewish — under a constitution which should protect, among other rights, the right of the Jewish national home to grow by immigration and settlement "to the full extent of the economic absorptive capacity of the country."

The circumstances of the postwar period of the late 1940's were such that this non-Zionist position had little chance of acceptance and hardly more chance of gaining a hearing. No martyrdom in the long history of Jewish suffering rivals the slaughter of entire Jewish communities in which the Hitler era culminated. Nor did any previous catastrophe exceed it in violence of shock. The vicious determination of the exterminators and the fact that this monstrosity arose out of the organic corruption of a modern Western European nation which was considered a paragon of civilization, particularly perhaps by Jews, had a true traumatic effect. No Jew anywhere in the world was permitted to escape its immediate impact. Those who lived beyond the direct menace of the Nazis had to stand by impotently while Jewish refugees were shunted from port to port and, often enough, turned back from their very own doors. Nor was their horror only a sympathetic emotion, for in those years the Nazis wove an international net of hatred that left no Jewish community without its own organized anti-Semitic enemy in its own country. The calculated destruction of all Jews in Nazi Europe was felt by Jews throughout the world as, in the most direct way, aimed at themselves.[82]

In this extremity, instincts of self-defense would brook no barriers of ideology or established usage. The expedients which the Jewish consensus was emotionally prepared to respond to exceeded not only what the non-Zionist American Jewish Committee but what the Zionists, operating in established relationships with governments, were likely to suggest. The Revisionist Organization which had broken the discipline of the World Zionist Organization and then abandoned it altogether in rebellion against the restraint of its tactics, now itself became insufficient to give full expression to Jewish resentments. Loosely attached or completely separated Revisionist splinter groups carried out a policy of armed "activism" in Palestine and of independent propaganda and diplomacy in the Diaspora.[83] In America, their campaigns for a Jewish Army, for various measures of opposition to Great Britain, and for expedients calculated to save Jews from the Nazi executioners, not only attracted widespread support but consolidated around them a group of adherents, including many who had not previously shown an active concern with Jewish affairs but now adopted a tone of bitter partisan contempt for the official Zionist bodies and their half-hearted demands.[84]

In such a climate of opinion, the Zionists found that every step they took toward more militant tactics and a more decisive formulation of their aims consolidated rather than weakened the support given them by the communal consensus. In the years after American Zionism adopted the Biltmore program, it also experienced a threefold increase in its registered membership.[85] Public opinion polls conducted in 1945 showed that the attitudes of the Jews in America were strongly favorable to the idea of a Jewish state, and Gentile opinion was also strongly sympathetic.[86]

The dominant view in Jewish communal organizations that were not officially Zionist also became forthright and unreserved in support of the Zionist demands. In Britain, the Board of Jewish Deputies was controlled by a Zionist majority and favored the Jewish commonwealth proposal.[87] In the less tightly organized American community, authoritative opinion was shared by a variety of fund-raising and functional agencies: the Welfare Funds and Federations, the large fraternal orders, the national religious "unions" and "assemblies" of the three Jewish "denominations," and the "civic protective" and "community relations" agencies. To the extent that these were membership organizations and thus reflected the communal consensus, they followed the impulse which was apparently dominant among their members. They joined in the American Jewish Conference and adopted the demand of a Jewish commonwealth in Palestine.[88] To the extent that they were more functional in aim and bureaucratic in structure, as in the case of the communal fund-raising bodies, a long background of cooperation in aid for Jews abroad had bound them as directly to the ideologically Zionist as to the ideologically non-Zionist organizations. In the circumstances that were anticipated for the postwar period, the overwhelming importance of free immigration to Palestine was as obvious to Jewish social workers as to the Jewish community at large.[89]

Once before, in the closing years of the First World War, the resistance of ideological non-Zionists to Zionist demands had set them against the communal consensus. Nevertheless, in the years after, the claim of non-Zionist notables, in particular the leaders of the American Jewish Committee, to "represent" the Jewish community was given virtually official recognition by the Zionists through the negotiations leading to the enlargement of the Jewish Agency.[90] But, in the wave of feeling that swept the Jewish community in the West during the Hitler era, the reservations of ideological non-Zionism were simply swept out of court. When the American Jewish Committee left the Conference in which the communal consensus had endorsed the idea of a Jewish commonwealth, they did so as a dissident minority; and they underscored this fact by undertaking almost at once to reorganize on the basis of individual membership and more substantial numbers.[91] That they left the Conference, nevertheless, indicates the strength of their ideological opposition to the restoration of political sovereignty to the Jews.

But one of the factors which had been most powerful in converting Western anti-Zionism into non-Zionism after the First World War now came into play. Governments began to come to the conclusion that the partition of Palestine was the only rational and feasible solution of the difficulties in that area. One important reason why non-

Zionism replaced anti-Zionism and practical cooperation succeeded ideological dispute in the 20's had been — as Louis Marshall stressed — that the Western governments stood behind the Mandate. Now, too, when the American government indicated in 1946 that further Jewish immigration to Palestine depended on such a final political solution as partition, the American Jewish Committee could no longer oppose the idea.[92]

History repeated itself ever more precisely. Once committed to a Jewish state in part of Palestine, the American non-Zionists remained loyal to that decision even when the American government, whose indicated approval had been a crucial factor in winning their own acceptance of the idea, began to waver. Before the partition plan was finally put into effect, the American non-Zionists had occasion to stand firm with the Zionist-minded community against an attempt to turn the wheel back to a trusteeship, the kind of solution originally favored by the American Jewish Committee. After the Jewish state was established, too, the non-Zionists had to cooperate with the other representatives of the community in efforts to persuade their government to assure the sovereign integrity of the State of Israel.[93]

But the existence of the State of Israel precipitated those very issues of ultimate ideological import which the non-Zionists had striven so long to suppress. The non-Zionists were now faced with the problem of obtaining from the government of Israel such official interpretations and policies regarding the meaning of Jewish sovereignty as might help to lay their old fears to rest.

The rise of the State of Israel much more unexpectedly raised problems of a similar nature for Diaspora Zionists. All at once they saw that their own special status had become problematical as a result of their crowning success.

As for the Israelis, they, too, were now confronted with the problem of formulating the nature of their relationship, as not only a sovereign but a Zionist state, to the Jewish people at large, which, in its great majority, still lived in the Diaspora.

7 ISRAEL AND THE DIASPORA

SINCE the rise of Israel, outright opposition to the existence of a Jewish state is no longer recognized by the consensus of the Jewish community as a legitimate attitude. This does not mean that Jewish anti-Zionism has disappeared entirely. Ideological opponents of the very idea of the Jewish state did not undergo a total conversion simply by virtue of its legal establishment. But it is natural that when the State of Israel was recognized internationally, it was also accepted by the consensus of the Jews throughout the world. Ideological opponents had to adjust themselves in one way or another to the new situation.

Even the most intransigent anti-Zionists, who hardly abated their hostility to the state at all, nevertheless found themselves, as a result of the war, in a new position which necessarily altered their attitudes. An extreme case was that of the Bundists. Diaspora nationalism had lost all bearing upon contemporary affairs. In the mild Bundist form of cultural autonomy, this program had enjoyed a vigorous if not a full realization in only one area, Eastern Europe. The natural environment for such an ideology had disappeared, for what the Nazis had not destroyed, the Soviets and their satellites now submerged through a policy that became violently hostile to all expressions of Jewish nationalism. Many of the surviving leaders of the Bund became refugees in Western countries where their kind of anti-Zionist Jewish nationalism had never taken root, and they remained feeble, isolated voices. While they made sincere efforts to readjust their ideas and apply them to the new situation of a global Diaspora Jewry, they succeeded only in consolidating part of their old adherents scattered in small groups throughout the world.[1]

The ultra-Orthodox anti-Zionists of Eastern Europe had never based their principles on the specific situation that obtained in Eastern Europe, for, as traditionalists, they considered no status in the Exile definitive. Moreover, they were strongly represented in the older,

pre-Zionist Jewish community in the Land of Israel, and had prominently contributed to its continuing growth.[2] After the rise of the
State of Israel, some diehards among them, the Natorei Karta,
("Wardens of the City") continued to repudiate the very idea of the
State and acted in defiance of its legitimacy.[3] By this attitude, they
placed themselves in a position of illegitimacy: not outside the law,
but beyond the pale of the Jewish consensus, in somewhat the same
way as the Jehovah's Witnesses are placed in relation to American
society. However, the main organized body of ultra-Orthodox anti-
Zionists, the Agudat Israel, could not allow itself to take such an
attitude of fanatical dissidence. The validity of the State of Israel
was no longer a matter upon which the Jewish consensus permitted
legitimate differences of opinion, and no body that valued its recognition by the community could ignore this fact.

Much the same situation developed in regard to the Western non-
Zionists and anti-Zionists. The political crisis through which the State
of Israel was established brought about a temporary reversion of many
non-Zionists to anti-Zionism. Once Israel proclaimed itself a state
and was internationally recognized, however, the Jewish consensus
no longer tolerated an anti-Zionist repudiation of Jewish sovereignty
in Israel. Nor did the most implacable Western anti-Zionists belong
to the same breed of fanatical legitimists as the Natorei Karta, who
could defy both the Jewish and the international consensus and set
their own voice up as the organ of law to which all Jews must submit.
Even the American Council for Judaism, the most rigid Western anti-
Zionists, acknowledged the State of Israel as a legal entity. Their
anti-Zionism persisted, however, expressing itself in active hostility
to the Jewish state of a kind and intensity which could not be accepted
as a legitimate attitude within the Jewish consensus.[4] The American
Council for Judaism was militant enough to court ostracism. Such a
position could not, of course, appeal to the major representative of
non-Zionist opinion, the American Jewish Committee. The Committee,
instead, adopted a position of friendly support for the Jewish state
which was well within the limits approved by the consensus.[5]

Fringe phenomena like the Natorei Karta and the American
Council for Judaism could obviously have no effect on Israel's
definition of its sovereignty. But some of the underlying reasons for
their hostility to Israel and Israel's policies involved issues in which
their opposition was shared by other groups, acting on lines considered legitimate by the Jewish consensus. Traditionalist opposition
to secularist policies presented no more than a police problem when
it took the form of outright defiance of authority among the Natorei

Karta. Opposition to the same policies had to be met on political grounds when it was expressed by the joined forces of Agudat Israel and Mizrachi, employing tactics already used to good purpose by the Orthodox party in the World Zionist Organization. The fears of Western anti-Zionists that a *Jewish* state would place their own allegiances in question represented no more than a problem in public relations for the American Jewish community when put forward in the obsessional style of the American Council for Judaism. The same misgivings had to be met diplomatically by the State of Israel when presented by the sober and friendly American Jewish Committee.

But another source of controversy in regard to the scope of Israel's sovereignty arose essentially from within the Zionist movement, from its own ideas and institutions. A debate began concerning the relations of the state, once established, to the Diaspora community and especially to the Zionist Organization, which had hitherto embodied the will of the Jewish people to determine its own destiny. A fanatical view, popularly called Canaanitism, denied any relation whatever of the Jewish community in the State of Israel to Jews in the Diaspora or to Judaism. This was a logical outgrowth and, one may say, a *reductio ad absurdum* of the Zionist thesis that the Jewish state would solve the Jewish problem by a mass transfer of Jews, "liquidating" the community in Exile. While this attitude, too, was placed beyond the pale of the Jewish consensus, the underlying Zionist thesis from which it was derived was shared, in a more balanced version, by leading Israelis and, in fact, by the consensus of Israeli opinion.[6] The opinion of Diaspora Zionists and particularly of American Zionists, on the other hand, favored setting up new, clear and enduring relations between the Zionist Organization and the State. The difference between these approaches raised problems in regard to the meaning and effects of Israel's sovereignty.

In the short period since Israel's foundation, the State has, accordingly, been compelled to concern itself with conflicting views concerning the significance of its sovereignty. Some of the issues that arose were, perhaps, more verbal than real and were resolved by little more that formulas; but others seem to have had a more substantial effect upon the ways in which Israel's sovereignty has actually been realized.

I

Throughout the history of the opposition to Zionism among Western Jews, anti-Zionists had left themselves loopholes for becoming reconciled to the existence of the Jewish state, if they should not succeed in shaping history so that its emergence might be avoided. After all, the ethnic character of Jewish history in the past was so clear that only heedless fanatics could deny or disavow it totally, however much one might desire that Jewish history take a different course in the future.[7] In the same way, "reasonable" Western anti-nationalists — that is, anti-nationalists sensitive to the moods of the Jewish consensus — could not refuse to support the demands of their own contemporaries for "national minority rights," or even for a Jewish state, if they seemed indispensable for Jewish communities in a different situation from their own. Even before the pattern of cooperation with Zionists in the Jewish Agency had been worked out, British and French anti-Zionists, as we have seen, had rather grudgingly conceded that a Jewish restoration in Palestine need not necessarily have the dire consequences they feared. This clearly implied that if the creation of a Jewish state could not be avoided, these opponents would find a way to put up with it. The American Jewish Committee's cooperation with Zionism in the final stages of the political battle for a Jewish state certainly does not deserve to be called grudging. But on the morrow of Israel's rise they found themselves very much concerned about the effects of the new state upon their own community, and began at once to seek assurances on this point.[8]

To have significant effects upon the Diaspora was, of course, precisely the purpose for which Zionism had sought to establish Jewish sovereignty in Israel. Zionist theories of different types postulated a variety of such effects.[9] Of these, not all proved to be actual, and not all those actually confirmed by events were of the kind against which a body like the American Jewish Committee would wish to obtain assurances, or the State of Israel be likely to give them.

In Zionist theory, the mere existence of the Jewish state, or else the achievement of the highest level of social and cultural excellence that its existence made possible, would serve to solve certain aspects of the Jewish problem. Anti-Semitism, it was believed, was a kind of ghost-fear aroused among the Gentiles by the anomalous survival of the Jews in conditions of dispersion which had caused all other nations to die a natural death. The same cause which called forth anti-Semitism among the Gentiles produced self-hatred and inferiority complexes among Jews who thought themselves emancipated. Both types of malady would be cured by the very existence of the Jewish state, for then Jewish national survival would no longer be an anomaly, but a normal historical process which would cause no morbid anxieties. Thus the psychological aspects of the "problem of the Jews" would be solved.[10] So, too, by making possible the social and cultural development of the Jewish national genius to the highest pitch of its capacities, the state would eventually provide a solution for crucial aspects of the "problem of Judaism." For in dispersion among the Gentiles, Jewish cultural individuality could be maintained only by a kind of rigid separatism which caused it to lose its attraction for minds opened to modern Western thought and expression. After a normal, independent, socially and economically self-subsistent Jewish community was created in Palestine, its revival and realization of Jewish ideals would create forms of culture that would appeal to Jews throughout the world as expressing their own highest and inmost tendencies.[11]

Ideological non-Zionists, unless obsessed with antagonism to Israel, had no reason to object to such effects of the Jewish state, if they were shown to exist. On the other hand, the anti-Zionists had always assumed that a Jewish state would have quite different collateral effects, and, specifically, would increase rather than decrease the danger of anti-Semitism. The non-Zionists, accordingly, were particularly concerned with ascertaining what, in fact, was the effect of Israel's creation.

The evidence was mixed. Inquiries conducted by the American Jewish Committee after the establishment of Israel were reassuring as to the psychological effect of the new independence and militancy of the Jews, for, after acts of terrorism and reprisal by Israelis, the opinion of Jews and Gentiles alike in America continued favorable to the State of Israel.[12] The non-Zionists themselves had long appreciated the "public relations" value of the Zionist society in Palestine, based on a solid core of Jewish farmers and workers: it gave the lie to the anti-Semitic image of the Jew as a congenital middleman, a people made up of Fagins and Shylocks. And a Western non-Zionist could hardly fail to be as moved as the Zionists when the startling demonstrations of enthusiasm for Israel by Soviet Jewry proved that the restoration of Jewish sovereignty had revived what many had thought to be virtually a dead branch of the Jewish people.[13] As for the cultivation of social idealism and cultural excellence, the non-Zionists had regarded this as the special ideological basis of their own interest in Palestine.[14]

On the other hand there was evidence that hostility to the Jews, whether in Israel or in Diaspora countries, had risen sharply or threatened to rise precisely because of the establishment of the state. The chronic difficulties under which the Jews had labored in Moslem countries and, in different forms, in the Soviet zone were made acute and critical by the creation of Israel and its involvement in international politics. Not only were Jews in those lands subjected to new and sharper oppression because of the anti-Zionist and anti-Israel policies of their governments, but the campaign against Israel revived familiar, anti-Semitic motifs and — in the case of the Arabs, at least — was backed by a world-wide anti-Jewish campaign in which the international fraternity of anti-Semites were active partners.[15]

The pairing of anti-Semitism with anti-Zionism was nothing new, of course. It is worth noting that the classic "document" of modern anti-Semitism, the "Protocols of the Elders of Zion," purported to be the records of secret meetings held in Basle on the occasion of the First Zionist Congress in that city. But when the creation of Israel brought Zionism into active conflict with British policy, or when, after its creation, Israel came into lesser collision with American policy, the impetus this gave to anti-Semitic agitation in those lands was a much more serious matter. The non-Zionist bogey of dual loyalties became a tangible menace. Not only was the loyalty of Jews who supported Israel questioned by people who openly declared themselves anti-Semites, as might have been expected. Christian friends of Arab nationalism and critics of Israel who repudiated the name of anti-Semite did not hesitate to predict that Jewish support of Israel could cause the American people to become more actively anti-Semitic.[16]

This was a threat to which non-Zionists must have been especially sensitive, for it was one of the very arguments with which they had opposed the Balfour Declaration, the Biltmore program, and the partition of Palestine. Yet, after the rise of Israel, non-Zionists disregarded the threat and rejected the argument, on the grounds of a well-defined principle. They, too, like the Zionists before them, stood by their right as free citizens in a democratic land to differ with policies of the government in power, including its foreign policies.[17] Holding to this principle, they could not accept the implication that, because of their natural and legitimate sympathy with Israel as Jews, they must disqualify themselves as American citizens from any legitimate political activity involving the interests of Israel. Nor, as self-respecting Jews, could they bow to the threat that such activity on their part would cause a greater number of Americans to become actively anti-Semitic and anti-Semitism to assume more drastic forms. Neither the argument nor the threat could be effective once the non-Zionists had accepted as legitimate the natural Jewish sympathy for the Jewish state. If such a body as the American Jewish Committee were to concede, as a general principle, that it had no right to pursue political activities in any case where its sympathies with Jewish interests were involved, or if it were to submit to threats that such activities would stimulate the growth or intensification of anti-Semitism, then consistency would require it to disband altogether. For the *raison d'être* of the Committee was the defense of Jewish rights, both in the United States and throughout the world.

Two logically separable attitudes, however, were required in order to take this position. It involved not only tacit recognition by the American Jewish Committee that the State of Israel was a legitimate fact, but also the conviction that the natural sympathy of the Diaspora Jews for Israel, shared by the Committee itself, was equally legitimate. The fringe organization of anti-Zionists, the American Council for Judaism, did not contest the legitimacy of the State of Israel, after it was established, as did the Natorei Karta in Jerusalem. But theirs continued to be an anti-Zionist rather than a non-Zionist attitude, because they took the position that it was not legitimate at all for the Jewish community in America to manifest a sympathetic interest in the State of Israel. They distinguished sharply between the State of Israel and the Jewish religious community in Israel, and would only recognize a natural interest in the latter to be proper for American Jews.[18] Taking this view, they themselves imputed a taint of disloyalty to Jews who expressed their natural sympathy for the Jewish state through political channels; though, to be sure, when placed on the defensive by the indignant Jewish consensus, they guarded these charges with a wall of technicalities. So, too, they argued that American Jewish support for Israel would make America more actively and more extensively anti-Semitic, and by their example encouraged Christian anti-Zionists to employ this threat; while, on the other hand, in defense against the indignant Jewish consensus, they urged Arab and Christian anti-Zionist propagandists in America to keep within the bounds of a professedly non-anti-Semitic campaign.[19]

Despite these sharp differences between the attitudes of non-Zionists and anti-Zionists to Israel, their ideological premises were identical. They differed, however, in one vital mythic element: the non-Zionists accepted a natural Jewish sympathy for the Jewish state as proper and hence were able to share it within limits determined by their ideological premises; while the anti-Zionist fringe denied its legitimacy and did not share it at all. Hence, the non-Zionists remained within the general Jewish consensus, while the anti-Zionists placed themselves outside it.

At the same time, in order to maintain their complex position with conviction and persuasiveness, the non-Zionists needed some token that their assumptions were valid. The limits within which they were prepared to accept Jewish sympathy for Israel as being legitimate as well as natural bore upon the question of dual loyalties. They were prepared to defend a spontaneous, free sympathy of Jews with the Jewish state as legitimate. But the charge of dual loyalties implied something quite different: that Jews in the Diaspora supported Israel under a kind of obligatory attachment amounting to political allegiance. The American Jewish Committee not only denied this on its own behalf and on behalf of the whole community of American Jews, but desired to have the denial certified by the Israeli government.

The Western non-Zionists were not alone in this desire, for Diaspora Zionists were equally eager to make the matter quite clear. Zionist organizations themselves issued statements declaring that Jews in the Diaspora had only one political allegiance, their allegiance to the countries of their citizenship, while Israel claimed the political allegiance only of its own citizens.[20] The State of Israel, too, had its own good reasons for making a sharp and formal distinction between its relation to its own citizens and to the Jews of the Diaspora, and it stressed that only Israelis enjoyed the rights and were subject to the obligations of citizenship in the Jewish state.[21] But the American non-Zionists, anxious to hammer the point home, made a number of trips to Israel in order to secure additional, specific and formal avowals that the Jewish state "represents" only its own citizens and that it neither "represents" nor "speaks on behalf of" Jews of any other country.[22]

Such statements merely formulated what was necessarily implied in the establishment of the Jewish state within its political boundaries, and what was well understood in the case of any other state. Even though the statements that were made implied no restriction or qualification of the area of sovereignty logically involved in the very act of creating the State of Israel, the stress laid on this matter by all ideological groups within the Jewish consensus is easy to understand historically.

If the creation of Israel did, indeed, provide psychological solutions for certain aspects of the problem of the Jews, and if the development of a free and elevated Jewish culture and social ethic in Israel would, indeed, solve crucial aspects of the problem of Judaism, such effects must flow from the very being and character of the Jewish state. No government policy was needed or could help Israel to liquidate the ghost-fear and the inferiority complexes that were assumed to result from the anomalous condition of the Jews before the Jewish state arose; and, on the other hand, no policy Israel could adopt, short of abolishing itself, could prevent it from having the supposed effect, if the theory were true. So, too, if Israel were to make a deliberate effort to develop a high order and authentic style of Jewish culture in order, by this means, to maintain Judaism in the Diaspora, such a procedure could only defeat both purposes. Elevation and individuality in a culture, if they can be deliberately fostered as the ends of policy at all, are unquestionably ends in themselves, not means to ulterior ends. A policy designed to produce a high culture packaged for export would only turn out an adulterated product that could have no more than a superficial effect upon the Jewish community abroad. On the other hand, if it is true that Jewish culture possesses basic values which appeal intimately to all who have been significantly formed by its tradition, then vital and authentic expressions of these values, realized in full freedom, would have a mythic force that would evoke a response wherever Jews could participate in them, whether directly or vicariously. If Israel created such values by a genuine dedication, no other policies that it adopted, short of cutting off communication, could prevent it from having this effect on the Diaspora.

The only way in which opponents could reject such Israelian influence, in principle, would be to deny or destroy its legitimate position in relation to world Jewry, or, at any rate, to withdraw themselves entirely from any consensual communication with it. These ways were open only to fringe groups of anti-Zionists who were ready to exclude themselves from the consensus of the Jewish community as a whole. Non-Zionists who were effectively within the community could not reject such effects and influences of Israel upon the community at large or, according to the form and degree of their participation in the general consensus, upon themselves.

However, besides the effects inherently connected with Israel's very existence and free self-expression in culture, Zionist theory had forecast other effects of the Jewish state upon the Jews in the Diaspora which depended upon specific activities that the state might deliberately plan and execute. Opponents of Zionism, for their part, had been concerned not only about the harmful effects which the very existence or the essential character of a Jewish state might have upon the Jewish position in the Diaspora. They were also concerned with the effects of particular policies that the State of Israel might be expected to adopt. On these questions, too, there were negotiations between non-Zionists and the State of Israel, which bore in some respects upon the question of Israel's sovereignty.

Zionist theory had anticipated that the Jewish state could help

solve the Jewish problem by adopting suitable policies in at least
three fields: by organizing the transfer to its territory of all Jews
who could not or would not remain in the Diaspora; by using the
diplomatic and political channels open to a state, in defense of the
rights of Jews remaining in the Diaspora; and by giving assistance
to the Jewish and Hebrew education of Jews in the Diaspora in
preparation for their transfer to Israel, or for maintaining the continuity of Jewish culture in the Diaspora.[23] Opponents of Zionism, on
the other hand, had feared that the policies the Jewish state might
adopt in these very fields would have damaging effects upon the
Diaspora.

The American Jewish Committee, therefore, as a friend and an
interested party likely to be affected by Israel's decisions, did not
hesitate to suggest lines of policy and seek formal assurances on
these matters. There was, of course, a significant distinction between
subjects on which the Committee felt it could properly do no more
than venture a suggestion and those on which it felt entitled to expect
formal assurances. The latter were issues in which Israelian policies
directly applied to the Jews of other countries; and the Committee
was anxious to make it clear, at any rate, that no grounds would be
given for hostile interpretation of such policies as an extension of
Israel's sovereignty to the Diaspora. Thus the Committee sought and
obtained formal assurances that, whatever Israel might do through
channels open to it as a sovereign state in order to protect Jewish
rights abroad, it did not act with any authority "on behalf of" the
Diaspora;[24] and whatever special status might be conferred on the
Jewish Agency, or the Zionist Organization, for conducting its work
in Israel, it did not signify a recognition of that body as the authorized
representative of the Jewish people, or of Diaspora Jewry, considered
as an integral unit with a kind of sovereign will of its own.[25] This
assurance, by the way, denied to the Jewish Agency a status which
it had enjoyed with general, though sometimes tacit, consent under
the Mandate for Palestine.

Even if it were clear beyond question that an Israelian policy
applied only to its own territory and citizens and thus represented
an exercise of sovereignty strictly confined to the normal jurisdiction
of any similar country, the Committee still felt obliged to suggest
that such policies be framed with consideration for the Diaspora
Jews who might be indirectly affected by it. But here the Committee
acted in a different capacity and spirit. The Committee felt entitled
only to offer suggestions for inclusion in the projected constitution
of Israel; to raise questions concerning the marriage and the nationality

laws of Israel; and to argue for liberality in the general Arab policy of Israel.[26] In all these matters Israel's policy was likely to have an indirect effect on Diaspora Jews. It might make some citizens of other countries living in Palestine become at the same time citizens of Israel; and it gave all Jews in the Diaspora the right to come to Israel and become citizens there. Even Israel's policies which affected Diaspora Jews still less directly — for example, its Arab policy — were of potential concern to them, for Israel's treatment of its minorities could reflect on Jewish demands for equality in countries where Jews were a minority. But these were matters so clearly within Israel's unquestioned jurisdiction that an ideological non-Zionist body like the Committee, anxious to keep absolutely clear the line between the sovereign Jewish state and the consensual Jewish community, could not present its proposals in the form of legitimate demands. And it could expect no more from the Jewish state than to listen sympathetically to its suggestions.

When Israel was founded, ideological non-Zionism was no longer the only important expression of Jewish opinion, outside Zionism, that the Jewish state had to take into account in its relations with the Diaspora. Jewish agencies and organizations which had no occasion, because of their restricted purposes, to formulate a position on the issues between Zionists and non-Zionists, or which deliberately refrained from doing so because they comprised a membership including adherents of both views, found themselves interested in and affected by the policies adopted by the Jewish state. Such organizations did not hesitate to seek institutionalized channels for controlling the influence of Israel upon the Diaspora and the Diaspora upon Israel. The general statements issued by all sides stressing that only Israelis enjoyed the rights and bore the obligations of citizenship in Israel were not interpreted by these groups as meaning that the claims of the Diaspora upon Israel, or of Israel upon the Diaspora, had no element of obligation in them. On the contrary, the attempts to organize and channel these reciprocal influences implied a conviction that the claims of each upon the other could be legitimate demands and not merely justified requests.

One would have to dig deep, to be sure, in order to find any implication remotely ideological in the new relationship with Israel of Jewish philanthropic agencies outside the Jewish Agency. Such organizations as the JDC, HIAS, or ORT, who had been concerned with relief and rehabilitation, assistance to emigrants, vocational training and other welfare activities in emergencies affecting Jewish communities throughout the world, found that one of the most important areas for their postwar work was the massive stream of immigration to Israel.[27] The fact that they were now able to conduct Jewish philanthropic activities by agreement with a Jewish government instead of by arrangement with non-Jewish governments altered the nature of the relationship in no respect, either legally or in principle; but it undoubtedly gave it the backing of a consensus instead of merely a contract. Other Jewish agencies and organizations, such as the lay and rabbinical associations of the three Jewish denominations, were concerned not with overseas aid but with the welfare of the Diaspora communities at home. They, too, discovered that the restoration of Jewish sovereignty in Israel — and, on the other hand, the drastic change in the global Jewish situation after World War II — significantly affected the conditions of their own work, presenting altogether new perspectives. They then took up the problem of instituting a stable pattern that would control the relationship between Israel and the Diaspora in pertinent ways. Thereby they opened up questions of appreciable ideological import.

II

The direct and indirect influence of Eastern European Jewry had powerfully affected the orientation of many other Diaspora communities towards their own problems in the prewar period. Its destruction created a divide in Jewish history of such crucial significance that all landmarks had to be shifted.[28] This was the effect upon those large communities, now the major part of all Jewry, which were mainly the offshoots of the Eastern European Diaspora — the Jews of the United States, of the British Commonwealth, and of Latin America. It was true in an even more significant way of the shattered communities in Western Europe now augmented by a refugee mass left by the ebb of Nazi oppression. To a greater or lesser extent, these groups of Jews had been increasingly made up, even before the war, of men and women who were recent immigrants from Eastern Europe, and whose patterns of thought were formed by the situation and attitudes of the Eastern European Diaspora. The disappearance of Eastern European Jewry as a living force and a frame of reference threw them abruptly upon their own resources. It forced them to try charting their historic course toward the future by the unusual method of analyzing the immediate situation and determining its needs in its own terms, without reference to the past.

The genocide of Eastern European Jewry built up a massed force of Jewish revulsion and humiliation throughout the Diaspora for

which Zionism offered some positive emotional outlet. The support in
Jewish communities for the struggle to establish the State of Israel
and defend it against overwhelming attack was so wide and deep
because it was the only remotely adequate, available reply to a vicious
challenge which had compelled European Jewry to die helplessly and
other Jews to stand helplessly by. Subjectively, then, the Zionist
undertaking had profound meaning for all Jews, whether they had
been Zionists before or not. Zionism claimed also to be an objectively
relevant solution for the Jewish problem, a claim which became of
immediate significance when the state was founded and opened its
gates to all Jews. But in making this offer, the Jewish state became
objectively irrelevant from the point of view of the very groups in
the West who, as immigrants from Eastern Europe or as Western
Zionists identifying with the Eastern European consensus, had accepted the Zionist myth and ideology.

The basis for Western Zionism had been the assumption that the
situation of Eastern Europe was the authentic situation of contemporary Jews. What had happened under Hitler left no question, in
the consensus of Jewish opinion, that for the survivors of Eastern
and Central European Jewry transfer to Israel was the only safe and
effective solution of the Jewish problem. Nor was there any significant
ideological difference over the need to remove Jews *en masse*, to the
extent possible, from Arab and Moslem lands or the Soviet zone,
where the aftermath of the war left critical dangers for the community; even though there were differences over tactical questions
and particular diagnoses.[29] The major situation about which ideological controversy was still possible remained that of the Jews in the
free, Western countries themselves.

For Western Jews, mass transfer to Israel seemed an objectively
unreasonable idea, considered as a solution for their particular
problem.[30] Theirs was not "the problem of the Jews" in that drastic
form of acute oppression from which only evacuation could provide
escape; in fact, they did not feel particularly oppressed at all. Their
immediate problem, it was now realized all the more sharply, was
"the problem of Judaism." The disappearance of Eastern European
Jewry threw that problem in high relief; and the restoration of Jewish
sovereignty in Israel was now seen to have a new, critical significance
for its solution, precisely because of the destruction of the Eastern
European Diaspora.

As long as the solid core of Eastern European Jews maintained
its own way of life and, by the unceasing flow of emigration, trans-
planted its values and attitudes to the large Western communities,

there seemed to be a reasonable prospect that the problem of Judaism could be "contained," if not solved, in terms of the probable development of the community. Even in the East, of course, the strict religious tradition of Judaism was no longer universally accepted, but the cultivation of a secular Jewish culture in Yiddish and Hebrew took place within an effective consensus and seemed to foster its continued growth. The Reform and Conservative deviations from Orthodox tradition and the dominance of European languages and non-Jewish schooling in Western countries did not seem to carry enough centrifugal force to overcome the nuclear attraction of the massive Jewish ethnic community of Eastern Europe.

With the destruction of Eastern European Jewry, the nuclear center was destroyed and Western Jews lost the comforting sense of maintaining an orbit around it. Western denominationalism and adaptation to the languages and cultures of diverse European traditions no longer were mere deviations from a central tendency determined by a solid Jewish ethnic tradition. Instead, each such force threatened to become a governing principle determining by itself the direction in which Jewish communities would be impelled. In that case, Latin American Jewish communities, with very little left of Jewish religious tradition and with Spanish beginning to replace Yiddish as their language of discourse, could conceivably be drawn completely out of contact with the Jews of the United States, who defined themselves as a tridenominational religious community and understood each other in English. Similar reflections were in order about the divergencies between the various European and African Diaspora communities where the problem of Judaism had also to be faced. The problem was all the more acute in a generation that had undergone the trauma of the Hitler era, for such men could not escape the sense that Jewish unity was the only resource upon which Jews could safely rely in the face of the always possible ultimate threat.

The problem was felt most sharply by persons and agencies engaged in Jewish education in the Diaspora communities. The solution which most frequently commended itself to them was to seek in Israel a new center that could exert the centripetal attraction once supplied by Eastern Europe. In countries like Argentina and Brazil, or France and Belgium, where Eastern European immigration was recent enough to maintain the tradition of Jewish ethnic unity and secular culture, the direct aid of the Israelian government or of Israelian teachers was welcomed.[31] In the United States, on the other hand, a generation had passed without substantial immigration, and

religious affiliation was the accepted public face of Jewishness. Moreover Jewish education had already developed in established channels
of its own. Consequently, it was preferred to build "cultural bridges"
to Israel from the other direction. Plans were made to encourage,
or even require, rabbis and Hebrew teachers to obtain part of their
training in Israel, and to organize visits, tours, and pilgrimages to
Israel by American Jews, particularly the young.[32] The educational
leaders in the Western Jewish communities, in other words, not only
appreciated a need but recognized an obligation for themselves and
their communities to share to some degree in the developing culture
of Israel and maintain a consensus with it.

Even more significant, perhaps, was the conviction of Western
Jews that Israel must recognize an obligation upon itself to maintain
a consensus with the Diaspora, and to develop such a culture as could
be expected to appeal to all Jews. This was more than a pious formula,
for the kind of demand Western Jewish groups made upon Israel in
this regard implied a quasi-constitutional restriction upon the exercise
of Israel's authority in questions of cultural policy.

These demands were made not only by Diaspora Zionists but by
nominally non-Zionist organizations as well. They were made most
significantly by religious groupings, whether Orthodox, Conservative,
of Reform.

The rise of the State of Israel did not quiet the qualms of Orthodox
Jews which, in the extreme case of the Natorei Karta, resulted in a
denial of its legitimacy. However, ever since the proposal of partition
in 1937, Agudat Israel had known that a Jewish state might well be
established without regard to its wishes, and begun to think that it
might have to accord it "*de facto*" if not "*de jure*" recognition. When
this actually occurred they had negotiated an agreement to establish
a united religious front with Mizrachi, based on the kind of policy
which the latter had adopted within the Zionist Organization and
Jewish Agency, and which Agudat Israel hitherto had rejected as a
basis for joining those organizations. They undertook to accept, as
a minimum, provisions for the full exercise of traditional requirements
in questions of personal status, in groups and localities dominated
by the Orthodox, and in all public facilities which the Orthodox Jews
were entitled to use — in order to be able to fight, through the
political institutions of the Jewish state, for the full domination of
traditional Jewish law in all of Israel, as a maximum objective.[33]

This change of attitude led the Agudat Israel not only to accept
the Jewish state but to join the governmental coalition, which cer-

tainly implied *de jure* as well as *de facto* recognition of the state. Yet, even then, it was a recognition subject to certain reservations. The Orthodox parties continued to regard Jewish tradition as a constitution which Israel must ultimately be brought to respect in full. Existing law not subject to the rule of the Torah was accepted under a kind of general protest, without prejudice to legitimist claims. But not only in Israel did Orthodoxy feel entitled to take such a position. Orthodox groups in the Diaspora, too, felt they had a right to protest vigorously whenever some policy of the Jewish state violated what they regarded as the legitimate constitution of Israel, the same code which they recognized as the divinely instituted law of their life as Jews in the Diaspora. Moreover, this attitude was taken not only by the Diaspora sister parties of the Israelian Mizrachi and Agudat Israel, but also by Orthodox organizations without affiliates in Israel, such as the various associations of Orthodox rabbis and Young Israel, an American organization of Orthodox laymen.[34]

It may be said, as a general statement, that all of Orthodox Jewry, whether Zionist or anti-Zionist before the rise of Israel, or officially Zionist or non-Zionist today, feels itself intimately affected by the character of Israel, as determined by its policies. Not only respect for the learning of Israel's rabbis, but the existence of a compact community able to apply Jewish law more fully and freely than in the Diaspora, make some Western Orthodox Jews hopeful that new religious rulings and examples may emerge there which might help them maintain a traditional way of life in the Diaspora.[35] But the obverse side of this relationship is that violation of Orthodox demands in Israel directly concerns the Diaspora, too; and no Orthodox organization has ideological scruples in exerting whatever pressure it can, within conscience, to influence the policies Israel may follow in such matters.

The Reform and Conservative denominations of American Jewry are concerned with the policies of Israel in certain respects hardly less intimately than are the Orthodox. Their attitude is a more complicated one and, as some of the assumptions upon which it rests have scarcely been formulated, they must be derived from implications.

Nothing would seem less in need of explanation than the dislike of the Conservative and Reform denominations of American Jewry for the legal arrangements that gave Orthodoxy a monopoly of Jewish religious authority, under government sanction, in Israel. At the same time, the recognition by Israel of the jurisdiction of the Orthodox rabbinical courts in marriages, divorces, and other questions of the personal status of members of the Jewish community in Israel introduced nothing radically new. More or less the same legal position, based on Ottoman precedents, already existed under the Mandate,[36] and it aroused no great opposition until it was sanctioned by the Jewish state. The new seriousness with which this matter was regarded by non-Orthodox denominations is a consequence of the new situation in which Western, particularly American, Jewry found itself after World War II.

Those who until then had thought that the Jewish problem was most authentically understood in terms of the situation of Eastern Europe, now were compelled to analyze their own situation, as we have seen, and to consider their own particular problem. The situation of Western Jews — or, at any rate, of the major community in the West, American Jewry, which lived under a constitutional system of strict separation of church and state and was, after a whole generation without immigrants from the East, becoming increasingly a community of native-born Americans — was one in which religious rather than ethnic identification was favored as the formal principle of Jewish cohesion.[37] But precisely this fact raised, as a critical question, the problem of Judaism.

The very rise of Israel made quite untenable any belief that, by sloughing off ethnic elements of Jewish identification and proclaiming religious faith to be the bond that defined a Jew, one would have brought Judaism into harmony with contemporary conditions and solved the Jewish problem. The most impressive single feature of the contemporary situation of world Jewry outside America was the State of Israel. There, Jewishness was largely ethnic; while the Jewish religious tradition, if not ignored, was accepted only in the Orthodox form. American Jewry, on the other hand, not only defined itself as a religious community but was chiefly Conservative and Reform in its composition. If American Jews had made a rigid ideological principle of defining Jews by religious affiliation and denying their ethnic ties (instead of defining Jews publicly by religion and letting their ethnic bond be tacitly understood), it might have precipitated a series of public clashes on religious issues that could easily make the problem insoluble.[38]

It had never been characteristic of America to make an ideological fetish of the *pro forma* definition of the Jews as a religion and thus undermine the ethnic qualities of their cohesion.[39] But even in European countries where this did happen, there were unavoidable ethnic implications (arising ultimately from the fateful fact that Judaism never effectively converted other peoples than the Jews) [40] in the very ideology which denied that the Jews were a national entity. This thesis was most likely to be defended by protagonists of the Reform, or sometimes the Conservative, variety of Judaism, which departed from the strict tradition. They sought warrant for their deviations from Orthodoxy in a historical definition of Judaism. Pharisaism, in its time, they said, had freed Judaism from rigid adherence to petrified codes by insisting on the validity of continuous interpretation. Theorists of Reform Judaism, and later of Conservatism, claimed to be true followers of the Pharisees when they reinterpreted or revised the findings of Orthodox tradition in accordance with the new historical conditions.[41]

But an appeal to history implies the acceptance of a concrete organ through which history voices its judgments; and an appeal to Jewish history by a "progressive" movement means reliance on the verdict of the contemporary Jewish consensus. In the period before the Second World War, the judgment of the Jewish consensus on the Reform and Conservative claims to be valid Jewish beliefs was never made an urgent issue. In spite of ideological controversy over these questions, Reform, Conservative, and Orthodox beliefs and practices dwelt together in some sort of mutual toleration made possible by the ethnic elements of the Jewish consensus. But after the war, American Jewry, plunged into denominational polemics at home because of its own heightened religious awareness,[42] awoke to the challenge implied in Israel's exclusive recognition of Orthodoxy. By this measure, Israel had, in effect, formally denied the validity of Reform and Conservatism as Jewish religious expressions. Relying as they did on history as an organ of religious revelation, Reform and Conservative Judaism necessarily had to appeal against the verdict which the Israel government seemed to be making on behalf of the global Jewish consensus, of which Israelian Jewry was so significant a voice.

But it was not the Israelian government alone which had implicitly rendered a historic verdict invalidating Reform and Conservatism. The same verdict was given by the Israelian Jewish community, which tacitly recognized Orthodoxy as the only genuine expression of Judaism. Reform and Conservatism not only were without legal status in Israel, they were also virtually without adherents. This was, in a way, a far more serious matter for the American denominations than the legal monopoly granted to the Orthodox. For while their doctrine held that changes in religious belief and practice in response to historic situations were valid, it also held that they were valid because — and, hence, insofar as — history served as an organ of revelation. That is to say, it was necessary to distinguish between trivialities and fads of transient circumstance and new universal insights which were occasioned by historic changes. Changes by Conservatism or Reform in religious belief and practice, although made in response to the evident demand of history, nevertheless claimed universal validity no less than did the Orthodox doctrines, attributed to a single exclusive revelation. Such a claim to universal validity demands general recognition. No religious movement of any depth and sincerity could rest satisfied with the recognition of its validity by so narrowly confined, so provincial an organ of historic revelation as the American Jewish community alone; nor could any belief claim universal significance, if it merely expressed the very special and obviously impermanent demands of the midtwentieth century in North America. The least that such a Jewish movement could demand of itself would be the acceptance of its validity by some Jews in all communities within the full range of its historic context. The fact that two major American Jewish denominations remained virtually unrepresented in so significant a community as Israel confronted them with a critical challenge to prove themselves. That challenge could not be ignored without sapping the confidence of Reform and Conservatism in their own validity — a result from which the whole of American Jewry, believed by the Reform and Conservative leaders to depend increasingly upon themselves, would suffer both spiritual and institutional damage.

Three ways suggested themselves as possible methods for obtaining Israelian recognition for the validity of Reform and Conservatism. The first and most direct was to adopt the same approach as the Orthodox Jews in the Diaspora and press the claims of non-Orthodoxy upon the Israelian government as a matter of legitimate right. To some extent, this was the method adopted. Rabbinical investigators, sent by the American denominations, vigorously criticized the Orthodox monopoly in Israel as a breach of the principle of freedom of worship, which, they argued, was best served, in spirit, by the separation of church and state, as in America.[43]

The weaknesses in such a tactic are obvious. The principle of separation of church and state is a specifically American principle, not a traditional Jewish principle like the dominance of Torah, to which the Orthodox legitimists appealed. Freedom of worship, on the other hand, seemed to offer more promising grounds, for it is a basic legal principle to which Israel is formally committed.[44] But in order to make a legal appeal to this principle with conviction and effect, American Reform and Conservatism would have had to rely on some significant group in Israel to complain of religious oppression because it was unable, for example, to be married or divorced by non-Orthodox rabbis. Most Israelis did not regard this as a *religious* grievance.

The second possible method was, accordingly, to seek to stimulate the development of non-Orthodox religious groups in Israel. This could be achieved either by the settlement in Israel of American Reform and Conservative Jews, dedicated to the establishment of their doctrine in the Jewish state, or by the organization of new religious groups among Israelis who, having been estranged from the strict tradition, sought some way of return to Judaism in a non-Orthodox version. Both approaches were recommended and explored by American Reform and Conservative leaders, but naturally it was the possibility of encouraging non-Orthodox religious stirrings among Jews already in Israel which was chiefly considered. In either case, this general approach implied an assumption that, although Israel's recognition of the validity of non-Orthodox expressions of Jewish religion might be vital for the Diaspora — above all, for America — it was, after all, a matter to be determined under Israelian sovereignty, and only Israelis could make such demands effectively, or perhaps even legitimately, upon their government.

A third approach, however, was to seek to use or to create institutional channels whereby the Diaspora could make its own demands effectively and legitimately upon Israel regarding this matter. This, of course, assumed that the religious institutions of the Jewish state were not a matter to be considered exclusively within the jurisdiction of Israel, but, insofar as they affected Diaspora Jewry, were subject to some form of authority to be exercised by all Jews throughout the world. The one who advocated such views most articulately was Dr. Mordecai M. Kaplan. He proposed that the organizations of Reform and Conservative Jews, which already cooperated with the Jewish Agency as officially non-Zionist bodies ready to support the existence and growth of Israel, should now join the Zionist Organization and through its channels seek to advance the acceptance of non-Orthodox Judaism in Israel.[45] As for the Zionist Organization itself, he sought to reshape it as the vehicle of a world-wide covenant of Jews, both in Israel and the Diaspora, in which not only Conservatism and Reform and his own Reconstructionist doctrine, but the "secularist" way of the life of non-Orthodox Jews in Israel would be given religious sanction as valid expressions of Judaism.[46]

III

Whether Diaspora Jews could make legitimate demands regarding the policies of the Israelian government or whether this remained the prerogative of Israelis alone was a question which arose far more sharply in the World Zionist Organization itself. Before the Jewish state was created, there had already been some ideological differences vaguely involving this very point, but there was no reason to formulate the implicit oppositions openly.

The principle that the national home constituted an obligation of the mandatary to the Jewish people throughout the world was stoutly defended, as we shall see, by all Zionist groups in the face of tendencies among the British to restrict the obligation to the Jewish community already established in Palestine. On the other hand, the growing Zionist settlement in Palestine began to occupy an increasingly important and privileged position in the policy-making of the national home. To grant wide autonomy to the worker-settlers in determining the social structure and economy of their settlements was a natural decision in a project which depended so greatly on the pioneering initiative of its front-line forces.[47] It was, perhaps, equally natural to adopt the principle of doubling the representation granted to Palestinian settlers in comparison with that of most Diaspora electors to the Zionist Congress.[48] Thus while the "sovereignty" of the Jewish people, as expressed in the Zionist Congress, was shared by Jews throughout the world, it was shared in double measure by Palestinian Jews.

This "sovereignty," of course, was internationally recognized solely for the restricted purpose of cooperating with the mandatary in building the Jewish national home. The privileged position granted to Palestinians suggested that, once the national home was built, the implied principle of distinction might become a principle of division. Instead of a fractional share of sovereignty, Diaspora Jews might be granted none, and instead of a privileged share, the Jews in Israel might claim the exclusive right of determining the destiny of the Jewish state.

Such a possibility was latent in one of the two lines of reasoning which could justify granting a share to Diaspora Jews in determining the destiny of the Jewish national home. If the Zionist Organization was considered to be composed of those who could not or would not assimilate in the Diaspora, then, in voting on matters of national home policy, Diaspora Zionists were only helping to determine the character of what would one day be their own country. For this reason, their right to a share in the sovereign decisions of the Jewish Agency rested on a stronger and more valid claim than that of non-Zionists in the Jewish Agency, just as the settlers who already lived in Palestine had a greater right to share in such an exercise of sovereignty than they. But this implied that, once the Jewish state was established, sovereignty in all its decisions — perhaps after a reasonable period of transition to permit everyone to come there who was destined to do so — would rest exclusively with those in the country. And, in fact, in the very first Zionist Congress after the establishment of the state, the Israeli Zionists strongly argued for a revision of the Basle program, still the official program of the Zionist Organization. They proposed to replace it with a formula that would make it obligatory on all Zionists to immigrate to Israel, now that the doors of the Jewish state were open to them.[49] This clearly implied that in a reasonably limited period all those who were entitled to participate in the sovereign decisions of the people returning from Exile would be gathered together in Israel; and then instead of the Zionist Organization's functioning like a kind of Government-in-Exile, sovereignty would be exclusively exercised by the Jewish state, in the normal way.

This line of thought presented no problem when only theories were involved, for it implied the assumption that, following the establishment of the state, the Jewish communities in the Diaspora would disappear by emigration or assimilation. But conditions after 1948 did not meet the requirements of this theory. Not only did large Jewish communities seem likely to persist in the Diaspora after the rise of the state. It was an even greater difficulty that Zionists from the free West found it quite unreasonable to be expected to go to Israel as a duty. The new question arose, whether Zionist ideology could permit not only Jewish communities but Zionists to remain in the Diaspora, and, if this were possible, what sort of sovereign will would be embodied in the Zionist Organization in relation to Israel. An alternative doctrine existed, of course, which could justify the continued existence of Diaspora communities as well as the continued exercise of authority in certain matters in Israel and the Diaspora by the Zionist Organization. There had always been a strand of doctrine which implied that the Jewish people was a national entity whose sovereign will should be exercised not only in seeking to establish the Jewish state but in seeking, at least as an immediate aim, to secure its survival in the Diaspora as well. On these grounds, one could argue that the creation of the State of Israel, or even the ultimate completion of the ingathering of exiles, would not end the Zionist Organization's task and its need for authority. For Jewish communities would continue to exist both in Israel and in the Diaspora, and a world-wide national organization of Jews would have to assume a kind of sovereign responsibility for their survival.

However, in the generation from the Balfour Declaration to the creation of Israel events had taken a course inconvenient for such a theory. For, the two major activities capable, in the Zionist view, of assuring the survival of a Jewish national entity in the Diaspora had, in the interval, been committed to the care of other organizations. The defense of the rights of Jewish Diaspora communities was undertaken by the World Jewish Congress, in which Zionists who leaned to the theory of Diaspora "survivalism" were active leaders. The advancement of Hebrew culture and Jewish education was the concern of well-established local and international agencies outside the Zionist Organization in which, too, Zionists were active. There was some support, to be sure, for the rather vaguely expressed notion (similar to the already noted proposals of Mordecai M. Kaplan) that these functions, together with the remaining functions of the Zionist Organization within Israel, should be reorganized under the aegis of a single democratically organized body expressing the will to survival of the bulk of the Jewish people.[50] But not only did established patterns and vested interests prevent this idea from having much attraction. Anything reminiscent of Jewish sovereignty, an idea that was necessarily examined far more closely after the rise of the Jewish state, no longer seemed applicable in reference to a global organization of Diaspora Jewry. American Jewry, which had never been able to agree on a unified representative agency of its own, began to take its situation as the norm of Diaspora Jewishness. From the American point of view sovereignty was proper, in a Jewish context, only to the State of Israel. A voluntary, contractual, limited relationship seemed a more appropriate form of organization for Jewish agencies devoted to the interests of Jews in the Diaspora.

The possibility of formulating a full and defensible ideological justification for continuing the Zionist Organization as the authorized representative of world Jewry in Palestine even after the rise of Israel was thus precluded. Only a few leaders, like Nahum Goldmann, were prepared to support some of the ideological theses which this might imply.[51] An alternative ideological position, also rejected by the Diaspora Zionists, was proposed by the Israelis. While foreseeing the absorption of all Jewish sovereignty together with all Jewish exiles in Israel, they nonetheless suggested a defensible ideological basis for the exercise of a kind of provisional authority by the Zionist

Organization. It would be natural to concede such rights to prospective Israelis, still making their way, for a period of years, to the national home. But this theory, too, was impossible for Zionists who regarded the Diaspora as their permanent home. Yet, with both conceivable approaches to an ideological justification blocked, the Zionist Organization, in actuality, continued to exercise certain quasi-governmental powers in much the same way that the Jewish Agency had done under the Mandate. The fundamental ideological problem could be evaded or overlooked; but there was no way to avoid the practical problems, and the ideological perplexities they contained.

The rise of the Jewish state relieved the Jewish Agency of some of its most significant functions together with the status inherent in them. In the United Nations discussions leading to the 1947 Partition Resolution, the Agency had reached its peak as a kind of government-in-exile of the Jewish people seeking sovereignty in Palestine. It had conducted the crucial political struggle for the Zionist aim as the "legally and publicly" recognized representative of a sovereign national will.[52] This function and status was taken over by the Jewish state. While there continued to be urgent need for supporting the cause of the new state in the political emergencies that repeatedly beset it, the Zionists in all parts of the world had no recognized jurisdiction to act in this field which could distinguish them from the non-Zionists in the Jewish community who were also ready to extend sympathy and aid. On the other hand, by title and description the Zionists were singled out as being especially concerned with Israel's welfare. Consequently, it was natural for the Jewish Agency to take the initiative in rallying other Jewish organizations in America when a political crisis arose for Israel, even though it might no longer feel obliged or empowered to act as the authorized representative of the Jewish people in all the political concerns of Israel.[53]

The responsibilities of the Agency in organizing the immigration and resettlement of Jews in Palestine, on the other hand, suddenly underwent an extraordinary expansion. The rate of immigration and settlement far exceeded all previous experience, and so, too, did the contributed funds channeled through the Jewish Agency by the Diaspora communities. However, the expanded resources of the Jewish Agency did not, by far, suffice to provide for the existing needs; a major part of the burden fell upon the fiscal capacity of the state itself.[54] Moreover, the planned development necessary to absorb the great increase of population and eventually make it self-sustaining was pursued far more vigorously by the government of Israel than it had been by the Mandatory government. Under the Mandate the

Jewish Agency had assumed virtually complete responsibility in these matters because of the default of the government. Now it became necessary to establish a specific form of coordination between the two authorities.

In another field where the conditions after the rise of Israel suggested an expansion of activities by the World Zionist Organization, the Jewish state for the most part was not a factor. This field was the promotion of Jewish education and Hebrew culture in the Diaspora. Those Diaspora Zionists who were not ready to accept an obligation to go to Israel and who nevertheless insisted that they were Zionists had a special ideological interest in this area, for it could provide a distinction proving them to be something more than the non-Zionist "friends of Israel." It seemed to be a doctrine particularly appropriate for Zionists rather than non-Zionists that not only abstract religious beliefs but an active social and cultural consensus made Jews one people throughout the world. To preserve and foster that consensus by educational and cultural work was a natural function that could give ideological definition to the Zionist movement in the Diaspora.[55] The Israelis were equally interested in an expansion of Zionist cultural and educational work in the Diaspora, and they generally agreed that the Jewish Agency rather than the Jewish state must take the lead in this field. For they began to concede that, since Jews in the free democracies feared no oppression, only deep roots in Jewish culture would impel them to immigrate to Israel, where they could give their Jewish values fuller expression. And they understood that, with minor exceptions, the Jewish Agency rather than the Jewish state was the appropriate instrument for coordinating and stimulating efforts to disseminate Jewish values in accordance with Zionist objectives.[56]

But, as it turned out, the increased activity of the Jewish Agency in promoting Jewish education and Hebrew culture in the Diaspora did not take forms that made it possible to claim or advantageously exploit the responsibilities and prerogatives of a central authority in the Jewish community. The Agency was able to work, with some effect, largely by extending to existing bodies responsible for education and culture auxiliary services which they welcomed. It gave them excellent facilities for contact and communication with the rapidly developing Israelian culture and society, helping them to organize trips and cultural exchanges. The expanded functions of the Agency in this field, far from requiring a status of general authority on behalf of the Jewish people, often demanded a disclaimer of such status.[57] For the educational institutions welcomed the services offered by the

Jewish Agency only when they were implied no claim to control educational aims and methods.

Only in one field did the responsibilities of the Jewish Agency seem to many Zionists, particularly Diaspora Zionists, to require a quasi-sovereign status. Such demands were made on behalf of the Jewish Agency in connection with its functions in governing the flow of immigration and progress of resettlement in Israel in cooperation with the Jewish state.

The authority retained by the Zionist Organization and its subordinate bodies in Israel is symbolically quite impressive. The Jewish National Fund shares under Israelian statute extensive powers to preempt and develop abandoned lands in Israel; and the Fund is an agency supported by contributions of Jews everywhere and governed ultimately by the Zionist Organization.[58] The State of Israel, moreover, has committed itself to a symbolic entity, the Jewish people throughout the world, to admit freely any Jew who wishes to enter its gates.[59] This is, of course, a moral rather than a legal commitment, for the immigration law quite obviously represents a sovereign decision of Israel's legislature; and it establishes a policy of free immigration, subject to the exclusion of individual Jews, by exception, on grounds of endangering public security or public health. Moreover, when immigration must be encouraged, as in recent years, by providing tax relief, job placement, and similar inducements to professional experts or investors, or to Israeli students remaining abroad, government agencies are of course the major controlling factors. But the bulk of immigration to Israel came in *en masse*, as refugees with no means of support or immediately required skills. In their case, the effective limitation on the number and kind of immigrants was not imposed by the Israelian government, which simply allowed free entry. The controlling element was the Jewish Agency's ability or willingness to transport and shelter all those who wished to come and the priorities and selective principles it adopted to regulate the flow.

This body of laws and institutional relationships is an emphatic demonstration of the extent to which, symbolically at any rate, the State of Israel is willing to recognize the Jewish people as possessed of a sovereign will to which it is prepared to dedicate its own sovereignty in important respects. Whether the recognition is more than symbolic depends on the kind of authority exercised by the Zionist Organization, the only body that has some pretension to act in Israel specifically on behalf of world Jewry — not merely symbolically (as the Jewish state itself may do), but with a certain representative power.

Whatever its limitations, the power structure of the Zionist Organization is independently constituted. In determining its policies it is not in theory subordinate to the Jewish state, however much it may depend, in practice, upon the policies independently arrived at by the state, with which its own most important functions must be coordinated.

No other testimony to the significant independent power of the Zionist Organization is needed than the debate which took place after 1948 between Israelian and Diaspora Zionist groups concerning the internal structure and electoral procedures of the Organization. Apart from the complicated and not entirely consistent ideological theses of this debate, it was based on the hard fact that substantial political advantages were at stake. Before the destruction of Eastern European Jewry, the strength of the various parties in Palestine had been roughly paralleled by their strength abroad. The effects of the war, however, led to a great increase in the relative strength of Western communities within the World Zionist Organization. As a result, the dominantly left-of-center Israeli government parties were faced by dominantly right-of-center Diaspora Zionist parties in the Zionist Organization.

Consequently, two issues were long and bitterly discussed. The major Diaspora Zionist parties strongly argued that the double weight granted to Israeli electors as compared with Diaspora electors in the Zionist Organization was no longer justified after the rise of the Jewish state. The major Israeli parties, however, were long reluctant to give up this privileged status, which enabled them to keep the same rough parallelism of power relationships between the Israel government coalition and the Zionist Executive as had been guaranteed by Eastern European votes before the war.[60]

They took the offensive, for their part, by pressing the demand that the Zionist movement in the Diaspora be reorganized in such a way that it could attract sympathizers not willing to identify themselves with one of the existing Zionist parties, linked, as they generally were, to sister parties in Israel that were involved in the internal political struggles of the Jewish state. If this Israeli demand were effectively carried out, the Zionist movement might be expected, under the influence of newly affiliated groups and individual members, to observe self-imposed limitations in the exercise of its authority. Such a reorganized and expanded Zionist movement would undoubtedly follow a general rule of avoiding controversial issues between Israeli parties in order to be able to cooperate with any Israeli government that might arise.[61]

Resolutions demanding the reorganization of the Diaspora Zionist movement along such lines were very slow in taking effect. But, in the meantime, the Israeli government cultivated an increasingly important network of relationships that brought it into direct contact with agencies and institutions of the Diaspora Jewish community, particularly in the United States, outside the Zionist Organization. Such a threat to its traditional prerogatives impelled the Zionist Organization to seek a statutory definition of its rights.

These underlying differences can be traced in the documents and discussions bearing directly on the question of the status of the Zionist Organization in Israel and the Diaspora. The "Zionist Organization-Jewish Agency for Palestine Status Law" of November 24, 1952, contains the following pertinent paragraphs:

(1) The State of Israel regards itself as the creation of the entire Jewish people, and its gates are open, in accordance with its laws, to every Jew wishing to immigrate into it.

(2) The World Zionist Organization, from its foundation five decades ago, headed the movement and efforts of the Jewish people to realize the age-old vision of the return to its homeland, and with the assistance of other Jewish circles and bodies, carried the main responsibility for establishing the State of Israel.

(3) The World Zionist Organization, which is also the Jewish Agency for Palestine, takes care, as before, of immigration and directs absorption and settlement projects in the State.

(4) The State of Israel recognizes the World Zionist Organization as the authorized agency which will continue to operate in the State of Israel for the development and settlement of the country, the absorption of immigrants from the Diaspora and the co-ordination of the activities in Israel of Jewish institutions and organizations active in those fields.

(5) The mission of gathering in the exiles, which is the central task of the State of Israel and the Zionist Movement in our days, requires constant efforts by the Jewish people in the Diaspora; the State of Israel, therefore, expects the co-operation of all Jews, as individuals and groups building up the State and assisting the immigration into it of the masses of the people, and regards the unity of all sections of Jewry as necessary for this purpose.

(6) The State of Israel expects efforts on the part of the World Zionist Organization for achieving this unity; if, to this end, the Zionist Organization, with the consent of the Government and the approval of the Knesset, should decide to broaden its basis, the enlarged body will enjoy the status conferred upon the World Zionist Organization in the State of Israel.[62]

These provisions gave the World Zionist Organization, or the Jewish Agency, much the same general position and functions as it had had under the Mandate. However, on two points the Zionist Congress desired a more specific grant of authority. That the Jewish Agency was referred to in the Mandate as authorized to cooperate with the mandatary in matters of Jewish immigration and settlement and to receive concessions for the development of waste lands implied a preferential if not an exclusive status over against other bodies that might wish to conduct similar activities. The Zionist Organization now desired the Jewish state to make this explicit. So, too, it was implicit in the Mandate's references to the World Zionist Organization and the Jewish Agency that these bodies were recognized as representing the Jewish people and expressing its sovereign will. This, again, the Zionists wished to have explicitly stated by the Jewish state.

To grant the first request did not mean the same thing as to grant the second. The Jewish state could, in principle, grant the Jewish Agency the same kind of exclusive or paramount rights in order to bring people in and settle them as it granted to oil companies in order to explore or develop a specified part of its economic resources,[63] without certifying that the Jewish Agency, any more than the oil company, represented an ethnic body and expressed its sovereign will. The provision included in paragraph 4 of the Status Law, granting the Jewish Agency the right to "coordinate" the activities of other Jewish organizations active along parallel lines in Israel, enabled it to plan on a large scale, without fear of other, minor operations that might otherwise work at crosspurposes. It did not recognize the desired status of the Agency as the authorized representative in Israel of the will of the Jewish people.

The Twenty-Third Zionist Congress had formulated its own view on this point in a resolution proposing that the Zionist Organization be recognized as the "representative of the Jewish people in all matters that relate to organized participation of Jews the world over in the development and upbuilding of the land and the rapid absorption of newcomers." [64] The Zionist demand had strong support in Israel. It was accepted in a draft bill which proposed to recognize the World Zionist Organization as the "representative organization" of the Jewish people, and which passed a preliminary reading in Israel's parliament, the Knesset.[65] On the other hand, the formulation proposed by the Twenty-Third Zionist Congress had been strongly opposed by non-Zionists like the American Jewish Committee.[66] The government of Israel, accepting the view that it was neither wise nor warranted for it to recognize by statute a "representative organization" for world Jewry, finally withdrew from consideration the draft in which this phrase had been used. When resubmitted, the law (paragraph 4) recognized the Zionist Organization only as an "authorized agency," not as a "representative organization," in carrying out its defined responsibilities.

To be sure, historical references in the law to the part played by the Jewish people in building the national home and the need for organized unity of all Jews for the same purpose in the future, as well as to the crucial responsibility of the Jewish Agency in both connections, could well be construed as encouragement for the Zionists. These phrases were surely calculated to strengthen the Zionist conviction of having expressed the will of their people in the past and assure them that they still represented it in spirit. But the State of Israel had refused the Zionist demand to give formal recognition to this implied relationship between the Zionist movement and the Jewish people, suggesting instead that the Zionists seek such recognition elsewhere, by enlarging the Jewish Agency to include the non-Zionists. The total effect was to discourage, rather than encourage, the Zionist feeling that they really were entitled to represent the Jewish people.

The fact is that more fundamental, if less obvious, reasons than the refusal of the Israelian government to sanction by statute a "representative organization" for world Jewry underlay the Zionists' loss of the sense that they expressed the sovereign will of the Jewish people. The assurance that the Jewish people *had* a sovereign will and that the Zionist movement was its authentic expression, just as the Zionist Organization was its legitimate embodiment, was not something which arose when the Balfour Declaration was addressed to the Zionist movement; nor was it established by the references in the Mandate to the Jewish Agency. Zionism itself evoked this new political reality when it created the myth of auto-Emancipation, and gave the living consensus of the Jewish people an active, historically specific direction. The Diaspora Zionists who demanded that the Jewish state recognize the Zionist Organization as the representative organ of World Jewry were no longer borne up by a mythic conviction that united them all and gave them assurance in speaking for the Jewish people. The Israeli proponents of this demand did have a mythic foundation for claiming to voice the historic will of the Jewish people. They were passionately convinced that what had happened to Jews in Europe could happen anywhere, that destruction or assimilation would liquidate the remaining Jewish communities throughout the Diaspora, and consequently all who wished to survive as Jews must prepare themselves to immigrate to Israel. In the name of this desperate necessity, they demanded that the Zionists assume, and Israel recognize, the right to act on behalf of the Jewish people throughout the world. The Israelis, however, were of less importance as representatives of the will of world Jewry than were the Diaspora Zionists, for it was the problem of the Diaspora that Zionism still desired to solve. Diaspora Zionists were far from accepting the idea of total Jewish ingathering to Israel either as a personal obligation or as a mythic foundation for their movement — and they had no alternative myth from which to draw any assurance of an historic mission. If the State of Israel did not enact a representative status for them, they no longer had the assurance to act as the legitimate agent of a sovereign Jewish will. They were reduced to spokesmen of established organizational interests and vested rights, seeking to reach a new arrangement with the Jewish state that would meet new needs while causing the least possible disturbance to existing institutions.

IV

The symbolic or effective restrictions upon Israel's sovereignty involved in the obligations it assumed toward world Jewry also had appreciable effects upon Israel's relations with other countries. The Zionist functions which it was the duty of the Jewish state to perform were constantly referred to in debates on foreign policy. As in the economic, social, and cultural policy of Israel, so, too, in its foreign policy, the interests of the already settled population, their security and well-being, were more immediately effective forces than the Zionist ideal. Much that was symbolically justified on Zionist grounds was accepted because it also seemed to serve the interests of the Israelis themselves. On the other hand, as in domestic policy, so, too, in foreign policy, there were things done out of a commitment to Zionism which were hard to justify in terms of the immediate interests of the Israelis themselves. This real, and not merely symbolic, subordination of the exercise of Israel's sovereignty to the imputed historic will of the Jewish people was sometimes defended on not very convincing grounds as consonant with the interests of the Israelis themselves. Sometimes, however, it was openly avowed as a Zionist duty whose cost must be gladly borne. Such an argument, whether merely symbolic or quite material, had a persuasive effect upon the Israelian consensus, in spite of the fact that it was not always enough to override domestic interests. Only the small fringe group whom the hostile consensus called "Canaanites" adopted an open ideological position calling upon Israel to sever its tie with Judaism and renounce the duty of solving the Jewish problem in order to seek the integration of its settled population within a regional political and social-cultural system.[67]

There are two Zionist functions involving Israel's foreign policy and international relations which the ideology had expected the Jewish state to perform. The first is the protection of Jewish rights in the Diaspora through international diplomatic channels; the second is the ingathering of the exiles. Israel has not been able to do a great deal about the first of these functions, but Israel's immigration policy has been an important factor in shaping Israel's foreign policy and an argument constantly used in debating it.

The idea that Israel could use international channels open to it as a state on behalf of Jews in other countries, a doctrine frequently heard in early Zionist arguments, is by no means unparalleled. India used the United Nations persistently and with effect as an agency to bring pressure on South Africa in regard to its race policies. So, too, the Arab nations appealed effectively to this forum on the rights of Arab nationalism in North Africa. Israel, however, did not find it possible to appeal with the same degree of confidence on the oppression of Jews in the Soviet Union and its satellites, or in Arab countries.

If there was little success, it was not for want of effort.[68] On January 7, 1960, Israel's Foreign Ministry intervened to some effect in a series of notes to governments of countries touched by the wave of swastika smearings of the end of 1959. In the following spring, the Eichmann seizure and trial was boldly carried out, as Ben-Gurion said, on the grounds that only Israel, as "a Jewish State in actuality, and . . . potentially the State of the victims, could be the rightful plaintiff . . . [in] an act of historic justice to the entire Jewish people." But an attempt in 1964 to include a specific reference to anti-Semitism in a draft convention for the elimination of racial discrimination was defeated in the United Nations Commission for Human Rights when the Soviet Union demanded that Zionism should also be specifically condemned, along with "Nazism, neo-Nazism, and all other forms of colonialist policy and ideology, hatred, nationalist exclusiveness and racialism." Since then the Communist bloc countries have developed the theme of a "Zionist world conspiracy" into a propaganda weapon of equal virulence and widespread effect with the notorious Protocols of the Elders of Zion. Following the Six Day War, June 5–10, 1967, Israel was similarly frustrated in its attempt to secure international aid for Jews imprisoned and oppressed in Arab countries. This, indeed, evoked a backlash reaction from none other than the

United Nations Secretary General himself. Not only has Israelian intervention often been unimpressive in its success: Israel has had to beware of endangering Diaspora Jews by too active a campaign in their behalf.

The reasons, if obvious, are instructive. The position of Israel in the United Nations is one of relative weakness and isolation. Far from having influence to exert on behalf of fellow Jews abroad, it must constantly defend itself, relying frequently on the influence of Diaspora Jewish communities. On the other hand, the international position of the countries whose treatment of the Jews gives cause for complaint is exceedingly strong. The Soviet Union can and does disregard the opinion of the United Nations on matters of considerably greater interest in global *Hochpolitik* than the treatment of Jews. The Arab countries occupy so strategic a bargaining position in the balance between East and West that only the most direct threat to their own interests can cause other nations to act or speak against them.[69] But this is only half of the account. For not only are the diplomatic facilities of Israel of little use to alleviate these sufferings. The acute phase of Jewish oppression in the Arab and Soviet bloc countries was brought on by the creation of Israel. Arab hostility to the new state and Soviet interest in exploiting Arab nationalism against the West — these are causes of anti-Jewish policies in the countries in question which only the destruction or defeat of Israel could eliminate.

There could be no question, then, of adjusting Israel's foreign policy or international relations in order to carry out more effectively the Zionist duty of defending Jewish rights in the Diaspora countries where they are most threatened. This obligation was not brought up as a significant consideration in foreign policy debate. On the other hand, the Zionist duty of ingathering the exiles is an argument that both defenders and critics of government policy resorted to continually, each in his own interpretation of its international implications.

The mass migrations to Israel have come in large part from countries hostile to the Jewish state or even technically at war with it. Under the circumstances, in order to make the movements of population possible, diplomatic negotiations, usually of a highly indirect sort, were required.[70] But unlike similar cases where hostile peoples negotiated population movements between them, the intricate international dealings which produced the flow of Jews from Yemen and Iraq or from Russia and Poland to Israel did not lead to peace or to permanently improved relations between the parties. Because of this

Israel could never make provisions for the kind of immigrant flow
that would meet its Zionist obligation while at the same time regulating the rate and character of immigration according to the requirements of economic and social stability. Turkey's treaties with the Balkan
countries are an example of the kind of gradual transfer of large
groups which might have been arranged for if Israel had been able
to consult its own immediate interests in negotiating the mass migrations.[71] But lacking a basis of good will — or even, in many cases,
direct contact — Israel was forced to accept its migrants from zones
of acute oppression under conditions which completely ignored and
often violated such normal considerations.

The Israeli public in the beginning was itself overwhelmingly
impressed by the desperate need for immigration. It was convinced,
moreover, that the demands of Israel's security, no less than the
perilous situation of the imimgrants, dictated as rapid and massive
an ingathering as could be managed by opening the doors of Israel
wide and by straining the resources of all world Jewry to their utmost.
Faced with the immense odds of five or six armies and forty million
foes, they saw any accession of numbers as an accession of strength.
But when the fighting ceased and economic problems came into the
foreground, the immediate interests of the Israelis seemed far less
compatible with the Zionist urge for rapid and indiscriminate ingathering.

Public opinion polls conducted in 1949 showed a significant confusion in attitudes about the question. The consensus of opinion,
by an overwhelming majority, was still against limiting the extent
of Jewish immigration; but an even larger majority was in favor of
planning and regulating it, and bringing immigration and the economic absorptive capacity of the country into conformity with each
other. Most Israelis took the position that such conformity could be
brought about, without cutting down immigration, by expanding the
absorptive capacity of the country.[72] The Israeli public was shown
to be prone, like other publics, not only to wishful thinking but to
conclusions based on ignorance of the facts in regard to a major
ideological issue like immigration; but at the same time there was a
clear awareness of the threat to Israel's social and economic stability
of an undirected and unselected as well as unlimited immigration.

In the years that followed, immigration into Israel was placed
under more effective regulation by the policy of the World Zionist
Organization.[73] It was selected, directed to settlement areas, and, in
regard to certain countries, limited, according to plans which took

into account the balanced development of Israel's economic and social structure, and not only the pressure of emergency needs and Zionist duties. But at the same time, all such plans were subject to sudden, drastic revisions, since Zionist duties could at any time become paramount. The decisive factor in these changes were not the immediate interests of settled Israelis, but the shifts in policy of countries like Morocco and Egypt or Russia, Poland, and Hungary. Israel's, or, for that matter, the Zionist Organization's, policy of orderly immigration was likely to be set aside at any time by such emergencies.

The clash with immediate social and economic interests can only be obscured, not effaced, by arguing that Israel gains security from increased population. Speculation that Russia might release a mass of Jewish emigrants spread simultaneously with the habit of saying that Israel would be secure against attack, given a population of five million.[74] It is impossible to deny the burdens of a small people faced with Israel's security tasks. The Six Day War in 1967, with its legacy of large new areas and Arab populations, sharply increased the efforts involved. But obviously no conceivable rise in Jewish immigration could seriously alter the disparity in numbers between Israel and its sworn foes. The argument of increased security as the reason for favoring Jewish immigration represents an attempt to justify on grounds of self-interest what is, in fact, accepted as a Zionist duty, regardless of self-interest.

There is, on the other hand, an equally prevalent Israelian habit of arguing in terms of Zionist duty over differences on foreign policy which are actually motivated by, and decided on grounds of, interpretations of the requirements for Israel's self-preservation. These differences are focused, of course, on the crucial issue of all international politics in our day, the global conflict between East and West.

The political parties in Israel, running the usual gamut of contemporary ideologies from Left to Right, had the usual ideological reasons for favoring an association of Israel with either the Communist East or the Western democracies. They also usually estimated the chances of Western or Eastern victory in the global war in accordance with their ideological leanings. But the policy to which the consensus of Israeli opinion most naturally leaned, in the beginning, was a policy of neutrality or "nonidentification." This reflected not only the most feasible basis for a government coalition, given the division of opinion with which Israel started, nor just the instinctive prompting of prudence to avoid entanglement in the struggle of the titans. It also seemed, at first sight, to be most in accord with the Zionist duty of the Jewish state towards a Diaspora divided between Eastern and Western countries.

Diaspora Jewry, as Israel saw it, could be classed in three groups. There was the uprooted or crisis-afflicted mass of Jews in Europe, Africa, and Asia that made up the vast ingathering of exiles into Israel. There was, on the other hand, the powerful Jewish community in Western countries that did not yet recognize its need to be ingathered, but gave indispensable financial assistance, technical aid, and political support without which the ingathering would have been impossible. In addition to these, there was the great Russian Jewry, kept apart for a generation from the fellowship of Jews throughout the world. This community was especially dear to the Israeli leaders, the pioneers who themselves had come from the Russian Empire and its successor states a generation earlier to establish the institutions of Israel. The hope of reunion with Russian Jews, when they would be permitted at last to come to Israel, was never allowed to die among these old Zionists. In the days of mass migration from strange and backward countries, they looked with redoubled desire to the Soviet Zone. They hoped that doors might be opened there that would bring them a fresh stream of young, active, technically skilled Jewish immigrants, sharing the traditions of European socialism and the ardor for Jewish auto-Emancipation that had been built into the institutions of Israel.[75]

Another element, of mythic character, that entered into the situation was the wish to be free at length of the characteristic plight of the Jew in Exile, who was forced to assume actively or suffer passively his involvement in quarrels which pitted him always against his brother Jews across the border. Only the revolutionaries among Eastern European Jews felt a true personal involvement in the politics of the Gentiles; and in the wars of the Gentiles the others were loyal to their sovereign out of customary obedience, not out of a real devotion. This was not an attitude that could do anything to dull the edge of the tragedy of fighting other Jews. Zionists hoped that in coming to Israel they would find in their loyalty to the Jewish state an allegiance based on deep commitment and, at the same time, inherently unable to bring them into battle against the other Jews.[76] The struggle between East and West involved precisely this danger. Israel had brethren on both sides of the barriers between the contending blocs, and it had Zionist obligations that, in principle, encompassed both. The natural inclination of the Israelian consensus was toward a position that would not involve the country on either side.

The realities of Israel's situation, however, were against a rigidly neutral policy. The aid which Israel was able to obtain only from the West — from Western Jews and Western governments — as well as the strategic dominance of the West in the Mediterranean area; and then, on the other hand, the greater ruthlessness and success with which Russia was able to play a pro-Arab game: these determined the dependence of Israel on the West for its self-preservation. The foreign policy of Israel was soon defined as one not of "neutrality" but of "nonidentification." Nor did the trend stop there, for increasingly Israel was forced to turn to the West (often with indifferent success) for the means of self-defense and assurances of survival that it was hopeless to seek in the East after Moscow committed itself to rearming Egypt and Syria.[77]

Leftist groups in Israel, not only believing in the ultimate socialist salvation of Russia if not in its contemporary socialism but believing also in its probable victory over the West, feared and disapproved this tendency. But (apart from the Communists — and even they were split by the Six Day War) they were forced by events to understand that no policy Israel adopted could win over Russia from its cold calculation of the advantages of a pro-Arab and anti-Israel policy. The Russian willingness to hint transparently at Israel's destruction [78] left no practical alternative to an attempt to seek some security in Western aid.

The strategic and political arguments of the non-Communist Left against a Western orientation were no longer defensible, but the Zionist argument remained. The rise of official as well as vulgar anti-Semitism in the Soviet Union gave the customary threats of the Russians against relying on the West a particular point when made against Israel.[79] The safety of Soviet Jewry, not only the security of Israel, was at stake. If not the dictates of self-preservation — for the Zionist Left shared the myth of reliance only on Israel's own strength, and would not lay down Jewish arms obtained from the West to rely on the hope of Russian forbearance — then the hope of one day receiving the Russian Jews should make Israel cautious about offending Russia by its foreign policy.

The increasingly pro-Western parties in Israel, on the other hand, also appealed not only to self-preservation but to Zionist duty as the grounds for their foreign policy. Indeed, since there was little difference of opinion on the first score any longer, ideological discussion of foreign policy was formulated even more frequently in terms of Zionism. Since Israel had Zionist obligations, it was argued, it was naturally bound to the West. In the Western democracies immigration to Israel was not prohibited and the Jewish community was free not only to maintain cultural bonds with Israel and share the burden of settling mass immigration but also to protest against anti-Israel trends in government policy and seek to alter them.[80]

The real determining factor in Israel's foreign policy remained, nevertheless, the sheer requirements of self-preservation. Neither Zionist principles nor other ideological factors, neither long-range geopolitical calculations nor a clever grasp of short-range tactical opportunities were truly decisive. The external pressures on Israel were so severe, and the country was forced into so tight a corner, that the basic principles of its foreign policy became hardly an exercise of sovereignty at all, but rather an acceptance of necessities to which there was no alternative. In this respect, of course, Israel shares the common fate of many other countries in the modern world.

Part Three

ZIONISM AND THE INTERNATIONAL COMMUNITY

8 ZIONISM AND WORLD POLITICS FROM NAPOLEON TO BALFOUR

THERE were Gentile projects to resettle the Jews in Palestine and to restore their sovereignty in their ancient homeland long before the Zionist movement began to pursue these ideas as practical, political possibilities. In this sense, one may say that the earliest Zionists were Christian Zionists; and, moreover, until late in the nineteenth century the long succession of Christian Zionist projects met with no significant Zionist awakening among the Jews.

Zionism, however, means before all else the national awakening of the Jews. To speak of Christian Zionism at all is to use a metaphor, and to speak of it as a continuous phenomenon antedating true Zionism by a hundred years or more is undoubtedly paradoxical. Yet such a "Christian Zionism," developing before true Zionism and independently of it, is a fact of some historical significance for the formulation and achievement of the idea of Jewish sovereignty in Palestine.

The ideas of "Christian Zionism," moreover, were different in important respects from those of the Zionist movement. Zionism is essentially a theory which sees in the restoration of Jewish sovereignty in Palestine the solution of the Jewish problem in its manifold aspects. It proposed to end not only the oppression and cultural insecurity of the Jews, but also the burdens of guilt and *malaise* which the anomalous existence of the Jews imposed upon the Gentiles. Such doctrines were not necessarily involved in Christian Zionism. Some Gentiles who were sensitive to the Jewish question appreciated the fact that the removal of the Jews to Palestine might be a way to avoid admitting them to social and political equality, with all the perils they feared from this; others thought that Palestine or some other undeveloped territory could offer an alternative for Jewish immigrants and refugees unwanted in London or New York. Such motives did not necessarily lead to Zionism, however. Nor were the Christian Zionists characteristically concerned with the Jewish problem, in its contemporary political, social, and economic aspects.

The religious problem of the Jews, their place in the Christian eschatological myth, was the cultural complex which chiefly inspired Christian Zionism before Jewish Zionism arose.[1] On the other hand, in an opposed interpretation, it was also this cultural complex that aroused Christian anti-Zionism after true Zionism became a concrete reality. The political idea of national liberation and, above all, political calculations concerning the strategic importance of Palestine, were another complex of motives that led to Christian Zionist projects and ideas, before Jewish Zionism arose.[2] In opposed interpretations, the same complex of motives also led to Christian anti-Zionism after Jewish Zionism became a concrete reality. Neither the political nor the religious sources of Christian Zionism and anti-Zionism had much to do with the Jewish problem, as a concrete historical question requiring a solution; indeed, the countries in which Christian Zionism and anti-Zionism were most conspicuous were often those in which the Jewish problem was considered least serious.

The Zionist movement had to take the opinions and motivations of Christian Zionists and anti-Zionists into account in reaching the successive formulations of the idea of Jewish sovereignty for which it sought to obtain international recognition. The intellectual history of the idea of the Zionist state must include, accordingly, the history of Christian Zionism and anti-Zionism. We must consider, first, what the Zionists themselves thought were the formulations of their idea that would make it generally attractive or acceptable to non-Jews concerned with Palestine. Then, too, we must consider how the idea was successively reformulated to meet actual demands made by individual nations or by the concert of nations in negotiations for the recognition of Jewish claims.

I

Jewish history can list innumerable Jewish "anticipations" of Zionism in the attempts of religious enthusiasts and political adventurers, ever since the Second Exile, to bring about the Restoration. But in the century or two preceding the rise of Zionism, the historians of "proto-Zionism"[3] record a considerably greater proportion of Christians than of Jews among the promoters and advocates of such millennarian projects and fantasies. Moreover, the Jewish consensus regarded with great caution, not to say suspicion, the appeals made to them from time to time to participate in schemes to set up a Jewish polity again in Palestine. This reserve, first shown towards the obviously impractical plans of enthusiasts and adventurers, continued to be shown towards proposals with a much greater appearance of practicality.[4]

The course taken by the Sabbatian movement in the seventeenth and the Frankist movement in the eighteenth century caused representative Jews in the years after to dread anything that smacked of pseudo-Messianism. There was a marked rise in the Jewish settlement in Palestine, beginning at that time, owing to a succession of immigrant groups stimulated by religious enthusiasm. But the duty and merit of settling in the Holy Land were sharply separated from attempts to achieve such aspects of Redemption as Jewish sovereignty in Palestine. These bore the stigma of sacrilegious pseudo-Messianism.

Christian proponents of such ideas also aroused suspicions among the Jews. The religious enthusiasts among them openly aimed at conversion, which, naturally, prevented Jews from cooperating freely with them. Nor could the Jews be expected to flock to the banners of prophets of a new world religion like Oliger Paulli, promoters of a Moslem-Jewish crusade against the Pope like the Marquis de Langallerie, or royal adventurers like the bastard Count of Saxony, who sought to gain a crown and a people for himself by setting up a Jewish state in South America.[5]

The idea of sending the Jews back to Palestine — or at least the thought that it might have been better if they had never left there — occurred to Gentiles of a more practical cast, too; though these men should hardly find a place in a chronicle of Christian Zionism. When the Enlightenment and the democratic revolution posed the problem of accepting the Jews into full citizenship, opponents of the emancipation proposed instead that the Jews be segregated in thinly populated regions or resettled in new territories, even in Palestine. There was nothing in the logical content of these proposals which made them inconceivable for Jews; and, as we have seen, some Christian friends as well as opponents of emancipation accepted the premises upon which this "proto-Zionism" was based. Moreover, whatever else might be said about the motives of the proponents of Jewish resettlement, they were neither missionaries seeking to convert the Jews nor adventurers seeking to profit by them, but they were concerned directly with the Jewish problem. On the other hand — and this consideration was uppermost in the minds of contemporaries — these were chiefly the opponents of the Jews; their purpose was to forestall the proposed solution of the Jewish problem by emancipation through a false and meaningless advocacy of Jewish resettlement elsewhere. Not being advanced with serious intent, the idea of resettle-

ment was not taken seriously by Jewish contemporaries, except as a
serious threat. As a defense, therefore, the Jews who sought emancipation renounced the hope of restoration to sovereignty in Palestine and
declared Berlin or Paris to be their Zion. These new principles,
widely adopted by Jews in Western Europe in the early nineteenth
century, could hardly be maintained if, at the same time, they lent
themselves to schemes for their resettlement in Palestine.

The idea of resettling the Jews in Palestine began to be advanced,
at the same time, on new grounds which made it seem a matter of
real practical significance to many statesmen and political amateurs
among the Christians. By the latter half of the eighteenth century
the Eastern question, which has played a prominent part in European
foreign policies to the present day, had already emerged. The Ottoman
Empire, corrupted within, began to be shaken by rebellion at its
extremities. Nationalist movements soon arose among its Christian
subjects on the north and east, and local Moslem potentates asserted
their independence on the south and west. European powers, whose
attention was increasingly drawn to the Eastern Mediterranean, began
to consider the possible collapse of the Ottoman Empire. Each power
had to weigh its potential gains in new territories or in dominant
influence if it encouraged rebellion in the weakened Empire. It had
also to consider its losses if a rival power should play the same game
successfully. In either case, some action was required: whether to
support nationalist or provincial movements against the Turks or,
on the other hand, to strengthen the Ottoman Empire against com-
peting European influences by helping to reform the Turkish administration, bolster the economy and repopulate waste territories.[6]

As the notion of restoring the Jews to Palestine was current at
the time (particularly in the Evangelical movement in Britain), it
began to be woven into the stratagems devised by some European
politicians to deal with the Eastern question. The Jews were thought
of both as possible pawns in schemes to dispossess the Turks of
Palestine and, on the other hand, as new settlers who could help to
bolster up the Turkish power. In 1771–1773, when Russia was acting
in concert with the rebellious Mameluke, Ali Bey, against the Turks,
officers of the Russian fleet sought to employ the Jews as an additional
source of strength for their alliance. They mediated an abortive
agreement between the Bey and Jews of Leghorn, where the Russian
fleet was based, for the purchase of Jerusalem.[7] In 1798–1799, when
France was speculating on the possibilities that might open up
through Napoleon's expedition to the East, the Jews were again
thought of as a source who, because of their perennial hope to return

to the Holy Land and revive their ancient state, might prove a political as well as financial ally of importance for the French forces.[8]

In 1839, when Mohammed Ali was in rebellion against the Sultan, and his son, Ibrahim Pasha, held Palestine, the European powers met in London to deal with the crisis. British proto-Zionists bombarded the conference with proposals for creating a buffer zone between Egypt and Turkey with the aid of Jewish settlers.[9] One year earlier, Sir Moses Montefiore had concluded an oral agreement with Mohammed Ali for rights to purchase land and settle Jewish colonists in Palestine under a regime of relative autonomy. The agreement collapsed before it was committed to writing, because of the onset of the crisis.[10]

The Crimean War from 1853–1856 and the crisis in Lebanon in 1860 kept the Eastern question before the European public. Christian Zionists in France now suggested that the French and the general European interest would be best served by a Jewish state in Palestine.[11] The continuing warfare between Russia and Turkey caused the European powers once more, at the Congress of Berlin in 1876, to deal with the Eastern question. While the powers came to an agreement among themselves, the Ottoman situation grew even more vexed. The idea again cropped up of using Jewish settlement in Palestine as a means of stabilizing the Turkish regime. At the end of the seventies, two British gentlemen, Laurence Oliphant and Edward Cazalet, were trying to negotiate such plans in Constantinople.[12] Only now were they joined by the first significant Jewish group, from whose appearance the rise of Zionism is often dated, the BILU delegation that appeared in Constantinople in 1881.[13]

Christian proto-Zionists, from the Earl of Shaftesbury (1801–1885) to Laurence Oliphant, often realized that it was advisable to suppress their religious motives for wishing the restoration of the Jews, whatever they might be, if they hoped to gain the necessary support of European statesmen and cooperation of potential Jewish settlers. Therefore, the more practically they approached the problem, the more they tried to talk to Jews and foreign secretaries without millennarian or conversionist propaganda. Shaftesbury notes in his diary:

How singular is the order of Providence! Singular, that is if estimated by man's ways! Palmerston had already been chosen by God to be an instrument of good to His ancient people, to do homage, as it were, to their inheritance, and to recognise their rights without believing their destiny. And it seems he will yet do more. But though the motive be kind, it is not sound. I am forced to argue politically, financially, commercially; these considerations strike him home; he weeps not like his Master over *Jerusalem*, nor prays that now, at last, she may put on her beautiful garments.[14]

So, too, Oliphant says,

It is somewhat unfortunate that so important a political and strategic question as the future of Palestine should be inseparably connected in the public mind with a favorite religious theory . . . The mere accident of a measure involving most important international consequences, having been advocated by a large section of the Christian community, from a purely Biblical point of view, does not necessarily impair its political value. On the contrary . . . as far as my own efforts are concerned, they are based upon considerations which have no connection whatever with any popular religious theory upon the subject.[15]

Considering Oliphant's extraordinary religious enthusiasms, one can take such a statement at face value only if it is read with emphasis on the word "popular"; for it is true enough that Oliphant's religious theories were anything but popular.

Presenting their case in this way, Christian Zionists were able from 1840 to 1880, to gain a sympathetic hearing among statesmen, particularly in the British Foreign Office. They even gained the confidence and cooperation of important Jewish circles.[16] But in adapting their exposition to a neutral and practical style that could enlist the necessary interest, the Christian proto-Zionists separated the idea of Jewish sovereignty from the idea of Jewish resettlement.

It was essential to make this distinction. After 1840 the ruling principle of Western European, and especially British, policy on the Eastern question was to bolster up the Ottoman Empire; it was Russia that hoped to gain territorial advantages from a collapse. Thus, no British Christian Zionist could propose the restoration of the Jews as a successor state to part of the Ottoman Empire. On the other hand, it struck a responsive chord to suggest them as an industrious and efficient body of settlers who would be loyal subjects of the Sultan and could protect the Empire by establishing a strong buffer zone on its exposed southern frontier. As for the prophesied sovereignty of the Jews in Palestine, this was presented as an ultimate or even millennarian possibility, not an immediate objective. The immediate requirement was only that degree of self-rule implied in local autonomy. The position was stated in these words by Col. George Gawler, one of the most active proto-Zionists: "I should be truly rejoiced to see in Palestine a strong guard of Jews established in flourishing agricultural settlements, and ready to hold their own upon the mountains of Israel against all aggressors." At the same time, he added these provisos:

To give Jews in Palestine the means of maintaining themselves and their families by honest and healthy industry would be the best preparation of the way for better things, to the Jewish nation and to the whole human race, that could be desired. In maintaining such projects I am not at all proposing faithlessness to "our allies" the Turks. So long as the empire stands, Jewish civilised settlement in Syria would be a strength and a blessing to it. It is only in the event of its ever falling that I should be glad to see the claim boldly enforced in reference to Palestine, "This portion belongs to the God of Israel, and to his national people." [17]

Such formulas were required in order to conform with the established terms of Western foreign policy. They also fell in with the established terms in which representative Jews of the East and West were each predisposed to think of resettlement in Zion, if they could be brought to favor it at all. The Eastern European Jews and the Jews of the Ottoman Empire looked on contemporary settlement in Palestine as a positive religious act, while they were suspicious of the idea of contemporary sovereignty as pseudo-Messianic. The Western Jews, particularly as the practical necessity for Jewish emigration from Eastern Europe and North Africa became apparent, could be induced to support schemes for resettlement in Palestine, but to connect such schemes prominently with the idea of national sovereignty would arouse their resistance. For, as we have seen, in their "apperceptive field," sovereignty for the Jews in Palestine was bound up with the denial of civil rights to Jews in Europe.

It may be added that in suppressing the theme of Jewish sovereignty, British proto-Zionists made the idea of Jewish resettlement in Palestine acceptable, from time to time, to the Turks. Indeed, in the years from 1840 to 1880, when Turkey was sustained by Britain and was largely amenable to British influence, there were occasions when Turks seemed more to wish for Jewish settlers than Jews wished to sponsor settlement.[18] Ironically, it was after a serious impulse to resettlement developed among the Jews that the Turks, in turning against the British, turned firmly against the idea of Jewish colonization.

It appears, then, that from the time when Napoleon's Egyptian expedition revived the Eastern question for European diplomacy until late in the nineteenth century, proto-Zionist ideas and projects were more often than not originated by Christians and held under suspicion by the Jewish community. Moreover, the contemporary Jewish problem was not the major source of such Christian Zionism. In part it arose from religious enthusiasm which saw the Second Advent of Christ foreshadowed by Jewish settlement in Palestine; and in part it arose from the general enthusiasm for the liberation of oppressed nations, which found expression in the generous impulse to see the

Jews, too, restored to sovereignty in their ancestral homeland. Neither of these sources of Gentile Zionism, but a third source — the concern of European powers with the state of the Ottoman Empire — gave the idea of Jewish resettlement in Palestine some substance as a political possibility. The enthusiasts of Christian Zionism were able, on several occasions throughout the nineteenth century, to "sell" their idea to cool-headed politicians and diplomatists by stressing its "geopolitical" aspects — and by suppressing their eschatological and romantic aims centering on the restoration of Jewish sovereignty. So, too, by suppressing the missionary or the nationalistic aspects of their idea and concentrating on the more sober attractions of aid for increased Jewish immigration into Palestine, some Christian Zionists were able to arrive at a degree of cooperation with the rather suspicious Jewish community.

After the Zionist movement arose in the eighties and nineties, many of the above general statements were sharply reversed. The rise of a nationalist movement among the Jews made Zionism a cause promoted upon Jewish initiative, and Christian Zionism now became an expression of sympathy with ideas for whose formulation Jews were responsible. In those formulations great prominence was given to the contemporary Jewish problem, with whose complexities Christian Zionists were often only vaguely familiar.

From the middle of the nineteenth century, certain aspects of the Jewish problem claimed general attention as matters of international concern. The chronic oppression of the Jews in the Balkans and the Russian Empire began to take the spasmodically acute form of expulsions and other extreme measures that precipitated a rising tide of Jewish emigration into the Western World. The deliberate intent to get rid of the Jews, which declared itself as openly in Rumania in the 1860's as it did in Russia in the early 1900's and in Poland and Germany in the 1920's and 30's, was not at first (or even in the end, except under pressure of extreme urgency) met by an organized Jewish movement to transfer the Jews wholesale from these danger spots. In the 1860's, the idea of agreeing to the forced evacuation of Jews from Rumania appealed only, temporarily, to individuals like Benjamin Franklin Peixotto (1834–1896), the American consul in Bucharest, and was roundly condemned by leaders of the Jewish community. Even after the rise of Herzlian Zionism, with its idea of a compact with the Gentiles to rid them of the Jewish problem by an organized mass transfer to Palestine, the consensus of Zionist as well as of Jewish opinion strongly resisted any notion of acquiescing in forced movements arbitrarily produced by anti-Semitic governments. When threatened with such calamities the Jewish consensus reacted by appealing to the governments of the enlightened West to protect the human rights of Jews. Only in the Hitler era did many Jews, and above all Zionists, lose hope in such expedients, and themselves attempt the emergency operation of rescuing Jews by transfer to Palestine, by whatever means possible. Before then, from the middle of the nineteenth century on, Jewish intercessions against the persecution which was driving Jewish refugees to Western countries had become a recurrent and substantial feature of international and Western political affairs. But even though Jewish appeals were answered by Western governments individually and in concert — for example, through America's denunciation of its commercial treaty with Russia because of anti-Jewish discrimination or through the provisions of the Treaty of Berlin safeguarding Jewish rights in countries like Rumania — conditions were not improved and the stream of emigrants grew continually stronger.

The flow of immigration from Eastern Europe to the West caused the rise of restrictionist proposals in Western bastions of liberalism like Great Britain and the United States. Moreover, a specific feeling against Jewish immigrants, with an unpleasant affinity for the virulent anti-Semitism of Continental reactionaries, showed itself in the propaganda and debates leading to Britain's Alien and America's successive Immigration Acts. The Western countries began to have a direct interest in the Jewish question, arising from qualms of conscience at their own behavior, and not only a remote interest, arising out of indignation at the acts and sympathy for the sufferings of others. These circumstances made Western countries more responsive when Jews now proposed measures intended to alleviate or solve the Jewish problem.

On the other hand, the development of the Eastern question, toward the end of the nineteenth century, made them much less likely to favor bold plans regarding Palestine. Yet much more boldness and persistence were required for any plan of Jewish resettlement which was proposed as a solution of the Jewish problem than for transient ventures inspired by missionary sentiments or humanitarian enthusiasm. The Zionists, in particular, advanced a project involving both Western sponsors and the Ottoman Empire in a long-range policy committed to legal forms. However cautiously formulated, the commitments they demanded had serious and far-reaching implications. In the past, when a Western country had interceded at the request of its own citizens for the rights of unorganized Jewish groups to enter or live in Palestine, it made no serious commitment itself and demanded nothing unusual of the Ottoman Empire.

After the Congress of Berlin, moreover, Turkey grew increasingly restive under the traditional privileges Western powers enjoyed in its realm. Even the kind of protection they extended to Jews, among others, under the capitulations, which was quite usual from 1840 to 1880, was felt now by the Turks to be a serious imposition. And in view of the delicate diplomatic balance of relationships (especially after Germany entered into the rivalry for influence in Constantinople), a country like England began to consider its protection of Jews in Palestine an encumbrance in seeking smoother relations with the Porte.[19]

When the Zionists began seriously to test the chances of achieving their goal in the political circumstances of Palestine at the end of the nineteenth century, they found a balance not only of political but of religious and sentimental interests which they themselves estimated as strongly opposed to their design. The Christian Zionism manifested among the British Evangelicals in the middle of the century was still regarded by the Zionists as a powerful, though rather diffuse, influence which they could count on in their favor. On the other hand, they felt the weight of a more pervasive and at least equally powerful Christian religious anti-Zionism. The mythic belief of the Evangelicals and other Protestant enthusiasts in the Jewish Restoration as a portent of the Second Advent and the End of Time was a sectarian myth. The broadest mythic consensus of all Christendom was evoked by the legend of the Wandering Jew, rejected of God because of his "perfidy" and doomed to reside in Exile, subject to the Christians, to the end of time. In strongly Roman Catholic or Eastern Orthodox countries this myth, and not the sectarian variant, determined the Christian attitude; and, hence, there was a strong undercurrent of religious resistance to the idea that the Jews might emerge, still unconverted, from Exile.[20]

In addition to this broad foundation, there was a more specific ground for Christian anti-Zionism. Two major European powers, France and Russia, had made the defense of Catholic and Orthodox positions an occasion for promoting their political interests in the Bible Lands. If the Ottoman Empire collapsed and the question of a successor should arise, these powers would probably be far more inclined to claim this title for themselves rather than support a Jewish claim. Under the circumstances, the Zionists anticipated resistance from these quarters even if Ottoman suzerainty were still maintained. A major diplomatic task was to persuade French and Italian Catholics, at least, that Christian interests would not suffer as a result of Zionist activity in Palestine.[21]

While seeking to allay the religiously grounded opposition feared from France and Russia, Zionist diplomacy hoped to win active support from the Protestant powers, Germany and England, particularly the latter. To preserve the Ottoman Empire was, generally speaking, a ruling principle of British policy from the first half of the nineteenth century, and, later, of Germany as well. The support of these powers could be hoped for, under the circumstances, only if Zionism undertook to be loyal to the Ottoman Empire, and to seek only such national status as was compatible with the suzerainty of the Sultan. But in the period after the Congress of Berlin, assurances of loyalty were no longer acceptable to Constantinople if they were combined with reliance on the backing of Western powers. The Turks viewed with suspicion any scheme which, it seemed to them, might extend European influence in their realm under the guise of protecting a religious minority. In the interests of good relations with Turkey, the Protestant powers were inclined to limit their protection of Jews rather than extend it.

Consequently, when Zionists sought British support for their plans in Palestine, the British tentatively suggested alternatives, much as the Turks themselves did when they continually offered to let Jews settle as Ottoman subjects in other parts of the Empire, instead of as a national community in Palestine. The suspicion of designs on Palestine extended to its outlying areas. A philanthropic, non-Zionist project financed by Paul Friedmann, a converted Jew, for a Jewish settlement in Midian in the Sinai was rejected by Egypt because Turkey did not wish any colonization on the disputed borders of the Holy Land; and the Zionist idea of settling in El Arish — this, too, on the Sinai side of the Palestine border — was also rejected by Egypt.[22] The final result of Zionist diplomacy in this period was the British East African offer, when serious negotiations were undertaken for Jewish settlement in a colonial area far removed from Palestine. Other projects, along the same lines, were negotiated by the ITO, only to collapse in each case. Thus, the political activity of this period involved European powers, and particularly Britain, in serious consideration of plans to solve the Jewish problem by concentrated resettlement. The prevailing political conditions also led the same powers to be far more cautious about advocating and assisting Jewish resettlement in Palestine, at a time when the emergence of the Zionist movement demanded much bolder advocacy and assistance.

II

From its beginning, then, the Zionist movement had to reckon with the fact that, in the given circumstances, what it could achieve diplomatically depended on its own success with Turkey. Herzl conducted a widespread search for diplomatic support in all quarters, using every motive that could induce any power to look favorably on his project and seizing every slightest opportunity to make capital of even purely symbolic expressions of good will. But his major strategy, too, was centered on a plan to win over the Sultan. The outlines of his scheme resemble closely those of earlier negotiators like Montefiore and Oliphant. The basic elements of the situation in the Eastern Mediterranean, the three analysts agreed, were the economic decline and insecurity of Palestine, a strategic outpost of the Ottoman Empire (or, if Mohammed Ali had seized it, of the Egyptian Empire). The specifications for a satisfactory solution, then, were Western capital and skills, together with an increased population, based on immigrants who could be counted on to be loyal to the suzerain power, and not to serve as an entering wedge for foreign interests. Such a solution, said Oliphant, in an argument that might have served as a brief for Herzl, was provided only by Jewish resettlement.

It was manifest [after the conclusion of the Treaty of Berlin] that the . . . treaty would . . . render inevitable an external interference in the domestic affairs of Turkey, of a more pronounced character than had ever existed before; and that this interference was calculated, sooner or later, to produce most serious complications, unless it could be averted by reforms in the administration springing from the initiative of the Sultan, which should anticipate any such forcible intrusion from without . . . As, however, it was scarcely to be expected that the Turkish Government would . . . adopt a radical measure . . . and apply it throughout . . . its vast Asiatic dominions, it occurred to me that an experiment might be made on a small scale, and that an evidence might thus be afforded to the Porte of the advantages which would attend the development of a single province, however small, under conditions which should increase the revenue of the empire, add to its population and resources, secure protection of life and property, and enlist the sympathy of Europe, without in any way affecting the sovereign rights of the Sultan . . . It appeared to me that this object [to bring in foreign capital without obnoxious foreign supervision] might be obtained by means of a Colonization Company, and that one of those rich and unoccupied districts which abound in Turkey might be obtained and developed through the agency of a commercial enterprise which should be formed under the auspices of his Majesty, and have its seat at Constantinople . . .

The next questions which naturally presented themselves to my mind were — first, the locality to be selected for the experiment; and secondly, the class of people who should be invited to come as colonists. The objection to foreigners who were at the same time Christians seemed insurmountable, as by the existing colonization law it was made a *sine qua non* that any colonists permanently settling in Turkey in Asia should become Ottoman subjects — a provision with which foreign Christians were extremely unlikely to comply . . . The possibility of finding, under the auspices of such a company, an asylum for the thousands of Moslem refugees, who, driven from their homes in Bulgaria and Roumelia, were starving in various parts of the empire, also suggested itself; but the difficulty in this case arose from the extreme improbability of finding the capital in Christian Europe which would be required . . . There was, in fact, only one race in Europe who were rich, and who did not, therefore, need to appeal to Christian capitalists for money to carry through the whole undertaking; who were not Christians, and to whom, therefore, the objections of the Porte to the introduction of more rival Christian sects did not apply; who had never alarmed the Turkish Government by national aspirations, but, on the contrary, had always proved themselves most loyal and peaceable subjects of his Majesty; who were nevertheless strongly attached by historical association to a province of Asiatic Turkey, and to whom the inducement of once more becoming proprietors of its sacred soil might prove strong enough to tempt them to comply with the probable conditions of the Turkish Government; more especially as the persecution to which they were subjected by some Christian governments in Europe, contrasted with the toleration with which they were treated in Turkey itself. It was thus that I found myself, by a process of deduction, compelled to turn for the locality of the colony to Palestine, and for the colonists to the Jews.[23]

To Oliphant's formula, Herzl added one major inducement for Turkey to grant him a Charter. He offered loans by the Jews to relieve Turkey's chronic financial difficulties. His scheme, as outlined in the form of a draft charter for a "Jewish-Ottoman Land Company," [24] contained the following proposals, which were echoed as late as 1908 in a similar offer that David Wolffsohn, Herzl's successor as President of the World Zionist Organization, made to the Sultan: First (par. VIII), the Company would loan 4 million Turkish pounds to the Sultan (in Wolffsohn's time, the sum had risen to 26 million). Second (par. VIIA), in return, the Company would be permitted freely to bring into the region of Palestine and Syria (Wolffsohn: Palestine and neighboring lands) Jewish immigrants and employees, who would acquire Ottoman citizenship. Third (par. I–III, V), the Company would have an option to acquire crown lands and waste lands in the designated area, and to purchase, as tenant of the Sultan, needed private lands — except holy places and land in Jerusalem — on condition that the owners were provided with equivalent land elsewhere. Fixed annual fees would be paid to the Sultan in lieu of taxes, while the Company would collect all taxes and customs in its area. (Wolffsohn: Crown lands and waste lands would be purchased, and paid for in debentures of the Company.) Fourth (par. I, IV, VI), the Jewish-Ottoman Company and the settlement it established would be granted full autonomy in their designated area (Wolffsohn: Rights and liberties needed for carrying out the full economic development of the land). Fifth (par. VII B–E), Jewish military and naval corps would be organized within the Ottoman Army for the defense and internal security of the designated area, and for limited use beyond it, when necessary for the defense of the Empire. Sixth (par. IX), the Governor and Chief Justice of the designated area would be Jews or Moslems selected by the Jewish-Ottoman Company and approved by the Sultan, and the Governor would represent the Sultan in the area with full authority and be directly responsible to him.

The bait of a potential loan was sufficiently effective to cause Sultan Abdul Hamid II to grant interviews to Herzl and Wolffsohn. But no agreement could possibly be attained since the Zionists were unable — even if they had been willing — to make what the Sultan considered the essential first step. Neither Herzl nor Wolffsohn had the 4 million or 26 million Turkish pounds they were offering to loan Turkey. The Jewish bankers whom Herzl approached told him to come back when he had some concrete agreement with the Sultan. Herzl and Wolffsohn, in turn, were convinced that if they could get an agreement with the Sultan, they might indeed get the money from Jewish bankers or the Jewish people. But the Sultan took much the same bargaining position as the bankers; he indicated that if the loan were provided first, he might then be inclined to negotiate in a friendly spirit about the desired charter. Between the two demands, Zionist diplomacy from Herzl to Wolffsohn floundered in a series of feverish endeavors that always led to an impasse.[25] But so long as the Sultan remained in power, there were always court favorites who could be induced by the time-honored method of dispensing *baksheesh* to take steps toward obtaining interviews for Zionists; while the autocratic character of the regime, together with its always impending bankruptcy, made it always seem within the bounds of possibility to strike a bargain.

Zionist hopes of a charter in return for solving the Ottoman financial problem steadily receded, however, and other strategies — territorialism or "Practical Zionism" — began to replace it in popularity. The Young Turk revolution gave the death-blow to the Herzlian strategy. A popular movement, fiercely opposed to the corruption of the old regime and even more to the foreign influences whose incursions had been facilitated by the Sultan's autocratic methods and weakness, could not be approached in this way. The status the Zionists wanted had now to be obtained with the consent of a government responsible to the public. To ask such a government for the kind of powers proposed for the chartered company was to invite an indignant refusal.

In his address to the Ninth Zionist Congress (Hamburg, December 26–30, 1909), Max Nordau publicly renounced the "charter" idea for which Wolffsohn had been hopefully negotiating less than two years before in Constantinople.

But the most disheartening development of the past months has been the clamor from many sides for a revision of our program. Have those who raised this cry fully realized the meaning and implications of their demand? . . . . What is to be altered in the Basle program? "The idea of the charter has become obsolete," they cry. That can be admitted without further ado. (Applause.) But there is not a word about the charter in the Basle program. The charter was a personal idea of our immortal Herzl's, an idea that could be defended at the time the creator of our movement formulated it. He could not carry it into effect, and under present-day conditions it no longer has any justification. (Quite right.) We can drop it quite calmly, all the more calmly inasmuch as it is not of the essence for our movement, it does not go to the heart of it at all. (Applause.) . . . In an absolutist Turkey we had to demand liberties which, in conditions of general unfreedom, necessarily assumed the character of special rights and required formal contractual guarantees. In a constitutional state, in which all citizens enjoy liberty under the law, we need no privileges and no special guarantees. The law for all suffices. (Applause.) So let us place Herzl's charter idea respectfully in the archives of modern political Zionism and speak no more of it.[26]

While renouncing the quest for the charter, Nordau defended the text of the Basle program against proposals for revision. But he did so in such a way as to rule out another tactical approach to the Zionist goal which, too, Herzl had not only left open but repeatedly attempted to use.

But what is the objection to the Basle program? It should no longer read: "Zionism aims to establish a home for the Jewish people secured by public law." "Public law" disturbs you. "Public law" seems to you to be useless or even dangerous. Honored Congress! I believe I may say I am qualified to speak on this point. It is perhaps not entirely forgotten, in spite of the fast pace of life and the short memory of mankind today, that I was mainly responsible for the concrete formulation, that is, for the literal text of the Basle program. I did not originally employ the expression "public law." It seemed unnecessary to me. I contented myself with the expression "a legally assured home.". . . . You see, I have no personal reason to champion the term "public law." I do so, however, because if we suppress the term now we shall give it retrospectively a signification that would gravely distort its real, original meaning. (Loud approval.) A small minority of the First Congress attached to the term "public law" the conception of Jewish immigration into Palestine under the auspices of the great Powers, who should recognize this Jewish resettlement of the Holy Land as an integral part of the European law of nations. But the vast majority of the Congress was free of any such far-fetched fantasy. By "public law" as by "legally assured," all they wanted to indicate was that the Zionists reject the idea of sneaking into Palestine, that they wish to come into the Ottoman political union only on the basis of expressly granted rights, as parties to a mutual agreement. (Loud applause.) That is the meaning of the term "public law." This meaning has been confirmed by our President [Wolffsohn] in a formal public declaration . . . . We have been told: "Just come to us in Turkey, you shall be welcome. You will find everything you could ask for, fertile, cheap, perhaps free land, security against persecution, the freedom that is assured to every citizen of the Ottoman realm; but you must become Turkish citizens, adopt the Turkish language, merge with the Turkish people so that you cannot be distinguished from other Turks. And in order to be quite sure that you actually observe these conditions, we shall not allow you to settle together in large numbers and compact groups . . . . nor shall we admit you into Palestine at all. This is the only one of all the provinces of the Empire that remains closed to you." In the face of such views, it is a duty of honor and self-respect to refer to the Basle program (approval and applause) and declare that we maintain it unaltered and will permit not a single word to be obsequiously retouched.[27]

Thus, not only the charter but the idea that Jewish resettlement in Palestine should be part of an internationally covenanted general settlement was dropped by the tacticians of political Zionism. The text of the Basle program was militantly defended by Nordau in order to make clear that the irreducible aim of Zionism, to reestablish an autonomous Jewish national entity in Palestine, should be neither abandoned nor misunderstood. In the years immediately following Herzl's death, the means to this end had already been reconsidered and practical Zionism was replacing political Zionism. The rise of the Young Turks now altered even the terms in which political Zionism was understood. Attention was more fully centered on the Ottoman authorities rather than the chancelleries of Europe; and it was no longer the European courts but the Turkish parliament, not Viziers and Foreign Secretaries but the leaders of Ottoman political parties, both Turks and Arabs, whose cooperation was considered decisive.

A Zionist office for small-scale practical work had been established in Jaffa shortly before the Young Turk revolution. Not long after it, another Zionist office was established in Constantinople in order to do political work.[28] The new channels used by Zionist diplomacy were characteristic: contacts with both political parties in the new democratic Turkey, discussions and negotiations with the Arab members of the parliament from Syria and Palestine and with Arab leaders in both Ottoman parties, and a general approach to the younger Ottoman intellectuals through a newspaper issued by the Zionist office.[29]

In the short period between the Young Turk revolution and the First World War, no great results were obtained. Indeed, some of those engaged in the work, notably Vladimir Jabotinsky, came to despair of success so long as the Ottoman Empire controlled Palestine, and they thenceforth pinned their hopes on its collapse. The Palestinian Jews at first thought they might advance the Zionist cause under the new democratic regime by various electoral combinations in the polls for parliament, in spite of the fact that so few of them were Ottoman citizens entitled to vote. But this line of action led to a steady retreat. First, the Jewish community attempted to elect a Palestinian Jewish deputy in 1908. At the next election in 1912, they limited themselves to seeking better terms from the majority Union and Progress party of the Young Turks in return for Jewish electoral support. In 1914, they were forced into virtual abstention from electoral politics in the hope that by such a policy they might foster friendlier relations with the Arabs of the liberal Decentralization Party without openly offending the Young Turks.[30]

In Constantinople, too, Zionist attention shifted gradually from the Young Turks to the Arab parliamentary delegation. In a period marked by continual warfare in the Balkans, the Turkish nationalist revolutionaries showed a growing hostility to any expression of minority nationalism in the Ottoman realm. Thus the mild sympathy the Young Turks had shown for Zionism in the beginning was replaced by cold suspicion. Arab politicians, on the other hand, had been the chief anti-Zionist force in the first years of the Turkish parliament. In the later years, they began to think of Zionism as a possible makeweight against the Turks. Zionist policy shifted to meet these conditions. In the beginning, the hope was that a constitutional Turkey, in accordance with its own essential principles, would necessarily drop the restrictions against Jewish immigration, land purchase, and settlement. On the other hand, the sixty-odd Arab parliamentary delegates in Constantinople and the newly active Arabic press kept up a drumfire of complaints and defamations against the Jewish settlers on precisely these subjects; and it was necessary for the Zionist political office to seek to placate them. The necessity became more evident when the Young Turks bowed to the demands of the Arab delegations and reinforced the old bans, advising the Zionists that they must first make their peace with the Arabs. But Zionists soon observed that their reception by Arab leaders grew warmer as the Arabs were disappointed in their hopes of gaining concessions from the Turks, while it cooled swiftly when these hopes revived. In the years immediately preceding the First World War, Arab opposition to the Young Turks grew cautiously bolder and the contacts with the Zionists became more definite in character. Preliminary drafts for an agreement were even composed, and in the summer of 1914, Arab representatives were asking for a top-level meeting to discuss the proposals. The Zionists were prepared only for a preliminary discussion: first, because the ideas of the newly met parties were still too vague and too far apart to hope for conclusive results; second, because they had justified qualms about the suspicions that might be aroused among the Turks (who were kept informed of the talks) about possible disloyalty. But before anything was decided, the war broke out which was to alter all the terms of political thinking about Palestine.[31]

III

The first effect of the war upon Zionist politics was to make impossible any concerted activity or agreed policy of the World Zionist Organization as a whole. The dispersion of the Jews among many warring countries destroyed the assumption upon which the Zionist Organization was based: that it was free to express the sovereign will of the Jewish people. The Zionist agencies authorized by the Congress — the Executive, located in Berlin, and the Zionist offices in Jaffa and Constantinople — were in a position which gave them no choice but to follow the prewar Zionist policy of loyalty to the Ottoman Empire. In this, however, they could not bind the Zionists living in Allied countries, with whom indeed they could no longer communicate with complete freedom. Zionists in Allied countries, on the other hand — and also in neutral countries — found themselves considering new alternatives to the prewar policy. Since they were free to assume that the Ottoman Empire would collapse, they hoped that the postwar settlement would finally give Zionism the most complete recognition under public law that its program could require. An alliance between Zionism and Britain, the major Western power likely to bring down the Turks, seemed the most direct road to this end. But as the war drew to a close, it became clear that such an alliance would be only one of the factors that might determine the postwar fate of Zionism. A new element, the international community which was organizing around the Western Allies as a nucleus, became an independent factor of critical significance.

In the prewar years when "practical Zionism" took the upper hand over "political Zionism," there had been far-reaching changes not only of tactics but of mood in the Zionist camp. At Herzl's death, the

conclusive rejection of territorialism by the Zionist Congress closed
the only avenue which the Zionists might have found open for more
or less serious diplomatic negotiations. Zionist political work in the
Young Turk period, too, was necessarily a matter of laying the groundwork for future agreement by allaying suspicions and seeking to create
a friendly atmosphere. The most modest formulations of Zionist demands were so far removed from the programs of either Turkish or
Arab politicians that it was obviously impossible to expect any serious
discussion looking toward an agreement on the crucial issues. At the
Ninth Zionist Congress, Max Nordau, the spokesman of political Zionism, assessed the immediate prospects in the following manner:

I do not know if I shall be involving myself in opposition to the so-called
practical Zionists, but I feel that our most important task is still not that
of entering into official relations with the Turkish government, but the
dissemination of the Zionist idea, of Zionist conviction among the Jewish
people . . . So, if you are told: "We will not admit you into Palestine,
you may not live as a Jewish nationality, Turkey is ready to receive you
only if you give up Zionism," then you endeavor to say no word in reply
that could provoke enduring hostility but break off a correspondence that
promises no results at this time. The Zionists have waited so long, they
will wait a while longer until their elucidations, the effect of time, political ·
developments, and greater maturity will have changed the attitudes of
authoritative Turkish circles.[32]

But militancy and not patience, action and not waiting were the
myth images that gave the Zionist movement its *élan*. The turmoil
that opened the twentieth century in Russia — the Kisheneff pogrom
on the one side and the Russo-Japanese War and the 1905 upheaval
on the other — kept the mood of militancy at a high pitch in Eastern
European Jewry. And at that time, if political Zionism could give no
sustenance to the militant mood, practical Zionism, in unique ways of
its own, did. Those were the years when the Jews realized, to their
own astonishment, that some among them, the Zionist pioneers, were
successfully achieving unprecedented aims: Hebrew was again a
spoken language, and the elements of a secular Hebrew culture were
arising overnight; Jews from the towns and schoolbenches of the Pale
of Settlement were being converted not simply into planters but into
farm laborers and peasants.

Such were the revolutionary achievements that made the doctrine
of practical Zionism not just a counsel of despair dictated by the
failure of political Zionism — reduced as it was to tactics of passivity,
or at most of active preaching — but a gospel of hope. Yet there was
a certain vagueness about the mechanisms by which practical Zionism
was to solve the Jewish problem. For, large-scale Jewish immigration

to Palestine, at the proper time, was considered essential to the full solution of the problem by all Zionists, including those who thought that the problem of Judaism, not the problem of the Jews, was the first item, and under existing circumstances still the only item, on the current Zionist agenda. The program of practical resettlement and cultural revival which absorbed the energies of these Zionists gave far more adequate expression to Zionist militancy than Nordau's proposals that the movement devote itself to increasing the strength of its organization. But while practical Zionism launched a direct attack on the problem of Judaism, it too merely counselled patience in regard to the equally essential problem of the Jews. Some of the theorists of the new Zionism, moreover — and especially Aaron David Gordon, the most notable of all in his mythic appeal — gave such a rigorous form to their doctrine that it became difficult to imagine how, in practice, the mass resettlement of the Jews in Palestine could ever take place.

Gordon opposed the immigration to Palestine of Jews whose only motive was to escape persecution, and preferred them to find safety in America. He wished the Jewish nation in Palestine to be built up solely by those who were prepared to devote themselves to manual labor on the soil and disposed to live together in total brotherhood in the spirit of his Utopian nationalism. Naturally, he expected the number of these idealists to be small, at least in the beginning. But even if the mass of Jews could be inspired by the example of the beginners to abjure the "parasitism" of their Exile existence and become primary producers in a cooperative Zion, Gordon set such stringent tactical requirements that one finds it difficult to imagine how they could gain admittance to Palestine. In his radical doctrine of auto-Emancipation, concentrated entirely on the transformation of the individual, Gordon repudiated every outside condition that could help the community grow. Not only funds contributed to ease the workers' lot and not only Jewish participation, as a quasi-ally, in the military effort of one side or another in the war, but even the acquisition through diplomacy of legal titles to build the Jewish national home in Palestine seemed pointless, if not worse, to this visionary.[33] If, nevertheless, he looked forward to a full-scale national restoration in Palestine, and if his vision was shared by many of the most ardent Zionist youth, this can only be explained on mythic grounds. That the mass of Jews could and would in the fulness of time be ingathered in Palestine under the conditions specified by Gordon's doctrine was a belief of the same character as the Messianic doctrine of traditional Judaism. Yet the doctrine, no less than the

example, of A.D. Gordon was among the most effective forces uphold-
ing Zionist *élan* in those days.

Chaim Weizmann and the other leaders of Practical Zionism at
the congresses were not visionaries of this order. They frequently
preferred to call themselves "synthetic" or "organic" rather than
"practical" Zionists, precisely in order to show that they did not
repudiate political methods. They argued that just as legal titles
gained by political activity could facilitate practical resettlement, so
practical resettlement could establish the substantial claims in Palestine which alone could lead to real and permanent political victories.
With such views, they could satisfy neither themselves nor their
critics by sheer messianic faith, but were implicitly required to show
concretely how, on their premises, the full solution of the Jewish
problem would come about. To such a question, Weizmann in the
days before the First World War could have given no other answer
than the unsatisfactory advice of Nordau: Patience; wait for the
appropriate opportunity. It is not surprising, then, that, finding himself in England when the war broke out, Weizmann, the "practical"
Zionist, immediately grasped the significance of the political opportunity which now arose.

The simplest way in which to conceive of the nature of the new
opportunity was to assume that an alliance might be concluded between Britain and the Jewish people in terms of their direct, mutual
interests. The notion of such a compact had been a persistent theme
in the tradition of British Christian Zionism. Even after it became
the accepted policy to bolster the Ottoman Empire, and Jewish resettlement was advocated as a means of strengthening rather than
supplanting Turkey, it was implied that if the Ottoman Empire should
nevertheless collapse, a strong Jewish community as its successor in
Palestine would serve England as a reliable and grateful ally and a
suitable buffer state for the defense of Suez. When Turkey's adherence
to the Central Powers finally destroyed the traditional British policy,
this line of argument was picked up and presented with great vigor
by C. P. Scott and Herbert Sidebotham of the *Manchester Guardian*.[34]
It also appealed not only to a man like Jabotinsky, who preferred to
think in simplistic, categorical terms, but also, at first, to the subtle
Weizmann. But, as Weizmann speedily discovered, it was not a line of
argument that succeeded universally with the British, whose view
of their own interests was, after all, decisive. As Weizmann said in
reply to critics at the Twelfth Zionist Congress in Carlsbad:

Two assumptions mainly determined the construction of our policy. The first . . . was a coincidence of Jewish interests with the interests of that Power which today stands as Mandatory for Palestine, Great Britain. And since I am on this point, which I fear has been misunderstood by many, I should like to add a brief elucidation. If you think that this coincidence of interests is strategic, then you are building on a false assumption. If you think that we have undertaken to act as agents of English imperialist policy in Palestine and the Near East, then you are building on a false assumption. I will be even plainer. If it had helped, if it had helped the Jewish Palestine for us to serve English imperialist policy, I would have done so; and I believe that I could demand absolution for it from this Congress with a clear conscience. If you ask spokesmen of the English Navy or the English Army today, in ninety-five out of a hundred answers they will be against holding on to Palestine. So, let us not imagine ourselves to be the defenders of the Suez Canal. England has provided for that otherwise.

But there is a different coincidence of interests . . . England, with its world-embracing view, understood sooner and more fully than any other nation that the Jewish problem lies like a shadow over the world and can become a tremendous force either for construction or for destruction . . . That is why it was not the English generals but the English intellectuals who were directly the foundation of our policy.[35]

It is possible to state Weizmann's point in another way, which casts a somewhat different light on it. The Zionists, it may be said, went through a course of diplomatic education divided into three stages of sophistication. At the very first ventures into diplomacy of Weizmann, the practical Zionist, his pursuit of an agreement à deux between the Jewish people and the British Empire ran into the hard fact that British interests were tied up with intricate and extensive international combinations. To negotiate an agreement with Britain meant that the Zionists must take account of or come to some understanding with many other interested parties.

The effect of this realization, at first disconcerting, was then exhilarating. Not only did the Zionists find themselves credited with significant influence in America and in the Russian revolutionary movements. The old Zionist myth of a global reconciliation of the Jews with all the Gentiles revived with new vigor when the Zionists were required to win the agreement to their demands not of a single nation, but of a concert of nations, and thus to prepare their entry as a normal nation into the international family. In those days when it seemed that an international conscience would soon address itself to the liberation of all suppressed nationalities, the Zionists hoped that through the international solution of the Jewish problem they, too, would begin to share in a new global consensus.

But the awakening was as rude as it was rapid. The Zionists found that the diplomacy to which they were invited consisted in a management of the balance of power much more than in an appeal to the common conscience of mankind. They entered this arena, moreover, tagged as the client of Britain — even though Britain was ready to grant them no concessions, in the beginning, for which they did not first themselves obtain the assent of its Allies, and, above all, of France. The positions they won in this way subsequently became legal titles which they had to defend against Britain herself through an appeal to Western public opinion and to international tribunals.

The first stage of sophistication began at a crucial meeting between Sir Mark Sykes and nine Jewish and Zionist leaders on February 7, 1917. Two years of general propaganda and preliminary contacts had culminated months earlier in a kind of negotiation by which the British Cabinet had begun to take the Zionist aim seriously. Now the Zionists were shown a fairly detailed contour map of the diplomatic terrain they must traverse in order to reach their goal. Following is Weizmann's account of Sir Mark Sykes' presentation:

Sir Mark began by revealing that he had long considered the question of Palestine and the Jews, and that the idea of a Jewish Palestine had his full sympathy; moreover, he understood entirely what was meant by "nationality," and there was no confusion in his mind on that point. His chief concern, at the moment, was the attitude of the Powers. Sir Mark had been in Russia, had talked with the Foreign Minister, Sazonov, and anticipated little difficulty from that quarter. Italy, he said, went on the principle of asking for whatever the French demanded. And France was the real difficulty. He could not understand French policy. The French wanted all Syria and a great say in Palestine. We (the Zionists) would have to discuss the question very frankly with the French — and at this point we interrupted to say that "we" did not at all relish having to conduct such negotiations: that was the business of the British Government. Mr. James de Rothschild pointed out very correctly that if British Jews approached the French Government, the latter would get French Rabbis to press for a French Palestine.

Sir Mark then went on to speak of the Arab problem, and of the rising Arab nationalist movement. Within a generation, he said, the movement would come into its own, for the Arabs had intelligence, vitality and linguistic unity. But he believed that the Arabs would come to terms with us — *particularly if they received Jewish support in other matters*; Sir Mark anticipated the attitude of the greatest of the Arabs, the Emir Feisal.[36]

The Zionists may not have relished at first the task Sykes assigned them, but they soon developed great enthusiasm for it. They did not, of course, enter upon this undertaking alone or unguided. The path of the Zionist emissary, Nahum Sokolow (1860–1936), in Paris and Rome, with French diplomats and Vatican authorities, was outlined and smoothed at every step by the advice and preliminary contacts freely supplied by Sykes. The Zionists discovered that when they appeared as protégés of England, they met with quite a different response than when they had gone to European chancelleries alone. At first, it was the great advantages of this connection which impressed themselves upon them most forcibly; the disadvantages were to emerge later. Backed by England, the Zionists found themselves able to persuade France, Italy and the Vatican to make concessions about the territory of Palestine which the British were not ready to negotiate directly, whether in their own name or even on behalf of the Jews.[37] Moreover, the recognition thus given to Zionism by the Gentile world reinforced the Zionist position in the Western Jewish community, for outright opposition to Zionism began to look like opposition to the wartime policies of Western governments. Lastly, there was some confidence even in regard to those factors in the situation whom Weizmann and his colleagues were unable to reach as yet — the Russians and, above all, the Arabs; for Sykes gave assurance that he had taken preliminary measures, and made sure of probable consent. In the more doubtful case, that of the Arabs, he said he had already prevented incipient opposition to Zionism from being openly expressed; so that the way was clear for the Zionists to come to an agreement regarding Palestine by offering their help in regard to other Arab interests.[38]

The relationship between the Zionists and Britain, then, was anything but a clear bilateral agreement based on a well-defined *quid pro quo*. The Zionists soon realized that it was to be a relationship crucially affected by the whole web of agreements, ententes, and tacit understandings which united Britain with so many other interests; that the service Zionists could offer the British was as vague as the reward they could expect in return, both being best formulated in discreet generalities; and that it was a service not so much in relation to the direct war effort as to the strategic — that is, the moral — position of Britain vis-à vis its own Allies or potential Allies. Entering into the tangle of these relationships little by little as they learned about them through the effect on their own special interest, the Zionists found much to dismay them. But they also found that Britain looked favorably upon their efforts to change certain established relationships; for Britain was involved in compacts concerning Palestine which it also disliked but was unable to oppose effectively, either because it had originally agreed to them or because they concerned a foreign sovereignty.

Thus the most obvious strategic gain to be hoped for from an understanding with the Zionists was a strengthening of pro-Allied feeling among Jews in America just before and just after its entry into the war, or among Jews in Russia just before and just after the collapse of the Czar. In both countries, the Jewish community, from the British point of view, held positions of unofficial or even of official power that could be used, as Weizmann put it, "either for construction or for destruction." The pro-German, anti-Entente sentiments which, it was feared, might prevail among Jews because of their feeling against Czarism could perhaps be counteracted or even overborne by a pro-Zionist declaration; and a Jewish consensus favorable to the Allies might have a significant effect upon the whole war effort of Russia and America. To be sure, such an analysis of Jewish influence was anything but certain, just as it would have been hard later to demonstrate conclusively the effect of the Balfour Declaration upon general public opinion in those countries. Even though Lloyd George was very generous — overgenerous, indeed — in his appraisal of the effect of the Balfour Declaration,[39] this was hardly the kind of clear, concrete service for which the Zionists could expect a clear, concrete reward.

But there were more specific demonstrations of the importance Zionist initiative might have in improving the position of Britain in the Alliance. Weizmann has described one such incident as an *opera bouffe* intermezzo,[40] but, at the same time, it must have been a revelation to him of the nature and strength of his own position. In June 1917, while the negotiations for the Balfour Declaration were at their height, Weizmann learned from Brandeis of an American mission to the Near East. On inquiring at the Foreign Office, Weizmann was told that "attempts were being made to detach Turkey from the Central Powers." [41] At about the same time, the Armenian nationalist, James Malcolm, heard it announced at a public meeting of the British pro-Turkish party in London that through the efforts of this group it was proposed "to approach certain Turkish politicians in Switzerland, with a view to a separate peace." [42] Putting two and two together, Weizmann and Malcolm went to the Foreign Office in a vigorous joint protest against any idea of falling back on the old British policy of protecting the territorial integrity of the Ottoman Empire. Weizmann, in particular, pointed out that there had already been German proposals to the Zionists to obtain broader rights within the Ottoman Empire, and if the British were to propose no more, the balance of Jewish sentiment might swing toward the German, not the British, side. As a result of these representations, Weizmann received satisfaction in a peculiarly significant manner. Not only was any British initiative toward a separate peace with Turkey within its old frontiers firmly disavowed both privately and publicly, but the Foreign Secretary, Mr. Balfour, sent Weizmann himself to join the American commission as the British representative. His instructions were to "talk to Mr. Morgenthau, [the American commissioner], and keep on talking till I had talked him out of this mission." [43]

Even before this, the Zionists had had proof, on a far more significant point, that by exerting the strength they now learned they possessed they could, in certain matters, alter the shape of the postwar settlement to their own advantage. Whatever the facts of the case, it was the retrospective — and, for that matter, the contemporary — opinion of other interested parties that the Foreign Office used the Zionists as a convenient instrument by whose means (as Lawrence put it in a different connection) they could "biff" the French out of Palestine.[44] George Antonius makes the categorical assertion that British imperialistic designs on the territory adjoining the Suez Canal were the essential reason for the Balfour Declaration.[45] Against this thesis Christopher Sykes marshals impressive evidence to show that up to and even after the issuance of the Declaration, leading British statesmen involved in the negotiations suggested America as a mandatary and even countenanced talk of France as a possible alternative to Britain.[46] But if Antonius proves too much, Sykes overdoes the disproof. The whole tradition of British policy firmly opposed the entrenchment of France in Palestine, and the evidence cited by Christopher Sykes does not suggest any change in this attitude. On the other hand, it is clear that for Britain to set up its own claim to Palestine in direct opposition to the French was a matter of extreme delicacy at the moment. The British undoubtedly preferred to have such a demand come from the Zionists; and Balfour, it seems, would really have liked to interpose America. At any rate, the Zionists themselves had obviously become aware by the time of Sykes' February 1917 briefing, that they could venture to question any arrangements that might have been discussed between Britain and France for the postwar administration of Palestine. They no longer feared that it would be regarded as *ultra vires* for them to make independent suggestions, as an interested party, in this matter, and, in particular, to propose Britain as the new power administering Palestine.

Thus, the first Zionist memorandum, of October 1916, had not ventured to propose any arrangement of its own but merely assumed, in its introductory paragraph, that "Palestine will come under the Suzerainty or the protection or within the sphere of influence of Great Britain or France or under the joint control of both governments." [47] But the Jewish negotiators at the February 7, 1917 meeting each in turn addressed Sir Mark Sykes with insistent arguments against an international administration or a Franco-British condominium in Palestine, and strongly urged British control of Palestine and protection of the Jewish National Home. They proposed that only the Holy Places should be internationalized, and that French and Russian influence extend over these religious sites alone. They were already able to argue then, as they continued to do afterwards, that Zionists in other countries, and above all the influential American Zionists, were "in favour of a British protectorate, and utterly opposed to a condominium." [48] This attitude the Zionists, alone among all parties concerned in the postwar disposition of Palestine, maintained publicly and consistently from that day to the day Britain assumed the Mandate. They were convinced that their attitude had been a factor of critical importance in giving Britain a legal foothold in Palestine, an area where it was evident that, whatever its public professions, Britain desired not only to deny control to the French but to exercise control itself for as long as possible.

Of course, the Zionists throughout the world did not raise their voices on behalf of Britain as the administering power in Palestine simply because they wished to gain an advantage for the British Empire that London was too shy to claim for itself (nor, for that matter, did the British actually obtain the Mandate without hard bargaining with the French on their own behalf).[49] The Zionists had what they considered good and valid reasons for objecting to an international administration, with the insuperable complications that could be expected from such an arrangement, or to French administration, which they openly said probably would be less than efficient and would favor the assimilation of the territory to the culture and community of France. The American Zionists, too, knew quite well how little their own country was really inclined to undertake colonial responsibilities so far afield.[50] England, with its already well-established tendency toward indirect rule and loose ties permitting diverse nationalities to find room for free development under the Crown, seemed to the Zionists objectively the most suitable power for their own aims, quite apart from the fact that British arms would probably occupy the country at the war's end. Thus, when the Zionists took and maintained the initiative in seeking Britain as the ruling power in Palestine, it was their own purposes, and not merely Britain's, they felt they were serving.

They also found that they must, and, what is more, that they could with good effect, fight for their own interests against British commitments that stood in the way of Zionist needs. At the February

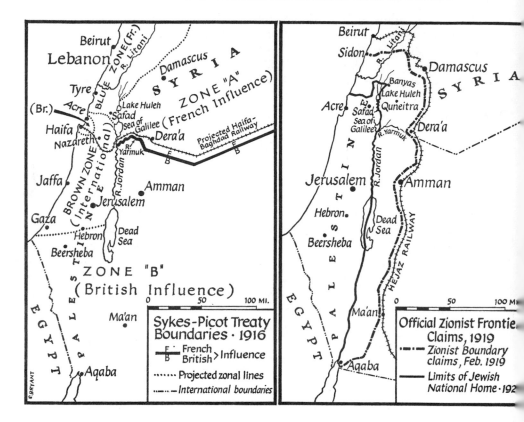

7, 1917 meeting neither Sykes nor Herbert Samuel would say anything specific about the already concluded Sykes-Picot agreement, but the geographical boundaries which Sykes proposed for the Jewish National Home reflected its provisions. The Jewish representatives at once reacted strongly against northern boundaries, adapted from the Sykes-Picot agreement, which would have cut Jewish settlements in the Galilee out of the territory of Palestine. They also objected to Sykes' proposal to salvage for international administration not only the Holy Places but the city of Jerusalem together with a corridor from Jaffa to Jerusalem containing even older Jewish agricultural settlements.[51] Two months later the Zionists obtained specific information on the Sykes-Picot agreement. Dr. Weizmann found an occasion soon afterwards for a full discussion of the matter with Lord Robert Cecil, the Assistant Secretary for Foreign Affairs. He explained in emphatic terms the Zionist objections to the territorial boundaries laid down in the Sykes-Picot agreement and to the internationalization of Pales-

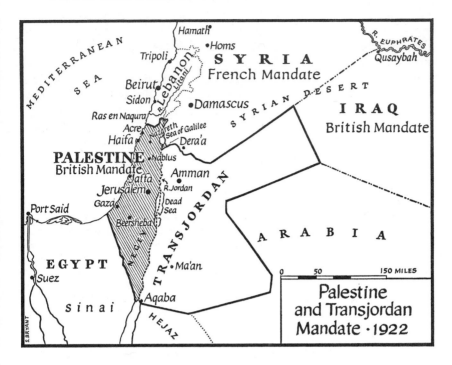

Palestine and Transjordan Mandate · 1922

tine, which in effect meant establishing an Anglo-French condominium. He argued for a single Power, and specifically for a British Protectorate; and, in reply to Cecil's leading question, he went into detail about the reasons which caused the Zionists to reject France and prefer Britain as the protecting Power. The upshot of the interview was a suggestion by Cecil that Weizmann go to Palestine and Syria. Weizmann reports:

> I answered that I was prepared to make the trip — if my work at the Admiralty would permit it — but only with the understanding that I was to work for a Jewish Palestine under a British protectorate. Lord Robert Cecil agreed to this view. He saw the difficulties of the situation, but suggested that it would help a great deal if the Jews of the world would express themselves in favour of a British protectorate; to which I answered that the task of mobilizing this opinion was exactly what I was prepared to undertake; and it would be in pursuance of such a task that I would go to Palestine.[52]

In 1917, leading Arabs had long been aware in a general way of Franco-British negotiations for the postwar disposition of Ottoman territory. The terms of the proposed agreement were drawn up, from the beginning, in a way which the British hoped, on the basis of continuing contact with Arabs, would meet the demands of their projected Arab alliance.[53] At the very time of Weizmann's compact with Cecil to undo the Sykes-Picot treaty, Sykes and Picot were visiting Cairo and Jeddah together, in order to acquaint Syrian and Sherifian Arab leaders more specifically with their agreement. The Arabs made no move at that time to contest the proposed division of the Ottoman realm, but rather came to an understanding with the French about the method of its application. This did not mean, however, that they were ready to accept it as anything more than a provisional arrangement. Thus, according to an Arab report:

There came to Cairo in [April–May 1917] one of the Arab leaders who were with the Amir Faisal. We found him convinced that the King had agreed with the English and the French over their plans for Syria and Iraq. I again heard the same story a month later from another Muslim who was connected with the secret societies. Others who were in Amir Faisal's *entourage* have informed us that they saw a letter from his father to him, mentioning the same thing and giving as a reason for his consent that France would guard the Syrian coast for him till the Arab state could acquire a navy capable of defending it, and that France would pay a stipulated sum to the Arab state every year so long as she occupied the coast.[54]

When reminded by Hogarth in January 1918, that England's policy in the Middle East was based on its alliance with France as well as with the Arabs, King Hussein merely made a joking reference to the Fashoda incident. His acceptance of the Sykes-Picot terms, as he had no hesitation in suggesting to the British emissary, was given in the expectation that France and Britain would fall out sooner or later, and the Arabs would gain even better terms from their friends, the British.[55] It was an expectation in which Hussein must have been encouraged by the anti-French spirit he could easily have observed among his British advisers.

The interest of the Zionists in revising the Sykes-Picot arrangements and their readiness to take the initiative in this matter was no doubt the basis for the British belief that, under their tutelage, Jews and Arabs could come to terms. The British and the Arabs, too, were dissatisfied with the treaty, though neither were prepared to oppose it openly at that time. As the war drew to a close and all concerned with the disposition of the Ottoman Empire began a feverish jockeying for position, this common interest of the British, the Zionists, and the British-sponsored Arabs was developed into a rough-and-ready agreement for cooperation in the postwar peace conferences.

IV

The maneuvering which was required of the Zionists in order to gain their ends in the peace conference was, then, a standard exercise in political tactics. But none of those who worked together to undermine the Sykes-Picot agreement regarded this enterprise as an ordinary matter of *Realpolitik*. On the contrary, the Sykes-Picot treaty itself was condemned as a piece of old-style power politics which had prejudiced the postwar settlement. The campaign to revise it was conducted in a spirit of reform, and everyone who cooperated in it felt that he was defending not merely a selfish interest but the principles of a new and better world order. This was true not only of the Americans, who could offer their Fourteen Points in blithe disregard of secret agreements to which they had never been a party. Sykes and other British Arab experts, who had had much to say in the evolution of the Franco-British-Arab understandings, were equally enthusiastic about upsetting them in favor of grand new designs all their own.[56] The Zionists, too, while seeking their immediate ends, shared in the visions both of a Wilson and a Sykes, so akin to their own idealized myth.

In America the Zionists under Brandeis felt themselves to be part of a world-wide movement of national liberation arising under the aegis of Wilsonian democracy. Brandeis actively aided the causes of Czech, Polish, Armenian, and other suppressed nationalities who fought for their freedom.[57] In cooperation with Eastern European Jews, the Zionist-minded leaders of the American Jewish Congress sought national minority rights for ethnic groups residing in countries outside the center of their national sovereignty; and Jewish delegations became a leading force in the early postwar cooperation of small nationalities interested in minority rights.[58] Brandeis' influence was powerful enough in American postwar planning, in which he was one of Wilson's closest advisers, so that the scholars who briefed the American delegation drew up a plan for Palestine fully in accord with Zionist demands.[59] The American Zionists, then, had reason to feel that their own cause, the repatriation of an exiled people and the restoration of its sovereignty in its ancient homeland, was a natural and well-established part of the general design for national liberation that was to emerge in the peace.

On the British side, too, the Zionists had no sooner begun seriously negotiating with Whitehall than they found themselves associated with other suppressed nationalities in a broad design for a better postwar world. Moreover, the design was more concretely tailored to the specific area of the Middle East than the general principles of the Americans. Weizmann came to the Foreign Office with Malcolm, an Armenian nationalist, in order to discuss matters of fundamental importance to both liberation movements. Through Sykes, and later through Ormsby-Gore, Clayton, Storrs, Lawrence, and other Britons they found themselves discussing with Arab leaders not only their claims on Palestine but the future prospects of the Arab kingdom and the way to overcome the obstacles, such as the Sykes-Picot agreement, which confronted both Jews and Arabs at the Peace Conference. The letters and protocols which record the *rapprochement* between Weizmann and Frankfurter and the leader of the Arab delegation, Feisal, not only outline an agreement for establishing Jewish and Arab "areas" and jointly demarcating the boundaries between them, nor do they simply seal a compact for mutual support in the Peace Conference. There are also statements of the affinity that was felt to exist between the two movements. When Feisal said, "We are working together for a reformed and revived Near East, and our two movements complete one another. The Jewish Movement is national and not imperialist. Our Movement is national and not imperialist, and there is room in Syria for us both. Indeed, I think that neither can be a real success without the other," [60] a sanguine Zionist could be excused for hoping that what had been achieved was not only a political but an ideological understanding with the Arabs. The theses of such an understanding included these propositions: that the Jews were not a foreign Western element, but brother Semites returning to their home in Asia; that the form of their resettlement, not as an upper stratum of administrators, planters, and exploiters but as a working community aiming to become native, guaranteed that they bore none of the taint of imperialism and its associated ills; and that consequently they could serve as a bridge to convey to the Arab East the skills and resources of Western civilization, in a form already assimilated to a Semitic culture, instead of as a bridgehead for depositing its raw, undigested mass as an incubus upon the Arabs.

The euphoria of such vague and sentimental generalities could hardly survive the first contact with the Peace Conference in Paris. The victorious Alliance was breaking apart into barely suppressed rivalries, while its erstwhile foes showed a surprising capacity to regain lost ground at the expense of one or another of the contending Allies. Americans, who held aloof from these rivalries and fought nobly for their vision of a Wilsonian new freedom for the world, were without the authority of solid support in their own country. And instead of the meek — the aggrieved and silenced oppressed nationalities with nothing but their just claims to lean upon — the bold, the shrewd, and the realistic seemed likely to inherit the earth.

The Balfour Declaration and the supporting statements by Allied governments gave the Zionists an uncommonly strong semilegal, semimoral basis for claiming a more concretely legal charter for their further work. But when they came to press this claim they found that the circle of those upon whose political favor they could depend had shrunk alarmingly. The general ideology of a global liberation of suppressed nationalities proved an unreliable support for Zionist demands. The suppressed nationalities whose cause prevailed were those who proved able to defend what they effectively occupied, while others who had no more to rely on than the sympathy of the world, or of some of the Allies, like the Georgians, the Armenians, the Kurds, or Assyrians, were unable to make good their claims.[61] The Zionists, moreover, had a claim which made more than ordinary demands upon the imagination as well as the conscience of the world. They asked to be restored to a land on the basis not of effective occupation but of an ancient historic title. The doctrine of self-determination, on the face of it, opposed rather than supported such a demand; unless, of course, one were prepared for the effort of imagination required by the extraordinary case of a landless people whose opportunity for self-determination depended on being restored to a country of which not they but others were in effective occupation. The Zionists found that such imagination, though not lacking when the problem was posed in a general way before the peace settlement had become an immediate problem, faltered when put to the test of final decisions. The pro-Zionist sentiments of the Americans, for example, proved vague; and a sharp anti-Zionist tendency developed among them justified precisely in terms of the doctrine of self-determination. The Americans, in any case, soon eliminated themselves as a dominant force in framing the terms of the Palestine Mandate (except in defense of their own commercial and other direct interests) when the American Senate and electorate successively repudiated Wilson.[62] As for the French — or, for that matter, the Italians — the tie between Zionism and Britain made them distinctly unfriendly to the cause of the Jewish homeland.[63]

Least effective of all was the relationship the Zionists hoped to build between themselves and certain of the Arabs. The Hejaz leaders who were presented by the British as spokesmen of the Arab cause commanded nothing like solid support among their supposed constituents. Even before the war ended, the British Foreign Office, in

June 1918, had to issue a statement in order to allay fears that the rule of the Sherifian dynasty would be imposed upon Syria against the popular will.[64] At the Peace Conference France was able to produce a Syrian delegation of its own which opposed the rule of British-sponsored Feisal in Damascus and demanded an independent Syria, including an autonomous Jewish national home in Palestine, under French protection.[65] In the following year, while the Mandate for Palestine was still being drafted, the Hashemite dynasty was ejected from Damascus by the French. The assumption upon which the Zionists, no less than the British, had relied, that Feisal could speak as the authoritative voice of Arab nationalism, was thus totally destroyed. But even before the collapse, Feisal's position was sufficiently insecure so that he had to consider carefully the effect of his compacts with the Jews upon his prestige among the Arabs. Accordingly, the documents to which he signed his name were exceedingly cautious and imprecise, and he contradicted in one breath what he implied in the last. Thus, to the formal agreement concluded with Weizmann on January 3, 1919, Feisal added (as an afterthought?) a condition written in his own hand:

If the Arabs are established as I have asked in my manifesto of January 4th addressed to the British Secretary of State for Foreign Affairs, I will carry out what is written in this agreement. If changes are made, I cannot be answerable for failure to carry out this agreement.[66]

Hashemite representatives, as we have seen, had taken a similar attitude in accepting Franco-British agreements which they expected would probably be set aside at a later stage of political development. The Arab position on Palestine was defined by Hashemite spokesmen from an early time in terms of more or less the same implied reservations. In the Sykes-Picot agreements Palestine is set aside as an area of international interest in whose administration the Sherif of Mecca, as well as Russia and the other Allies, were to be consulted.[67] In the same vein, Feisal at the Peace Conference declared that Palestine, because of its universal character, was not to be included in the area for which the recognition in principle of Arab independence was then demanded. Its administration was to be considered as a separate matter by all parties interested; including, of course, the Arab nationalists.[68] Thus while it was conceded that Palestine should not at the outset be declared a part of the Arab Kingdom that was to be established, at the same time a continuing interest of Arab nationalists, among others concerned, was asserted. This left open the possibility of claiming Palestine for the Arab State if the appropriate occasion arose at a later stage of development. Such a claim had already been implicitly asserted by King Hussein in the reservations concerning Palestine which he hinted to Commander Hogarth when the latter called to explain the Balfour Declaration in January 1918. Hogarth undoubtedly knew what was in the Arab monarch's mind when he "agreed enthusiastically" to the Jewish national home formula. Since, as Hogarth noted in his report, he was not instructed to tell Hussein the British had determined to create a Jewish state in Palestine, he could let the Arab hope that the Jewish national home would end as part of the Arab Kingdom, just as the Jews could hope it would end as an independent commonwealth.[69]

The rivals of the Sherifians among Arab representatives in the early postwar period, and particularly the Syrian nationalists, were by no means so circumspect on the subject of Palestine. The French-sponsored Syrian committee demanded that a clear political connection between Palestine and Arab Syria be proclaimed at once, instead of being held in reserve as an Arab claim not specifically ruled out by the proposed Mandate.[70] This kind of demand was easier for French-sponsored Syrians or for Syrians renouncing all mandates, British or French, than it was for the British-sponsored Feisal. If Palestine were to be attached politically to an Arab state in 1919, it would have to be to Syria, whether under French mandate or under an independent Arab regime. For Palestine to be assigned otherwise, one had to argue, in opposition to these Syrian Arab nationalist claims, either that its "universal character" demanded an international administration or that the Jewish national home required Britain as a mandatary. Nevertheless, Arab nationalist opposition to the Jewish demands he had recognized caused Feisal after only two months to record his reservations as explicit rather than tacit conditions. He gave an interview to a French newspaperman in which he was reported as saying that "if the Jews desire to establish a state and claim sovereign rights in the country, I foresee and fear very serious dangers and conflicts between them and other races." The Zionists at once protested, and were reassured by Feisal's secretary who said the interview was in error, since the Emir had only stated his fears that "if the Zionists wished to found a Jewish state at the present moment, they would meet with difficulties from the local population." [71] However, in subsequent years when the Hashemite position was progressively weakened, Hussein reverted to a position similar to that of the Syrian nationalists. Not long before his expulsion from the Hejaz by Ibn Saud, the King of the Arabs rejected a proposed Anglo-Hejaz treaty, because the British refused to substitute the wording of Hogarth's interpretation of the Balfour Declaration to him (stipulating that the Jewish national home policy must be "compatible with the freedom of the existing population, both economic and political") for the wording of the Declaration itself ("nothing shall be done which may prejudice the civil and religious rights of existing non-Jewish communities in Palestine"). In order to make quite clear what he meant, King Hussein offered a counterdraft, in which

. . . he proposed that Palestine be constituted into an independent state with a national government representing all the inhabitants, including the Jews; that it be expressly allowed the faculty of joining a federation of Arab states; and that its "political and economic freedom" must in no sense or degree fall short of that of the other Arab states.[72]

If such a position had been taken at the Peace Conference, it would have made utterly impossible the cooperation of Arab and Jewish opponents of the Sykes-Picot agreement that was there arranged with British advice. The Zionists might, for the sake of cooperation, agree to a formula that did not specifically guarantee the creation of a Jewish Commonwealth if only it did not rule it out. They could, therefore, not agree to a formula that specifically destined Palestine to be attached to an Arab state, because this meant to preclude a Jewish state at the outset. It was only because both Jews and Arabs were allied to the British that an acceptable formula was obtained. That formula was suited above all to make the British task at the moment easier: for by suppressing the question of the ultimate political destiny of Palestine and gaining agreement between Jews and Arabs on a provisional basis, it promised to give the immediate task of governing Palestine a foundation in the consent of the governed. It was an agreement, moreover, which presumed the indefinite continuation of Britain as a mediator between the two, for to leave the two parties to manage their relationship alone meant to raise ultimate questions on which they were not agreed.

Thus, in the period of the Peace Conference, the Zionists found themselves thrown back more and more upon the British. It was a position whose disadvantages they speedily realized. It meant that, with the subsidence of the wartime urgency for assuring Jewish sympathy with the Allies, not only did the fundamental Christian and particularly Catholic antipathy to Jewish restoration in the Holy Land revive; but added to it was suspicion of the Jews in Palestine as British agents that estranged the French, Italians, and others. Even more oppressive was the sense of being at the mercy of the British in arrangements where the British had other than Jewish claims to satisfy. As early as March 20, 1917, Weizmann wrote to Scott, concerning his relations with Sir Mark Sykes:

> I cannot help feeling that he considers the Zionist scheme as an appendage to the bigger scheme with which he is dealing, the Arab scheme. Of course, I understand that the Arab position is, at present, much more important from the point of view of the immediate prosecution of the war than the Jewish question, which requires a rather long view to appreciate its meaning; but it makes our work very difficult if, in all the present negotiations with the Arabs, the Jewish interests in Palestine are not well defined.[73]

The anxiety expressed here became more rather than less acute at the end of the war. In Palestine the Zionists saw their claims resisted by British authorities on the legalistic grounds of the Hague Convention, that required a military occupation to respect the *status quo ante*.[74] No such scruples prevented the same occupation authorities from encouraging similar Arab claims in Damascus in spite of vehement protests from the French. Not only Lawrence but Allenby and the Foreign Office as well cooperated in the military and political arrangements that sought to convert into specific commitments and secured positions the general promises to the Arabs.[75] It became essential, then, for the Zionists, too, to convert the general phrases of the Balfour Declaration into something more specific and more binding. This was accomplished during the Peace Conferences by the negotiations through which the terms of the Mandate were hammered out; and in these negotiations the Zionists had to obtain, primarily with the support of Britain, specific legal titles for the claims they would subsequently have to make, primarily against Britain, before the tribunals of international organization and public opinion.

9 THE MANDATE FOR PALESTINE: FORMULATION AND INTERPRETATION, 1918-1936

THE Jewish national home, whether as a strict legal conception or a symbol rich in the associations of the Zionist myth, is inherently connected with the aim of solving the Jewish problem. But only the Zionists, even among Jews, fully accepted the idea that the restoration of some form of Jewish sovereignty in Palestine would solve the Jewish problem; and they, too, had different conceptions of what the primary significance of the problem was and how, consequently, it was to be solved. Jewish non-Zionists doubted that the Jewish national home need, or could, solve the Jewish problem, but they could not deny, with total consistency, that there was a positive relationship between the two. In moments of critical ideological controversy, to be sure, they propounded anti-Zionist arguments to prove that the national home was a threat to Jewish interests rather than a solution of the Jewish problem. But upon the conclusive settlement of the controversial issues, they reverted to the position adopted by the consensus of the Jewish community: the value of the national home for solving immediately pressing aspects of the Jewish problem could not be denied; nor could its mythic appeal as an expression of immemorial Jewish longings be repressed.

The international Gentile consensus which vaguely recognized that there was a Jewish problem, and that the Jewish national home was an act of justice because it was designed to solve that problem, was essentially the consensus, or the conscience, of the Western World. Even in 1918–1919, when a shared search for national status made Jews and Arabs talk in terms of Semitic brotherhood and political cooperation, the Arab and Moslem world never perceived the Jewish question as a question of conscience: that is, as its own problem. Arab spokesmen declared their sympathy for Jewish sufferings the like of which they averred they, too, had suffered; but this was by no means an act of contrition. It meant no recognition of a duty to redeem the Jews from the unhappy position of a subject minority in the Islamic world. The suffering that evoked Arab sympathy was conceived as something that Christians, and not Moslems, inflicted upon the Jews. When they had to describe their own treatment of the Jews, the Arabs would refer to their generous grant of Islamic protection to a people persecuted by European unbelievers, thus appropriating a stereotype based on Ottoman history.[1] Such a view of the relations between Jews and Moslems made it difficult to accept Jewish sovereignty in Palestine as the solution of a *universal* Jewish problem, since that involved recognizing an *Islamic* Jewish problem. While a *European* Jewish problem was recognized by the Arabs, they denied the justice of solving it by granting Jews sovereignty in Palestine where it would derogate from Arab sovereignty.

Accordingly, even when special political circumstances induced Feisal to enter into an agreement with Weizmann, the understanding did not assume the Jewish problem as its ethical, mythic framework. There was no implication, as there was in Christian endorsements of the Balfour Declaration, that a reconciliation was achieved that atoned for the injuries one side had suffered at the hands of the other. The framework was that of a consensus between brother peoples, both seeking from men of good will in the Christian world their liberation and revival. Only the Jews tacitly assumed that the Jewish problem existed in the Moslem world, too, and consequently expected that the scope of the national home would be measured by the need to solve the Jewish problem universally. The Arabs tacitly assumed that the welcome they extended to the Jews was not an act of reparation, obligatory under conscience, but an act of gratuitous benevolence. The measure of the Jewish national home for them was the extent to which it served or at least did not hamper their own national aims. But, the clauses of the Palestine Mandate inherently contained as their measure of the national home its relation to the Jewish problem. Consequently, when Arab national aims were specifically confined to Palestine, they could no longer accept this document as the basis of any possible agreement with the Jews.

It is true, of course, that an attitude in many respects similar to that of the Arabs was common among Europeans as well. The Jewish problem which the national home was expected to solve was quite frequently conceived as the problem not of one's own Jewish compatriots but of Jews in other European countries. But a feeling of guilt accompanied the view that other Christian nations, even if not one's own, were abusing the Jews; for the roots of the abuse, and of the Jewish problem, could not be separated from the Christianity which was the common heritage of all of Europe. Thus even when disavowing direct responsibility for the Jewish problem that the national home was intended to solve, European nations perceived the restoration of Jewish sovereignty in the ancestral Jewish home as an act of contrition and of reparation to which they were justly, even if vicariously, obligated.

Acts of contrition and reparation in political history, when reduced to legal forms, often lose touch with their original ethical frame of reference. In Palestine, moreover, the Jewish claim upon the conscience of the mandatary could be neutralized by another claim of conscience, the duty to the Palestinian Arabs, which, too, was embodied in the legal forms of the Mandate. By cancelling out the reference to the Jewish problem in this way, the Mandate government could reduce its task — in conception, at any rate — to the normal dimensions of a locally defined administrative situation. The history of the Mandate, accordingly, became, from the Jewish point of view, a continual struggle to reassert, by an appeal to international opinion, the relationship of the Jewish national home to the global Jewish problem. The mandatary, on the other hand, tended to suppress that relationship by interpretation and the Arabs by outright rejection of the provisions of the Mandate.

I

The yardstick by which it is natural to measure the legal titles provided in the Mandate for the development of the Jewish national home is, of course, the draft for a charter drawn up long before by Herzl. Taking this as their model in 1918–1920, the Zionists would have found a number of significant changes which the altered situation immediately suggested. First, there was no longer any need to include provisions for relieving the financial embarrassments of the suzerain of Palestine, for it was not a *quid pro quo* of this kind that had induced Great Britain and its Allies to promise to establish the Jewish national home. Secondly, the authority of the new mandatary in Palestine was not conceived as permanent and unconditional, like Ottoman rule, but was of a provisional kind; as was, for that matter, the theoretical suzerainty over the territory which, according to some, was reposed in the new League of Nations.[2] Consequently, it was not only possible but necessary to make far bolder Jewish claims to ultimate sovereignty in Palestine — for, if not the Jews, then the Arabs would ultimately fill the legal vacuum caused by the provisional suspension of the anticipated national sovereignty in Palestine.

Thus, the earlier negotiators — Montefiore and Oliphant as well as Herzl and Wolffsohn — stressed the recognition of Ottoman suzerainty and conceived Jewish sovereignty in Palestine in terms of a far-reaching local autonomy. The general object of these programs was to give the proposed Jewish Company freedom of action to develop Palestine, unhampered by the insecure tenure of power common to the Ottoman system or by the exactions of officials whose authority from time to time extended over the Holy Land. This general purpose was adequately secured, in 1919–1920, by the very plan to establish Palestine as a separate Mandate. Accordingly, while the political provisions desired in the Mandate instrument reflected the earlier drafts in other respects, they were framed from a different perspective. Time, not space, was the important dimension. The object was to define the status toward which Palestine must ultimately be raised, rather than to single out for it a special status within a territorial complex to which it belonged.

These two changes — the elimination of one of Herzl's provisions and the inclusion of a provision he had omitted — were demanded by the new situation even in terms of the most rigorous political Zionism. But Weizmann and his friends were Practical Zionists; and they had witnessed the effective revival of spoken Hebrew and the beginnings of a rounded Jewish community anchored in a new Jewish farming and workers' class. They sought Mandate provisions which would safeguard these achievements, too, as valuable instruments and expressions of the Jewish will to sovereignty. With these additions and omissions, the Zionists, in their negotiations conducted with Britain concerning the clauses of the Mandate, attempted to obtain powers that closely resembled the Herzlian idea of the charter.

A new emphasis was evident in the efforts to obtain satisfaction on one matter to which Herzl had given little real weight when he included it as a point in his negotiations with the Sultan. In arguing against the small-scale colonization conducted by his predecessors, Herzl employed a striking illustration of the difference between their conceptions; he said that the kind of settlement he had in mind was such as would naturally be defended by its own armed forces.[3] And, indeed, he included Jewish armed forces among the proposals he wished to lay before the Sultan. But he did so in a spirit which makes this demand appear far from essential to his immediate tactical design. He noted in his diary that he made this demand precisely because he expected it to be denied. Herzl feared that the Sultan might accept all the major elements of his plan, and that the Zionists would then find they could not, after all, produce the funds they promised. But if, at the same time, the Sultan rejected the minor demand for Jewish armed forces, this would give Herzl an opportunity to withdraw from the arrangement more gracefully and with more credit than if he had to admit his own financial incapacity. When he was in a position to reopen negotiations with assured financial backing, he could then present it as a concession on his part to waive the demand, in the beginning, for the creation of a Jewish armed force.[4]

The ideas of a Jewish army and a Jewish militia had greater significance in Zionist diplomatic designs during the First World War. When Jabotinsky and Weizmann or Pinchas Rutenberg (1879–1942) and David Ben-Gurion took up the idea of a Jewish Legion in the Allied armies, they had the same tactical model in mind as did some of the Britons who organized the Arab Revolt, or the French and Italian leaders who pressed for the inclusion of their units in the army that was to drive the Turks out of the Levant. Cavour's maneuver to gain representation and rewards for Italy at the peace conference by sending a small force to participate in the Crimean War was the classic pattern which they all sought to emulate. In the case of the Jews, moreover, maintaining a Jewish battalion as an organized force in Palestine after the war was important not only for the implied political recognition but for sheer security in the face of threatened Arab violence.

Only the Arabs were able, with the full cooperation of the British, to follow Cavour's example with any significant success. The Italians and French were represented at the Peace Conference, since they had had a major share in the fighting in other sectors. But their relatively feeble efforts to bolster up their claims in the Levant by a show of military participation in that arena were rebuffed and their token forces were kept well in the background by British policy.[5] The Jews, too, were able to present their demands at the Peace Conference and to obtain important rights and titles. But this, it was made clear, was the result of Zionist diplomacy in England and America and of the international situation in the spring of 1920 that made Britain desire a continued entente with the Zionists. On the other hand, the fate of the Jewish armed forces in the Mediterranean theater served only to demonstrate to the Zionists the weakness of their position in the combinations of British policy, both during the war and, even more sharply, after it.

The first attempt at a Jewish Legion, made in 1915 by a group of Jewish refugees in Alexandria who had been expelled from Palestine by the Turks, led to results that could not be accepted by politically oriented Zionists. The British would agree only to establish a

Jewish unit not specifically assigned for service in Palestine and constituted in the modest form of a labor corps. Since he had hoped to obtain political credit by a symbolically striking military demonstration, Jabotinsky rejected the plan. The Zion Mule Corps was founded, nevertheless, through the efforts of Joseph Trumpeldor (1880–1920) and participated in the Gallipoli campaign with credit to its members. It could have no significant political effect, despite a certain amount of publicity given it.[6]

Jabotinsky's campaign to organize a more impressive Jewish Legion was finally approved by the British in the summer of 1917, when the government was also considering its intended pro-Zionist Declaration. Jewish battalions were organized in Britain and America in time to participate in Allenby's Palestine campaign and in Palestine in time to participate in the postwar occupation. The appearance of these Jewish units, with their political implications, was no more welcome to the staff and political officers of the Egyptian Expeditionary Forces than the prospect of French and Italian army units with similar implications; for the local staff strategy had adopted the Arab Revolt as its chosen instrument whereby to gain British objectives in the area. They did not bear gladly the folly, as it appeared to them, of the politicians in London who wished to fasten the Jewish units upon them as a political encumbrance. The men and officers of the Jewish battalions were made to feel staff displeasure in the most pointed fashion, particularly by the suppression of any notice of them calculated to stress their connection with Zionist aims.[7]

The impression which then took root among Zionists, and particularly Palestinian Jews, that they had an enemy in the staff officers of the British army in Egypt and in the Arab experts delegated from service in Egypt to administer Palestine became a fixed opinion in the period of the military government in Palestine. Having failed to manage Jewish participation in the Palestine campaign in such a way that it would achieve political goals, like the Arab Revolt, the Zionists hoped for greater success in the postwar period. They worked hard to maintain the Jewish battalions as a force-in-being that could support the promise of the Balfour Declaration and also provide a more effective defense for the Jewish community than the prewar organization of settlement guards. Circumstances seemed to favor such plans. With the approval of the government in London, an international Zionist Commission had been despatched to Palestine in the spring of 1918. This, together with specific instructions from the War Cabinet, seemed to make the staff in Egypt more responsive to the official Zionist policy.[8] Also, the demobilization of older units at the end of the war left the Jewish battalions, especially the Americans and Palestinians, a significant fraction of the dwindling force available for occupation duties. However, such use of the Jewish battalions in Palestine was resisted on political grounds by the staff in Cairo, just as it was pressed on political grounds by the Zionists.[9] During the unsettled and violent days of military rule in 1919 and 1920, and in the first year of civil administration, the Jewish battalions did contribute to the safety of the community on repeated occasions, but only in the face of staff opposition. The political consequence was that the idea of a Jewish military force as a part of the Mandate scheme was officially repudiated through such measures as the disbandment of the battalions, and the forced departure of the Jewish officers who most prominently defended the Legion as a symbol and guarantee of the ultimate political significance of the Balfour Declaration.[10]

The three-day pogrom behind the walls of Jerusalem in April 1920 sealed with mythic effect the conclusion drawn by the Jewish consensus that the military government was anti-Zionist and more than slightly anti-Semitic. Not only the attitude of the authorities to the Arab rioters before, during and after the attacks but their attitude to the attempted Jewish self-defense reinforced this impression. The Jewish legionaries were confined to barracks during the attack and those who had already arrived in Jerusalem were rounded up by military police. The Jewish militia then being organized in Jerusalem, with the knowledge of the authorities, was barred from entering the Old City during the pogrom; and Jabotinsky and others of its leading members were arrested and, after a secret trial before a military tribunal, were sentenced to long-term imprisonment.[11]

Another event, shortly before, also made an impression of mythic force. This was the desperate defense of the Jewish settlements in the Upper Galilee, where the withdrawal of British occupation forces and the failure of the French to substitute effectively had left conditions of anarchy. This, too, was a defeat for the Jews, but in effect it was a moral victory. The 1920 Jerusalem pogrom and the 1921 Jaffa riots had essentially negative effects. The Jewish consensus learned not to rely on official goodwill in pursuit of its aims. Thus, the community despaired of achieving an officially recognized militia as part of the Jewish national home policy under the Mandate. From the defense of Tel Hai, crowned by the heroic death of Trumpeldor, the Jewish consensus derived a legendary positive example of pride and self-reliance. The mythic effect of this episode was not impaired by the fact that the settlements in Upper Galilee beyond the line of

British occupation had to be abandoned after the fight at Tel Hai. At the first opportunity, months later, the area was resettled as a point of honor. The emotional conviction behind the doctrine of self-defense, with or without official recognition, which was inspired by the myth of Tel Hai was reinforced by an ideological rationale. The community became convinced that only because of the existing Jewish settlements in Upper Galilee and the independent Jewish defense of Tel Hai was the northern boundary of Palestine finally fixed so as to include the eastern source of the Jordan River.[12]

One effect of these events was to turn the Jewish consensus against Jabotinsky's rational ideology. His views became a minority opinion, capable only of voicing the resentments of the people against the hardships encountered in its chosen way but not of leading them in a different way. The British refusal to set up a Jewish garrison for all of Palestine or an official Jewish police force for the defense of the settlements meant that the Palestine police force which *was* set up became overwhelmingly Arab instead. The same was true, for that matter, of virtually all the government services, especially health and education. The government not only used the relative proportions of the Arab and Jewish populations as a guide in apportioning its services, but budgeted for a scale of wages and a level of services adapted to an Arab rather than a Jewish standard of living. Few Jews could be employed and few Jews served at such a level. The official Zionist spokesmen protested against this outcome, demanding a fairer proportion of government employment and government services and an administrative policy geared to what Palestine had to become, not to the backward conditions it had to overcome. The Revisionists, for their part, gained the applause of an irritated public by voicing the same demands more radically, and also by blaming the official Zionist policy for the development of the existing situation. But at the same time, the consensus of Jewish opinion in Palestine after 1921 consistently relied on its own independent efforts and autonomous institutions to do whatever the Mandate government failed to do for the education, health, and defense of the community, and for the growth of the Jewish national home. The same attitude was adopted as a more or less articulate line of policy by the Zionist leadership in response to the position taken by the British in the formative years when the Mandate was drafted and the boundaries of Palestine marked out.

Whether or not it is true that the inclusion of one of the sources of the Jordan within Palestine's frontiers was a consequence of the defense of Tel Hai and the resettlement of the Jewish colonies in the north, there is ample evidence that the boundary in question was claimed and obtained by the British in virtue of their undertaking to establish the Jewish national home. When Lloyd George struck his bargain with Clemenceau in November 1918 for a British instead of a Franco-British regime in Palestine, he demanded the Biblical boundary "from Dan to Beersheba";[13] and this, too, was the phrase used by Lord Curzon to delineate the proper bounds of the Holy Land. The Jewish national home was to be a modern replica of the Promised Land; and on the strength of this historical argument the boundary of Palestine would have to be extended northward beyond the demarcation line of the Sykes-Picot agreement. Balfour at the Peace Conference considered that the British demands concerning the northern boundary of Palestine could not and should not be defended against the French on strategic grounds. The convincing arguments for a boundary including the whole of the Jordan in Palestine were the needs of the Jewish national home. In order to have resources sufficient to allow it to perform its proper function in solving the Jewish problem, Palestine needed control of the Litani and Jordan waters as well as agricultural land east of the river, short of the Hejaz railway line.[14] The point was made even more significantly by Forbes Adam, one of the British experts at the Peace Conference charged with preparing a draft Mandate. The differences between the British and French over the Palestine boundary, he said, came to a difference over the definition of the Jewish national home.

(2) From the general tenour of these discussions it seems obvious that the French and British conflict of opinion on this matter fundamentally arises from their different interpretations of the declaration as to a national home for the Jews, to which both Governments, in company with the Italian and U.S. Governments, have subscribed. The French Government interpret this declaration as a promise to protect and somewhat extend the existing Zionist colonies (M. Berthelot repeatedly spoke of "les colonies Sionistes existantes") . . . .

(4) On the other hand the British Government by their support of Zionism have to a much greater degree accepted the natural implications which Zionists give to the declaration of a National Home, i.e., an attempt to make Palestine a state in its natural geographical and historic frontiers and by gradual immigration and special economic facilities to turn this state into a Jewish state. Only time and experience can show how far the Zionist aspiration is realisable; while it is not expected that Palestine will ever be able to give a home to all the Zionists in the world, it is thought that eventually some three (3) million instead of the present 60,000 Jews may be able to settle, and that hope and self-respect may be given to a large part of Eastern Jewry who can never actually go to live in Palestine.

Behind British policy, therefore, is the recognition of the principle of Jewish nationality, which is the essence of Zionism and the intention to lay in the Turkish Peace Settlement the foundation for the reconstruction of a Jewish Palestine, as of an Armenia for the Armenians.

(5) If this aspect of British policy is to be fulfilled it is obvious that the frontiers of Palestine must be drawn on the same sort of principles as those of other reconstructed countries. It also seems clear that some such frontiers are required in order to give that impetus and encouragement to Zionists, at this crisis of their fortunes, which will enable them to secure the right number of suitable immigrants and the large sums of money essential to the success of their cause.[15]

The British position, as defined above, reflected the letter and spirit of the memorandum submitted to the Peace Conference by Zionists. Under the heading of "The Historic Title of the Jews to Palestine," this Statement of the Zionist Organization regarding Palestine declared:

The claims of the Jews with regard to Palestine rest upon the following main considerations: (1) The land is the historic home of the Jews; there they achieved their greatest development; from that centre, through their agency, there emanated spiritual and moral influences of supreme value to mankind. By violence they were driven from Palestine, and through the ages they have never ceased to cherish the longing and the hope of a return.

(2) In some parts of the world, and particularly in Eastern Europe, the conditions of life of millions of Jews are deplorable. Forming often a congested population, denied the opportunities which would make a healthy development possible, the need of fresh outlets is urgent, both for their own sake and in the interest of the population of other races, among whom they dwell. Palestine would offer one such outlet. To the Jewish masses it is the country above all others in which they would most wish to cast their lot. By the methods of economic development to which we shall refer later, Palestine can be made now, as it was in ancient times, the home of a prosperous population many times as numerous as that which now inhabits it.

(3) Palestine is not large enough to contain more than a proportion of the Jews of the world. The greater part of the fourteen millions or more scattered through all the countries must remain in their present localities, and it will doubtless be one of the cares of the Peace Conference to ensure for them, wherever they have been oppressed, as for all peoples, equal rights and humane conditions. A Jewish National Home in Palestine will, however, be of high value to them also. Its influence will permeate the Jewries of the world, it will inspire these millions, hitherto often despairing, with a new hope; it will hold out before their eyes a higher standard; it will help to make them even more useful citizens in the lands in which they dwell.[16]

The same Britons who so pointedly recognized the connection

between the Jewish national home and the Jewish problem when seeking to gain more generous boundaries for Palestine from the French were extremely cautious about the use of terms that would suggest a British guarantee for the actual realization of the Zionist goal in Palestine. If we may abuse a phrase that was popular in Zionist debates on a similar topic, they considered Britain responsible for creating *Bedingungen* but not *Dinge*: the conditions for a Zionist solution of the Jewish problem, not the solution itself. In defining the boundaries of Mandated Palestine, the powers of the Jewish Agency, and the rights of the Palestine Jewish community and the global Jewish people, the British statesmen were prepared to bear in mind the requirements necessary for mass immigration and for an ultimate Jewish majority and Jewish state in Palestine. They would undertake to provide the necessary conditions. But Britain would not explicitly commit itself to bring about the mass immigration and resettlement of Jews in Palestine and the creation of a Jewish majority and a Jewish state in Palestine. That was for the Jews to attempt and for time and events to determine.

The distinction that it was sought to establish here was a difficult and, as it turned out, a slippery one. If the Mandate were to specify only the conditions for achieving the Zionist goal, not the goal itself, then only the means would appear as the letter of the law. Respect for the spirit of the law would then depend on continued British sympathy with the unspecified end, the Zionist goal. Weizmann and his colleagues, even while negotiating the terms of the Mandate, already knew enough of the anti-Zionist temper of the local adminis-tration in Palestine to fear this prospect. They wanted the letter of the law to be sufficiently explicit to make the Zionist goal unmistakable in the Mandate. At the same time, their pro-Zionist British friends not only insisted on a Mandate which specified conditions rather than results, but they also expected official Zionists to ease the task of the local British administration by restraining the Jewish people and especially the Palestine community from what they considered exces-sive demands. Only on these terms would they agree to a British Mandate at all. These were the most important counterbalanced pres-sures whose resultant — only achieved after years of revision — was the Palestine Mandate.

The excessive Zionist demands that Weizmann was expected to suppress were nothing but a direct logical application, in terms of instruments, of the fundamental Zionist principles that statesmen like Balfour — or Wilson — were themselves ready to accept as a valid goal. The ethical basis of the Balfour Declaration, transposed into

Wilsonian terms, might be stated in the following manner: The Jewish people, like other historic nationalities, has a right to self-determination. The Jews, having been exiled from their ancestral homeland, cannot effectively exercise their right to self-determination until restored to sovereign possession of their country. *Ergo*, the Jews are entitled to the sovereign possession of Palestine. The subordinate clauses that were appended to the Balfour Declaration had the following significance, in terms of this scheme: Other legitimate rights existed which might conceivably be affected by restoring Jewish sovereignty in Palestine. The restoration should be so conducted that these would not in fact be adversely affected. This was entirely possible, moreover, since the rights in question, by definition, were not incompatible with Jewish sovereignty in Palestine.

These were the principles which some Zionists, particularly the Palestinians, sought to embody in proposals that would directly symbolize, as well as implement, the fundamental intentions of the Balfour Declaration. They proposed accordingly that Palestine be governed, under British authority, by a representative council in which the Jewish people throughout the world, ultimately to constitute a majority in Palestine, should have a voice, side by side with the delegates of the settled Jewish and the Arab population; that the country be referred to by its Hebrew name *Eretz Israel* and its flag be the Jewish flag of the Zionists; and that Hebrew and Arabic be the official languages.[17]

None of these hopes could be countenanced by the British; and there was nothing the pro-Zionists among them wished more ardently than to have Zionist demands of this kind silenced. Western pro-Zionist public men, though not yet attacked as subservient to a Zionist electorate, even then had to defend themselves against the charge that sentimental sympathies for the Jews were blinding them to the cold realities of their own national interest. Colonel Meinertzhagen, posted to Cairo as political officer with Zionist support, felt obliged to preface one of his reports with a frank statement proving himself conscious of what others might consider his bias. He began, he indicates, as something of an anti-Semite, like anyone else, but was won over by what he saw in Palestine and became an ardent Zionist: an avowal of possible bias and a suggestion of willingness to guard against it which were much appreciated by the chill intelligence of Lord Curzon.[18] Lord Balfour himself was provoked at the Peace Conference to an indignant protestation that his Declaration had not been an act of sentiment but a war measure; and in despatches he follows the admission that he is "an ardent Zionist" with instructions to defer Zionist requests.[19] Lloyd George, while always attesting a genuine sympathy for the Zionist idea, ascribes the timing, if not the origin, of the Balfour Declaration to the need for Zionist services (which he rated as highly effective) in rallying Jewish support for the Allied war effort.[20]

The Britons in official positions who were friends of Zionism found themselves on the defensive. It follows that they could not withstand protests from the man on the spot in Palestine contending that Zionist demands and demonstrations were arousing the Arab populace and making their task of governing the country acutely difficult. The pro-Zionist Britons in London and Paris expected men like Weizmann and Brandeis to silence such inconvenient demands and demonstrations. They had proved their friendship for Zionism by forcing the local administration to give recognition to moderately formulated Zionist demands. The most emphatic demonstration of this attitude was the replacement of the Military by a Civil Administration in the spring of 1920, shortly after Britain was named mandatary but before the Mandate itself was approved. Sir Herbert Samuel, a Jew and a friend of Zionism, became High Commissioner, and Norman Bentwich and A. M. Hyamson were nominated to high positions in the Administration. The British expected the Zionist leaders, in return, to come to terms not only with the British officials in Palestine but also, as far as possible, with the Arabs, and to silence whatever Zionist demands and demonstrations they had to in order to achieve this.[21]

These were tasks that Zionist leaders like Weizmann and Brandeis did, indeed, accept. Weizmann began very early to discourage demands for an explicit promise of a Jewish state, and Brandeis after San Remo virtually declared the political era of Zionism to be suspended. Weizmann managed to transfer liaison with the government from more doctrinaire to more elastic Zionist officials, and Brandeis proposed a clean sweep of the old-line Zionist leadership, including especially those who were most rigid in their demands. Weizmann also went to great pains to appease the Arab leaders and assure them that the Zionists did not demand immediate preponderance in the government of Palestine.[22] The Jewish officers in the British administration in Palestine also strove to accomplish a task for which as Jews they were well qualified: to hold in check the pressure which Jews might bring to bear against the administration. They took this assignment seriously enough not only to win the applause of a veteran of the Military Administration like Sir Ronald Storrs but to incur the criticism of a moderate official Zionist like Colonel Frederick Kisch, who was equally intent on holding the Jewish public in check in order to achieve harmonious cooperation with the Mandate government.[23]

The Zionist leaders were simultaneously engaged in a protracted campaign of negotiation with British statesmen and of pressure against them in order to establish definitively a political framework for the Jewish national home which would permit it, not only in name but in fact, to solve the Jewish problem. The growing opposition to Zionism in the immediate postwar era made it obvious that specific safeguards in the Mandate were necessary for this purpose. All those who had concurred in issuing the Balfour Declaration now began to waver. The French were hostile, and the Italians, on behalf of the Vatican, raised objections to Zionism itself in connection with their demands for satisfactory Mandate provisions regarding the Holy Places. The same Wilson who had been so useful, in his offhand way, in obtaining the Balfour Declaration now caused a quasi-plebiscite to be organized by an American Commission, a procedure which implied that the Zionist policy announced for Palestine was anything but a *"chose jugée."* The local British administration could only be brought to permit the publication of the Balfour Declaration in Palestine by specific instructions from above. Consequently, the Zionists had to seek positive indications, if not guarantees, in the Mandatory instrument that Jewish sovereignty was the aim of the Mandate; or at least to avoid formulas which either explicitly or by their potential application foreclosed this aim.

The history of these negotiations falls into two parts. During the first period, until the San Remo conference, the nomination of Britain to be the mandatary in Palestine still remained uncertain. In the second period, the bargaining position of the Zionists was weakened because this point was already decided.

II

Proposals for the Palestine Mandate were drafted by American and British Jewish leaders like Felix Frankfurter and Herbert Samuel, working with committees of Zionists from all over the world assembled in Paris and in London. At the specific demand of the British — and American experts who annotated one document were equally hostile — certain proposals demanded by the Zionist public were omitted from the official draft. Among these were provisions calling for an ultimate Jewish majority and a Jewish flag in Palestine, for representation of the world Jewish people, and for a Jewish chief and a majority of Jewish officials in the Palestine government.[24] On the other hand, the official Zionist drafts tried persistently to insert new phraseology, supplementing the wording of the Balfour Declaration, and clearly disavowing certain restrictive interpretations of the Declaration which were already being voiced. Efforts were made to indicate that the whole of Palestine, and not some part of it, was to be the site of the Jewish national home; that what was contemplated was *the* national home of the Jews, and not *a* national home such as they might be said to have in Poland, if granted national minority rights; and that this home should ultimately take the form of an autonomous Jewish commonwealth. To establish the basis for such demands it was sought, moreover, to have the Mandate state that the international community recognized the historic title of the Jewish people to Palestine.[25]

The Zionist drafts also concerned themselves with the specific rights and powers needed for carrying out an aim such as theirs. If they wished to follow precedent, the Zionists had two logical alternatives. They could center their demands on a wide grant of authority to themselves, following Herzl's conception of the chartered company; or they could rely on the Mandatory administration and its laws, in the way they had thought might be done during the Young Turk days. In neither case could the historical model be closely followed. Even in miniature, the achievements of the era of Practical Zionism had suggested new uses for Jewish autonomy and different forms of Jewish autonomy to add to the Herzlian conception. On the other hand, if the general policy of the Mandatory government were to be relied on (as Jabotinsky proposed), not merely abstract principles of liberal democracy but a regime of sponsored development could surely be demanded from the country that had issued the Balfour Declaration, and was now to put it into effect as the trustee of the Jews and representative of the international community.

The official Zionist proposals for a Mandate instrument did not choose one or the other abstract possibility, for the situation they faced allowed for no clear choice. Britain would neither agree to permit such dominance of a Jewish Agency in the government of Palestine as was contemplated in Herzl's idea, nor would she specifically obligate herself to create a Jewish majority and a Jewish state in Palestine. Under the circumstances, the Zionist drafters sought to obtain as much scope as possible for Jewish autonomy in furtherance of their national aim and, at the same time, to commit the Mandatory government as far as possible to cooperate toward the same end.

Since it was impossible to claim a share for world Jewry in the government of Palestine as a whole, the autonomous rights conceded to the Jewish community in Palestine became even more important, symbolically as well as materially. The embryonic commonwealth doubly represented by the Palestine community and the world-wide Zionist movement needed recognition of its historic legitimacy, and it needed, also, the conditions for fostering its national individuality and its rapid growth. Accordingly, the Zionist drafts demanded recognition of Hebrew as an official language and of the Jewish Sabbath and Holy Days as legal days of rest; progressive recognition of local self-government as communities proved able to exercise it, and autonomy for Jewish educational institutions to be administered by the Jewish community and the world Zionist movement; and, especially, recognition of a Jewish agency, entitled to cooperate with the government in bringing in and settling Jewish immigrants and authorized to obtain concessions on a preferred basis for developing waste lands and other natural resources.

At the same time, the Zionist drafters sought to commit the mandatary itself to policies which, without guaranteeing it, would provide suitable conditions for the achievement of their aim. They proposed that the Mandate government be obliged to promote the immigration and resettlement of Jews in Palestine, in cooperation with the Jewish Agency, and to facilitate the acquisition of Palestinian citizenship by Jewish settlers. The government was to be instructed in the Mandate to adopt economic policies such as would favor the intensive development of the country, as required by the Zionist plan; and when Zionist development had made this possible, the mandatary was to transfer all authority to the people of Palestine as a self-governing commonwealth.

A final major provision which the Zionist drafters proposed at an early stage was a specific delineation of Palestine's frontiers. This was still another question on which Herzl had permitted himself to be both elastic and vague, concentrating as he did on the primary question of the recognition in principle of Jewish sovereignty over some territory. Under the postwar conditions, it was necessary to have firm and definite assurances on this point. Not only did the Zionists now face the problem of actually accommodating from three to six million Jews in a country poor in land, water, and mineral resources. They also had to devise specific plans for accomplishing this without detriment to the rapidly multiplying Arab population. Whether Palestine would ever become a Jewish commonwealth at all or whether the Jewish national home would remain no more than another Jewish national minority, seemed to depend on success or failure in dealing with both tasks simultaneously.

The Zionists approached the question of boundaries with a background of forty years of colonizing under the Turks. The following, they had concluded, were the conditions which determined what boundaries were needed to make possible the Jewish commonwealth: The country was poor and unbalanced in land and water resources, and had no significant minerals or fuels. Moreover, Jewish resettlement had been accompanied by an unprecedented growth of Arab population in the same restricted area. This had already led to a sharp rise in the price of land and to political clashes, going beyond the accustomed quarrels between neighbors or between settlers and Bedouin in Palestine. Under these conditions, the successful establishment of the Jewish commonwealth without detriment to the Arab population could only be achieved by a far more intensive use of Palestine's cultivated land, requiring greater water and power resources, and by opening up new, unused tracts of land capable of producing cereals economically.

More specifically, it required that Palestine include on the north the outlet of the Litani River, as well as the entire Jordan River, from its sources in the southern slopes of Mount Hermon. It required the cereal growing lands from Mount Hermon south, east of the Jordan, including the falls of another stream, the Yarmuk. This area might make Palestine self-sufficient in bread grains, and provide a land reserve for the expansion of the farming population and the resettlement of tenants from lands west of the Jordan which the Zionists might wish to convert to irrigated or other intensive crops. For the same reasons, and in order to exploit the commercial potentialities of a land bridge between the Mediterranean and the Red seas, a southern boundary from Akaba to El Arish in Sinai was required. In this southern area, as in the Hauran and Transjordan plains and the Jordan Valley, were to be found unused state lands which could be developed by the Zionists without exorbitant payments to absentee landlords and without arousing the resistance of tenants, whom even compensation and the prospect of resettlement on equivalent lands elsewhere could not always persuade to leave their holdings peaceably.[26]

In the first phase of the drafting of the Mandate, up to the San Remo Conference of April 1920, the Zionist negotiators found their British counterparts quite understanding, in spite of the generally adverse political conditions under which Zionism labored. In the second phase, after Britain had been accorded the Mandate for Palestine, the Zionists had to appeal to public opinion and use other available pressures in order to salvage as much as possible of their draft.

Weizmann himself valued the recognition of the "historic connection" of the Jews with Palestine as a decisive achievement. It was not recorded in the Mandate without difficulty, however, nor without modifications of the Zionist draft. The Zionist drafters repeatedly asked for recognition of the "historic title" of the Jews, which justified reconstituting Palestine as their National Home. According to Weizmann's report, Curzon rejected this phrasing, "remarking dryly: 'If you word it like that, I can see Weizmann coming to me every other day and saying he has a *right* to do this, that or the other in Palestine! I won't have it!' As a compromise, Balfour suggested 'historical connection,' and 'historical connection' it was." [27]

But it did not go quite so simply. In the drafting suggestions of Forbes Adam, composed as an alternative to the Zionist draft of 1919 several months before the San Remo Conference, there was a reference to the Jewish "historical connection" with Palestine.[28] In the San Remo Conference no more was decided than the assignment of the Palestine mandate to Britain with the proviso that the mandatary would put into effect the Balfour Declaration, whose main clauses were repeated, and appoint a special Commission, under a chairman named by the Council of the League of Nations, for "all questions and claims relating to the different religious communities." [29] In spite of this renewed international commitment to the Balfour Declaration in the very instrument that awarded the Mandate to Britain, agitation against Zionism continued, culminating about two years later in a vote by the House of Lords (though not, of course, the Commons) to revoke the Balfour Declaration. The chill in the atmosphere surrounding Zionism had already made itself felt much earlier and in more influential quarters. On June 10, 1920, shortly after the San Remo Conference, the Foreign Office, with Curzon rather than Balfour as the final arbiter, issued the first official British draft for the Palestine Mandate. It omitted reference not only to the "historic title" but to the previously acceptable "historic connection" of the Jews with Palestine. Only through long and strenuous efforts were the Zionists able to restore the acknowledgment of an "historic connection" in the Preamble of the Mandate as submitted to the League of Nations on December 6, 1920.[30]

Other Zionist proposals had a history of similar vicissitudes. The Zionist drafters repeatedly proposed phrases like the "establishment" or "reconstitution of Palestine as the Jewish national home," and statements recognizing that a Jewish commonwealth was the ultimate aim of the Mandate, or even a specific stipulation that the Mandate must be so administered as to achieve this goal. By these provisions they sought to rule out hostile interpretations, based on the Balfour Declaration's wording — *a* national home for the Jewish people *in* Palestine — which might restrict the national home to part of Palestine or to autonomy instead of sovereignty as an ultimate status. So, too, they drafted provisions which tended to oblige the mandatary to establish local self-government and communal autonomy at once, expanding them progressively, and to recognize the country as a self-governing commonwealth when Jewish immigration and development had created the necessary conditions for a Jewish state.

In the negotiations before San Remo, the British accepted a clause which stated that a recognized "historic connection" gave the Jews a claim "to reconstitute Palestine as their national home (*Erez Israel*)." [31] The Zionist provision calling for a self-governing commonwealth to develop out of the growth of the Jewish national home was also accepted, though mention of a "*Jewish* commonwealth" had to be suppressed on pain of British refusal of the Mandate. After San Remo, the whole paragraph in which the Zionists sought to revise the wording of the Balfour Declaration was simply dropped. Concerted Zionist efforts succeeded only in restoring, in the Preamble of the Mandate, the original wording of the Balfour Declaration (not the proposed revision), together with a reference to the "historical connection of the Jewish people with Palestine and to the grounds for reconstituting their national home in that country." As for self-government, the British confined their commitment to "the development of self-governing institutions," not a "self-governing commonwealth." They also changed the construction of the sentence to take this clause out of its significant relationship with the establishment of the Jewish national home and leave it hanging midway between the Mandatory obligations to establish the Jewish national home and to safeguard "the civil and religious rights of all the inhabitants of Palestine, irrespective of race and religion."

The Zionist drafters fared somewhat better in those sections where they proposed to create conditions for autonomous cultural institutions and economic organizations that should constitute and enlarge the framework of the Jewish national home. Before San Remo, Zionist demands for an option for the Jewish Agency to take up concessions for waste lands, water and power development and other utilities, and for the recognition of Jewish cultural autonomy and the Jewish holidays were well received. In the British official draft drawn up after San Remo all these provisions were suppressed. But the final text of the Mandate recognized in more or less general terms the obligation to facilitate immigration and resettlement and the acquisition of citizenship by Jews, and to safeguard at the same time the civil and religious rights and general welfare of the non-Jewish communities.

In all drafts for the Palestine Mandate, the rights of the non-Jewish communities were more or less plainly distinguished from the rights of self-determination and the promise of national sovereignty characteristic of other "A" Mandates, which were outlined in the fourth paragraph of Article 22 of the Covenant of the League of Nations. Article 22 itself was drawn up by some of the same men who were chiefly responsible for the Jewish national home policy. Its general purpose was to proclaim the principles of ultimate self-determination and of government by consent of the governed for the benefit of the mandated peoples and to establish the rules of trustee-ship as a guiding principle for the mandataries.[32] In the Palestine Mandate, Article 22 is referred to generally in the Preamble as the occasion for granting a Mandate for Palestine, and its eighth paragraph is referred to specifically as the basis for the right of the Council of the League of Nations to define explicitly "the degree of authority, control or administration to be exercised by the Mandatory." [33] But both Article 22 and the references to it in the Palestine Mandate were phrased, certainly by design, in a way which could forestall an appeal against the Balfour Declaration on the grounds that the existing majority of the population was entitled to veto the establishment of the Jewish national home.

Article 22 was formulated in what have been called "studiedly" general terms. Some of its paragraphs referred in particular to countries stated to be virtually ready for self-government, others to areas stated to require Mandatory supervision for an indefinite time. The general clauses of the Article, and especially its third and eighth paragraphs, made ample provision for such exceptional cases as the Jewish national home or the nation of Armenia, which were of particular concern to one of the authors of the Article, J. C. Smuts.[34] These cases required a form of self-determination that recognized the superior claim of an exiled or refugee nation whose extremity of national need and recognized historical connection with a country ought to override the opposition of hostile neighbors in and around it or of the established majority in it. In spite of the relative political maturity of the populations involved, the grant of territorial self-government in such countries would have to await the solution of the primary problem.

When Article 22 was referred to in the instruments governing the postwar disposition of liberated parts of the Ottoman Empire, it was done in a way which expressed the intentions of the authors to make it cover radically different cases. Thus, the Treaty of Sèvres made a pointed distinction in referring to Article 22 in its provisions concerning Syria and Mesopotamia, on the one hand, and Palestine, on the other. In the former case, the fourth paragraph of Article 22 was specifically cited, and, in language echoing that paragraph, it was stated that Syria and Mesopotamia were to be "provisionally recognised as independent States subject to the rendering of administrative advice and assistance by a Mandatory until such time as they are able to stand alone." The provision regarding Palestine refers generally to Article 22, without mentioning its fourth paragraph, and instead incorporates the language of the Balfour Declaration (as had the agreement of San Remo) in its instruction for the future constitutional arrangements of the country.[35] So, too, in the Mandates for Syria and Lebanon and for Mesopotamia, the Preamble cites the fourth paragraph of Article 22 specifically; and the body of these Mandates provides for carrying out the aim of this paragraph as a primary objective. In the Palestine Mandate, on the other hand, Article 22 is referred to twice in the Preamble — one general and one specific reference, but to the eighth not the fourth paragraph. Provisions for carrying out the Balfour Declaration appear as the primary objective in the body of the Mandate.[36] Lord Balfour, then, was well justified when he replied on June 21, 1922, in the House of Lords to contentions that Article 22 of the League Covenant stood opposed to the terms of the Palestine Mandate.

When my noble friend tries to maintain the paradox that the Powers who adopted the Mandatory system, the Powers who laid down the lines on which that system was to be carried out and have embodied it in the League of Nations, and have set going Governments in different parts of the world, who are at this moment carrying out the mandatory system, are so ignorant that they do not know their own child, and are violating all their principles when they establish the policy of a Jewish Home in Palestine, I think my noble friend is not only somewhat belated in his criticism, but is asking us to accept a proposition which, as men of common-sense, we should certainly repudiate.[37]

If, then, the British draft and the final approved text carefully avoided anything in the nature of a guarantee that the Mandate would culminate in a Jewish state or a Jewish commonwealth, they were framed with equal care to avoid any guarantees to non-Jewish political claimants that could preclude the ultimate establishment of a Jewish state or a commonwealth. The Palestine Mandate has been accused both of mutually contradictory provisions in favor of Jews and of Arabs and of being obscure and ambiguous in its terminology. The first of these charges is evidently unwarranted; but precisely in order to avoid contradictions, without giving the Jews the specific guarantees that they desired, the British draft necessarily resorted to obscure and ambiguous phrasing of the provisions in favor both of the Jewish people and of the non-Jewish communities in Palestine. The unequivocal meaning of these phrases could only be made clear experimentally, in the course of Zionist efforts to take advantage of the opportunities offered them.

One vital condition which would determine what the Zionists could make of the national home, and for which they had proposed specific provisions to be included in the Mandate, was the extent of Palestine's boundaries. These were left undetermined in the Mandate text approved by the League of Nations on July 24, 1922. However, negotiations between France and Britain and political developments from 1918 to 1921 had established the major outlines of the area. Events had also led to an administrative division between the parts of the Mandate east and west of the Jordan River, which withdrew Transjordan from the application of the Balfour Declaration. The final text of the Mandate authorized this measure in its Article 25. The basis for such a delimitation of the Jewish national home was set out in a White Paper issued on July 1, 1922, which was recognized as an authoritative comment on the Mandate formally approved a few weeks later.

In their boundary discussions with the French, the British succeeded in achieving their own major aims. They acquired frontiers between Syria and their own Mandates, Mesopotamia and Palestine, which, together with certain transit rights, left room for British road and rail transport and oil pipelines between the Mediterranean and the Persian Gulf. They were not as successful in arguing the Zionist case for an adequate northern frontier for Palestine. The French recognized the Zionist need for water, but they seem to have felt that the national home could easily turn out, and might well be confined to, a more modest affair than the Zionists imagined. They agreed only to allow the eastern source of the Jordan, the area of the existing Zionist settlements defended at Tel Hai, to remain in Palestine. The French argued that on historical grounds, too, the Jewish national home was not entitled to more. The other sources of the Jordan flowing from Mount Hermon, as well as the outlet of the

Litani River, were retained in the French mandated area, on the understanding — never carried out, however — that the French would favor an arrangement permitting the Zionists to use these streams for irrigation and power development. So, too, the Zionist claim to land in the Hauran plain south of Mt. Lebanon was rejected.[38]

For its eastern and southern frontier, the Jewish national home was primarily dependent not on French but on British goodwill. The consideration for Zionist territorial needs in order to accommodate millions of immigrants which was shown by the British in 1919 and 1920, when it was a question of the northern frontier with a French Mandate, was not in evidence in 1921 and thereafter, when it was a question of Transjordan, which like the rest of the Palestine Mandate was under British control. The fortunes of the Hashemite dynasty and not the requirements of the Jewish national home had the upper hand in British calculations. The east bank of the Jordan, where Zionists had hoped to find land reserves only thinly occupied by cultivators, was denied both to Jewish settlers and to the expanding Arab rural population west of the Jordan.[39] However, the need to defend the Hashemites against the claims of Ibn Saud, as well as the need for a supply route from the Red Sea for Britain's forces in Palestine, led, subsequently, to the inclusion of the Negev, Palestine's semiarid southern half, in the area to which the Jewish national home clauses of the Mandate continued to apply.

The Churchill White Paper of 1922, which explained the basis for the division of the Palestine Mandate into areas open and areas closed to Zionism, also laid down other principles which controlled the interpretation of the Mandate thereafter.[40] The White Paper took the significant form of a dual reply to complaints from the Arabs, on the one hand, and the Jews, on the other.

To the Arabs, it explained that His Majesty's Government did not think it practicable to create a wholly Jewish Palestine and had no such aim in view. Nor was "the disappearance or the subordination of the Arabic population, language or culture in Palestine" contemplated at any time. It called attention to the phrasing of the Balfour Declaration, which did not say "that Palestine as a whole should be converted into a Jewish National Home, but that such a Home should be founded *in Palestine.*" It also noted a resolution of the 1921 Zionist Congress, which had indicated the Zionist desire to "live with the Arab people on terms of unity and mutual respect, and together with them to make the common home into a flourishing community, the upbuilding of which may assure to each of its peoples an undisturbed national development." In addition, the White Paper noted that the Zionist Commission in Palestine "has not desired, and does not possess, any share in the general administration of the country," and that the powers of the Jewish agency referred to in Article 4 of the draft Mandate did not "entitle it to share in any degree in its Government"; and, also, that "the status of all citizens of Palestine in the eyes of the law shall be Palestinian." It referred to the plans of the mandatary for the gradual introduction of self-governing institutions and for safeguarding the civil and religious rights and improving the position of all the inhabitants and particularly the Moslem community in Palestine. Finally, it defended the application of the Balfour Declaration and the suspension of independence west of the Jordan River (and by implication, the exclusion of Transjordan from the area subject to the Jewish national home provisions) as consonant with British promises to the Arabs in the McMahon correspondence.

To the Jews, the White Paper gave the assurance that the policy of the Balfour Declaration, reaffirmed at San Remo and in the Treaty of Sèvres, was "not susceptible of change." It interpreted the Jewish national home as existing in nuclear form in the Jewish community built up in Palestine over the past two or three generations and already possessed of "national" characteristics in "its town and country population, its political, religious and social organisations, its own language, its own customs, its own life." The "development" of this national home did not imply "the imposition of a Jewish nationality upon the inhabitants of Palestine as a whole, but the further development of the existing community, with the assistance of Jews in other parts of the world, in order that it may become a centre in which the Jewish people as a whole may take, on grounds of religion and race, an interest and a pride." This aim required that the Jewish community "should know that it is in Palestine as of right and not on sufferance," and hence that "the existence of a Jewish national home in Palestine should be internationally guaranteed and . . . formally recognised to rest upon ancient historic connection." Furthermore, the Jewish community must be able to grow by immigration, subject to the exclusion of politically undesirable persons such as the administration was already keeping out. The limit of Jewish immigration should be "the economic capacity of the country at the time to absorb new arrivals," and the guarantee that "the immigrants should not be a burden upon the people of Palestine as a whole, and that they should not deprive any section of the present population of their employment."

The White Paper was presented as a summary of the "essential parts" of correspondence between the Colonial Secretary and the Moslem Christian Society of Palestine. It was transmitted both to the Arabs and the Jews for their acceptance. The Zionists, still nervously awaiting the final approval of the Mandate, reluctantly agreed to be guided in their activities by its principles. The Arabs rejected it.

III

The Churchill White Paper of 1922, and the extensive correspondence with Palestinian Arab representatives that preceded it, represented an attempt to define the legal situation under the Mandate through negotiations with Palestinian Arabs as well as with Jews. It was a singularly one-sided sort of negotiation, to be sure, for the Arab spokesmen simply rejected the Mandate, based, as it was, on the Balfour Declaration. They founded their claims, instead, on Paragraph 4 of Article 22 of the Covenant of the League of Nations, although the Mandate was written not only without citing this paragraph but in deliberate exception to it. It remained for the British Colonial Secretary to suggest how far Arab claims could be legitimately presented on the basis of the clauses of the Mandate as it stood. Rejecting this approach, the Arabs in the following years repeatedly appealed from the mandatary to the League of Nations. Here, too, they cited Article 22 as the legal foundation of their claim to invalidate the Mandate as a whole, adding a series of specific complaints concerning the administration of the Mandate. The dilemma of the Permanent Mandates Commission in the face of such a position was like that of the mandatary itself; and the Commission found a similar way to solve it. The Commission declared itself incompetent to consider petitions against the Mandate as a whole, while it sought to consider specific allegations in terms of the Mandate as it stood.[41]

Thus, the legal possibilities for defending Arab claims which were inherent in the Mandate as formulated were not at first exploited by the Arabs themselves, for they argued from a basis of outright opposition to the Mandate. It was the mandatary and the Permanent Mandates Commission that first indicated the possibilities of an Arab case in terms of the Mandate.

Two Articles of the Mandate in particular, Articles 2 and 6, invited interpretation as legal supports for Arab grievances without going outside the accepted constitutional framework of government in Palestine.

Article 2. *The Mandatory shall be responsible for placing the country under such political, administrative and economic conditions as will secure* the establishment of the Jewish national home, as laid down in the preamble, and *the development of self-governing institutions*, and also for safeguarding the civil and religious rights of all the inhabitants of Palestine, irrespective of race and religion.

Article 6. The Administration of Palestine, while *ensuring that the rights and position of other sections of the population are not prejudiced*, shall facilitate Jewish immigration under suitable conditions and shall encourage, in cooperation with the Jewish agency referred to in Article 4, close settlement by Jews on the land, including State lands and waste lands not required for public purposes.[42]

The history of the italicized clauses in Article 2 has been referred to before. In the original Zionist draft, "self-governing institutions" had been referred to as a "self-governing Commonwealth," or even as a "Jewish Commonwealth," and the clause as a whole signified a promise to recognize the sovereign independence of the Jewish national home when it had reached the position of a preponderant part of the population in Palestine. This phrasing and signification were accepted by British negotiators before San Remo. Afterwards, however, when the plans for a transfer to a Civil Administration in Palestine were being completed, the British, on second thought, revised the phrasing. "Self-governing institutions" appeared in place of a "self-governing Commonwealth," signifying that the political status promised might well be less than sovereign independence. Moreover, the connection between the promise of self-government and the promise of the Jewish national home, which had been unmistakable in the Zionist draft, was obscured by the new draft. As the paragraph finally read, self-government could easily be interpreted as a promise to "all the inhabitants of Palestine" rather than a final stage of the establishment of the Jewish national home. The British Civil Administration, established in July 1920, cited this clause of the draft Mandate when it began immediately to attempt the institution of limited self-government for all Palestinian inhabitants. It seems likely that the official draft of June 1920, which introduced the revision of the Zionist draft, intended to provide a legal basis for this new British policy.[43]

While they were aware of the implications, the Zionists, in their comments on the revision, did not refer to the fact that the promise to develop self-government had been torn out of its Zionist context. They remarked that "self-governing institutions" did not necessarily mean full self-government, as did "self-governing Commonwealth"; and they said that even though they recognized that the Jewish national home must grow gradually into full sovereignty, it would be unfortunate if the Mandate phraseology left any doubt that full self-government was the ultimate status that was intended. They showed no apprehension that the promise to develop self-governing institutions would be interpreted as an obligation separate from the Jewish national home policy and perhaps in some conflict with it, on the grounds that its intended beneficiary was rather the present Arab majority than the potential Jewish majority.[44]

In the 1922 White Paper, Winston Churchill denies that the claim of an independent Arab Palestine could be based on the McMahon-Hussein agreements, just as in earlier correspondence he had denied that it could be based on paragraph 4 of Article 22 of the Covenant.[45] But he then indicates on what legitimate grounds Arab claims for a greater share in self-government could be considered and gradually satisfied.

Nevertheless, it is the intention of His Majesty's Government to foster the establishment of a full measure of self-government in Palestine. But they are of the opinion that, in the special circumstances of that country, this should be accomplished by gradual stages and not suddenly. The first step was taken when, on the institution of a civil Administration, the nominated Advisory Council, which now exists, was established. It was stated at the time by the High Commissioner that this was the first step in *the development of self-governing institutions* . . .[46]

But Winston Churchill, it seems, no more felt that the italicized clause was a special obligation towards the Arabs in Palestine than did the Zionist drafters. He apparently interpreted it, as they did, as a basis upon which a Jewish state, too, could ultimately emerge if the Jews responded to the opportunity granted them by becoming a preponderant part of the population of Palestine. Reporting to the Cabinet shortly after he had set Emir Abdullah up as ruler of Transjordan in 1921, Churchill said that when Palestine, by a gradual development, became mature for full self-government, Jews and Arabs would participate on a *pro rata* basis in its rule, according to the population ratio at that time.[47] In testimony before the Royal Commission of 1937, he said that this remained his interpretation of the Mandate in the following years too, after the 1922 White Paper was published.[48]

It was the Mandates Commission which first unmistakably indicated the use of the "self-governing institutions" clause as the legal grounds for asserting a special obligation to the Arabs. The first extensive discussion of the Palestine administration before the Commission took place at its Fifth Session, held in Geneva, from October 23 to November 6, 1924. The Commission had before it not only the mandatary's regular report and reply to its questionnaire, but a memorandum of protest from the Palestine Arab Congress forwarded by the British Foreign Office.[49] The Commission, having considered certain particular grievances mentioned in the latter document, passed over without comment other Arab complaints which called the Mandate itself into question. At the Seventh Session, from October 19 to October 30, 1925, the Arabs, adopting the procedure suggested by the action of the Commission at the Fifth Session, sent two memoranda. The first, attacking the Mandate itself, was directed to the Council of the League of Nations. The second memorandum presented a list of grievances which could be argued on the basis of the Mandate itself.[50]

One of the major Arab grievances which the Permanent Mandates Commission at its Fifth Session recognized as admissible under the Mandate was the halting development of "self-governing institutions." The Arab memorandum to the Fifth Session, to be sure, had raised this issue not as a grievance under the terms of the Palestine Mandate but as part of their fundamental objection to that Mandate. They based their legal argument on an appeal from the particular terms of the Palestine Mandate to the general spirit of the mandatory system, and specifically to paragraph 4 of Article 22 of the Covenant.

[The Palestine Arab] case may be summed up in the following words: The injustice of creating a Jewish National Home for the Jews in Palestine, which is the well-established home of the Palestinian Arabs (Moslems and Christians), and the impracticability of training its inhabitants in self-government and preparing them for independence, which is the principal aim of the mandatory system, as long as the Jewish National Home policy is in progress.[51]

Nowhere in this memorandum do the Arabs explicitly claim a grievance under Article 2 of the Mandate in the failure of the government to set up "self-governing institutions." Nor is such an argument to be found in the Arab correspondence with the Colonial Secretary preceding the issuance of the 1922 White Paper. On the contrary: Article 2 is mentioned only as a legal basis for establishing the Jewish national home, and the Arab complaint is that the "self-governing institutions" referred to in it could only mean, under the circumstances, the eventual self-government of a Jewish majority.[52] After having read the minutes and reports of the Fifth Session, however, the Arabs adopted the line suggested by the Commission, and in their memorandum listing grievances admissible under the terms of the Mandate, they complained vigorously of the failure to develop self-governing institutions.[53]

In its comments, direct and indirect, on Arab grievances, the Commission Report on the Fifth Session considered two legal points. The first, which was the major argument of the Arab memorandum, concerned the Arab claim under Article 22 of the League Covenant. On this point the Commission reported as follows:

Whereas all the other mandates the application of which it has hitherto examined were only intended to give effect to the general principles laid down in Article 22 of the Covenant, the Palestine Mandate is of a more complex nature. As is expressly stated in the Preamble of the Mandate, and as is clearly shown by several of the clauses of this document, the Council, in drawing up its terms, desired, while giving effect to the provisions of Article 22 of the Covenant, to carry out also the plan of establishing in Palestine a National Home for the Jewish people . . .

It is not in any way for the Commission . . . to contrast the two principles which the Council sought to embody in the terms of the Mandate for Palestine. But, as this Mandate of necessity reflects the dual nature of its inspiration, and as its application has given rise to complaints by persons basing their case on one or other of these principles to the exclusion of the other, the Commission would not be fulfilling its task if it refrained from making any reference to the facts which have come to its notice in this connection.[54]

In addition, however, another legal consideration was inserted into the discussion and the report. The Chairman of the Commission, Marquis Theodoli, who had Arab connections by marriage, said in the discussion that Arab rejection of the proposed Legislative and Advisory Council was based on Article 2 of the Mandate, which provides for self-governing institutions; and he insisted on an explicit reference to this legal point in the report.[55] Thus the report says:

The divergences which bring Zionism and the Arab majority into conflict . . . produced particularly unfortunate results when an attempt was made to create an Advisory or Legislative Council. The Arabs, appealing to Article 2 of the Mandate, which guarantees the development of self-governing institutions, declined to cooperate . . .[56]

Thereafter, Article 2 was regularly referred to as a basis for Arab complaints in regard to self-government. However, in considering the complaints in substance, the Permanent Mandates Commission did not tend to sustain the Arab position. In his defense of the administration of Palestine before the Fifth Session, Sir Herbert Samuel explained how the government was forced to fall back on an Advisory Council made up entirely of officials because of the Arab boycott of the elections and their insistence on the right to nullify the Balfour Declaration. Although the mandatary was hard pressed by Commission questioners, the Commission in the end tacitly accepted the view that self-government should, for the time being, be advanced on the level of local and municipal autonomy. In subsequent sessions, the Commission concluded that the Palestine government was bound by the terms of the Mandate to develop self-governing institutions in such a way that the Jewish national home could be simultaneously developed. In 1928, one of the members, William E. Rappard, even proposed a report stating explicitly that

In the present instance, it seems obvious that a form of democratic and parliamentary government is not provided for either by the Covenant or by the Mandates, and that it is not even compatible with the obligations devolving upon the Mandatory Power under those engagements.[57]

This view was not shared by all the Commission members, nor did those who were inclined to agree think it advisable to formulate the point so explicitly. There was general agreement, however, that if one defined the Arab demand as territorial self-rule in Palestine without regard to the Balfour Declaration and the Jewish demand as the continuation of direct rule by the mandatary in pursuance of the Balfour Declaration, then the Jews had the law on their side.[58]

But this, it was felt, constituted a legal privilege for the Jews, and resulted in the inability of the Arabs to enjoy rights which were promised them under the terms of the Mandate as formulated. For it appeared to members of the Commission that even if one accepted — as they did — the observations of the British in reply to Arab complaints, then Arab rights to local autonomy under Article 3 of the Mandate were being reasonably well fulfilled, but Arab rights to territorial self-government under Article 2 remained in suspension. There were undoubtedly good legal and political grounds for so suspending the exercise of Arab rights to self-government, but the suspension was a grievance which both the Palestine government and the Zionists should seek to remove by conciliatory policies.

An idea that grew increasingly appealing was that since no direct political understanding with the Arabs seemed possible, an indirect method might be adopted by seeking to eliminate Arab dissatisfaction in regard to nonpolitical matters, such as their economic position. On this subject, too, a legal basis was sought, under the Mandate as formulated, for Arab complaints that their civil and religious rights (Preamble) or their rights and position (Article 6) were being prejudiced.

On the question of the welfare of the non-Jewish population in Palestine, a common understanding of the legal requirements of the Mandate was shared in the beginning by the mandatary and the Mandates Commission and by the Zionists as well. The legal position was defined not only by the pertinent clauses in the Mandate, but by the Churchill White Paper of 1922 which declared "economic absorptive capacity" to be the ruling principle for determining the scale and rate of Jewish immigration into Palestine. This does not mean that there were no Arab petitions complaining of economic injury, or that the topic was not frequently discussed by the British accredited representatives and the members of the Mandates Commission. But these discussions did not revolve about the recurrent theme of a conflict in legal rights which were possibly incompatible, as did the discussion of self-government. For the most part, it was assumed that Jewish and Arab economic welfare could be promoted together, if only the accepted legal principles of the Churchill White Paper were properly administered. The discussion centered chiefly on a question not of law but of fact: whether the actual administration of the country had conformed to the principles laid down in the White Paper.[59]

Of all the parties concerned, the Arabs alone refused to recognize that the economic benefits which might be conferred by Jewish resettlement could be a pertinent fact in assessing the situation. Their favorite position was to reject with scorn this mess of pottage with which it was proposed to purchase their birthright. Even when their protests referred to economic injuries, what was most likely to provoke their wrath was the political or the social threat seen in the professed economic loss. Thus in their memorandum to the Fifth Session of the Permanent Mandates Commission (and in evidence before the Haycraft Commission investigating the 1921 Jaffa rioting) the Arabs made complaints such as these: Jewish Bolshevist immigrants were taking work that could be done by Arabs, and, moreover, the unemployed among them were carrying on violent agitation which could spread subversive notions to unemployed Arab workers; the government's new land regulations purporting to protect Arab tenants from eviction (as well its alleged use of a Turkish law calling for the reversion to the State of land left uncultivated three years) were really intended to make farming unprofitable and force Arab landlords to sell to Jews at a low price; and the employment of Jewish officials and the official use of the Hebrew language burdened the tax payers with unnecessary expenses.[60] So, too, they protested to the Fifth and Seventh Sessions that certain land and public utility concessions were granted to Jews when they might have been granted to Arabs.[61] The complaints were of economic injury, but the emphasis was on a threatened loss of the position occupied by the Arabs in prewar days and the potential creation of a superior Jewish position — a situation which would not be acceptable to the Arabs even if they were shown that it had actually brought them material advantages rather than injuries.

In the first decade of the Palestine Mandate, both the Permanent Mandates Commission and the mandatary were aware of this Arab attitude, and both were inclined to consider at times whether it might not be politic to make some concessions to it. Thus, in deference to Arab opinion, the mandatary was decidedly generous in granting land concessions to Arabs even when they had little or no prospect of developing them effectively, and, in fact, subsequently sought to profit by reselling them to Jewish companies.[62] On the other hand, despite the specific clauses of the Mandate providing that concessions might be granted to the Jewish agency and that close settlement of Jews was to be facilitated, the land concessions granted to Jews were surrounded with severe restrictions [63] and fell far short of what they anticipated in extent. The criterion used here was not that of maximum economic development, but of maintaining the Arab "position" as a sort of *status quo ante*. So, too, M. Beau, a member of the Permanent Mandates Commission, in the Fifth Session, suggested that it might be good policy to confine the close settlement of Jews to areas relatively unpopulated by Arabs and so avoid disturbing the Arab position.[64] But in none of these cases was there any clear idea of a legal right to maintain the *status quo ante*; the policy was a pragmatic one of avoiding Arab irritation.

Indeed, it was a recurrent theme in the whole discussion of Palestine that there were two distinct grounds upon which the mandatary was bound to give consideration to the Arabs. In addition to their legal rights under the Mandate, the Arabs had a certain "sociological" claim based on their status in the past, which it would be both politic and equitable for the mandatary, as well as the Zionists, to bear in mind.[65] It was logically possible to adduce a legal basis, too, for this claim in the clause in Article 6 of the Mandate which said that the "rights and position" of the Christian and Moham-medan Arabs should not be prejudiced. Nevertheless, the Mandates Commission, which had discovered a certain legal justification for Arab claims to territorial self-government in Article 2 of the Mandate, did not suggest or recognize the possibility of a legal argument under Article 6 of the Mandate which would preserve the relative social and economic positions of the several sections of the population more or less as they had existed in Turkish times.

This was perhaps due, among other reasons, to a general bias inherent in the theory of mandates. Progress to a more advanced stage of freedom and social welfare was the keynote of the system. Hence, the Arab claim to independent self-government, which they had not had under the Turks, was in harmony with the general principles of the mandates system, and it was natural to seek a legal basis in the Mandate to justify it. Their claim to be undisturbed in traditional social privileges that were associated with conditions of economic backwardness and deprivation was contrary to the general intent of the mandates. The example of Egypt, where Western order, efficiency, and medical service had brought great economic expansion together with social change, was held to be a generally suitable model for Palestine. Thus, while suggesting that the peculiar circumstances in Palestine required particular tact and care to reduce the shock of similar changes, the Mandates Commission did not think of finding clauses in the Mandate which would give the Arabs a legal guarantee for the *status quo ante*. On the contrary, the economic expansion brought about by Zionism was in accord not only with the Balfour Declaration but with the general purpose of the mandates system. The legal right of the Arabs under the Mandate was the right to share in the benefits of such expansion, under an appropriate policy of the mandatary calculated not only to control but to encourage economic development and to see that its benefits were equitably distributed.

The mandatary, on the other hand, eventually developed the theory that it was obliged under the Mandate to protect an established relative position of the Arab population in Palestine. Many reasons, which go beyond the scope of this study, no doubt contributed to this turn of events. The strategic importance of Palestine grew more rather than less impressive after the war, especially when the British plans for road and rail communications, sea and air port development, and the oil pipeline from Iraq began to be carried out. And if the tie with the Jews seemed vital when it was a question of getting the Mandate, holding the British position in Palestine during the Mandate and in the period after the Mandate would be succeeded by independence, seemed, on any sober calculation, to depend more on the goodwill of the Arabs than of the Jews. The former were so large a majority that it was very doubtful at first whether the Jews could ever outnumber them. And when this prospect became something more than a chimera, it seemed obvious that if it wished to sponsor the Jewish commonwealth, Britain risked losing its hold on the surrounding Arab countries, which were at least equally essential to imperial strategy. Apart from all these considerations, there were also certain inherent possibilities of interpreting the Jewish national home policy which could be harmonized with the idea of a British obligation to maintain the relative position of Jews and "other sections of the population" essentially as it was in the prewar period. From the very beginning of the Mandate, the Palestine Administration, because of its composition and because of the kind of problem it faced in governing the country, was predisposed to take advantage of any such possibility.

The vague and more or less tacit understanding worked out between Jews and Britons in drawing up the Mandate — and accepted both confidentially and publicly in even vaguer terms by Arab representatives — involved agreeing on explicit provisions for the development only of what was called the "Jewish national home," and on the suppression of all but the most obscure suggestions of the "Jewish commonwealth." In order to make the agreement work, the Zionists were expected not only to accept the elimination from the Mandate of phrases which specifically recognized their full and final aim of Jewish sovereignty. They were also required to endorse the Churchill White Paper, which instead of merely remaining obscure on this point, as the Mandate did, explicitly denied that Britain undertook, as its own obligation, to bring about the Zionist aim. They were expected to state publicly that their own activities would conform to the policy thus laid down by Britain — which, if it meant anything, could only mean an undertaking not to press Britain with regard to the ultimate political demands of a Jewish majority and Jewish sovereignty; and, accordingly, they were obliged to keep the Jewish community as far as possible from voicing its ultimate demands.

Those responsible for this compact, the British authorities at the highest levels and the reluctant Zionist leaders, could accept it in the awareness that nothing in it prevented the Zionists from quietly hoping for a Jewish commonwealth and earnestly working away to achieve a situation, by immigration and resettlement, which would make it the natural form of political sovereignty in Palestine when the time came for bringing the Mandate to a close. On the other hand, the compact was open to a different interpretation — one which could reconcile British officials on lower levels to their job, even though many of them had been far from sympathetic, from the beginning, to the Zionist complication. These men, under the Military Administration, had resisted any application of the Balfour Declaration on the grounds that the Hague Convention required an occupying power to observe the *status quo ante* with scrupulous care. With the inception of Civil Administration some of the adherents of this point of view were removed and others resigned. Still others, according to Sir Ronald Storrs, should have resigned but did not, continuing to serve under an administration committed to the Balfour Declaration, a document to which they could not reconcile themselves.[66] But there was an additional group, notably represented by Storrs himself, who found a way to interpret the Mandate and the Balfour Declaration so that these documents, too — like the maintenance of the *status quo ante* during the Military Occupation — were capable of protecting to a large extent the relative position of the Arabs *vis-à-vis* the Jews. It had the additional advantage that it promised to establish permanent British positions in Palestine.

All that was necessary in order to evolve such a point of view was to ignore the tacitly conceded right of the Jews to expect suitable conditions in which to work for the Jewish commonwealth as the culmination of the Jewish national home. Part of the compact accepted by the Zionists, as we have noted, was their undertaking not only to give up the demand of British guarantees for the emergence of a Jewish commonwealth, but to silence Zionist demands for the immediate or rapid achievement of this goal. The Zionists, moreover, were expected to state explicitly that they did *not* demand the immediate or rapid achievement of such a goal. They were helped by men like Storrs himself to deliver such avowals directly to Arab leaders in order to appease them, and make the British task of government easier and — if possible — to gain for it the consent of Arabs as well as Jews. The hope of men like Winston Churchill and Sir Herbert Samuel, as well as Weizmann, may have been that the Palestine Arabs would adopt an attitude like that adopted earlier by Feisal and Hussein. They might agree to cooperate in the progressive development of the country through Zionist investment and the *pax Britannica*, while quietly hoping that in the final political accounting Palestine would be a dominantly Arab state or part of a larger Arab state. But the Palestine Arabs accepted these British and Zionist assurances only momentarily, during Weizmann's visit in 1918. In the ensuing years of general Arab unrest, the Palestine Arabs, too, became recalcitrant and violent. The Zionists blamed the disturbances that followed on the unwillingness of British administrators to enforce the Balfour Declaration wholeheartedly, or, in some cases, to accept it at all. The British administrators counterattacked by blaming the Zionists. The Zionists, they held, were supposed to appease the Arabs with moderate statements of their policy. They had not succeeded. The reason was obvious, and to anyone not himself favorably disposed to the Zionist aims, it was a reason discreditable to the Zionists; and consequently, by a natural association of ideas, it was a legitimate reason to blame the Zionists for the failure to gain Arab consent for the Mandate, and for the resulting unrest. The reason why the Zionists had not gained Arab consent, as they were expected to, was that when the Zionists disavowed any intention of establishing (immediately or rapidly) a Jewish state, they did not mean it. "Immediately" and "rapidly" were quibbles meant to deceive. In order to conform to the Mandate as authoritatively interpreted by the 1922 White Paper, and certainly in order to make the Mandate "workable," the Zionists would have to do more than they had hitherto been ready to do. The view now emerged that the Zionists must renounce not only for the immediate moment or the foreseeable future but absolutely and for all time any hope of a Jewish commonwealth in Palestine. Not only had the mandatary refused to guarantee this as its own direct obligation under the Mandate and the White Paper, but these documents, it was now held, were a final rejection of such aims.

Not only certain anti-Zionist officers, but the British Government as a whole, eventually adopted this new interpretation of the British-Zionist compact outlined in the Churchill White Paper. Without tracing the full history of this change, we may indicate some of its stages.

After the riots of May 1921, the Haycraft Commission was appointed to conduct an investigation. The report of the Commission concluded [67] that while the Arabs had been generally the aggressors in the racial strife, Zionist charges that the attacks were premeditated and planned had no foundation; that the general body of Jews in Palestine were anti-Bolshevist — a partial denial of Arab charges; and that "the fundamental cause of the riots was a feeling among the Arabs of discontent with, and hostility to, the Jews, due to political and economic causes, and connected with Jewish immigration, and with their conception of Zionist policy as derived from Jewish exponents." The "political and economic causes" specifically cited included Arab charges that a disproportionate number of Jews were coming in as workmen, public servants, and investors, and that Arabs were, or would be, dominated or displaced by these aliens, with their alien ideas. The "conception of Zionist policy" which was regarded as provocative was illustrated by the statement before the Commission of Dr. M. D. Eder, (1865–1936), Acting Chairman of the Zionist Commission and head of the Zionist Political Department:

The Balfour Declaration provides for a National Home for the Jewish people in Palestine. The interpretation we have put upon this is that Jews should be free to enter Palestine to build up their own civilization and culture, and eventually when the Palestinians are fit for it by their experience and political judgment, representative Government shall be conferred upon Palestine by His Majesty's Government. We look eventually to Palestine being in the position of one of the free dominions, inhabited by Arabs and Jews, and that both will play their part, the only difference being that the League of Nations has a certain control over the Government . . . .

The country has to be built up by the Jews and the Arabs. Jews do not come here for domination. I claim predominance. My own view is this: in the remote future there could be a Federate State of the Near East. Syria, Mesopotamia, Hedjaz, Palestine, Transjordania, could all be independent. Palestine would be predominantly Jewish . . . . I do not say that they [the Arabs] are foreigners. Every respect would be paid to their civil and religious rights in this country. We do not think there is room for an Arab National Home in Palestine. Their National home is in Syria, Transjordania, Mesopotamia and Hedjaz . . . . We could have them both [Jews and Arabs] united in one home.[68]

These views were reported and commented upon by the Haycraft Commission:

[Dr. Eder] gave no quarter to the view of the National Home as put forward by the Secretary of State and the High Commissioner. In his opinion there can only be one National Home in Palestine, and that a Jewish one, and no equality in the partnership between Jews and Arabs, but a Jewish predominance as soon as the numbers of that race are sufficiently increased . . . . As acting Chairman of the Zionist Commission Dr. Eder presumably expresses in all points the official Zionist creed, if such there be, and his statements are, therefore, most important. There is no sophistry about Dr. Eder . . . . it is relevant to our report to show that the acting Chairman of the Zionist Commission asserts on behalf of the Jews those claims which are at the root of the present unrest, and differ materially from the declared policy of the Secretary of State and the High Commissioner for Palestine.[69]

And in its closing paragraph, the Commission made the following recommendation, no less free from "sophistry" than Dr. Eder's declarations:

Much, we feel, might be done to allay the existing hostility between the races if responsible persons on both sides could agree to discuss the questions arising between them in a reasonable spirit, on the basis that the Arabs should accept implicitly the declared policy of the Government on the subject of the Jewish National Home, and that the Zionist leaders should abandon and repudiate all pretensions that go beyond it.[70]

The Haycraft Commission report, as it developed later, did not accurately reflect official opinion at the level of the Secretary of State and the High Commissioner. Feeling their way, no doubt, through the jungle trails of political possibility, these authorities took an attitude, if not more sophistical, at any rate more sophisticated than the forthright recommendations of the Commission. Naturally they too, showed a disposition toward a specifically British ultimate solution for Palestine different from the ultimate political form of the country favored by either Jews or Arabs. The ideas that there should be a Palestinian people, neither dominantly Jewish nor dominantly Arab, and that British intermediating rule and the British language and civilization should bind the two disparate elements together were voiced not only by a representative British officer on the spot like Storrs, but by a representative British officer in the metropolis like Ormsby-Gore.[71] However, the principles on which Palestine was governed after the Churchill White Paper did not demand that either Jews or Arabs accept this ultimate political solution, or that either renounce their own aspirations concerning the ultimate form of sovereignty in Palestine. They simply laid down an interpretation of the Balfour Declaration which postponed all decisions on these questions, leaving the way open for the "development of the Jewish national home, as defined in the preamble, and of self-governing institutions" — both conceived as intermediate, not final phases, of the Mandate.

The country was governed under this compact for about six years in relative calm, with the Jews and the Britons cooperating by going their separate ways, and the Arabs abstaining both from cooperation and from active resistance. Because of Arab abstention, nothing was done to advance the aim of self-governing territorial institutions; and even in the sphere of local self-government it was the Jews who forced the pace.[72] The Arabs complained of the abandonment of the prewar status, which had recognized Moslem predominance, and were less than eager to take up new forms of local self-government based on Western principles and involving unfamiliar forms of taxation. The British were quite ready to make haste slowly, in line with the general policy of the Colonial Office to disturb native institutions as little as possible. As to the "other part of the Mandate," the Jewish national home, here progress was made by independent Jewish effort as swiftly as was allowed by the erratic flow of Jewish capital and the setbacks resulting from unplanned investment in a country with a narrow economic base. The British government confined itself to the social policy outlined by the first High Commissioner, Sir Herbert Samuel:

It is the clear duty of the Mandatory Power to promote the well-being of the Arab population, in the same way as a British Administration would regard it as its duty to promote the welfare of the local population in any part of our Empire. The measures to foster the well-being of the Arabs should be precisely those which we should adopt in Palestine if there were no Zionist question and if there had been no Balfour Declaration.[73]

With the Jews more than ready to speed the growth of the Jewish national home, the Palestine government left this task to them and conceived its own Mandatory role more and more as that of protecting the social and economic interests of the Arabs, if it could not, under the Mandate, accede to their political claims.

However, the idea that such a policy could be carried out without reference to the Jewish national home or to the effects of its growth upon Arab society was obviously baseless. Even without the Zionist complication, the duty of a British Administration "to promote the welfare of the local population" could not easily be carried out free from political involvements "in any part of [the] Empire." The effect of any colonial welfare policy, as well as of the investments made by the administration in pursuit of imperial interests, had been to disturb the existing social balance practically everywhere from India to Egypt. The "presence" of England increased the agrarian population density, raised up new discontented urban classes — and thus accumulated new political grievances to add to the primary hostility against a foreign regime. In Palestine, however, the original hostility and the newly accumulated grievances were directed against the Zionists as well as the British. The disturbance of the local balance was caused not only by activities which Britain was forced to introduce for reasons of imperial policy, but also by Zionist activities in which Britain was concerned only out of altruism. Moreover, the Zionists proposed to disturb the local social and economic balance far more extensively and far more rapidly than the British needed to do for their strategic purposes. Not only was it hard to bear the onus of responsibility, in the eyes of the Arab majority, for changes not required by British security, but this rapid pace of Zionist development was directly contrary to the policy and practice generally adopted with a view to securing a stable imperial position. While any British imperial administration had to build roads and harbors and maintain hygiene and security, and consequently set in motion social changes that bred the seeds of unrest, the latter results were considered unfortunate; for it had long since become the set British policy to rely on native authorities and institutions as the best means for maintaining a British position at the lowest cost and with the longest life expectancy.

Accordingly when the Arabs complained that Jewish development of the national home threatened to disturb their traditional social relationships and their position of dominance in the native population, it was a plea towards which British colonial practice inculcated sympathy. Accordingly the Palestine Administration in its daily routine and the British government, through new proposals of constitutional character, tried to find legal guarantees for the relative social and economic position of the Arabs. But the attempts to interpret the Mandate as protecting social and economic *status quo* in Palestine by its references to the "rights and position" of the non-Jewish population met opposition not only from the Jews but from the Permanent Mandates Commission as well.

In 1928, upon the appointment of a new High Commissioner, Sir John Chancellor, the regular reminders by the Permanent Mandates Commission were heeded and the British once more began to seek a way to govern Palestine with the consent, in some form, of the Arab majority. At the same time, a period of unrest over collateral issues ensued. This was touched off by Arab-Jewish-British clashes over the religious *status quo* in the Old City of Jerusalem. The momentum of conflict was kept up and heightened by the founding of the Jewish Agency, with the prospect of more intensive Jewish resettlement; by the sharp rise in the flow of Jewish refugees; and by the international situation, rapidly deteriorating into the preliminaries of World War II, which caused foreign powers to fish in Palestine's troubled waters. Violence in 1929 and 1936 was the occasion for despatching new British inquiry commissions and experts to Palestine. Their investigations now centered not on the ultimate political aims but on the immediately foreseeable economic and social effects of Zionism, which were designated as the causes of Arab unrest.[74]

Calculations were made that, on the basis of the agricultural techniques of Arab cultivators, there was already rural overpopulation in Palestine; the *fellaheen*, it was deduced, were already underemployed and gradually being forced to leave the land. To Jewish counterarguments that with other techniques smaller acreages would support a farm family, so that there was a large margin for agricultural settlement even within Palestine west of the Jordan, there was the more or less tacit reply that such a program involved disturbing the traditional Arab "position" guaranteed in Article 6 of the Mandate. Even more pointed calculations were made showing that, at the current rate of immigration, Jews could probably attain a majority in spite of the higher Arab natural increase; and that whether or not Jewish development brought advantages to the Arabs, it created a sector more or less isolated from the Arab economy and removed from it by a growing disparity of economic level. All these, it was implicitly or explicitly stated, were legitimate Arab grievances under

Article 6 of the Mandate. The British government now planned to fulfill its obligations towards the Arabs under the Mandate by financing a plan for the more intensive development of Palestine's agricultural and other resources, starting from the position of the Arab, not the Jewish, economy. But in the meantime it had to do its duty towards the Arabs by holding back any Jewish development that claimed resources which would sooner or later be needed to maintain the existing Arab position.[75]

Such a justification for the new British policy in terms of the Mandate was put forward in the Passfield White Paper of October 20, 1930. The proposed policy met at once with sharp criticism from men who had themselves helped frame the Balfour Declaration, the Mandate, and the White Paper of 1922. These critics denied that, in rescinding the promise to the Jews that they would be free to develop Palestine so long as it was done at their own expense, the Labor Government could claim to be fairly interpreting the documents that defined its Mandate.[76] In its consideration of the Shaw Commission Report, the Permanent Mandates Commission had been equally severe. The way to reconcile the obligations to Jews and Arabs, the Commission members said, would have been for Britain to devote itself more actively to the economic development of the whole country in cooperation with the Zionists. Under this barrage from so many sides, the government retreated from its position and undertook to continue to administer Palestine on the old basis. At the same time, it was stressed that the government was bound to take into account "considerations of balance" in its obligations towards Jews and Arabs.[77] It was clear that if these came into conflict the British government would not be bound indefinitely by the accepted interpretation of the Mandate.

The inquiry commission which followed the next major clash, in 1936, took a different tack. The Peel Commission was as emphatic as its predecessors in stating that the British government could no longer go on permitting the Jews to develop their national home on the old basis. But they did not claim any right under the Mandate to prevent this development. Such a policy, they concluded, was ruled out by the terms of the Mandate.[78] That they came to this conclusion was not only the result of their close study of the legal issues involved. It also reflected the acute stage of the global Jewish problem in the late 1930's.

The theory that the Mandate required that Jewish development should be held back in order to protect the Arab relative or traditional position could be defended logically only if a certain view of the

Jewish national home — and, hence, of the Jewish problem — were accepted. A strongly entrenched Hebrew-speaking community amounting to almost a third of Palestine's population could be considered a satisfactory fulfillment of the promise to set up a national home in which Jews the world over could take pride as an expression of their racial individuality and cultural tradition. Thus, in reversing the agreement to keep Palestine open to Jewish immigration up to the limit of its economic capacity, the British could claim that they were faithful to their Mandate only if they also defined the Jewish problem culturally, as the problem of Judaism alone, ignoring the problem of the Jews. But in the moral and political climate of world opinion in the years of Hitler's rise to power such a definition of the Jewish problem seemed worse than arbitrary. It seemed so, certainly, to Jews, and it seemed so to the Permanent Mandates Commission and to an important part of British opinion as well.[79] But if it was part of the meaning of the Jewish national home to solve the problem of Jews suffering the extreme of oppression, then it followed that closing the doors of Palestine to them in order to maintain the Arabs' relative position was inconsistent with the Mandate. Accordingly, the Peel Commission came to the same conclusion as the Permanent Mandates Commission, that the Mandate provided no guarantee of the Arabs' relative position. But they came to another conclusion as well: the Mandate was politically unworkable. Thus they placed on the international agenda the question concerning which the Mandate instrument remained most deliberately blank: the form of sovereignty in Palestine upon the liquidation of the Mandate.

IV

The question of a final political resolution of the conflicting claims to sovereignty in Palestine was one that lay essentially between the Jews and the Arabs. That such a position would eventually arise was, of course, realized from the beginning. Consequently, the Zionists throughout the Mandate period had to concern themselves with Arab claims and Arab interests in formulating the immediate and, above all, the ultimate forms of their aspirations for sovereignty in Palestine.

The attempts by official Zionist quarters to come to an understanding with the Arabs were channelled, during this time, by the overriding political fact of British dominance in Palestine, just as the dominant position of the Turks had been a major factor in the Ottoman period. The British, moreover, like the Young Turks before them but with far more consistency and emphasis, demanded that the Zionists adopt a policy looking toward an agreement with the Arabs.

During the period of the Peace Conference, major emphasis was laid both by the British and the Jews on a broad regional agreement with the leaders of the whole Arab national movement. A conditional private understanding with Feisal, the terms of which were neither made public at the time nor later given effect, and the public cooperation of the British-sponsored Arab and Jewish representatives at the Peace Conference were the fruits of that effort.

There were also some vague thoughts on both sides about a Jewish-Arab diplomatic *entente* which would not be dependent on the overriding British interest. The idea that Palestine might be given a special status of Jewish predominance and Jewish autonomy within a greater Arab federated state — on the lines suggested by the already established political tradition of Lebanon — was put forward at the Peace Conference, as we have seen, by French-sponsored Syrian rivals of Feisal. At that time when the downfall of Feisal began through the withdrawal of the British from the over-all responsibility for military occupation in Syria, T. E. Lawrence thought that Feisal might use the Jews as a weapon held in reserve against the French: instead of accepting French advice and assistance in his administration of inland Syria, he could strike a bargain with the Zionists and get diplomatic support as well as technical advice and assistance from them.[80] After Feisal was driven out of Syria, non-Palestinian Arab nationalists once more negotiated with Zionists. They proposed that neither the Balfour Declaration nor the McMahon-Hussein agreement — that is, the documents which established a relationship between each of the parties and a third party, Britain — should be considered the basis of negotiation. The Arabs and Jews alone, as nation to nation, were to discuss their mutual interests and see how their respective aims of a federal Arab state from the Mediterranean to the Persian Gulf and of the Jewish national home in Palestine could be combined in support of each other.[81]

The Arabs and Jews seemed to feel that their daring to negotiate directly about the future of the area without the mediation of a European power might be a cause of suspicion. The Arabs made a pointed declaration that "it was not their intention to ask the Jews to declare themselves against any foreign power, even as it was not their intention to inaugurate their political work by a manifestation of hostility towards those very governments."[82] The Jews, for their part, kept the British informed of the negotiations. It was the conviction later on of some of those who had conducted the talks that they

were frowned on by Britain and that this was why they were brought
to no conclusion. But there were enough other reasons to bring about
the same result whether Britain actively discouraged the talks or not.
If the creation of a federal Arab state, covering both the French and
British mandated territories, were to be a condition of Arab acceptance of the Jewish national home — as it had been in the case of the
Feisal-Weizmann agreement — it was a condition that the Jews had
no power to meet. On the other hand, the Jews could hardly accept
the suggestion that they abandon legal titles like the Balfour Declaration and the Mandate, which were effectively in force and backed
by the League of Nations and by Britain, for a still-to-be-defined title
to Jewish autonomy in Palestine that depended on Arab success in
establishing a single federal state from Palestine to Mesopotamia.
Finally, the authority of the Arab negotiators to speak for a united
pan-Arab national movement was not beyond question. Under the
circumstances no more could have been expected as a result of the
negotiations, even given the most favorable auspices, than to maintain
friendly contact in anticipation of a time when the plan for a form
of Jewish sovereignty in Palestine, as part of a greater federal state,
should become more realistic.

In any case, by the end of 1922 the division of the Middle East
into distinct political entities was too final a fact for Jewish-Arab
negotiations to be conducted with a view to reversing it. Even talks
with Abdullah for uniting Palestine and Transjordan under a single
regime with the Balfour Declaration applying to both were rather
pointless, in view of Britain's set policy of keeping Abdullah on one
side of the Jordan and the Zionists on the other.[83] Zionist endeavors
to achieve any tangible *rapprochement* with the Arabs had to be confined essentially to Palestine west of the Jordan. And in that area
the Zionists had to work within the fixed limits of British policy and
primarily through British channels, rather than by direct contacts
with Arabs, so long as they hoped to further the growth of the Jewish
national home under the terms of the Mandate.

The attempt at an understanding with Palestinian Arabs, mediated
by Britain, was begun as early as the attempt at a regional understanding with the whole Arab nationalist movement. In 1918, shortly
before his visit to Feisal's headquarters, Weizmann was able to meet
leading Arab notables in Jerusalem through the good offices of Sir
Ronald Storrs and to seek, not without some superficial success, to
persuade them of the friendly intentions of the Zionists.[84] These
efforts were not only supported by the British far more consistently

than the attempts at a Jewish-Arab understanding covering the whole region; they were more or less demanded of the Zionists by the mandatary. For, one object that could be obtained by their success would be to make possible the administration of the Mandate with the consent of all the governed, a situation not only desirable in itself but capable of sparing Britain untold expense and trouble. But if the British felt that an Arab-Jewish *rapprochement* was something they could legitimately demand of the Jews, and if it became a British grievance that the Zionists did not achieve the required understanding, the Zionists, for their part, were always aware how much an Arab-Jewish understanding in mandated Palestine depended on the mandatary's policy, and they made a grievance of policies which, in their opinion, discouraged rather than favored its emergence.

A crucial question was the participation of the Arabs in the gradual development of self-governing institutions in Palestine. For the British, success in this field meant gaining a cardinal proof of the consent of the governed. For the Jews, it meant Arab acceptance of the Balfour Declaration, however the Arabs might wish to interpret it, and the creation of a political meeting place where Jews and Arabs, with British assistance, might gradually work out a mutually acceptable interpretation of the status of Palestine. Consequently the Zionist Executive watched with critical concern the way in which the first High Commissioner dealt with this question. The diary of Col. Frederick Kisch, (1888–1943), the head of the Zionist Political Department at the time, is unsparing in its frequently repeated objections to the policy adopted.[85] The Palestine administration, he felt, was following a course calculated to discourage Arab moderates and give the Arab extremists every reason to persist in their stubborn rejection of the terms of the Mandate. When the Husseini clan, who dominated Arab councils, refused to participate in the proposed Advisory Council or when their faction boycotted the elections, the Government should have gone ahead and established the Council with the cooperation of rival clans and leaders with more moderate views. So, too, Kisch lamented the administration's lack of energy in trying to advance municipal self-government, which was the most suitable area for developing Arab-Jewish "grassroots" collaboration. His general conclusion was that Herbert Samuel, under the guidance of British partisans of Arab extremism like Ernest T. Richmond, seemed to think that the way to appease Arab opposition to the Mandate was to give its most violent opponents positions of government-sanctioned power, on the theory, no doubt, that authority makes responsible men out of rebels. This policy, he felt, not only failed of its purpose but involved discrediting Arab moderates in their own community and destroyed the basis on which one might hope to win over the Arabs for cooperation within a political framework with the Jews.

The Palestine administration may or may not have been working on some such theory as the Zionists attributed to them in the recognition they granted to the extremist Husseini clan and in their general policy regarding "self-governing institutions" and local self-government. A British intelligence report on factions among the Arabs in the days of the military administration suggests that the Husseinis may have been favored over their rivals in the Arab nationalist movement because it appeared at the time that they were so anti-French that they would accept Zionism in order to get Britain, not France, as their mandatary; while some of the Nashashibis (later considered moderates by Britons and Jews alike) were among the group that would accept a French Mandate over a united Palestine and Syria rather than the division of the area and the establishment of a Jewish National Home in Palestine.[86] In any case, after the first tide of postwar Arab uprisings from Egypt to Syria swept over Palestine as well, ending everywhere in defeat, whoever led the resentful Arab community could only hope to keep his position by riding the wave of nationalist extremism. If the faction not in control voiced more moderate opinions, it may have been because of their weakness. The British alone, if they wished, could oust the Husseinis from their central positions of communal and political power and install the Nashashibis in their place; while Jewish votes could perhaps decide the issue of power in the municipal elections. But the Jews soon discovered — as they had in Turkish days — that an appearance of moderation, which won their support before a municipal election, was speedily dropped by the successful candidate, who sought to restore his credit among his Arab constituents by a display of nationalist partisanship.[87]

In the light of their experience, the Zionists ceased to complain against British failure to bring Jews and Arabs together in self-governing institutions. They learned in the mixed Jewish-Arab municipalities that talking over or even collaborating in minor matters did not necessarily lead to *rapprochement* on fundamental issues, but instead, under the conditions of Palestine, the major differences sometimes carried over into minor questions where they were irrelevant. The task remained of finding some basis for agreement between Jews and Palestinian Arabs on their major differences.

When the stakes in the game were a federal Arab state covering a whole region, on the one hand, and Jewish sovereignty in Palestine, on the other, it was possible for the Zionists to hope for agreement on the lines of the Balfour Declaration without further specification. For help in gaining and developing a large Arab commonwealth from the Mediterranean to the Persian Gulf, the Arabs might agree to a small Jewish commonwealth in part of the area. But if the stakes were limited to Palestine alone, the Zionists knew from the outset that they would have to convince the Arabs of their willingness to guarantee certain *desiderata* which went beyond what was already explicit in the terms of the Mandate. This document already assured the Arabs, in specific terms, that their civil and religious rights and their "position" — authoritatively interpreted to mean their economic prosperity — would not be prejudiced by the development of the Jewish national home. The Zionists had one possible additional bargaining counter with which to gain Palestinian Arab acquiescence to the Balfour Declaration and the Mandate. This was to recognize that the Arabs had legitimate rights in Palestine not only as individual citizens or as the Moslem and Christian religious communities, but also as a national community.

The Jews were predisposed, for many reasons, to the view that Arab rights in Palestine were not only those of individuals and of religious communities but of a nationality. They were among the leaders in the movement to gain recognition in the postwar settlement for the autonomy of minor nationalities in countries dominated by others. They were quick to see, therefore, that the formulas adopted in the Balfour Declaration not only could be interpreted on legal grounds, but should be interpreted on grounds of equity, as providing national rights for the Arabs, as well as for the Jews, in Palestine. This view was formulated by Ahad Ha'am in a classic analysis of the legal and political implications of what had actually been granted to the Jews in the British drafts of the Mandate, in comparison with formulations they themselves had proposed.

"To facilitate the establishment in Palestine of a National Home for the Jewish people" — that is the text of the promise given to us by the British Government. But that is not the text suggested to the Government by the Zionist spokesmen. They wished it to read: "the re-establishment of Palestine as the National Home of the Jewish people"; but when the happy day arrived on which the Declaration was signed and sealed by the Government, it was found to contain the first formula and not the second . . . . There were some who understood at once that this had some significance; but others thought that the difference was merely one of form. Hence they sometimes attempted on subsequent occasions, when the negotiations with the Government afforded an opportunity, to formulate the promise in their own wording, as though it had not been changed. But every time they found in the Government's reply a repetition of the actual text of the Declaration — which proves that it is not a case where the same thing may be put equally well in either of two ways, but that the promise is really defined in this particular form of words, and goes no further.

It can scarcely be necessary to explain at length the difference between the two versions. Had the British Government accepted the version suggested to it . . . its promise might have been interpreted as meaning that Palestine, inhabited as it now is, was restored to the Jewish people . . . ; that the Jewish people was to rebuild its waste places and was destined to rule over it . . . without regard to the consent or non-consent of its present inhabitants. For this rebuilding (it might have been understood) is only a renewal of the ancient right of the Jews which over-rides the right of the present inhabitants, who have wrongly established their national home on a land not their own. But the British Government, as it stated expressly in the Declaration itself, was not willing to promise anything which would harm the present inhabitants of Palestine . . . The Government thinks, it would seem, that when a people has only the moral force of its claim to build its national home in a land at present inhabited by others, and has not behind it a powerful army or fleet to prove the justice of its claim, that people can have only what its right allows it in truth and justice and not what conquering peoples take for themselves by armed force, under cover of various "rights" invented for the occasion. Now the historic right of a people in relation to a country inhabited by others can mean only the right to settle once more in its ancestral land, to work the land and develop its resources without hindrance . . . But this historic right does not over-ride the right of the other inhabitants, which is a tangible right based on generation after generation of life and work in the country . . . . This position, then, makes Palestine common ground for different peoples, each of which tries to establish its national home there; and in this position it is impossible for the national home of either of them to be complete and to embrace all that is involved in the conception of a "national home" . . . . national homes of different peoples in the same country can demand only national freedom for each one in its internal affairs, and the affairs of the country which are common to all of them are administered by all the "householders" jointly if the relations between them and their degree of development qualify them for the task, or, if that condition is not yet fulfilled, by a guardian from outside, who takes care that the rights of none shall be infringed.[88]

Ahad Ha'am wrote his analysis for the express purpose of damping the enthusiasm of those Zionists who saw in the confirmation of the Balfour Declaration at San Remo a prospect that a Jewish state would soon arise in Palestine. He obviously considered that his view of the legal and political as well as the moral implications of the Mandate, if accepted, necessarily involved abandoning fantastic hopes of rapid, massive immigration to Palestine and of far-reaching powers for the Jewish people, in and out of Palestine, to influence its development

and administration. But it would be incorrect to infer that the Zionists
at the opposite pole of the movement, who entertained just such
fantastic hopes, were indeed forced by the logic of their position to
deny any kind of national rights to the Arabs in Palestine. Like other
contemporary observers, Zionists did not consider Palestinian Arabs
a distinct nationality apart from the general Arab national body; and
some of them even had believed, in an earlier period, that the Levan-
tine mixture of the whole Eastern Mediterranean littoral was so
heterogeneous and so susceptible to outside influences that instead
of developing their own nationalism, they would be assimilated in
the Jewish national home.[89] But the same people who made these
assertions or accepted these tacit premises were also strong adherents
of the principle of national minority rights and believed in the preservation and fostering of any nationalist ideal that was real enough
and strong enough to assert itself. Those who wanted rapid, massive
Jewish immigration and a share for the Jewish people in governing
Palestine were as ready as Ahad Ha'am to accept the principle that
the Jewish commonwealth would have to permit and encourage the
development of national individuality among its Arab citizens, if the
latter showed a real desire for it. Ahad Ha'am, for his part, was as
convinced as his opponents that the national rights of Arabs in Palestine did not include the legal or moral right to prevent Jewish
immigration and resettlement to the point of Jewish numerical
dominance, if the economic possibilities of the country permitted.
Where the two differed was in their rating of contemporary Arab
nationalism as a political force and in their tactics in relation to it.
The "maximalists" did not believe that Arab nationalism was a serious
obstacle in the early days of the Mandate, but they feared that if
a Jewish majority were not speedily established it might become so.
The "moderates," who took a position similar in many ways to that
of Ahad Ha'am, felt that Arab nationalism was already so significant
a factor that it must be treated with, and they hoped that, with British
cooperation, it might be possible to gain the acquiescence of the
Arabs to the intermediate phase of immigration and resettlement, and
eventually to the final phase of the creation of the Jewish commonwealth.

There was, accordingly, no ideological dispute over the doctrine
propounded in the resolution of the Carlsbad Congress in 1921 (and
quoted with approval by the Churchill White Paper) which spoke
of Palestine as "the common home" of Jews and Arabs whose upbuilding was to "assure to each of its peoples an undisturbed national

development." It was an idea common to all Zionist shades of opinion, moreover, that the kind of colonization which they represented, as a national movement of permanent settlers, must be more beneficial and more acceptable to the Arabs, by its very nature, than the colonial methods of foreign imperialists. In the negotiations with Syrian or Hejazi Arabs for a settlement of regional scope, this Zionist doctrine had been accorded a sympathetic reception by the Arabs. They agreed, in effect, that a Jewish commonwealth with a "good neighbor" policy would make possible the necessary adjustments of the Arab countries to the modern world — a task inherent in the rise of Arab nationalism — without the threat of foreign domination. Stated in the regional context, moreover, there was nothing in the doctrine of the compatibility of Jewish and Arab nationalism which ruled out a demand (which might or might not be accepted by the Arabs in the course of negotiation) for the immediate recognition of the right to a Jewish majority and a Jewish commonwealth in Palestine. But when the Carlsbad Congress declared that Arab nationalism as well as Jewish nationalism had a place in Palestine, the tactical situation and, consequently, the pragmatic meaning of the principle enunciated were somewhat different. In theory, the Carlsbad Arab policy was proclaimed primarily in an attempt to gain consent by the Palestinian Arabs for the terms of the Balfour Declaration and the Mandate. In that context it signified Zionist renunciation of demands for an immediate recognition that Jews were to become a majority and establish a Jewish state in Palestine.

There can be no clearer illustration of the tactical objectives of Zionist pronouncements of that time than Weizmann's famous statement before the Supreme Council at the Peace Conference, in which he stated that he expected to build up in Palestine "a nationality which would be as Jewish as the French nation was French and the British nation British." This statement was made in answer to a question by the American Secretary of State, Lansing, whether the Zionists meant by a Jewish national home to demand an autonomous Jewish government.

Dr. Weizmann replied in the negative. The Zionist Organization did not want an autonomous Jewish Government, but merely to establish in Palestine, under a Mandatory Power, an administration, not necessarily Jewish, which would render it possible to send into Palestine 70,000 to 80,000 Jews annually. The Zionist Association would require to have permission at the same time to build Jewish schools, where Hebrew would be taught, and in that way to build up gradually a nationality which would be as Jewish as the French nation was French and the British nation British.

Later on, when the Jews formed the large majority, they would be ripe to establish such a Government as would answer to the state of the development of the country and to their ideals.[90]

The reply was a fairly precise definition of the moderate Zionist view. The Zionists did not ask for immediate Jewish dominance in governing Palestine nor for unlimited mass immigration capable of installing a Jewish majority there in a short time. Arab fears of their lands' being "expropriated" and their institutions being "dominated" might be assuaged, it was implied, by this assurance that Jewish economic expansion and the development of new political forms would be gradual, and that the Zionists would be considerate of the rights and position of the already settled population. Moreover the Jewish national character of the Jewish national home was defined with emphasis on the development of Hebrew culture, implying the parallel right of the "non-Jewish population" to develop its Arabic culture. And when the Jewish national home was fully developed, the Jewish character of Palestine would be like the national character of any democracy; which implied that the Arabs would have rights and facilities to develop their own national culture and would be represented in the political institutions of the country as citizens fully equal to any other in the eyes of the law.

This explanation, said Weizmann, satisfied Lansing.[91] But the declaration that "Palestine should be just as Jewish as America is American and England is English" had just the opposite effect on the Arabs. It was interpreted by Arabs not in the moderate sense that Weizmann intended, but as a claim for the establishment of Jewish dominance in Palestine immediately. It might be more correct, perhaps, to say that in their combative mood, the Arabs were not interested at all in distinctions between the ultimate and immediate or swift and gradual achievement of the Zionist aim. They opposed Zionism in any formulation. To have recognized this, however, would have been to concede at the very beginning of the Mandate that the Arabs were unalterably opposed to its terms, and that the Mandate would have to be administered without hope of their consent until its aim was accomplished. This was not an admission, naturally enough, that Britain was ready to make at the inception of its Mandate, nor a conclusion which the Zionist consensus was ready to face without attempting to overcome it by compromise. Consequently, the Churchill White Paper, on the assumption that Arab objections were based on a maximalist interpretation of Weizmann's statement, took the Weizmann formula as its text in pledging in positive and unmistakable form the very assurances to the Arabs which were only implied and hence subject to misinterpretation in Weizmann's remarks.

Unauthorised statements have been made to the effect that the purpose in view is to create a wholly Jewish Palestine. Phrases have been used such as that Palestine is to become "as Jewish as England is English." His Majesty's Government regard any such expectation as impracticable and have no such aim in view. Nor have they at any time contemplated, as appears to be feared by the Arab Delegation, the disappearance or the subordination of the Arabic population, language or culture in Palestine. They would draw attention to the fact that the terms of the Declaration referred to do not contemplate that Palestine as a whole should be converted into a Jewish National Home, but that such a Home should be founded *in Palestine*.[92]

It would be hard to find a document which, for reasons which can be readily understood, compounded so many errors within so brief a text. A few of them are pertinent here and must be examined. The Weizmann statement was misinterpreted as a maximalist rather than a moderate Zionist formula, and Zionist maximalism was misinterpreted as contemplating "the disappearance or the subordination of the Arabic population, language or culture in Palestine." In this, of course, Churchill was responding not to Weizmann's statement itself, in its proper context and interpretation, but to its restatement by the Arabs in the light of their own fears and tactical concerns. On the other hand, Mr. Churchill also misinterpreted the Arabs' mood when he implied that they were probably opposed not to the kind of Zionism he favored himself but only to maximalist Zionism in the form described — that is, to the immediate or rapid creation of a Jewish state and of a Jewish majority, with the prospect of submerging the individual tradition of the Arabs. Their opposition applied, in fact, to the creation of a Jewish majority and a Jewish state at whatever speed, and not only to the submergence but to any relative alteration of their traditional position in Palestine. But despite this fundamental opposition, it was natural to hope that Arabs and Jews might be brought to a form of agreement — like the Weizmann-Feisal treaty — which left it to time to settle these issues, and that they could be induced to cooperate with the British during an intermediate phase with the ultimate questions held in abeyance. The Churchill White Paper was an attempt to achieve this by guaranteeing the Arabs against demands the Zionists were not, in fact, making, and by assuming that the Arab grievance was something other than what it, in fact, was.

Considering that the Churchill White Paper was formulated in close consultation with Herbert Samuel, and that he was, in a way, a representative of Zionism in the Mandatory government, the pretenses or pious misrepresentations alluded to may be reasonably attributed to the Zionists as well; at least to the moderates among them who sought to cooperate with the mandatary. They could no more concede than could the British, at the beginning of the Mandate, that the Arabs were irreconcilably opposed to the Balfour Declaration; not, at least, without trying to reconcile them to it. Their early success in negotiations of regional scope, moreover, gave them grounds to suppose that the Arabs, like themselves, might be willing, under proper conditions, to let ultimate issues rest while cooperating in an intermediate phase of the Mandate. The British, in any case, were not prepared to enforce the Mandate without an attempt to gain Arab consent, and there was no choice but to try the assumption that Arab acceptance of the Balfour Declaration could be gained. Such an assumption implied that if Arab consent were not forthcoming it was not the fault of Zionist aims inseparable from the Declaration, but of certain interpretations of Zionist aims which were either not held by Zionists at all or which most Zionists were ready to disavow. Thus, while they might criticize the way in which the Churchill White Paper formulated the matter, the Zionists were prepared, in substance, to agree. And, indeed, the White Paper was able to back up its interpretation of the Balfour Declaration by citing the resolution of the Carlsbad Congress a year earlier, which recognized that Arabs had not only individual and communal but national rights in Palestine.

But this was not enough. Despite the White Paper and Zionist declarations in the same vein, the Arabs continued to reject the Mandate. Even in Europe, the status of a national minority remained a minority status; and to propose it to mainly Moslem Arabs in Palestine meant, in their terms, to reduce them to a *millet* — that is, to place them in the subordinate position occupied by Jews and Christians in Turkish times. If the policy of moderate Zionism were to be continued, more assurances would have to be offered to the Arabs. The refusal of the Arabs to defer ultimate issues would have to be faced. The solution offered by the Zionist Organization for this problem was its proposal — maintained through the late 20's and early 30's — that there be parity between the two nations in Palestine: neither was to dominate or be dominated by the other in the self-governing institutions of the country.[93] This principle was to apply under the Mandate, when Arabs were the majority, and it was to apply in the independent Palestine when it was hoped that Jews would be the majority.

As a solution of the political difficulties of the Mandate, the proposal of parity remained blatantly academic. Put forward repeatedly by the Zionists, it was ignored by the Arabs and the British alike. And if the idea were to have had any practical significance, it needed to attract the interest not only of the Arabs but of the British as well. For the idea of political parity without regard to numbers had one fatal defect in common with the idea of postponing the ultimate political solution of their differences. Conceived as a method to gain goodwill, it could also, given ill-will, cause existing differences to be prosecuted with even greater rigidity. In a legislative council based on Jewish-Arab parity, major issues involving their national rivalry might invariably result in a deadlock. Consequently, an impartial umpire – Britain during the Mandate, and some international agency, perhaps, after Palestine attained independence – was likely to be indispensable. The Zionists might hope – and, indeed, argued – that in the future Commonwealth of Palestine, a legislature in which Jews and Arabs were represented equally in spite of Jewish predominance in the population would not be deadlocked on important issues, because the social and economic interests represented would cut across national lines.[94] But, certainly, if such a legislature were to be set up during the Mandate, when the growth of the Jewish population towards a majority in accordance with the Balfour Declaration would constitute the major political issue, it could only be saved from deadlock by the casting vote of the British umpire.

It is clear why neither this nor the British plans for self-governing institutions with restricted authority had any appeal to the Arabs. Considered in terms of political advantage alone, the Arabs were being asked, under the British proposal, to consent to a form of government which gave only a certain symbolical recognition to their existing predominance without authority to maintain it in the future. Under the Jewish proposal of parity regardless of numbers, they were being asked to surrender their claims to political predominance based on their existing majority in return for the Jewish promise to do the same in the future, when they might rise to a majority. In the latter case, they were being given the proverbial offer of a bird in the bush for the bird in their hand; while in the former it was suggested that they set free the bird in their hand on the theory that it might prove to be a homing pigeon.

It is equally clear why the British showed no inclination to substitute the Zionist proposals of parity for their own plans concerning self-governing institutions under the Mandate. Their primary concern was not with the ultimate political structure of an independent

Palestine but with obtaining the consent of the Arabs — who alone remained recalcitrant — for their administration of Palestine under the Mandate. Moreover, in the effort to obtain Arab consent their published proposals were leaning more and more toward recognition of the Arab claim to a constitutional predominance in Palestine. To adopt the Jewish suggestion of constitutional parity would have meant lowering their bid when the Arabs were demanding that it be raised still higher. Even in the earliest proposals made by the British concerning self-governing institutions in Palestine, there were some exceptions to the principle that anything touching the promise of the Jewish national home, and hence bearing on the ultimate political status of Palestine, was reserved for the mandatary and withdrawn from the competence of the representative bodies to be created. The White Paper of 1922 noted that the question of immigration, a central issue in determining the ultimate predominance of Jews or Arabs and the political character of the future Palestine Commonwealth, would not be withdrawn entirely from the competence of the proposed legislative council.[95] In subsequent revisions of the British offer during the 30's, the legislative council, now altered to give the elected Arab members a virtual majority, was to be given the fullest opportunity to discuss, if not decide, immigration and other strategic questions of Mandate policy. Moreover, during this time the British themselves adopted increasingly restrictive measures regarding immigration and land settlement designed to preserve the endangered predominance of the Arabs in Palestine. They also began to draft plans for the termination of the Mandate which, they hoped, would satisfy the Arabs, but which doomed Zionist hopes. And, when these plans did not gain full Arab approval, they began to put them into effect piecemeal.[96]

In view of this *volte-face* of British policy, it was impossible any longer for the official Zionist group, or for any group that wished the support of the Zionist consensus, to rely on the academic formula of parity. Even if there had been any sign that either the British or the Arabs would agree to accept this offer as a basis for discussion, it could no longer be accepted by the Jews because of its major inherent defect. A political structure built on the principle of binational parity meant having recourse to an impartial arbiter in case of deadlock. The Jews in the 20's had been willing to rely on Britain's good faith in implementing the Balfour Declaration, and to accept self-governing institutions subject to a British official majority or to a British veto or casting vote. In the 30's they no longer had this confidence; and lacking faith in Britain, the Zionist consensus knew of no other impartial arbiter, either, to whom it would be willing to entrust the casting vote in a binational deadlock on issues of such importance as the admission of Jews to Palestine. The binational idea vaguely expressed in the official Zionist offer of parity regardless of number was carried on, accordingly, only by groups of partisans who occupied peripheral positions in the sphere of permissible attitudes sanctioned by the Zionist consensus.

More representative Zionist opinion and the official groups with a more central and intimate relation with the Zionist consensus could not accept proposals to rely on Britain or submit the rights granted once by the international community to a new international arbitration. The Jewish problem, as it presented itself in the days of Hitler and in their aftermath, was no longer one on which the Jewish community could submit to Solomonic judgments. Regardless of the final form of a political solution for Palestine, the problem of Jewish refugees was one which Jewish opinion insisted Palestine must solve.

The imminence of a final political resolution of the Palestine problem was a reality, however, which Jewish opinion, from the late 30's on, could no longer avoid facing. Hence, the Jewish consensus held itself open for a reformulation of its basic demands. It insisted only that whatever the final political solution of the Palestine problem, which was soon to be expected, it must make it possible to solve the postwar problem of the Jews in Palestine. This implied a readiness to abandon both the demand for carrying out the letter and spirit of the Balfour Declaration and the proposal for Jewish Arab parity, regardless of number. The first position could no longer be maintained once it was recognized that neither Britain nor any other international trustee could be expected to carry out the Mandate. The second was equally impossible once it was recognized that the position of impartial umpire between Jews and Arabs required exactly the qualities demanded in vain of a mandatary. Only the Jews themselves, was the necessary conclusion, could be relied on to administer Palestine — or a part of it entrusted to them — for the purpose of solving the problem of the Jews. And an agreement with the Arabs, it was concluded, would come only after the essential Jewish political demands were firmly established; it was not a feasible method for achieving the indispensable Zionist political goals.[97]

10 TERMINATION OF THE MANDATE: EVOLUTION OF THE PLAN FOR PARTITION

W E have considered in earlier chapters of this book the unusual conceptions of sovereignty which grew up out of the myth of auto-Emancipation. The special circumstances under which the Palestine Mandate was terminated and Israel arose have also had the effect of producing unusual attitudes towards and conditions for the exercise of sovereignty in the Jewish state.

Israel is a state with peculiar bonds to the international community, bonds of filiation in one sense and of subjection in another. It had its legal origin, in some degree, in an act of the United Nations, and its first, basic proclamation refers explicitly to this as a source and inspiration.[1] But Israel is also bound in a web of international commitments, involvements, restrictions and dependencies. To Israel these appear not as a source of institutional inspiration but as a fate which it feels to be irritating and in some cases capricious.

Moreover, Israel was born after an extraordinary travail. For ten years before the rise of the state, its founders were exposed not only to the strain of political uncertainty but to the trauma of Hitler's persecution of the Jews, which renewed with overwhelming force the basic Zionist myth of auto-Emancipation and activism. During that period the Zionist myth image of sovereignty extended its dominant influence to the entire Jewish consensus, while its intensity reached ultimate limits among the Zionists themselves.

In Israel today, consequently, there exists a tension, a sense of precarious balance, between the impulses to make sovereignty absolute and the conditions which require a sovereignty moderated and restricted as the Zionist conception of sovereignty had been in its earlier history. A decade during which the liquidation of the Palestine Mandate remained probable, but never certain, created this unstable tension of opposed forces; after two decades of Israel's existence, the institutional forms in which they could be permanently balanced had not yet been fully established.

I

One of the major ambiguities in the Mandate for Palestine consisted in the provisions for its termination. The Mandate, as we have seen, sought to gain the consent of the governed by leaving the ultimate form of sovereignty open and defining only the conditions of the intermediate phase of development in Palestine. Hence, it could not establish a clear criterion by which to determine its own successful completion. The other "A" Mandates, by citing and quoting the fourth paragraph of Article 22 of the League of Nations Covenant, specified that they were to be terminated when the people under mandate were "able to stand alone." Even in these cases, the question of the manner in which mandates might be terminated presented a complex issue; and it was considered appropriate that the League of Nations be given commitments about certain future policies of the proposed new state, assuming international obligations contained in the mandate, before a mandate was ended.[2] The Palestine Mandate, as we have seen, deliberately omitted citations which could define the proper moment for its termination; though it did contain, in Articles 8, 13, 14, and 28 stipulations which would be binding in the event of termination. A member of the Permanent Mandates Commission sought to supply the deficiency by interpretation, in the following manner:

The Arabs claimed that the Palestine mandate was incompatible with paragraph 4 of Article 22 of the Covenant, and that they were therefore justified in regarding the mandate as non-existent . . . . It was true that the Covenant referred to "the advice and assistance" of a Mandatory and that these terms were not to be found in the mandate, which, in Article 1, conferred on Great Britain full legislative and administrative powers. As, however, these full powers were limited to Article 1 by the terms of the mandate, and as Article 2 provided for the development of self-governing institutions, it followed that the provisions of Article 1 had only a transitory character. The duration of the transitory period must depend, in the first place and in principle, on the Arabs themselves. As soon as they were prepared to contribute to the establishment of a free Government in a form which respected the international obligations of Great Britain, paragraph 4 of Article 22 of the Covenant would have its full effect for Palestine as for the other mandated territories.[3]

It would seem, from this statement, that the condition for the development of self-governing institutions, leading towards independence, was acceptance by the Arabs of the Balfour Declaration as a British international obligation; and, consequently, the condition for the creation of an independent Palestine and the termination of the mandate would be a declaration by the new state assuming an appropriate variant of the same international obligation, and so committing itself to the idea of the Jewish national home.

But the legal framework of the Jewish national home, as provided in the Mandate, defined a process of growth rather than a terminal status. There were authorities on international law and diplomatic history who concluded from this that the Mandate was to be of indefinite duration, ending only when there no longer remained any economic absorptive capacity in Palestine for the further development of the Jewish national home.[4] This was a rather academic goal, which hardly constituted a feasible criterion for determining the end of a Mandate. On the other hand, from the beginning it was obvious to those who drafted the Mandate that political, if not legal, criteria must be expected at some time to make it clear that the term of the Mandate was concluded, and that the final form of Palestine's sovereignty must be decided, "pro-rata," in accordance with the proportions of national elements in the population.

Political pressures for the termination of the "A" Mandates built up even before the Mandates were formulated and approved, and grew progressively stronger. Soon after, the Arab mandated territories or treaty-bound states surrounding Palestine were going forward rapidly to fuller independence. Foreign powers like Italy, Germany, or even Russia, which had not figured seriously in the British and French contest for Middle Eastern power and influence in the 1920's, put in a threatening appearance.[5] The British policy of building up an Anglo-Arab entente began to seem a pressing need, not merely wise counsel for a rather remote future. In Palestine, this led to a policy of restricting the Jewish national home to proportions that would preserve the *status quo* of Arab predominance; to renewed proposals for self-governing institutions, with diminishing concern for the effect upon the Jewish national home of Arab votes; and to projects for terminating the Mandate under conditions of Arab predominance.

Considering these new British proposals for Palestine in their legal context, the Permanent Mandates Commission repeatedly pointed out inconsistencies with the provisions of the Mandate. The Commission, as we have noted, seems to have been the first to suggest that the inability of the mandatary to go forward with the creation of self-governing institutions constituted an Arab grievance under Article 2 of the Mandate. It began now to express doubts concerning proposals to create a Legislative Council under conditions which would make it seem a reward for intransigeance in opposing the Balfour Declaration.[6] The exemption of Transjordan from the terms of the Balfour Declaration formed a specific provision (Article 25) of the Mandate, but the Permanent Mandates Commission repeatedly questioned the manner in which this was carried out. The exclusion of Jewish settlers from Transjordan was decried as contrary to the Mandate provisions against discrimination on grounds of race or religion. Members of the Commission also criticized the British policy of preventing land sales to Jews even when the Emir Abdullah and his parliament were in favor, as well as the unwillingness to plan the settlement of Western Palestinian Arabs, if not of Jews, in Transjordan.[7]

The question of a procedure for terminating the Mandate — or, at least, of basic changes in it — arose early in connection with Transjordan. The Mandates Commission questioned the validity of the procedure by which quasi-independence was granted to Emir Abdullah under an Anglo-Transjordan Treaty. This measure was only announced to the League of Nations and not effected after consultation with the League and with its consent and approval. M. Rappard even pointed out the difficulty that the Palestine Mandate had no provisions concerning the proper time and manner for advancing to independence, so that the Treaty might appear to be without any foundation in the terms on which the country was entrusted to the mandatary. But the Council of the League, unwilling to concern itself with the Commission's legal scruples, endorsed the British act and, by implication, its procedure.[8]

Thus, when Britain began, in the late thirties, to suggest forms for the termination of the Palestine Mandate or, in the meantime, to restrict the further development of the Jewish national home, both the Jewish petitioners and the Permanent Mandates Commission were aware that their legal objections to such measures might not be effective in the superior, political forum of the League, the Council. In spite of this, the Permanent Mandates Commission sharply criticized the anti-Zionist turn of British policy at its successive stages. This judicial support of their case strengthened the Jews in their appeal from the British government to public opinion, and hardened their determination to defend their cause against the fixed policy of the mandatary. Their morale was heightened by the conviction that their own attitude was formally as well as essentially legitimate, while the laws directed against the growth of the Jewish national home were constitutionally illegitimate.

Suggestions that the growth of the Jewish national home should be restrained in order to maintain Arab predominance in Palestine were made in a vague form in the inquiries, reports, and official

Colonial Office statements that followed the 1929 outbreak in Palestine.[9] When the Permanent Mandates Commission met in extraordinary session about a year afterward, two different views on the constitutional questions involved were voiced by the members, the British-accredited representative maintaining an interested silence. The chairman, Marquis Theodoli, indicated that the Palestine Mandate seemed to contain mutually contradictory provisions. Like all Mandates, and particularly all "A" Mandates, it was required under Article 22 of the League Covenant to bring the country to independence; but it also contained the special obligation to establish the Jewish national home. The latter obligation, he felt, should be subordinate to the former and carried out only to the extent consistent with it. He strongly suggested that the Jewish national home might be considered already established. In sharp disagreement, M. Rappard began by stating the principle that the Permanent Mandates Commission, by its very function as a quasi-judicial body, must consider the Mandate a consistent document. If the Mandate were not held consistent, two interpretations of it were indeed possible: a pro-Arab interpretation would make self-governing institutions the primary obligation and let the growth of the Jewish national home depend on the consent of the existing Arab majority — which meant, in effect, to prohibit its growth; and a pro-Jewish interpretation would rule out all intermediate stages of development and allow the institution of territorial self-government only in the ultimate form of the Jewish commonwealth. Assuming the Mandate to be an inconsistent document, each interpretation would try to resolve the difficulty by giving preference to one obligation over the other. If, as the Commission must do, the Mandate were interpreted as a consistent document, then both obligations should be pursued; and, hence, self-governing institutions should be gradually established to the degree and in forms consistent with the growth of the Jewish national home.[10]

The report of the Commission which followed this discussion defined the position in the following terms: the Mandate must be interpreted as a consistent document, and both of its obligations much be considered of equal weight and equal priority. It was necessary to distinguish between the *objects* and *immediate obligations* of the Mandate. Its *objects* were to create the Jewish national home and to bring Palestine to the stage of self-government. No term was set for the achievement of these objects, and no complaint could be made against the mandatary if it had not accomplished them fully at any given time. The *immediate obligations* of the mandatary were only to *facilitate the development* of the Jewish national home and of self-governing institutions.

The policy of the Mandatory would not be fairly open to criticism unless it aimed at crystallising the Jewish National Home at its present stage of development, or rigidly stabilising the public institutions of Palestine in their present form.[11]

The Peel Commission, investigating the Arab revolt of 1936, confronted the Permanent Mandates Commission with a new and startling set of conclusions. On the legal side, it carried the analysis of the Mandate a radical step further than the Commission had gone. The Mandate, it concluded, if held consistent, was a consistently pro-Zionist document. The Jewish national home clauses were the primary purpose of the Mandate, and the safeguards for the non-Jewish population could be applied, consequently, only in so far as consistent with the primary obligation. But this purely theoretical consistency rested upon a pragmatic assumption. Those who drafted the Mandate assumed that Jewish and Arab interests in Palestine were reconcilable in practice; that by a tactful approach and demonstrated economic benefits, the Zionists and the government would gain Arab consent for the Jewish national home policy. Events had shown, however, that the rival national interests were not, in fact, reconcilable; so that the Mandate, whether consistent or inconsistent, was at any rate impracticable. Thus, the Peel Commission disposed of the legal argument and passed to the decisive political problem. Its favored solution involved terminating the Mandate and giving both Jews and Arabs as much as possible of their demands, under existing circumstances, by means of a partition. Pending such a solution, they proposed that the Mandate be administered henceforth in accordance with what was politically expedient rather than what was legally required. The growth of the Jewish national home should be crystallized at its existing relative position in respect to population and land holdings. Emphasis should henceforth be laid on preparing the two nations in Palestine for eventual self-government in a common state; but how little faith the Commission reposed in this prospect is indicated by the fact that they did not recommend the establishment of a Legislative Council under existing circumstances.[12]

The problem which these findings presented to the Permanent Mandates Commission was one of unanticipated difficulty. As the Commission's report tartly noted, if a mandatary stated officially that its Mandate was unworkable that in itself was sufficient to make it so. The question of terminating the Mandate was, thus, forced upon the Commission, even though it found itself without clear legal criteria for considering it. Considering the political feasibility of the proposal, the Commission pointed out the enormous difficulties that any plan for partitioning Palestine faced, in view of the existing circumstances in the country and the attitude of the peoples concerned. It recommended, however, that the proposal be studied in terms of the following principle:

Any solution to prove acceptable should therefore deprive the Arabs of as small a number as possible of the places to which they attach particular value, either because they are their present homes or for reasons of religion. And further, the areas allotted to the Jews should be sufficiently extensive, fertile and well situated from the point of view of communications by sea and land to be capable of intensive economic development and consequently of dense and rapid settlement.[13]

At the same time, the Commission opposed any attempt to achieve a partition by setting up two separate states without preliminaries. They suggested that partition be approached gradually by dividing the country into cantons, some open and some closed to Jewish development, or by setting up two separate mandates, with the League of Nations to decide when each was ready for independent statehood.[14]

The British government made its own investigation of partition as a solution in Palestine, with the result that it abandoned the idea. Instead it adopted the alternative of retaining the Mandate for an additional period of at least ten years,[15] while restricting Jewish immigration and land purchase in order to crystallize the growth of the Jewish national home at its existing relative position.

The justification now resorted to was no longer a frank avowal that the Mandate could not be carried out and that overriding political considerations demanded a speedy terminal solution. Instead, the British government presented its policy as an interpretation of its legal obligations under the Mandate, whose termination, consequently, might be deferred. The new policy was, therefore, judged by the Mandates Commission in accordance with legal criteria first of all. The Commission unanimously declared that "the policy set out in the White Paper was not in accordance with the interpretation which, in agreement with the Mandatory and the Council, the Commission had always placed upon the Palestine mandate." However, it went on to consider whether, under existing political circumstances, "the Palestine mandate might not perhaps be open to a new interpretation which, while still respecting its main principles, would be sufficiently flexible for the policy of the White Paper not to appear at variance with it." On this ground, no unanimity was possible, and the Commission had to refer the Council to its minutes for an exposition of the views of individual members.

(14) As will be seen therein, four of the latter did not feel able to state that the policy of the White Paper was in conformity with the mandate, any contrary conclusion appearing to them to be ruled out by the very terms of the mandate and by the fundamental intentions of its authors.

(15) The other members, three in number, were unable to share this opinion; they consider that the existing circumstances would justify the policy of the White Paper, provided the Council did not oppose it.

(16) All the members agree in thinking that the considerations put forward in the report of the Royal Commission of 1937 and in the preliminary opinion presented by the Mandates Commission in August of the same year have not lost their relevance: the solution [of partition] envisaged in those two documents (excluding the setting-up of two independent States withdrawn at the outset from mandatory control) should be borne in mind at the appropriate moment.[16]

Only a few months after this discussion, World War II broke out. Britain, having no opportunity to seek Council approval for its policy, simply proceeded to put the policy into effect. For the whole tragic period of the war and its aftermath until 1948, Palestine was governed on the principle, adopted as a provisional measure in 1937 and made permanent by the 1939 White Paper, that the Jewish national home was to be crystallized at its existing relative position. This was a policy which the Jews rejected as a repudiation of the international trust undertaken in the Mandate, and which they held to have been disavowed by international legal opinion. They drew the conclusion that they had the right to refuse their cooperation to the execution of that policy and to act in defiance of it. Legal rationalizations gave them conviction in this attitude, but its emotional motivation was the unparalleled urgency of the "problem of the Jews" in those days, and the fury aroused by Britain's fixed resolve not to consider this problem as pertinent to the administration of its mandate in Palestine.

II

The fundamental connection between the Jewish national home and the Jewish problem was interpreted by Zionists in different ways, as we have seen, some stressing the problem of Judaism, some the problem of the Jews as the prior and paramount problem to be solved. But, the Zionist movement did not develop major groupings that defined either the problem of Judaism or the problem of the Jews as the exclusive task, ruling out any obligation to solve the other. From the beginning, there were British spokesmen who, for reasons of imperial policy, were predisposed to make such a distinction. They gradually came to define not only the purpose of the Mandate, but also the intent of a "moderate" Zionism, working within the legitimate framework of the Mandate, as being to solve only the problem of Judaism, not of the Jews. In the end they, or rather events, persuaded the British government to deny its sanction to any Zionism but an essentially imaginary "moderate" Zionism which would concern itself exclusively with solving the problem of Judaism, and not at all with the problem of the Jews. Such an arbitrary definition of Zionism was not the official British attitude in the early days of the Mandate, when the Jewish situation permitted moderation to be preached to Zionists. It became the official British attitude in the later years, when the critical turn of the problem of the Jews made it impossible for any Zionist, however much predisposed to such a philosophy, to be satisfied with an attempt at the solution of the problem of Judaism alone in Palestine.

The negotiators who cooperated in drawing up the Mandate, Britons and Zionists alike, thought in terms of a rate of immigration of fifty to eighty thousand a year and a total of three to six million Jews to be settled in Palestine. These were figures that signified a clear purpose, which was, in any case, explicitly avowed: not only to set up a viable social context for a revived Jewish culture in Palestine, but to take care of a major part of the anticipated Jewish emigration from Europe and to ease the "Jewish problem" for those who remained. On the other hand, the flow of emigrants to America, in preceding decades reaching a peak annual rate in excess of a hundred thousand, had not produced a net decrease in the Jewish population in Europe. Natural increase had more than taken up the slack. Thus, what was hoped for was not, in any sense, the Herzlian vision of a mass migration of entire communities out of areas of acute anti-Semitism. Even Nordau's proposal for an immediate transfer of six hundred thousand Jews to Palestine was more clearly related to the political problem of establishing a Jewish majority at the outset than to an envisaged surgical solution of the Jewish problem.

The expected rate of immigration generally referred to in the beginning was reduced in the light of experience, as the British and the Jews learned that realism as well as prudence dictated a more modest flow. The formal criterion which was applied as an authoritative interpretation of the law of the Mandate was that Jewish immigration should not exceed Palestine's economic absorptive capacity at a given time, and that the Jews should be able to finance it. But the British and the Jews each had an important additional test by which they were disposed to measure the rate of Jewish immigration.

The British felt that a gradual rather than rapid influx of Jews into Palestine was desirable on political grounds, as it would probably be less irritating to the Arabs and entail less difficulty and expense in the administration of Palestine. This was a principle which only was put forward as a precise, legal measure of Jewish immigration in the later period, but which acted from the beginning as a diffuse motivation predisposing the British to a cautious assessment of Palestine's economic absorptive capacity.[17]

The Jews, too, had their own reason for favoring a regulated and moderate flow of Jewish immigration in the earlier period. They wanted to create a national entity that would strike root and grow in the country. They wished to avoid a one-sided social and economic composition of the Jewish settlement, such as had resulted from the immigration of the 1880's and 1890's, which had failed to establish a Jewish working class or a community that could sustain a living Jewish secular culture. They also wished to avoid a boom and bust cycle of speculative investment and settlement such as occurred with dire effects in 1926 and 1927.[18] Herzl had belittled the problems of economic development and vocational and social readjustment involved in the transfer of Jews to Palestine, considering them to be mere details of administration that he need not concern himself about unduly.[19] The Zionists now regarded them as crucial.

The special reasons of the British and the Jews for favoring a regulated and moderate immigration predisposed both to accept economic absorptive capacity as a measure of the flow. But as each motivation worked itself out in the course of events, there developed not a greater accord but a growing divergence between the British and Jewish views. The crux of the difference was the question of labor immigration to Palestine.

The employment of labor immigrants depended to a considerable extent on the funds the Zionists had available for agricultural settlement; and since these funds were derived from the voluntary contributions of Diaspora Jewry, they, in turn, were expected to expand or shrink in response to Zionist success or failure in obtaining immigration certificates for laborers. For, if a large quota of certificates was granted, it encouraged the supporters of Zionism as a token of the approach of their goal and, at the same time, spurred them to greater effort by demonstrating a larger specific budget of needs and activities.[20] Moreover, the number of applicants in Eastern Europe who urgently needed visas as labor immigrants and who met the qualifications set by the Jewish Agency continually outnumbered the number of certificates granted, more seriously so as time went on. The official Zionist policy of selective immigration was itself fiercely attacked by opposition groups in the movement. They demanded a mass evacuation of the poverty-stricken, crowded, oppressed Jewries of Poland and Rumania, or at least a distribution of immigration certificates according to the need in Europe rather than according to qualification for farm labor in Palestine.[21] But even in applying its own criteria, the Zionist Organization found itself under pressure. It was faced with thousands and tens of thousands of young, disciplined, Hebrew-speaking men and women, organized in collective farm or industrial groups in Eastern Europe, who waited with increasing impatience year after year for lack of sufficient certificates for immigrants to Palestine. Within two years of Hitler's accession to power, an organized movement of similar scale also stood waiting for permission to move in Germany.[22]

But it was just this category of immigration to which the British found, on behalf of the Arabs, the gravest political objections, not only because of their number but because of their aims and methods. The creation of a rounded and, as far as possible, self-contained Jewish economy based on its own working population was regarded as a greater threat to the Arab position than, for example, the investment of Jewish capital employing Arab labor.[23] This reaction on the part of the Arabs — and the British, as well — was considered disappointing and ill-founded by the Zionists. In their negotiations with Feisal and other Arab statesmen, they seemed to have encountered an understanding of what they were convinced was a valid point: that the settlement of a Jewish workers' society aiming to strike root in Palestine would bring Arab nationalism the necessary advantages of Western civilization without the dangers of an absentee imperialism, represented by a thin ruling stratum of administrators, garrison troops, and capitalists. They later interpreted the hostile Arab reactions as reflecting the economic and social interests of the ruling class of landowners and moneylenders, not of the whole Arab people.[24] But whatever the Zionist interpretation, the fact remained that Arab nationalism voiced a sharper opposition to Jewish labor immigration and labor settlement than to any other aspect of the Jewish return to Zion. The British officials were interested chiefly in gaining Arab consent for their own rule and, besides, were more than cool to the antitraditional, innovating spirit of secular Zionism and particularly to the socialist experimentation of the labor settlers.[25] The "schedule" of labor immigration certificates seemed to them the most natural point at which to apply policies of restriction, whether intended, as at first, to make the relative growth of Zionism gradual, and hence presumably more palatable to the Arabs, or to crystallize it at a given ratio.

Despite these diverging motivations, there was a working agreement between the official Zionists and the official Britons so long as the Mandatory policy was one of keeping Jewish immigration and resettlement gradual. The Zionists realized that even if the British had yielded to all their demands for larger quotas for labor immigration, their own policy in the twenties could not provide adequately for the contemporary problem of the Jews. By setting up their selective criteria for labor immigrants — youth, knowledge of Hebrew, willingness to be life-long laborers, preferably in collective farm settlements — they knew that they were, in a sense, condemning many older or less adaptable Jews to live in the hopeless and increasingly constricted dead end of the Eastern European Jewries. Whether by policy or by history, these, they knew, were doomed, and the Zionist policy of selective immigration to Palestine could not solve the problem of all Jews but only — like the Messiah himself — redeem the saving remnant.[26]

In the thirties, when the divergence in underlying motivations revealed itself openly, other conditions also had changed. Not only had political exigencies caused the British to abandon the interpretation of the Mandate previously agreed on in regard to Jewish immigration; the problem of the Jews in Europe took such a turn that the previous Zionist attitude could no longer be maintained. Not slow decay under conditions of grinding poverty and official discrimination, but the immediate menace of destruction faced whole communities. In the face of this, the Jews themselves had to be prepared to depart from their previous criteria for regulating immigration selectively. What was now needed was not a slow sifting of the saving remnant, but a swift campaign of rescue, a straining of every resource to save whoever could still be saved among the Jews of Europe.

The Zionists argued, and were convinced, that, at the stage of development of the Jewish national home already arrived at, opening the doors of Palestine to all Jews who could be brought in by an organized effort would not place impossible demands upon Palestine's economic absorptive capacity. But even if this were not the case, they insisted, it was inherent in the idea of a Jewish national home that Jews in the extremity of danger should be able to seek a haven there as of right and not on sufferance.[27] The British, on the other hand, now took a quite different view. Not only did they defend their own policy of a political high-water mark for the growth of the Jewish national home as a valid interpretation of the Mandate. They also rejected the Jewish demands as incompatible with the Mandate. It was never contemplated, they said in effect, that Palestine should solve the problem of the Jews; only the problem of Judaism. Certainly, it was never contemplated that Palestine should be expected to admit such a flood of Jews as was let loose by Hitler.[28]

The issue was now joined in a direct opposition of principles. The pragmatic agreement on an immigration policy based on an agreed interpretation of the Mandate was now replaced by a categorical disagreement in which the emotions of the disputants became most bitterly involved.

III

The 1930's and 1940's were a long crisis in the affairs of world Jewry from which two perceptions of mythic force arose and impressed themselves upon the people. The Mandatory policy in Palestine from 1937 to 1947, based on the claim that the Jewish national home was not meant to solve the problem of the Jews, and Hitler's program for a "final solution" of the Jewish problem by extermination combined to constitute a single traumatic experience. Out of the anguish of those days, the Jewish consensus learned that only Jewish efforts and sacrifices could be relied on unreservedly in the rescue of Jews — and then, too, only where Jews were free to act as though they exercised a national sovereignty. The Jewish consensus learned also that a threat could arise so total and so ruthless that no temporizing with it was possible. Only the psychology of the all-or-nothing choice, only total risks and total resistance were possible and possibly effective against totalitarian Hitlerism. It was a time when the psychology of partisan resistance developed among European Jews out of a situation where no form of submission could save life; and it developed also in Palestine where alone Jews really felt they had the right to act as though there were a Jewish national sovereignty.[29]

In the years after Hitler's rise, the Jewish consensus found that many Christian and humanitarian governments, apart from the British in Palestine, could not be relied on to do what was needed for rescuing European Jewry.[30] The Mandate government was able to point to the inactivity of others — the barred gates of America, in particular — in extenuation of its restrictive policy in Palestine; in fact, it did not hesitate to extol its humanitarianism in admitting so many Jewish refugees to Palestine, in comparison with larger countries. It could argue that if only other countries did their fair share, the administration of the Mandate would not be made so difficult by unwarranted demands to solve the whole problem of the Jews in Palestine.[31] It was true, indeed, that, in the first years of Hitler, Palestine admitted more Jewish refugees from Central Europe than all other countries combined. Not until the late thirties did the emergency programs initiated by the United States divert a large part of that stream and rob the British excuse for restrictions in Palestine of its moral sting.[32] But the asylum granted in all countries of the world together, even in the later period when the enormity of the problem caused doors to open in the West, was glaringly inadequate. It did not spare Jews the brutal spectacle of their unwanted brethren shunted back and forth across hostile borders or turned back from port after port throughout the civilized world. Nor did it spare them the demonstrations at the Evian Conference on Refugees in 1939 or the wartime Bermuda Conference that there was not enough hospitality in all the world to save European Jews from murder, and that the Jewish national home would not be permitted to welcome them to safety so long as Britain retained the Mandate.[33]

That all the nations in the world could not, or would not, rescue European Jewry meant that the duty fell on the Jews alone, for they could not evade it. But what the Jews could do usually depended on the extent to which they could sway their governments, or even dared to attempt this; for when Diaspora Jews urged that the rescue of European Jewry be treated as a war aim, or an immediate military objective, they had to do so knowing of the widespread propaganda which branded the war as a Jewish war and themselves as warmongers.[34] The Jews in Palestine, however, felt that they embodied a sovereign national will themselves. They neither feared nor scrupled to take all risks to rescue European Jews, whether with the agreement of the Mandatory power or in defiance of it.

Before the Second World War broke out, active Jewish resistance had already begun in Palestine. It took the form, first, of smuggling Jewish immigrants from Europe to Palestine in disregard of British regulations, and — on the part of Revisionist "activists" — of one or two retaliatory actions against Arabs following Arab attacks on Jews. During the war, demands for a Jewish Army and for specific measures intended to rescue Jews from Europe and bring them to Palestine continued to bring Palestinian Jews and world Zionism into conflict with British policy. Yet the war against Hitler was one in which any

Jew necessarily felt involved. Thus the policy of Palestinian Jewry, as formulated by Ben-Gurion, was to fight with Britain against Hitler as though there were no White Paper and to fight against the White Paper as though there were no war.[35] After the war, only the fight against the White Paper remained. This struggle involved Palestinian Jewry and world Zionism in a conflict with Great Britain that was waged over a large part of the globe and by the most direct as well as the most subtle methods. The British used every resource of diplomatic pressure and propaganda in the capitals of half the world to cut off the flow of immigrants. The Jews lobbied and pleaded over as wide an area to force Palestine's doors open, while they organized an intricate blockade-running apparatus to collect the immigrants, transport them by sea, and land and distribute them under armed guard through Palestine.[36]

Nor was it any longer possible to hold the line of resistance short of outright rebellion against the mandatary. While Hitler still ruled Europe, only the small group of extremists most heedless of public opinion, the Fighters for Freedom of Israel ("Stern group"), was willing to be at war with England itself and not just with its White Paper policy.[37] Afterward, the National Military Organization (Irgun), the other, larger activist group rejecting the discipline of the organized community, in turn declared war on the mandatary.[38] Both rebel groups took the position that, having violated its trust by adopting the White Paper, the mandatary had forfeited its right to rule in Palestine and was now to be considered an illegitimate, foreign occupying force. Against its tyranny, the Hebrew rebels were conducting a war whose aim was the independence of Palestine as a Jewish commonwealth comprising its present Jewish population and the Diaspora Jews prevented by the White Paper from living in their own country.

On emotional grounds such a position had a powerful appeal to the community as a whole. It responded to the deep revulsion which predisposed Jews, despairing of help in their need from the Gentile world, to welcome the emotional release of risking the all-or-nothing choice in a fight for their own survival. But the consensus of the community, and its official policy, rested on a long-tried commitment to quite different attitudes. The view that the British White Paper policy was a breach of trust was combined with another working assumption — that the pending Jewish appeal to the international community, interrupted by the war, might still cause the mandatary to abide by the formerly accepted interpretation of its obligation to the Jewish national home. The moral need to rescue the survivors from the intolerable position in which they were still caught in Displaced Persons' camps on German soil, or in the pogrom atmosphere of postwar Eastern Europe, dictated a policy of flouting the White Paper in order to bring Jews to Palestine. But there was no inclination to concede in advance that the old legal claims under the Mandate were now hopeless and to resort to force in the name of a status of political sovereignty not specified in the Mandate. At the San Francisco United Nations Conference in 1945, the Zionist movement succeeded by assiduous diplomacy in obtaining stipulations in Article 80 of the Charter which could be interpreted to mean that the rights of the Jewish people, and not only of the Jews already resident in Palestine, were to remain intact in any transition from the Mandate to the UN trusteeship system.[39] Out of mere consistency, the active opposition of the Zionist movement to the White Paper had to observe certain limits. For, the position defended in San Francisco implied that the Mandate remained in force, and consequently the authority of the mandatary had to be respected except in its constitutionally illegal White Paper policy.

Rational consistency — an elastic criterion — was, no doubt, less important in defining the limits of resistance to Britain than another traditional attitude of the Zionist consensus: its deep commitment to slow, organic growth of the still embryonic Jewish national home.[40] The consequent reluctance to risk the gradually accumulating strength of the community in a total conflict with Britain was supported by obvious considerations of prudence. On the other hand, events gave no encouragement to traditional policies.

Coming into power after the war, the British Labor Party reversed the strong stand against the White Paper it had adopted while in opposition and began to follow the anti-Zionist policy of its predecessor. The Jewish consensus could no longer hope that international pressure would force the British to revert to the pre-1939 interpretation of the Mandate. The critical question now became what form of settlement would be imposed in Palestine after the termination of the Mandate, for no one could place much hope in its continuance. Not only the dissident activists, but groups within the organized Zionist movement began to demand civil disobedience and other measures of resistance that would not constitute reactions to specific acts under the White Paper policy but a challenge to British authority as such. They were rejected, with much debate, because even in the expectation of a final political solution in Palestine the community preferred not to risk its whole strength too early, or against Britain. If the international community could not make Britain carry out the

Mandate, it might nevertheless determine the political status of Palestine upon the termination of the Mandate. The Jewish community preferred to guard its strength against that day rather than expose itself to repression by the British while the Mandate remained in force.[41]

But what the Jewish community considered a limited resistance to authority was not necessarily accepted as such by the mandatary. The British refused to accept the official disavowal of the two dissident activist groups as sufficient and demanded that the community give information and the Jewish Agency take action against them. There were moments when the Zionist movement did proceed against the terrorist groups, but only to maintain the campaign of resistance within the limits of its own strategy. Generally, however, the Zionist officials refused to turn over dissident activists to the British so long as Britain provoked Jewish terrorism by the White Paper policy; and the community was induced neither by appeals to respect the law nor by lengthy punitive curfews to lay information against them. Moreover, the British rejected *in toto* the Zionists' distinction between dissident and disciplined resistance. In the end, they concentrated their efforts to repress resistance upon the most representative groups in the Jewish community. Countrywide raids were conducted for almost two weeks in June and July 1946, in an effort to round up the activist cadres of the Hagana. The leaders of the Jewish Agency who were in Palestine at the time were arrested. In the political discussions conducted by Britain in London during that summer, an attempt was made to find opponents of the Zionist consensus who were ready to represent the Jewish community. The failure of this effort proved to the British that their anti-Zionist policy was going to founder on the same difficulty which had caused them to abandon the Balfour Declaration. They could not gain the consent of the (Arab) governed for an administration of the Mandate based on the Balfour Declaration; and now, they concluded, they could not gain the consent of the (Jewish) governed for an administration based on the White Paper, which annulled the Balfour Declaration by interpretation.[42]

This conclusion resulted in the British decision, announced on February 14, 1947, "to refer the whole problem to the United Nations." [43]

IV

When Britain submitted "the whole problem" of Palestine to the United Nations, it did not signify that His Majesty's Government had decided the time had come to terminate the Mandate and was asking the UN to make a final settlement of the political issues. As the Colonial Secretary said,

We are not going to the United Nations to surrender the Mandate. We are going to the United Nations setting out the problem and asking for their advice as to how the Mandate can be administered. If the Mandate cannot be administered in its present form we are asking how it can be amended.[44]

If this statement is to be taken at face value, Britain hoped to gain UN support — and especially, through the UN, American support — for some version of the kind of settlement for Palestine that it had been applying under the White Paper and seeking to negotiate with Jews and Arabs. On this interpretation, the recourse to the UN was one of a chain of efforts by which Britain, since the end of the war, had sought the participation of America in enforcing a British-designed solution for the problem of Palestine. What the British wanted was a joint Anglo-American scheme following as closely as possible the essential provisions of their 1939 White Paper: guaranteeing, that is, that, after a final period of refugee immigration, Jews should no longer be admitted to all of Palestine in accordance with its economic absorptive capacity, but only to part of it and only with the consent of the Arabs or of some impartial referee between Jewish and Arab claims; and guaranteeing, also, that Arab predominance would be preserved in Palestine, in one way or another, while the chance of establishing an Arab state dominating the whole area would at least remain open. The Americans, for their part, were concerned with the Jewish refugee problem. As a concession to American demands, it was thought that, if a trusteeship were set up to replace the mandate temporarily, 100,000 Jewish DP's might be admitted into Palestine on humanitarian grounds. British agreement to continue governing Palestine in spite of the change in policy involved in such a solution of the Palestine problem would depend on America's willingness — whether by a direct understanding with Britain or under a UN resolution — to share the responsibility and burden of imposing it on Arabs and Jews alike.[45]

So long as a bilateral understanding with America on the Palestine problem was its goal, Britain had put forward its plans quite explicitly and worked hard to gain American support for them. But when they referred the Palestine question to the UN, the British studiously avoided making any recommendations. Moreover, they stated that they would refuse to be solely responsible for any solution proposed by the UN which was not accepted by both Jews and Arabs.[46] Such a solution had never been found by Britain herself in all the days of the Mandate; and the immediate occasion for the referral to the UN was the failure to find a solution acceptable to *either* Jews or Arabs at the London Conference of 1947.[47] What the British were saying, then, was that the UN was to advise them how to administer the Mandate, but that they would not undertake alone to put into effect any advice that the UN could conceivably give them. Thus it was up to the UN, either collectively or through one of its members — preferably America — to share with England the responsibility for putting its advice into effect; if, that is, it proved to be advice Britain would willingly associate itself with at all.[48] If, on the other hand, the UN gave different advice from that which Britain would like to receive — and which it now refrained from suggesting — then the international organization might have to devise its own means of enforcement without any help from Britain. Thus, the referral of the Palestine issue to the UN implied a British promise, or threat, to withdraw from Palestine under certain conditions.

The difference in Britain's approach to the UN as a whole from its approach to the United States alone in seeking international guidance and aid in the Palestine problem is easy to understand. Britain could assume a community of strategic interests with America in regard to Palestine which it could not assume in the case of the world organization; consequently, it could *propose* solutions required in the interests of Western strategy in the one case while it could only *await* them in the other. But the effect of approaching the UN was also different in another way from the effect of approaching America. Britain had not received its mandate from America. When London considered with Washington what to do about Palestine, it did not signify a final accounting of its trust by Britain in anticipation of a new settlement. The referral to the UN did have this significance in effect, whether Britain fully intended it or not. Whatever advice the UN might offer, it was virtually certain to be given in the form of proposals for governing the country after the termination of the Mandate.

Of the other major powers whose views would probably be decisive in the UN, Russia made its general position clear at once while the United States kept its own counsel. The Russian motives were transparent. They made no bones about their desire to get Britain out of Palestine. Independence for the area was what they aimed at, and the form of independence a secondary matter. If a unitary binational state could be set up, they preferred it. If no unitary state could be set up — and now that Jews as well as Arabs had shown themselves capable of fighting, this seemed all too likely — then the country should gain its independence by partition.[49]

In the two postwar years before the UN was confronted with "the whole problem," the United States had generally favored a continuation of Britain's mandate. The great difficulty was the "problem of the Jews"; or, more specifically, of the 100,000 — and later 200,000 — Jewish DP's in the camps of occupied Germany. If the White Paper were a valid interpretation of the Mandate, as Britain held, then it was only a gratuitous humanitarian act, but by no means a legal obligation, to admit the Jewish refugees to Palestine. But the White Paper of 1939 was not only an interpretation of the Mandate; it was also a political promise made by Britain to the Arabs. To admit 100,000 Jewish DP's to Palestine might appeal to Britain as humanitarian, but it would be a breach of that political promise; and, unless America shared with Britain in the burden of enforcing a new, mutually acceptable policy, or the Arabs (and Jews) agreed on some policy which included admitting the DP's, England would not risk it.

To this attitude of the British, the Americans on such a body as the Anglo-American Committee of Inquiry of 1946 might take exception on legal and political, as well as humanitarian, grounds. The Committee, in fact, including its British as well as American members, implicitly denied that the "problem of the Jews" could be separated from the purposes of the Palestine Mandate. They recommended that free land sales and Jewish immigration up to absorptive capacity be resumed, at least until a new trusteeship agreement was formulated, and they concluded that there was no apparent solution for the acute problem of 100,000 of the Jewish DP's in European camps except that they be immediately allowed to enter Palestine. As to the final political solution for Palestine, the Committee favored the prewar Zionist formula of parity regardless of numerical preponderance. They accordingly recommended that, under the trusteeship agreement which was to succeed the Mandate, immigration to Palestine be regulated (without discriminating against Jews as such and while allowing for the growth of the national home) in some way or other calculated to make a binationalist political solution ultimately feasible.[50]

Confronted with these recommendations, clear only in their rejection of the White Paper and their humanitarian plea for the 100,000 DP's but excessively vague in their proposals concerning a trusteeship agreement and an ultimate political settlement to succeed the Mandate, President Truman enthusiastically accepted the former and proposed to take the latter under consideration. In an angry retort, Prime

Minister Attlee doomed this attempt to find a mutually acceptable Anglo-American policy for Palestine. He made it plain that Britain would not make any gestures of humanitarianism until it was satisfied on its political demands from the Zionists — to abandon resistance — and from America — to agree to, and to help enforce, not only the immediate recommendations of the Committee, but also the long-range proposals for a trusteeship and a non-Jewish, non-Arab Palestinian state.[51]

In the ensuing period — as was usually true in the history of American policy in regard to Zionism — Washington spoke with two voices and was concerned with two different sets of political considerations. In order to restore Anglo-American cooperation in a strategy for the Middle East, an American Cabinet Committee was appointed to negotiate with a similar British Committee concerning a joint plan following upon the Inquiry Committee's investigation. Since America was unwilling to asssume military as well as financial responsibility in Palestine, the American negotiators had little bargaining power, and the "joint plan" — the so-called Morrison-Grady plan — turned out to be a modified version of the White Paper policy.[52] To have agreed to this would have been to flout other political considerations to which Washington was also sensitive. The Jews' conviction of the justice of their cause, so intense that they resorted to tactics of partisan resistance in Palestine and in Europe, had aroused American Jewish voters to the point of making this an open political issue. It would involve substantial repercussions to approve a policy that would rob the Jewish national home of its right to solve, as far as possible, the problem of the Jews. Consequently the Morrison-Grady plan was not carried further.

But one conclusion was certain from that time on: that no large number of Jews would be admitted into Palestine on humanitarian grounds alone, for not until some definite political decision was made in the country would the bars be let down. In the election campaign of that fall, President Truman spoke out openly in approval of partition as a possible solution for the Palestine problem.[53] But when the issue reached the United Nations half a year later, the Americans refrained from defining their position, pending the report of the UN Special Committee on Palestine (UNSCOP) that was then set up.[54]

The UNSCOP investigation and report, which paved the way for the political settlement of the Palestine problem, brought to bear the opinions of so-called "neutral" powers: nations considered not to be directly involved in the Palestine dispute or in the global strategies that were in conflict there.[55] The countries represented — Australia,

Canada, Czechoslovakia, Guatemala, India, Iran, Netherlands, Peru, Sweden, Uruguay, and Yugoslavia — include a wider range of opinion than entered into the consensus of the League of Nations. The consensus which had originally granted international recognition "to the historical connection of the Jewish people with Palestine and the grounds for reconstituting their national home in that country" — that is, the bond between Zion and the Jewish problem — was represented in UNSCOP by the smaller Christian powers of Europe, the Americas, and the British Commonwealth. In addition, however, there were two representatives of the colonial world — Iran, a Moslem nation, and India — who did not share the special involvement of Christendom with the Jewish problem.

Every approach to a renewed international consideration of the Palestine problem after the Second World War began with attempts by interested parties to cancel, in the very approach to the question, its connection with the Jewish problem. The Arabs had tried in vain to accomplish this in 1945 at the United Nations Conference on International Organization in San Francisco, in the debate over the formulation of Article 80 of the UN Charter.[56] The terms of reference worked out between the Americans and the British for the Anglo-American Committee of Inquiry were broad enough, at any rate, to permit considering the Jewish problem in connection with the Palestine question; but Foreign Secretary Bevin at once issued interpretive comments calculated to preclude a solution for the latter which would also be designed to solve the former problem.[57] In submitting "the whole question" of Palestine to the UN, Britain said only that it was seeking advice concerning "the future government of Palestine." The terms of reference devised for UNSCOP by the Special Session of the General Assembly were phrased more broadly in order to include the Jewish problem and its connection with Palestine within the purview of the proposed Committee. The detached attitude assumed by the British on this occasion precluded outright opposition to such terms of reference. But Sir Alexander Cadogan did indicate his government's attitude by requesting the deletion of the phrase stating that the question was raised at the request of the mandatary. Solving the Jewish problem together with the Palestine problem was not the question, one infers, upon which Britain had asked for UN advice. The Arabs did not content themselves with hints. They waged a determined but unsuccessful battle against any phrasing that admitted a possible connection between the problem of the Jews and the question of Palestine; and they fought with equal stubbornness and with the same lack of effect for an agenda item of their own, stating that the question at issue was "the termination of the Mandate and the proclamation of the independence of Palestine." On these points, the Arabs had the full support of other Moslem peoples and of such a country as India. The support of the Soviet bloc was less complete, for while they backed any formulation that would commit the investigating committee to speedy independence for Palestine — that is, to British withdrawal — they also favored terms of reference that would include the problem of the Jews as pertinent to the inquiry. The bulk of the Assembly, however, refused to accept the Arab formulations at all, as they seemed intended to rule out the Jewish question and prejudge the major issues.[58]

While Christian conscience forced recognition of the connection between Palestine and the problem of the Jews, this recognition had strikingly ambivalent aspects and was by no means complete. Andrei Gromyko repeatedly stressed the point that the problem of the Jews existed in Western Europe, not in the Soviet zone.

The fact that no western European state has been able to ensure the defence of the elementary rights of the Jewish people, and to safeguard it against the violence of the Fascist executioners, explains the aspirations of the Jews to establish their own State.[59]

The postwar international efforts to analyze the linked problems of the Jews and of Palestine ended with strikingly inconclusive findings on this point. The Anglo-American Committee's Recommendation No. 1 states:

We have to report that such information as we have received about countries other than Palestine gave no hope of substantial assistance in finding homes for Jews wishing or impelled to leave Europe.

But Palestine alone cannot meet the emigration needs of the Jewish victims of Nazi and Fascist persecution; the whole world shares responsibility for them and indeed for the resettlement of all "displaced persons." [60]

It might be possible to explain this as a politic compromise between American and British proposals. But it becomes clear that some more general cause is at work when we note the similar finding of the UN Special Committee. In its twelfth statement of principles, the Committee proposed (Uruguay and Guatemala dissenting) that "it be accepted as incontrovertible that any solution for Palestine cannot be considered as a solution of the Jewish problem in general." [61]

It is easy to understand that Christian powers could not easily accept — let alone share — the mythic attitude that exercised such a powerful influence on the Jewish consensus. They could not assume the principle that no full confidence could be felt in Jewish life among any people of the Gentiles, and that once the always-to-be-feared catastrophe had befallen them, the Jewish victims could seek no future anywhere but among their own brethren and in their own national home. But there was a more telling — at any rate, a less ambivalent — reason for attaching reservations to the recognition that the Jewish national home must help solve the problem of the Jews, by absorbing the bulk of Jewish emigrants. The time had gone by when it was possible to consider marking out the boundaries of an area for the Jewish national home in terms of the territorial requirements for solving the problem of the Jews, or, for that matter, in terms of historical connections. If there were to be any effective relationship at all between Palestine and the solution of the contemporary problem of the Jews, it would have to be through the creation of a Jewish state; but the only possibility for creating a Jewish state in 1947 depended on the partition of mandated Palestine west of the Jordan River. And the boundaries of such a partition would have to depend not so much on the needs for solving the problem of the Jews as on the existing distribution of populations in the territory to be partitioned.

v

From the moment partition was proposed as a solution of the Palestine problem, it was subject to sharp criticism. But all alternative suggestions had come to seem even less reasonable or capable of enforcement. The members of UNSCOP were unanimous in declaring, as their first principle, that, in whatever form, the independence of Palestine would have to be granted without delay. The UNSCOP minority proposal of a single federal state of Palestine, in which the Jews would be a recognized minority with some regional autonomy, gained the votes not only of Iran and India, but of Yugoslavia.[62] When an alternative to partition had to be worked out in the General Assembly, however, only one non-Moslem state, Colombia, could be found to join the subcommittee to draft it; and, before the subcommittee finished its labors, Colombia, too, had dropped out. The subcommittee drew up a plan for an Arab state, with a vague minority status, but no regional autonomy, for Jews. The proposal was rejected in the General Assembly's Ad Hoc Committee on Palestine by a vote of 29 to 12, only Cuba and Liberia joining the ten Arab and Moslem states in support of their plan.[63] For, the Jewish national home — even apart from anticipated Jewish armed resistance — had grown too big to be easily digested by an Arab state of Palestine; and a solution which promised neither to solve the problem of the Jews nor to be enforceable at the outset and workable in the long run provided no grounds for arriving at an international consensus. Partition was a lesser evil, it seemed, than any available alternative.

However, before partition could gain international approval the obvious difficulties involved in it had to be met by a number of complicated special arrangements. The Jews accepted both partition and the attendant arrangements because it gave them the sovereign right to seek to solve the problem of the Jews, their main purpose; but the sovereignty which they were ready to accept under the plan was subject to many, far-reaching limitations.

The most obvious and the most serious difficulty in any proposal to partition Palestine lay in the distribution of the Jewish and Arab populations of the country. The two principles originally formulated by the Permanent Mandates Commission were agreed upon as essential to an acceptable plan for partition: that the Arabs should be deprived of "as small a number as possible of the places to which they attach particular value, either because they are their present homes or for reasons of religion" — or, to put it differently, the Arab population of the proposed Jewish state should be a minority, and as small a minority as possible; and, on the other hand, "the areas allotted to the Jews should be sufficiently extensive, fertile and well situated from the point of view of communications by sea and land to be capable of intensive economic development and consequently of dense and rapid settlement." But in the course of Jewish settlement in Palestine since 1880, the areas where they had concentrated were also the areas to which the densest Arab population had been attracted. This meant that any conceivable division of Palestine into Jewish and Arab states would leave the Jewish state, initially at least, with almost as many Arab as Jewish residents. And in order to have any reserve lands for the resettlement of the large influx of Jews which the Jewish state expected, and needed, it was essential to add to the area of greatest Jewish and Arab population density two underdeveloped zones in which neither Jews nor Arabs were thickly settled, but in which there were even fewer Jews than Arabs. These were the northern zone of the Galilee, that part of Palestine in which there was an appreciable water surplus, and the arid southern half of Palestine, the Negev, a portion of which might be placed under regular cultivation by piping water to it. Proceeding along these lines, the UN Special Committee drew up a partition plan in which Jews (not counting 100,000 Jews in the Jerusalem area who, while living outside the Jewish state, were entitled to citizenship in it) had a small majority of the settled population. In fact, if one added the Beduins of the Negev, the Jewish majority almost disappeared — but the majority would be rapidly increased by the release of the Jewish internees in Cyprus and the DP's in Germany.[64]

The second difficulty which was seen in all partition plans from the time the Peel Commission first officially proposed one was the dubious viability of the states to be established in Palestine.[65] The term "viability", as employed in the debate about partition, had a rather special meaning. From the outset it was clear that if one applied the criteria of partition which seemed most nearly equitable in a rough and ready way — the division of the country as far as possible according to the preponderance of existing Jewish and Arab populations — then one could never lay out boundaries that were "viable" in the sense of providing easily defensible strategic frontiers.

The question of economic viability was also a very murky one. The requirements of territory and natural resources needed to maintain a marketing economy like that of the Jews, which was deeply involved in foreign trade and which anticipated large scale immigration, could be worked out in some detail. Only part of the Arab economy, on the other hand, was significantly involved in commodity exchange and foreign trade and that part was largely concentrated in the proposed Jewish area. The Arab villages were to considerable extent economically self-contained within the ecological frame of small local areas and the subsistence farming they pursued would not be significantly affected by state boundaries. Thus, subject to all the reservations that might be made in special cases, partitioning Palestine in accordance with economic viability became a matter of carving out the absolute minimum for Jewish purposes, and declaring all other areas an Arab state. In the residual Arab state, the interests of a certain number of farmers and city dwellers who depended on the Jewish market and the international traffic in commodities and services might then be adversely affected, but this would only be the case if partition meant shutting off access to the Jewish state or, through it, with the outside world. It was possible to solve this special problem by arrangements for access to the Jewish state and to its ports, no matter how the boundaries were drawn.

Another complication was the chief problem referred to whenever the viability of the proposed Arab state was discussed. This was the question of the taxable resources from which to supply an appropriate budget for the proposed Arab state. The difficulty stemmed from the fact that, under the Palestine Mandate, government budgets largely devoted to serving the Arab population had been based to a great ex-

tent on the growth of the Jewish economy. In all partition schemes the
budget of expenditures for an Arab state was calculated on the level
of services that had been thus provided; but partition would necessarily deprive it of its major revenue sources. But here again was a
problem not to be solved by particular changes in the partition boundaries. Special arrangements would be needed to deal with it no matter
how the partition into Jewish and Arab states were drawn in detail.

The third difficulty was the question of the Holy Places and, above
all, of the city of Jerusalem.[66] If Palestine were to be partitioned under
the auspices of the United Nations, not only the two nations who lived
in the country but a third claimant, the Christian religious interest,
would have to be provided for in the division. The question of the
Holy Places was to have been dealt with under the Mandate by a
special commission, but the League of Nations was never able to
unite on its composition.[67] When it was proposed to partition Palestine, the problem of the Holy Places again arose. Since Christian holy
places were to be found throughout Palestine, both proposed states
were to guarantee free access and respectful care for all places of
worship and devotion. But, in addition, the partition was to set aside
as an area for international administration the city of Jerusalem —
for over a century predominantly Jewish — together with Bethlehem
and a number of adjacent Arab areas, making an enclave containing
over 200,000 people evenly divided between Jews and Arabs.[68] Only
on condition that this special claim of the Christian world were accepted could the necessary two-thirds majority be obtained in the UN
General Assembly for any plan for the creation of independent Jewish and Arab states in a partitioned Palestine.

VI

After they had agreed to all the special arrangements introduced
into the partition plan in order to meet the difficulties involved in
such a solution of the Palestine problem, the Jews found that the
price of the sovereign right to solve the postwar problem of the Jews
in their part of Palestine was the renunciation of authority in many
other respects. The great difference between the partition plan, as
finally formulated, and all other plans for regional autonomy or can-
tonization, within a federal state or under a new trusteeship of Palestine, was that no authority was set up over the Jews themselves in
regard to their immigration policy. They were not obligated to limit
the admission of Jews in the Jewish part of Palestine according
to the political interests of the non-Jewish population of their region

or of Palestine as a whole or according to the absorptive capacity of their region as judged by a predominantly Arab federal government, a British governor-general, or some impartial international arbitrator of Jewish and Arab differences. They were to have full, sovereign freedom to devote the area allotted to them, according to any principles and criteria they themselves chose, to the solution of the postwar problem of the Jews. But in order to obtain the sanction of the international consensus for the acquisition of such sovereignty they had to agree to a partition drawn on lines that deliberately ignored the question of defensible boundaries; that denied them full, sovereign freedom in economic matters by tying the Jewish to the Arab areas of Palestine in an economic union; and that placed 100,000 Jerusalem Jews, entitled to citizenship in the Jewish state, in an internationalized enclave containing an equal number of Arabs and totally surrounded by the Arab state.

The map of partition drawn up by the UN divided Palestine into six segments, three Jewish, three Arab (with additional enclaves) by splitting the country in half vertically, and into three sections horizontally.[69] The Jewish and Arab areas were interlocked in a checkerboard design by this division. In the top horizontal section the Arab state lay to the west of the Jewish state; in the middle horizontal section, the Jewish state lay to the west of the Arab state — with Jerusalem as an internationalized enclave in the middle of the Arab state and Jaffa as an Arab enclave in the Jewish state; and in the bottom horizontal section, the Arab state again lay to the west of the Jewish state. Moreover, the two points of intersection between the boundaries of the Jewish and Arab states, connecting the middle and top sections and middle and bottom sections of the partition, were deliberately designed to make it possible to pass either from any part of the Arab state to any other part of it, or from any part of the Jewish state to any other part of it, without crossing the territory of the interlocking state. Such a partition demonstrated by its very design that it was founded on the assumption that neither the Jewish nor the Arab state would ever wish or need to defend itself against the other. During a transitional period in preparation for independence, each of the states was to organize its militia in strength sufficient to maintain internal security and prevent border outbreaks, and the United Nations was to exercise a supervisory authority, with the right to approve the High Command of each militia.[70] In accepting a partition plan of this sort, the Jewish state, for the sake of the sovereign right to seek to solve the problem of the Jews, renounced, for all practical purposes — though, of course, not formally — the sovereign right of self-defense, on the understanding and condition that the Arab state that was to be set up would do likewise.

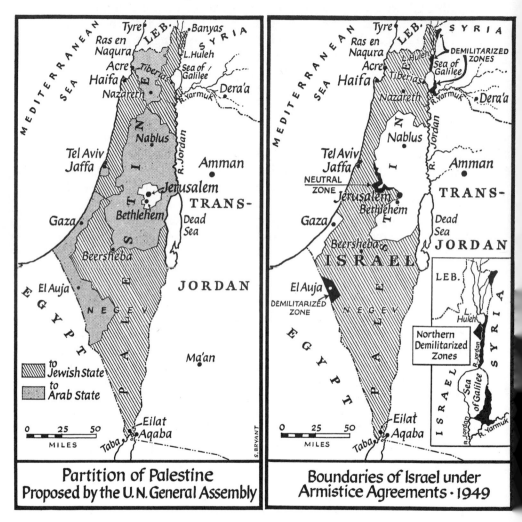

Partition of Palestine Proposed by the U.N. General Assembly

Boundaries of Israel under Armistice Agreements · 1949

The plan for economic union required a similar suspension of sovereign rights usually exercised by states.[71] While accepting this plan, the Jews showed greater concern for drawing the partition boundaries in terms of economic requirements than had been possible in regard to their strategic defensive requirements. Under the plan for economic union, the Jewish and Arab states had to bind themselves for ten years to share in a common currency and a joint customs and foreign exchange pool. Their joint income was to be dispensed by a joint economic board, with UN members casting the decisive votes, in such a way that a minimum standard of services would be maintained in the Jewish and Arab states and in internationalized Jerusalem — meaning that the Jewish state would be expected to subsidize the other two partition areas up to a stated maximum. Also there was to be a common tariff policy, free transit and communications, and cooperation, organized by the Joint Economic Board, on irrigation and other development projects in the whole Palestine area. In spite of these substantial concessions, restricting the economic sovereignty of the proposed Jewish state, the Zionists felt that partition, with economic union, could give them the essential minimum of freedom in economic planning to enable them to absorb the expected mass influx of Jews. This is implied in their careful negotiations concerning the partition boundaries. They aimed at including within the proposed Jewish state all the essential water and land resources and land sites needed for combining the surplus water of northern Palestine and the arid land of southern Palestine in a country-wide development plan.

Perhaps the most difficult decision the Jews had to face in agreeing to the partition plan was to accept the provision for internationalizing Jerusalem. This was the one place in Palestine that had been dominantly and increasingly Jewish in population since well before the Zionist resettlement began in the 1880's. If the criterion of equity in dividing Palestine were to be the existing population distribution, and, if in the name of this principle, the city of Jaffa had to be made an Arab enclave in the heart of the Jewish state, then it was a pointed injustice to prevent the inclusion of Jewish Jerusalem in the Jewish state by internationalizing it. Even more irritating were the attitudes regarding historic ties to places sanctified by religious sentiment which seemed to be involved. A Jewish state without Jerusalem seemed a mockery of the historical connection to which the Balfour Declaration and the Mandate had granted recognition. Hardly less painful to Zionist feeling was the historical Christian animus they could not help but sense in this inequity. There were other Christian holy places, mainly in the proposed Arab state, which it was not thought essential to internationalize. In regard to Jerusalem itself, there was a sort of traditional tacit agreement that, in view of the violent disagreements of Christian sects over the holy places, Moslem custodianship might be the best way to keep the peace there. If such a view did not prevail when the prospect arose of Jewish custodianship of Jerusalem and its holy places, it bespoke, to the Zionist instinct, the same theological odium in which a current of Christian opinion held the whole enterprise of the restoration of Jewish sovereignty in Zion.[72] Symbolically, this meant to deny the historic legitimacy of renewed Jewish sovereignty in the very act of granting it as a mark of political justice. But without the internationalization of Jerusalem, inequitable as it might appear to Jews, there could be no two-thirds majority establishing an international consensus in favor of partition. In order to gain the most essential sovereign rights needed to solve the postwar problem of the Jews, the Zionist swallowed not only the substantive restrictions on their authority in other respects but the symbolic denial of their historic claim to restoration in Zion represented by the proposed internationalization of Jerusalem.

The UN partition plan for Palestine assumed not only that the proposed Jewish and Arab states would dispense with defensive frontiers and arms against each other. It also assumed, quite knowingly, that the new arrangement would require no substantial enforcement in order to come into effect, but that, upon the proclamation of its judgment by the United Nations, all parties concerned — at least all UN members — would accept it and cooperate in carrying it out. Long discussions over provisions to enforce the UN solution for Palestine, all leading to nothing, preceded the decision to rely solely on the moral force of a UN resolution; so that it was not naiveté but something like resigned desperation that brought about such a position.[73] But the assumption of ready compliance and cooperation by UN members proved unwarranted; and the main intent of the UN partition plan was achieved, amid chaos and conflict, by the willingness of Israel to stake its existence and independence on the all-or-nothing choice of a war for survival.

Most calamitous for the UN plan was the refusal of Britain to cooperate in any way in putting it into effect. Not only did Britain fail to transfer any authority or facilities in Palestine to the UN or to coordinate its withdrawal with the planned gradual assumption of authority by the UN Commission that was to supervise the partition; it even prevented the Commission from coming to Palestine until just before the last stage of its own withdrawal. The British concerned themselves almost exclusively with the safety of their own personnel, and made only such provisions for the transfer of authority upon their departure as did not interfere with this object or seemed likely to help in achieving it. Sometimes they handed over authority, before leaving, to whichever group — Jews or Arabs — was locally dominant; sometimes they left the two to fight it out. The result was described by Jews as "Operation Chaos" and by a British observer as "anarchy."[74]

The Arabs, as they had warned they would, took the offensive against partition and attacked the Jews at all possible points. While the full-scale Arab attack by the regular armies of the neighboring states was delayed until May 15, the day the British main forces left Haifa, the Palestinian Arabs together with irregular forces from other countries, groups detached from the Iraqi army and, in the end, the Transjordan Arab Legion, began the attack earlier. From the day partition was announced on November 29, 1947, to the day the Mandate was ended, May 15, 1948, the Jews in Palestine had to fight a peculiar, desperate battle for their own survival and for the survival of the partition plan, with its recognition of Jewish sovereignty. After May 15, 1948, this became an all-out war of the new Jewish state against the armed forces of the combined Arab states, who refused to recognize the existence of the state they were attacking.[75]

From November 29, 1947, to May 15, 1948, the United Nations did nothing of consequence to carry out the partition plan it had adopted for Palestine. The provisions made in the plan itself for execution by UN organs depended completely on British cooperation. Since this was denied, the Palestine Commission that was appointed could only submit gloomy reports of growing chaos and of their own helplessness.[76] Moreover, after exerting itself to obtain approval of partition, one of the major sponsors, the United States, backed down in the face of difficulties. When the Palestine Commission reported in February 1948 that it could not carry out its responsibilities without armed assistance, the United States, taking a legal position opposed to that of the UN Secretary General, stated that the Security Council could not intervene to impose partition in Palestine, but only to preserve the peace.[77] Later the United States completely abandoned partition, urging that efforts to put it into effect be suspended and a temporary UN trusteeship be resorted to. For such a solution in Palestine, it was suggested, some American forces might even be available. But the prospect of enforcing a trusteeship against the combined opposition of Jews and Arabs was even less appealing to the UN consensus than of seeking to enforce partition; nor did Britain show any signs of reversing its position and agreeing to stay in Palestine in response to the American reversal.

As the UN session was drawing to a close, simultaneously with the British mandate in Palestine, without a new decision, Israel, on May 14, took matters into its own hands and proclaimed its existence as a sovereign state. Boldness had its instant reward. Without warning even to the State Department officials who, to the last minute, were seeking to stave off partition and Jewish independence together with all their consequences, the White House immediately announced recognition of the new Jewish commonwealth. The Soviet Union swiftly picked up its cue, recognizing Israel *de jure* three days later.[78]

11 ISRAEL AND THE UNITED NATIONS

THE Jews had been willing to accept an extremely restricted sovereignty as part of an orderly solution of the Palestine problem under the aegis of the United Nations. But the UN solution was neither carried out in an orderly fashion nor enforced at all by its authors. A bold assertion of sovereignty by Israel itself, at the risk of desperate war, was responsible for the ultimate solution of the Palestine problem.

Israel's independence was fiercely contested from the outset by sworn foes. Even the original sponsors of the new state, the United Nations — as a body, bloc by bloc, or individually — did not always grant to Israel's sovereignty the same measure of recognition normally accorded to less controversial states. But having won its very right to exist by an assertion of independence, Israel carefully examined all new suggestions to abridge its sovereignty in order to see whether they were not, in actuality, threats to its existence. Against such threats it is even today inclined to defend its rights in an all-or-nothing mood.

I

In the period between November 29, 1947, and May 14, 1948, the Jews, alone among all the parties concerned, worked in close collaboration with the United Nations Palestine Commission.[1] As Abba Eban pointed out, when he appeared before the Ad Hoc Political Committee of the General Assembly to defend Israel's application for membership in the UN, the General Assembly, in its partition resolution, had specifically requested cooperation from six different sources: the Jews, the Arabs, the mandatary, the Security Council, the Trusteeship Council, and the Economic and Social Council. Only the Jews extended their cooperation. The Arabs opposed the resolution by violence. The mandatary not only refused cooperation but prevented execution of the General Assembly's instructions by its Palestine Commission. The Security Council rejected clauses in a resolution offered by the United States which would have accepted the tasks assigned to the Security Council by the partition resolution. The Trusteeship Council considered but did not adopt a draft statute for the internationalization of Jerusalem, and the Economic and Social Council did not appoint a joint economic board as required by the partition resolution.[2]

If this were not sufficient to prove how dubious the General Assembly's political solution of the Palestine problem had become, other developments underscored the point. Among these we have mentioned the American reversal of policy after November 29, 1947 — to be reversed in its turn by the presidential recognition of Israel on May 14, 1948. American hesitancy had its effect on the General Assembly. The UN consensus was not persuaded to replace partition by a trusteeship for Palestine nor did the United States push this proposal beyond the stage of a working paper. However, even as Israel was proclaiming its independence, the UN did disband the Palestine Commission appointed to carry out partition and replaced it with a Mediator. This measure was interpreted at least by one of the great powers most interested in Palestine, Great Britain, as a mandate to the Mediator to seek new political solutions other than partition for the situation in Palestine.[3] Count Folke Bernadotte, appointed as Mediator, took the same view of his instructions, and was rather impatient with any action of UN quarters that might tie his hands.[4] He made, or considered, new proposals for the demilitarization or international control of Haifa; the surrender of large blocks of territory in Southern Palestine which had been allocated to Israel by the UN partition in return for Western Galilee, which had been allocated to the Arabs; the incorporation of the proposed Palestine Arab state — including the Negev in the south (and, at one time, the Jerusalem area originally to have been internationalized) — in the Kingdom of Transjordan; and the joint control of immigration into Israel by Jews and Arabs through the union of the two territories in a dual state.[5] These proposals, which were in accord with British strategic requirements, were generally understood, by Israel among others, to have been drawn up in agreement with the foreign affairs policy planners of Britain and the United States.[6]

The proposals had no practical significance at the time, since most Arab states were as firmly opposed to them — though, of course, for different reasons — as was Israel. But merely by making such plans public, the UN Mediator gave the Israelis an unmistakable demonstration of two facts pertinent to their situation. First, they were put on notice that the delineation of boundaries by the UN resolution of

November 29, 1947, could not be regarded as decisive. The Western consensus, backed by the Soviet bloc for its own convenience, had worked out partition boundaries which took account of the Zionist aim to solve the problem of the Jews. Many of these same countries were now inclined to mediate — that is, to split the difference — between their own adjudication of the issues on their merits and the Arab refusal to accept the existence of Israel in any shape. Secondly, and following from this, Israel perceived that only by another assertion of its sovereign will — for no other court of appeal remained — could it preserve itself within boundaries that made it a viable instrument for the functions it had undertaken as a Jewish state.

The framework within which Israel had to act was the developing UN regime of cease-fire orders and truces regulating the Arab-Israeli war. The regulations that grew up, and the tactical and strategic situations that arose in relation to them, were another demonstration to the Israelis of the nature of the dangers to which they were exposed and, consequently, of the kind of method which alone held out any hope for survival.

In the last days of the Mandate, the Jews in Palestine already had occasion to learn that the UN resolution offered no protection for their lives or political survival. On the other hand, both could be successfully defended by the independent action of the Jews themselves, if they were ready to fight against apparently desperate odds. Since the British generally stood aside, the Jews and Arabs, both of whom were most densely settled in the same regions in mixed or neighboring rural and urban concentrations, were left to fight a bitter civil war on the roads and streets, in the citrus groves and from house to house. Fighting raged throughout the area marked out for the Jewish state as well as in Jerusalem and its environs and approaches. The Arabs, having the initiative of attack and bolstered by men and arms from neighboring Arab states, began by cutting off the communications between major Jewish settlements. They were also able to destroy by May 15 several villages in the area destined for the Arab state or the *corpus separatum* of Jerusalem. In the course of time, however, it became clear that the Jewish defense would not merely hold fast in most of the towns and villages. The Jews in their campaign to maintain dominance over the whole area of the proposed Jewish state, as well as of the new city of Jerusalem and its approaches,[7] were also able to destroy Arab strongholds that commanded the roads or threatened Jewish settlements.

The situation was sharply reversed on May 15, 1948, the day the Mandate was officially terminated and the day after Israel came into being. Detachments of the regular armies of Egypt and Saudi Arabia, Transjordan, Iraq, Syria, and Lebanon marched into Palestine, seeking to cut off the major areas of Jewish settlement from each other and to converge on Jerusalem, Haifa, and Tel Aviv. Until it received delivery of heavy arms ordered abroad, sometimes in evasion of an embargo against arms shipments to Palestine, Israel had nothing to match the equipment of its foes, who had long been and were still receiving modern armaments from Britain and other countries. The Arab incursions, of course, were not only contrary to the intent of the General Assembly's partition resolution but directly opposed to a series of Security Council resolutions of March 5, April 1, April 17, and May 22, calling on all parties involved to end the fighting in Palestine. It needed a new Security Council resolution for a temporary cease-fire, passed on May 29, and a period of negotiation even after that to secure the first truce, which went into effect on June 11.[8] In the meantime, the Arab forces had penetrated far beyond the frontiers laid down in the partition plan, except in those places, like the Jordan and Jezreel valleys and the Sharon Plain, where Jewish settlements presented a more or less continuous front. Elsewhere, in the Negev in the south and Jerusalem in the east, isolated Jewish settlements maintained themselves in a "hedgehog" defense, while Arab armies marched freely around and between them to occupy strategic positions practically at will within the area allotted to the state of Israel under the UN plan. In the rear of the Egyptian forces, Israeli mobile units operated.[9]

This was the situation which was to be regulated by the negotiation of a truce. The resort to a truce as a means for dealing with the Palestine situation had been from the beginning an alternative employed by the Security Council upon failing to undertake the direct enforcement of the General Assembly's partition plan. A truce was first proposed by the American delegation following the policy shift from support of the partition plan to the expedient of a temporary trusteeship. When the Security Council, in lieu of action enforcing the partition, did issue a call for a truce on April 1, 1948, it called at the same time for the special session proposed by the American delegation to consider "further the future government of Palestine." [10] The Zionist representatives at the UN plainly expressed their fear of two possibilities inherent in a truce inaugurated under such conditions.[11] They were suspicious of any agreement for which there was no agency of enforcement except the mandatary, and they successfully demanded that the UN establish its own supervisory agency. In addition, they obviously felt that, even under UN supervisory auspices, the resort to a truce without enforcement of the partition resolution might have political as well as military implications. Consequently, they tried to have the political and military aspects of the problem separated. Here, too, they were successful, formally at least, and the Consular Truce Commission and subsequent truce supervisory bodies were charged with maintaining a purely military equilibrium, and were without any competence in regard to the political issues. Yet, it was clear enough that, whatever might be the formal provisions that applied, in fact the status existing under the truce arrangements must necessarily have crucial political effects; and it could be used as a weapon against the sovereignty or existence of the Jewish state.

Thus whenever a truce was under discussion, the Arabs sought to ban Jewish immigration from entering Palestine on the grounds that this would constitute a breach of the military *status quo*.[12] Israel, on the other hand, asserted its sovereign right to admit immigrants to its shores, yet had to agree that the UN might supervise the admission of men of military age in order to ensure they would not be placed under arms. Also, of course, there were UN observers in Israel to enforce the ban on arms imports under the truce — a condition which complicated the position of the government when the *Altalena* had to be sunk off Tel Aviv beach.[13]

At the end of the first truce, which at British and Arab insistence had been limited to four weeks, a UN resolution called for an extension of the cease-fire.[14] This was ignored by the Arab armies, who reopened hostilities, only to be sharply set back in a ten-day Israeli offensive that substantially widened the area under Jewish control. A second truce was imposed, intended this time to be permanent. But the positions occupied by the Jewish and Arab forces at the onset of the truce still cut across each other's communications. As a result, new fighting broke out continually, sometimes provoked by different interpretations of the complex truce provisions.[15]

The cease-fire orders of that time began to contain paragraphs stipulating that the forces must retreat to their lines as they existed before the outbreak.[16] The political implications of such a clause were unmistakable, for at that very time the UN Mediator, with British support, was proposing to scrap the partition resolution and allot to Transjordan areas of Southern Palestine in which isolated Jewish strongpoints were surrounded by the armored forces of Egypt. The justification for abandoning the UN partition plan in this way was that the UN resolution was based on an assumption of universal compliance which had been proven illusory. Once the plan was resisted by violence, a new solution, taking into account the political realities represented, for example, by the line of battle between Israel and the Arabs, would have to be sought.

But the attempt to stabilize a military *status quo* relying on the kind of truce lines that existed was itself based on an unreal assumption. This was recognized in Count Bernadotte's report:

It would be dangerous complacency . . . to take it for granted that with no settlement in sight the truce can be maintained indefinitely. Each side contends that the indefinite truce works to the advantage of the other. The strain on both sides in maintaining the truce under the prevailing tension in Palestine is undoubtedly very great. I am convinced that neither side really wishes to resume the fighting but, on the other hand, neither side appears to be prepared, openly or voluntarily, to surrender its position or to make fundamental concessions. There is the constant danger, which must be faced, that the accumulated irritation from daily incidents, war nerves, the economic strain of maintaining large armies in the field, the pressures of public opinion, and the tendency to despair of any peaceful settlement, may provoke one or the other party to take the foolhardy risk of resuming hostilities in the vain hope of a quick victory. There is also the danger that under the constant pressure of tension, mutual suspicion and recrimination, and in the absence of any enforcement ability by the United Nations representatives, the truce, if too long prolonged in its present indefinite form, will deteriorate into a virtual resumption of hostilities through a mounting number of local incidents widely spread.[17]

It became obvious that the only way to establish a military *status quo* that could endure was not to demand, after each outbreak, withdrawal to untenable truce lines but to disentangle the foes and regroup them along continuous demarcation lines accepted by both under an armistice. A Security Council resolution of November 16, 1948 called upon the parties to come to an agreement for this purpose.[18]

During this period Israel was given another object lesson in the inefficacy of the UN partition resolution as a support for its existence. That resolution had specifically provided that the UN should give "sympathetic consideration" to applications for membership from a Jewish or Arab state if either should make its independence effective as envisaged in the partition plan.[19] Israel submitted its application for UN membership on November 29, 1948, the anniversary of the passage of the partition resolution, together with a declaration committing itself to accept all the obligations of the UN charter.[20] If the provisions of the UN partition resolution relating to this application had been respected, the sovereign existence of Israel, denied by the Arabs, would have been reaffirmed by the UN as a whole at that time.

Circumstances seemed favorable for such an application. Not only had Israel been granted diplomatic recognition by a considerable number of states by the end of 1948,[21] but the progress of the fighting had made it clear that the Arab armies could not crush the Jews. By the middle of November, it was Egyptian forces who were being encircled by the Jewish advance. Even though no armistice negotiations had yet begun, the General Assembly was discussing draft resolutions which were to lead, on December 11, to the creation of a conciliation commission in order to assist the parties to take the next step, from armistice to peace.[22] The effective establishment and international acceptance of Israel's independence seemed clear enough to encourage Israel in its hope for UN membership as a conclusive sign of recognition.

But encouraging omens were not the only reasons for the application. Even more to the point were the strong, persisting opposition to Israel's very existence among the Arabs, and the evidences of readiness among powerful European countries to endanger the viability of Israel in order to give at least partial and provisional satisfaction to the Arabs. Israel made its application for membership at a time when Egyptian forces were still widely deployed over Southern Palestine. Even though their position was already precarious, these Egyptian troops consituted an argument in favor of placing Southern Palestine under Arab rule in the name of political realism. Moreover, Count Bernadotte's murder by Jewish terrorists had converted his plan to award this area to an Arab state into a kind of testament of a man martyred in the cause of the United Nations.[23] Thus the discussion in the General Assembly was based on British draft resolutions providing that the Bernadotte boundary proposals be adopted by the UN instead of, or at least in addition to, the original partition boundaries as the basis for defining the appropriate limits of the Jewish state.

That such a delimitation placed in question the very existence of Israel was implicitly recognized by the Australian delegation when it suggested adding to the British draft a clause approving Israel's application for UN membership, no doubt in order to indicate that the severe loss of viability entailed by the proposed boundary revisions did not mean the denial of Israel's existence in principle.[24] In the end, the resolution of December 11 did not give formal endorsement to the Bernadotte boundaries — nor did it provide for Israel's admission to the UN. That issue was later decided in a Security Council resolution; and on December 17, 1948, Israel's application for UN membership was set aside by the negative vote of Syria and the abstention of such pillars of the European and UN consensus as Belgium, Canada, France, and the United Kingdom, together with China.[25]

The situation was altered radically when Israel, in renewed fighting, asserted its claims by an act of sovereign will. As 1948 ended, Israeli forces swept through Southern Palestine and over into Egyptian Sinai at El Arish, gathering in the Egyptian armies as they rode. In a later swoop, an Israeli column drove down to the Red Sea, securing the port of Eilat. In both instances, the British considered their interests endangered and they threatened to invoke their treaties of alliance with Egypt and Jordan. In the earlier outbreak, things went so far that British reconnaissance planes were shot down over the battle lines.[26]

This chain of events brought about decisive changes in attitude in Egypt and England. The former country had virtually lost its army in a battle where its Arab allies gave it no support. It now had to choose between the evil of an armistice with Israel and the evil of invoking an alliance with Britain which it ardently sought to annul. It chose the armistice with Israel.[27] In Britain, where the mounting consequences of the anti-Israel policy called forth growing opposition, the spectacle of British planes shot down over the Egyptian-Israeli battle lines provoked a sharp reaction of public opinion. Thus, the withdrawal of Israeli troops from across the lines in Sinai was met, on the British side, by the final agreement to extend diplomatic recognition to the new Jewish state.[28]

The Egyptian armistice was soon followed by armistices with other Arab states. The British recognition, too, was accompanied by a flood of similar recognitions by states which until then had held back. On January 15, 1949, Israel had held its first elections and in March 1949, replaced its Provisional Government by the first regularly constituted government of the Jewish state.[29] The time seemed ripe for renewing the Israeli application for UN membership.

But the outcome demonstrated to Israel once more that its claim to independence within viable boundaries could not rest on a reliable foundation if it depended on the UN consensus alone. The Israelis found, on the other hand, that when they asserted the prerogatives of sovereignty, such an approach proved effective. Before Israel was admitted to UN membership, as it eventually was on this second application, it had to submit to an unprecedented examination in the Ad Hoc Political Committee of the General Assembly.[30] The kind of question asked, not only by Arabs who were opposed to the very existence of Israel but by states whose votes had helped call it into existence, implied that Israel might legitimately be required to make political concessions infringing on the normal prerogatives of sovereignty as the price of its admission to the international organization.

But Israel made responses which, for all the tact with which they were phrased, left no doubt that the Jewish state claimed all the legal rights normally exercised by all states, and it succeeded through this approach in obtaining UN membership.

Some of the Scandinavian countries seemed inclined to reserve the right to deny Israel the full recognition implied in UN membership if the methods and results of Israel's investigation of Bernadotte's assassination did not satisfy them.[31] Some Roman Catholic countries seemed inclined to demand, as the price of Israel's admission to the UN, that it accept without question the internationalization of Jerusalem as laid down in the original partition plan.[32] Arab and Moslem states argued against Israel's right to be a UN member on the grounds that it refused to give immediate, total, and unconditional consent to that part of UN Resolution 194 (III) which envisaged the eventual repatriation on certain conditions of some Arab refugees to Palestine as one of the methods for the solution of that urgent problem. Some of their questions and arguments directed against Israel's application also implied that acceptance of the boundaries laid down in the original partition plan was a legitimate condition which might be imposed before Israel's right to be an equal member of the family of nations could be confirmed.[33]

To all these questions the Israeli representative answered courteously and patiently, but without conceding in any case that the points raised were legally valid criteria by which Israel's qualifications for UN membership could be properly judged.[34] Resolutions of the General Assembly, he contended, should be respected by UN members not because of their legal force — for they were not legally binding — but because of their moral force, and consequently what was important was to interpret correctly the spirit of the resolution in changing circumstances. Israel undertook to respect the purposes of the UN and, on the lines indicated, to give due consideration to its resolutions. Upon such a presentation of its case, Israel won admission to the UN without yielding on any point the position it had taken up in the interests of its sovereign existence and national security.[35]

But while Israel successfully resisted the view that particular political demands favored by small or large UN blocs or included in one or another UN resolution could be made legally binding upon it, and that its recognition as a UN member could be made conditional on unquestioning acceptance of such demands, this was far from the end of the matter. The Roman Catholic countries, with considerable support elsewhere, continued to insist on the internationalization of a Jerusalem enclave. The Arab countries continued to insist on the full and immediate repatriation of the Arab refugees to their old homes. They also began with increasing emphasis to take recourse to the very partition resolution they had at first violently opposed in demanding that Israel give up territory beyond the original partition lines which it had incorporated as a result of the fighting. These were issues on which Israel not only remained in conflict with influential blocs in the UN but, from time to time, found itself unsupported, if not opposed, by the UN consensus. Since, moreover, the conflict with the Arabs involved the question of Israel's very right to independence and sovereignty, the failure to obtain the support of the UN on other matters also casts doubt, to the Israeli mind, even after admission to UN membership, on the full acceptance by the international community of Israel as a legitimate political entity.

There was hardly an aspect of the UN partition plan which was so repugnant to the Jews as the internationalization of Jerusalem.[36] The elimination of the symbolic Zion from the Jewish state placed in question the success of Zionism, if its goal were to solve the problem of Judaism; but it was part of the price that had to be paid for international aproval of the minimum conditions for solving the more urgent problem of the Jews. However, the internationalization of Jerusalem was accepted on certain assumptions: that the partition would be carried out in an orderly and peaceable fashion; that, consequently, the Jews in Jerusalem would be secure in their lives and property; that the economic viability of the community would be assured by the freedom of transit and the division of the income of the economic union provided in the partition plan; and that not only would the Jews of Jerusalem be able to opt for citizenship in Israel at once, but after ten years the city might possibly be joined to Israel through a referendum.[37] The fighting which immediately broke out destroyed those assumptions. It exposed the Jews of Jerusalem, from the first moment, to attack and siege, sniping and shelling, hunger and thirst. The UN could do nothing effective either to protect the population of Jerusalem or to carry out its plan for the city. Only by force of arms were the Jews able to save the community in the New City from being destroyed together with the community in the Old City. The control they exercised over the city and its communications with the coast were the only guarantees the Jews henceforth were willing to rely on for the continued safety of Jewish Jerusalem.[38]

The history of the Jerusalem question in the UN was not calculated to alter but rather to confirm this attitude. In the period before the terminal date of the Mandate, when the Security Council, appealed to by the Palestine Commission for measures to enforce partition, replied instead by rejecting this responsibility, the Trusteeship Council also found itself unable to give final approval to a plan for an international regime in Jerusalem. Arab opposition to the draft statute that the Trusteeship Council had drawn up in accordance with the partition resolution, and the American desire to replace that resolution by new arrangements, made the Council hesitate to carry out its instructions from the General Assembly. Instead, it reported the inconclusive stage of its efforts and asked for instructions — and the General Assembly tacitly approved inaction by failing to instruct the Council to adopt its statute formally, but instead asked it to make some interim proposal to deal with the bloodshed there.[39] The next suggestion regarding Jerusalem to emanate from UN quarters was the Mediator's proposal, during the first truce in June 1948, to turn the city over to Transjordan, because the Jewish military position seemed precarious. This abandonment of the idea of the internationalization of Jerusalem did not survive the subsequent fighting, in which Israel gained a secure line of communications to the New City. In September 1948, Count Bernadotte, recognizing the changed situation, reverted to the idea of internationalizing the city.[40] The General Assembly resolution of December 11, 1948, following the Mediator's suggestions, instructed the projected Palestine Conciliation Commission to draw up a specific plan for internationalizing Jerusalem, providing, however, for maximum municipal autonomy for the two populations involved.[41]

The Conciliation Commission had to face the fact that the city of Jerusalem was divided between two hostile armed nations, facing each other across a newly defined armistice line, and that the populations and supply lines of the two parts of the city were integrally connected with Israel, on the one hand, and Transjordan, on the other. Its plan for an international regime in the city sought to recognize this division as far as possible, while still providing for UN authority over the area.[42]

In an interview with the Chairman of the Commission during negotiations prior to the formulation of the plan, Prime Minister Ben-Gurion firmly rejected internationalization. He said that, upon becoming a member of the UN, Israel would propose that the originally adopted approach to the problem be revised.[43] Abba Eban, under questioning upon Israel's application for UN membership, explained that there had been no real determination of Jerusalem's position, as the Trusteeship Council had failed to carry out its assignment, and the whole partition plan, to which the internationalization of Jerusalem was integrally related, had never been enforced by the UN. He recognized, however, that Israel was morally, if not legally, bound to respect the conclusions the UN might still arrive at on the question, and indicated that Israel would propose an alternative plan of its own for the approval of the UN.[44] When the Conciliation Commission's plan came out, with its provisions for UN authority over a Jerusalem divided, along the armistice line, between two states, to one of which each half was administratively linked, it was subjected to scathing criticism on legal, economic, and security grounds by Israel. In its place, Israel proposed an agreement between the two states controlling the city respectively and the UN, in order to establish international control of the Holy Places, but not of the whole area.[45] (Jordan, for its part, consistently rejected any form of internationalization, considering its own promise to respect the *status quo* in regard to the Holy Places as sufficient.) [46] While the question was being considered in the General Assembly's Ad Hoc Political Committee, with the Israeli delegation seeking to make its point by diplomacy, the Prime Minister intervened, under pressure of public opinion and of the opposition parties. He declared outright, in a statement made in the parliament but directed to the General Assembly, that Israel would reject any proposal to remove Jewish Jerusalem from its sovereign control.[47] The response of the Ad Hoc Committee to this challenge was to report out an excessively severe and impracticable resolution. The Trusteeship Council was instructed to prepare and put into effect immediately, in spite of any action by an interested government, a plan for the international control of the Jerusalem area as a *corpus separatum*, along the lines of the original partition resolution. No provision was to be made, however, for economic union with the Arab or Jewish state, nor was there any mention of "municipal autonomy" and administrative ties with the two states, as in the Conciliation Commission's plan. The resolution — Resolution 303 (IV) — was adopted on December 9, 1949, by the necessary two-thirds majority.[48]

Given this assignment, the Trusteeship Council duly brushed up and formally adopted its plan for internationalizing Jerusalem, though, of course, with no hope of putting it into effect in view of the stand of both states that ruled the area. The position of Israel, in particular, was made clear by the progressive concentration of government offices in the city, which public opinion united in considering "the only conceivable capital of a Jewish state." [49] After some negotiation with Israel and Jordan, the Trusteeship Council was forced to report that it was unable to put its plan into effect, since the consent of neither of the governments in control could be obtained.[50]

The Chairman of the Trusteeship Council and the delegations of several leading UN members tried to find a reasonable way out of the situation by taking a similar line to that proposed by Israel. Such a solution had been contemplated by a Bolivian and a joint Netherlands and Swedish draft resolution which were presented at the Fourth Session of the General Assembly. These drafts provided that Jerusalem would not be withdrawn from the jurisdiction of Israel and Jordan, but that international control of the Holy Places and the demilitarization of the city would be established with the consent of the two states at the invitation of the UN.[51] In the Fifth Session, a similar resolution was again introduced by Sweden, but was rejected by the Ad Hoc Political Committee.[52] However, an attempt to reaffirm the intention of the UN to internationalize Jerusalem as such, and not only its Holy Places, and proposing to continue negotiations with Israel and Jordan to that end, failed in the plenary session to receive the two-thirds majority required for passage.[53] Two years later, a similar proposal attracted even less support.[54] An increasing number of delegations recognized the impracticality, if not the injustice, of a plan that ignored the economic dependence of Jerusalem on the states to which it was tied, that made singularly light-hearted assumptions about responsibility for the security of life in the city, and that had neither a clear legal basis nor a feasible political combination of forces to help the UN make good its claim to authority. Their number was large enough, after 1952, to block a renewal of the consensus in favor of internationalization. On the other hand, the combination of last-ditch defenders of the plan remained large enough to make the adoption of any more reasonable and more equitable arrangement a very remote possibility.

For Israel, the history of this problem was a particularly pointed reminder of the uncertain and far from complete recognition of its sovereignty by the concert of nations. The inconsistencies in the attitude of the Western Protestant powers, bulwarks of that international consensus which had originally recognized the Jewish claim to a national home and then to a State, were painful enough. When Jerusalem was entirely cut off by Arab forces, they were prepared to award the city to Transjordan on the grounds of strategic rationality. But after Israel had firmly attached the New City to itself by conquering a strong land bridge to the coast, the Western powers did not apply the same criteria to the case and would not recognize formally the fact of Israel's control. This was particularly resented because the part of Jerusalem held by the Jews contained hardly any of the Holy Places, almost all of which were in the Old City.[55] In the course of time, America and other powers became convinced that internationalization was impossible and a new arrangement acknowledging Israel's sovereignty would have to be sought; yet even while recognizing this, they responded to Israel's transfer of its seat of government to the capital by ordering a diplomatic boycott of the city.[56]

More ominous still was the use the Arab bloc was able to make of the Jerusalem issue in the UN. Themselves firmly opposed (in the beginning) to the internationalization of Jerusalem, as to all other aspects of the partition plan, the Arab states (with the exception of Jordan, which held the Old City) eventually agreed to internationalization of the whole city as "a lesser evil" than Israel's retention of part of it. In 1952, as we shall see, this won them enough support from Roman Catholic countries to defeat a UN resolution which declared it a responsibility primarily of the Jews and Arabs to make peace. Through voting for the right of the Roman Catholics to demand Israel's acceptance of the internationalization of Jerusalem in a rider to a UN resolution proposing peace negotiations, the Arabs successfully asserted their right to impose their own conditions before agreeing to discuss peace. If Jerusalem were internationalized, it would be a severe blow to the integrity of Israel, as a people and a territory, and it would symbolically cripple it as a state dedicated to solving the problem of Judaism. But Israel might still go on to solve the more urgent problem of the Jews, and to exercise sovereignty of sufficient scope for this purpose. The Arab conditions regarding the return of refugees and the revision of boundaries, on the other hand, struck at the very heart of Israel's viability as a sovereign entity pursuing Zionist goals. The attitude of a large part of the UN on the Jerusalem question thus became an implement whereby the road to a conclusive recognition of Israel's sovereign existence could be blocked in the UN.

From this record, Israel was inclined to draw certain conclusions as to its situation. It could conclude that in facing the Arab threat to its existence it could not rely implicitly on the support of the UN consensus. It could conclude also — a conclusion bolstered by the pragmatic union of Arabs and anti-Semites in a joint propaganda campaign throughout the world — that the rise of Israel had not caused some of the fundamental sources of anti-Semitism to disappear but instead had given them a new target upon which to concentrate hostility. In a case like the issue of Jerusalem, the pervasive Christian opposition to a symbolic restoration of Israel was aroused, and it could be carried to the length of placing in question indirectly Israel's very right to exist as a conclusively recognized member of the world community.

On the other hand, the several resolutions to internationalize Jerusalem remained ineffective. To be sure, Jordanian opposition as well as Israelian opposition was encountered by the plan. But it was Israel that bore the brunt of the diplomatic battle. Consequently, the people and government of Israel had an exhilarating, myth-generating sense of having successfully resisted massive international pressure in their assertion of sovereignty. While still formally contested by many nations, the fact that Jerusalem functioned effectively as Israel's capital under its full sovereignty was being recognized more widely every year. This, too, was an object lesson in the efficacy of an exercise of the rights of sovereignty which has had its effect in Israel.

II

The same issue and rather similar conclusions arose in a context where Israel did not occupy the familiar Jewish position of the aggrieved party, but was itself charged with injustice. The context was, of course, that of the Arab refugee problem.

It is true that the Israelis had sufficient reason to feel that theirs was not by far the sole or primary guilt for the displacement and continued suffering of so many Arab refugees. The fact that there would have been no Arab refugee problem if the Arabs had not fought partition by force of arms could in itself serve as an effective self-justification. The Israelis also knew that even after the outbreak of violence they had not planned the evacuation of the Arabs. The mass flight had come as a surprise to them and had, at first, filled them with misgivings.

In Haifa, to name only one example, they had pleaded with the Arabs to stay, partly out of regard for the tradition of good relations with Arab fellow-workers of which the Haifa socialists were so proud; partly out of the conviction that the evacuation had been ordered by Arab military leaders in order to clear the city for an anticipated assault that was to bring the Arabs back in triumph after the Jewish community was destroyed.[57] Not only the Arab states but, in the final period of their Mandate, the British, too, had adopted policies which largely contributed to the flight of Arabs. They had done nothing to make possible an orderly transfer of authority after their retirement; but in certain places where Arabs or Jews were dominant, they had recognized the control exercised by local bodies, and, to Arabs at least together with authority they handed over Palestine police armaments as well.[58] With the areas of densest Jewish and Arab settlement so closely intermingled, this policy — or lack of policy — led to a violent struggle for control in each place abandoned in the gradual British withdrawal. Some British officials, in their concern for the side that seemed to be losing in the ensuing local battles, thought that helping to evacuate the weaker side was their way out. Such proposals, made to both Jews and Arabs, were more than once rejected by Jews. In Tiberias, the Arab community was apparently evacuated simultaneously with the British forces, while in Haifa, on the other hand, the British commander supported the Jewish plea that the Arab community remain, and helped organize the exodus only after the Arabs nevertheless decided to leave.[59]

Arabs in towns and villages like Abu Ghosh near Jerusalem or Nazareth and the Druse villages in the Galilee, who responded to Jewish overtures or who — often, no doubt, because of feuds with other Arabs — had long before decided on friendly relations with Israel, remained unharmed in Israel and did not join the refugee mass. The same could be said of Arab areas which were transferred to Israel by the armistice agreements rather than by combat.

Nevertheless, the Israelis were acutely conscious of their own actions that had swelled and speeded the Arab exodus. It was not merely a question of the terror provoked by the "dissident" groups of Jewish fighters who did not bow to communal authority, and whose capture of the village of Deir Yasin was accompanied by such wanton bloodshed. This action could be, and was, condemned by Jewish representatives.[60] But the disciplined forces of the community had to adopt tactics, in the last days of the Mandate and in the early fighting afterwards, which were opposed to the policies of which the community had been so proud in the earlier outbreaks of 1936–1939; and where the new tactics were successfully applied, many of the defeated Arabs necessarily became refugees. In 1936–1939 the Jews had defended themselves against Arab attacks in accordance with a policy of self-restraint (havlaga), guarding themselves against attack but not taking the offensive in retaliation. This was a line of tactics which was only possible, just as it was necessitated, because the British exercised responsibility for law and order in the country. Its tactical disadvantages were resented even then — and when the British sought Jewish cooperation in defensive night forays and patrols against Arab raiders, the opportunity was welcomed — but it carried the immense moral advantage, of which the Jews were quite conscious, of clearly defining who the aggressor was. But in 1947–1948, there was no British willingness to maintain order. To sit behind sandbag barricades in defensive positions was impossible, for with the roads cut, Jewish settlements were threatened with starvation. The only possible defense, in places where Jews lived side by side with their foes, was to seize and hold the ground from which the Arab attack came — or, as was very often the case, if a place that was raided could not be held for long, it was necessary to deny the enemy its use as an offensive base by destroying strong points. When such a Jewish raid was launched, or even feared, one immediate effect was often the flight of the Arab population; and where the raids succeeded and demolition was carried out, the Arabs could not very well return, at least until the fighting ended.

The moral loss which these new tactics entailed was as well-understood by the Jews as the military gain. But there was a clear choice which had to be made between the two. There was hardly any dissent or hesitation in choosing the course which alone offered a chance for survival.

The loss of their moral advantage was soon felt by the Israelis in its political consequences. In the first truce, Count Bernadotte proposed almost as a matter of course that the Arabs who had fled from their homes should return at once. This was at a time when the Arab countries had agreed to suspend hostilities for a period of four weeks only and obviously intended to renew the fighting at the end of the period. At that very time, moreover, Count Bernadotte was sounding Israel out on plans for a revision of the partition of Palestine which might give Jerusalem to the Arabs and deprive Israel of its essential land reserve and entree to the Red Sea in Southern Palestine, and thus of the chance to undertake the solution of the problem of the Jews; while if Arab demands had any effect, Bernadotte's proposals for demilitarizing Haifa might end in barring Jewish immigration through the country's major port.[61] If they were wise, Bernadotte argued, the Israelis should accept such sacrifices because the result of a renewal of war was uncertain and might well lead to even worse terms for Israel. Under the circumstances, it would have required political blindness not to have seen the effect on Israel's security if Arabs were to return into the small stronghold which was held intact as the base of Israelian defense against the soon to be reopened attack. Bernadotte renewed his proposal for the immediate return of large groups of refugees during the second truce, arguing that since the truce was of indefinite duration the security risk could be discounted. This view was not accepted by the Israelis, who took the position that Israel could not consider the return of Arab refugees to its territory until there were negotiations for a peace settlement.[62]

This, however, placed the Israelis, as they well knew, in a moral position the reverse of that which had been theirs previously, and from which they had formerly derived certain imponderable political advantages. It had been the Arab or the British argument until now that political considerations made it impossible to admit into Palestine refugees whose suffering aroused the humanitarian sympathy of the world — in spite of their asserted legal claims to enter this haven. Against this position a powerful current of public opinion in all Christian countries had strongly rebelled. Forces friendly to Britain and disinclined to drive hard bargains on legal and political issues concerning the Mandate in Palestine — for example, the American government and non-Zionist Jewish organizations — had insisted that the humanitarian issue of the Jewish refugees be separated from the political issues and treated as a matter of urgency.

The Zionists themselves could hardly agree, in those days, that the 100,000 or 200,000 DP's assembled at a given moment in camps represented the entire postwar problem of the Jews that Palestine must solve. Nor did they believe that the refugees would, in fact, be given priority and special treatment apart from a solution of the political issues. Yet the humanitarian, as distinct from the political, aspect of the Jewish refugee problem had a significant effect upon them too. Outrage at the Arabs' and especially the Britons' icy determination not to be deflected from political aims by humanitarian considerations served more than anything else to harden the Zionists' own resolution. On the other hand, whenever it seemed that the British might, after all, heed the humanitarian plea, the Zionist consensus became accessible to suggestions of reducing or deferring political demands, if necessary, in order to secure the concession. Now, however, it was Israel that refused an absolute priority to humanitarian pleas because of their political implications. The Jews could not do this with the same wholeheartedness that had been theirs when the positions were reversed; nor could they do it without incurring a shift in the pressure of political imponderables.

The Arab refugee question was one of the main issues debated in the session of the General Assembly at the end of 1948 that led to the creation of the Palestine Conciliation Commission. The conclusions of that session regarding Palestine were summed up in Resolution 194 (III) of December 11, 1948, of which paragraph 11 dealt specifically with the Arab refugee question. The resolution, continually referred to in later UN determinations as well as in the subsequent polemical literature, defines the position of the international consensus in the following terms:

THE GENERAL ASSEMBLY, HAVING CONSIDERED FURTHER the situation in Palestine . . . .

(11) RESOLVES that the refugees wishing to return to their homes and live at peace with their neighbours should be permitted to do so at the earliest practicable date, and that compensation should be paid for the property of those choosing not to return and for loss of or damage to property which, under principles of international law or in equity, should be made good by the Governments or authorities responsible;

INSTRUCTS the Conciliation Commission to facilitate the repatriation, resettlement and economic and social rehabilitation of the refugees and the payment of compensation, and to maintain close relations with the Director of the United Nations Relief for Palestine Refugees and, through him, with the appropriate organs and agencies of the United Nations.[63]

The terms of the resolution were considered at a time when Israel was not yet a member of the UN, but representatives of Israel were permitted to state their views. Their presentation of the legal and political aspects of the case, of the prerogatives of Israel as a sovereign state and the objective requirements for its security, was reflected in the final text adopted, and in clarifying statements by various delegations during the debate.

Paragraph 11 of Resolution 194 (III) derives originally from the following conclusions of the Mediator:

(i)   The right of the Arab refugees to return to their homes in Jewish-controlled territory at the earliest possible date should be affirmed by the United Nations, and their repatriation, resettlement and economic and social rehabilitation, and payment of adequate compensation for the property of those choosing not to return, should be supervised and assisted by the United Nations conciliation commission . . . . [64]

The draft for paragraph 11, proposed by Great Britain, had a preamble endorsing the "principle" stated in the quoted portion of the Mediator's progress report, while its operative clauses reflected the language of the report, with certain changes.[65] The discussion of the draft introduced further significant changes.

First, the proposed endorsement of the principle stated by the Mediator ("the right of the Arab refugees to return") and, indeed, all references to the Mediator's report were omitted. The phrasing employed by the Mediator carried the implications that the Arab refugees had an absolute, individual right to return, and that the UN had authority, unlimited by national sovereignties, to "affirm" such rights of the Arab refugees and to "supervise and assist" directly the measures proposed for solving the refugee problems. Even in the British draft, which had proposed to endorse in its preamble the principle stated by the Mediator, the language of the remainder of the paragraph carried quite different implications. Instead of "affirming the right to return," the UN was to "resolve that the Arab refugees should be permitted to return"; and instead of "supervising and assisting," the UN Conciliation Commission was to "facilitate" the proposed measures for alleviating and solving the refugee problems. These drafting changes took account of the fact that measures for repatriating, resettling, rehabilitating, or compensating the refugees were essentially within the sovereignty of the several states upon whose territory they were to be carried out. Consequently, the Conciliation Commission could not very well be instructed to "supervise and assist," but only to "facilitate" them. So, too, the effect of a UN resolution could only be to recommend to Israel that, as a matter of equity and policy, it "should permit" the Arabs to return, thus recognizing their moral, if not their legal rights. The UN was not competent to state with authority that a legal right existed and must be respected. But after these drafting changes, it would have been inconsistent to "endorse the principle" stated in the Mediator's report, where a quite different view, sharply at variance with the text finally adopted, had been proposed.

So, too, the final text included a number of conditions relating to the proposed repatriation of a part of the Arab refugees which took account of the representations of the Israeli spokesman. The resolution agreed that certain political conditions must be observed before the readmission of those "wishing to return to their homes" could be recommended when it added the qualification that they must also wish to "live at peace with their neighbours." In addition a wide range of pertinent conditions was recognized in changing the phrasing from "return . . . at the earliest *possible* date" to "permitted to do so at the earliest *practicable* date."

The British delegate introduced the latter alteration, as he said, "in accordance with the remarks of the representative of Israel. He hoped this would make clearer the intention of the proposal." [66] The remarks here referred to were the following:

Large movements of population were not ordinarily envisaged during war when considerations of military security must prevail. The return of Arab refugees before peace had been established would place upon Israel the burden of maintaining large internal security forces . . . . The facts had been taken into consideration by the representative of the United Kingdom when he said that measures to remedy the situation should be taken as soon as possible after stable conditions had been established. Mr. Eban believed that some such qualifying phrase might be inserted in the resolution to emphasize to the parties that the consequences of the war could only be settled at the end of the war.[67]

The meaning of "stable conditions" referred to by the British and Israeli representatives was fairly well defined by the discussion. A Guatemalan amendment to the British draft, proposing to add after "as soon as possible" the phrase "after the proclamation of peace between the contending parties in Palestine, including the Arab States," would have made the recommendation to repatriate refugees depend on the full conclusion of peace.[68] The rejection of this amendment signified that Israel was asked to permit the return of refugees before the conclusion of peace. At the same time, even the phrasing "as soon as possible" recognized that repatriation of hostile Arabs during war, or during the truce then in force, was not yet possible. In commenting on the Guatemalan amendment, the British delegate gave an authoritative comment on the intention of his own wording, and of the revised form finally adopted.

Referring to the Guatemalan amendment, he stated that the Committee must face the fact that it might be many years before a formal peace was established in Palestine. One of the possibilities, however, was that conditions of stability might be re-established in fact without any agreement on the terms of a formal peace and his delegation considered that as soon as such reasonable stability had been restored in Palestine, the problem of the return of those unfortunate people should be given urgent consideration.[69]

This meant that it was hoped that the armistice agreements then being negotiated might turn out to be effective enough ("one of the possibilities") that Israel could reasonably — that is, without serious danger to her security — be asked to consider the repatriation of Arabs before all other issues were definitively settled. The Lebanese delegate signified his understanding of the point in saying that "it was, however, true that the refugees could not return in the present circumstances and would have to wait until the situation was more normal."[70] And the Israeli representative, from his own point of view, placed the same interpretation upon the resolution when he appeared before the Ad Hoc Committee at a later date, in connection with Israel's application for UN membership.

Similarly, the reference in the resolution of 11 December 1948 to the "earliest practicable date" was also a definite acknowledgement of the fact that the restoration of normal conditions was essential to any fruitful discussion on the proportion of refugees willing and able to return, as against those eligible for resettlement and compensation.[71]

Israel had succeeded in obtaining a wording that formally respected her sovereignty and her need for reasonable security, but in practice it did not prevent continued pressure for the immediate and virtually unconditional readmission of the Arab refugees. In view of the unresolved humanitarian problem, not only the Arabs, who used selected phrases of paragraph 11 of Resolution 194 (III) as a polemical weapon against Israel, but other UN circles, too, reverted, from time to time, to the position of the Mediator.

In the UN debate on Israel's admission to membership, the Danish delegate pointedly asked whether Israel recognized the right to return as an individual right and legal claim of each refugee.[72] Without going into a full legal argument, Israel maintained that the refugee problem was a matter that should be negotiated between the governments involved and included in a general peace settlement. Not only was such an approach in accord with the sovereign rights of the parties, but the only practical method to solve the problem was through collective measures.[73] On this statement, Israel was admitted into the UN, but not without comments by delegates from Western Europe that they considered Israel not to have taken a fully satisfactory attitude on the "outstanding issues." [74]

Moreover, the Conciliation Commission no sooner entered upon its work than it expressed, in general terms, its agreement with the Arab premise that the Arab refugees had an absolute, individual right to return to their homes.[75] This attitude was altered when the Commission encountered Israel's resistance, based not only on authoritative interpretations of the Commission's terms of reference but on the undoubted objective conditions that made wholesale repatriation of Arab refugees dangerous to Israel and of dubious advantage to the refugees themselves. Nevertheless, the impossibility of carrying out in any large measure the mandate to facilitate the return of refugees "wishing to live at peace with their neighbours" was taken by the Commission, as well as by public opinion, as a quasi-legal claim still outstanding in favor of the Arabs against Israel.

The tactics adopted by the Arabs were designed to derive the greatest possible political advantage from the humanitarian and quasi-legal claims of the refugees. They were even better equipped to pursue such a course than the Zionists had been when the cases were reversed, for, unlike the Zionists, the Arab states could not be influenced toward political moderation by concessions on humanitarian issues. Relying on the monolithic support of the refugees themselves, they consistently opposed and successfully prevented the application of any method, other than repatriation to Israel, which might take substantial numbers out of the camps — this, in spite of the provisions in paragraph 11 of Resolution 194 (III) and in succeeding UN resolutions for the "resettlement" of refugees, and in spite of the increasing pressure from UN quarters to recognize that repatriation became less suited to the interests of the refugees with each passing year.[76] By rejecting any method which would solve the humanitarian problem of the refugees without achieving Arab political aims in regard to Palestine, the Arab states kept the humanitarian pressure upon Israel at a high pitch.

They sought also to press a legal point by interpreting paragraph 11 of Resolution 194 (III) as establishing an absolute right of return and a sole method — repatriation — for the solution of the refugee problem. To be sure, there was a certain difficulty in using this resolution as an argument against the position adopted by Israel: it involved isolating paragraph 11 from the whole context of the resolution, which was an effort to reach a general peace settlement between Israel and the Arab states. Hence, Egypt attempted in December 1950 to obtain a new resolution establishing a separate agency specifically instructed to repatriate the Arab refugees and to administer the payment of compensation to those who did not wish to return. These instructions were not only to be carried out without reference to the other objectives of the Conciliation Commission created by Resolution 194 (III); they were also to be imposed on Israel under threat of sanctions by the Security Council. Israel, for its part, offered a draft resolution calling upon the parties in conflict to enter into direct negotiations for peace between them, treating the refugee problem as an urgent matter in their discussions. The Egyptian draft had no hope of passing and was eventually withdrawn, as was Israel's draft; and the resolution adopted added nothing of substance to Resolution 194 (III).[77] Failing to obtain a resolution which would plainly recognize their contention that repatriation was an absolute right unrelated to peace, the Arabs then interpreted paragraph 11 of Resolution 194 (III) — originally opposed by them — as having precisely this meaning.

The political purpose and significance of these tactics was quite clear. The Arabs wished above all else to avoid recognizing the legitimate existence of Israel. By keeping the refugees in camps on Israel's borders and by refusing all invitations to discuss a general peace settlement unless Israel accepted in advance a position on the refugee question which meant, in effect, agreeing to repatriate any and all refugees unconditionally, the Arabs reduced the political possibilities to alternatives either of which would suit their purpose. If Israel should take the suicidal alternative of unconditional mass repatriation, it might easily destroy itself thereby. If it refused, the Arabs could refuse to move from the armistice agreements to a peace settlement. And the "technical state of war" which was maintained under the cloak of the armistice might perhaps, in more gradual attrition of Israel, eventually produce an opportunity for the destruction of the hated state.

III

The question of the boundaries of Israel was another issue which, intimately tied up with the refugee question, served like the latter to place Israel under political and quasi-legal pressures and to restrict the possibilities of dealing with the Palestine question. The abortive efforts of the Mediator were based, as we have mentioned, on the assumption that the existing military positions of the parties might induce them to accept the new boundaries he proposed. Similarly, the military positions won by Israel determined the demarcation lines of the four armistice treaties of 1949. These frontiers, however, were described as determined by the needs of a durable military truce, and it was indicated that a subsequent peace settlement would establish permanent political boundaries. The Conciliation Commission set up under Resolution 194 (III) was to facilitate such a settlement between Israel and the Arab states; while it was also to facilitate the solution by those states of the refugee problem through the various methods specified in the resolution: by repatriation of Arabs willing to live at peace in Palestine when stable conditions made repatriation practicable; or by resettlement with compensation, where compensation was due, for those who chose not to return; or, in any case, by rehabilitating the refugees through measures of relief and reemployment.

The initial difficulty encountered by the Commission was to bring about a meeting between the parties for consideration of all the issues referred to in its terms of reference. In the Israeli view, part of the Commission's difficulty arose from the difference between the procedure it adopted and the procedure successfully applied in the armistice negotiations.[78] Under the patiently insistent guidance of Dr. Ralph Bunche, Israel had met separately with each of its antagonists in discussions that sooner or later became direct. The Conciliation Commission began by accepting, or even facilitating, the separate presentation of demands before it by the Arabs as a solid bloc, which in the Israeli view placed a premium upon intransigence and stifled at the outset any inclinations to be moderate that one or another state might evince. Suspicion in Israel of a tendency to appeasement on the part of the Commission — two members of which, France and Turkey, had not recognized Israel at the outset — was not lessened by the kind of reception the Commission gave to the initial Arab demands, nor by the nature of those demands. Israel had grounds for expecting that, just as the Acting Mediator did not consider it a question for discussion or compromise whether or not there should be negotiations for an armistice, so the Conciliation Commission would not consider it a question for discussion or compromise whether or not a full peace settlement, including the question of boundaries as well as of refugees, should be negotiated. But the Commission began by discussing with the Arabs on what conditions they would agree to negotiate anything more than the repatriation of refugees; and won their consent to discuss the boundary issues too only by a statement of its own endorsing, as an isolated principle though in general terms, the right of the refugees to return to the territory controlled by Israel.[79]

The actual negotiations began — though only through separate meetings between the Commission and Israel and the Commission and the Arab bloc — when Israel, despite its distrust of the procedures adopted, undertook to give the refugee problem top priority, and the Arabs undertook to discuss boundaries and other issues without waiting for the conclusion of the discussion on refugees. They foundered, however, on the rock of Arab refusal to advance to direct discussion of the points at issue through mixed Arab-Jewish committees under UN chairmanship, except on one condition: that Israel accept in advance the virtually unconditional right to return, and that the mixed committees concern themselves solely with carrying out first this and subsequently other predetermined principles in detail.[80]

On the question of the refugees the Commission adopted the procedure of asking each state to estimate how many refugees it was prepared to accept as a contribution toward a solution; and, on the question of boundaries, it obtained agreement to take the UN partition map as a basis of discussion, with the two opposed parties to indicate what revisions they thought were necessary.[81] The two topics were closely tied together in the proposals made both by Israel and the Arab states.

The first specific Arab proposal was *not* that all Arab refugees should return immediately to their homes. They proposed the return only of those Arabs who had lived in territory not assigned to Israel in the original partition; and, of course, the eventual withdrawal of Israel from such territory. Moreover, in order to make possible the resettlement of the remaining Arab refugees on Arab soil, the Arab states proposed that Israel give up the Negev in the south and Eastern Galilee in the north — Western Galilee having already been claimed as Arab under the original partition.[82] Such proposals departed considerably from the bare principle that the refugees must be returned to their homes, since they claimed territorial concessions from Israel in order that Arab refugees might be resettled in new homes on Arab soil in preference to repatriation to their old homes on soil that would remain Jewish. But if, as the Arabs proposed, Israel were reduced to a tiny coastal strip between the Haifa and Tel Aviv areas, with Jaffa an Arab enclave and Haifa a free and open city, this would achieve the main political aims of the Arabs as effectively as the return of a mass of hostile Arabs to Israel. If the new Arab plan were accepted, the Jewish state would be unable to solve the problem of the Jews and thereby grow in strength. It would be confined to a narrow, untenable area that would place it entirely at the mercy of the Arabs, and it could then be disposed of at the next opportunity.

The Jews, for their part, considered both the refugee and the boundary question in the light of their own security needs in the situation created by the undeclared war that had followed the partition resolution. At the same time, they had to take into account the outside political pressures upon them, particularly when exerted by a country like America upon whose aid, in various forms, Israel so largely depended. Since they felt that appeasement of the Arabs was a more important factor determining Western policy than concern for the security and Zionist functions of Israel — and since the Conciliation Commission, made up of American, French, and Turkish representatives, reflected Western policy — the Israelis sought to avoid Western pressure by demanding direct negotiations with the Arabs. Direct negotiations however, were firmly refused by the Arabs, and the negotiations through the Conciliation Commission became a method which, in the Israeli view, helped the Arabs to extort concessions dangerous to Israel's security while at the same time avoiding any discussion of peace.[83]

The Israeli view had been that the repatriation of refugees to the territory of the Jewish state should be considered part of over-all peace negotiations and take place, under procedures and conditions compatible with Israel's sovereignty, upon the conclusion of peace. The UN resolution had not fully accepted this view but had proposed that repatriation, as one of the specified solutions of the Arab refugee problem, be facilitated by the Conciliation Commission, the same body that was to help the Jews and Arabs make peace; and that it was to begin as soon as relations between the Jews and Arabs were normal enough for the readmission of Arabs to Israel to be safe, even though formal peace treaties might not yet have been concluded. The Conciliation Commission, while stressing at all times that it had a mandate to deal with the refugee question in connection with all outstanding issues, seemed to the Israelis to retreat well below the requirements of its mandate in relation to the Arab states and go well beyond them in relation to Israel. As we have noted, it began with a statement that singled out repatriation from the other solutions of the refugee problem — especially resettlement — and it continued to imply that paragraph 11 of Resolution 194 (III) created a legal right to return to Israel enjoyed by all Arab refugees individually. Apart from the legal argument, however, the commission members, and the diplomatic officers of the Western powers, took the view that it would create an atmosphere favorable to peace negotiations if Israel made immediate concessions on the refugee question. It was clear that failure to make such concessions would not only invite condemnation by the Western public for callousness on a humanitarian issue, but would be regarded by Western diplomats and by the Conciliation Commission as obstructing a peace settlement. Under these pressures, Israel agreed not only to discuss the refugee question, through the Conciliation Commission or directly in mixed committees, before any other issues of the peace settlement were taken up, but to readmit immediately substantial numbers of refugees in order to alleviate the problem and create a suitable atmosphere for peace negotiations.

The first offer made by Israel, following insistent suggestions from United States and Conciliation Commission quarters, was based on the assumption that the readmission of Arab refugees could be treated as a solely humanitarian problem, not as a tactical means for undermining Israel's security. To solve a humanitarian and a security problem at one and the same time, Israel undertook to accept the quarter of a million Arab refugees in the Gaza strip if this area were included in the Jewish state.[84] After the rejection of this offer, Israel undertook to admit a specified number of Arab refugees immediately into the territory it already controlled. The following were the terms of the offer:

> The Israel representative informed the Commission on 3 August 1949 that his Government was prepared to make its contribution to the solution of the refugee problem. This contribution would be limited by considerations affecting the security and the economy of the State. Thus, the refugees would be settled in areas where they would not come in contact with possible enemies of Israel; moreover, the Government of Israel reserved the right to resettle the repatriated refugees in specific locations, in order to ensure that their reinstallation would fit into the general plan of Israel's economic development. Subject to these conditions, the Government of Israel would be prepared to accept the return to Israel, in its present limits, of 100,000 Arab refugees beyond the total Arab population existing at the end of the hostilities (including those who had already returned), thus increasing the total number of that population to a maximum of 250,000. This repatriation would form part of a general plan for resettlement of refugees which would be established by a special organ to be created for the purpose by the United Nations.[85]

As to the boundary question, Israel's proposals were based on the requirements for a viable Jewish state which, unlike the state contemplated in the partition resolution, would have to be strategically defensible against its neighbors and would not be bound to them in an economic union. In battle and in the armistice negotiations, Israel had achieved, and the Arabs had been forced to accept under treaty, a boundary demarcation that gave minimum assurance of viability, both strategic and economic, and allowed Israel a minimal scope for the development required by its Zionist purposes. Israel proposed that these boundaries be confirmed in the final peace settlement, subject to revisions of mutual interest to Jews and Arabs, which were best determined by direct negotiation between the parties. Among such adjustments, specifically proposed at various times, were the inclusion of the Gaza strip in Israel — by which the most intractable part of the refugee problem would be solved, and both Israel and Egypt would gain in security — and the revision of the armistice line with Jordan to reunite (Arab) villages with their agricultural lands.[86]

The Conciliation Commission, in one of its later reports, spoke of three stages in its unsuccessful attempts to settle the issues between Israel and the Arab states: first, it failed as a simple intermediary, second, as a conciliator, and third, as a mediator between the two parties.[87] At the several stages, the Commission made comments which, in diplomatic style, assigned what it considered proportionate shares of the blame for its failure to the Israelis and to the Arabs.

Thus, when Israel stated that it would admit 100,000 Arab refugees within its existing frontiers, the Commission labelled this an unsatisfactory statement. In its Progress Report for 1951, the Commission blamed the Israelis for noncompliance with paragraph 11 of Resolution 194 (III), through rejecting repatriation,[88] and the Arabs for noncompliance with paragraph 5, through rejecting a peace settlement. In spite of agreeing to discuss all issues, not merely the refugee question, the Arabs, the Commission implied, were using their demand for Israel's prior agreement to repatriation as an excuse for evading full compliance with the UN's resolution calling for peace negotiations.[89]

On the boundary issue, the Commission, toward the end of its Lausanne conference in 1949, made a statement declaring the positions taken by both parties to be unsatisfactory.[90] The reasoning behind this conclusion is not given in the official report, but it may be assumed that the Commission took the partition lines of the original UN resolution to be not only a basis for discussion, as both parties had agreed to do, but ascribed to it some validity on grounds of both law and equity. This, of course, had not been the position taken by UN quarters when Count Bernadotte proposed to settle the Palestine issue in terms of boundaries based on the existing military *status quo*, or on a prudential discounting of the military prospects of the parties, and when the British piloted resolutions through the Security Council seeking to force Israel back to cease-fire lines unrelated to the partition boundaries. Nor could the needs for strategically viable borders, which had been deliberately ignored by the partition resolution, have entered into whatever calculation of the equities the Commission may have made. In any case, the Israeli position, taking its departure not from the original partition but from the armistice lines, and the Arab position, leaving Israel only one of the three sections of the Jewish State under the original partition, were now both considered excessive.

Failing to bring Jews and Arabs together in mixed committees, the Commission in 1950 abandoned its efforts to make peace between the Jews and Arabs in Geneva, reopening them on a new basis and under new conditions in Paris in 1951. The Lausanne-Geneva cycle of negotiations had begun before the armistice negotiations were concluded and, even afterwards, had been continued on the assumption by the Commission that the armistice would speedily be replaced by a peace settlement. But it was now understood that the armistice must be considered far more seriously as the *status quo* upon which to build toward peace. As for the Israelis and the Arabs, their appreciation of the new circumstances had advanced considerably farther than that of the Commission. The Arab blockade against Israel demonstrated that the *status quo* of the armistice agreements could, in fact, be used for the continuation of the undeclared war, without major hostilities, under the guise of a technical state of war. The issue had only recently been considered by the Egyptian-Israeli Mixed Armistice Commission and the Security Council, and despite the objection of both bodies and a Security Council determination that Egypt could not legitimately assert belligerent rights to bar Israeli shipping from the Suez Canal, Egypt persisted in its policy.[91] Thus, at a time when the Commission hoped to build a permanent peace upon the structure of the armistice agreements, the Arabs came into the conference determined to continue using the *status quo* of the armistice as a basis for belligerency and the Israelis came to insist, as a matter of priority, upon the abandonment of Arab belligerency.

At Paris, the Conciliation Commission appeared in the role of a mediator between the two parties and initiated the discussions by presenting its own proposals. In adopting this role it acceded to the demand made by the Arab states following the Lausanne Conference. But the Commission proposals did not, as the Arabs might have hoped, present the boundaries of the UN partition resolution or the right of Arab refugees to be repatriated as virtual decisions of the UN which Israel must accept in order to be entitled to obtain peace. Instead, the Commission assumed that the armistice agreements constituted the only more or less solid legal basis determining the relations between Jews and Arabs and proposed to begin with this and build cautiously. It suggested, by way of preamble, that both parties initiate the conference by committing themselves to use only pacific procedures to settle the disputes between them. It then proposed five specific measures: first, the mutual cancellation of war damages claims; second, "that the Government of Israel agree to the repatriation of a specified number of refugees in categories which can be integrated into the economy of the State of Israel and who wish to return and live in peace with their neighbours"; third, that the Government of Israel undertake to pay in compensation a global sum based on UN evaluation of the refugees' assets; fourth, that there be a mutual release of blocked bank accounts; and fifth, that, instead of attempting a final peace settlement, progress be made by revising or amending the armistice agreement, including territorial adjustments — especially with reference to demilitarized zones — the creation of an international water authority for the development of Jordan and Yarmuk water resources, border regulations to facilitate access to Holy Places, and joint health and contraband controls at the frontiers.[92]

The Arab reaction to the Commission's efforts to mediate was emphatic. They saw no need to commit themselves to pacific procedures in beginning the conference, but simply made reference to the armistice agreements. In this way, they upheld the Egyptian claim to belligerent rights under the armistice. They also rejected emphatically the recognition of any conditions upon the absolute right of repatriation. They now referred to the UN partition resolution and the map initialled by the parties at Lausanne, not as a basis for discussion but as having established the boundaries to which Israel must be confined.[93]

Israel, welcoming the Commission's call for a statement that none but pacific procedures would be used, not only issued the requested statement but proposed to give it the status of a formal nonaggression pact. The Commission rejected the latter proposal as premature and excessive. The Israelis for their part strongly objected to the Commission's decision — that the Arabs' refusal to commit themselves to strictly pacific procedures was a satisfactory basis for going on with the conference. As for the other points, while accepting some fully or partly and rejecting others, Israel altered the position it had taken at Lausanne and would no longer commit itself to readmit a specified number of Arab refugees.[94] That proposal had been accepted a year before by Israel on the Commission's argument that to make such a gesture might produce an atmosphere conducive to a peace settlement. Its cool reception by both the Arabs and the Commission was a disillusioning experience with regard to the effect of such gestures. Moreover, the Israelis saw no need to defend themselves at the Paris meeting against a possible charge that they were hampering conciliation by their unbending views. The attitude adopted by the Arabs on the issue of belligerency would make it difficult to blame the Jews for the lack of a conciliatory atmosphere at the Conference. In any case, with the passage of time the objective case against repatriation, in view of the rapidly changing conditions in the places where Arabs once had lived in Israeli territory, had grown continually stronger.

The Commission brought the Paris Conference to a close and, with it, its attempts to make peace, having exhausted the possibilities of its roles as intermediator, conciliator, and mediator. Its report to the UN placed upon both Israel and the Arabs the onus of being unwilling to comply fully with the UN resolutions which were intended to solve the outstanding issues between them.[95]

This reference to the UN resolutions was relied on by the Arabs in raising as an agenda item for the Seventh Session of the UN General Assembly the complete failure reported by the Conciliation Commission.[96] At this session the Arabs developed in full their new case against Israel, based on the contention that the boundary lines set out in Resolution 181 (II) and the reference to the "right to return" in Resolution 194 (III) were legal requirements towards which Israel stood in defiance.

This Arab argument did not succeed in gaining the approval of the UN consensus. The Israeli rebuttal of it was even more successful in the General Assembly than it had been with the members of the Conciliation Commission. In the discussion Arab delegates were asked to define and specify what they meant by the UN resolutions which Israel was required to respect. As the French delegate (and Chairman of the Conciliation Commission), M. Pierre Ordonneau, pointed out, "there were a great many resolutions, some of them contradictory, and for practical reasons it was impossible to carry them completely into effect." [97] In reply to a direct question on the same point, an Arab delegate classified all the fifty-odd resolutions adopted to that time and rejected everything as irrelevant except the boundaries set out in Resolution 181 (II) and the phrase referring to a "right to return" in paragraph 11 of Resolution 194 (III). [98] The conclusion of his questioner, Mr. David Johnson of Canada (who also put the same question to the Israeli delegate), was the following:

Mr. Eban had been quite right in taking the view that the Canadian representative had not been interrogating him on certain particular resolutions. . . . Mr. Eban had . . . made it clear that, . . . the principal objectives of the United Nations in the Palestine question were to be kept in mind in the proposed negotiations. That reply disposed of the charge that it was the intention of one of the parties to brush aside all United Nations resolutions. Discussions in the Committee had made it clear that one party had narrowed down its attention to two particular General Assembly resolutions, while the other had agreed that the principal objectives of the United Nations were to be borne in mind in the negotiations.[99]

The development of the debate took a turn very far from the intentions of those who had initiated it. How much support had been gained for the Israeli view that peace — to which every UN member was committed by the fact of membership — must be sought by direct negotiation in terms of existing conditions, was shown by such statements as M. Ordonneau's:

[the parties] must . . . refrain from attempting to bind themselves in advance by recommendations of the General Assembly. His delegation was concerned at the insistence with which some representatives sought to confine the proposed negotiations to the framework of the General Assembly resolutions. If the delegations which took the view sought to prevent the parties from departing from the decisions of the General Assembly, even in cases where they agreed to do so, and wished to lay down that no negotiations were possible except on the basis of the General Assembly resolutions, they were advocating a course which would lead nowhere. Negotiations in which the parties could not compromise on any point ceased to be negotiations.[100]

This point of view was reflected in a resolution submitted by eight powers which — like the resolution adopted at the preceding session of the General Assembly but in more positive terms — declared that "the Governments concerned have the primary responsibility for reaching a settlement of their outstanding differences." [101] This unexpected outcome so disturbed the Arabs that they sought unsuccessfully to withdraw the item, originally proposed by them, in order to forestall action.

However, not only the Arabs but also Catholic countries were interested in pinning Israel down to a particular arrangement included in one or another earlier UN resolution adopted under different circumstances, before they would take so unexceptionable a step as voting for peace negotiations. The Ad Hoc Committee, in order to meet their demands, had included a general injunction that, in negotiating peace, the parties should bear in mind "the resolutions as well as the principal objectives of the United Nations on the Palestine question, including the religious interests of third parties." This phrasing was not fully satisfactory to such a country as Mexico, which consequently abstained in the Ad Hoc Committee voting.[102] Only after the draft resolution was adopted by the Ad Hoc Committee was the full force of Catholic pressure brought to bear. A Philippine amendment was introduced for consideration in the plenary meetings, seeking to bind the proposed peace negotiations to previous UN resolutions, "and, in particular, [to] the principle of the internationalization of Jerusalem." This amendment, like a similar proposal two years earlier, failed to secure the necessary two-thirds vote for passage. On the other hand, by insisting on it the Catholic countries gave the Arab states the margin they needed to prevent a renewed two-thirds vote in favor of the principle that it was the primary responsibility of the parties in conflict to negotiate peace between them.[103]

So ended the major efforts of the Conciliation Commission and of the United Nations as a whole to make peace in Palestine. A chapter had closed from which Israel drew its own conclusions. It became clear that Israel could rely neither on the UN consensus nor on the major powers to uphold consistently, let alone enforce, what the Israeli consensus felt to be the minimum essentials for its security and viability, and, least of all, its ability to carry out its Zionist functions. Special interests of individual nations or blocs of nations in the UN — the religious interests of Catholic countries, the political and religious interests of Moslem countries, and the strategic interests of the major powers, East and West — might override the motives of humanitarianism and conscience which had created a UN consensus in favor of founding a Jewish state. Moreover, the successful establishment of Israel had lightened the weight of guilt in regard to the Jews which had affected the attitudes of Christian countries in relation to Zionism, while the simultaneous creation of an Arab refugee mass had established a new humanitarian pressure which bore against Israel. On the other hand, there was another set of pertinent factors in the situation upon which, as experience had shown, Israel could more confidently rely. Political realism, which accounted Israel as "expendable" in many calculations of global strategy, now also had to recognize Israel as a hard and stubborn fact in local strategies of the Middle East. The will to sovereignty of Palestinian Jewry was a major factor which had forced the partition resolution, in the first place; and the assertion of sovereign will had maintained Israel's existence and its control over the minimum essentials for security, viability, and the ability to carry out Zionist functions in the face of war by the Arab states and political pressures by Western states, both directly and through the UN.

In the period that followed, Israel learned that in the limbo between war and peace, between security and destruction, where it resided under the armistice argrements, sovereignty was still its most reliable weapon — but also the most dangerous weapon in the arsenal of its enemies.

IV

Each of the four Israel-Arab armistice agreements declared explicitly in its preamble that it was designed to implement the Security Council resolution of November 16, 1948, and that the parties had entered into the agreement in response to that resolution.[104] The agreements, then, represented acts of compliance with the Security Council's resolution, which called upon Israel and the Arab states to negotiate these treaties "as a further provisional measure under Article 40 of the Charter of the United Nations." Article 40 of the Charter authorizes the Security Council, before applying punitive measures in case of a threat to the peace, "to call upon the parties concerned to comply with . . . provisional measures" in order "to prevent an aggravation of the situation." If the provisional measures called for — namely, the negotiation of the armistice — had not been complied with, the Security Council was obliged under Article 40 to "duly take account of failure to comply"; or, in other words, the Security Council, having determined the existence of a threat to the peace in Palestine and having unsuccessfully called upon the parties to comply with provisional measures to prevent the aggravation of the situation, would then consider the drastic action provided in Articles 41 and 42, under Chapter VII of the UN Charter.[105]

The armistice agreements were not only made at the behest, or under the menace, of the UN and negotiated with the assistance of the Acting UN Mediator, but they provided for the use of UN officials and good offices in many respects. The regulation of incidents affecting the agreements took place through Mixed Armistice Commissions, each presided over by a UN official wielding the decisive vote. In the demilitarized zones set up in some of the armistice treaties, the UN chairman of the Mixed Armistice Commission was given certain powers. The UN Secretary General in 1957 appointed a special officer to help adjust the situation in regard to the demilitarized zones in the Jerusalem area.[106] An additional measure taken by the Secretary General in 1956 sought to strengthen the legal position of the UN in regard to the armistice agreements. After an outbreak of fighting on the Israeli-Egyptian armistice lines, Mr. Hammarskjold negotiated an exchange of letters in which Israel and the neighboring

Arab states respectively committed themselves to the UN to give a special status to the cease-fire provisions of the armistice treaties.[107]

Despite the imposing extent of UN involvement, the legal force of the armistice treaties derived not from UN pronouncements but from the fact that they represented contracts between sovereign states.[108] On the other hand, the involvement of the UN was of sufficient significance to make possible substantial restrictions on the exercise of sovereignty by the parties to the armistice, on those occasions when the UN chose to intervene. Such intervention has more than once been effective against sovereign acts of Israel. But neither the UN nor the major powers who claim prerogatives of a similar order have been willing or able to guarantee Israel its security, viability, and ability to carry out its Zionist functions. In the name of these objects, Israel has accordingly continued to rely, in the case of critical issues, upon the assertion of its sovereign rights, even in the face of UN or great power opposition.

In all the armistice agreements there are certain provisions that are given a special and quite unusual status. While all other clauses of the treaties could be "suspended" by mutual consent of the parties, these were to remain in force, even if both parties should agree to their "suspension," until replaced by a peace treaty. The provisions in question read as follows, in the case of the Israeli-Jordanian agreement (Articles I and II in the Egyptian treaty):

Article I

With a view to promoting the return of permanent peace in Palestine and in recognition of the importance in this regard of mutual assurances concerning the future military operations of the Parties, the following principles, which shall be fully observed by both Parties during the armistice, are hereby affirmed:

. (1)   The injunction of the Security Council against resort to military force in the settlement of the Palestine question shall henceforth be scrupulously respected.

(2)   No aggressive action by the armed forces — land, sea or air — of either Party shall be undertaken, planned or threatened against the people or the armed forces of the other; it being understood that the use of the term "planned" in this context has no bearing on normal staff planning as generally practised in military organisations.

(3)   The right of each Party to its security and freedom from fear of attack by the armed forces of the other shall be fully respected.

(4)   The establishment of an armistice between the armed forces of the two Parties is accepted as an indispensable step toward the liquidation of armed conflict and the restoration of peace in Palestine.

Article III

(1) In pursuance of the foregoing principles and of the resolution of the Security Council of 16 November 1948, a general armistice between the armed forces of the two Parties — land, sea and air — is hereby established.

(2) No element of the land, sea or air military or para-military forces of either Party, including non-regular forces, shall commit any warlike or hostile act against the military or para-military forces of the other Party, or against civilians in territory under control of that Party; or shall advance beyond or pass over for any purpose whatsoever the Armistice Demarcation Lines set forth in . . . this Agreement; or enter into or pass through the air space of the other Party.

(3) No warlike act or act of hostility shall be conducted from territory controlled by one of the Parties to this agreement against the other Party.[109]

In the view of an Israeli commentator,[110] the above articles of the armistice established a permanent cease-fire along agreed frontiers, together with a nonagression pact of unlimited duration. They also committed the parties to a transition from a state of open war, left behind by the conclusion of the armistice, to the "return of permanent peace" which the armistice was to promote. All these commitments the parties were not free to renounce even by mutual consent.

Under the Hague Convention of 1907, in an armistice of limited duration either party was entitled to reply to a serious violation by the other by denouncing the treaty and even "in case of urgency, . . . recommencing hostilities immediately." If an armistice had no definite term, it was perhaps less secure, for either party was entitled to resume military operations simply by warning the enemy within an agreed time.[111] The Israeli-Arab armistice treaties were, thus, quite unusual in their unalterable provisions. The permanence attributed to them, together with the reference to the Security Council's resolution of November 16, 1948 which they contain, imply a kind of surrender of sovereign rights by Israel and the Arab states to the realm of international law.

On the other hand, in agreeing to abide by a cease-fire, abstain from aggression, and move through the armistice to peace, none of these states, obviously, renounced the right to self-defense. Article 51 of the UN Charter specifically refers to the inherent right of self-defense which may be exercised by Members in case of armed attack, until the UN is able to act in order to maintain international peace and security.[112] What the Israeli-Arab armistice agreements added to Article 51 of the Charter was, in effect, to set up fairly elaborate provisions by which the UN could concern itself continuously, until the conclusion of peace, with the security situation along the Israeli-Arab frontiers. This led to two developments, not always in harmony with each other. Since United Nations offices were perpetually involved in settling one or another question regarded as involving the security of the parties, any failure on its part — or anything so considered by one of the parties — continually suggested the alternative of a resort to the right of self-defense. On the other hand, whenever a party exercised its right to protect itself against threats against its security which were not effectively controlled under the armistice, it might be the occasion of immediate reaction in the UN. The net effect of these two circumstances, and of the policies adopted by Israel and the Arab states, was to nullify many of the provisions of the armistice treaties. The UN then tried to replace them by various *ad hoc* arrangements whereby it attempted at least to prevent, as far as possible, the resumption of full-scale war. Such arrangements were far more political than legal in their effect. Thus, in spite of the provisions of the Israeli-Arab armistices which seem to make exceptional concessions to the realm of international law, the actual development has been from a relatively secure legal situation of contract between the parties towards an insecure political control of the situation under *ad hoc* arrangements improvised by the UN.

This course of events was favored by the deliberate policy of the Arab states. Their agreement to the armistice treaties did not signify acceptance of the existence of Israel as an irreversible or legitimate fact. To seek the destruction of a sovereign state is not, of course, a policy which can be carried out with the direct sanction of the international legal order. The Arab states signed the armistices because the military situation forced them to submit to a legal arrangement. But they continued to proclaim that, when able to do so, they would have recourse to arms again, in a "second round," in order to destroy Israel. Their acceptance of the international legal order of the armistice was, then, a temporary measure which they expected would end in the destruction of Israel by arms or other methods. Nor did they feel obliged, in the period before the second round of hostilities, to leave Israel at peace. While accepting the protection afforded by the armistice treaties, they not only evaded the provisions of their contracts in international law which sought to promote peace; they also used the armistice and the UN provisions and machinery themselves in order to weaken Israel.

Israeli policy, on the other hand, was concerned initially to stress the legal validity of the armistice. Those treaties had two great virtues in the eyes of Israel: first, they created a *status quo* which seemed not only realistic but healing, for it included commitments to seek peace as well as boundaries conforming more or less to the strategic realities of the situation; and second, they were built upon the principle of direct, bilateral negotiation between the parties. However, as in the case of other UN principles Israel had accepted, the armistice agreements were regarded as an integral whole, all elements of which had to be respected if it were to be maintained. The Arab nullification of major portions of the agreements and the tendency for the remaining portions, interpreted by the Arabs in accordance with their own purposes, to be made an occasion to interpose the UN between the parties were resisted by Israel with little success. But the irritation of Israel and its consequent resort to the exercise of sovereign rights in defense of its security effectively demonstrated that, in departing from a basis of bilateral contract, the armistice agreements were being reduced to dead letters.

Among the unalterable provisions of the armistice agreements, as Israel saw it, were a definite renunciation of all varieties of war and aggressive intentions between Israel and the Arabs and an unequivocal commitment to negotiate peace. This was, in general, also the interpretation favored by the UN consensus but by no means the interpretation accepted by the Arab states. However, UN acceptance of the Israeli interpretation on this point was not made effective by any action. This had a fateful consequence: the failure to enforce the obligation to seek peace undermined respect for other unalterable obligations under the treaties — in particular, the cease-fire.

Although the Arab states had refused to consider themselves at war when they invaded Palestine on May 15, 1948, since they denied that Israel was a sovereign state and claimed they were merely engaged in a police action against terrorist bands at the request of the Palestinian Arabs, they resorted, after signing the armistice, to the argument that there was a technical state of war between them and Israel.[113] Accordingly, they claimed certain rights of belligerency and conducted a cold war of boycott, blockade, and blacklisting against Israel and many of those who traded with Israel. These measures, enforceable by Arab military and police forces,[114] were accompanied by openly proclaimed plans for military reorganization looking towards a second round of hostilities in which Israel would be wiped out. In the Israeli view, all these activities were clear violations of the fundamental armistice provisions that the "return of permanent peace" was to be promoted, that "no aggressive action by the armed forces . . . of either Party shall be undertaken, planned, or threatened against the people or the armed forces of the other," and that "the right of each

Party to its security and freedom from fear of attack" should be re-spected. Appealing to these clauses, the Israelis brought a protest against the Egyptian blockade of the Suez Canal before the Egyptian-Israeli Mixed Armistice Commission. This complaint was adjudged to be justified in substance, but action on it was regarded as beyond the competence of the Commission, for lack of proof that armed force had been employed in the blockade.[115] On its appeal to the Security Council, Israel won a decision that Egypt had no belligerent rights during the period of the armistice; and an order was issued on September 1, 1951, for the removal of the ban on Israeli traffic in the Suez Canal.[116] The order was ignored by Egypt, and no action by the Security Council followed. When further incidents, involving the use of armed force in the blockade, caused Israel to complain again to the Security Council in 1954, its political position had grown even weaker, since the USSR had begun to exploit Arab nationalism as a means for intervening in the Middle East. Egypt's assertion of belligerent rights against Israel could now not even be condemned by the Security Council, for the resolution to this effect was vetoed by the Soviet Union.[117]

While Israel found that the mixed armistice commissions (and, for that matter, the Security Council) were ineffective in preventing violations of the armistice by aggressive and hostile acts behind the frontiers on the Arab side, it soon discovered that Arab states were able to employ the UN machinery under the armistice agreements in order to interfere with peaceful acts behind the frontiers on the Israeli side. To achieve this purpose, the Arab states — particularly Syria — made use of the provisions establishing certain demilitarized and "neutral" zones along the armistice demarcation lines.

The first such zones were established in the Jerusalem area. The religious interests and philanthropic institutions concentrated there, together with the presence of the consular and truce headquarters, did not spare the Holy City fierce fighting, but certain attempts to mitigate the conflict were made. An agreement to demilitarize the Hebrew University and Hadassah Hospital area on Mount Scopus brought an early cease-fire for this point, and on November 30, 1948, a stable cease-fire for the whole Jerusalem front was established by agreeing on truce lines which placed a continuous "No-Man's Land" between the two forces. These lines were then incorporated into the Israeli-Jordanian armistice agreement. In the remaining portions of the Israel-Jordan armistice demarcation line, it was not thought necessary to establish demilitarized zones. An agreement to maintain troops in defensive strength only in the vicinity of the demarcation lines was considered a sufficient precaution.[118]

Nor was it thought necessary to do more than make a similar agreement in the case of the Israel-Lebanon armistice treaty. On this front, there had been active hostilities during the autumn of 1948, and Israel had carried its military drive beyond the international frontier, after destroying all opposition. Israel then carried out a unilateral withdrawal behind the international frontier, which became the armistice demarcation line.[119] The political rather than military significance of this arrangement was obvious, since there was no question of disengaging fighting forces in this case.

Disengagement of forces was an important consideration in the Israeli-Egyptian armistice. The autumn campaigns had carried Israeli forces over the international frontier and left Egyptian units surrounded on the Palestine side. The threat of British action under the Anglo-Egyptian treaty of defense, which applied, of course, to the territory defined by the international frontier, had forced Israel's withdrawal behind that line, but the problem of Egyptian troops encircled or endangered on the other side remained. Israel agreed to Egyptian occupation of the Gaza strip with its large refugee population, but Egypt — for reasons which were probably political as well as strategic — wanted more. To accept the international frontier as a demarcation line would be a public admission of defeat and an omen of a final peace settlement on the same line. Also at Auja on the international frontier was a strategic crossroads from which attacks could be mounted by either side against the other. If Israel occupied it, the position of Egyptian forces in Gaza was threatened, while if Egypt occupied it together with the position in Gaza, a new attack on Israel would be facilitated. The solution of the problem was the agreement to make the international frontier the demarcation line from Eilat in the south to the Gaza strip, but to demilitarize Auja in Israel, while imposing severe restrictions on military activity on a similar area on the Egyptian side facing Auja.[120]

The last armistice to be signed, after long and tedious negotiations, was the armistice with Syria. In this area, after the initial Syrian penetrations had been contained and some inconclusive fighting occurred in July, both sides remained inactive. Accordingly, Syrian troops remained on the Palestine side of the international frontier. The Israelis demanded a Syrian withdrawal behind their frontier, just as they themselves had withdrawn unilaterally from Lebanese territory. The Syrians resisted stubbornly, but faced with the possibility of a concentrated Israeli attack upon them alone, ultimately agreed. However, here again demilitarized zones were established, chiefly in the areas evacuated by the Syrians.[121]

It appears, then, that the major function of the establishment of demilitarized zones in the armistice agreements was to secure certain withdrawals behind the international frontier. For Israel, this meant marking out the area in which it asserted its national sovereignty; and just as it withdrew from Egyptian and Lebanese territory beyond that line, it insisted that the Syrians withdraw from territory within it. Since the provisions of the armistice treaty could only be altered — if at all — by the mutual consent of the parties, the Israelis considered the demarcation line relatively permanent and regarded the demilitarization of areas along the frontier as of temporary significance. In the case of the Syrian armistice, the Israelis accepted the establishment of these zones on the express understanding that civilian development there would not be hampered.[122]

For the Arabs, on the other hand — and above all for Syria — it was the demarcation line along the international frontier that was considered temporary, while the rules regarding the demilitarized zones offered a permanent opportunity to contest Israel's sovereignty over the territory it controlled. The UN chairman of the Israeli-Syrian mixed armistice commission was given certain powers to supervise the withdrawal of troops and the correlative return of civilians, together with "limited numbers of locally recruited civilian police," to the demilitarized zones.[123] The Syrians relied upon these and other provisions of the armistice agreement in asserting the right to hamper civilian development of the area. This was a matter of critical importance, because the demilitarized zones in the north contain those sources of surface water upon which depended plans for intensive agricultural and power development affecting virtually the whole range of Israel's territory.

The period after the conclusion of the Syrian armistice was then marked by repeated outbreaks of fighting, when Syrian artillery opened fire or infantry and armored forces advanced into the demilitarized zone to seek to prevent Israeli drainage and irrigation projects. The reaction of the UN to these activities was, of course, closely watched by the Israelis. They noted, first, what was done in response to the breach of the cease-fire and crossing of demarcation lines by the Syrians. They observed not only that nothing effective was done against the party which first resorted to arms, but that the Syrians each time obtained an advantage by their aggressiveness. The UN, and its major Western members, invariably yielded to the Syrians to the extent of insisting, under severe pressure, that Israel temporarily suspend its peaceful development of the area in return for a renewal of the cease-fire — which, according to the armistice, had never been subject to suspension, even by mutual consent of the parties.[124]

The Israelis observed with care, secondly, the interpretation placed by the UN on the exercise of Israeli sovereignty and UN control in the area. That interpretation was worked out from crisis to crisis under pressure of the respective Syrian and Israeli positions and the varying attitudes of third parties, including the several UN chairmen themselves. The Israeli position from the beginning was that the Mixed Armistice Commission was not granted any competence under the treaty to deal with the affairs of the demilitarized zone. The provisions regarding the UN chairman's powers of supervision in the zone referred only to the withdrawal of Syrian troops and the restoration of civilian life. Thus, the Israelis contended that Syria had no right under the armistice to make complaints in regard to civilian activities in the demilitarized zones either in its own behalf or on behalf of the Arabs who lived there.[125]

Syria, on the other hand, contended, quite generally, that Israeli development projects were not allowed under the armistice because they gave Israel military advantages; and they also contended that they were entitled under the armistice to exercise a veto over such projects in behalf of either Syrian or Palestinian Arabs whose interest might be affected. Moreover, they argued that Israel had no sovereign rights in the area, and that the UN chairman had authority to disapprove Israeli actions affecting Arab interests.[126]

The UN chairmen ruled, in the particular instances that arose, that no military advantages such as were forbidden by the armistice agreements were obtained by Israel under any of the projects. One chairman, General Vagn Bennike, held that he had the right, under the powers granted him by the armistice in regard to the civilian population, to issue cease and desist orders to Israel years after the restoration of normal civilian life in the demilitarized zones. He also held that before Israel could carry out development projects in the zones it must obtain Syrian agreement. The UN consensus, when the issue arose before it, denied Syria such a right of veto or right to complain to the Mixed Armistice Commission on behalf of Palestinian Arabs in the zone. To be more precise, a Security Council resolution indicating these conclusions had a large majority, but a Soviet veto led to the adoption of no resolution at all. However, the several UN chairmen maintained they had the right to bar Israel activity in the zones if

Arab property rights were affected. The Security Council, advised by Dr. Bunche that questions of sovereignty in the demilitarized zone had been intentionally avoided in the armistice agreement, confined itself to political rather than legal issues; yet its action often seemed to assume that sovereignty in the area had been suspended. Moreover, it was the UN position that the Mixed Armistice Commission should itself convene in order to interpret the meaning of the agreement on such controverted points.[127]

Even though Israel never accepted the interpretation of the armistice agreements under which such UN authority was asserted and its own full sovereignty in all civilian spheres denied in respect to the demilitarized zones, it frequently bowed to the UN decision. It did so only in the face of severe pressure and on one occasion only because the United States had cut off all aid. But Israel opposed with unyielding firmness the view that the Mixed Armistice Commission should itself interpret the treaty clauses concerning the demilitarized zone. This, in effect, would have authorized the UN chairman to adjudicate the issue of Israel's sovereignty in the zone. Israel therefore refused from 1951 on to attend meetings where such questions were proposed for the agenda. This led to the total inactivity of the Israel-Syrian Mixed Armistice Commission from 1960 on.[128]

The initial purpose of the armistice agreements was to establish and maintain a military *status quo* in the area of an agreed armistice line between Israel and her Arab neighbors. This had become essential because of the breakdown of the Security Council's efforts, even under the threat of the sanctions of Chapter VII of the Charter, to stop the war in Palestine by imposing a truce. For, despite all that the UN could do through its large staff of truce supervisors and the increasingly peremptory tone of the Security Council resolutions, the truce was continually punctuated with sharp outbursts of full-scale fighting. Considering how the opposed forces were placed during the truce, it is extremely difficult to imagine how anything else could have been expected; and, as we have seen, Count Bernadotte reported that only by advancing to an armistice could the situation be controlled.

The military *status quo* which was established by the armistice agreements achieved a major improvement over the situation under the truce. By mutual agreement, the parties set up a continuous border between them, corresponding (with the exception of the Jordan frontier and the Gaza strip) to the international frontiers of Palestine, and they withdrew their respective forces behind this line. But even with these improvements, it was clearly realized and implicitly stipulated by the parties that the armistice, like the truce before it, could be no more than a provisional arrangement which must lead to, and be replaced by, a final peace settlement. For if a development toward peace did not take place, then everything Count Bernadotte had said about the situation under the truce applied with equal force to the situation under the armistice.

It is needless to recount in detail the collapse of the armistice agreements in the matter of maintaining peaceful borders between Israel and her Arab neighbors. In the first year or more of the life of the armistice agreements, conditions were certainly far from satisfactory, but in respect to the border situation, at least, the Chief of Staff of the Truce Supervision Organization, General Riley, felt able to express moderate satisfaction:

I personally believe that the Mixed Armistice Commissions have outserved their usefulness, as far as the military portions of the Armistice Agreements are concerned. During the past twelve or fourteen months we have had three or four violations, from a military point of view, with something like 200 complaints, which were police complaints, particularly involving the stealing of cattle, sheep, goats and waterpipes. . . . In addition to that number of complaints, I would say that there were 300 or 400 complaints which have been solved on the spot by sub-committees . . . without the necessity of either side submitting a formal complaint to the Chairman. If the parties themselves desire to act in good faith, there is no subject that cannot be handled before these Mixed Armistice Commissions. I would suggest that these Mixed Armistice Commissions have their bases broadened by means of conversations or conferences between the parties themselves in accordance with [the pertinent clause in the several agreements].[129]

In line with these comments, the staff of truce observers had been reduced from five hundred to thirty. General Riley felt, then, that it was incumbent upon the parties, having more or less stabilized the border situation, as he thought, to get on to their main obligation under the armistice, the approach to a final peace settlement through the Mixed Armistice Commissions.

But General Riley, of course, relied upon a good faith which proved lacking. There was nothing the Arabs wanted less than to get on with the task of making a final peace settlement. Under the circumstances, the supposedly stabilized border situation began to deteriorate sharply and steadily, and, instead of the mixed armistice commissions taking on peace-making functions because border violations were too petty and few to require attention, the border situation became so grave and troubled that not only the commissions but the UN Chief of Staff was felt to be insufficient to deal with it. The UN Security Council was continually called into session and the UN Secretary General was pressed into service to obtain the agreement of the parties to plans for removing the tensions resulting from recurrent incidents — and all this without any remarkable success.

The tendency to discount thievery and sabotage by relatively small groups or "infiltrators" was natural enough in the first year of the armistice, especially if it was hoped that the efforts of the mixed armistice commissions could be enlarged in scope and turned toward advancing a final peace settlement. But it soon became clear that infiltration was an instrument of guerrilla war deliberately encouraged and employed. Where the Arabs wished to stop border raiding, as on the Lebanese frontier and, at times, the Jordan frontier, they were able to do so effectively. A proper respect for the armistice agreements would have reduced the raiding to a minor police matter indeed, for the treaties state that "rules and regulations of the armed forces of the Parties, which prohibit civilians from crossing the fighting lines or entering the area between the lines, shall remain in effect after the signing of this Agreement with application to the Armistice Demarcation Line. . . . "[130] The rules and regulations referred to were quite rigid, and more than amply effective for controlling infiltration if applied in good faith. But time showed that "infiltration" was often only another name for guerrilla bands pressed into service and trained for minelaying, ambushing, spying, and simple killing expeditions. The mixed armistice commissions proved quite ineffective against this kind of miniature war, and its total effect, if unchecked, threatened to make civilian life on Israel's borders impossible. In the end, the Israelis refused to put up with this situation and began to police the borders on their own by retaliation raids.[131] It cannot be denied that these raids more often than not proved effective as regards their limited police objective, but they caused Israel to be censured on each occasion by the UN Security Council. The publicity that attended them underscored, as nothing else could, how close to collapse the armistice agreements had come.

The armistice agreements contain a provision for the revision or suspension, by mutual consent, of all but their major objectives, as we have already noted. Moreover,

In the absence of mutual agreement and after this Agreement has been in effect for one year from the date of its signing, either of the Parties may call upon the Secretary-General of the United Nations to convoke a conference of representatives of the two Parties for the purpose of reviewing, revising or suspending any of the provisions of this agreement other than

Article I and II [in the case of the Egyptian treaty; I and III in the others]. Participation in such conference shall be obligatory upon the Parties.[132]

These clauses were undoubtedly inserted in the hope that the armistice agreements would indeed pave the way for peace and would have to be altered in order to facilitate successive stages of the advance toward that goal. Eventually these clauses had to be invoked by Israel *vis-à-vis* Jordan for just the opposite reason: the agreements were obviously in need of revision because they were unable to prevent the steady deterioration of the situation.

It is instructive to note the fate of Israel's attempt to invoke this provision of the agreement. Secretary General Hammarskjold soon found himself in the position of asking the Israelis for assurances, which were calculated to soothe and reassure the Jordanians, that the demand for a conference was not an attempt to raise points looking toward peace, but only to discuss the arrangements for policing the borders. Despite these extraordinary assurances, Jordanian suspicion persisted, and after long and fruitless negotiations the Secretary General abandoned his efforts to carry out the terms of the armistice.[133] This in spite of the express statement in the treaty that "participation in such conference shall be obligatory upon the Parties."

The final acknowledgement of the collapse of the armistice agreements and an attempt to salvage at least its cease-fire provisions took place after a pitched battle between Israelis and Egyptians at the El Auja demilitarized zone on the Sinai border. Following this explosion, Dag Hammarskjold himself made an emergency trip to the Middle East and renegotiated the cease-fire clause of the armistice. He obtained agreement from Israel and the Arab states concerned, affirmed in letters to the UN, that even if other provisions of the armistice were violated, the parties would not consider this grounds for considering the cease-fire invalid. However, this agreement — which, to be sure, did not add but detracted from the scope of the armistice treaties — was only secured by an elaborate procedure which made it clear that it was itself based on reciprocity. Each side renewed its commitment to the cease-fire upon assurance of simultaneous acceptance by the other. Thus it was obvious that even though the cease-fire — but not, as previously, the commitment to seek peace and avoid aggressive acts, plans, or threats — was independent of other provisions of the armistice, it was not independent but specifically dependent on the respect for the cease-fire observed by the other side.[134]

In other words, the armistice had not only been reduced to a cease-fire, but to a conditional cease-fire. Each side very clearly implied that if the other shot, it would shoot back; that if the other crossed the border, it would retaliate; and that if the other threatened its security by major military measures, it would resort to its rights of self-defense. These implications were not stressed by the UN Secretary General, who emphasized instead the new position enjoyed by the UN in virtue of the fact that the new agreement was embodied in letters addressed to the UN Secretary General. In fact, he declared that any recourse had by either side to its "inherent" rights of self-defense under Article 51 of the UN Charter was subject to approval by the UN.[135] But the Secretary General's statement was without effect in preserving the cease-fire, for, soon after, the "second round" of the Arab-Israeli war broke out through the Israeli campaign into the Sinai Peninsula. This incident was closed by the withdrawal of Israeli troops upon the understanding that UN forces posted on the Sinai frontier and at the Red Sea would restrain Egypt from infiltration and blockade at those vital points. The UN now stood between the two parties to keep the peace, not having been able to bring them together to achieve it.

12 ISRAEL AND WORLD POLITICS

I F an Israeli were to consider, some years after the creation of his state, how far it was established securely under the sanctions of international law, he could only come to grim conclusions. Neither the armistice agreements nor action by the United Nations had been able to give Israel peace. The Arabs had been able to commit acts of patent hostility in defiance of their obligations. Both under the armistice agreements and under provisions of UN resolutions, the Arabs contested Israel's sovereignty over strategically and economically vital parts of its territory and over aspects of its domestic policy. While Israel was able to assert its rights as a sovereign state effectively in reply to such attacks, and did so in matters of critical importance, on other issues it was forced by the pressure of Western powers and UN officials, who were anxious to conciliate the Arabs, to submit to what Israelis considered infringements of sovereignty. The Arabs had not been conciliated, however, but were pressing their campaign for the total destruction of Israel or for cutting it back to a non-viable condition, and using both the armistice and the UN resolutions for these purposes.

Against these designs, Israel relied for defense more and more upon the exercise of its sovereignty and less and less upon the international consensus. When it assessed its position in the global power struggle, the picture looked even more forbidding. And here, too, Israel's primary reliance had to be on its own sovereignty and will to survive.

The "colonial" and Asian world, of which Israel was a member by location and previous condition of dependency, gave little weight to Israel's right to exist. The Arab and, in general, the Moslem countries denied it and fought it, or at best were willing to make terms with it provisionally only if Israel would accept such conditions that it could neither serve its Zionist purpose nor survive a second occasion to attack it. Countries like Turkey, who early recognized Israel partly out of self-interest, or Iran or India, who recognized it for lack of a specific hostility, were easily moved by their greater interest in their good relations with the Arab and Moslem world to restrict temporarily or never to initiate full diplomatic relations. The new African and East Asian excolonial areas saw Israel through the myth images neither of Christian Europe nor the Moslem East, but they might easily be persuaded to see it under the image of a Western imperialist colony. They showed little resistance to Arab marshalling of the Afro-Asian bloc against Israel except where determined Israeli efforts demonstrated concrete advantages in friendly relations.[1]

As for the European countries, Israel's position in terms of their *Realpolitik* was only slightly better. The whole UN consensus, based on Christian Europe and its extensions overseas, had asserted Israel's right to exist, but hardly any segment fully accepted Israel's right to exist for the purpose to which it had autonomously dedicated itself — the Zionist ingathering — or to exist within boundaries and with a scope of sovereignty sufficient to make it viable. The Roman Catholic countries, hoping to make Israel bow to the internationalization of Jerusalem, had joined the Arab-Asian bloc in rejecting a UN resolution calling for direct peace negotiations. Many of these countries were part of the Latin American "bloc" in the UN and in the first years of the international organization had a certain interest in voting agreements with the Arabs in order to derive minor advantages from their balance of power position.[2] In those early years, the Soviet bloc remained relatively passive on the Palestine question. But after a while the Communist countries began to support every Arab demand in the UN and, in return, to enjoy the general support of many Arab countries, as they did, in many matters, of the Afro-Asian group as a whole. These new allies were ready to go along with the Arabs in opposition to Israel much further than the Roman Catholic-Latin American grouping had been. In a period when the Soviet Union was waging a grand campaign of threats of atomic war against all countries allied with the West, it issued repeated and pointed denunciations of Israel and its rulers, and said they were courting the extinction which they, indeed, deserved.[3]

The Western, mainly Protestant, European countries who were locked with Russia in a global struggle were the major prop upon which Israel's economic viability leaned. Among them resided the western Christian conscience that had been successfully invoked from the beginning in support of Israel's right to exist. But they, too, were far from recognizing Israel's right to exist within viable frontiers and with a scope of sovereignty equal to that of other sovereign nations and sufficient for the Zionist functions Israel was designed to carry out. The British had not only, in the beginning, done everything short of participating openly in the Israeli-Arab war in order to make the creation of Israel difficult. In later years they continued to support the excision from Israel of areas which might be of strategic importance for a projected Arab military grouping in some sort of friendly relationship with themselves. The Americans, from whom Israel derived a major part of its financial support, did not hesitate to use this fact as a club to force Israel to comply with measures that the new state considered in derogation of its sovereignty. A blatant illustration of the limits within which some officials felt that Israel's sovereignty should be confined was given in a series of speeches, and statements in explanation of the speeches, by Henry Byroade, Assistant Secretary of State, in 1954. In the face of protests not only by American Jewish organizations but by the Israeli Ambassador, Mr. Byroade maintained, while denying any intention to question Israel's sovereign right to regulate immigration, that the Zionist ideology of Israel and its free admission of Jews were a legitimate matter of concern both to the Arabs and to the Western countries, and should be reconsidered by Israel in favor of "integration" into the (Arab) Middle East.[4] America also took drastic steps to enforce Israeli submission to restrictions of its sovereignty in the civilian development of the demilitarized zones, and it maintained a stiff avoidance of Israeli Jerusalem after it became the effective and proclaimed capital of the country. In addition, America from time to time expressed a vague sympathy, if not support, for plans to cut back Israel's territory in vital areas; although American officials also suggested the inclusion of the Gaza strip in Israel on condition that the refugee population there be absorbed in the Jewish state.[5]

The most critical involvement of Israel with global politics arose, however, not from the varying attitudes different nations took, in line with their interests, to the problems represented by Israel itself and its claims to the conditions of a viable existence. The gravest challenges to Israel's sovereign existence arose from the clash between the global powers, East and West, and the measures each took to strengthen its position in the Middle East.

I

In the first years of Israel's existence, the Soviet Union was virtually excluded from influence in the Middle East and, apart from occasional gestures, maintained a relatively passive attitude toward developments there. The Western powers, on the other hand, began very early to plan for the organization of the area under their aegis as a defensive bloc designed to contain Soviet expansion. After initial vagueness, specific plans consistently left Israel out of consideration, owing to Arab hostility to that country, and sought to combine Arab countries with other Moslem countries opposed to Russia.[6]

Western planners, whose military potential dominated the Middle East, did not totally ignore the Israeli-Arab problem, to be sure. America, Britain, and France, through their 1950 Tripartite Declaration, were a more effective force controlling this explosive issue than was any UN measure. Through this Declaration the three Western powers declared it their purpose to maintain a balance of armaments between Israel and her Arab neighbors and to oppose any aggressive action, from whatever side, in violation of the borders established by the Palestine armistice.[7] A clear legal basis upon which the Western powers could intervene, or indeed really undertook to intervene, existed, however, only in the treaties by which Britain, with its military bases and forces in Egypt and Jordan, was committed to protect the borders of those countries against attack. During the fighting in 1948, Britain had let it be seen that she took seriously her rights and obligations under the two treaties. Israel had no similar treaty with any of the Western powers. Moreover, the territory of Israel — unlike Egypt, Jordan, or Syria — was so small that, if not adequately armed for speedy defensive action of its own, the country could be totally overrun and largely destroyed before the Tripartite agreement could become effective, even if it were successfully invoked in Israel's favor. Nor was the attitude of the Western powers on the question of Israel's borders such that, if it were occupied by the Arabs, Israel could hope that the Western powers would require a withdrawal to the original lines — as would certainly happen if the case were reversed — or to any boundaries that would leave Israel a viable and not merely a nominal political unit.

In 1953, pleading exhaustion, Ben-Gurion retired from leadership to a desert retreat in Sde Boker in order to reassess Israel's strategic position.[8] Among the signatories of the Tripartite Declaration only the United States, under Harry Truman, had for a time shown friendship; but this, too, once more became questionable in 1951–1952, when the Americans so readily consented to exclude Israel from their projected Middle East defense organization. The Republican administration inaugurated at the beginning of the year had indicated special interest in removing Arab suspicions of American partiality to Israel. Israel's relations with Eastern Europe were severely troubled in 1952 by the

Slansky trial in Prague, by that late flare-up of Stalinist anti-Semitism, the alleged "doctors' plot" in Moscow, and by Russia's temporary severance of diplomatic relations with Israel following a bombing attempt on the Soviet Embassy in Tel Aviv. Moreover, one could already see the omens of a new Russian anti-Israel stand on UN issues when the Communist countries joined with the Muslim-Catholic opposition on December 18, 1952, to block a resolution favoring direct peace talks between Israel and the Arab states. There was thus ample evidence that international moral and political support for Israel's threatened existence was waning and new defense measures had to be taken.[9]

Yet if any major power had been interested in diverting Israel policy from a military to a diplomatic focus, the rise to Prime Minister of a veteran diplomat, Moshe Sharett (Shertok, 1894–1965), seemed to offer just such an opportunity. But the actual course of events strongly suggests that no one thought such a change sufficiently important to be worth encouraging. The Jewish state did not count enough to be wooed, as did Egypt. It was apparently thought better to keep Israel in line by occasional applications of pressure. Precisely in the year and a half of Sharett's ministry, international (not excluding Western) pressures against Israel rose to a point of clear and present danger.

The new revolutionary regime in Egypt, welcomed at first in Israel as elsewhere, turned not to peace but to heightened belligerency, repeatedly tightening the Suez and Tiran Straits blockade against Israel's commerce. The Israelis examined the traces and effects of Arab terrorist attacks and concluded that units sent from Gaza and Jordan showed growing signs of military training and organization. Now, also, the Soviet veto was applied against Security Council resolutions seeking to restrain Syria or Egypt from belligerent acts in violation of the armistice agreement. The UN was thus effectively precluded from responding to any Israeli appeals; but it continued with mounting emphasis to condemn the reprisals Israel resorted to, under its sovereign right of self-defense, in order to contain and deter the sabotage and terror campaign. Britain was negotiating its withdrawal from the Suez Canal without stipulating for Egyptian guarantees of freedom of passage for Israel's commerce. As for the United States, it began to rearm Iraq, as its contribution to Dulles' "northern tier" defense strategy. America was also prepared to negotiate terms for selling arms to Egypt which, of course, together with Jordan, had long-standing arms supply arrangements with the British. In contrast Israel's urgent applications for a balancing arms supply were consistently rejected or evaded. The result was a sharp decline in popular support for the Sharett government in Israel.[10]

Reprisals continued to be taken by Israeli forces, acting on their established doctrine of border defense. But with the departure of Ben-Gurion, who had served as both Prime Minister and Minister of Defense, smooth working relations in the defense establishment and with other government offices were badly disrupted. Ben-Gurion was called back as Defense Minister in February 1955, in order to repair the damage, and returned as Prime Minister in November after the election of Israel's third Knesset. Although his return was welcomed by the public, it did not save his party from a painful setback at the polls or prevent a marked rise in relative strength of Herut, the militant Revisionist opposition party. As Ben-Gurion saw it, not only the public but Israel's increasingly constricted strategic situation demanded a different policy from Sharett's. Instead of a defense policy restrained by diplomacy, he demanded diplomacy subordinated to and supporting a consistent Israeli policy of strength. In June 1956 Sharett's departure from the Foreign Ministry signalized the definite Israeli acceptance of this line of policy.[11]

In Egypt, where Colonel Nasser was exploiting his unfolding opportunities with bold initiative, Ben-Gurion's return did not produce greater caution. However, if Nasser's later comments may be relied on, the coincidence of Ben-Gurion's reappearance as Defense Minister with a major Israeli reprisal raid against Egyptian forces in Gaza brought home the urgent need for military preparedness. In April 1955, at the Bandung Conference, the Egyptian ruler set out in earnest on his dazzling new adventure as a neutralist leader of the "third world." He entertained with interest Chou En-lai's suggestion that the Russians might sell him more arms, more cheaply, than the Americans, and without irritating restrictions on their use. In September, Nasser startled the world by confirming publicly his arms deal with the Soviets (through the nominal agency of Czechoslovakia), the first of a series of rapid maneuvers that culminated in the nationalization of the Suez Canal in July 1956. With that step the fat was in the fire: Nasser had added to his determined foes France and Britain, along with Israel.[12]

Upon the conclusion of the Soviet-Egyptian arms deal the alignment of military forces progressed rapidly to the point of imminent explosion. In September 1955, Egypt tightened the blockade of the Tiran Straits, extending it to air traffic. In November, the Egyptians were driven from their encroachment on the El Auja demilitarized zone in a pitched battle. Following this, Israeli intelligence observed with interest a redeployment of Egyptian troops in Sinai to forward positions where they threatened attack on Israel — but were also exposed to encirclement. When, as was soon expected, Britain finally withdrew troops from the Canal Zone, Egypt's invasion road would be unimpeded, but Israel, too, could strike without an intervening barrier of British troops. The mounting pressure of Arab raids from Jordan and Gaza deep into Israel was now virtually acknowledged as an Egyptian-sponsored project, amid open boasting of the feats of the fedayin. Hammarskjold's renegotiated cease fire in April 1956 was followed by stepped-up fedayin raids.

The disparity in armaments remained unchanged. Eden responded to this situation with proposals that Israel cede land to the Arabs. A modest breakthrough in regard to Western arms for Israel, through agreement for French and Canadian supplies of fighter planes, occurred only in the beginning of 1956. Even then Dulles advised Israel to seek its security in the UN rather than by arming itself.[13] The Western powers still concentrated on wooing Egypt with discussions of arms sales and loans for the proposed Aswan Dam. But by the spring of 1956, Egyptian tactics had irritated Dulles to the point of terminating these negotiations. Nasser then replied by the seizure of the Suez Canal.

By September, Israel staff officers were alerted to the possibility of a regional war upon receiving information of a Franco-British decision to retake the canal by force. Accelerated pilot training programs were introduced in order to absorb speedily the increased delivery of jet aircraft. As for Arab military planning, it went forward quite publicly. English-sponsored plans to post Iraqi troops in Jordan produced a disconcerting result after a bitter parliamentary election campaign in October: Jordan now decided to join a joint Egyptian-Syrian military command. By this time Israeli plans to wipe out the fedayin in Gaza and end the blockade in the Tiran Straits had been coordinated with the French and, rather distantly and distrustfully, with the British.

On October 29, the five-day war began.[14]

The Israeli attack on Egyptian army concentrations and raiders' bases threatening its borders was the occasion for an Anglo-French move to seize the Suez Canal. The differences in the military methods and results of the two campaigns are familiar and need not detain us. What should be noted, however, are the differences in the avowed objectives of the two campaigns and in the spirit in which the Israeli public, on the one hand, as compared with the French and British publics, on the other, received the announcement of the actions taken and the consequences which were then incurred.

The Israelis did not, of course, go through any such formal procedure as Mr. Hammarskjold had virtually suggested in order to obtain advance approval from the Security Council for declaring the armistice with Egypt inoperative and asserting their rights to self-defense under Article 51 of the UN Charter. The Sinai operation was kept a close secret not only from the outside world but from members of the government as well as the public of Israel until the last possible moment in order to ensure its success. But no one was left in any doubt as to the grounds on which Israel asserted its rights of self-defense and the real reasons why it resorted to them. In launching its offensive Israel indicated that the Armistice with Egypt had died because of its ineffectiveness, and that the Jews intended to defend their security by destroying the military threat which Egypt had assembled against them in Sinai and in Gaza.[15]

The French and British, on the other hand — in particular, the latter — did not say they were acting against the Egyptians at all or in self-defense against the threat to their security inherent in the nationalization of the Suez Canal. They claimed that they were acting under the Tripartite Declaration, and that their intervention was a response not to the internationalization of the canal but to the Israeli campaign into Sinai. It was a legal attitude which not only betrayed its unreality to the most superficial observer but recoiled against the Anglo-French planners with disastrous effect. For, the third party to the Tripartite Declaration, the United States, came out in flat opposition to the Franco-British intervention, as to the Israeli offensive which had served as its pretext.[16]

While the nature and intensity of the public response to the collapse of the Suez campaign and to the repercussions in the UN differed in France and Britain, in neither country did the government enjoy the solid support of the public. Such solidarity as was displayed quite often came as a reaction of resentment against the United States for turning against its allies. But the direct response to the government's policy, in both cases, was critical and antagonistic, on balance. This was true both in the first phase, of Anglo-French intervention, and in the second phase, of Anglo-French withdrawal under UN pressure. In Israel, on the other hand, the government enjoyed the solid support of the public, which showed enthusiasm for the successes of the military offensive and high morale and confidence in the government in its slow, negotiated withdrawal in the face of UN pressure. Of all the governments which attacked Egypt in the fall of 1956, only the Israeli government emerged from the crisis and its aftermath strengthened rather than weakened in its hold on the popular consensus.[17]

The Israelis, moreover, held their ground in the face of UN pressure longer and with more conviction than the British or the French, and consequently at much greater risk of penalties both through international action and the unilateral action of one or another great power. The British and French suffered severe penalties — as did the rest of Western Europe — through the blockage of the Suez Canal, but America did nothing to add to their difficulties. Indeed, it sought to ease them by arranging for alternative supplies of oil. Against Israel — as against Egypt for its earlier offenses — the United States took financial measures by blocking funds at once. Russia for its part cancelled the shipments of oil by which it paid for its large-scale purchases of Israelian citrus fruits. The insistence by Israel that its withdrawal behind its frontiers must not result in a restoration of the *status quo ante*, and its demand for new and effective assurances of security before it would comply with the UN order to retire, led the American Secretary of State to threaten that the sanctions provided in the UN Charter would be imposed. The outcry against this statement in the United States, leading to a softening of the American attitude, helped no less to end the crisis than did Israel's decision to withdraw on the basis not of "guarantees" but of "assumptions" that its frontiers would be kept at peace and its gateway to the Red Sea kept open by UN action.[18]

It was noted as a mark of confidence in its leaders that the Israeli public accepted quietly the final decision to withdraw from Sinai and from the Gaza strip. The obvious implication is that the Israeli public was believed ready to face the imposition of sanctions which would have threatened the shaky Israeli economy with collapse and confronted the Israeli public with an austerity regime that might bring the whole country as close to the starvation level as Jerusalem had been during the siege of 1948. The policy the Israel government followed, until a compromise between its own position and the position of leading UN powers broke the crisis at the last minute, was possible only because it could count on the solid support of the Israelian consensus. The people was ready to back the government to the point of all-or-nothing risks in which Israel would withstand not only the Arab and Moslem world, or the ruthless Soviet bloc, but even the invocation of extreme sanctions against it by Western powers through the UN — closing a circle of worldwide hostility to the Jewish state.

II

If boundaries were the measure, Israel emerged from the 1956 Sinai campaign no better off than before it. As Jordan, Syria, and Lebanon were not involved, relations remained as difficult (or, in the case of Lebanon, as smooth) as before. Under pressure, Israeli troops had withdrawn behind the old Israeli-Egyptian armistice demarcation line. In Gaza, Israel's expectations regarding the "understandings" and "assumptions" of its withdrawal were speedily disregarded. Egyptian military and civil personnel were rushed in when Israel left instead of the UN administrators who were to have been installed, pending a peace settlement. After this object leson, Israel firmly resisted a repetition at the more strategic location of Sharm el-Sheikh, which commands the Tiran Straits entrance to the Gulf of Akaba. Ben-Gurion refused to be satisfied with American promises to "exercise the right of free passage" through the Straits and "to join with others to secure general recognition of this right"; nor was he content with President Eisenhower's public statement of assurance:

We should not assume that, if Israel withdraws, Egypt will prevent Israel shipping from using the Suez Canal or the Gulf of Aqaba. If, unhappily, Egypt does hereafter violate the Armistice Agreement or other international obligations, then this should be dealt with firmly by the society of nations.

Israel waited until, late in March, Hammarskjold obtained Nasser's tacit agreement to have a contingent of the UN Emergency Force posted in Sharm el-Sheikh. In this matter, Israel relied on a privately recorded interpretation by Secretary General Hammarskjold that an Egyptian order to remove the UN force before the "completion of [its] tasks" would entail an immediate referral of the question to the General Assembly.[19]

In spite of a clear diplomatic defeat, Israel then enjoyed ten years undisturbed by the border belligerency of its major and most dangerous foe, Egypt. The Negev, along the Sinai-Gaza frontier, was quiet, busy with civilian development. The continuing Suez blockade could be ignored because traffic flowed freely to and from Akaba. While the UN Emergency Force was sketchily represented by troops in Gaza and Sharm el-Sheikh and by a light patrol along the Negev-Sinai line, no one — certainly not Israel — considered the Emergency Force a major factor in securing the border peace. Its chief function was to give the Egyptians an excuse for not reopening hostilities at a time when they felt unprepared. Israeli analysts explained this restraint in terms of the strategic calculations of Egypt herself and, above all, those of the major world powers. On such grounds they, in common with most expert commentators in the West, expected the Israeli-Egyptian conflict to remain a relatively stable form of the cold war, Middle Eastern style.[20]

The global cold war during this period increasingly spread in the Eastern Mediterranean even at times of developing détente in other matters. As a result of this, and also of a chain of political upheavals in the neighboring countries which Israel's victory provoked in 1956, as in 1948, the Arab world began to divide along lines of cleavage related to the global power struggle. In these circumstances Israel, openly written off as a liability and a class enemy by Russia by 1952 but having proven its substantial strategic significance in the Sinai campaign, began to figure more seriously in Western calculations.

The special Franco-Israeli understanding initiated by the 1956 war was fostered by both sides, even after De Gaulle began in the 1960's to reestablish the French position among the Arabs. During the 1958 crisis which was touched off by the union between Syria and Egypt (and, remotely, Yemen) and exploded in the Iraqi coup and Lebanese rebellion, Britain and the United States relied on tacit Israeli cooperation in restoring stability to their spheres of concern and interest in Jordan and Lebanon. A moderate arms supply to Israel, paralleled by efforts to strengthen the defensive capacity of the Western-oriented Arab states, Jordan and Saudi Arabia, became part of American policy.[21]

After 1956 it was clear that to allow Israel to be driven to the point of desperation simply meant tempting the embattled nation to take desperate measures. A limited arms supply to Israel recommended itself as a prudent balancing operation, in view of the lavish, politically motivated Soviet rearming of the left-leaning Arabs. It might permit the Israelis to observe growing Arab strength in relative calm, and give their Western suppliers levers of influence wherewith to enforce patience on the military planners in Tel Aviv. Also, if Israel's strength were known to be keeping pace with Arab rearmament, at least in quality, this in turn might inhibit the Arab chiefs from rash revanchist adventures.

All this assumed a tacit agreement by the Russians to follow a similar policy vis-à-vis their clients in Cairo and Damascus. To anxious and impatient demands from Jerusalem for more or better supplies, Washington might reply that Israel was better prepared than it pretended to meet the Arab threat, and, in any case, its best ultimate defense was the Sixth Fleet stationed in the Mediterranean. Russia, for its part, could contribute to avoidance of a greater power clash by cautioning the Egyptians and Syrians not to suppose they were ready to risk actions that Israel would be bound to view as a *casus belli*.[22]

Israel might not agree with the Western analyses offered in justification when its applications to buy arms were rejected. It did, however, accept the prevailing view that Russia, on the whole, was a cautious and restraining influence in Egypt, and did not intend to be involved in a major clash. Notwithstanding Bulganin's brutal threats in 1956, the Israelis assumed that Russia was not interested in liquidating the Jewish state. It was a generally accepted theory that Moscow considered Israel's existence, and Arab resentment of it, to be valuable assets in its campaign to penetrate West Asian and African areas. For this reason among others, Israeli strategists believed in the spring of 1967 that Egypt would continue to avoid acts that would predictably lead to war.[23]

Leftist Syria from the beginning was the one element of high uncertainty in such calculations; and in the end it confounded them completely. Syria demanded immediate, unconditional militancy against Israel, particularly from the Egyptians. Entrenched on heights overlooking the Israelian border, it launched continual bombardments and pinprick raids upon the exposed Jewish farmers, fishermen, and military posts below.

At this point Israeli reprisals, which followed on a mounting scale, could no longer be planned within the confines of a purely local strategy. Syria provided at Latakia one of the intended bases for the fleet Russia was concentrating in the Mediterranean to challenge the Americans. The Baathist regime, turning increasingly leftist, was regarded by the Russians as a near-socialist fraternal party and thus implicitly taken under the wing of Soviet protection.

Long before the Czechoslovak crisis of 1968, which produced the formal statement of a Soviet-style Monroe Doctrine, guaranteeing to maintain by force approved regimes in the "Socialist Commonwealth," Israel was given to understand that pressures likely to collapse the unstable Damascus government would not be tolerated. Israeli reprisals against persistent Syrian provocations were interpreted as part of an imperialist scheme to roll back the proletarian revolution: an interpretation echoed, among others, by Marshal Tito. In October 1966, following a series of incidents on the Syrian frontier, Russia adopted a tactic that it used repeatedly thereafter. Refusing to listen to Israeli denials, or to UN confirmations that the charges were unfounded, Soviet sources reported nonexistent troop concentrations against Syria and warned of an allegedly imminent Israeli invasion. In November, after a raid from the Jordan side, Israel reacted swiftly and massively with an attack on the Jordanian village of Samua. There seemed to be an implied message for the Russians: Israel's counter-attacks were not part of the cold-war strategy of any global power, but independent acts of self-defense. They were applied no less swiftly and forcefully against clients of Washington, when they threatened Israel's security, than against Moscow's clients. On the other hand, Israeli leaders thereafter intimated on several occasions that they would hardly regret it if the Baathist regime were to fall, and they obviously had no intention of withholding the penalty of reprisals in order to prop up Damascus.[24]

By the spring of 1967, it appeared that Russia felt it urgently necessary to save the Syrians from the consequences of their own policy. A Russian mission to Cairo at the end of March probably produced agreement to activate the mutual defense pact concluded in November 1966 between Syria and Egypt and thus transfer the responsibility for confronting Israel to Egypt. In May, for the third time in less than a year, Russia again made unfounded charges of Israeli mobilization against Syria. But this time a loudly publicized, open Egyptian troop mobilization took place, while calm descended on the Israel-Syrian lines.[25]

What happened then, according to most observers of the incredible scene, was not part of a strategic scenario favored by Moscow. For several years, Nasser had been observing the puzzling behavior of an Israeli government no longer headed by Ben-Gurion. Now, when pushed into a corner by Russia and his Arab allies, he decided to gamble — and for big stakes. He peremptorily ordered the UN Emergency Force to leave Sinai and Gaza, posted his troops in offensive positions in Sinai, and then, have occupied Sharm el-Sheikh, he declared the Tiran Straits blockaded. These acts deliberately produced the conditions long known to be regarded by Israel as a *casus belli*. Openly referring to this, Nasser invited Israel to fight; in which case, he promised his exultant subjects, he would proceed to wipe out the Jewish state.[26]

In all the subsequent developments, which have been the subject of much controversy among analysts, one thing at any rate was immediately clear: those "understandings" and "assumptions" upon which Israel finally withdrew its troops from Sinai and Gaza were quite valueless and virtually without effect.

The shield of the UN Emergency Force was removed at Nasser's instant demand. Hammarskjold's interpretation of his agreement with Nasser (which, UN circles noted, was not contained in their official files) was not applied by U Thant in order to delay the impending bloodshed. Of the nations supplying troops to the Emergency Force,

India and Yugoslavia, who provided half the strength as well as the Indian UNEF commander, were plainly determined to comply immediately with Nasser's orders, whether or not the question were referred to the General Assembly. As for the American undertaking to exercise the right of free passage in the Tiran Straits, or to have the matter "dealt with firmly by the society of nations," it was handled in a dilatory way that looked very much like Dulles' maneuvers of 1956, following the nationalization of the Suez Canal. The Israeli public, at any rate, regarded it as a mere device to evade by diplomatic verbiage the need to take any action at all. Nor did Israeli leaders see how any steps belatedly taken on this issue could remove the threats being mounted on the land frontiers against the Jewish state. By this time the French attitude was a new danger. De Gaulle vied with Moscow in seeking a solution of the crisis by the global powers, including, of course, himself. Such a procedure would necessarily begin by freezing a *status quo* defined by Nasser's newly established stranglehold on Israel's lifelines.[27]

The conflict was now truly irrepressible — unless Israel had been inclined to suicidal meekness. The Israeli public's sense of extreme peril (shared by spectators the world over, as they witnessed with rapt concern the impending possible obliteration of a second major Jewish community within a single generation) now produced a drastic internal political change. On May 30, King Hussein had suddenly flown to Cairo and signed a mutual defense pact with Egypt; on the next day Iraqi troops had moved into Jordan; and meanwhile the Egyptians steadily advanced their border positions. Taut with the suspense of their own mobilization and fretful at the dubious course of diplomatic delay, the Israelis applied party pressure and organized demonstrations in order to force the majority coalition to expand to a broadly national government. They also compelled the recall of Moshe Dayan (1915–   ), the victorious leader of 1956, who was now named Minister of Defense. On June 4, Iraq too joined the Egyptian-Syrian-Jordanian military compact. But on June 5 Israel began the six-day offensive that nullified all such Arab preparations on each of its embattled frontiers.[28]

This was a war fought under far different circumstances from the 1956 campaign. Israel now fought alone. The Arabs, on the other hand, fought together: Egypt, Syria, and (in spite of persistent Israeli overtures urging Hussein to stay out and thus preserve his realm) Jordan all were fully and directly engaged, while Iraqi troops, too, took a hand in the fighting. In one of the more comic interludes of the swift conflict, a much publicized Algerian airborne contingent failed to appear while there was still a war. The total defeat of all the Arab states, taken together, by Israel, completely on its own — a repetition of the 1948 struggle — was so violent a blow to the legends by which those regimes lived that, as is notorious, stories of American airstrikes were put about by Nasser and Hussein in order to explain it away. But even those defenses against reality had to be abandoned: the Arabs were compelled to withdraw these accusations in the face of stiff and indignant American reactions.

It appeared that Israel now held the position from which, since the 1930's, its leaders had assumed the Arabs might be brought to make peace with a viable Jewish state. Now, if never before, it should be obvious that Israel was a fact too firmly established for the Arabs to eliminate or overthrow. But the Arabs still had a reserve weapon: their overwhelming advantage in the diplomatic battles that must follow. Israelis were all too aware of this fact. They awaited with grim anticipation the coming struggle.

Apart from the decisiveness of their tactical victory, the Israelis had a further advantage, gained in the war, which they meant to use in the bargaining. They now held territory which totally altered the strategic position. Israeli towns and villages formerly exposed to attack across the border were now, with the exception of a small bloc at the northwest frontier of Jordan, protected by broad buffer zones under Israeli control. Damascus, Amman, and even Cairo, on the other hand, were now within striking distance of Israeli forces on the Golan heights, the Jordan river, and the Suez Canal. Israel at once indicated its willingness to trade back portions of these military gains for peace treaties directly negotiated with the Arabs which would establish new, permanent, and secure political boundaries between the several neighboring states.

The UN debate started with an Israelian success of a negative sort. The only action which could be taken, after several efforts both in the Security Council and the General Assembly, was the unanimous adoption of a British-sponsored compromise resolution by the Security Council on November 22, 1967.[29] This provided in deliberately vague terms for the following:

i) Withdrawal of Israeli forces from territories of recent conflict;
ii) Termination of all claims or states of belligerency and respect for and acknowledgment of the sovereignty, territorial integrity, and political independence of every state in the area and their right to live in peace within secure and recognized boundaries, free from threats of acts of force.

A special representative was to be designated by the Secretary General "to establish and maintain contacts with the states concerned in order to promote agreement and assist efforts to achieve a peaceful and accepted settlement."

A Swedish diplomat, Gunnar Jarring, was named UN special representative and began a series of contacts with Israel and with Jordan and Egypt; Syria and Iraq had rejected the UN resolution as well as the special representative designated under its terms. It was immediately obvious that a struggle would ensue over the meaning of the UN resolution which served as Jarring's terms of reference. Israel read it to mean endorsement of their long-standing demand for direct negotiations leading to peace treaties with the Arabs, whereupon Israel would be ready to withdraw from "territories of recent conflict" to "secure and recognized boundaries." The Arabs read it as meaning first and foremost the "withdrawal of Israeli forces from [all the] territories of recent conflict"; upon which they would be prepared to renounce "claims of belligerency" and even, perhaps, respect Israel's existence "within secure and recognized boundaries." But under a position defined at a conference in Khartoum, they would not recognize Israel's legitimacy, sign peace treaties, or negotiate directly with the Jewish state. They took the Security Council resolution to represent a decision defining terms which must be imposed forcibly upon the parties by the major powers, and not merely a decision in favor of "efforts to achieve a peaceful and accepted settlement."

No one in Israel was under any illusion about the way in which the true meaning of the UN resolution would, in the end, be determined. Preponderant power, not intrinsic meaning, would decide whether the Arab or Israeli interpretation would prevail. Since 1952, the Israeli insistence on direct peace talks with the Arabs, hardly an extravagant demand between fellow members of an international peace-seeking body, had been treated as an impracticable, extremist position. Whenever advanced by Israel it was immediately discounted — among others, by the American UN mission — as a mere bargaining move.[30]

The Arab demand, as a minimum initial step, for total, unconditional Israeli withdrawal from all territories it had gained in 1967 and for "no recognition, no negotiation, and no peace treaty" but only a declaration of nonbelligerency by the Arabs, was never treated by the powers as quite so unreasonable as they appeared to find the demand for direct talks between the foes. There was not enough support for the Arab position to gain it a two-thirds majority in the UN in spite of insistent Soviet pressure. But Western opposition to it was nonetheless sharply eroded. France, at least, took up a new line distinctly opposed, if not hostile to Israel. A one-sided embargo against delivery of planes ordered and paid for by Israel was continued. France pressed particularly for a great power settlement imposed by agreement between the United States, Russia, Britain, and France instead of an agreement negotiated by the recent combatants. The French concern was primarily, and quite blatantly, for the access of *grandeur* it would enjoy as a result of playing such a role. The British followed rather reservedly in the wake of the United States. America alone, of the great powers, plainly stated that Israel was entitled to an agreement on recognized and secure frontiers and could not be expected simply to retreat to the *status quo ante* June 5, 1967, before this object was achieved or even negotiated about. But no Israeli, remembering the record of American inconstancy in supporting Israel, could have great confidence that there would not be another turn of policy away from Israel's position and toward the Arab line.[31]

The only secure reliance of Israel, apart from the sympathy of Jews abroad, was in the determination of its own citizens to resist all pressures. This, however, was a force that foreign powers had learned to rate at a high value. Some, to whose interests Israel's existence and fitness seemed adverse, would have to consider very carefully the cost of eliminating this hindrance. Some, inconvenienced in certain aspects, were significantly compensated in other ways by Israel's ability and resolve to hold its own ground. The pressures they might use against Israel in order to reestablish their credentials as governments well disposed toward Arabs were often quite ambiguous. They sometimes seemed to rely on Israel's determination to defend its vital interests even against its friends, when the interest of such friends caused them to disregard dangers to the Jewish state.

The character of the Jewish state and the way in which it conceives its own sovereignty today must be understood in the light of the position taken by Israel in these crises. The idea of a Jewish state, as we have seen, was susceptible of all kinds of restrictions, modifications, or deferments of sovereignty so long as the central purpose and myth image of auto-Emancipation was served, or at least not blocked by them. But to seek to impose such restrictions as would deny this central purpose provoked a resistance, and an insistence on the prerogatives of sovereignty, which was as fierce as it was determined.

In the exercise of its sovereignty in the face of such challenges, Israel was prepared to risk all extremities and to stake its very existence on an all-or-nothing choice. Israel, moreover, was quite self-conscious about its own willingness to resist to the uttermost extreme. It considered this not merely a last resort to which it might be driven, but an effective weapon which might be used by policy. Such an attitude is not unexampled, of course, for countries like Japan or Russia have also considered it a calculable strategic or tactical advantage that the kind of morale, or the kind of objective circumstances, were to be found on their side which would make their people risk more or endure more than would the enemy. The Israeli version of this doctrine — almost a military principle — is the maxim *Ein breira:* "We have no choice." Israel is conceived as the last stand of the Jewish people, for the Hitler era had shown they had no safety they could rely on elsewhere. The Hitler era had also taught the Jews the lesson that survival can be bought in some situations only by seemingly suicidal resistance. And while the Jewish state arose out of rebellion against the Jewish situation in the Diaspora, the prospect of having to resist, even in Israel, an entire world made the Israelis see the continuity of their own situation and their own tactics with those of the Exile. In a formula used repeatedly at the time of the Sinai campaign, Mrs. Meir, Israel's Foreign Secretary, said that the Jews had survived in the Exile by asserting their right to survive even when it was denied by all others; and, if necessary, they would survive as a sovereign state in Israel by asserting their sovereign freedom even when it was denied by all others.[32]

To live by such desperate expedients is, of course, not a positive ideal possible for any people. For a small and relatively weak nation like Israel, it is a reliable tactical model only on condition that it is not opposed by a great power capable of acting with utter ruthlessness. The suicidal determination of Israel could serve them against the Arabs only because, given Arab weakness, it made them the stronger party. It could not serve them in the same way against Russia, as they are fully aware. Only the risk of involvement in a third World War which Israel could create for the Soviets by its resistance was a safety factor that the Israelis could count on during the Sinai campaign. In spite of threats of obliteration, Israel did not feel that atomic bombs would drop on Tel Aviv to enforce Russian demands: for this evoked the dread possibility of global atomic war. Nor could Israel's determination to resist pressure help the Israelis to stave off starvation or economic collapse, if UN sanctions were rigidly enforced against them. Only the belief that Western public opinion would not tolerate measures that clearly threatened the very survival of Israel could have given Israel the confidence that they could challenge such a test with a margin of safety.

The war of June 1967 left Israel confronting even greater risks, and even more firm in its resolution. There could no longer be full confidence that Russia would not directly intervene, and Israelis had to contemplate becoming the objects of a Soviet "Vietnamese" adventure. Nor could anyone in 1968 rely on long-continued Western forbearance from pressing Israel, let alone expect reliable support. But the new strategic position and, above all, the demonstrated strength of Israel, anchored in the total commitment and disciplined ingenuity of its people, made its exercise of sovereignty a more formidable weapon than ever before.

No government weak in the exercise and defense of sovereignty would be permitted by the people of Israel to stand. But a government that had proved its firmness could also win the Israeli public for concessions to outer pressure which Israel's interests made essential and possible. For if Israel is ready to take an incredibly rigid and, it may seem, a suicidally risky stand in defense of its right to exist on terms it considers as right and just, it also has accepted recognition of its demands in the vaguest, most noncommittal and informal of terms. The "assumptions" on which Israel withdrew from Sinai in 1957 were, in fact, effective for a decade in securing its objective of peaceful conditions on the Egyptian frontier and free access to the Red Sea. Their legal quality, however, was of the most tenuous nature; and they collapsed as soon as Nasser actively challenged them.

The creation of a stabler balance and of a legal relationship of peace would require recognizing the customary restrictions on sovereignty which make possible the modicum of order that exists in normal relations between peoples. To accept this kind of restriction upon sovereignty — even in unusual degree — has always been compatible with the idea of the Jewish state. To accept a reciprocal relationship of the Jewish state and the Arab states respecting these limits on sovereignty would obviously be welcomed by Israel as a crowning recognition of its sovereign existence.

BIBLIOGRAPHY

NOTES

INDEX

BIBLIOGRAPHY

The purpose of this bibliography is not to provide a comprehensive guide to the literature on the idea of the Jewish state, but to supplement the abbreviated references in the notes with necessary bibliographical details. Where the notes are sufficiently detailed to identify the source cited, no further information is given here.

Accordingly, the records of the proceedings of continuing public and semipublic bodies, such as the United Nations General Assembly or the Zionist Congress, are not here listed. Similarly, encyclopedias and periodicals are not listed, nor are particular articles in such sources.

Aaronsohn, Alexander. *With the Turks in Palestine*. Boston: Houghton Mifflin, 1916.

Adamow, E. A., ed. *Die Europaeischen Maechte und die Tuerkei waehrend des Weltkrieges*. 5 vols. Dresden: C. Reisner, 1930–1932.

Adler, Cyrus. *Lectures, Selected Papers, Addresses*. Philadelphia: privately printed, 1933.

Adler, Cyrus and Aaron M. Margalith. *With Firmness in the Right: American Diplomatic Action Affecting Jews, 1840–1945*. New York: American Jewish Committee, 1946.

Agus, Jacob B. *Guideposts in Modern Judaism*. New York: Bloch, 1954.

Ahad Ha'am (Asher Ginzberg). *Al Parashat Drakhim*. 4 vols. Berlin: Juedischer Verlag, 1930.

————— *Igrot Ahad Ha'am*. 6 vols. Tel-Aviv: Yavne, 1923–1925.

————— *Selected Essays* (tr. Leon Simon). Philadelphia: Jewish Publication Society, 1912.

————— *Ten Essays on Zionism and Judaism* (tr. Leon Simon). London: G. Routledge, 1922.

Alcalay, Judah and Zvi Hirsch Kalischer. *Rabbi Yehuda Alkalay — Rabbi Tz'vi Hirsh Kalisher, Mivhar Kitveihem*. G. Kressel, ed. Tel-Aviv: Sifriat "Shorashim," 1945.

Alliance Israélite Universelle. *L'Alliance Israélite Universelle, 1860–1895*. Paris: Siège de la Société [1895 ?].

American Council for Judaism. *An Approach to an American Judaism*. n.p., 1958.

————— *The President's Annual Report . . . April 27, 1956*. New York, n.d.

————— *This is the Council* (statement by Lessing J. Rosenwald). n.p., n.d.

American Jewish Committee. *To the Counsellors of Peace, Recommendations of the American Jewish Committee*. New York, 1945.

——— *Toward Peace and Equity; Recommendations of the American Jewish Committee*. New York, 1946.

Andrews, Fannie Fern. *The Holy Land under the Mandate*. 2 vols. Boston and New York: Houghton Mifflin, 1931.

Antonius, George. *The Arab Awakening*. Philadelphia: Lippincott, 1939.

Arlosoroff, Hayim. *Yoman Yerushalayim*. n.p.: Mapai, 1948/1949.

Babbitt, Irving. *Rousseau and Romanticism*. New York: Meridian, 1955.

Baer, Yitzhak Fritz. *Galut*. New York: Schocken, 1947.

Barer, Shlomo. *The Magic Carpet*. London: Secker and Warburg, 1952.

Barkay, R. M. *The Public Sector Accounts of Israel, 1948/49–1954/55*. 2 vols. Jerusalem: Falk Project and Central Bureau of Statistics, 1957.

Baron, Salo W. *The Jewish Community*. 2 vols. Philadelpiha: Jewish Publication Society, 1957.

Bar-Yaacov, Nissim. *The Israel-Syrian Armistice: Problems of Implementation, 1949–1966*. Jerusalem: Magnes Press, 1967.

Begin, Menahem. *The Revolt* (tr. Samuel Katz; ed. Ivan M. Greenberg). New York: Schuman, 1951.

Bein, Alex. *The Return to the Soil*. Jerusalem: Youth and Hechalutz Department, Zionist Organization, 1952.

——— *Theodore Herzl* (tr. Maurice Samuel). Philadelphia: Jewish Publication Society, 1940.

Belkind, Israel. *Di Ershte Shrit fun Yishuv Erets-Yisroel*. 2 vols. New York: "Hame'ir", 1917–1918.

Ben-Gurion, David. *Ba-Ma'arakha*. Vol. III. Tel Aviv: Mapai, 1947/1948.

——— *L'Siyum Perek*. Tel Aviv: Ayanot, 1953/54.

——— *P'gishot im Manhigim Arvi'im*. Tel Aviv: Am Oved, 1967.

Ben-Zvi, Yitzhak. *Eretz-Israel v'Yishuva bi-Y'mei ha-Shilton ha-Ottomani*. Jerusalem: Mosad Bialik, 1955.

Bentwich, Norman. *Israel*. New York: McGraw-Hill. 1952.

Bericht ueber die Konferenz der Amerikanischen Nichtzionisten ueber die Frage der Jewish Agency fuer Palaestina. Jerusalem: Keren Hayesod, 1929.

Bernadotte, Count Folke. *To Jerusalem* (tr. Joan Bulman). London: Hodder and Stoughton, 1951.

Bialik, Hayyim Nahman. *Complete Poetic Works*. Vol. I (tr. from Hebrew, ed. Israel Efros). New York: Histadruth Ivrith, 1948.

Bieber, Hugo and Moses Hadas. *Heinrich Heine: A Biographical Anthology*. Philadelphia: Jewish Publication Society, 1956.

Bodenheimer, Hannah. *Toldot Tokhnit Bazel*. Jerusalem [1947].

Boehm, Adolf. *Die Zionistiche Bewegung*. 2 vols. Berlin: Juedischer Verlag. 1935–1937.

Bonar, Andrew A. and Robert M. M'Cheyne. *Narrative of a Mission of Inquiry to the Jews from the Church of Scotland in 1839*. Phildelphia: Presbyterian Board of Publication [1843].

Bonsal, Stephen. *Suitors and Suppliants: The Little Nations at Versailles*. New York: Prentice-Hall, 1946.

Borochov, Ber. *Nationalism and the Class Struggle*. New York: Poale Zion-Zeire Zion, 1937.

——— *Poale-Zion Shriftn*. 2 vols. New York: Poale Zion Organization, 1920.

Brenner, J. H. *K'tavim*. 3 vols. Tel Aviv: Am Oved, 1946–1950.

Breuer, Isaac. *The Jewish National Home* (tr. Miriam Aumann). Frankfurt a.M.: J. Kauffmann, 1926.

—————— *Messiasspuren.* Frankfurt a.M.: R. L. Hammon, 1918.

—————— *Der Neue Kusari: Ein Weg zum Judentum.* Frankfurt a.M.: Verlag der Rabbiner-Hirsch Gesellschaft, 1934.

Buber, Martin. *Israel and Palestine: The History of an Idea* (tr. S. Godman). New York: Farrar, Strauss, and Young, 1952.

Burstein Moshe. *Self-Government of the Jews in Palestine since 1900.* Tel-Aviv, 1934.

Byrnes, Robert Francis. *Antisemitism in Modern France.* New Brunswick, N.J.: Rutgers University Press, 1950.

Cahan, Abraham. *Bletter fun Mein Leben.* 5 vols. New York: "Forverts" Association, 1926–1931.

Campbell, John C. *Defense of the Middle East: Problems of American Policy.* New York: Praeger, 1960.

Chouraqui, André. *Les Juifs d'Afrique du Nord.* Paris: Presses Universitaires de France, 1952.

Cohen, Aaron. *Israel v'ha-Olam ha'Aravi.* Merhavia: Sifriat Poalim, 1964.

Cohen, Israel. *Zionist Work in Palestine.* London: T. F. Unwin, 1911.

Conjoint Foreign Committee of the Jewish Board of Deputies and the Anglo-Jewish Association. *Correspondence with His Majesty's Government Respecting the Eventual Peace Negotiations.* London, 1917.

Dayan, Moshe. *Diary of the Sinai Campaign.* New York: Schocken, 1967.

De Haas, Jacob. *History of Palestine.* New York: Macmillan, 1934.

—————— *Louis D. Brandeis.* New York: Bloch, 1929.

Dinaburg, Ben-Zion. *Sefer ha-Zionut.* Vol. I, bk. 1. Tel-Aviv: Mosad Bialik, 1938.

Doniger, Sundel, ed. *A Zionist Primer.* New York: Young Judea, 1917.

Draper, Theodore. *Israel and World Politics: Roots of the Third Arab-Israeli War.* New York: Viking, 1968.

Druyanow, A. *Pinsker u-Z'mano.* Jerusalem: R. Mass, 1953.

Dubnow, S. M. *Die Neueste Geschichte des Juedischen Volkes, 1789–1914.* 3 vols. (Alexander Eliasberg tr. vols. I and II, Elias Hurwicz, tr. vol. III). Berlin: Juedischer Verlag, 1920–1923.

Dugdale, Blanche E. C. *Arthur James Balfour.* 2 vols. London: Hutchinson, 1936.

Esco Foundation for Palestine, Inc. *Palestine: A Study of Jewish, Arab, and British Policies.* 2 vols. New Haven: Yale University Press, 1947.

Essays in Honour of the Very Rev. Dr. J. H. Hertz. London: E. Goldston, 1944.

Eytan, Walter. *The First Ten Years: A Diplomatic History of Israel.* New York: Simon and Schuster, 1958.

Finer, Herman. *Dulles over Suez: The Theory and Practice of His Diplomacy.* Chicago: Quadrangle Books, 1964.

Forster, Arnold and B. R. Epstein. *Cross-Currents.* New York: Doubleday, 1956.

Franco, Moise. *Essai sur l'Histoire des Israélites de l'Empire Ottoman depuis les Origines jusqu'à Nos Jours.* Paris: A. Durlacher, 1897.

Frankenstein, Ernst. *Justice for My People.* New York: Dial, 1944.

Friedlaender, Fritz. *Das Leben Gabriel Riessers.* Berlin: Philo-verlag, 1926.

Frischwasser-Ra'anan, H. F. *The Frontiers of a Nation*. London: Batchworth Press, 1955.

Frumkin, A. L. and Eliezer Rivlin. *Toldot Hakhmei Yerushalayim*. 3 vols. Jerusalem: "Darom," 1928–1930.

Galanté, Abraham. *Turcs et Juifs: Etude Historique, Politique*. Stamboul: Haim, Rozio, 1932.

Gelber, Nathan Michael. *Hatzharat Balfour v-Toldoteha*. Jerusalem: Zionist Executive, 1939.

────── *Zur Vorgeschichte des Zionismus; Judenstaatsprojekte in den Jahren 1695–1845*. Wien: Phaidon-verlag, 1927.

Goodman, Paul. *Zionism in England: English Zionist Federation, 1899–1929*. London: English Zionist Federation, 1929.

Goodman, Paul and Arthur D. Lewis. *Zionism: Problems and Views*. London: T. F. Unwin, 1916.

Gordon, Aaron David. *Kitvei A. D. Gordon*. 5 vols. Tel Aviv: Ha-Poel ha-Tza'ir, 1925–1929.

Gordon, Judah Leib. *Kol Shirei Judah Leib Gordon*. 2 vols. St. Petersburg: Agudat-Anashim Ohavei S'fat Ever, 1884.

Glick, Edward B. *Latin America and the Palestine Problem*. New York: Theodor Herzl Foundation, 1958.

Graetz, Heinrich. *History of the Jews*. 6 vols. Philadelphia: Jewish Publication Society, 1891–1898.

Granott, Abraham. *Agrarian Reform and the Record of Israel*. London: Eyre and Spottiswood, 1956.

Graves, Richard Massie. *Experiment in Anarchy*. London: Gollancz, 1949.

(Great Britain, Parliamentary Papers). Cmd. 1499: *An Interim Report on the Civil Administration of Palestine during the Period 1st July, 1920–30th June, 1921*. London, 1921.

────── Cmd. 1540: *Palestine: Disturbances in May, 1921. Reports of the Commission of Inquiry with Correspondence Relating Thereto*. London, October 1921.

────── Cmd. 1700: *Correspondence with the Palestine Arab Delegation and the Zionist Organisation*. London, June 1922.

────── Cmd. 3530: *Report of the Commission on the Palestine Disturbances of August, 1929*. London, 1930.

────── Cmd. 5479: *Palestine: Royal Commission Report*. London, 1938.

────── Cmd. 5354: *Palestine: Partition Commission Report*. London, 1938.

────── Cmd. 6019: *Palestine: Statement of Policy*. London, May 17, 1939.

Haber, Julius. *The Odyssey of an American Zionist*. New York: Twayne, 1956.

Ha-Kinnus ha-Olami l'Mada'ei ha-Yahadut (Papers read in Jerusalem, July 6–10, 1947). Jerusalem: Hebrew University, 1952.

Hallez, Théophile. *Des Juifs en France*. Paris: chez G. A. Dentu, 1840.

Halperin, Samuel. *The Political World of American Zionism*. Detroit: Wayne State University Press, 1961.

Halpern, Ben. *The American Jew*. New York: Theodor Herzl Foundation, 1956.

Halpern, Israel. *Ha-Aliyot ha-Rishonot shel ha-Hasidim b'Eretz-Israel*. Jerusalem and Tel-Aviv: Schocken, 1946.

Handlin, Oscar. *Adventure in Freedom*. New York: McGraw-Hill, 1954.

Hanna, Paul L. *British Policy in Palestine.* Washington: American Council on Public Affairs, 1942.

Hecht, Ben. *A Child of the Century; An Autobiography.* New York: Simon and Schuster, 1954.

Henriques, R. D. Q. *A Hundred Hours to Suez.* New York: Viking, 1957.

Herberg, Will. *Protestant, Catholic, Jew; An Essay in American Religious Sociology.* New York: Doubleday, 1956.

Herzl, Theodor. *Tagebuecher.* 3 vols. Berlin: Juedischer Verlag, 1934.

—— *Theodor Herzl: A Portrait for this Age* (ed. Ludwig Lewisohn). Cleveland and New York: World Publishing, 1955.

Hess, Moses. *Moshe Hess u-V'nei Doro.* Tel-Aviv: Am Oved, 1947.

—— *Rome and Jerusalem* (tr. M. Waxman). New York: Bloch, 1918.

Hirsch, Samson R. *Neunzehn Briefe ueber Judentum,* 4te aufl. Frankfurt a.M.: Kauffmann, 1911.

Holdheim, Samuel. *Geschichte der Enstehung und Entwicklung der Juedischen Reformgemeinde in Berlin.* Berlin: J. Springer, 1857.

Hurewitz, J. C. *Diplomacy in the Near and Middle East.* Vol. II: *A Documentary Record, 1914–1956.* Princeton: D. Van Nostrand, 1956.

—— *The Struggle for Palestine.* New York: W. W. Norton, 1950.

Hyamson, Albert M. *The British Consulate in Jerusalem in Relation to the Jews of Palestine 1838–1914.* 2 vols. London [Jewish Historical Society], 1839–41.

—— *Palestine under the Mandate, 1920–1948.* London: Methuen, 1950.

Hyman, Joseph C. *The Activities of the Joint Distribution Committee (JDC): A Summary Report, March 22, 1931.* American Jewish Joint Distribution Committee: n.p., 1931.

Ihud Association of Palestine. *Palestine a Bi-National State.* New York, August 1948.

—— *Palestine — Divided or United? The Case for a Bi-National Palestine before the United Nations.* Jerusalem, 1947.

Israel and the United Nations (National Studies on International Organization). New York: Carnegie Endowment for International Peace, 1956.

Jabotinsky, Vladimir. *Ba-Derekh la-M'dina.* Jerusalem: Eri Jabotinsky, 1953.

—— *Ne'umim, 1905–1926.* Jerusalem: Eri Jabotinsky, 1947.

—— *Ne'umim, 1927–1940.* Jerusalem: Eri Jabotinsky, 1948.

Jaffe, Leib. *T'kufot,* Tel-Aviv: Masada, 1948.

Janowsky, Oscar I. *Jews and Minority Rights, 1898–1919.* New York: Columbia University Pres, 1933.

Jeffries, Joseph M. N. *Palestine: The Reality.* London: Longmans, Green, 1939.

Joint Palestine Survey Commission. *Report of the Joint Palestine Survey Commission.* New York, 1928.

—— *Reports of the Experts Submitted to the Joint Palestine Survey Commission.* Boston: Daniels, 1928.

Joseph, Bernard. *British Rule in Palestine.* Washington: Public Affairs Press, 1948.

Joseph, Samuel. *History of the Baron de Hirsch Fund.* Philadelphia: Jewish Publication Society, 1935.

Kaplan, Mordecai M. *A New Zionism.* New York: Theodor Herzl Foundation, 1955.

Kastein, Josef (Katzenstein, Julius). *Das Geschichtserlebnis des Juden.* Wien: Loewit, 1936.

———— *History and Destiny of the Jews.* New York: Viking, 1933.

Katznelson, Berl. *Kitvei Berl Katznelson.* 12 vols. Tel-Aviv: Mapai, 1946–1949.

Kaufman, Yehezkel. *Gola v'Nehar.* 2 vols. Tel-Aviv: D'vir, 1930.

Kedourie, Elie. *England and the Middle East.* London: Bowes, 1956.

Kisch, Frederick Hermann. *Palestine Diary.* London: Gollancz, 1938.

Kimche, Jon and David Kimche. *The Secret Roads.* New York: Farrar, Straus, Cudahy, 1955.

Kirk, George E. *A Short History of the Middle East from the Rise of Islam to Modern Times.* Washington: Public Affairs Press, 1949.

Klausner, Israel. *Hibbat Zion b'Rumania.* Jerusalem: Ha-Sifria ha-Zionit, 1958.

Kohler, Kaufmann. *Hebrew Union College and Other Addresses.* Cincinnati: Ark, 1916.

Krochmal, Nahman. *Kitvei Rabbi Nahman Krochmal* (ed. S. Rawidowicz). Berlin: Ayanot, 1924.

Kuk, A. I. *Eretz Hefetz, Imrot al Eretz-Israel u-Vinyana.* Jerusalem: "Darom," 1930.

Laqueur, Walter. *The Road to Jerusalem: The Origins of the Arab-Israeli Conflict, 1967.* New York: Macmillan, 1968.

Lassalle, Ferdinand. *Tagebuch.* Breslau: Schlesische Buchdruckerei, 1891.

Lawrence, T. E. *The Letters of T. E. Lawrence* (ed. David Garnett). New York: Doubleday, Doran, 1939.

Leroy-Beaulieu, Anatole, *L'empire des Tsars et les Russes.* 3 vols. Paris: Hachette, 1881–1889.

Lessing, Theodor. *Der Juedische Selbsthass.* Berlin: Juedischer Verlag [c. 1930].

Lestschinsky, Jacob. *Dos Natsionale Ponim fun Golus Yiddentum.* Buenos Aires: Kium, 1955.

Leven, Narcisse. *Cinquante ans d'histoire.* 2 vols. Paris: Librairie Felix Alcan, 1911–1920.

Levin, Harry. *Jerusalem Embattled.* London: Gollancz, 1950.

Lewin, Isaac. *Homer l'Sh'elat Hitkonenut v'Sidur ha-M'dina ha-Yehudit al pi ha-Tora.* New York: Research Institute for Post-War Problems of Religious Jewry, 1947.

Lichtheim, Richard. *Die Geschichte des Deutschen Zionismus.* Jerusalem: R. Mass [ca. 1954].

Lie, Trygve. *In the Cause of Peace.* New York: Macmillan, 1954.

Lilienblum, M. L. *Mivhar Ma'amarav.* Tel-Aviv: Sifriat Shorashim, 1943.

Lipman, Vivian D. *Social History of the Jews in England, 1850–1950.* London: Watts, 1954.

Liptzin, Solomon. *Eliakum Zunser.* New York: Behrman House, 1950.

Lloyd George, David. *The Truth about the Peace Treaties.* 2 vols. London: Gollancz, 1938.

Loeb, Isidore. *Biographie d'Albert Cohn.* Paris: Durlacher, 1878.

———— *La Situation des Israélites en Serbie et en Roumanie.* Paris: A. Chaix, 1876.

Mahler, Raphael. *Divrei Y'mei Israel ba-Dorot ha'Ahronim.* Vol. V. Merhavya: Sifriat Poalim, 1956.

—— *Der Kampf tsvishn Haskoleh un Khasides in Galitzie in der Ershter Helft fun 19 ᵗᵉⁿ Yorhundert.* New York: YIVO, 1942.

Maimonides, Moses. *The Book of Judges.* Bk. 14 of *The Code of Maimonides* (Abraham M. Hershman, trans.). New Haven: Yale University Press, 1949.

Manuel, Frank E. *The Realities of American-Palestine Relations.* Washington: Public Affairs Press, 1949.

Marshall, Louis. *Louis Marshall, Champion of Liberty: Selected Papers and Addresses* (ed. Charles Reznikoff). 2 vols. Philadelphia: Jewish Publication Society, 1957.

Marx, Karl. *Zur Judenfrage.* Berlin: Rowohlt, 1919.

McDonald, James G. *My Mission in Israel, 1948–1951.* New York: Simon and Schuster, 1951.

Mendelssohn, Moses. *Moses Mendelssohns Gesammelte Schriften.* 8 vols. Leipzig: F. A. Brockhaus, 1843–1845.

Miller, David Hunter. *My Diary at the Conference of Paris.* Vol. 14. New York: privately printed, 1924.

Montefiore, Claude G. *Liberal Judaism and Hellenism, and Other Essays.* London: Macmillan, 1918.

Montefiore, Sir Moses. *Diaries of Sir Moses and Lady Montefiore.* 2 vols. London: Griffith Farran Okeden and Welsh, 1890.

Naiditch, Isaac. *Edmond de Rothschild.* Washington: Zionist Organization of America, 1945.

Nordau, Anna and Maxa Nordau. *Max Nordau.* New York: Nordau Committee, 1943.

Nordau, Max. *Zionistische Schriften.* 2nd ed. Juedischer Verlag, 1923.

Noy (Neustadt), Melech. *Zionism Today and Tomorrow.* London: Jewish Vanguard, 1956.

O'Ballance, Edgar. *The Arab-Israeli War, 1948.* London: Faber, 1956.

Oliphant, Laurence. *Haifa.* 2nd ed. Edinburgh: Blackwood, 1887.

—— *The Land of Gilead.* New York: Appleton, 1881.

Parkes, James. *The Emergence of the Jewish Problem, 1878–1939.* London: Oxford University Press, 1946.

—— *A History of Palestine from 135 A.D. to Modern Times.* London: Gollancz, 1949.

—— *The Jewish Problem in the Modern World.* London: Thornton Butterworth (Home University Library), 1939.

Patkin, A. L. *The Origins of the Russian-Jewish Labour Movement.* London: F. W. Cheshire Pty., 1947.

Patterson, John Henry. *With the Judeans in the Palestine Campaign.* New York: Macmillan, 1922.

—— *With the Zionists in Gallipoli.* New York: Doran [ca. 1916].

Petegorsky, David W. *The Jewish Community. Reprint of articles in Congress Weekly,* December 6 and 20, 1948. New York, American Jewish Congress, 1948.

Philipson, David. *The Reform Movement in Judaism.* New York: Macmillan, 1907.

Pines, Dan. *He-Halutz b-Khur ha-Mahapekha*. Tel-Aviv, 1938.

Pinsker, Leo. *Road to Freedom*. New York: Scopus, 1944.

Pollak, Gustav. *Michael Heilprin and His Sons*. New York: Dodd, Mead, 1912.

Rabinovitz, A. S. *Toldot ha-Yehudim b'Eretz Israel*. Jaffa: Eitan and Shoshani, 1921.

Rabinowicz, Oskar K. *Fifty Years of Zionism: A Historical Analysis of Dr. Weizmann's "Trial and Error."* London: Anscombe, 1951.

Rackman, Emanuel. *Israel's Emerging Constitution, 1948–1951*. New York: Columbia University Press, 1955.

Robinson, Jacob. *Palestine and the United Nations: Prelude to Solution*. Washington: Public Affairs Press, 1947.

Robinson, Jacob et al. *Were the Minorities Treaties a Failure?* New York: Institute of Jewish Affairs, 1943.

Rosenheim, Jacob. *Ausgewaehlte Aufsaetze und Ausprachen*. 2 vols. Frankfurt a.M.: J. Kauffmann Verlag, 1930.

Rosenne, Shabtai. *Israel's Armistice Agreements with the Arab States* (pamphlet). Tel-Aviv: International Law Association, Israel Branch, 1951.

Rotenstreich, Nathan. *Ha-Mah'shava ha-Yehudit ba-Et ha-Hadasha*. 2 vols. Tel-Aviv: Am Oved, 1945–1950.

Ruppin, Arthur. *Three Decades of Palestine*. Jerusalem: Schocken, 1936.

——— *The Jewish Fate and Future*. London: Macmillan, 1940.

Sacher, Harry. *Israel; The Establishment of a State*. New York: British Book Centre, 1952.

Sacher, Harry, ed. *Zionism and the Jewish Future*. New York: Macmillan, 1916.

Samuel, Herbert L. S. *Memoirs*. London, Cresset Press, 1941.

Schechtman, Joseph B. *The Arab Refugee Problem*. New York: Philosophical Library, 1952.

——— *European Population Transfers, 1939–1945*. New York: Oxford University Press, 1946.

——— *Rebel and Statesman*. New York: Thomas Yoseloff, 1956.

Scheib, Israel. *Ma'aser Rishon*. [Tel-Aviv]: "Ha-Matmid." 1950.

Schiff, Jacob H. *Jacob H. Schiff: His Life and Letters* (ed. C. Adler), 2 vols. New York: Doubleday, Doran, 1928.

Scholem, Gershom G. *Major Trends in Jewish Mysticism*. 3rd ed. New York: Schocken, 1954.

Schwarz, Joseph. *Das Heilige Land*. Frankfurt a.M.: Kaufmann, 1852.

Sefer ha-Mizrahi (ed. J. L. Fishman). Jerusalem: Mosad Ha'Rav Kuk, 1946.

Sefer Toldot ha-Hagana. Vol. I, 2 bks. [Tel-Aviv]: Am Oved, Zionist Executive, Tzahal, 1954.

Sicron, Moshe. *Immigration to Israel, 1948–1953*. 2 vols. Jerusalem: Falk Project and Central Bureau of Statistics, December and August, 1953.

Sidebotham, Herbert. *Great Britain and Palestine*. London: Macmillan, 1937.

Silberner, Edmund. *Ha-Sozialism ha-Ma'aravi u-Sh'elat ha-Yehudim*. Jerusalem: Mosad Bialik, 1955.

Sklare, Marshall. *The Jews: Social Patterns of an American Group*. Glencoe, Ill.: Free Press, 1958.

Smilansky, Moshe. *Prakim b'Toldot ha-Yishuv*. 3 vols. Tel-Aviv: Dvir, 1943–1948.

Smuts, J. C. *The League of Nations: A Practical Suggestion*. London and New York: Hodder and Stoughton, 1918.

Sokolow, Nahum. *History of Zionism, 1600–1918*. 2 vols. London: Longmans, Green, 1919.

Stein, Leonard. *The Balfour Declaration*. New York: Simon and Schuster, 1961.

———— *Zionism*. London: E. Benn, 1925.

Stember, Charles Herbert et al. *Jews in the Mind of America*. New York, London: Basic Books, 1966.

Storrs, Sir Ronald. *Orientations*. London: Nicholson and Watson, 1937.

Stoyanovsky, J. *The Mandate for Palestine*. London: Longmans, Green, 1928.

Straus, Oscar S. *Under Four Administrations: From Cleveland to Taft*. Boston: Houghton Mifflin, 1922.

A Survey of Palestine: Prepared in December 1945 and January 1946 for the Information of the Anglo-American Committee of Inquiry. 3 vols. Jerusalem: Palestine Government, 1946.

Sykes, Christopher. *Two Studies in Virtue*. New York: Alfred A. Knopf, 1953.

Syrkin, Marie. *Way of Valor*, New York: Sharon Books, 1955.

Tartakower, Aryeh and Kurt Grossman, *The Jewish Refugee*. New York: Institute of Jewish Affairs, 1944.

Teller, Judd L. *The Kremlin, the Jews, and the Middle East*. New York and London: Thomas Yoseloff, 1957.

Temperley, H. W. V., ed. *A History of the Peace Conference of Paris*. 6 vols. London: Frowde, Hodder and Stoughton, 1920–1924.

Tuchman, Barbara W. *Bible and Sword*. New York: New York University Press, 1956.

Va'ad Le'umi. *Tazkirim Historiyim*. (Memoranda on Historical Connection of Jews with Palestine Submitited to Anglo-American Inquiry Committee) Jerusalem, 1947.

Vitta, Edoardo. *The Conflict of Laws in Matters of Personal Status in Palestine*. Tel-Aviv: S. Bursi, 1947.

Vlavianos, B. J. and Feliks Gross. *Struggle for Tomorrow: Modern Political Ideologies of the Jewish People*. New York: Arts, Incorporated, 1954.

Volney, C. F. C. *Travels through Syria and Egypt*. 2 vols. London: G. Robinson, 1805.

von Propper, S. M. *Was Nicht in die Zeitung Kam*. Frankfurt a.M.: Frankfurter Societaets-druckerei, 1929.

Waxman, Meyer. *A History of Jewish Literature*. 4 vols. New York: Bloch, 1933–1941.

Weizmann, Chaim. *Chaim Weizmann, Reden und Aufsaetze, 1901–1936* (ed. Gustav Krojanker). Berlin: Juedischer Buchverlag Erwin Loewe, 1937.

———— *Trial and Error*. Illus. London: Harper Brothers, 1950.

Wilhelm, Kurt. *Roads to Zion: Four Centuries of Travelers' Reports*. New York: Schocken, 1948.

Wischnitzer, Mark. *To Dwell in Safety; The Story of Jewish Migration since 1800*. Philadelphia: Jewish Publication Society, 1948.

Woodward, E. L. and Rohan Butler. *Documents on British Foreign Policy, 1919–1939*. London: H. M. Stationery Office, 1946–.

World Zionist Organization. *Book of Documents Submitted to the General Assembly of the United Nations Relating to the Establishment of the National Home for the Jewish People.* New York: Jewish Agency for Palestine, 1947.

———— *Hazut.* Vol. IV, 5718 — Records of the Ideological World Conference in Jerusalem. Jerusalem: Executive of the Zionist Organization, 1958.

———— *The Jewish Case before the Anglo-American Committee of Inquiry in Palestine; Statements and Memoranda.* Jerusalem: Jewish Agency, 1947.

———— *Memorandum Submitted to the Palestine Royal Commission.* London: Jewish Agency, 1936.

———— *Y'sodot la-Hinukh ha-Ivri bi-T'futzot ha-Gola* (Report of World Conference of Teachers at Tzofit, Elul, 5715 [1955]). Jerusalem: Executive of the Jewish Agency, Department of Education, 1958.

Ya'ari, Abraham. *Igrot Eretz-Israel.* Tel-Aviv: Youth Department, Zionist Executive, 1943.

Yavne'eli, Samuel. *Sefer ha-Zionut.* Vol. II, bk. 2. Tel-Aviv: Mosad Bialik, 1943/1944.

Yellin, Joshua. *Zikhronot l'Ven Yerushalayim.* Jerusalem: privately printed, 1924.

Young, George. *Corps de Droit Ottoman.* 7 vols. Oxford: Clarendon Press, 1905–1906.

Zitron, S. L. *Toldot Hibbat-Zion.* Odessa: Va'ad Hovevei-Zion, 1914.

Zionist Organization of America. *Report of the Commission on the Future Program and Constitution of the World Zionist Organization.* New York, 1949.

Zlocisti, Theodor. *Moses Hess, der Vorkaempfer des Sozialismus und Zionismus, 1812–1875.* Berlin: Welt-Verlag, 1921.

NOTES

The following abbreviations have been used throughout the notes:

ACJ	American Council for Judaism, Inc.
AJCommittee	American Jewish Committee
AJConference	American Jewish Conference
AJCongress	American Jewish Congress
CCAR	Central Conference of American Rabbis
Esco	Esco Foundation for Palestine, Inc.
Ihud	Ihud Association of Palestine
JA	Jewish Agency for Palestine
LN.PMC.	League of Nations, Permanent Mandates Commission
UNCIO	United Nations Conference on International Organization
YIVO	Yiddishe Vissenshaftlikhe Institut
ZOA	Zionist Organization of America

AJYB	*American Jewish Year Book*
AZJ	*Allgemeine Zeitung des Judenthums*
GB.Cmd.	Great Britain, Command Paper
JADigest	*Jewish Agency's Digest of Press and Events*
JE	*Jewish Encyclopedia*
JL	*Juedisches Lexikon*
JPPP	*The Jewish People, Past and Present* (Jewish Encyclopedic Handbooks)
LN.OJ.	League of Nations, *Official Journal*
LNPublications	League of Nations, *Publications*
PAJHS	*Publications of the American Jewish Historical Society*
UN.GA.OR.	United Nations, General Assembly, *Official Records*
UN.SC.OR.	United Nations, Security Council, *Official Records*
UN.TC.OR.	United Nations, Trusteeship Council, *Official Records*
ZC.Din v'Heshbon Stenografi	Zionist Congress, *Stenographic Record* (Hebrew)
ZC.Ha-Protokol	Zionist Congress, *Protocol* (Hebrew)
ZC.Protokoll	Zionist Congress, *Protocol* (German)
ZGDJ	*Zeitschrift zur Geschichte des Deutschen Judentums*

Chapter 1: The Setting of Modern Jewish History

1. Arthur Ruppin, *The Jewish Fate and Future* (1940), p. 25ff.
2. *Ibid.*, p. 28.
3. *Ibid.*
4. Cf. James Parkes, *The Jewish Problem in the Modern World* (1939), pp. 50–73; Ben Halpern, *The American Jew* (1956), pp. 4–20.
5. Israel Klausner, *Hibbat Zion b'Rumania* (1958), pp. 17–27.

Chapter 2: Zionist Conceptions of Sovereignty

1. *Theodor Herzl: A Portrait for This Age* ([ed. Ludwig Lewisohn], 1950), p. 246ff.
2. A. Druyanow, *Pinsker u-Z'mano* (1953), pp. 179ff., 184ff.
3. *Ibid.*, pp. 182ff., 191ff., and 230 n52.
4. *Theodor Herzl*, pp. 242ff., 248, 253ff., 309–311.
5. ZC.I. *Ha-Protokol*, p. 102. (Published by R. Mass, Jerusalem, 1946.)
6. *Theodor Herzl*, pp. 241–242, 311, 315.
7. ZC.I. *Ha-Protokol*, the remarks by Motzkin, pp. 100, 102; see also the speeches by Farbstein p. 90, Schnirer p. 145, Kaminka p. 150, and Rosenberg p. 151.
8. Adolf Boehm, *Die Zionistische Bewegung* (1935), I, 254–266, 307–315.
9. Israel Cohen, *Zionist Work in Palestine* (1911), pp. 13–20, 86–98, 137–142; Paul Goodman and Arthur D. Lewis, *Zionism: Problems and Views* (1916), pp. 115–119, 157–170; Harry Sacher, ed., *Zionism and the Jewish Future* (1916), pp. 99–116, 138–189, 214–234; Sundel Doniger, ed., *A Zionist Primer* (1917), pp. 53–61; Boehm, *Zionistische Bewegung*, I, 407–484, 504–520.
10. Boehm, *Zionistische Bewegung*, I, 662–676.
11. Theodor Herzl, *Tagebuecher* (1934), I, 420ff., 425ff., 427ff., 431–435, 439, 440, 452–455, 460–462.
12. ZC.I. *Ha-Protokol*, p. 97.
13. *Ibid.*, p. 98.
14. Vladimir Jabotinsky, *Ba-Derekh la-M'dina* (1953), pp. 283–302; B. J. Vlavianos and Feliks Gross, *Struggle for Tomorrow* (1954), pp. 86–99.
15. *Theodor Herzl*, pp. 298–300, 307–312, *et passim*.
16. *Ibid.*, p. 252ff.
17. Joseph B. Schechtman, *Rebel and Statesman* (1956), pp. 110–125, 137–149, 169–194.
18. Vladimir Jabotinsky, *Ne'umim, 1905–1926* (1947), pp. 183–207, 271–290, 311–325.
19. Vladimir Jabotinsky, *Ne'umim, 1927–1940* (1948), pp. 167–193, 305–326.
20. Chaim Weizmann, *Trial and Error* (illus. ed., 1950), pp. 156ff., 419.
21. *Ibid.*, pp. 369–375.

22. Goodman and Lewis, *Zionism*, pp. 48–68, 197–204, 223–227, *et passim*.

23. *Jewish Frontier*, IV, no. 1 (January 1937), pp. 15–16; no. 3 (March 1937), pp. 5–7.

24. GB.Cmd.6019 (1939); J. C. Hurewitz, *Diplomacy in the Near and Middle East* (1956), II, 219–226. (The full titles of the Command Papers, abbreviated in these notes as GB.Cmd. are listed in the bibliography under the heading [Great Britain, Parliamentary Papers].)

25. Aryeh Tartakower and Kurt Grossman, *The Jewish Refugee* (1944), pp. 412–420.

26. See Samuel Halperin, *The Political World of American Zionism* (1961).

27. Vlavianos and Gross, *Struggle for Tomorrow*, pp. 88–90, 93.

28. Hurewitz, *Diplomacy*, II, 234–235.

29. Vlavianos and Gross, *Struggle for Tomorrow*, p. 100ff.

30. Ihud, *Palestine — Divided or United?* (1947), pp. 26ff., 37ff.

31. Esco, *Palestine* (1947), II, 1014–1020.

32. Ihud, *Palestine — Divided or United?*, p. 71f.

33. Jabotinsky, *Ba-Derekh la-M'dina*, p. 298f.

34. *AJYB*, XLIV, 132f.; XLV, 210f., XLVII, 331.

35. Israel Scheib, *Ma'aser Rishon* (1950), pp. 70ff., 302ff., 321–336.

36. Richard Massie Graves, *Experiment in Anarchy* (1949), pp. 220–238.

37. Menahem Begin, *The Revolt* (1951) pp. 47–58.

38. Hayim Arlosoroff, *Yoman Yerushalayim* (1948/1949), pp. 333–342.

39. David Ben-Gurion, *Ba-Ma'arakha* (1947), III, 18.

40. Weizmann, *Trial and Error*, p. 360ff.; Hurewitz, *Diplomacy*, II, 105f., 111 (art. 25), 156ff.

41. ZC.XX. *Din v'Heshbon Stenografi*, p. 359ff.; translation from Esco, *Palestine*, II, 854–856.

42. Arlosoroff, *Yoman Yerushalayim*, p. 341.

43. Abraham Granott, *Agrarian Reform and the Record of Israel* (1956), pp. 29–38.

44. Edgar O'Ballance, *The Arab-Israeli War, 1948* (1956), pp. 31–86.

45. Reprinted in Norman Bentwich, *Israel* (1952), pp. 206–208.

46. *Ibid.*, p. 209 (Law of Return); *Israel Government Year Book*, 5713 (1952), pp. 207–210 (Nationality Law).

Chapter 3: The Rise and Reception of Zionism in the Nineteenth Century

1. Karl Mannheim, *Ideology and Utopia* (1949), p. 206ff.

2. Halpern, *American Jew*, pp. 119–123.

3. S. M. Dubnow, *Die Neueste Geschichte des Juedischen Volkes* (1920), I, 66–74; Oscar I. Janowsky, *Jews and Minority Rights, 1898–1919* (1933), pp. 22–29.

4. Ben-Zion Dinaburg, *Sefer ha-Zionut* (1938), vol. I, bk. I, pp. 133–137.

5. *Ibid.*, pp. 125f., 144f.

6. *Ibid.*, pp. 116–118, 130–132, 136, 155ff., 158–161.

7. Nathan Michael Gelber, *Zur Vorgeschichte des Zionismus* (1927), pp. 56–61, 90ff.

8. Dinaburg, *Sefer ha-Zionut*, vol. I, bk. I, pp. 142–144, 152–154.

9. Samuel Holdheim, *Geschichte der Entstehung und Entwickelung der Juedischen Reformgemeinde in Berlin* (1857), pp. 1–25.

10. Dubnow, *Neueste Geschichte*, I, 125–153; Théophile Hallez, *Des Juifs en France* (1840), pp. 180–229, 297–348.

11. Dinaburg, *Sefer ha-Zionut*, vol. I, bk. I, p. 85.

12. Jacob Katz, "L'Virur ha-Musag 'M'vasrei ha-Zionut,' " *Shivat Zion*, I, 91–105.

13. Moses Hess, *Rome and Jerusalem* (1918), pp. 118–126, 141–159.

14. Gelber, *Vorgeschichte*, pp. 176–201.

15. M. L. Lilienblum, *Mivhar Ma'amarav* (1943), p. 63. Unless otherwise indicated, translations in this volume are by the author.

16. Abraham Cahan, *Bletter fun Mein Leben* (1926), I, 500.

17. *Ibid.*, pp. 435, 501ff.

18. A. Liessin, "Epizodn," in YIVO, *Historishe Shriftn*, III, 196–200.

19. Boehm, *Zionistische Bewegung*, I, 100–113; S. L. Zitron, *Toldot Hibbat-Zion* (1914), I, 166–172, 251–263.

20. Dubnow, *Neueste Geschichte*, I, 315–332; II, 136–144, 190–205, 237–254, 372–383, 427–453.

21. Z.C.I.*Ha-Protokol*, pp. 161–162; see also Klausner, *Hibbat Zion b' Rumania*, pp. 61ff., 77.

22. Hess, *Rome and Jerusalem*, p. 70ff.; cf. Jacob Katz, "L'Virur ha-Musag," *Shivat Zion*, I, 100; G. Kressel, in Moses Hess, *Moshe Hess u-V'nei Doro* (1947), Introduction, p. 75ff.

23. *Theodor Herzl*, p. 321ff.

24. *Moses Mendelssohns Gesammelte Schriften* (1844), V, 494.

25. Ferdinand Lassalle, *Tagebuch* (1891), p. 160f; cf. Theodor Zlocisti, *Moses Hess, der Vorkaempfer des Socialismus und Zionismus* (1921), p. 283f.

26. A. M. Klein trans., in Hayyim Nahman Bialik, *Complete Poetic Works*, I (1948), 133–134.

27. *Partisan Review*, XXIII (Spring 1956), pp. 180f., 182.

28. Meyer Waxman, *A History of Jewish Literature* (1936), III, 78–81, 114–118, 123f., 141, 164–194.

29. *Theodor Herzl*, p. 253ff.

30. Heinrich Graetz, *History of the Jews* (1895), V, 414–422; Dubnow, *Neueste Geschichte*, I, 197–204.

31. Waxman, *History of Jewish Literature*, III, 164–170.

32. Judah Leib Gordon, *Kol Shirei Judah Leib Gordon* (1884), I, 91–93.

33. Druyanow, *Pinsker u-Z'mano*, p. 54ff.

34. Boehm, *Zionistische Bewegung*, I, 89–95.

35. *Ibid.*, p. 504ff.

36. Ahad Ha'am (Asher Ginzberg), *Selected Essays* (1912), p. 186f.

37. *Ibid.*, p. 183f.

38. *Ibid.*, p. 193f.

39. Nathan Rotenstreich, *Ha-Mahshava ha-Yehudit ba-Et ha-Hadasha* (1945), I, 90ff., 114ff.

40. Richard Lichtheim, *Die Geschichte des deutschen Zionismus* (1954), pp. 40–43; S. L. Zitron, "Zur Geschichte der Zionsliebe," *Der Jude*, II, 347–353, 670–677; III, 116–121.

41. Jacob Katz, "L'Virur ha-Musag," *Shivat Zion*, I, 91–105.

42. *Cambridge Modern History* (1909), VI, 834–836; VIII, 772–776; Irving Babbitt, *Rousseau and Romanticism* (1955), pp. 16–90.

43. Hugo Bieber and Moses Hadas, *Heinrich Heine: A Biographical Anthology* (1956), pp. 79ff., 102ff., 107ff., 114ff., 118–134.

44. Siegfried Ucko, "Geistesgeschichtliche Grundlagen der Wissenschaft des Judentums," *ZGDJ*, V, 1–34.

45. Lichtheim, *Geschichte des deutschen Zionismus*, pp. 77–85; Parkes, *The Jewish Problem in the Modern World*, pp. 50–73.

46. Theodor Lessing, *Der Juedischer Selbsthass* (ca. 1930), pp. 55–79, 101–131; Bieber and Hadas, *Heinrich Heine*, pp. 238–245, 418–445.

47. Halpern, *American Jew*, pp. 14–20; Robert F. Byrnes, *Antisemitism in Modern France* (1950), pp. 137–178; Edmund Silberner, *Ha-Sozialism ha-Ma'aravi u-Sh'elat ha-Yehudim* (1955), pp. 303–312.

48. Karl Marx, *Zur Judenfrage* (1919), p. 42ff.

49. David Philipson, *The Reform Movement in Judaism* (1907), pp. 197–316; Jacob B. Agus, *Guideposts in Modern Judaism* (1954), pp. 56–70; Rotenstreich, *Ha-Mahshava ha-Yehudit*, I, 52ff., 90ff.

50. ZC.II.*Protokoll*, p. 5f.

51. Boehm, *Zionistische Bewegung*, I, 291–305.

52. *Ibid.*, pp. 522–548.

53. Lichtheim, *Geschichte des deutschen Zionismus*, pp. 164–171.

54. *Sefer Toldot ha-Hagana*, vol. I, bk. I (1954), pp. 155–175; Julius Haber, *The Odyssey of an American Zionist* (1956), pp. 49–52.

55. A. Liessin, "Epizodn," in YIVO, *Historishe Shriftn*, III, 182–185; Jacob H. Schiff, *Life and Letters* (1928), II, 122, 125, 126, 131, 138, 141f.

56. Lichtheim, *Geschichte des deutschen Zionismus*, pp. 110–121, 139, 148ff.; Boehm, *Zionistische Bewegung*, I, 202f; Ahad Ha'am, *Al Parashat Drakhim* (1930), II, 86–88.

57. Bein, *Theodore Herzl*, pp. 201f., 205ff., 451f.

58. Azriel Shohet, "Ha-Shekel," *Shivat Zion*, I, 221–224; "Shemot, S'malim," *ibid.*, II–III, 228–250.

59. S. Tchernowitz, *B'nei Moshe u-T'kufatam* (1914), p. 61.

60. Solomon Liptzin, *Eliakum Zunser* (1950), pp. 153–192.

61. Tchernowitz, *B'nei Moshe*, p. 40ff.

62. Moshe Smilansky, *Prakim b'Toldot ha-Yishuv* (1943), I, 5–23, 111ff.

63. Tchernowitz, *B'nei Moshe*, pp. 60ff., 93ff.

64. *Theodor Herzl*, p. 287ff.

65. Boehm, *Zionistische Bewegung*, I, 203ff.

66. *Ibid.*, p. 205f.

67. Judah Leib Fishman, "Toldot ha-Mizrahi," in *Sefer ha-Mizrahi*, pp. 89–101.

68. Vlavianos and Gross, *Struggle for Tomorrow*, pp. 200–206; *JL*, I, 124–131; Boehm, *Zionistische Bewegung*, I, 588–590.

69. Dubnow, *Neueste Geschichte*, II, 334–344, 372–376.

70. Isaac Breuer, *The Jewish National Home* (1926), pp. 20–59, 80–89, 95ff; Moshe Burstein, *Self-Government of the Jews in Palestine since 1900* (1934), pp. 157–160.

71. *JPPP*, II, 119–143.

72. *Theodor Herzl*, pp. 241ff.

73. *JL*, I, 129ff.

74. Moses Maimonides, *The Book of Judges* (1949), p. 241.

75. *JPPP*, I, 328–347.

76. *Rabbi Yehuda Alkalay — Rabbi Tz'vi Hirsh Kalisher, Mivhar Kitveihem* (1945), pp. 43ff., 127ff.

77. See A. I. Kuk, *Eretz Hefetz, Imrot al Eretz-Israel u-Vinyana* (1930).

78. *JPPP*, I, 338–347.

79. Samson R. Hirsch, *Neunzehn Briefe ueber Judentum* (ed. 4, 1911), p. 87.

80. Jacob Rosenheim, *Ausgewaehlte Aufsaetze und Ausprachen* (1930), I, 89–99, 118–124, 159–173, 209–217.

81. Breuer, *Jewish National Home*, pp. 60–62; *Der Neue Kusari, ein Weg zum Judentum* (1934), pp. 434–437; *Messiaspuren* (1918), pp. 15f., 18–20, 88–110.

82. Abraham G. Duker in the introduction to Ber Borochov, *Nationalism and the Class Struggle* (1937), pp. 17–20.

83. *Ibid.*, pp. 33–36; see also pp. 135–166, 183–205.

84. *Ibid.*, pp. 44–46.

85. A. L. Patkin, *The Origins of the Russian-Jewish Labour Movement* (1947), pp. 124–191.

86. Fritz Friedlaender, *Das Leben Gabriel Riessers* (1926), pp. 37–78.

Chapter 4: Attachment to Zion: Traditional Bonds and Involvement of Jewish Organizations

1. Lichtheim, *Geschichte des deutschen Zionismus*, pp. 11–25.

2. Cf. Josef Kastein (Julius Katzenstein), *Das Geschichtserlebnis des Juden* (1936) and *History and Destiny of the Jews* (1933); also Yitzhak Fritz Baer, *Galut* (1947).

3. *JPPP*, I, 328–347.

4. Martin Buber, *Israel and Palestine: The History of an Idea* (1952), pp. 89–108; Gershom G. Scholem, *Major Trends in Jewish Mysticism* (3 ed., 1954), pp. 327–330.

5. *Kitvei Rabbi Nahman Krochmal*, pp. 34–112; Rotenstreich, *Ha-Mahshava ha-Yehudit*, II, 151–163.

6. Maimonides, *The Book of Judges* (1949), pp. xxiiif.; Jacob Katz, "L'Virur ha-Musag," *Shivat Zion*, I, 105, n. 33.

7. Claude G. Montefiore, *Liberal Judaism and Hellenism and other Essays* (1918), pp. 284–306; Kaufmann Kohler, *Hebrew Union College and other Addresses*, pp. 161–172.

8. Montefiore, pp. 293–298; Kohler, pp. 184–194.

9. *Ibid.*, pp. 192–194.

10. Raphael Mahler, *Der Kamf tsvishn Haskoleh un Khasides* (1942), pp. 170–250.

11. Dubnow, *Neueste Geschichte*, I, 114; Naomi Wiener Cohen, "The Reaction of Reform Judaism in America to Political Zionism (1897–1922)," *PAJHS*, XL, 375–383.

12. Waxman, *History of Jewish Literature*, III, 267–278; Mahler, *Haskoleh un Khasides*, pp. 75–79.

13. *Theodor Herzl*, p. 254.

14. Borochov, *Nationalism*, pp. 197–204.

15. J. H. Brenner, *K'tavim* (1950), III, 28–81; *Kitvei Berl Katznelson*, V, 379–393.

16. Ahad Ha'am, *Al Parashat Drakhim*, I, 1–19, 144–161, 169–177; II, 22–35, 111–143.

17. Aaron David Gordon, *Kitvei A. D. Gordon* (1925–1929), I, 216; II, 43f.; III, 15f.; IV, 86f.; 303f.

18. Yehezkel Kaufmann, "Bikoret," *Moznayim*, XVII, 191–193.

19. Yehezkel Kaufmann, *Gola v'Nekhar* (1930), II, 466ff.

20. Jacob De Haas, *History of Palestine* (1934), pp. 298–370.

21. Israel Halpern, *Ha'Aliyot ha-Rishonot shel ha-Hasidim b'Eretz-Israel* (1940), pp. 20–37; A. L. Frumkin and Eliezer Rivlin, *Toldot Hakhmei Yerushalayim* (1930), III, 138ff.; Abraham Ya'ari, *Igrot Eretz-Israel* (1943), pp. 324ff.

22. Kurt Wilhelm, *Roads to Zion* (1948), p. 78ff.

23. Vaad Le'umi, *Tazkirim Historiyim* (1947), pp. 7–17; Bernard Lewis, "Ottoman Cadaster," *Eretz-Israel*, IV, 171–173; C. F. C. Volney, *Travels through Syria and Egypt* (1805), II, 306; Consul J. G. Willson, in U.S. (Department of State), *Reports from the Consuls of the United States*, I (1881), 223f.

24. Yitzhak Ben-Zvi, *Eretz-Israel v'Yishuva bi-Y'mei ha-Shilton ha-Ottomani*, pp. 244, 383ff., 173, 278f.

25. *Ibid.*, pp. 150, 365; Vaad Le'umi, *Tazkirim Historiyim*, pp. 21–66.

26. Wilhelm, *Roads to Zion*, p. 71.

27. Halpern, *Ha'Aliyot ha-Rishonot*, p. 22f.

28. *JE*, *s.v.* "Halukkah."

29. Ben-Zvi, *Eretz Israel v'Yishuva*, p. 365.

30. U.S., *Reports from the Consuls*, I, 223–224.

31. James Parkes, *A History of Palestine from 135 A.D. to Modern Times* (1949), pp. 226ff., 261ff.

32. Ben-Zvi, *Eretz Israel v'Yishuva*, pp. 354–368.

33. Albert M. Hyamson, *The British Consulate in Jerusalem* (1939), I, xxxiii–xlvii.

34. Oscar S. Straus, *Under Four Administrations: From Cleveland to Taft* (1922), pp. 79–86.

35. Sir Moses Montefiore, *Diaries of Sir Moses and Lady Montefiore* (1890), II, 106–107; Isidore Loeb, *Biographie d'Albert Cohn* (1878), pp. 115–150.

36. *Ibid.*, p. 147ff.; André Chouraqui, *Les Juifs d'Afrique du Nord* (1952), pp. 88ff., 97–124.

37. Isidore Loeb, *La Situation des Israélites en Serbie et en Roumanie* (1876), pp. 18–40, 93–138.

38. Moise Franco, *Essai sur l'Histoire des Israélites de l'Empire Ottoman* (1897), pp. 158–161, 220–233.

39. *JE*, *s.v.* "Alliance Israélite Universelle."

40. Max J. Kohler, "The Board of Delegates of American Israelites, 1859–1878," *PAJHS*, XXIX, 84.

41. *JE*, *s.v.*, "Anglo-Jewish Association" and "Israelitische Allianz zu Wien."

42. *JL*, *s.v.* "Hilfsverein der deutschen Juden."

43. Salo W. Baron, *The Jewish Community*, I, 304–307; II, 333–339.

44. Chouraqui, *Juifs d'Afrique du Nord*, pp. 102–108.

45. Franco, *Histoire*, pp. 143–151.

46. Max J. Kohler and Simon Wolf, "Jewish Disabilities in the Balkan States," *PAJHS*, XXIV, 2–39.

47. *JE*, *s.v.* "Alliance Israélite Universelle" and "Anglo-Jewish Association"; *JL*, *s.v.* "Hilfsverein der deutschen Juden."

48. Montefiore, *Diaries*, I, 197; cf. 167.

49. Andrew A. Bonar and Robert M. M'Cheyne, *Narrative of a Mission of Inquiry to the Jews from the Church of Scotland* [1843], pp. 392f., 394f.; Israel Klausner, "Ha-Rav Yehuda Bibas," *Ha'Olam*, XXXII, 69.

50. *Rabbi Yehuda Alkalay — Rabbi Tz'vi Hirsh Kalisher*, pp. 54–81.

51. Montefiore, *Diaries*, I, 162–168, 178f.; II, 178ff.

52. Dubnow, *Neueste Geschichte*, II, 190–209, 372–378.

53. Baron, *Jewish Community*, II, 190–200.

54. Nathan Michael Gelber, "Yisud Bet ha-Sefer Laemel," *Yerushalayim* (quarterly published by Mosad Ha-Rav Kuk, 1920–), I, 95–108, 199–220.

55. Montefiore, *Diaries*, II, 48–51, 77f.; A. S. Rabinovitz, *Toldot ha-Yehudim b'Eretz Israel* (1921), pp. 150–154; Hyamson, *British Consulate*, II, 583f.

56. Rabinovitz, *Toldot;* Joshua Yellin, *Zikhronot l'Ven Yerushalayim* (1924), pp. 135–163; Tchernowitz, *B'nei Moshe*, pp. 111–115.

57. Nahum Sokolow, *History of Zionism, 1600–1918* (1919), I, 176–183.

58. See Charles Netter's report in the *Bulletin* of the Alliance Israélite Universelle, 1868, 1 er semestre, p. 4; 2 ieme semestre, pp. 55–66; Narcisse Leven, *Cinquante ans d'histoire* (1920), II, 265–319.

59. Israel Belkind, *Di Ershte Shrit fun Yishuv Erets-Yisroel*, I, 17ff.

60. Yellin, *Zikhronot*, p. 128ff.; Cohen, *Zionist Work*, pp. 86–98.

61. Harry Sacher, ed., *Zionism and the Jewish Future* (1916), pp. 171–189.

62. *JE*, *s.v.* "Wissotzky, Kalonymos Zeeb Wolf."

63. Sacher, *Zionism*, p. 181ff.

64. Montefiore, *Diaries*, I, 164–168.

65. Belkind, *Ershte Shrit*, I, 152ff., 167ff.

66. Montefiore, *Diaries*, II, 106ff., 260–265, 283–286.

67. Hyamson, *British Consulate*, II, 569–571; Parkes, *History of Palestine*, pp. 261–276.

68. Hyamson, *British Consulate*, I, l–liv; De Haas, *History of Palestine*, p. 441ff.

69. *Ibid.*, pp. 388–398, 402ff., 412–417.

70. Loeb, *Situation des Israélites*, pp. 1–18, 423–428; Abraham Galanté, *Turcs et Juifs: Etude Historique, Politique* (1932), pp. 13–16.

71. De Haas, *History of Palestine*, pp. 424–425, 430–431.

72. Montefiore, *Diaries*, II, 107, 285f.

73. *Ibid.*, p. 51ff., cf. Hyamson, *British Consulate*, I, doc. no. 11, p. 24.

74. Montefiore, *Diaries*, II, 51–54, 68f., 74, 103ff., 107, 109; Rabinovitz, *Toldot*, p. 151.

75. Joseph Schwarz, *Das Heilige Land* (1852), pp. 344f.

76. Laurence Oliphant, *Haifa* (2 ed., 1887), pp. 19ff.

77. Smilansky, *Prakim*, I, 11ff., 17f., 23, 26, *et passim*; *Sefer Toldot ha-Hagana*, vol. I, bk. I, 48–92.

78. George E. Kirk, *A Short History of the Middle East from the Rise of Islam to Modern Times* (1949), pp. 86–90.

79. Oliphant, *Haifa*, pp. 59–67, 204–212, 285–289, 309–313, 325ff.

80. George Young, *Corps de Droit Ottoman* (1905), II, 155ff.

81. Zosa Szajkowski, "Emigration or Reconstruction," *PAJHS* XLII, 157–188; Isaac Naiditch, *Edmond de Rothschild* (1945); Samuel Yavne'eli, *Sefer ha-Zionut* (1943/1944), vol. II, bk. 2, intro., p. 19ff.

82. Mark Wischnitzer, *To Dwell in Safety: The Story of Jewish Migration Since 1800* (1948), pp. 37ff., 39ff.

83. Zosa Szajkowski, "Attitude of American Jews," *PAJHS* XL, 221–280.

84. Vivian D. Lipman, *Social History of the Jews in England 1850–1950* (1954), pp. 134–144; Oscar Handlin, *Adventure in Freedom* (1954), p. 174ff.; *Louis Marshall, Champion of Liberty: Selected Papers and Addresses* (ed. Reznikoff) (1957), I, 109ff.

85. *The Times*, London, January 11, 1882, p. 4; Anatole Leroy-Beaulieu, *L'Empire des Tsars et les Russes* (1889), III, 615; Dr. Gerard Salinger has called my attention also to S. M. von Propper, *Was nicht in die Zeitung kam* (1929), pp. 106–115.

86. *Theodor Herzl*, pp. 238, 240, 242ff., 254, 314.

87. Wischnitzer, *To Dwell in Safety*, pp. 32ff., 44ff., 70–76, 113–130.

88. *Ibid.*, pp. 58–66, 85–93, 130–140; Perlmann, "Paul Haupt," *PAJHS*, XLVII, 154–175.

89. *L'Alliance Israélite Universelle, 1860–1895* (1895), p. 28ff.

90. Zitron, *Toldot Hibbat Zion*, I, 374ff.

91. Druyanow, *Pinsker u-Z'mano*, pp. 149–159, 167f.

92. Tchernowitz, *B'nei Moshe*, pp. 81–86; Wischnitzer, *To Dwell in Safety*, pp. 86–88.

93. Alex Bein, *The Return to the Soil* (1952), pp. 6f., 27ff.

94. Paul Goodman, *Zionism in England: English Zionist Federation 1899–1929* (1929), pp. 7ff.; Tchernowitz, *B'nei Moshe*, pp. 81–86.

95. Belkind, *Ershte Shrit*, I, 65–126; Ahad Ha'am, *Al Parashat Drakhim*, I, 26–67; II, 144–283.

96. Wischnitzer, *To Dwell in Safety*, pp. 60–64, 78ff.

97. Herzl, *Tagebuecher*, I, 15–28, 30–36, 128–130, 144–210, 216–218, 221–223, 248–249.

98. Alex Bein, *Theodore Herzl* (1940), pp. 179–187.

99. Alex Bein, "Gilgulei ha-Ra'ayon," *Ha-Kinus ha-Olami l'Madaei ha-Yahadut* (1952), I, 469–476.

100. *Theodor Herzl*, p. 344.

Chapter 5: Anti-Zionism and Non-Zionism: Effects upon Policy from First Zionist Congress to Balfour Declaration

1. Hannah Bodenheimer, *Toldot Tokhnit Bazel* (1947), p. xxxv.
2. Lichtheim, *Geschichte des deutschen Zionismus*, pp. 140ff.
3. *Theodor Herzl*, pp. 304–306.
4. Sokolow, *History of Zionism*, I, 228–236.
5. Bein, *Theodore Herzl*, pp. 202–225.
6. Frankel, "Bein Herzl l'vein Guedemann," *Shivat Zion*, IV, 100–113.
7. Herzl, *Tagebuecher*, I, 43, 579ff., 614.
8. *Theodor Herzl*, pp. 241ff., 304–306.
9. Herzl, *Tagebuecher*, I, 159ff.
10. Leib Jaffe, *T'kufot* (1948), pp. 62 ff.
11. Bodenheimer, *Tokhnit Bazel*, p. xxxiv.
12. *Ibid.*, pp. xviii, xxxiii.
13. *Ibid.*, pp. xiii, xv.
14. *Ibid.*, pp. v, xxxvi, xl.
15. *Ibid.*, p. 24.
16. *Ibid.*, p. xi.
17. *Ibid.*, pp., viiff., xi, xxvf., xxixff., xxxii, xxxivff., 76–78.
18. *Ibid.*, p. ii.
19. *Ibid.*, p. 76.
20. *Theodor Herzl*, p. 308.
21. Bein, *Theodore Herzl*, pp. 243ff.
22. *Theodor Herzl*, pp. 308–309.
23. *Ibid.*, p. 311.
24. Lichtheim, *Geschichte des deutschen Zionismus*, pp. 147ff., 164–169; Boehm, *Zionistische Bewegung*, I, 199ff., 291ff.
25. Cf. "The New Ghetto," in *Theodor Herzl*, pp. 152–193.
26. *Theodor Herzl*, pp. 238ff.
27. Lichtheim, *Geschichte des deutschen Zionismus*, pp. 92–98.
28. *Theodor Herzl*, pp. 304–305.
29. See ACJ, *An Approach to an American Judaism* (1958), pp. 3–11.
30. *AJYB*, XXXVII, 434–440; XXXIX, 820; XLIX, 781.
31. Jacob Robinson et al., *Were the Minorities Treaties a Failure?* (1943), pp. 35–41.
32. AJCommittee, *Toward Peace and Equity, Recommendations of the American Jewish Committee* (1946), pp. 13ff., 28, 50ff.; Morris Waldman, "Beyond 'National Self-Determination,'" *Contemporary Jewish Record*, VII, 227–238.
33. Gustav Pollak, *Michael Heilprin and His Sons* (1912), pp. 205–220; Samuel Joseph, *History of the Baron de Hirsch Fund* (1935), pp. 48–183.
34. A. Levy, "Zur russischen Auswanderung," *AZJ*, LV, 398.
35. *AZJ*, LV, 554–555. The records of this conference were called to my attention by my friend and colleague, Dr. Moshe Perlmann.
36. *Ibid.*, p. 556, col. 2.
37. *Ibid.*, p. 557, col. 1.
38. *Ibid.*, pp. 566–567.

39. Bein, *Theodore Herzl*, pp. 377–382, 386–391; Moshe Perlmann, "Paul Haupt," *PAJHS*, XLVII, 160–165.

40. Bein, *Theodore Herzl*, pp. 411ff.

41. *Ibid.*, pp. 412–420.

42. *Ibid.*, pp. 361ff., 378f.

43. *Ibid.*, pp. 438ff.

44. *Ibid.*, pp. 455ff.

45. Cf. J. Stoyanovsky, *The Mandate for Palestine* (1928), pp. 61–69; Ernst Frankenstein, *Justice for My People* (1944), pp. 85ff.

46. Bein, *Theodore Herzl*, pp. 464f.

47. David Isaac Marmor, "Ha-Massa v'Mattan ha-Diplomati shel ha-Histadrut ha-Territorialistit ha-Yehudit (ITO) u-M'sibot Kishlono," *Zion* (Hebrew, quarterly published by the Palestine Historical and Ethnographical Society; n.s., October, 1935–), vol. XI, nos. 1–3, p. 110, n.7.

48. *Ibid.*, pp. 110f.

49. *Schiff, Life and Letters*, II, 96–113.

50. David Isaac Marmor, "Ha-Massa v'Mattan," *Zion* (n.s.), vol. XI, no. 4, pp. 190–194.

51. See Vlavianos and Gross, *passim*.

52. Boehm, *Zionistische Bewegung*, I, 320–349.

53. Cyrus Adler and Aaron M. Margalith, *With Firmness in the Right, American Diplomatic Action affecting Jews, 1840–1945* (1946), pp. 261–291.

54. Boehm, *Zionistische Bewegung*, I, 626–632.

55. ZC.XII, *Reports of the Executive, Palestine Report*, pp. 20–32; Alexander Aaronsohn, *With the Turks in Palestine* (1916).

56. ZC.XII, *Reports of the Executive, Palestine Report*, pp. 33–34; Jacob De Haas, *Louis D. Brandeis* (1929), pp. 72–74, 79–82; Frank E. Manuel, *The Realities of American Palestine Relations* (1949), pp. 119–159.

57. David Mowshowitch, "A Bletl Neie Yiddishe Geshikhte," YIVO, *Historishe Shriftn*, II, 549–562; "Hinter di Kulissen fun der Balfour Deklaratzie," *Zukunft*, XLII, 392ff.

58. Schechtman, *Rebel and Statesman*, I, 224–226.

59. Sokolow, *History of Zionism*, II, 38ff.; Nathan Michael Gelber, *Hatzharat Balfour v-Toldoteha* (1939), pp. 153ff.; Weizmann, *Trial and Error*, p. 253.

60. David Mowshowitch, "Hinter di Kulissen," *Zukunft*, XLII, 393; Zosa Szajkowski, "L'korot ha-Ma'avak ha-Zioni b'Ve'idat ha-Shalom," *Shivat Zion*, IV, 241f.; "Resumés des lettres de Victor Basch," in Lucien Wolf file (AM 306/1), Central Zionist Archives, Jerusalem.

61. David Mowshowitch, "Hinter di Kulissen," *Zukunft*, XLII, 394; see memorandum in file AM 306/1, no. 30, pp. 7ff., Central Zionist Archives, Jerusalem; see Leonard Stein, *The Balfour Declaration* (1961), ch. xiv.

62. Christopher Sykes, *Two Studies in Virtue* (1953), pp. 173–188.

63. Herbert L. S. Samuel, *Memoirs* (1941), p. 140.

64. *Ibid.*, p. 139; cf. Weizmann, *Trial and Error*, pp. 191ff. and Oskar K. Rabinowicz, *Fifty Years of Zionism: A Historical Analysis of Dr. Weizmann's Trial and Error* (1950), pp. 65ff.

65. Samuel, *Memoirs*, pp. 140–142.

66. Weizmann, *Trial and Error*, p. 209ff.; Rabinowicz, *Fifty Years*, pp. 71ff.

67. Weizmann, *Trial and Error*, pp. 139–141, 215–216, 231–232, 262, *et passim*.

68. Zosa Szajkowski, "L'Korot ha-Ma'avak ha-Zioni," *Shivat Zion*, IV, 240.

69. Gelber, *Hatzharat Balfour*, p. 270ff.; Weizmann, *Trial and Error*, p. 199ff.

70. Zosa Szajkowski, "L'Korot ha-Ma'avak ha-Zioni," *Shivat Zion*, IV, 240–263.

71. De Haas, *Brandeis*, pp. 75–78; Boehm, *Zionistische Bewegung*, I, 635–643.

72. Sykes, *Two Studies*, pp. 220f.

73. Ahad Ha'am, *Igrot Ahad Ha'am* (1923–1925), V, 201–205.

74. Conjoint Foreign Committee, *Correspondence with His Majesty's Government respecting the Eventual Peace Negotiations* (1917), enclosure III, 31.

75. E. A. Adamow, ed., *Die Europaeischen Maechte und die Tuerkei waehrend des Weltkrieges*, V, document no. 78, 64ff.; cf. Esco, *Palestine*, I, 84 and n. 47; Leonard Stein, *Zionism* (1925), pp. 138f.

76. Zosa Szajkowski, "L'Korot ha-Ma'avak ha-Zioni," *Shivat Zion*, IV, 241; cf. Blanche E. C. Dugdale, *Arthur James Balfour* (1936), II, 227.

77. E. A. Adamow, ed., *Die Europaeischen Maechte*, V, document no. 80, 66.

78. Sykes, *Two Studies*, p. 178.

79. Gelber, *Hatzharat Balfour*, pp. 52f.; cf. "Resumés des lettres de Victor Basch," p. 6, Lucien Wolf file (AM 306/1), Central Zionist Archives, Jerusalem.

80. Sykes, *Two Studies*, pp. 187ff.; Dugdale, *Balfour*, II, 227ff.

81. ZC.XII, *Reports of the Executive, Political Report*, pp. 9f.

82. Accounts of this meeting, *ibid.*, p. 10f.; Weizmann, *Trial and Error*, pp. 238ff.; Gelber, *Hatzharat Balfour*, pp. 59ff.; Esco, *Palestine*, I, 90ff.; Sykes, *Two Studies*, pp. 194ff.

83. Dugdale, *Balfour*, II, 230ff.

84. Sokolow, *History of Zionism*, II, 56.

85. Sykes, *Two Studies*, pp. 214ff.

86. *Ibid.*, pp. 212ff.

87. Gelber, *Hatzharat Balfour*, p. 295, n. 239.

88. *Ibid.*, pp. 109–113, 293–295; Esco, *Palestine*, I, 101–107; cf. Herbert Sidebotham, *Great Britain and Palestine* (1937), pp. 51–66.

89. Dugdale, *Balfour*, II, 225.

90. Esco, *Palestine*, I, 102ff.

91. ZC.XII, *Reports of the Executive, Political Report*, Appendix 2, pp. 71–72.

92. David Lloyd George, *The Truth about the Peace Treaties* (1938), II, 1137.

93. *Ibid.*, 1138f.; GB.Cmd.5479 (1937), pp. 24f.

94. Esco, *Palestine*, I, 101–107.

95. *Ibid.*, p. 105; Sokolow to Sacher, July 10, 1917, quoted in Stein, *Balfour Declaration*, p. 465.

96. Stein, *Balfour Declaration*, pp. 468ff.; cf. Gelber, *Hatzharat Balfour*, p. 112; cf. also p. 110, and p. 294f.

97. Weizmann, *Trial and Error*, p. 257; cf. Lloyd George, *Peace Treaties*, II, 1117ff.

98. Facsimile in Weizmann, *Trial and Error*, plate 80, facing pp. 256 and 257.

99. *Ibid.*, pp. 256ff.

100. Lloyd George, *Peace Treaties*, II, 1132–1134.

101. Sykes, *Two Studies*, Appendix A, pp. 236–240.

102. David Mowshowitch, "Hinter di Kulissen," *Zukunft*, XLII, 394.

103. Sokolow, *History of Zionism*, II, 67ff.

104. Sykes, *Two Studies*, pp. 210ff.; cf. Zosa Szajkowski, "L'Korot ha-Ma'avak ha-Zioni," *Shivat Zion*, IV, 243f., 259–263; Naiditch, *Edmond de Rothschild*, pp. 26ff.

105. Zosa Szajkowski, "L'Korot ha-Ma'avak ha-Zioni," *Shivat Zion*, IV, 253.

106. Sokolow, *History of Zionism*, II, 62f.

107. *Ibid.*, p. 66.

108. Lloyd George, *Peace Treaties*, II, 1123, 1137.

109. Gelber, *Hatzharat Balfour*, p. 62.

110. George Antonius, *The Arab Awakening* (1939), pp. 267ff.; cf. Elie Kedourie, *England and the Middle East* (1956), p. 151ff. and Lloyd George, *Peace Treaties*, II, 1142.

111. Cf. *Essays in Honour of The Very Rev. Dr. J. H. Hertz* (1944), pp. 261–270; Sykes, *Two Studies*, pp. 222ff., 229f.

Chapter 6: The Jewish Agency and the Jewish State

1. Weizmann, *Trial and Error*, p. 381.

2. Hayim Fineman, "Jews in World Congress," *Jewish Frontier*, III, nos. 9–10, pp. 17–22.

3. *AJYB*, XXXV, 301–303; XXXIX, 820.

4. Cf. Scheib, *Ma'aser Rishon*, pp. 239–245.

5. *LNPublications*, VI.A.18, p. 2; cf. E. L. Woodward and Rohan Butler, *Documents on British Foreign Policy, 1919–1939*, series I, vol. IV, pp. 431, 572f.

6. *ZC.XIII.Protokoll*, statement by Soloweitschik, p. 237.

7. *Louis Marshall*, II, 719.

8. Vlavianos and Gross, *Struggle for Tomorrow*, pp. 144–149, 201, 236–243.

9. See annual tables of "JDC funds appropriated for relief of war sufferers," *AJYB*, XXII–XXVII.

10. Joseph C. Hyman, *The Activities of the Joint Distribution Committee* (1931), pp. 14, 17, 24ff.

11. *ZC.XIV.Protokoll*, remarks by S. S. Wise, pp. 174ff.; Dan Pines, *He-Halutz b'Khur ha-Mahapekha* (1938), pp. 272ff.

12. Vlavianos and Gross, *Struggle for Tomorrow*, pp. 133–196.

13. *Ibid.*, pp. 249–268.

14. Cf. Borochov, *Nationalism*, pp. 94–108.

15. Anna and Maxa Nordau, *Max Nordau* (1943), pp. 280–286.

16. De Haas, *Brandeis*, pp. 233ff.

17. *Ibid.*, p. 260.

18. ZC.XI.*Protokoll*, p. 242.

19. De Haas, *Brandeis*, pp. 260ff.

20. *Max Nordau*, pp. 243f., 250, 258, 260, 262ff., 265, 267ff., 270, 274–288.

21. De Haas, *Brandeis*, p. 128f.

22. Weizmann, *Trial and Error*, pp. 326–336.

23. De Haas, *Brandeis*, pp. 233–259.

24. *Ibid.*, p. 249.

25. *Chaim Weizmann, Reden und Aufsaetze, 1901–1936* (1937), pp. 68ff.

26. Cf. Weizmann, *Trial and Error*, pp. 332ff.

27. *Ibid.*, p. 227.

28. *Chaim Weizmann*, pp. 72ff., 214–217; cf. Rabinowicz, *Fifty Years*, pp. 36ff., 98ff.

29. Weizmann, *Trial and Error*, pp. 330ff., 376ff.

30. ZC.XIV.*Protokoll*, remarks by Jabotinsky, pp. 248ff.

31. ZC.XIII.*Protokoll*, remarks by Mereminski, pp. 137ff.

32. ZC.XII.*Protokoll*, p. 771.

33. *Ibid.*, p. 756.

34. Weizmann, *Trial and Error*, pp. 330–342, 356–360; Boehm, *Zionistische Bewegung*, II, 115ff., 193ff., 227ff.

35. Weizmann, *Trial and Error*, p. 379f.

36. ZC.XIII.*Protokoll*, p. 521.

37. *Ibid.*, (Paragraph 6).

38. ZC.XV.*Protokoll*, remarks by Jabotinsky, pp. 128–131.

39. ZC.XIII.*Protokoll*, remarks by Gruenbaum, pp. 117ff., 415ff.

40. Pines, *He-Halutz b'Khur ha-Mahapekha*, pp. 8–12, 69–75.

41. ZC.XIII.*Protokoll*, remarks by B. Kaznelson, pp. 268ff.

42. See the pamphlet by Bar Avraham, "Herut: Avar, Hoveh, Atid"; translated (incomplete) in *Jewish Frontier*, XXV, no. 5, pp. 5–8.

43. ZC.XVI.*Protokoll*, remarks by Arlosoroff, pp. 96–102.

44. *AJYB*, XXVII, pp. 470–472; XXVIII, pp. 510–513.

45. Translation quoted from ZC.XV, *Report of the Executive*, pp. 35–37.

46. *Report of the Joint Palestine Survey Commission*, "Terms of Reference," Annex I, pp. 115–121.

47. ZC.XVII.*Protokoll*, Second Jewish Agency Council Meeting, remarks by Senator, pp. 548ff.

48. J. C. Hurewitz, *The Struggle for Palestine* (1950), pp. 40ff., 110f.

49. On this and the preceding paragraph, see Halperin, *Political World of American Zionism*.

50. Frederick Hermann Kisch, *Palestine Diary* (1938), pp. 309, 312ff., 392f.; ZC.XVII.*Protokoll*, Second Jewish Agency Council Meeting, remarks by Jung, p. 569ff.

51. *Bericht ueber die Konferenz der Amerikanischen Nichtzionisten ueber die Frage der Jewish Agency fuer Palestina* (1929), p. 64f.; ZC.XVI.*Protokoll*, First Jewish Agency Council Meeting, remarks by Shiplacoff, pp. 622f.

52. Naomi Wiener Cohen, "Reaction of Reform Judaism," *PAJHS*, XL, 361–394.

53. *Louis Marshall*, I, 351–353; II, 719–723.

54. Naomi W. Cohen, "Reaction of Reform Judaism," *PAJHS*, XL, 391ff.

55. *Bericht ueber die Konferenz*, pp. 30ff., 35–39, 41–43.

56. CCAR *Yearbook*, XLV, 102ff., 110–112.

57. *Ibid.*, LII, 169–182; LIV, 145ff.

58. Weizmann, *Trial and Error*, p. 253.

59. Rabinowicz, *Fifty Years*, pp. 36ff., 98ff.; cf. also Sykes, *Two Studies*, pp. 221, n.2, 225 (and note 2 there), 229f.

60. *Louis Marshall*, II, 745.

61. *Ibid.*, p. 726.

62. Rabinowicz, *Fifty Years*, p. 99.

63. *Louis Marshall*, II, 710.

64. *Ibid.*, pp. 728, 737ff., 746, *et passim*.

65. Paul L. Hanna, *British Policy in Palestine* (1942), pp. 92–108.

66. Esco, *Palestine*, II, 614–648.

67. *Ibid.*, pp. 648–660.

68. Hurewitz, *Diplomacy*, II, 107.

69. Hurewitz, *Diplomacy*, II, 108.

70. *Report of the Joint Palestine Survey Commission*, pp. 40–45, 83ff.; *Reports of the Experts to the Joint Palestine Survey Commission*, reports of Dr. Elwood Mead and Associates, pp. 37f.; Sir John Campbell, pp. 451ff.; Dr. Leo Wolman, pp. 496–499, 512, 517f., 522f.

71. ZC.XVII.*Protokoll*, Second Council Meeting, pp. 529f.; Cyrus Adler, *Lectures, Selected Papers, Addresses* (1933), p. 339.

72. GB.Cmd.1700 (1922), p. 19.

73. As quoted in Adler, *Lectures*, p. 339; cf. Bentwich, *Palestine*, p. 101.

74. GB.Cmd.5479 (1937).

75. GB.Cmd.6019 (1939); Hurewitz, *Diplomacy*, II, 218–226.

76. Esco, *Palestine*, II, 909–915, 1008–1018.

77. GB.Cmd.3530 (1930), p. 109.

78. Esco, *Palestine*, II, 620ff.; cf. GB.Cmd.3530 (1930), p. 110ff.

79. See "What Zionism Stands For," *American Jewish Chronicle*, June 20, 1940; quoted in Esco, *Palestine*, II, 1135.

80. *New Judea*, XIII, 233–236; cf. *AJYB*, XL, 586ff., 619f., 625–628.

81. AJCommittee, *To the Counsellors*, pp. 5–8, 68–87.

82. Parkes, *Emergence of the Jewish Problem*, pp. 216–229.

83. Begin, *Revolt*, pp. 38–46, 55.

84. Ben Hecht, *A Child of the Century* (1954), pp. 515–625.

85. *New Palestine*, XXXII, no. 18, p. 6; XXXVI, no. 3, p. 3.

86. *AJYB*, XLVIII, 243ff.

87. *Ibid.*, XLVII, pp. 342–344.

88. AJConference, *Organization and Proceedings, 1st Session*, pp. 39–51.

89. See annual surveys of overseas relief programs, *AJYB*, XLV *et seq*.

90. Weizmann, *Trial and Error*, pp. 381f.

91. Ben Halpern, "The American Jewish Committee," *Jewish Frontier*, X, no. 12, pp. 13–15.

92. *AJYB*, XLIX, 785–788; XL, 813ff.

93. *Ibid.*, pp. 815ff.; XLI, 553ff.; XLIII, 551; XLV, 506; XLVII, 637f.

Chapter 7: Israel and the Diaspora

1. Vlavianos and Gross, *Struggle for Tomorrow*, pp. 150ff.

2. *Louis Marshall*, II, 745.

3. Nathan Eck, "The N'turei Karta," *Jewish Frontier*, XVII, no. 2, 23–26.

4. ACJ, *President's Annual Report* (April 27, 1956), pp. 4–9.

5. Ben Halpern, "The Impact of Zionism on American Jewish Ideologies," *Jewish Social Studies*, XXI, 65–71, 74–77.

6. S. Ephraim, "The Canaanites," *Jewish Frontier*, XIX, no. 8, 26–26.

7. Lessing J. Rosenwald, "This Is the Council" (ACJ pamphlet); ACJ, *An Approach*, pp. 1–11.

8. *AJYB*, L, 817; LI, 554.

9. *Hazut*, IV, remarks by Halpern, 156ff.

10. Leo Pinsker, *Road to Freedom* (1944), pp. 77ff.; Nordau, *Zionistische Schriften*, pp. 43–54.

11. Cf. Ahad Ha'am, *Selected Essays*, pp. 253–305.

12. Marshall Sklare, *The Jews: Social Patterns of an American Group* (1958), pp. 437–450; *AJYB*, LVI, 278ff.; see Charles H. Stember et al., *Jews in the Mind of America* (1966), ch. viii, *et passim*.

13. Marie Syrkin, *Way of Valor* (1955), pp. 243–260; Judd L. Teller, *The Kremlin, The Jews, and The Middle East* (1957), pp. 98–135.

14. *Louis Marshall*, II, 742ff.

15. Arnold Forster and B. R. Epstein, *Cross-Currents* (1956), pp. 301–382.

16. *Jewish Frontier*, XXII, no. 11, 4–6; XXIII, no. 2, 5–7.

17. *AJYB*, LI, 554ff.

18. ACJ, *An Approach*, pp. 18ff.

19. Halpern, "Impact of Zionism," *Jewish Social Studies*, XXI, 70ff., 76.

20. ZOA, *Report of the Commission on the Future Program and Constitution of the World Zionist Organization*, p. 9; "Declaration," *Jewish Frontier*, XVI, no. 7, 21.

21. UN.GA.III.Pt. II, *OR.,Plenary*, 11 May, 1949, p. 332.

22. *AJYB*, LII, 527ff.; LIII, 552, 564ff.

23. *Hazut*, IV, remarks by Halpern, 156ff.

24. *JADigest*, X, 1274.

25. *AJYB*, LV, 506.

26. *Ibid.*, LI, 554; AJCommittee, *Report of the 47th Annual Meeting*, p. 103; *Report of the 48th Annual Meeting*, p. 21.

27. *AJYB*, LI, 179.

28. Jacob Lestchinsky, *Dos Natsionale Ponim fun Golus Yiddentum*, pp. 11–127.

29. Hal Lehrman, "North Africa's Dilemmas for American Jewry," *Commentary*, XIX, 225–235; "Morocco's Jews between Islam and France," XX, 393–402.

30. Hayim Greenberg, "Zionism and Diaspora," *Jewish Frontier*, XVIII, no. 9, 7–9.

31. JA Department of Education, *Y'sodot la-Hinukh ha-Ivri bi-T'futzot ha-Gola*, pp. 150ff., 156ff., 173ff.

32. Moshe Davis, "A Way to Win the Future," *The American Zionist* (January 5, 1954), pp. 9–12.

33. Cf. Isaac Lewin, ed., *Homer l'Sh'elat Hitkonenut v'Sidur ha-M'dina ha-Yehudit al pi ha-Tora* (1948).

34. Halpern, "Impact of Zionism," *Jewish Social Studies*, XXI, 73.

35. *Ibid.*

36. Edoardo Vitta, *The Conflict of Laws in Matters of Personal Status in Palestine* (1947), pp. 105–112.

37. Will Herberg, *Protestant, Catholic, Jew; An Essay in American Religious Sociology* (1956), pp. 18–35.

38. Halpern, *American Jew*, pp. 131–138.

39. *Ibid.*, pp. 11–33.

40. Kaufmann, *Gola ve-Nekhar*, I, 433–455.

41. Agus, *Guideposts*, pp. 53–60, 85–97.

42. Cf. Ben-Zion Bokser, "The Ketubah and Conservative Judaism," *Jewish Frontier*, XXI, no. 12, 17–20; Leo Pfeffer, "Secularizing the Ketubah," *Jewish Horizon* (June 1955), pp. 7–8.

43. Cf. Ben-Zion Bokser, "The Status of Religion in Israel," *Jewish Frontier*, XVII, no. 2, 20–24; Herbert Weiner, "The Liberal Religious Impulse in Israel," *Commentary*, XX, 38–49, 146–154.

44. Cf. "Proclamation of Independence," reprinted in Bentwich, *Israel*, pp. 206ff.

45. *Reconstructionist*, XXIII, no. 16, p. 3; no. 19, pp. 31ff.; XXIV, no. 2, pp. 31f.; no. 6, pp. 31ff.

46. Mordecai M. Kaplan, *A New Zionism* (1955), pp. 103–172.

47. Arthur Ruppin, *Three Decades of Palestine* (1936), pp. 153ff.

48. ZC.XII.*Protokoll*, pp. 781ff., 799 (Art. 25).

49. ZC.XXIII.*Din v'Heshbon Stenografi*, pp. 117f., 136ff., 148ff., 153ff., 164ff., 497–517.

50. David Petegorsky, *The Jewish Community* (AJCongress pamphlet, 1948).

51. *Hazut*, IV, remarks by Goldmann, 148ff.

52. UN.GA.1st.Sp.*OR.*, *Plenary*, pp. 12, 34, 44, 50ff., 52, 65–115; *General Committee*, pp. 16f., 22, 23–25, 35, 36, 38, 41ff., 46, 48, 63, 81–126.

53. *AJYB*, LVIII, 208.

54. R. M. Barkay, *Public Sector Accounts of Israel, 1948/49–1954/55* (1957), II, Tables 71–75, 80–83.

55. Halpern, *American Jew*, pp. 89–96.

56. Melech Noy, *Zionism Today and Tomorrow* (1956), pp. 59–65, 85–91, 99–119, 152–159, 240–250, 266–268.

57. *AJYB*, LII, 122.

58. Abraham Granott, *Agrarian Reform and the Record of Israel* (1956), pp. 103ff.; *Israel Government Year Book*, 5722 (1961/62), p. 47.

59. Cf. Proclamation of Independence in Bentwich, *Israel*, pp. 206–208; Status Law, p. 238 above.

60. Cf. Noy, *Zionism Today*, pp. 127–137, 160–163, 169–175, 192–194; ZC.XXIII.*Din v'Heshbon Stenografi*, pp. 444ff., 446, 495.

61. *JADigest*, III, 1165ff.

62. *Israel Government Year Book*, 5714 (1953/54), pp. 243ff.

63. *Ibid.*, pp. 244–260.

64. ZC.XXIII.*Din v'Heshbon Stenografi,* pp. 583ff.

65. *AJYB,* LIV, 155ff.; *JADigest,* IV, 1060ff., 1110ff.

66. AJCommittee, *Report of the 45th Annual Meeting,* pp. 19f.

67. S. Ephraim, "The Canaanites," *Jewish Frontier,* XIX, no. 8, 25–26.

68. *Israel and the United Nations,* pp. 173–180; *AJYB,* LXII, 119–213, 312ff.; *Israel Government Year Book,* 5722 (1961/62), p. L; *New York Times,* August 3, 1967, p. 5.

69. Cf. Walter Eytan, *The First Ten Years: A Diplomatic History of Israel,* pp. 138–191, 201–205.

70. Shlomo Barer, *The Magic Carpet* (1952), pp. 153–183.

71. Joseph B. Schechtman, *European Population Transfers, 1937–1945* (1946), pp. 488–496.

72. Israel Institute of Applied Social Research, publications nos. 5, 11.

73. Moshe Sicron, *Immigration to Israel, 1948–1953* (1953), pp. 35f.

74. *Hazut,* IV, remarks by Livneh, 61–63.

75. Cf. Noy, *Zionism Today,* pp. 235–239.

76. Cf. Britische Palaestina Komitee, *Politisches Memorandum,* ¶12, in Ettinger file (A111/21), Central Zionist Archives, Jerusalem; also, A. D. Gordon, *Kitvei,* I, 193ff.; II, 242ff.; IV, 149ff., 182, 193, 196.

77. Hal Lehrman, "Arms for Arabs — and What for Israel?" *Commentary,* XVIII, 423–433; "Western Self-Interest and Israeli Self-Defense," XXI, 401–408.

78. *JADigest,* X, 322f.

79. Cf. *Hazut,* IV, remarks by Livneh, 62ff.; Dorman, 84ff.; Mahler, 89ff.

80. *Ibid.,* remarks by Sharett, pp. 18ff.

Chapter 8: Zionism and World Politics from Napoleon to Balfour

1. Barbara W. Tuchman, *Bible and Sword* (1956), pp. 113–143.

2. Sokolow, *History of Zionism,* I, 63–66, 95ff.

3. Cf. Sokolow, *History of Zionism;* Gelber, *Zur Vorgeschichte des Zionismus,* vol. I; Dinaburg, *Sefer ha-Zionut,* vol. I, bk. I.

4. Gelber, *Vorgeschichte,* pp. 12–26, 49–55, 70ff., 92–124, 176–201.

5. *Ibid.,* pp. 12–26.

6. Kirk, *Short History,* pp. 71–97.

7. Raphael Mahler, *Divrei Y'mei Israel ba-Dorot ha-Ah'ronim* (1952), IV, 282ff.; Ben Halpern, "A Note on Ali Bey's 'Jewish State' Project," *Jewish Social Studies,* XVIII, 284–286.

8. Gelber, *Vorgeschichte,* pp. 38–48; Dinaburg, *Sefer ha-Zionut,* vol. I, bk. I, pp. 161–168, 194–198; Franz Kobler, "Napoleon and the Restoration of the Jews," *New Judea,* XVI, 189ff., XVII, 18ff., 36–38, 69f.; Abraham S. Yahuda, "Napoleon and a Jewish State," *Zion* (English monthly, published by the World Zionist Organization, Jerusalem, from August 1949 to June 1952), I, no. 7, 29–34, II, nos. 3–4, 48f.

9. Gelber, *Vorgeschichte,* pp. 124–165.

10. Montefiore, *Diaries,* I, 198–204.

11. Sokolow, *History of Zionism,* I, 176–183.

12. *Ibid.,* I, 206–209; II, 267–269.

13. Druyanow, *Pinsker u-Z'mano*, pp. 184, 192, 229–230.
14. Sokolow, *History of Zionism*, I, 123.
15. Oliphant, *Land of Gilead*, p. 26.
16. Tuchman, *Bible and Sword*, pp. 122–143, 173ff.
17. Sokolow, *History of Zionism*, I, 175.
18. Montefiore, *Diaries*, II, 105–107, 284–286.
19. Hyamson, *British Consulate*, I, xlivff.
20. Cf. Herzl, *Tagebuecher*, III, 540–547, 555–559.
21. Florian Sokolow, "Sokolow and Pope Benedict XV," *Zion* [English], I, nos. 5–6, pp. 48–52; Sykes, *Two Studies*, pp. 198–203.
22. Jacob M. Landau, "T'udot meha-Arkhionim ha-Britiyim al Nisyon ha-Hityashvut ha-Yehudit b'Midian (1890–92)," *Shivat Zion*, I, 169–178; Alex Bein, "Ha-Massa v'Mattan bein Herzl uvein Memshelet Britannia ha-G'dola al El-Arish," *ibid.*, pp. 179–220.
23. Oliphant, *Land of Gilead*, pp. 11–14.
24. Boehm, *Zionistische Bewegung*, I, 705–709.
25. Herzl, *Tagebuecher*, I, 321ff., 429–462, 467–479; Boehm, *Zionistische Bewegung*, I, 387ff.
26. ZC.IX.*Protokoll*, p. 21f.
27. *Ibid.*, pp. 22–24.
28. Boehm, *Zionistiche Bewegung*, I, 383–386, 392–397.
29. F. A. Ellsberg, "Ha-Sh'ela ha-Aravit," *Shivat Zion*, IV, 161–209.
30. *Ibid.*, pp. 163ff., 168ff., 174ff.
31. *Ibid.*, pp. 176ff.
32. ZC.IX.*Protokoll*, pp. 19f., 25.
33. A. D. Gordon, *Kitvei*, I, 11–16, 64–76, 182ff.; II, 243ff., 280, 286; IV, 149ff.
34. Weizmann, *Trial and Error*, pp. 190ff., 233.
35. ZC.XII.*Protokoll*, pp. 279ff.
36. Weizmann, *Trial and Error*, pp. 239f.
37. Sykes, *Two Studies*, pp. 198–203, 223f.
38. Esco, *Palestine*, I, 92f.
39. Lloyd George, *Peace Treaties*, II, 1116–1122, 1139ff.
40. Weizmann, *Trial and Error*, pp. 246ff.
41. *Ibid.*
42. Sykes, *Two Studies*, p. 206.
43. Weizmann, *Trial and Error*, p. 247.
44. Kisch, *Palestine Diary*, pp. 122–124; cf. T. E. Lawrence, *The Letters of T. E. Lawrence* (1939), pp. 193–196.
45. Antonius, *Arab Awakening*, pp. 261ff.
46. Sykes, *Two Studies*, pp. 196f., 203ff.
47. ZC.XII, *Reports of the Executive, Political Report*, Appendix I, pp. 67–71.
48. Weizmann, *Trial and Error*, p. 239.
49. H. F. Frischwasser-Ra'anan, *The Frontiers of a Nation* (1955), pp. 97ff.
50. Manuel, *Realities*, pp. 178ff.
51. Esco, *Palestine*, I, 93.
52. Weizmann, *Trial and Error*, p. 242.
53. Elie Kedourie, *England and the Middle East* (1956), pp. 33–40, 97–98.

54. *Ibid.*, p. 39. (Quoting Mohammed Rashid Rida, *Al Manar*, XXII, 452.)

55. GB.Cmd.5964 (1939), p. 4.

56. Kedourie, *England and the Middle East*, pp. 67–87.

57. De Haas, *Brandeis*, pp. 98ff.

58. Cf. Robinson et al., *Minorities Treaties*, pp. 18, 247ff.

59. Manuel, *Realities*, pp. 211–220.

60. ZC.XII, *Reports of the Executive, Political Report*, pp. 23f.

61. Cf. Stephan Bonsal, *Suitors and Suppliants: The Little Nations at Versailles* (1946), pp. 186–201.

62. Manuel, *Realities*, pp. 221–261.

63. Weizmann, *Trial and Error*, pp. 353ff., 360.

64. Kedourie, *England and the Middle East*, pp. 113ff.

65. Esco, *Palestine*, I, 141ff.

66. JA Memorandum to Palestine Royal Commission, p. 296; cf. Antonius, *Arab Awakening*, pp. 437–439.

67. Hurewitz, *Diplomacy*, II, 19 (2nd doc. par. 3.)

68. David Hunter Miller, *My Diary at the Conference of Paris* (1924), XIV, 230.

69. Esco, *Palestine*, I, 191ff.

70. Miller, *Diary at the Conference of Paris*, XIV, 414ff.

71. Esco, *Palestine*, I, 142.

72. Antonius, *Arab Awakening*, p. 333.

73. Weizmann, *Trial and Error*, p. 243.

74. *Ibid.*, pp. 270–281.

75. Kedourie, *England and the Middle East*, pp. 116–122.

Chapter 9: The Mandate for Palestine: Formulation and Interpretation, 1918–1936

1. Cf. Antonius, *Arab Awakening*, p. 268ff.; Galanté, *Turcs et Juifs*, pp. 5–16.

2. Stoyanovsky, *Mandate for Palestine*, pp. 163ff., 238, 261ff., 293ff.; Bernard Joseph, *British Rule in Palestine* (1948), pp. 42–52.

3. Herzl, *Tagebuecher*, I, 483.

4. *Ibid.*, p. 599.

5. Frank E. Manuel, "Diplomatia Italkit," *Shivat Zion*, IV, 211–224.

6. Cf. John Henry Patterson, *With the Zionists in Gallipoli* (1916).

7. John Henry Patterson, *With the Judeans in the Palestine Campaign* (1922), pp. 43–46, 49f., 53–55, 70–79, 99f., 148–156, 159–161, *et passim*.

8. Woodward and Butler, *British Documents*, series I, vol. IV, pp. 283ff., 295, 300ff., 323–327, 329–335, 355, 381f.

9. *Sefer Toldot ha-Hagana* (1954), vol. I, bk. II, pp. 517–532; Schechtman, *Rebel and Statesman*, pp. 271–284.

10. *Sefer Toldot ha-Hagana*, vol. I, bk. II, pp. 641–644; Patterson, *With the Judeans*, pp. 240–263.

11. *Sefer Toldot ha-Hagana*, vol. I, bk. II, pp. 603–625; Schechtman, *Rebel and Statesman*, pp. 320–342.

12. *Sefer Toldot ha-Hagana*, vol. I, bk. II, pp. 565–585.

13. Lloyd George, *Peace Treaties*, II, 1038, 1144, 1176–1181.

14. Woodward and Butler, *British Documents*, series I, vol. IV, pp. 346ff.

15. *Ibid.*, pp. 607–608, and crossreferences cited there; see also, Bonsal, *Suitors and Suppliants*, pp. 52–54.

16. ZC.XII, *Reports of the Executive, Political Report*, Appendix 7, pp. 75ff.

17. Esco, *Palestine*, I, 151ff.; Ha-Mo'etza ha-Klalit (15–19 Tevet, 5679 [1919]), *Heads of Scheme for the provisional Government of Palestine*, Ettinger file (A 111/21) Central Zionist Archives, Jerusalem; cf. proposals of May 1917 for a Jewish autonomous Province in Palestine north of Jerusalem, Mowshowitch file, A 77/3, Central Zionist Archives, Jerusalem.

18. Woodward and Butler, *British Documents*, series I, vol. IV, pp. 425–428.

19. *Ibid.*, pp. 329ff., 360, 381f.; Bonsal, *Suitors and Suppliants*, p. 61.

20. Lloyd George, *Peace Treaties*, II, 1116–1122, 1139f.; Sykes, *Two Studies*, pp. 231–233.

21. Woodward and Butler, *British Documents*, series I, vol. IV, pp. 272 (doc. no. 183, note 1), 281–285, 294ff., 299–301, 303–308, 310ff., 317ff., 323–327, 329–335, 338ff., 355, 360–365, 368ff., 381ff., 391ff., 425–428, 442, 469–473, 495, 499, 507ff., 525-527, 529.

22. *Ibid.*; cf. also Weizmann, *Trial and Error*, pp. 270–281, 284–286, 290–294, 311–324, 366–368.

23. Sir Ronald Storrs, *Orientations* (1937), pp. 433ff.; Kisch, *Palestine Diary*, pp. 85, 124, 142ff., 150, 209, 211ff., 299ff., 319.

24. ZC.XII, *Reports of the Executive, Political Report*, p. 20; Appendices, 7, pp. 74–83; cf. Manuel, *Realities*, p. 232ff.

25. ZC.XII, *Reports of the Executive, Political Report*, pp. 27–33; Esco, *Palestine*, I, 156ff.

26. Frischwasser-Raanan, *Frontiers of a Nation*, pp. 100–109.

27. Weizmann, *Trial and Error*, p. 348.

28. Woodward and Butler, *British Documents*, series I, vol. IV, p. 429.

29. Stoyanovsky, *Mandate for Palestine*, pp. 22–27.

30. Esco, *Palestine*, I, 172–174.

31. Woodward and Butler, *British Documents*, series I, vol. IV, p. 429; ZC.III, *Reports of the Executive, Political Report*, p. 29.

32. Cf. Joseph, *British Rule*, pp. 53–62.

33. Hurewitz, *Diplomacy*, II, 107.

34. *Ibid.*, p. 62; cf. J. C. Smuts, *The League of Nations: A Practical Suggestion* (1918), pp. 16–20; Joseph, *British Rule*, pp. 53–62.

35. Hurewitz, *Diplomacy*, II, 84.

36. *Ibid.*, pp. 106ff.; Joseph, *British Rule*, pp. 70–72; Stoyanovsky, *Mandate for Palestine*, pp. 30–47.

37. Quoted in Joseph, *British Rule*, p. 58.

38. Frischwasser-Raanan, *Frontiers of a Nation*, pp. 97–141.

39. Joseph, *British Rule*, pp. 73–75.

40. Hurewitz, *Diplomacy*, II, 103ff.

41. Fannie Fern Andrews, *The Holy Land under the Mandate* (1931), II, 114–122, 148–154.

42. LN*Publications*, 1922, VI.A.18, pp. 2, 3. (Italics supplied.)

43. Esco, *Palestine*, I, 262ff.

44. ZC.XII, *Reports of the Executive, Political Report*, pp. 30ff.

45. GB.Cmd.1700 (1922), pp. 5ff., 20.

46. *Ibid.*, p. 20. (Italics supplied.)

47. Lloyd George, *Peace Treaties*, II, 1193.

48. GB.Cmd.5479 (1937), p. 33.

49. LN.PMC.V(Extraordinary), *Minutes*, Annex 2, pp. 166ff.

50. LN.PMC.VII, *Minutes*, Annex 7, A (pp. 160–164), B (pp. 164–173).

51. LN.PMC.V(Ext.), *Minutes*, p. 166.

52. GB.Cmd.1700 (1922), doc. nos. 1, 3, 6.

53. LN.PMC.VII, *Minutes*, Annex 7, pp. 168ff.

54. LN.PMC.V(Ext.), *Report*, p. 4.

55. LN.PMC.V(Ext.), *Minutes*, pp. 63, 65, 71, 120ff.

56. LN.PMC.V(Ext.), *Report*, p. 4.

57. LN.PMC.XIV, *Minutes*, pp. 246ff.

58. LN.PMC.VII, *Minutes*, remarks by Palacios, p. 112.

59. LN.PMC.V(Ext.), *Minutes*, pp. 71–74; *Report*, pp. 4ff.

60. LN.PMC.V(Ext.), *Minutes*, Annex 2, pp. 168ff., 170ff.; GB.Cmd.-1540 (1921), pp. 50ff.

61. LN.PMC.V(Ext.), *Minutes*, Annex 2, p. 172; LN.PMC.VII. Annex 7, pp. 164–168.

62. Esco, *Palestine*, I, 309ff.

63. *Ibid.*, I, 366–368.

64. LN.PMC.V(Ext.), *Minutes*, pp. 68f.

65. LN.PMC.VII, *Minutes* (cf. especially remarks of Palacios and Rappard), pp. 110–112.

66. Storrs, *Orientations*, p. 425.

67. GB.Cmd.1540 (1921), p. 59.

68. Quoted from Esco, *Palestine*, I, 273.

69. GB.Cmd.1540 (1921), p. 57.

70. *Ibid.*

71. Storrs, *Orientations*, pp. 448ff.; LN.PMC.VII., *Minutes*, remarks by Ormsby-Gore, p. 105.

72. Albert M. Hyamson, *Palestine under the Mandate, 1920–1948* (1950), pp. 102ff.; cf. Graves, *Experiment in Anarchy*, pp. 11ff.

73. GB.Cmd.1499 (1921), pp. 7f.

74. Esco, *Palestine*, II, 595–660, 739–875.

75. Andrews, *Holy Land under Mandate*, II, 325–366.

76. Esco, *Palestine*, II, 644–650.

77. *Ibid.*, pp. 656ff.

78. GB.Cmd.5479 (1937), pp. 37–42, 304–307, 370–376.

79. Esco, *Palestine*, II, 909–928.

80. Woodward and Butler, *British Documents*, series I, vol. IV, pp. 421–423.

81. Moshe Perlmann, "Chapters of Arab-Jewish Diplomacy," *Jewish Social Studies*, VI, 148–152.

82. *Ibid.*, p. 149.

83. *Ibid.*, pp. 152f.; Kisch, *Palestine Diary*, p. 36.

84. Esco, *Palestine*, I, 129f.; Storrs, *Orientations*, p. 399f.

85. Kisch, *Palestine Diary*, pp. 26, 28–39, 42ff., 45f., *et passim*.

86. Woodward and Butler, *British Documents*, series I, vol. IV, pp. 360ff.

87. Kisch, *Palestine Diary*, p. 75.

88. Ahad Ha'am, *Ten Essays on Zionism and Judaism* (1922), pp. xv–xviii.

89. Ber Borochov, *Poale-Zion Shriftn* (1920), I, 267–272.

90. Quoted in Esco, *Palestine*, I, 161; cf., ZC.XII, *Reports of the Executive, Political Report*, p. 22.

91. Weizmann, *Trial and Error*, p. 305.

92. GB.Cmd.1700 (1922), p. 18.

93. Esco, *Palestine*, II, 744ff.

94. *Ibid.*, p. 1169.

95. Hurewitz, *Diplomacy*, II, 105.

96. Esco, *Palestine*, II, 621ff., 739ff., 782ff., 876ff.

97. *Ibid.*, pp. 1125ff.; see Aaron Cohen, *Israel v'ha-Olam ha-Aravi* (1964) and David Ben-Gurion, *P'gishot im Manhigim Arviyim* (1967).

Chapter 10: Termination of the Mandate:
Evolution of the Plan for Partition

1. Bentwich, *Israel*, Appendix A, pp. 206–208.

2. LN.PMC.XX, *Minutes*, pp. 195–210.

3. LN.PMC.XVII(Ext.), *Minutes*, p. 38.

4. Stoyanovsky, *Mandate for Palestine*, pp. 350–354; H. W. V. Temperley, *A History of the Peace Conference of Paris* (1924), VI, 174.

5. Hanna, *British Policy*, pp. 120f.; Hurewitz, *Struggle for Palestine*, pp. 85–90.

6. LN.PMC.XVII(Ext.), *Minutes*, remarks by Van Rees, pp. 37ff., Palacios, Rappard, and Theodoli, pp. 4ff.; Report to the Council (Annex 10), p. 143.

7. LN.PMC.XVII(Ext.), *Minutes*, remarks by Dannevig and Lugard, pp. 63ff.; LN.PMC.XXIII, *Minutes*, remarks by Lugard, Penha Garcia, Van Rees, and Rappard, pp. 98ff.

8. LN.PMC.XIII, *Minutes*, pp. 42–45; (Report, Annex 7) pp. 225ff.; LN.*OJ*.IX, pp. 1449–1453.

9. Esco, *Palestine*, II, 595–660.

10. LN.PMC.XVII(Ext.), *Minutes*, pp. 48–50.

11. *Ibid.*, p. 145.

12. GB.Cmd.5479 (1937), pp. 34–42, 357–368, 370–376.

13. LN.PMC.XXXIII(Ext.), *Minutes* (Annex 11, Report), p. 229.

14. *Ibid.*, pp. 229ff.

15. Esco, *Palestine*, II, 861–908.

16. LN.PMC.XXXVI, *Minutes*, p. 275.

17. Hyamson, *Palestine under the Mandate*, pp. 51–57.

18. Bein, *Return to the Soil*, pp. 3–11, 33–36, 330–338.

19. Herzl, *Tagebuecher*, I, 493.

20. Cf. Ruppin, *Three Decades*, pp. 107–112.

21. Rabinowicz, *Fifty Years*, pp. 37–41.

22. Ben Halpern, "Hekhalutz," *Jewish Frontier*, XII, no. 2, pp. 24–28.

23. Andrews, *Holy Land under Mandate*, II, 337–342, 346–349, 360–365.

24. GB.Cmd.1540 (1921), p. 43; JA, *The Jewish Case*, pp. 356–359.

25. Cf. Joseph M. N. Jeffries, *Palestine: The Reality* (1939), pp. 409–421.

26. *Chaim Weizmann*, pp. 271–275.

27. JA, *The Jewish Case*, pp. 312–325.

28. Cf. paragraphs 4–6, 12–15 of the 1939 White Paper and Foreign Secretary Bevin's Nov. 13, 1945 statement, in Palestine Government, *A Survey of Palestine* (1946), I, 91–93, 95–98, 99–103.

29. Begin, *Revolt*, pp. 26–46; cf. Ben Halpern, "The Partisan in Israel," *Jewish Frontier*, XV, no. 8, 6–9.

30. Wischnitzer, *To Dwell in Safety*, pp. 171–285.

31. Cf. Bevin statements quoted in Hurewitz, *Struggle for Palestine*, pp. 236ff., 253.

32. Tartakower and Grossmann, *Jewish Refugee*, pp. 52ff., 80ff.

33. Wischnitzer, *To Dwell in Safety*, pp. 200ff., 245ff.

34. Cf. Jerome Frank, "Red-White-and Blue Herring," *Saturday Evening Post*, Dec. 6, 1941, pp. 8, 83ff.; see Stember, *Jews in the Mind of America*, ch. v, *et passim*.

35. Ben-Gurion, *Ba-Ma'arakha*, III, 18.

36. Jon and David Kimche, *The Secret Roads* (1955), pp. 158–174.

37. Scheib, *Ma'aser Rishon*, pp. 65ff.

38. Begin, *Revolt*, pp. 42ff.

39. Jacob Robinson, *Palestine and the United Nations: Prelude to Solution* (1947), pp. 2ff.

40. Cf. Scheib, *Ma'aser Rishon*, pp. 87–89, 99–104.

41. Ben Halpern, "Haganah and the Terrorists," *Jewish Frontier*, XIV, no. 3, 13–24.

42. Hurewitz, *Struggle for Palestine*, pp. 196–201, 232ff., 240–243, 253–255, 259–262.

43. *Ibid.*, p. 273; cf. Robinson, *Palestine and the United Nations*, pp. 26–47.

44. *Ibid.*, pp. 43ff.

45. Hurewitz, *Struggle for Palestine*, pp. 274–278; Manuel, *Realities*, pp. 305–331.

46. Robinson, *Palestine and the United Nations*, pp. 59f.

47. Hurewitz, *Struggle for Palestine*, pp. 272f.

48. Robinson, *Palestine and the United Nations*, pp. 57–62.

49. *Ibid.*, pp. 184ff., 236–239.

50. JA, *Book of Documents submitted to the General Assembly of the United Nations relating to the Establishment of the National Home for the Jewish People* (1947), pp. 254–266.

51. Hurewitz, *Struggle for Palestine*, p. 249.

52. *Ibid.*, pp. 257–259; Manuel, *Realities*, pp. 324–326.

53. *Ibid.*, pp. 327–329.

54. Robinson, *Palestine and the United Nations*, pp. 233ff.; cf. Manuel, *Realities*, pp. 332ff.

55. Robinson, *Palestine and the United Nations*, pp. 144ff.

56. *Ibid.*, pp. 3–6.

57. Hurewitz, *Struggle for Palestine*, pp. 236–238.

58. Robinson, *Palestine and the United Nations*, pp. 167–196.

59. UN.GA.I.Sp.OR., *Plenary*, p. 132.

60. Hurewitz, *Diplomacy*, II, 264ff.
61. UN.GA.II.*OR.*, Suppl. 11, no. I, pp. 46, 63ff.; no. II, pp. 23ff., 48ff.
62. *Ibid.*, no. I, 59–64.
63. UN.GA.II.*OR.*, *Ad Hoc Committee*, pp. 206, 270ff., 302ff.
64. UN.GA.II.*OR.*, Suppl. 11, no. I, p. 54.
65. GB.Cmd. 5479 (1937), pp. 386–388; GB.Cmd.5854 (1938), pp. 179–212, 224–231; UN.GA.II.*OR.*, Suppl. 11, no. I, pp. 55ff.
66. GB.Cmd.5479 (1937), pp. 381ff.; GB.Cmd.5854 (1938), pp. 34–39; UN.GA.II.*OR.*, *Ad Hoc Committee*, pp. 260–263.
67. Stoyanovsky, *Mandate for Palestine*, pp. 291–301.
68. UN.GA.II.*OR.*, Suppl. 11, no. I, pp. 54–58.
69. UN.GA.II.*OR.*, *Ad Hoc Committee*, insert between pp. 264 and 265.
70. *Ibid.*, p. 250.
71. *Ibid.*, pp. 254–256.
72. Cf. Eytan, *First Ten Years*, pp. 77f.
73. Cf. Berendsen statement, UN.GA.II.*OR.*, *Plenary*, pp. 1357f.
74. Graves, *Experiment in Anarchy*, pp. 87ff.
75. O'Ballance, *Arab-Israeli War*, pp. 31–125.
76. UN.GA.II.Sp.*OR.*, Suppl. 1, pp. 10–14.
77. Trygve Lie, *In the Cause of Peace* (1954), pp. 166–171.
78. Manuel, *Realities*, pp. 334–350; Eytan, *First Ten Years*, pp. 8–15.

Chapter 11: Israel and the United Nations

1. UN.GA.II.Sp.*OR.*, Suppl. 1, pp. 5–9.
2. UN.GA.III.Pt.II.*OR.*, *Ad Hoc Political Committee*, pp. 349ff.
3. UN.SC.III.*OR.*, 333rd Meeting, pp. 12ff.
4. Count Folke Bernadotte, *To Jerusalem* (1951), pp. 3f., 5.
5. Harry Sacher, *Israel: The Establishment of a State* (1952), pp. 122–131.
6. *Israel and the United Nations* (1956), pp. 89ff.
7. O'Ballance, *Arab-Israeli War*, pp. 31–67.
8. Eytan, *First Ten Years*, pp. 20–24.
9. O'Ballance, *Arab-Israeli War*, pp. 68–140.
10. *Israel and the United Nations*, pp. 70–72.
11. *Ibid.*, p. 72.
12. UN.SC.III.*OR.*, no. 52, pp. 26ff., 28; no. 58, pp. 17, 19; no. 68, pp. 10, 24, 27, 43ff., 45; no. 70, p. 11ff.; no. 74, p. 44ff., 48; no. 75, pp. 12ff., 20; no. 77, p. 45.
13. Sacher, *Israel*, pp. 120–122, 132.
14. UN.SC.III.*OR.*, no. 93, p. 35.
15. O'Ballance, *Arab-Israeli War*, pp. 141–164, 173–206.
16. UN.SC.III.*OR.*, no. 107, pp. 50ff.; no. 118, pp. 36–38; no. 124, pp. 38–43.
17. UN.GA.III.*OR.*, Suppl. 11, p. 4.
18. UN.SC.*OR.*, no. 126, pp. 53–55.
19. Part I, Section F; Hurewitz, *Diplomacy*, II, 289.
20. UN.SC.III.*OR.*, Suppl. for Dec. 1948, p. 118.
21. Eytan, *First Ten Years*, pp. 9–12.

22. Paragraphs 2–6, Resolution 194 (III), UN.GA.III.Pt.I.*OR.*, *Resolutions*, pp. 22f.

23. Manuel, *Realities*, p. 352; Sacher, *Israel*, pp. 292ff.

24. UN.GA.III.Pt.I.*OR.*, *First Committee*, Annexes, pp. 55–65.

25. UN.SC.III.*OR.*, no. 130, p. 37.

26. O'Ballance, *Arab-Israeli War*, pp. 193–204.

27. Hurewitz, *Diplomacy*, II, 299ff.; Sacher, *Israel*, p. 307.

28. *Ibid.*, pp. 306–309.

29. Emanuel Rackman, *Israel's Emerging Constitution 1948–1951* (1955), pp. 65ff.

30. UN.GA.III.Pt.II.*OR.*, *Ad Hoc Political Committee*, remarks by Eban, p. 230.

31. See statements of UN delegates, *ibid.*, pp. 199 (Federspiel), 211 (Sunde), 227 (Grafstrom), 341ff. (Sunde), 344ff. (Federspiel).

32. *Ibid.*, pp. 186ff. (Castro), 192ff. (de Souza Gomes), 211 (Nisot), 272ff. (Castro), 286ff. (Nisot.

33. *Ibid.*, pp. 180ff., 219ff., 261ff., 266ff., 289ff., *et passim.*

34. *Ibid.*, pp. 227ff., *et passim.*

35. UN.GA.III.Pt.II.*OR.*, Plenary, pp. 330f.

36. Sacher, *Israel*, pp. 154–180.

37. UN.GA.II.*OR.*, *Resolutions*, Res. 184 (II), Part I, B9, B10e, D; Part III, C7, C8, C11, D (pp. 134, 135, 139–142, 148, 150).

38. Cf. Harry Levin, *Jerusalem Embattled* (1950).

39. UN.TC.II.Pt.III.*OR.*, pp. 1–8; Annex (Doc. A/544), pp. 1–3; UN.GA.IISp.*OR.*, Plenary, pp. 10–27.

40. UN.GA.III.*OR.*, Suppl. 11, pp. 7ff., 17–19, 24–26.

41. UN.GA.III.Pt.I.*OR.*, *Resolutions*, Res. 194 (III) 8, p. 23.

42. UN.GA.IV.*OR.*, *Ad Hoc Political Committee*, Annex I, pp. 10–16.

43. *Ibid.*, Annex II, p. 5 (Doc. A/838, paragraph 28).

44. UN.GA.III.Pt.II.*OR.*, *Ad Hoc Political Committee*, pp. 230–237, 253–260.

45. UN.GA.IV.*OR.*, *Ad Hoc Political Committee*, Annex I, pp. 32–44, 46–48.

46. *Ibid.*, p. 59 (Doc. A/AC.31/11: cf. paragraphs 12ii, 15, 16).

47. *Israel and the United Nations*, pp. 133f.

48. UN.GA.IV.*OR.*, *Resolutions*, p. 25; *Plenary*, pp. 605–607.

49. *Israel and the United Nations*, pp. 134ff.

50. UN.GA.V.*OR.*, Suppl. 9.

51. UN.GA.IV.*OR.*, *Ad Hoc Political Committee*, Annex I, pp. 60–62.

52. UN.GA.V.*OR.*, *Annexes*, Agenda item 20, pp. 2–8.

53. UN.GA.V.*OR.*, *Plenary*, p. 684.

54. UN.GA.VII.*OR.*, *Plenary*, p 413.

55. *Israel and the United Nations*, pp. 139f.

56. Ibid., pp. 140ff.; Eytan, *First Ten Years*, pp. 78–85.

57. Eytan, *First Ten Years*, pp. 121ff.

58. UN.GA.II.Sp.*OR.*, Suppl. 1, p. 17.

59. *New York Times*, April 19, 1948, p. 7; April 20, pp. 1, 7; April 23, pp. 1, 5; April 24, p. 4; cf. Joseph B. Schechtman, *The Arab Refugee Problem* (1952), pp. 12ff.

60. *New York Times*, April 12, 1948, pp. 1, 9.

61. UN.SC.III.*OR.*, Suppl. for July, 1948, p. 61.

62. UN.GA.III.*OR.*, Suppl. 11, pp. 27ff.

63. UN.GA.III.Pt.I.*OR.*, *Resolutions*, pp. 21, 24. My discussion of this text is indebted throughout to Dr. Jacob Robinson's unpublished legal analysis.

64. UN.GA.III.*OR.*, Suppl. 11, p. 18.

65. UN.GA.III.Pt.I.*OR.*, *First Committee*, Annexes, pp. 57, 60 (paragraph 10), 63ff.

66. UN.GA.III.Pt.I.*OR.*, *First Committee*, p. 910.

67. *Ibid.*, p. 906.

68. *Ibid.*, Annexes, pp. 69 (paragraph 6), 70 (paragraph 6), 70f.

69. UN.GA.III.Pt.I.*OR.*, *First Committee*, p. 905.

70. *Ibid.*, p. 908.

71. UN.GA.III.Pt.II.*OR.*, *Ad Hoc Political Committee*, p. 238.

72. *Ibid.*, pp. 282ff., 345.

73. *Ibid.*, pp. 237–241, 261–266, 282ff., 286ff., 300ff.

74. UN.GA.III.Pt.II.*OR.*, *Plenary*, pp. 309f., 317.

75. UN.GA.IV.*OR.*, *Ad Hoc Political Committee*, Annex II, p. 3 (esp. paragraph 7).

76. UN.GA.IX.*OR.*, Suppl. 17, pp. 1, 4, 5ff.; UN.GA.XI.*OR.*, Suppl. 14, pp. 1ff., 6ff., 9ff., 12ff.

77. UN.GA.V.*OR.*, *Annexes*, Agenda item 20, pp. 35 (Doc. A/AC.38/L.-30/Rev.1), 36, 44–46.

78. Eytan, *First Ten Years*, pp. 51ff.; James G. McDonald, *My Mission in Israel, 1948–1951* (1951), pp. 176–180.

79. UN.GA.IV.*OR.*, *Ad Hoc Political Committee*, Annex II, pp. 2–4.

80. UN.GA.V.*OR.*, Suppl. 18, pp. 2–9.

81. *Ibid.*, pp. 15 (para. 23), 19 (para. 5).

82. *Ibid.*, pp. 19 (para. 7), 20 (para. 15).

83. Cf. McDonald, *Mission in Israel*, pp. 181ff.; *Israel and the United Nations*, pp. 94ff.

84. UN.GA.V.*OR.*, Suppl. 18, pp. 13 (para. 13), 19f. (para. 9); Schechtman, *Arab Refugee Problem*, pp. 35ff.

85. UN.GA.V.*OR.*, Suppl. 18, p. 14 (para. 20).

86. *Ibid.*, p. 19ff. (paras. 9–11, 16).

87. UN.GA.VI.*OR.*, Suppl. 18, p. 10 (para. 80).

88. Cf. UN.GA.V.*OR.*, Suppl. 18, p. 14 (para. 21).

89. UN.GA.VI.*OR.*, Suppl. 18, p. 10.

90. UN.GA.V.*OR.*, Suppl. 18, p. 20 (para. 18).

91. UN.SC.VI.*OR.*, Suppl. for 1 April through 30 June, 1951, pp. 162ff. (Doc. S/2194); Suppl. for July, August and September, 1951, pp. 9ff. (Doc. S/2241); 558th meeting, p. 2 (para. 5).

92. UN.GA.VI.*OR.*, Suppl. 18, pp. 3ff. (para. 23).

93. *Ibid.*, pp. 7ff. (paras. 51–61), 9f., 19–24 (Annex C, Appendix II).

94. *Ibid.*, pp. 8f., 17–19 (Annex C, Appendix I).

95. *Ibid.*, p. 10.

96. UN.GA.VII.*OR.*, *Annexes*, Agenda item 67, p. 2ff. (Doc. A/2184).

97. UN.GA.VII.*OR.*, *Ad Hoc Political Committee*, p. 199 (para. 17).

98. *Ibid.*, p. 206. (paras. 32–34).

99. *Ibid.*, p. 221.

100. *Ibid.*, p. 199 (para. 17).

101. UN.GA.VII.*OR.*, Annexes, Agenda item 67, pp. 9ff.

102. *Ibid.*, pp. 17f. (paras. 10–12), 18 (para. 15); UN.GA.VII.*OR.*, *Ad Hoc Political Committee*, pp. 225, 236ff.

103. UN.GA.VII.*OR.*, *Plenary*, pp. 413ff.

104. UN *Treaty Series*, XLII, nos. 654–657, pp. 252, 288, 304, 328.

105. UNCIO, *Documents*, XV, 343.

106. *New York Times*, Dec. 17, 1957, p. 1.

107. UN.SC.XI.*OR.*, Suppl. for April, May and June 1956, pp. 1–25, 27–66.

108. Shabtai Rosenne, *Israel's Armistice Agreements with the Arab States* (1951), pp. 24ff.

109. UN *Treaty Series*, XLII, no. 656, pp. 304–308; Hurewitz, *Diplomacy*, II, 300.

110. Rosenne, *Israel's Armistice Agreements*, pp. 24ff., 42, 44ff., 70ff., 82ff.

111. *Ibid.*, pp. 24ff.

112. UNCIO *Documents*, XV, 344f.

113. UN.SC.III.*OR.*, Suppl. for May, 1948, pp. 83ff.; UN.SC.VI.*OR.*, 549th Meeting, pp. 8–11.

114. *Ibid.*, pp. 7ff. (paras. 25–27).

115. UN.SC.VI.*OR.*, Suppl. for 1 April through 30 June, 1951, pp. 162–164 (Doc. S/2194).

116. *Ibid.*, 558th Meeting, p. 2ff.

117. UN.SC.IX.*OR.*, 664th Meeting, p. 12.

118. O'Ballance, *Arab-Israeli War*, pp. 95ff.; UN *Treaty Series*, XLII, no. 656, pp. 308–314 (Articles IV–VII).

119. *Ibid.*, no. 655, pp. 290ff. (Articles IV, V).

120. *Ibid.*, no. 654, pp. 254, 258ff. (Articles III, VI–VIII); cf. Eytan, *First Ten Years*, pp. 34–36.

121. UN *Treaty Series*, XLII, no. 657, pp. 330–334 (Articles IV, V).

122. UN.SC.VI.*OR.*, 542nd Meeting, pp. 7–10.

123. UN *Treaty Series*, XLII, no. 657, p. 334 (Article V).

124. UN *Yearbook*, 1951, pp. 286–293; 1952, p. 243; 1953, pp. 216f., 224–233; 1954, pp. 73ff. (Documentary Notes); 1955, pp. 34ff.

125. UN.SC.VI.*OR.*, 542nd Meeting, pp. 3–19; see on all legal questions regarding this treaty Nissim Bar-Yaacov, *The Israel-Syrian Armistice* (1967).

126. UN.SC.VIII.*OR.*, 633rd Meeting, pp. 6–9.

127. UN.SC.VI.*OR.*, Suppl. for 1 April through 30 June, 1951, pp. 17–20; UN.SC.VIII.*OR.*, Suppl. for October, November and December, 1953, pp. 23–36 (Doc. S/3122); UN.SC.VI.*OR.*, 546th Meeting, pp. 2–10; UN.SC.IX.*OR.*, 656th Meeting, pp. 27–34; see Bar-Yaacov, *Israel-Syrian Armistice*, pp. 74–76, 95–100, *et passim*.

128. *JADigest*, VII, no. 6, pp. 110ff.; no. 7, pp. 130–135.

129. UN.SC.V.*OR.*, no. 59, p. 16.

130. UN *Treaty Series*, XLII, doc. no. 654, pp. 256–258 (See Article V, 4).

131. Moshe Dayan, "Keeping Peace," *Jewish Frontier*, XXII, no. 10, pp. 7–9.

132. UN *Treaty Series*, XLII, p. 268 (See Article XII, 3).

133. UN.SC.IX.*OR.*, Suppl. for January, February and March 1954, pp. 9–22 (Docs. S/3180, S/3180/Add. 1, S/3180/Add. 2).

134. UN.SC.XI.*OR*., Suppl. for April, May and June 1956, pp. 15–25 (Docs. S/3584, S/3585, S/3586, S/3587).

135. *Ibid.*, pp. 39–41 (paras. 39–47).

Chapter 12: Israel and World Politics

1. Eytan, *First Ten Years*, pp. 177–191.
2. Cf. Edward B. Glick, *Latin America and the Palestine Problem* (1958), pp. 11ff., 177ff.
3. Eytan, *First Ten Years*, pp. 71–79, 110–112, 144–176.
4. *AJYB*, LVI, 281–283.
5. Hurewitz, *Diplomacy* II, 339, 341ff., 397.
6. Eytan, *First Ten Years*, pp. 138–147.
7. Hurewitz, *Diplomacy* II, 308–311.
8. See David Ben-Gurion, *L'Siyum Perek* (1953/54).
9. *AJYB*, LV, 344–362.
10. *AJYB*, LVI, 466ff.; John C. Campbell, *Defense of the Middle East* (1960), chs. iv, v.
11. *AJYB*, LVII, 491ff.
12. Campbell, *Defense of the Middle East*, ch. vi; Herman Finer, *Dulles over Suez* (1964), pp. 24ff.
13. *JADigest*, IX, no. 9, p. 258; no. 10, pp. 290ff.; no. 11, p. 320; no. 12,
14. R. D. Q. Henriques, *A Hundred Hours to Suez* (1957), pp. 29–179; Moshe Dayan, *Diary of the Sinai Campaign* (1967), chs. i, ii.
15. *New York Times*, Oct. 30, 1956, p. 4.
16. *Ibid.*, Oct. 31, 1956, pp. 1, 16.
17. *New York Times*, Nov. 30, 1956, pp. 1, 4; Dec. 4, pp. 5, 6; Dec.
18. *Ibid.*, *passim*, issues of January, February, and March, 1957.
19. Theodore Draper, *Israel and World Politics* (1968), ch. ii.
20. *Ibid.*, pp. 33ff.
21. Campbell, *Defense of the Middle East*, pp. 139ff., 186ff., 200ff.
22. *Ibid.*, 316ff.; cf. Draper, *Israel and World Politics*, pp. 34, 36, 45f., 48ff., 78ff.
23. *Ibid.*, pp. 50ff.
24. *Ibid.*, pp. 37ff., 51ff.
25. *Ibid.*, pp. 46, 57ff.
26. *Ibid.*, ch. vi.
27. *Ibid.*, pp. 86ff.
28. *Ibid.*, pp. 96ff.
29. *New York Times*, November 23, 1967, pp. 1, 5.
30. *AJYB*, LXIV, 283ff.
31. See Walter Laqueur, *The Road to Jerusalem* (1968), chap. v and Appendix 10.
32. "Meet the Press," NBC television program, Dec. 2, 1956; also speech before the National Press Club, Washington, D.C., Dec. 11, 1956.

INDEX